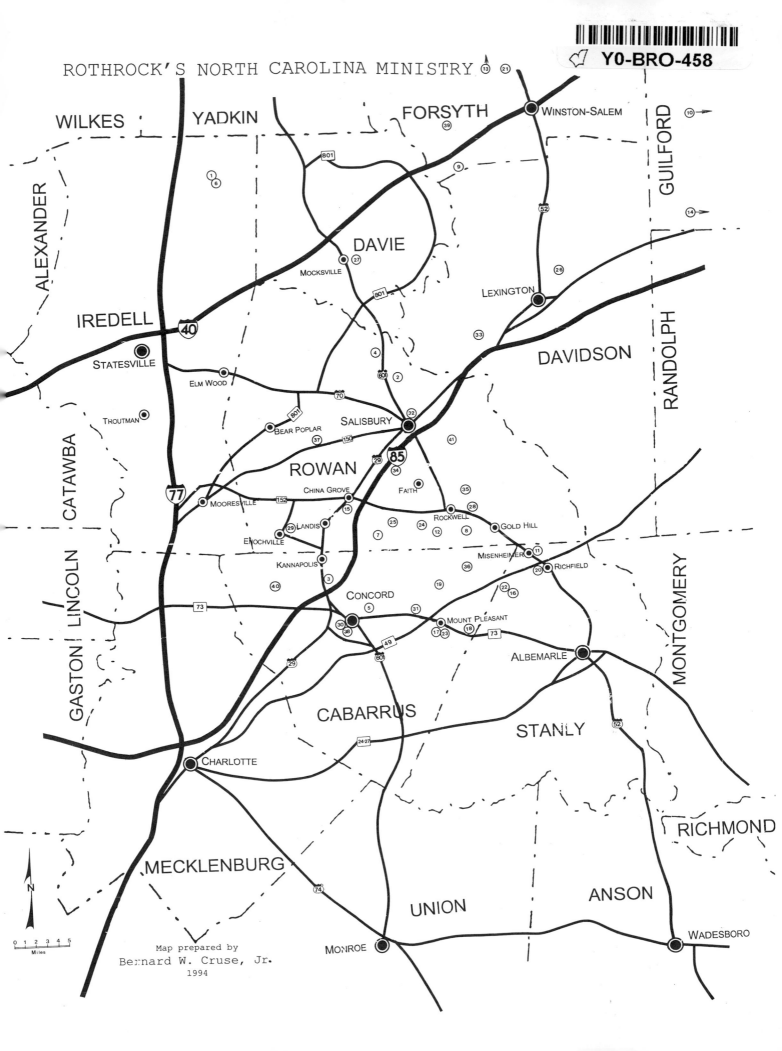

Y0-BRO-458

.WITHDRAWN

L. R. COLLEGE LIBRARY

The Samuel Rothrock Diaries

1834-1893

VOLUME I

Transcribed and Indexed by
Bernard William Cruse, Jr.

PUBLISHED BY THE AUTHORITY OF
HISTORICAL COMMITTEE
North Carolina Synod
Evangelical Lutheran Church in America

CARL A. RUDISILL LIBRARY
LENOIR-RHYNE COLLEGE

BX
8080
.R74
C77
1994
V I
March 2009

Published by North Carolina Synod, Evangelical Lutheran Church in America
1988 Lutheran Synod Drive
Salisbury, North Carolina 28144-5700

Copyright © 1994 by North Carolina Synod, ELCA

All rights reserved. No part of this book may be reproduced in any form or by
any means without the prior written permission of the publisher, except brief
quotes used in connection with reviews, written specifically for inclusion in a
magazine or newspaper.

Printed in the United States of America

First Edition, 1994

Library of Congress Catalogue Card Number: 94-066007

Transcribed and Indexed by

Bernard William Cruse, Jr.

ISBN Number 0-9641126-1-2
Rothrock Diaries Vol. I

This book was printed by Delmar Printing Company
Charlotte, North Carolina

HISTORICAL COMMITTEE
North Carolina Synod
Evangelical Lutheran Church in America
1988 Lutheran Synod Drive
Salisbury, North Carolina 28144-5700
(704) 633-4861

Rev. Samuel Rothrock, D. D.

A gift for the publication of
the Rothrock Diaries
was provided by
Archibald Caldwell Rufty
to the glory of God
and in memory
of his great-grandfather
Rev. Samuel Rothrock

ACKNOWLEDGEMENTS

THE SAMUEL ROTHROCK DIARIES, VOLUME I

Transcribed and Indexed by
Bernard W. Cruse, Jr.

NORTH CAROLINA SYNOD PARTICIPANTS DURING THE PREPARATION AND PUBLICATION OF THE DIARIES:

HISTORICAL COMMITTEE MEMBERS

CLERGY

Karl M. Park, Chairman
Mary Anna Bader
Paul D. Beatty, D. Min.
Ted W. Goins
Harry D. Hawthorne, D.D.
Luther L. Knauff

LAITY

Martha W. Agner
Robert Calhoon, Ph.D.
Bernard W. Cruse, Jr.
Gary R. Freeze
Bob L. Mowery
Catherine Safrit
Eleanor E. Sifford

1994 SUB-COMMITTEE

Karl M. Park
George L. Rhyne

Martha W. Agner
Bernard W. Cruse, Jr.

ADVISOR TO THE SUB-COMMITTEE

Martha Hines Morehead, Ph.D.

SYNODICAL STAFF LIAISON

George L. Rhyne

James A. Chesky

BISHOPS

Michael C. D. McDaniel, Ph.D.

Mark Wm. Menees, D.D.

CONTENTS

Samuel Rothrock   Amelia Arey Rothrock

The above photographs were reproduced with the name of the photographer, A.
Cronenberg, Wilmington, N. C., intact at the bottoms of the pictures. A number of
prints of this photo of Samuel Rothrock are extant. However, until August, 1982, no
one had been able to locate a photograph of Amelia Arey Rothrock. An old trunk had
been passed down through the Phebe Arey-Lewis Tobias Brown line to a descendant,
Boinest Brown. Originals of the above photographs were in that trunk. The trunk
contained a number of other photographs, but only the pictures of Samuel Rothrock
and the lady shown here bore the trademark of A. Cronenberg. Strong presumptive
evidence suggests the lady in the companion photograph is Amelia Arey Rothrock.
In her hand is a daguerrotype. It probably was a "likeness" of one of their children.
(Information from *Palatine Progeny* (p 150) by Harriet Arey Davidson, published by
Briarpatch Press, Davidson, NC, 1983)

REV. SAMUEL ROTHROCK, D.D.

The life of Samuel Rothrock is a study in humility, service, leadership, and love as Rothrock told the story of life through Jesus Christ to his parishioners in central North Carolina. His pastorate, begun in North Carolina at St. John's Evangelical Lutheran Church, Salisbury, was eventually to provide ministerial leadership for congregations not only throughout Rowan and surrounding counties, but also throughout the synod of North Carolina as well as in regional and national Lutheran organizations.

Samuel Rothrock was born on November 26, 1809, the fifth of nine children of Jacob and Esther Zeigler Rothrock. The family lived eight miles south of Salem in what was then Rowan, now Davidson County. They were members of Friedberg Moravian Church. Peter Rothrock, the grandfather of Samuel, had come to North Carolina from the York County area in Pennsylvania where a number of Rothrocks were located. The Rothrocks were said to be descendants of Huguenots, French Protestants who were persecuted in their homeland and sought refuge elsewhere. As did many other Protestants from bordering countries, the Rothrocks likely found refuge in the Palatinate before eventually finding religious freedom in America. The family name and burial ground are still evident in Leiselheim, Germany, a part of that section known as the Palatinate and now a suburb of Worms, the city where Martin Luther was tried.

Rev. F. W. E. Peschau, a friend and fellow pastor of Samuel Rothrock, was author of his biography, "Rev. S. Rothrock, D.D.," published in *American Lutheran Biographies; or, Historical Notices of Over Three Hundred and Fifty Leading Men of the American Lutheran Church, From Its Establishment to the Year 1890,* edited by Rev. J. C. Jensson and published in 1890 in Milwaukee, Wisconsin. No doubt Peschau had the privilege of personal information from Rothrock himself in describing events included in this story of the life of Samuel Rothrock.

Jacob, the father of Samuel, was a blacksmith until injured while shoeing a horse. Then he became a farmer. As a young boy, Samuel worked with his father as "striker" in the blacksmith shop and also with his father on the farm.

In addition to his work experiences of learning to survive in rural North Carolina, he attended "a regular old field school" for three months each year. The school was described as one in which "the cheapest teacher was the best, and his best aid was 'the birch,' and where every boy had to 'smart' when it pleased the teacher." From age six to fourteen he attended this school. While he worked on the family farm between his old field school days and his entry into Gettysburg Seminary, he probably had access to books from the nearby Moravian settlement. He did learn of the institution at Gettysburg from *The Lutheran Intelligencer,* the first English language Lutheran paper in the United States, and perhaps by word of mouth from travelers between the Moravian settlements at Salem, North Carolina, and Bethlehem, Pennsylvania, and also from family members who had remained in York, Pennsylvania.

It is likely that he applied and was accepted at Gettysburg before he set out on foot to walk the 400 miles from his home to the seminary. Rothrock was an inexperienced traveler at age nineteen years when he made a knapsack of home-made canvas, packed his home-made clothes, and his old Bible and started his long journey on Saturday, March 7, 1829, probably along the Great Wagon Road. On the journey he ate but twice a day, walking eight to ten miles before breakfast, and then walked until nighttime when he ate his evening meal. Along the road he walked through streams barefoot to keep his socks and shoes dry for the continued journey. On March 27, after twenty days, he arrived in Gettysburg to begin his theological education.

The two professors with whom he was most often associated at Gettysburg were S. S. Schmucker and E. L. Hazelius, two outstanding leaders in the Lutheran Church.

According to William Edward Eisenberg in *The Lutheran Church in Virginia 1717-1962* (p 150), Rev. Prof. Samuel Simon Schmucker (1799-1873), leader in establishing the Gettysburg Seminary, "began his ministry with the best and broadest educational foundation that any native born American Lutheran had received up to that time." He had attended York Academy in York, Pennsylvania, before enrollIng in the University of Pennsylvania in 1814 for two years. Later, in 1818 he entered Princeton for another two-year period.

Rev. Prof. Ernest Lewis Hazelius (1777-1853) was a professor at Gettysburg Seminary, 1830-1833. A biographical sketch in *A History of the Lutheran Church in South Carolina* (pp 862-63) provides further information regarding his background and accomplishments. He had been born in Prussia, educated at Barby, studied theology at Niesky under Moravian Bishop Anders, and received his Doctor of Divinity from Union College, Columbia, in 1824. He had come to America as Classical Teacher at Moravian School in Nazareth, Pennsylvania. He was licensed to preach prior to 1800 as a Moravian. The New York Lutheran Ministerium licensed him prior to 1809, the year in which the ministerium ordained him. Among his many biographical credits, including educator and author of note, is his leadership as professor at Southern Seminary for twenty years, 1834-1853, in the Lexington, South Carolina, location. A tablet in the chapel of Southern Seminary is thus inscribed to his memory: "He was a learned and consecrated servant of God. This Seminary is itself a memorial of his Spirit and of his faithful and self-sacrificing labors." This is the man for whom Samuel Rothrock would name his son, Lewis Hazelius Rothrock.

After Rothrock had been at Gettysburg for a year and a half, in the fall of 1830 he walked home again for an eighteen-day visit with his parents, returning to Gettysburg on foot.

In 1832, when he was twenty-three years of age, he had his first preaching experience; supplying the pulpit of Rev. Dr. John Daniel Kurtz at Chambersburg, Pennsylvania, where he preached for three weeks in German and in English during the springtime. Dr. Kurtz, a former director of the Lutheran Theological Seminary at Gettysburg, was a founder of the Maryland Synod and of the General Synod. Because of the illness of Dr. Kurtz, Rothrock also supplied the pulpit during the summer vacation.

Peschau wrote that Rothrock "borrowed some money to buy a horse and saddle, and reached home once more, at Christmas time, 1832. " Besides being in debt for the horse, he owed money to the Maryland Synod and The American Educational Society who had helped him through Seminary. It was in 1839 at the meeting of the General Synod at Chambersburg that he paid his debts and "returned South as he speaks of it, 'a free man.'"

At the end of his schooling in 1833, the North Carolina Synod, meeting at Friedens Church, licensed Rothrock to preach. In May 1834 he was ordained to the ministry by the North Carolina Synod, meeting in Wythe County, Virginia, then part of the North Carolina Synod.

As Peschau continued, from 1833 to mid-1835 Rothrock was pastor of "the old historical St. John's Church in Salisbury, N. C., in which the North Carolina Synod was organized in 1803." He also served Union Church and St. Paul's Church, then known as Holshauser's. He was called to Pennsylvania in 1835 where he served the churches in St. Thomas, Mercersburg, McConnellsburg, and Smoketown.

Dr. Martha Hines Morehead, one of the editors for *The Heritage and History of St. John's Evangelical Lutheran Church, Salisbury, North Carolina, through 1983*, noted the extent of Rothrock's ministry as follows when

... he returned to North Carolina in October of 1836, to serve once again "John's" and St. Paul's. In 1837 he was pastor of those churches and Union again as well. In 1839 he resigned from "John's," the "town church," but remained as pastor of St. Paul's and Union. Then in 1841, Luther's Church on the Stokes Ferry Road became another of the county churches in his care.

St. Paul's, Union, and Luther's comprised Rothrock's parish during 1842. He did not serve Union in 1843, but continued with St. Paul's and Luther's. In 1844, he remained with Luther's, left St. Paul's, returned to Union (just for that one year) and to "John's" in Salisbury, and also added Organ near Rockwell in Rowan County and St. Stephen's in Cabarrus County (three miles west of Gold Hill in Rowan County) to his pastoral responsibilities.

Thus in 1845 he was serving Organ, St. Stephen's, Luther's, and "John's"; however, from

1846 through 1853, he served only Organ and St. Stephen's, but in 1854 he added a third church, Lutheran (then called "Luther's") Chapel near China Grove. He continued with these three Rowan churches and in 1855 added a fourth, St. Peter's near Rockwell. Then from 1856 through 1866, he served only two churches — Organ and St. Peter's. To these, in 1867, he added St. Matthew's on the Bringle Ferry Road, Friedens in Guilford County, and St. Paul's in Alamance County. The next year he had all of these except St. Matthew's in his charge.

The year 1869 marked the end of this term of Rothrock's work as Organ's pastor, for in that year he began a new pastorate in west Rowan serving Salem on the Sherrill Ford Road and St. Luke's, which he organized at Bear Poplar. He served only these two churches until 1876 — with the exception of the time in 1872-73 when Bethel, also in Rowan, was in his charge as well. In 1876 he returned as pastor to Organ and St. Stephen's and in 1878 added New Bethel in Stanly County to this parish. In the following year, the size of this charge increased when a fourth church, Ebenezer on the Old Beatty Ford Road, was added to Organ, St. Stephen's, and New Bethel. From 1880 until 1885 Rothrock served only Organ and Ebenezer. He gave up Ebenezer in 1885, and St. Peter's was assigned to his care for 1885-86. In 1886 he resigned as pastor of Organ, the church he had served for a total of almost thirty-three years, the most time he had spent as pastor with any one church of the many in his entire ministry. He ended his active ministry after he returned to Luther's Church to serve as pastor in 1888 and 1889.

In addition to serving the many churches as pastor he also served as president of the North Carolina Synod in 1840, 1846, 1847, 1854, 1855, 1866, 1871, 1874, 1875, and 1880. He was secretary of Synod in 1837, 1838, 1839, 1844, and 1845 and treasurer 1834, 1876, 1877, 1878, and 1879. He was twice president of the Southern General Synod, 1849 and 1867. He also was a member of the Board of Western Carolina Male Academy which became North Carolina College.

The University of North Carolina at Chapel Hill awarded him the honorary degree of Doctor of Divinity in 1888. Throughout his lengthy pastorate Rev. Rothrock kept an almost daily record of his activities. The brief, informative entries, written in English, date from Saturday, February 1, 1834, to Sunday, July 2, 1893. Although some of the diaries are missing, those that are extant are published in this volume. *Life Sketches of Lutheran Ministers* (p 178) provides a view of Rothrock's work in the following summary:

It gives a good picture of a dedicated Lutheran pastor of the time in Piedmont North Carolina. Entries are short and factual. He preached in German and in English, sometimes in both at the same service. Text references are always given. He was diligent in catechizing, reconciling discord, visiting the sick, marrying couples (mostly in homes), and burying the dead. Four April confirmations at Organ Church (1851-57) were, respectively, of 46, 61, 53, and 62 persons. He mentions some 25-30 fellow pastors, in pastoral, official, or social relations, nearly all of whom served in N. C., and have sketches in this book. He taught school at times, farmed his land, took part in civic affairs, formed temperance and education-mission societies in churches, and served synod in official capacity. As a neighbor and good citizen, he helped regularly the local postmaster to prepare his quarterly reports, wrote wills, administered estates, conducted sales of property and "clerked" others, acted as guardian of minors, assisted with the mustering of troops, helped with house-rollings and barn-raisings, and did chores for neighbors. Voting in 1839 for the first time, he voted "for Charles Fisher for Congress and for free schools." In 1862 he made three trips to the war front to visit his son, who was wounded at Sharpsburg, and to preach to the troops and visit wounded ones in hospitals. He had bodies of some, presumably parishioners, exhumed and brought to Rowan Co., for burial.

At Synod Convention On May 3, 1883, Peschau wrote, the North Carolina Synod recognized Rothrock's fifty years in the ministry with "a special jubilee" and "presented him with a very handsome gold-headed cane." On that occasion Rothrock delivered "an interesting and able address in the Germanic part of the history of the North Carolina Synod."

Rev. Samuel Rothrock was first married to Miss Mary Hoke from Adams County, Pennsylvania. She and their newborn son died shortly after the birth in August 1836. With a broken heart but steadfast faith, Rothrock returned to Salisbury and Rowan County to begin anew his ministry to the Lutheran congregations in North Carolina.

In September 1837 Samuel Rothrock married Amelia Arey, daughter of Peter and Phebe Thomas Arey, and sister of his friend, Rev. Benjamin Arey. With his second wife, Amelia (1812-1890), as Peschau wrote, Rothrock "had the rare privilege, pleasure, and honor of celebrating his golden wedding."[1] Amelia and Samuel Rothrock had three children, but only their son Lewis lived past childhood. Their children were Lewis Hazelius (1839-1924), who served in the Confederate States Army, became a schoolmaster, taught at North Carolina College, and was principal of Mt. Pleasant Female Seminary 1876-1882; Milas Luther (1840-1842); and Charlotte Lucetta Jane (1847-1851).

In his 1890 biography of Rothrock, Peschau wrote,

> He resides in an elegant country residence of his own, near his son, Prof. Lewis Rothrock, at Gold Hill, N. C., an octogenarian who is universally esteemed, and whose name is a household word in hundreds of families, for he came in contact with many people of four generations, and always won golden opinions for himself. His pure life, his faithful services, his gentle manners, his Christian kindness, his rich experiences, and his full consecration to God and the Church have made this venerable Lutheran pastor, a man of whom our Church can be justly proud, for he brought us honor everywhere and in every way. May his last days on earth be his best.

Samuel Rothrock died on November 2, 1894,[2] at his home near Gold Hill and is buried at Union Lutheran Church, Rowan County.[3]

Martha W. Agner, Historical Committee
North Carolina Synod, ELCA

---

[1] See Appendix B.   [2] See Appendix C.   [3] See Appendix D.

WORKS CITED

Agner, Martha W. and Martha Hines Morehead. *The Heritage and History of St. John's Evangelical Lutheran Church through 1983.* Vol. 2, manuscript, 1994.

Brown, Backman S. *et al. Life Sketches of Lutheran Ministers, North Carolina and Tennessee Synods, 1773-1965.* Columbia SC: State Printing Co., 1966

Eisenberg, William Edward. *The Lutheran Church in Virginia, 1717-1962.* Lynchburg, VA: J. P. Bell, 1967.

Glatfelter, Charles H. *Pastors and People: German Lutheran and Reformed Churches in the Pennsylvania Field, 1717-1793.* 2 Vols. Breinigsville, PA: The Pennsylvania German Society, 1980. Vol. 1.

Jensson, Rev. J. C. *American Lutheran Biographies; or, Historical Notices of Over Three Hundred and Fifty Leading Men of the American Lutheran Church, From Its Establishment to the Year 1890.* Milwaukee: Rev. J. C. Jennson, 1890.

Morgan, Jacob L. *et al. History of the Lutheran Church in North Carolina.* Albemarle, NC: Press Printing Co., 1953.

McCullough, Paul G. *et al. A History of the Lutheran Church in South Carolina.* Columbia, SC: R. L. Bryan Co., 1971.

Wentz, Abdel Ross. *History of the Gettysburg Theological Seminary . . ., 1826-1926.* Philadelphia: United Lutheran Publication House, 1926.

PREFACE

In the past one hundred years, since the death of the Rev. Dr. Samuel Rothrock, several transcriptions have been made of the diaries he kept during his sixty years of ministry. These were typed and have been of great value to the genealogist searching in the Synod Archives and in the history room of the Rowan Public Library. This volume is the first actual publication of the diaries.

For the Synod Historical Committee to produce a near-perfect duplication of the entries in Rothrock's diaries has been a great joy and challenge. Using microfilm of the original diaries, Bernard William Cruse, Jr., of Concord, has meticulously transcribed and indexed with a computer the records as written in the 1800s by Rev. Samuel Rothrock. This project, accomplished indefatigably by Cruse over a period of several years, has truly been a labor of love, for which he is highly commended. These extant diaries are reproduced here in Volume I, along with appropiate appendixes and indexes, and a biography of the venerable pastor.

Harriet Arey Davidson, historian and genealogist, of Webster Groves, Missouri, generously volunteered to provide the annotations presented in Volume II. The annotations contain identification of pastors, places, people, and family relationships, plus pictures of people, houses, churches, tombstones, and sundry items — a genealogist's dream-come-true.

The initiation of the publication of these diaries came when Historical Committee Chairman Karl M. Park received a telephone call from Betty Dan Nicholas Gilliam in May 1990 stating that Archie Rufty might be willing to underwrite publication of the diaries of Rev. Samuel Rothrock if the North Carolina Synod would assume responsibility for the project. Pastor Park's letter to Mr. Rufty and the response in a telephone call from him confirmed this possibility, and the Synod Historical Committee agreed to the project. In July 1990, Pastor Park was in Las Vegas on other business but visited Archie and Frances Rufty to get their further ideas concerning the publication and confirmation of it. In August of that year, a sub-committee composed of Karl Park, Martha Agner and Eleanor Sifford was appointed to determine how to proceed. Permission was requested of Harriet A. Davidson to use the typescript copy of the Diaries she had provided for Mr. Rufty. He lent this typescript to us. Mrs. Davidson graciously agreed to the use of the typescript and volunteered to provide a biography and annotations. In addition to Mrs. Davidson's typescript, two other typescripts of the Diaries were located. The one by Bernard W. Cruse, Sr. is housed in the Synod Archives and the one by Edith Montcalm Clark is housed in the history room of the Rowan Public Library. These typescripts are valuable documents; however, for a publication of this magnitude we decided the original documents, now on microfilm, should be the source of the transcription by Bernard W. Cruse, Jr., as used here. Through the leadership of our commmittee chairman, Karl M. Park, this volume has been brought to completion. Pastor Park has also continued to oversee the preparation and publication of the *Annotations to the Samuel Rothrock Diaries* compiled by Harriet A. Davidson, soon to be published. We who are members of the Synod Historical Committee have been fortunate to serve with such a capable and dedicated leader.

These two volumes, the Diaries and the Annotations, will provide a treasury of historical information about life, religion, and relationships in central North Carolina for most of the nineteenth century. The publishing of this work has been made possible by the interest and generous support of Archibald Caldwell Rufty, a great-grandson of Pastor Rothrock. Mr. Rufty contributed valuable family documents in addition to assuming the entire cost of the publications.

Martha W. Agner
Historical Committee
North Carolina Synod
Evangelical Lutheran Church in America

THE SAMUEL ROTHROCK DIARIES

Dec. 1875.

Thurs. 9. In afternoon went to Mrs. Catharine Barringer's, & at night married Charles A. Miller & Ellen E. A. Barringer. After supper returned home.

Frid. 10. In forenoon called to see Eli ... being indisposed. In afternoon at home.

Sat. 11. Started for Salem Ch. Dinner at Phebe Brown's. All night at M. A. Bost's.

Sund. 12. Preached at Salem Ch. from Jam. 1:5. Dinner at ... At night preached in Salisbury from Acts 24:16. All night at Mr. O'Neal's.

Mond. 13. Returned home.

Tues. 14. At home. In afternoon sent my wagon to Mt. Pleasant with some flour &c for Lewis.

Wed. 15. Called in forenoon to see Eli Miller. In afternoon at home.

Thurs. 16. At home making a bridle.

Frid. 17. At home.

Sat. 18. A very cold day. Started for St. Luke's.

A Note to the Reader

To preserve the character and authenticity of the diaries we are not using the conventional system of annotation. To investigate the entries in Volume I, the reader should refer to the indexes to Volume I and the index to Volume II. To investigate the entries in Volume II, the reader should refer to the index in Volume II. Each of the annotations in Volume II refers the reader to a page number in Volume I.

The diaries are transcribed as they were written in the 1800s by Rev. Samuel Rothrock. There are variations in spelling, especially names and surnames; and variations in capitalization, abbreviation and punctuation within the framework of the diaries. Most of the spelling and capitalization variations result from the style of the time or a transitional blend of two languages, German and English. Some of the abbreviations he used are explained in annotations in Volume II.

Regrettably, a number of the original diaries are missing. The *Diaries* begin in this publication with "Diary No. 2nd" in 1834 and are arranged in chronological order to the final entry in 1893.

Diary No. 2$^{\underline{nd}}$

Sat. Feb. 1. This my day to preach at Hartman's, but the morning being very unpleasant, I did not go. Went to Mrs. Barringer's this evening and staid all night there. Attended a prayer meeting to night at Mr. Swink's & spoke some from John 5:40.

Sund. 2. Preached at Union English from 1 John 3:1.2. & german from John 3:16. to a large congregation. Preached in the afternoon at Mr. John Aronhart's from Josh. 24:15. Staid at Mr. Arey's to night.

Mond. 3. Went to town to day but left Mrs. R. at Mr. Arey's & at night returned again to Mr. Arey's.

Tues. 4. Went gunning some & shot several birds. To night married Mr. David Barringer to Miss Mary Arey.

Wed. 5. We returned to Salisbury. Had prayer meeting to night at Mr. Beard's & lectured from 1 John 3:1.2.

Thurs. 6. Visited some.

Frid. 7. At home.

Sat. 8. Preached at Wm. Foltz's from Rev. 2:4.5. & baptized 7 children, 6 of whom were his.

Sund. 9. Preached in Salisbury from Colos. 1:28. Did not go to Holshouser's ch. this afternoon in consequence of bad weather.

Mond. 10. Went to the country to visit the sick.

Tues. 11. Visited the sick in the country.

Wed. 12. At home. Had prayer meeting to night at Mr. Vogler's & lectured from Mark 1:35-45.

Thurs. 13. Visited the sick in the country.

Frid. 14. This afternoon went to the widow Peeler's together with Mrs. R.

Sat. 15. Preached the funeral of old Mr. Frick at Hartman's from Revl. 14:13. & baptized 2 children. Returned to Mrs. Peeler's.

Sund. 16. Preached at Union from Acts 17:30.31. to a large audience.

Mond. 17. This was a rainy day — Staid at Mrs. Peeler's — this evening Mrs. R. had the ague again very hard.

Tues. 18. We went to Mr. Arey's.

Wed. 19. This was a rainy day — amused myself some by shooting birds & for the first time shot a wild duck. The rain prevented me from attending my prayer meet. in town this evening.

Thurs. 20. Rode to town & at night returned to Mr. Arey's again.

Frid. 21. At Mr. Arey's.

Sat. 22. Preached at Mr. Corl's from Phil. 3:20.21. Returned to Mr. Arey's.

Sund. 23. Preached in Salisbury from Acts 24:25. & in the afternoon at Holshouser's from the same text. Returned at night to Mr. Arey's.

Mond. 24. At Mr. Arey's.

Tues. 25. Shot 3 wild ducks this morning, then went to Salis. Returned to Mr. Arey's again where I had prayer meeting to night. Mr. Jenkins being present addressed the people.

Wed. 26. Attended to the funeral of Mr. Geo. Kesler's child at Union — preached from Amos 4:12. Had prayer meet. to night at Mr. Murphey's & lectured from Amos 4:12.

Thurs. 27. Returned to the country to Mr. Arey's.

Frid. 28. Preached at Mr. Abraham Arey's from John 3:16.

Thurs. May 1. Went as far as Mr. Edwards' at the foot of the Blue Ridge. 43 miles. Entertainment very indifferent but horse fare good.

Frid. 2. Went to Mr. Ahart's in Wythe County, Va. fare very good.

Sat. 3. Arrived at St. Paul's ch. in Wythe Co., Va. where the Synod held its annual session.

Sund. 4. This was a rainy day. Preached a short sermon at the stand from John 8:36.

Mond. 5. Synod commenced its business. Preached 11 o'clock from Hosea 13:9.

Tues. 6. In Synod. To night the ministerium met in session at Revd J. Sherer's house. Was examined to night preparatory to ordination.

Wed. 7. Was solemnly ordained to day & set apart for the ministry. Preached to night at Mr. Wampler's in the neighborhood from Math. 8:2.3.

Thurs. 8. Preached at Mr. Naves from John 3:16.

Frid. 9. Went to St. John's church near Wythe Court-house & preached from John 3:16.

Sat. 10. Preached in the same place in german from Luke 13:24.

Sund. 11. Preached at the stand from Hebr. 2:3.

Mond. 12. Started for home & went to Edward's at the foot of the mountain. fare very indifferent.

Tues. 13. Went to Conrad's — delightfully entertained.

Wed. 14. Went to father's and took dinner. Staid all night at Jacob Sinks.

Thurs. 15. Arrived at home.

Frid. 16. At home.

Sat. 17. Went to the country to visit the sick & preached at Hartman's from Ephes. 5:18. on the subject of drunkenness.

Sund. 18. Preached at Union from Hebr. 2:3. to a crowded house. In the afternoon attended to the funeral of Mr. James Dun in Salisbury.

Mond. 19. Went to the country to visit the sick.

Tues. 20. Attended to the funeral of Geo. Smith's child at Jacob Smith's & preached from Ps. 97:11.

Wed. 21. Went to the country to see the sick. At night went to hear preaching in the Methodist ch.

Thurs. 22. At home.

Frid. 23. At home.

Sat. 24. At home.

Sund. 25. Preached In Salisbury from Prov. 14:32. & in the afternoon at Holshou. from the same text.

Mond. 26. Went to the country for butter &c.

Tues. 27. Had my stable raised.

Wed. 28. At home - had prayer meeting to night at Mr. Vogler's & lectured from Matt. 18:1-6.

Thurs. 29. Went to the country to day to Mr. Arey's, he having sent a horse for Mrs. R. to ride out.

Frid. 30. Had catechization at Union.

Sat. 31. At Mr. Arey's, made some preparation to preach on Sabbath.

Sund. June 1. Preached at Union from Prov. 1:24.25.26. In the afternoon had three funerals at the same place viz. Widow Cawble, Peter Aronhart's child, & Mr. Ruffta's child. Preached from 2 Cor. 5:1.

Mond. 2. Returned to Salisbury.

Tues. 3. At home.

Wed. 4. Had prayer meeting to night at Mr. Fraley's & lectured from Matt. 16:1-12.

Thurs. 5. At home.

Frid. 6. This morning Mother & Adam came to see us. At home to day.

Sat. 7. Attended to the funeral of Mr. David Brown ^{Senr} at his house & preached from Ps. 31:4.5.

Sun. 8. Preached in Salisbury from 2 Peter 3:9. & in the afternoon at Holshouser's from the same text and baptized 1 infant.

Mond. 9. To day I sent mother and Adam home in a private conveyance, the seats in the Stage having all been taken up on the preceding evening.

Tues. 10. Went to the country to Mr. Hartman's to get boards to cover my stable.

Wed. 11. At home. Had prayermeeting to night at Mr. Moses Brown's and lectured from Matt. 18:7-18.

Thurs. 12. At home.

Frid. 13. Had catechization at Union.

Sat. 14. Preached at Hartman's from 2 Peter 3:9. baptized one infant & then had catechization.

Sund. 15. Preached at Union from 1 Peter 4:18. & then German from the same text.

Mond. 16. At home. Tues. 17. At home.

Wed. 18. At home. Had prayermeeting to night at Mr. Beard's & lectured from the Epistle to Philemon.

Thurs. 19. At home.

Frid. 20. Went to father's to attend protracted meeting at Opossumtown.

Sat. 21. Preached at Opossumtown from Hebr. 2:3. All night at father's.

Sund. 22. Preached at the same place from Prov. 14:32. to a large concourse of people.

Mond. 23. Returned to Salisbury.

Tues. 24. At home.

Wed. 25. At home. Had prayermeeting to night at Mr. Vogler's & lectured from 2 Cor. 5:1-10.

Thurs. 26. At home.

Frid. 27. Had catechization at Union.

Sat. 28. At home.

Sund. 29. Had no preaching to day in Salisbury in consequence of a Sacramental occasion in the Presbyterian church. Attended the Presbyterian church. In the afternoon preached at Holshouser's from Ephes. 6:18.

Mond. 30. At home.

Tues. July 1. At home.

Wed. 2. Attended to the funeral of Mr. Andrew Brown at his residence & preached from Job. 14:14.

Thurs. 3. At home working at my stable.

Frid. 4. At home.

Sat. 5. Preached at Hartman's from Rev. 3:20. in German & after preaching had catechization at the same place.

Sund. 6. Preached at Union to day from Exodus 33:14. & in the afternoon had prayermeeting at Mr. Heilig's.

Mond. 7. Attended to the funeral of Adam Casper's child at the Germ. Reformed Church called the Stone church & preached from Rev. 14:13.

Tues. 8. At home till evening, then went to old Mr. Mull's to purchase some oats for my horse.

Wed. 9. Had prayermeeting to night at Mr. Mosses Brown's — lectured on no particular subject.

Thurs. 10. At home.

Frid. 11. Had catechization at Union.

Sat. 12. At home.

Sund. 13. Preached in Salisbury from John 20:20. & baptized 2 children. In the afternoon at Holshouser's from the same text & in the evening attended to the funeral of Mr. Harris' child in Salisbury preached from 1 Cor. 15:26.

Mond. 14. At home.

Tues. 15. To day Mrs. R. went to Lincolnton in company with Mr. Vogler & family, to night I staid at Mr. Crawford's.

Wed. 16. At home. Had prayermeeting to night at Mr. Beard's - lectured from no particular subject — all night at Mr. Crawford's.

Thurs. 17. Went to the country to Mr. Arey's.

Frid. 18. Had catechization at Union.

Sat. 19. This was my regular day to preach at Hartman's, but did not attend in consequence of the inclemency of the weather.

Sund. 20. Preached to day at Union from Prov. 22:6. on the duty of parents to children. All night at Mr. Vogler's.

Mond. 21. Preached to day at Savages Church from Luk. 13:24. All night at John M. Walcher's.

Tues. 22. Went on to Lincolnton. All night at Col. John Hoke's.

Wed. 23. Went to see the cotton factory 2 miles from town, which is indeed a great curiosity, displaying in eminent degree the ingenuity of man.

Thurs. 24. Started back to Salisbury, all night at Mr. Rose's — cost 62½ cts.

Frid. 25. Returned to Salis. & in the evening went to Mr. Arey's.

Sat. 26. Had catechization at Union in the afternoon had a temperance meeting at Wm. Smith's & met with considerable success. At night attended a prayermeeting at widow Krider's.

Sund. 27. Preached at Swicegood's church in Davidson Co. Luk. 13:24. Germ. John 3:16. English. To day Revd D. Jenkins preached for me in Salisbury & Holshouser's.

Mond. 28. Started for Lincolnton to bring Mrs. R. home — all night at Mr. Conner's, a fine old Presbyterian.

Tues. 29. Went to Lincolnton.

Wed. 30. Started back for Salisbury. All night at Mr. Conner's.

Thurs. 31. Arrived in Salisbury.

Frid. August 1. Had catechization at Union.

Sat. 2. Went to Loenard's ch. in Davidson Co. to attend a special conference appointed by our Synod. Preached from Luk. 13:24. all night a father's.

Sund. 3. At Loenard's ch. preached Germ. from John 3:16. English from Hosea 13:9. Then assisted in the administration of the Lord's Sup., after which preached Eng. again from John 3:16. At night attended a prayermeeting at Jacob Loenard's.

Mond. 4. Returned to Salisbury.

Tues. 5. Wed. 6. At home.

Thurs. 7. At home.

Frid. 8. Had catechization at Union.

Sat. 9. At home.

Sund. 10. Preached in Salisbury from Isaiah 55:7. & in the afternoon at Holshouser's from the same text.

Mond. 11. At home, having had company.

Tues. 12. Went to Mr. Barringer's to borrow some money to pay Mr. Mull for my house & lot. Obtained $60.

Wed. 13. Had prayermeeting to night at Mr. Vogler's & lectured on the subject of prayer.

Thurs. 14. Went to the country to day to Mr. Arey's, he having sent in a horse for Mrs. R. to ride out.

Frid. 15. Had catechization at Union.

Sat. 16. Preached at Hartman's from Isaiah 55:7. & after preaching had catechization. Returned to Mr. Arey's.

Sund. 17. Preached at Union to a crowded from Prov. 14:32. Returned to Mr. Arey's.*

Mond. 18. Wrote some articles of agreement for a school & in the afternoon went with Mrs. R. to Mr. Jacob Brown's - staid here all night.

Tues. 19. This morning borrowed of Mr. Brown $90 to pay to Mr. Mull. Returned again to Mr. Arey's.

Wed. 20. Returned to Salisbury, but Mrs. R. staid at Mr. Arey's. Had prayermeeting to night at Mr. Fraley's & spoke some on the duty of repentance.

Thurs. 21. Returned to Mr. Arey's & on my way out married Miss Catherine Heilig to Mr. Peter Peck.

Frid. 22. Had catechization at Union. In the afternoon we returned home to Salisbury.

Sat. 23. Attended the funeral of Mr. Henry Hohnbarger's son at the Organ church & preached from Math. 25:13. After the funeral called to see Revd Graeber & took dinner with him, then returned home.

Sund. 24. Preached at Salis. from Gal. 6:14. & in the afternoon at Holshouser's from the same text.

Mond. 25. To day Revd Graeber was with me & we together made a distribution of the Minutes of our Synod.

Tues. 26. Visited some in Salisbury.

Wed. 27. At home. Had prayermeeting to night at Mr. Moses Brown's & lectured briefly from Prov. 4:18.

Thurs. 28. Attended to the funeral of Mr. Samuel Fraley's child & preached from 2 Sam. 12:23.

Frid. 29. Had catechization at Union.

Sat. 30. Preached at Holshouser's preparatory to the Lord's Supper. Preached from 1 Cor. 5:8. baptized 4 children & admitted 7 to church membership by confirmation. Staid all night at Mr. Randleman's.

Sund. 31. This was a very rainy, inclement day. Had communion at Holshouser's ch., admitted one to church privileges by confirmation. Preached from John 7:37. & then administered the Lord's Supper to 67 communicants. After services returned home. Got wet with rain.

*Baptized to day 2 children at Union.

Mond, Sept. 1. At home. Wrote a letter to br. Jacob.

Tues. 2. At home. Wrote a letter to B. Arey at Gettysburg - not very well to day.

Wed. 3. Attended to the funeral of Mr. Beever's child at Holshouser's — felt very unwell to day - had prayer meeting appointed for to night but did not attend in consequence of indisposition.

Thurs. 4. At home & sick.

Frid. 5. This was my day to have catechization at Union, but being sick I could not attend.

Sat. 6. This was my day to preach at Hartman's, but could not attend in consequence of sickness.

Sund. 7. This was my regular day to preach at Union, but could not attend in consequence of sickness.

Mond. 8. At home & sick.

Tues. 9. Wed. 10. Thurs. 11. Frid. 12. Sat 13. At home & gradually recovering from my sickness.

Sund. 14. This was my regular day to preach in Salisbury & Holshouser's but was unable to attend, being yet too weak from my sickness.

Mond. 15. For the first time went up the street.

Tues. 16. At home.

Wed. 17. To day we intended going to the country but were disappointed.

Thurs. 18. Went to the country to Mr. Arey's with the intention of boarding.

Frid. 19. Had catechization at Union, then went to Salisbury & had our trunks brought out on Mr. Arey's waggon. On my way back was called to go to little John Cawble's to see his wife - found her very sick & baptized her the same evening, she having expressed a desire to receive this ordinance. Staid all night here.

Sat. 20. Cloudy & rainy. Returned to Mr. Arey's early this morning. To day a protracted meeting or special conference commenced at Union. Had the Revd Messrs. Graeber, Jenkins & Harris to assist me. To day Revd Graeber first preached in German, & Rev^d. Jenkins succeeded him in English. After which I baptized one adult viz. Camilla Earnhart. Then confirmed thirty three persons, viz 18 females & 15 males & also baptized & confirmed 1 colored man. Then attended to the services preparatory to communion. Baptized also 1 infant. Had prayermeeting to night at Mr. Arey's.

Sund. 21. Very rainy. Revd Graeber preached in German & Revd Harris in English. The clergy having communed, a large number lay persons communed also. Prayermeeting to night at Jacob Brown's, conducted by D. Jenkins.

Mond. 22. Preaching continued. Revd Graeber preached in English & was succeeded by Revd D. Jenkins, who flatly contradicted what had been said & thus caused much dissatisfaction & wounded the feelings of many, which caused the meeting to be discontinued. This evening in a private conference Mr. Jenkins was very impertinent & insulting towards Revd Graeber & evinced a great want of the Spirit of the gospel & a defective knowledge of the plan of salvation & the nature of conversion.

Tues. 23. Went to Salisbury & returned again in the evening.

Wed. 24. At home all day, it being a very rainy day.

Thurs. 25. Visited Mr. Trexler's, Harris & widow Barringer's.

Frid. 26. At home.

Sat. 27. Went to St. John's church in Cabarrus County, to attend a Special Conference appointed by the Synod - preached from Heb. 2:3. At night preached at Mr. Blackwelter's in German from Math. 8:1-3.

Sund. 28. It was the design to have communion to day at St. John's ch. but the rains poured down in such torrents that we could not get to the church. All night at Mr. Blackwelter's.

Mond. 29. Returned home to Mr. Arey's.

Tues. 30. Went to Salisbury - Returned in the evening.

Wed. Oct. 1. At home.

Thurs. 2. At home.

Frid. 3. At home.

Sat. 4. Went to Hartman's to preach there (it being my regular day) but it was not generally known & the people did not attend. Went to Henry Ludwig's in the afternoon & had a prayermeeting there & administered the Lord's Supper to his mother-in-law, Mrs. Eddleman who is very old & decrepit.

Sund. 5. Preached at Union from John 8:36. & baptized one child, after which the Revd F. F. Harris also preached an edifying sermon to the congregation.

Mond. 6. Commenced my school.

Tues. 7. In my school.

Wed. 8. In my school.

Thurs. 9. Went to Salisbury, & in the afternoon to the widow Rosemon's & married George Randleman to Eliza Rosamon. All night here.

Frid. 10. Returned to Mr. Arey's in the morning & then attended to my school.

Sat. 11. At home in my study.

Sund. 12. Preached in Salisbury from Acts 16:30.31. & baptized one infant. In the afternoon preached at Holshouser's from Rom. 6:23. a funeral. Returned home in the evening.

Mond. 13. In my school.

Tues. 14. Mrs. R. being very sick, I had to dispense with my school to day & stay at home.

Wed. 15. At home to day, Mrs. R. being very sick.

Thurs. 16. At home, Mrs. R. being very sick.

Frid. 17. Went to town to day.

Sat. 18. Preached at Hartman's to day from Ps. 73:1. & baptized one infant. Returned home at night.

Sund. 19. Preached at Union from Hosea 13:9. Mrs. R. still very sick.

Mond. 20. At home.

Tues 21. At home to day. I was taken sick with Ague & fever.

Wed. 22. At home & sick. Mrs. R. also very sick yet.

Thurs. 23. Very sick to day, sent for the doctor & obtained relief by bleeding. Mrs. R. still sick.

Frid. 24. Still sick & Mrs. R. also.

Sat. 25. Some better to day & Mrs. R. some better also. On to day I had appointed preaching at Union, but was prevented from attending by sickness.

Sund. 26. This was my regular day to preach in Salisbury & at Holshou. but was prevented by sickness.

Mond. 27. A good deal better to day both myself & Mrs. Rothrock.

Tues. 28. Very sick to day again.

Wed. 29. Felt some better — to day we went to Salisbury & staid all night at Mr. Vogler's.

Thurs. 30. Very unwell, staid at Mr. Vogler's till noon. Then went to Mrs. Fisher's & staid there till Sat. Nov. 1st.

Sat. Nov. 1st. Started to father's. Staid all night at Jacob Sink's & arrived at father's next day. Staid at father's & felt pretty well until the following friday. Then we went to Salem, & when we returned in the evening, we both took sick again, & were then obliged to stay at father's until the 3rd of December, when we started for Salisbury. Staid all night at Jacob Link's & next day arrived in Salisbury.

Frid. Decem. 5. We returned to Mr. Arey's.

Sat. 6. At home at Mr. Arey's.

Sund. 7. This was my regular day to preach at Union, but as I did not feel able to preach I did not turn out. Spent the day in reading the Bible.

Rowan County, N. C.
December 30, 1834
Diary No. 3rd

Mond. 8. At home & not very well. During this week I was sick with the Ague, in consequence of which I studied very little.

Sund. 14. I had allotted to preach on this day in Salisbury, as it was my regular day, but not being well enough, I staid at home.

Mond. 15. To day I commenced my school again & taught this the week out.

Wed. 17. This evening I had prayermeeting at Mr. Arey's & lectured from Ps. 27:4.

Sat. 20. Preached at Hartman's from Ps. 27:4. Returned home after service.

Sund. 21. Preached at Union from 2 Cor. 4:7. & baptized two children. After preaching attended to the funeral Services of Mr. Hartman's child.

Mond. 22. Attended to my school till Wednesday evening.

Thurs. 25. This was Christmas day – to day I preached at John Earnhart's from Matt 1:21. to a crowded house, & baptized 4 children for Elias Earnhart.

Frid. 26. To day I had a severe attack again of the ague.

Sat. 27. To day I went to Salis. & staid with Jeremiah Brown. To day I sold my house & lot to Mr. William Murphy.

Sund. 28. This was my day to preach in Salisbury, but having the Ague severely, I could not attend to it. In the afternoon attended preaching in the Court House by an independent Hinklehite.

Mond. 29. Returned home.

Tues. 30. At home. Had to dispense with my school to day in consequence of indisposition.

Wed. 31. At home.

Thurs. Jan. 1, 1835. This was New Year, but in consequence of sickness, I could have no appointment for to day. At home.

Frid. 2. Went to Salisbury with Mrs. Roth. & Mrs. Arey. Returned home in the evening.

Sat. 3. This was my day to preach at Hartman's, but not being well & weather threatening, did not turn out.

Sund. 4. This was an excessive cold day. Attended at Union church, but the congregation being small & the weather very cold, dispensed with preaching but gave the people an exhortation from Ps 73:1. & baptized one infant.

Mond. 5. At home.

Tues. 6. Wed. 7. Thurs. 8. Frid. 9. Sat. 10. At home.

Sund. 11. This was my day to preach in Salisbury, but not being well & the weather cold, did not turn out.

Mond. 12. Went to Salisbury.

Tues. 13. At home.

Wed. 14. Went to Salisbury. Had prayermeeting to night at Mr. Vogler's & lectured from Ps. 119:63.

Thurs. 15. Returned home, & then went to Nicholas Barringer's & married Ambrose Eddleman to Elizabeth Barringer. Returned home in the evening.

Frid. 16. Went to J. Barringer's, had prayermeeting there to night & lectured from Eph. 5:14. Staid all night here.

Sat. 17. Preached at Hartman's from Ps. 119:63. & there made an effort to form a Temperance Society.

Sund. 18. Preached the funeral of Mr. Hartman's child at Union from Job 14:14. & in the evening attended a prayermeeting at Mr. Arey's.

Mond. 19. Attended to the funeral of Philip Brown's wife, but did not preach for want of time.

Tues. 20. Went to Salisbury.

Wed. 21. At home.

Thurs. 22. Went to see Thom. Mull, who was very sick.

Frid. 23. Attended to the funeral of Wm. Smith's Junr child at J. Smith's but did not preach in consequence of being too unwell.

Sat. 24. Attended a meeting at Union ch. to consult on building a parsonage on the land belonging to the church.

Sund. 25. Preached in Salisbury from Matt. 11:28. & at 2 o'clock, preached Mr. Tho. Mull's funeral from Job 30:23. at his residence.

Mond. 26. At home.

Tues. 27. Attended to the funeral of Stuffle Lyerlie's child at Union ch. Preached from Luk. 12:37. at his residence.

Wed. 28. Thurs. 29. Frid. 30. At home, engaged in giving instruction to Mr. Arey's children.

Sat. 31. Preached at Hartman's from Luk. 18:9-14.

Sund. Feb. 1. Preached at Union from Isai. 55:7. & baptized one child.

Mond. 2. Went to Salisbury to the Post Office.

Tues. 3. Wed. 4. At home, giving instruction to Mr. A.'s children.

Thurs. 5. At home till 12 o'clock, then went to Mr. Wise's shop & had my horse shod.

Frid. 6. Went to Philip Brown's & preached the funeral of his wife Dec. from 2 Tim. 4:7.8. Had prayermeeting to night at Wm. Folts' & staid all night with him.

Sat. 7. Attended the Smith's Sabbath School Anniversary at Mrs. Krider's, afterwards returned home.

Sund. 8. This was my day to preach in Salisbury, but as the day was so excessively cold, did not turn out.

Mond. 9. At home, giving instructions to Mr. A.'s children.

Tues. 10. At home, giving instruction, &c.

Wed. 11. Went to Salisbury to the Post office & received a letter from brother Jacob, living in the State of Indiana. Also from Revd J. Sherer & Revd J. Ruthrauff.

Thur. 12. Frid. 13. At home giving instruction to Mr. Arey's children.

Sat. 14. Preached a Temperance Sermon at Hartman's from Rom. 13:13. and after preaching organized a Temperance Society, which 21 persons joined — was assisted to day by Mr. Lemly.

Sund. 15. Preached at Union on the subject of <u>Lewdness</u> from Ex. 20:14. & announced my valedictory.

Mond. 16. Went to Salisbury to the Post office & received a letter from Revd S. Harkey.

Tues. 17. Started to Salisbury but turned back again in consequence of the inclemency of the the weather.

Wed. 18. Went to Salisbury — returned home again in the evening.

Thurs. 19. At home reading.

Frid. 20. At home — had a severe attack of the ague to day.

Sat. 21. Was to have attended a Temperance meeting to day at Cochenours School house, but did not attend in consequence of indisposition.

Sund. 22. Preached in Salisbury to day from 2 Cor. 5:17. In the afternoon went to Holshouser's & commenced my Sermon, but could not get through in consequence of being too much indisposed.

Mond. 23. Went to Salisbury to make preparations to move back to town. Rented Mr. Crawford's house & issued Articles for a school. Met with Revd Jenkins in town & took him along home with me.

Tues. 24. At home sick with the ague.

Wed. 25. Went to Jacob Brown's in the afternoon to make some settlements with him & to purchase some grain.

Thurs. 26. At home sick with the ague.

Frid. 27. At home.

Sat. 28. This was my day to preach at Hartman's, but as the weather was inclement & feeling too unwell, did not turn out.

Sund. March 1. This was my day to preach at Union, but did not attend in consequence of indisposition & the inclemency of the weather.

Mond. 2. At home. Transcribed some old records for Mr. Arey, the remainder of the day sick with the ague.

Tues. 3. Went to Salisbury. Settled with some of my creditors, & exchanged some South-money for U. S. to send to the North, to square some of my accounts there.

Wed. 4. At home, sick with the ague.

Thurs. 5. At home. Transcribed some old records for Mr. Arey, & did some writing for myself.

Frid. 6. At home, & had the ague.

Sat. 7. Went to Mr. H. Trexler's on business but did not find him at home.

Sund. 8. This was my regular day to preach in Salisbury, but being indisposed & the weather inclement, did not attend.

Mond. 9. Went to Salisbury to the P. O. returned home in the evening.

Tues. 10. At home, making preparations to move to town.

Wed. 11. Moved to Salisbury into Mr. Crawford's house which I rented.

Thurs. 12. At home, putting things in order.

Frid. 13. Attended a while at the sale of Mr. Mull dec^d.

Sat. 14. At home & indisposed in consequence of the ague.

Sund. 15. Preached my valedictory at Union from 2 Cor. 13:5. Spoke with great freedom. Baptized 2 infants.

Mond. 16. Attended to the funeral of Mrs. Brown, consort of James Brown, at his residence. Preached from Amos 4:12.

Tues. 17. Went to Mrs. Steel's to hire a negro girl. Worked a little in the garden.

Wed. 18. At home. Worked a little in the garden.

Thurs. 19. Settled with some of my creditors.

Frid. 20. At home.

Sat. 21. Went to John Cawble's and baptized 3 of his children.

Sund. 22. Preached in Salisbury from Gal. 6:7. & in the afternoon at Holshouser's from 2 Cor. 5:17.

Mond. 23. Commenced my school in Salisbury.

Tues. 24. Had school till 12 o'clock, in the afternoon attended to the funeral of Wm. Loch's child in Salisbury.

Wed. 25. In school. Had prayermeeting at night at Mrs. Fraley's & lectured from Acts 24:1-21.

Thurs. 26. Frid. 27. In school.

Sat. 28. Preached my valedictory at Hartman's from 2 Cor. 5:17.

Sund. 29. Preached in Salisbury from 2 Kings 5:1-14. In the afternoon preached the funeral of John Kerns' child at Peter Kerns, from Heb. 4:9.

Mond. 30. Tues. 31. In school.

Wed. April 1. In school. Had prayermeeting to night at Mr. Vogler's & lectured from Math. 8:23-27.

Thurs. 2. Frid. 3. In school.

Sat. 4. At home.

Sund. 5. Preached at Holshouser's from Luk. 18:9-14. At night attended a prayermeeting at Charles Verble's & lectured from Rev. 2:4.5.

Mond. 6. Tues. 7. in school.

Wed. 8. In school. Had prayermeeting to night at Moses Brown & lectured from Math. 15:21-28.

Thurs. 9. In school. Frid. 10. In school.

Sat. 11. At home.

Sund. 12. Preached in Salisbury from Matthew 5:13-16. In the afternoon attended preaching in the Methodist church. At night attended a prayermeeting at Mr. Heilig's & lectured from Acts 17:30.31.

Mond. 13. Tues. 14. In School.

Wed. 15. In school till 12 o'clock, in the afternoon had the ague. This was the regular evening for prayermeeting, but dispensed with it in consequence of indisposition.

+Thurs. 16. In school till 12 o'clock in the afternoon at home.

Frid. 17. At home. Was to have attended the funeral of Philip Brown's child to day, but did not attend in consequence of indisposition — had the ague to day.

Sat. 18. At home.

Sund. 19. Preached in Salis. from John 7:37. In the afternoon was to have preached a funeral at Wm. Smith's Junr, but could not attend in consequence of indisposition. Had the Ague very hard this afternoon.

Mond. 20. Dismissed my school for this week, being too indisposed to attend to it.

Tues. 21. Wed. 22. At home

Thurs. 23. Went to Mr. P. Arey's & then to widow Butner's & married David Miller to Eliz. Butner.

Frid. 24. At home.

Sat. 25. Went to Mr. Crawford's & to Moses Brown's Senr.

Sund. 26. Attended to the funeral of Jacob Beaver at Holshouser's ch. Preached from Heb. 4:9.

Mond. 27. Having resolved to leave N. Carolina, I dismissed my school entirely. At home, making some preparations for Synod.

Tues. 28. Went to see Revd Sparrow & Revd Spears in the forenoon. In the afternoon at home & unwell.

Wed. 29. At home & sick.

Thurs. 30. At home, sick & took medicine from Dr. Mitchel.

+ Married to day Peter Trexler to Eliz. C. Miller. Also David Beaver to Abaline Hartman, all at my house.

Frid., May 1. to Wed. 6. Sick & in the Doctor's hands. During this time our Synod held it's session in the Luth. ch. in Salisbury, but in consequence of my indisposition I was unable to attend it — this appeared a great self-denial. On Wednesday the brethren all started for their homes again.

Thurs. 7. to Sund. 10. Able to be up in my room. Sunday I had promised to preach a funeral at Jerusalem ch. but was unable to go.

Mond. 11. Walked up street.

Tues. 12. Walked up street to make some settlements.

Wed. 13. At home.

Thurs. 14. Being about to trade with David Kerns for his horse to work in a carriage to the North, tried him in harness & found him very gentle & true, but did not agree in the trade.

Frid. 15. Went to see Mr. Kerns about his horse, but did not make a bargain.

Sat. 16. Assisted some in moving Wm. Murphy's house — exchanged horses with Mr. Kerns, gave him mine for his and 10 dollars.

Sund. 17. Preached my valedictory at Holshouser's from Matthew 5:13-16. & baptized five infants.

Mond. 18. Settling my business & attended a political meeting & heard some eloquent speeches, particularly by the Governor of the State.

Tues. 19. Settling my business.

Wed. 20. Settling my business & packed my books to move.

Thurs. 21. Had sale to day & disposed of all our property preparative to leaving N. Carolina.

Frid. 22. Went to Mr. Arey's in the country, to remain there until ready to start on our journey.

Sat. 23. At Mr. Arey's & not very well.

Sund. 24. Preached my valedictory in Salisbury from 2 Cor. 13:11. In the afternoon attended a prayer meeting at Widow Peeler's.

Mond. 25. Went to Jacob Brown's to settle with him.

Tues. 26. Went to Salisbury.+

Wed. 27. At Mr. Arey's.

Thurs. 28. Went to John Wise's & then to Salisbury & closed my settlements in town.

Frid. 29. Went to Jacob Brown's & closed my settlements with him. Then went to John Wise's & after some unpleasant occurrences, closed my settlements with him.

Sat. 30. Went to Salisbury & got ready to start & at 3 o'clock P.M. left town for Penn[a]. All night a Jacob Sinks.

Sund. 31. Went to Father's. Had promised to preach for Rev[d] Shuls in the Moravian ch. on this day, but could not reach there in time.

+ This evening married Charles Barringer to Elizabeth Arey.

Mond. June 1. Started from father's at 8½ o'clock A.M. for Penn^a and travelled 18 miles. All night at Mr. Thompson's supper & lodg. 75 cts.

Tues. 2. Travelled 24 miles. Breakfast at Kish Saunders 75 cts. horse fed at Braswells 25 cts. Rain in the afternoon, during which time stopped at Widow Sharp's fodder for horse 10 cts. All night at N. Wrights supper & lodg. 1.00 hostler 6¼.

Wed. 3. — 27 miles. Breakfast at Courts, 75 cts. accommodations bad. Dinner at Mr. Hesee's 75 cts. bad accommodations. All night at Sullevans in Danville. Supper & lodg. 1.25 hostler 6¼.

Thurs. 4. — 20 miles. Crossing Dan river 35 cts. breakfast at Wilkinson's 75 cts, good accom. all night at Carter's in Halifax Co., Va. Supper & lodg. 1.25. Tormented by the bed bugs.

Frid. 5. — 23 miles. Breakfast at Mr. Vaughn's 75 cts. bad accom, horse fed at Mr. Lewellin's, Halifax C. H. 25 cts, candy 31¼ cts. — all night at Mr. Youngers. supper & lodging 1.25. bat accom.

Sat. 6. — 18 miles. Breakfast at Mr. Harris' Mt. Laurel 75 cts. Dinner, supper & lodging at Mrs. Lewis' 1.50 — remained here from 2 o'clock till next morning in consequence of rain — ferriage at Staunton river to day 25 cts.

Sund. 7. — 31 miles. Breakfast at Mr. Smith's Charlotte C. H. 75 cts. good accom. — all night at Mr. King's Prince Edward 1.25 accom. tolerable.

Mond. 8. — 34 miles. Breakfast at Reyns' 1.00 — all night at Woodson's. Supper & lodg. 1.50 good accom.

Tues. Tues. [written twice] 9. — 33 miles. Breakfast at McKoy's in Cartersville 1.00 good accom. crossing James river 42 cts. horse fed at Mills' 25 cts. — all night at Walton's in Louisa Co., an old Baptist. Supper & lodg. 1.44, accom. tolerable.

Wed. 10 — 27 miles. Breakfast at Mr. Holladay's 75 cts. very good accom. all night at Mr. Wiglesworth's in Mt. Pleasant, supper & lodg. 1.50, accom. tolerable.

Thurs. 11. — 20 miles to Fredericksburg. Breakfast at Allsops 87½ cents. hog-jaw the principal diet. Stopped at Bowen & Ramsy's in Fredericksg. lodg. & breakfast 2.37½. Repairs to the carriage 37½ cts. Took the Steam boat here for Washington 65 miles in 3 hours. Fare for ourselves, horse & barouch 8.00. toll on turnpike 8 cts. Travelled 70 miles to day — all night at Mr. Loveless' D. C. Supper & lodg. 1.25.

Sat. 13. — 29 miles. Breakfast at Mr. Rabbits 62½ cts. all night at Mr. Cemps, supper & lodg. 50 cents. good accom.

Sund. 14. — 21 miles. Breakfast at Mr. Wertenbaker's New-Market, Md. 62½ cts. toll on turnpike 14 cts. all night at Mr. Bowersocks. Supper, lodg. & breakfast 00. good accom.

Mond. 15. — 20 miles. To day arrived at Mr. Conrad Hoke's.

Tues. 16. Went to Gettysburg & had the carriage repaired 1.50.

Wed. 17. Thurs. 18. At Mr. Hoke's.

Frid. 19. Went to Gettysburg on the way to York.

Sat. 20. Went to York to attend the meeting of the General Synod. Took up lodging in York with Mr. Klinefelter. very nice family.

Sund. 21. Mond. 22. Tues. 23. in York.

Wed. 24. In York till 12 o'clock, in the afternoon returned to Gettysburg.

Thurs. 25. Went to the country to Mr. Hoke's & remained there till Saturday.

Sat. 27. Went to Chambersburg, settled with Ludwig Heck, all night with Revd Hoffman.

Sund. 28. Preached from 2 Cor. 5:17. at 10 A.M. Preached at candlelight from Ps. 119:63. a good deal embarrassed.

Mond. 29. Went to St. Thomas — all night with Mr. Nead, Esq.

Tues. 30. Went to Mercersburg in company with Mr. Nead. Preached here at candlelight from 2 Cor. 5:17. All night with Mr. Fegly.

Wed. July 1. Went to Greencastle. Preached here in the Ger. Refor^d ch. at candlelight from Heb. 2:3. All night with Revd Ruthrauff.

Thurs. 2. Went to McConnellsburg. Preached here at candlelight form Heb. 2:3. All night with Mr. Hoke, Esqr.

Frid. 3. Went to the country to Mr. Flore's. Preached in town at night from 2 Cor. 5:17.

Sat. 4. Attended the celebration of the 4th of July in M'Con. opened & closed the meeting with prayer. in the afternoon returned to St. Thomas.

Sund. 5. To day Revd Babb preached in Ger. — in the afternoon I preached from Heb. 2:3.

Mond. 6. Went to Mr. Hoke's in Ad. Co.

Tues. 7. At Mr. Hoke's.

Wed. 8. Went to Mr. Gillan's — all night here.

Thurs. 9. Returned to Mr. Hoke's.

Frid. 10. At Mr. Hoke's.

Sat. 11. Went to Franklin Co. — all night at Major Heller's.

Sund. 12. Preached at Grindstone Hill ch. from Isa. 55:7. In the afternoon at Quincy from 2 Cor. 5:17. All night at Geo. Wertz.

Mond. 13. Went to John Tritles — all night here.

Tues. 14. Went to St. Thomas.

Wed. 15. A rainy day — at Mr. Nead's in great perplexity of mind relative to the place where I ought to labor.

Thurs. 16. Went to the country in company with Revd Babb.

Frid. 17. Went to Mercersburg.

Sat. 18. Visited some of the members of the congregation in company with Mr. Seller's.

Sund. 19. To day Revd J. Reck preach^d at 10 A.M. In the afternoon I preached from Is. 55:7. Attended a prayermeeting at night at Mr. Hoslar's.

Mond. 20. Went to McConnellsburg.

Tues. 21. Went up the cove to Mr. Waggoner's, who was too busy to keep us over night — returned to Mr. Flore's.

Wed. 22. Went to Mr. Kittle's.

Thurs. 23. Returned to M'Con. then went to Mr. Komerer's. All night here.

Frid. 24. Went to Mr. Rinedaler's and then to town.

Sat. 25. Went to J. Kern's — returned in the evening.

Sund. 26. Preached in M'Con. from Luk 13:24. Ger. & Engl. from the same.

Mond. 27. Went to St. Thomas.

Tues. 28. Went to Mr. Hoke's in Ad. Co.

Wed. 29. Went to Gettysb. — returned at even.

Thurs. 30. At Mr. Hoke's.

Frid. 31. Went to Gettysb. — purchased saddle & bridle — returned in the even.

Sat. Aug. 1. Went to St. Thomas.

Sund. 2. Preached in St. Thomas from Luke 13:24. Ger. from 2 Cor. 5:17. Engl. Prayermeeting at night in School house.

Mond. 3. At Mr. Nead's & wrote several letters.

Tues. 4. Went to Mr. Deckson's Esqr who had deceased & was buried to day. Went home with Mr. Butler & took dinner with him, returned in the ev^n.

Wed. 5. At home & wrote a letter to my companion.

Thurs. 6. Went to Mr. Butler's & had prayermeeting in the School house.

Frid. 7. Returned home & hat prayermeeting to night in town.

Sat. 8. Attended Rev^d M'Knight's preaching who had services preparatory to communion. Attended prayer meet. at night in the school house.

Sund. 9. Attended Rev^d M'Knight's preaching & joined with him in communion. Preached for him at night from Luk. 13:24.

Mond. 10. Went to Mr. Hoke's in Ad. Co.

Tues. 11. Went to Gettysb. retu. in evn.

Wed. 12. Went gunning without success.

Thurs. 13. At Mr. Hoke's.

Frid. 14. Returned to St. Thomas & had prayermeet. at night in school house.

Sat. 15. Went to Mr. Heilsman's near Mercersburg.

Sund. 16. Preached in Mercersburg from Luk. 13:24. Engl. & Ger. from the same. Returned home in ev^n.

Mond. 17. Went to Mr. Hoke's in Ad. Co.

Tues. 18. Went to Gettysburg.

Wed. 19. Attend the laying of the corner stone of the Engl. Luth. ch. in Gettysburg. Preached at night from 2 Cor. 5:17.

Thurs. 20. Started for home to St. Thomas all night at Mr. Bigham's.

Frid. 21. Arrived at home. Prayermeeting to night, lectured from 2 Cor. 4:7.

Sat. 22. Went to McConnellsburg.

Sund. 23. Preached in M'Con. from John 3:16. Ger. Isa. 55:7. Engl. In the evening married John Marshal to Sarah Spitle.

Mond. 24. Returned home.

Tues. 25. Went to Chambersburg — returned home in the evening.

Wed. 26. At home engaged in study.

Thurs. 27. At home in study.

Frid. 28. Went to Shippensburg & preached for Revd Stroh at 2 p.m. from Heb. 2:3. — at night from 2 Cor. 5:17.

Sat. 29. Attended a prayermeeting at 10 a.m. preached from Luk 13:24. Ger. at 12 from Isa. 55:7. Engl. In the afternoon returned home.

Sund. 30. Preached a harvest sermon in St. Thomas from Ps. 116:12-14. Ger. from the same in Engl.

Mond. 31. Went to Chambersburg — returned home in ev^n.

Tues., Sep. 1. At home, not very well.

Wed. 2. At home till evening, then went to the country & had prayermeet. in Butler's school-house, lectured from John 14:1-3. Returned home after meeting.

Thurs. 3. At home. prayermeet. to night in St. Thomas, lectured from 2 Kings 5:1-14. full house.

Frid. 4. Went to Scherer's ch. to assist Revd Stroh. preached this afternoon from John 3:16. Ger. — at night in a school-house at Mr. Snyder's from Rev. 3:20. Engl. — all night at Mr. Fetter's.

Sat. 5. Prayermeet. at the ch. at 9 A.M. Preached at 12 from 1 Peter 4:18. Engl. at night in Shippensburg from 2 Kings 5:1-14. Engl. All night at Mr. Wolf's.

Sund. 6. In Scherer's ch. at 10 from Ps. 116:12-14. Ger. at 12 from John 7:37. Engl. after which the Holy Supper was administered. At 4 P.M. at Mr. Keiner's school-house from 2 Cor. 5:17.

Mond. 7. Prayermeet. at the ch. at 10. in the afternoon returned home.

Tues. 8. Wed. 9. At home.

Thurs. 10. At home. Prayermeeting to night in St. Thomas, lectured from Acts 20:17-21.

Frid. 11. Sat. 12. At home.

Sund. 13. Went to Mercersburg and preached from John 3:16. Ger. from Acts 20:17-21. Engl. All night with Mr. Seller's.

Mond. 14. Returned home.

Tues. 15. At home.

Wed. 16. Received a letter from father to day. bringing the mournful information of the death of Brother Jacob, who departed this life on the 4th of August, 1835 at his residence in Indiana of the Billious fever, leaving a widow & one child. Prayermeet. to night at Butler's school-house, lectured from Eph. 5:14.

Thurs. 17. At home, prayermeet. to night in St. Thomas, lectured from Math. 8:28-34.

Frid. 18. Went to M'Connellsburg.

Sat. 19. Preached in M'Con. from 1 Cor. 5:8. Ger. preparatory to communion — rainy day.

Sund. 20. Preached in M'Con. from Ps. 116:12-14. Ger. & Engl. from the same & administered the Lord's Supper in both languages.

Mond. 21. Returned home & married Henry Swink to Barbara Gitz, both late from Europe.

Tues. 22. Went to Mr. Butler's, but did not find him at home.

Wed. 23. Attended the funeral of Mr. Seller's, the services being performed by Revd Rawhouser.

Thurs. 24. At home. Prayermeeting to night, lectured from Math. 5:13-16.

Frid. 25. To day Revd Stroh was to have preached for me, but did not come. Preached myself from Eph. 6:18. baptized an infant.

Sat. 26. To day Revd J. N. Hoffman preached twice for me.

Sund. 27. Preached in St. Thomas from John 7:37. Ger. & administered the Lord's Supper. In the afternoon from the same Engl. & the Lord's Supper. At night from Prov. 29:1. Engl.

Mond. 28. Went to Chambersburg. Attended the Ger. Reformed Synod. was sent for to return home, Mr. Arey having called to see me. Borrowed $100 to send by him to N. C. & then returned home.

Tues. 29. Went to Chambersburg — returned home in the evening.

Wed. 30. Started for Synod by way of Chambersburg. Staid all night with Revd Stroh in Shippensburg — lectured for him this evening.

Thurs. Oct. 1. Went to Mechanicsburg, the place for the meeting of Synod — was directed to take lodging at Mr. Lamb's.

Frid. 2. Synod was organized & proceeded to business — was received as a member of Synod.

Sat. 3. Preached this afternoon from Ps. 116:12-14. preparatory to communion.

Sund. 4. Services were performed in both languages & the Lord's Supper administered.

Mond. 5. Obtained leave of absence & started for home. All night at Mr. Ruply's.

Tues. 6. Arrived at home.

Wed. 7. At home.

Thurs. 8. Went to Mr. Walburn's & married Abraham Crider to Margaret Ann Hamilton. Prayermeeting to night in the academy, lectured from Rev. 2:4.5.

Frid. 9. Started for Mercersburg — all night at Mr. Cromer's.

Sat. 10. Preached in Mercersburg, preparatory to communion from Ps. 116:12-14. Engl. Revd Helfenstein preached for me in German — Ger. Ref^d Had prayermeeting at night & lectured from Math. 8:1-4.

Sund. 11. Preached from John 7:37. Engl. & gave a Germ. exhortation. Then administered the Lord's Supper in both languages. Preached at candlelight from 2 Cor. 4:7. Engl. Baptized one infant to day.

Mond. 12. Returned home.

Tues. 13. At home.

Wed. 14. Went to the country to Mr. Jones'. At night attended prayermeeting in Butler's school house, lectured from Gal. 6:14. Returned home after meeting.

Thurs. 15. Went to McConnellsburg & married Henry Unger to Susannah Hotzhe. At night at Jacob Hoke's.

Frid. 16. Went to John Komerer's.

Sat. 17. Had catechization at 2 o'clock in M'Con. — all night George Rinedaler's.

Sund. 18. Preached in M'Con. from John 7:37. Germ. & baptized 3 children, 2 of whom were of Rom. Cath. parents. In the afternoon from Acts 20:17-21. Engl. Returned home after preaching.

Mond. 19. At home. At night attended the debating Society as spectator and auditor.

Tues. 20. At home. At night attended the singing at Mr. Rothrauff.

Wed. 21. At home.

Thurs. 22. Went to Chambersburg to assist Revd Hoffman some in a protracted meeting.

Frid. 23. Preached from Acts 20:17-21.

Sat. 24. Preached from Ps. 116:12-14. In the afternoon returned home & had catechization in St. Thomas.

Sund. 25. Preached in St. Thomas from Rev. 3:20. Germ. from 1 John 3:2. Engl. Prayermeeting at night in the School-house, lectured from parable of ten virgins. Math. 25:1-4.

Mond. 26. Went to Chambersburg & brought Revd Kurtz to St. Thomas.

Tues. 27. To day celebrated anniversary of the Reformation, on which occasion Revd Kurtz preached. In afternoon took him back to Chambersburg.

Wed. 28. At home — had prayermeeting to night in Butler's School house — lectured from Isa. 55:6.7. — returned home after meeting.

Thurs. 29. Started for Adam's County — all night at Mark's tavern.

Frid. 30. Went to Mr. Hoke's.

Sat. 31. Went to Gettysburg — returned to Mr. Hoke's.

Sund., Nov. 1. At Mr. Hoke's to day as I had no appointment & there being no preaching convenient.

Mond. 2. Went to Gettysburg — returned in the evening.

Tues. 3. Went to Mr. Stuart's.

Wed. 4. Returned to St. Thomas.

Thurs. 5. At home — had prayermeeting to night in the School house.

Frid. 6. At home — not very well.

Sat. 7. At home till 12 o'clock. Then went to Mr. Unger's near Mercersburg.

Sund. 8. Preached in Mercersburg from Math 11:28. Germ. from 1 John 3:2. Engl. All night at old Mr. Hoke's.

Mond. 9. Returned home & wrote a letter to my dear wife.

Tues. 10. At home.

Wed. 11. At home till afternoon, then went to Mr. Butler's & had prayermeeting in the school-house, lectured from Eph. 6:18. Staid with Mr. B.

Thurs. 12. Returned home & had pmg in the School-house — lectured, from Math. 2 chap.

Frid. 13. Went to M'Connellsburg — all night at Mr. Flore's.

Sat. 14. Had catechization & at night prayermeeting at Mr. Flore's — lec^d from Math. 8:1-4.

Sund. 15. Preached in M'Con. from Math. 11:28. Germ. from Prov. 29:1. Engl. After preaching returned home.

Mond. 16. Went to Adams County.

Tues. 17. Went to Gettysburg.

Wed. 18. Went to Mr. Megaughy's.

Thurs. 19. At Mr. Hoke's.

Frid. 20. Returned to St. Thomas.

Sat. 21. At home.

Sund. 22. Preached in St. Thomas from John 3:16. Germ. from 2 Tim. 4:7.8. Engl. — prayermeeting at night in the School house, lec^d from Math. 7:12-14.

Mond. 23. Very cold & snowy — took Mrs. Wampler to Chambersburg.

Tues. 24. At home.

Wed. 25. At home till evening, then attended prayermeeting in Butler's School-house — lectured from Math. 11:28.

Thurs. 26. At home.

Frid. 27. At home.

Sat. 28. Went to M'Connellsburg — had catechization in the afternoon — prayermeeting at night at Mr. Flore's, lectured from Eph. 5:14.

Sund. 29. Preached in M'Con. from 2 Cor. 5:17. Ger. from 1 John 3:2. Engl.

Mond. 30. Returned home — baptized Mrs. Wunderlich & child.

Tues., Dec. 1. At home.

Wed. 2. Went to Chambersburg.

Thurs. 3. At home — Prayermeeting to night, lectured from Mar. 10:46-52.

Frid. 4. At home — attended preaching to night in the Meth. ch.

Sat. 5. Went to Mercersburg.

Sund. 6. Preached in Mercersbg from Math. 8:1-4. Germ. from 2 Tim. 4:7.8. & Mark 10:46-52. Engl.

Mond. 7. Returned home — at night attended preaching in Meth. ch.

Tues. 8. At home.

Wed. 9. Went to Chambersburg.

Thurs. 10. At home — prayermeet. to night, lectured from Mat. 4:1-11.

Frid. 11. At home.

Sat. 12. At home — had catechization this afternoon in the ch.

Sund. 13. Preached in St. Thomas from Mark 1:40-44. Germ. from Joh. 3:14.15. Engl. At night from Luk. 13:6-9. Engl.

Mond. 14. Went to the country to visit the sick Mrs. Wunderlich.

Tues. 15. Wed. 16. At home.

Thurs. 17. At home — prayermeeting to night, lectured from Math. 4:12-25.

Frid. 18. Sat. 19. At home.

Sund. 20. Preached in St. Thomas from Math. 11:28. Germ. from 1 Peter 4:18. Engl. At night from Hosea 13:9. Engl.

Mond. 21. At home — wrote several letters.

Tues. 22. Attended to the funeral of Mrs. Wunderlich in St. Thomas preached from Job 14:14.

Wed. 23. At home.

Thurs. 24. At home — pray. meet. to night in the School house, lectured from Math. 5:1-12.

Frid. 25. Christmas — Preached in Butler's School house from Math 1:21. Germ. & Engl. from the same.

Sat. 26. Went to M'Connellsburg — catechization in the afternoon — all night at Mr. Kittle's.

Sund. 27. Attended to the funeral of Mr. Arb's child — preached from Math. 1:21. Germ. & Engl. from the same. All night at Mr. Flore's.

Mond. 28. Returned home.

Tues. 29. At home & very low spirited.

Wed. 30. Thurs. 31. At home. Prayermeeting to night (31) & lectured from Math 5:17-26.

Frid., Jan. 1, 1836. Attended preaching in the forenoon by Revd Rahauser. In the afternoon a Temperance meeting & delivered a short address.

Sat. 2. Started for Mercersburg — all night at Mr. Heilman's.

Sund. 3. Preached in Mercersburg from Math. 1:21. Germ. from 1 Peter 4:18. Engl. Overstepped the mark in delivery — all night at Mr. Unger's.

Mond. 4. Returned home & got very wet with rain.

Tues. 5. At home.

Wed. 6. At home.

Thurs. 7. At home — pray^r meet^g to night — lectur^d from Math. 5:27-37. Baptized also to day Frederick's the barber's child.

Frid. 8. Sat. 9. At home.

Sund. 10. Visited the congregation at Grossman's & preached from Math. 1:21. Germ. Consented to take charge of the congregation.

Mond. 11. Went to Chambersburg in Mr. Baker's Sleigh.

Tues. 12. At home. Wed. 13. At home.

Thurs. 14. At home. Prayermeeting to night & lectured from Math 5:38-48.

Frid. 15. Sat. 16. At home.

Sund. 17. Preached in St. Thomas from Luk. 15:11-32. Germ. Ex. 33:14. English. At night attended preaching in the Methodist ch.

Mond. 18. Went to Mr. Butler's & brought my barouch home.

Tues. 19. Went to Mr. Hoke's in Adams County — night having overtaken us, we were ice-bound at the creek just before we got to the place of our destination — fortunately a friend came that way at that time & conducted us across.

Wed. 20. Left Mrs. Roth & started for home — all night in Chambersburg at Mr. Suesserot's.

Thurs. 21. Arrived at home & immediately started to the furnace in a sleigh & married John Bates to Barbara Bricken — in returning home the driver upset the sleigh — at night attended preaching in the church by Revd Smedmer — also to day baptized three children.

Frid. 22. At home.

Sat. 23. Went to M'Connellsburg — at night preaching in the Independent ch. by Revd Kerr. all night at Mrs. Fasnacht's.

Sund. 24. Preached in M'C. from Mark 1:40-44. Germ. In the afternoon Revd Smedmer preached for me & at night Revd Kerr.

Mond. 25. Returned home — snow in abundance.

Tues. 26. At home — wrote a letter to my beloved wife.

Wed. 27. At home.

Thurs. 28. At home — prayermeeting to night in the School-house — Thinly attended.

Frid. 29. At home.

Sat. 30. Went to Mercersburg — all night at Mr. D. Schaeffer's.

Sund. 31. Attended & addressed the Sabbath-School. Preached from 2 Cor. 5:17. Ger. from Ex. 33:14. Engl. returned home after preaching.

Mond. Feb. 1. At home.

Tues. 2. Went to see my companion at her parents' in Adams Co. — travelled in a sleigh — weather cold.

Wed. 3. Took Mrs. R. in a sleigh to Mr. Ferree's — hospitably entertained.

Thurs. 4. Returned to Mr. Hoke's — very cold weather.

Frid. 5. At Mr. Hoke's — not very well.

Sat. 6. Returned home to St. Thomas.

Sund. 7. Went to Grossman's church to preach, but being late in starting in consequence of a late breakfast at my boarding house, the people had well nigh all dispersed — preached however to a few remaining hearers from Mark 1:40-44. Germ. — Returned home after preaching.

Mond. 8. At home.

Tues. 9. At home.

Wed. 10. Went to Mr. J. Butler's — had prayermeeting to night in Butler's School house & lectured from Mark 10:46-52. All night at J. Butler's.

Thurs. 11. Returned home — in the afternoon married John Bechdole to Miss Sarah Sachman — prayermeet. at night and lectured from Math. 6:1-15.

Frid. 12. At home.

Sat. 13. At home had catechization in the afternoon.

Sund. 14. Preached in St. Thomas from 2 Cor. 5:17. Ger. Acts 26:17.18. Engl. At night attended preaching in the Meth. church by Revd Edwards.

Mond. 15. Went to Mr. Hoke's in Adams County to see my dear companion.

Tues. 16. Went to Gettysburg — returned to Mr. Hoke's in the evening.

Wed. 17. Thurs. 18. At Mr. Hoke's.

Frid. 19. Returned home to St. Thomas.

Sat. 20. Went to M'Connellsburg & had catechization in the afternoon. All night at Mr. Flore's.

Sund. 21. Preached in M'Con. from Luk 15:11-32. Germ. from Act. 26:17.18. Engl. All night Mr. Hoke's Esqr. Quite unwell in consequence of cold.

Mond. 22. Went to Mr. J. Camerer's. Still unwell.*

Tues. 23. Returned to M'Con. & attended a Temperance Meeting — was to have addressed the meeting in German, but felt too unwell — returned home in the evening.

Wed. 24. This morning finished a letter to my absent wife — at home to day — was to have attended a prayermeet. in the country to night, but felt to unwell.

Thurs. 25. At home — prayer meeting to night in the school house — lectured from Luk. 15:11-32.

Frid. 26. At home.

Sat. 27. Went to Mercersburg — at night attended preaching in the Methodist ch.

Sund. 28. Preached in Mercersburg from Luk. 15:11-32. Germ. Act. 26:17.18. Engl. returned home after preaching.

Mond. 29. Went to Adams Co. to Mr. Hoke's.

* This evening at Mr. Camerer's baptized 2 children.

Tues., March 1. At Mr. Hoke's.

Wed. 2. Went to Gettysburg — returned in the evening to Mr. Hoke's.

Thurs. 3. At Mr. Hoke's.

Frid. 4. Returned to St. Thomas, Mrs. Rothrock being with me.

Sat. 5. At home.

Sund. 6. Preached at Grossman's ch. from 2 Cor. 5:17. Germ. & English from the same text. Returned home after preaching — Revd Stroh having come to St. Thomas, preached in the School house.

Mond. 7. Tues. 8. At home.

Wed. 9. Went to the country to Mr. Butler's, Mrs. R. being with me — had prayermeeting to night in B's School house & lectured from the parable of the prodigal son — all night at Mr. B's.

Thurs. 10. Returned home — had prayer meeting to night in the School-house — few persons there the evening being very rainy.

Frid. 11. At home.

Sat. 12. Went to Shippensburg — all night at Mr. Wolf's.

Sund. 13. Having exchanged pulpits with Revd Stroh to day, preached in his stead in Shippensburg from 2 Cor. 5:17. Germ. afternoon from Acts 20:17-21. Engl. at night from Mark 10:46-52. Engl. all night at Mr. Wolf's.

Mond. 14. Returned home.

Tues. 15. Went to the country in search of corn & oats.

Wed. 16. Went to Rev^d M'knights.

Thurs. 17. At home. Prayermeeting at night in the School house and lectured from John 5:1-16.

Frid. 18. At home & prepared a Germ. skeleton.

Sat. 19. Went to M'Connellsburg & had catechization in the afternoon. All night at Mr. Stouer's.

Sund. 20. Preached in McConnellsburg from Joel 1:5. Germ. from Ex. 33:14. Engl. Returned to Loudon in the afternoon & preached there at candle-lighting from Acts 20:17-21. All night at Mr. Beaver's.

Mond. 21. Returned home.

Tues. 22. At home.

Wed. 23. Went to Rev^d M'knight's & purchased some articles preparatory to house-keeping. At night attended a prayer meeting at Butler's School house.

Thurs. 24. Went to Chambersburg, Mrs. R. having staid there from yesterday — purchased some articles from Mr. Sussonatt towards housekeeping — Returned home in the evening & attended a prayermeeting in the Schoolhouse lectured from Gal. 5:1.

Frid. 25. At home. Had catech^n in the afternoon in the church.

Sat. 26. Went to Mr. Breever's near Mercersburg — had a long argument with him on Universalism, he being a good deal tinctured with it.

Sund. 27. Preached in Mercersburg from 1 Peter 4:18. Germ. from Prov. 29:1. Engl. At candle lighting in Loudon from Prov. 29:1. Engl. All night at Mr. Baker's.

Mond. 28. Returned home.

Tues. 29. Went to the country & married John Bachman to Esther Krider.*

Wed. 30. At home.

Thurs. 31. At home — Prayermeeting to night in the school house & lectured from Math. 12:22-37.

* Baptized also to day one infant.

Frid. Apr. 1. At home — was to have preached for Revd Stroh to day, but the day being inclement did not turn out.

Sat. 2. Assisted Revd Stroh to day at Carper's ch. — Preached twice from 2 Cor. 5:17. Ger. Exod. 33:14. Engl.

Sund. 3. Preached at Grossman's ch. from 1 Pet. 4:18. Ger. from the same in Engl. Preached at 4 o'clock at the red School house from Rev. 2:4.5. Engl.

Mond. 4. Preached at Butler's school house from 1 Peter 4:18. Germ. from Rev. 2:4.5. Engl.

Tues. 5. Catechization to day in St. Thos.

Wed. 6. Went to Chambersburg.

Thurs. 7. Catechization at 10 A.M., at 2 P.M married John Croft to Miss Martha Wartz at Brindle's tavern.

Frid. 8. Catechization — to night Revd Stroh preached for me.

Sat. 9. Services in the church preparatory to communion — preaching by Revd Stroh — baptized one adult to day & admitted 13 persons to church membership by confirmation.

Sund. 10. Communion to day in the church — baptized one infant — house crowded. Preaching by Revd Stroh.

Mond. 11. At home. To day Revd B. Arey from N. C. was with us.

Tues. 12. Went to see Mr. Coble about feathers.

Wed. 13. Attended the funeral of Mr. Grossman, Senr. at Grossman's ch. Preached from Math. 25:13. Germ.

Thurs. 14. At home — prayermeeting to night in the School house & lectured from Acts 16:16-34. After meeting went to Mr. Vondersmith's & baptized his child.

Frid. 15. Baptized Mr. Cotz's child. Then went to M'Connellsburg and had catechization in the afternoon.

Sat. 16. Baptized Mr. Bermong's child — preached in the ch. from 1 Pet. 4:18. Germ. preparatory to communion. In the afternoon preached from the same text in Engl. and admitted 18 persons as members of the church by the rite of confirmation — baptized also 6 adults. Lectured at candlelighting in the church from Mark 10:46-52. Engl.

Sund. 17. Preached from Joh. 3:14.15. Germ. & administered the Holy Supper — In the afternoon from John 7:37. Engl. & administered the Holy Supper. Baptized Mr. Stouer's child. After preaching went to Loudon — had an appointment to preach there & candlelighting, being considerably indisposed, Revd Miller, Ger. Ref. preached for me.

Mond. 18. Returned home.

Tues. 19. Wed. 20. At home.

Thurs. 21. At home. Prayermeeting at night in the school house.

Frid. 22. At home. Attended preaching at night in the church by Mr. Keefer, a Reformed student.

Sat. 23. Went to Mercersburg & preached at 11 o'clock from Ps. 116:12.13.14. Germ. preparatory to Communion. At candlelighting from Rev. 2:4.5. Engl. All night at Mr. H. Smith's.

Sund. 24. Preached at 10 o'clock from John 3:14.15. Engl. to a full house — confirmed one person & administered the Lord's Supper. At candle lighting preached in Loudon from 2 Cor. 5:17. Engl. to a tolerably full house. All night at Mr. Baker's.

Mond. 25. Returned home.

Tues. 26. Went to Chambersburg — Returned home in the evening.

Wed. 27. Went to the country to purchase lard, meat &c. preparatory to housekeeping.

Thurs. 28. Moved our furniture &c. to Mrs. Hoffman's house. At candle lighting lectured in the school house from John 9:1-7.

Frid. 29. At home till in the afternoon then went to Chambersburg & preached at candlelighting from Exod. 33:14.

Sat. 30. Preached at Grossman's ch. from Luk. 13:24. Germ. preparatory to communion — baptized to day 2 infants — returned home in the afternoon.

Sund., May 1, 1836. Preached at Grossman's ch. from Psalms 116:12.13.14. Germ. after an intermission of a few minutes, preached Engl. from the same text. Then administered the Holy Supper in both languages — returned home in the afternoon & lectured at candle lighting in the school house from Col. 1:28.

Mond. 2. Left Mr. Nead's where we had hitherto been boarding & moved into a part of Mrs. Hoffman's house.

Tues. 3. At home.

Wed. 4. At home till evening, then went to the country & at candlelighting had prayer-meeting in Butler's school house.

Thurs. 5. At home — prayer-meeting at night in the school-house & lectured from Luk. 9:57-62.

Frid. 6. Went to Shippensburg and preached for Revd Stroh at 2 P.M. from 1 Pet. 4:18. Germ. at night from Rev. 2:4.5. Engl.

Sat. 7. At 9 A.M. attended pray^r meet^g. Preached at 11 from Ps. 116:12.13.14. Germ. at 2 from Exod. 33:14. Engl. after preaching returned home.

Sund. 8. This was my regular day in St. Thomas, on which occasion Revd Weider preached for me.

Mond. 9. Tues. 10. At home.

Wed. 11. At home.

Thurs. 12. Ascension Day. Preached to day at Butler's School-house from Mark 16:19. Germ. after which Revd Weider preached in English. Prayer meeting to night in the School house & lectured from Ps. 39:1.

Frid. 13. At home.

Sat. 14. Went to M'Connellsburg — all night at Mr. Hoke's Esqr.

Sund. 15. Preached in M'Connellsburg from Rev. 2:4.5. Germ. & Engl. from the same text — baptized to day 2 children. At candle lighting in Loudon from Rev. 2:4.5.

Mond. 16. Returned home — Rev. Kerr, an Independent preached to night in the school house.

Tues. 17. At home.

Wed. 18. Went to Chambersburg.

Thurs. 19. At home — prayermeeting at night in the school-house. Lectured form Isa. 34:16.

Frid. 20. At home.

Sat. 21. At home — made preparations for Sabbath.

Sund. 22. Went to Mercersburg & preached from Rev. 3:20. Germ. and Engl. from the same — Baptized 2 infants — Met with an accident, my horse stumbled & threw me off and sprained my ankle. Was to have preached in Loudon to night, but not being able to get there in consequence of my sprained ankle, had to disappoint the people. All night at old Mr. Hoke's.

Mond. 23. Returned home. Was to have preached to day in Butler's School house, but could not attend in consequence of not being able to walk.

Tues. 24. At home.

Wed. 25. Attended to the funeral of Mr. Schaeffer in St. Thomas — preached from Ps. 90:12. Germ.

Thurs. 26. At home — prayermeeting to night in the school house.

Frid. 27. Sat. 28. At home.

Sund. 29. Preached at Grossman's ch. from Rev. 3:20. Germ. & English from the same text. Baptized one infant. Preached at candlelighting in the school house in St. Thomas from Luke 23:39-43. Engl.

Mond. 30. Tues. 31. At home. Cloudy weather for the last ten days during which time there has been a great deal of rain. Had appointed a meeting this evening to organize a Bible Class, but was prevented by the rain.

Wed., June 1. At home.

Thurs. 2. At home — this was the regular night from prayermeeting but had to dispense with it in consequence of the rain.

Frid. 3. At home.

Sat. 4. At home — attended preaching in the Methodist ch. at 11 A.M. & at candlelighting.

Sund. 5. Preached in St. Thomas from Ex. 20:8. Germ. & Engl. from the same — at 3 P.M. attended preaching by Revd Kennedy, Presbyt^n. Attended the Sabbath School also in the morning.

Mond. 6. At home.

Tues. 7. Wed. 8. At home.

Thurs. 9. At home — prayermeeting at night in the School house & lectured from Ex. 23:2.

Frid. 10. At home.

Sat. 11. Went to M'Connellsburg — baptized Mr. Riechart's child near St. Thomas — all night at Mr. Flore's.

Sund. 12. Preached in M'Connellsburg from Ex. 20:8. Germ. & Engl. from the same text. At night attended Methodist preaching. Baptized also to day 3 children.

Mond. 13. Returned home.

Tues. 14. Went to the country & administered the Lord's Supper to Mr. Echert, a decrepit old man. Spent the afternoon at Mr. Nead's. At night attended Bible-class — Met for the first time & organized the class this evening.

Wed. 15. At home.

Thurs. 16. At 2 o'clock went in company with Revd Hoffman to Butler's school house where he preached. He, having been appointed by the Book Company of the Ev. Luth. ch. as agent to sell stock, came on business connected with his agency. At candle-lighting he preached in the church in St. Thomas.

Frid. 17. Took Revd Hoffman to Chambersburg in my barouch.

Sat. 18. At home.

Sund. 19. Went to Mercersburg & preached from Ex. 20:8. Germ. & Engl. from the same text. Returned home in the evening.

Mond. 20. At home.

Tues. 21. At home. Married Mr John Rensch to Miss Margaretta Miller both late from Europe. At night had bible-class in the school house.

Wed. 22. At home.

Thurs. 23. At home. Prayer meeting at night in the school house and lectured from Phil. 3:20.21.

Frid. 24. Sat. 25. At home.

Sund. 26. This was my regular day to preach at Grossman's, but did not attend in consequence of the inclemency of the weather — very rainy. At night attended preaching in the Meth. ch. by Revd Hayes.

Mond. 27. At home.

Tues. 28. Went to Chambersburg. In the afternoon went to Mr. Brech's in the country & baptized his child. At night had bibleclass.

Wed. 29. At home.

Thurs. 30. At home. Had prayermeeting at [Word missing] lectured from Mark 8:36.

Frid. July 1, Sat. 2. At home.

Sund. 3. Preached in St. Thomas from John 5:40. Ger. & Engl. from the same. At night lectured in the school house from Math. 26:41.

Mond. 4. At home.

Tues. 5. At home. At night married William Smith to Mary Morgan — afterwards had bible-class.

Wed. 6. At home. At had a Temperance meeting in the Meth. church which was addressed by Rev. Miller.

Thurs. 7. At home — prayermeeting at night in the school house.

Frid. 8. Sat. 9. At home.

Sund. 10. Went to M'Connellsburg & preached from Joh. 5:40. Ger. & Engl. from the same — returned home after preaching.

Mond. 11. At home.

Tues. 12. At home. At night was the time for the meeting of the bible-class but as none attended in time, dispensed with it.

Wed. 13. At home.

Thurs. 14. Attended to the funeral of Mrs. Chranister in St. Thomas who died of the small-pox. & preached from Hebr. 4:9. Germ. Prayermeeting at night in the School house.

Frid. 15. Sat. 16. At home.

Sund. 17. Went to Mercersburg & preached from Math. 1:21. Engl. & from Joh. 5:40. Germ. Returned home after preaching & lectured in the School house from Math. 1:21.

Mond. 18. Went early in the morning to Mr. Campbell's to see a travelling Presbyterian preacher — took breakfast at Mr. Campbell's.

Tues. 19. At home. Bible-class at night in the school house.

Wed. 20. Went to Mr. Houk's in the country to settle with him.

Thurs. 21. At home — prayer meeting at night in the school house.

Frid. 22. Went to Mr. Jones to purchase oats for my horse.

Sat. 23. At home.

Sund. 24. Went to Grossman's ch. and preached from John 5:40. Ger. & Engl. from the same text. Baptized 4 inf^{ts}. Baptized also Mr. Cradler's child in St. Thomas — prayer meeting at night in the School house & lectured from John 1:29.

Mond. 25. At home.

Tues. 26. Went to the country to see Mr. Kissel's to see his son who was sick. At night had bible-class.

Wed. 27. Went to see Mr. Kissel again, & to Mr. Wilson's to purchase corn. At candlelighting Rev^d Mr. Wilson was to have preached in St. Thomas, but as he did not come, lectured to the congregation from Acts 17:30.31.

Thurs. 28. Went to the country for corn & to the mill. At night married Nicholas Mourer to Sarah Ann Sellers.

Frid. 29. Sat. 30. At home.

Sund. 31. Preached in St. Thomas from Josh. 24:15. Germ. & Engl. from the same. Baptized Sarah Hemphill an aged & decrepit female — at night lectured in the school house from 2 Pet. 3:18.

Mond., Aug. 1. Went to Mr. Butler's to see Hanah Louecker, who was sick.

Tues. 2. At home. Bible-class at night in the School house.

Wed. 3rd. At home.

Thurs. 4. At home. Prayermeeting at night in the school house & lectured from Ps. 119:63.

Frid. 5. Sat. 6. At home.

Sund. 7. This was my regular day to preach in M'Connellsburg, but family duties required me to stay at home. Attended preaching by Revd Clearey, Meth. & Revd Kenneday, Presb.

Mond. 8. At home.

Tues. 9. At home. Bible class at night in the school house.

Wed. 10. At home.

Thurs. 11. At home. Prayermeeting at night in school house & lectured from Luk. 12:15-21.

Frid. 12. At home.

Sat. 13. Preached at Butler's school house from Luk. 12:15-21. German. Baptized one infant.

Sund. 14. Preached in Mercersburg from John 5:40. Engl. Returned home in afternoon. At night prayer meeting in the school house.

Mond. 15. At home.

Tues. 16. Went to Mr. Allemang's near Mercersburg to see his daughter who was sick & in great distress of mind. Had bible-class at night in the school house.

Wed. 17. At home.

Thurs. 18. At home till 12 o'clock. In the afternoon went in company with Geo. Heck to Mr. Moler's, his wife being sick & in distress of mind. Prayer meeting at night in the school-house & lectured from Rom. 5:1-5. Got very wet to day with rain.

St. Thomas
Franklin County, Pa.
August 26, 1836
Diary No. 4th

Frid. 19. At home. This evening before dusk or about the setting of sun, Mrs. Rothrock was taken sick. The time of her delivery being come – Brought Mrs. Nead & Mrs. Leady to her, Mrs. Hoffman being in the house also & with Mrs. Rothrock. After night awhile called in Dr. Humphrey's. During the night her sufferings were not more than usual at such times.

Sat. 20. This morning her labor pains became very great & about 8 o'clock was thrown into spasms – it was sufficient to melt a heart of stone to witness her sufferings now. Sent to Chambersburg for Dr. Love who arrived as soon as could be expected. During this time she had three spasms. Drs. Love & Humphrey had a short consultation, after which by the aid of instruments they delivered her of an infant son. Her sufferings during the whole time are indescribable. Her infant was very large. After the delivery, her bodily sufferings appeared to have subsided, but was very flighty in her mind. She spoke much of her "Sweet Jesus" – her "dear Redeemer" – Sometimes she would fall into a doze. In the evening she became perfectly rational – continued to talk of her "Sweet Jesus" – admonished all to love the Saviour, (O! that I could as I ought.) & wished to see her "sweet babe," but this was denied her as she was thought to be too weak. During the night she had apparently but little bodily suffering – appeared calm & tranquil & continued to speak of her "Sweet Jesus".

Sund. 21. This morning she was still tranquil & continued to speak of her "Sweet Jesus." This morning I sent a messenger with my horse & barouche for her mother. Between 7 & 8 A.M. she became very weak. I immediately called the doctor in & she revived a little – continued to speak of her "Sweet Jesus." She was thrown into a slight spasm & about 9 o'clock A.M. she expired very calmly. Her confidence in the Saviour was firm to the last, & now I trust she is singing his praises around his throne in the realms of eternal glory. Lord, prepare me for death & for a seat amongst all the sanctified around thy throne. Her friends were now sent for, who arrived next morning about 3 o'clock A.M.

Mond. 22. To day at 12 o'clock M. she & her little babe were buried in the same grave in St. Thomas, Franklin Co., Pa. There their bodies will rest till waked up at the resurrection day. "The Lord gave & the Lord taketh away & blessed be the name of the Lord. "The concourse of people which attended her funeral was large. A deep feeling of sympathy was manifested generally. The burial service out of the Liturgy was read by Rev^d Mr. Harpel of Greencastle. An Engl. funeral sermon was preached by Revd J. N. Hoffman of Chambersburg from James 5:10.11. A German one by Revd Ruthrauff of Greencastle from Phil. 1:21. Thus divine Providence has seen fit to take from me my beloved wife — my bosom companion. She is without doubt now in heaven, beholding the face of the Lord & praising the Redeemer of the world, whilst I am still an inhabitant of this world. An over-ruling Providence has so ordered it & for wise purposes. The Lord without doubt has something yet for me to do & wishes in this way to qualify me the better for the work. Lord, help me to receive the lessons of instruction which thou dost continually teach me by thy word & Providence, & make me willing to obey thee. Lord, what wilt thou have me do? & help to perform it.

Tues. 23. At home. Felt lonely.

Wed. 24. Went to Chambersburg in company with Mr. & Mrs. Nead. All night at Revd Hoffman's.

Thurs. 25. Wrote a letter to my parents informing them of my bereavements — returned home in the evening. All at Mr. Ruthrauffs.

Frid. 26. At home. Felt lonely. O! that God would lift upon me the light of his reconciled countenance. I am a great sinner, have been very unfaithful & am unworthy of God's goodness. God, be merciful to me a sinner.

Sat. 27. Went to Adams County to Mr. Hoke's.

Sund. 28. Went to Gettysburg to Rev^d M'Clean's preaching, but not being able to comprehend the thread of his discourse, was not edified any. At candlelighting attended preaching in the Luth. ch. by Mr. Dovey, student. All night with Professor Jacobs.

Mond. 29. Visited some & in the evening returned to Mr. Hoke's.

Tues. 30. Started for St. Thomas as far as Chambersburg. All night with Mr. Hoffman. Engaged a grave stone for the grave of my dear wife, with Mr. Denig, Merchant.

Wed. 31. Returned to St. Thomas.

Thurs., Sept. 1. At home, making some disposition of my furniture.

Frid. 2. Went to McConnellsburg in company with father Ruthrauff. All night at Mr. Kittles.

Sat. 3. At 10 o'clock Revd Ruthrauff preached in Germ. preparatory to communion. At 1 o'clock preached myself in Engl. from Prov. 25:13. At night Revd White, Presb., preached for me.

Sund. 4. Revd R. Preached in Germ. at 10 o'clock after which we administered the Lord's Supper in Germ. At one, preached myself in Engl. from John 3:14.15. after which administered the Lord's Supper in Engl. at candle lighting preached Engl. from Josh. 24:15. latter clause.

Mond. 5. Returned home. Wrote a letter to B. Fraley, Salisbury, N.C. informing him of my acceptance of the call from the congregations in & around Salisbury. At candle lighting attended preaching in the Meth. ch.

Tues. 6. Wrote several letters & attended preaching in the Meth. ch. At night, had bible-class.

Wed. 7. At home.

Thurs. 8. Moved to Mr. Nead's. Prayermeeting at night in the school house, lectured from John 14:22.

Frid. 9. Went to Mercersburg. Preached at candlelighting from John 14:22. Engl.

Sat. 10. Preached at 10 from 1 John 1:9. Germ. Preparatory to communion. In the afternoon & at night Rev^d Mr. Winter preached for me.

Sund. 11. Baptized one adult & one infant & confirmed three persons — Rev. Winter preached at 10, after which the Holy Supper was administered. At candle lighting preached my valedictory from 2 Peter 3:18. Engl. The congregation was large, silent, & attentive.

Mond. 12. Went to M'Connellsburg.

Tues. 13. Preached my valedictory in Germ. from John 14:22. & Engl. from the same. Preached a general valedictory at night from 2 Peter 3:18. Engl. The congregation was large, silent & attentive.

Wed. 14. Returned home.

Thurs. 15. Went to Mr. Coble's to meet Revd Hoffman, he having come there to attend a wedding. At candle lighting Revd Hoffman preached for me in St. Thomas.

Frid. 16. At home.

Sat. 17. Went to Chambersburg & settled with some of my creditors. In the evening went to Mr. Grossman's.

Sund. 18. Preached at Grossman's ch. from John 14:22. Germ. & Engl. from the same the same [written twice]. Baptized one infant to day. Prayer meeting at night in the school house in St. Thomas. Revd Babb lectured to the people.

Mond. 19. At home till the afternoon. Then went to Mr. Butler's in company with Revds. Stroh & Babb. returned home in the evening.

Tues. 20. At home till 12 o'clock, then went to Mr. Winter's in company with Revd Babb. Returned in the evening. At candle lighting had bible-class.

Wed. 21. Went to Mr. Tool's & baptized 2 children, of whom he has the raising. At night had meeting in Butler's school house. Preached from John 14:22. Engl.

Thurs. 22. Went to the mountain above Loudon in company with Revd Babb & married Geo. Dick to Cath. Keler. At night Revd Babb preached in St. Thomas.

Frid. 23. Went in company with Revd Babb to Chambersburg. Sold my horse, saddle & bridle to Mr. Sterret for $75. At night Revd Babb preached in St. Thomas.

Sat. 24. This forenoon Revd Ruthrauff from Greencastle preached in St. Thomas in Germ. preparatory to communion. In the afternoon Revd Babb preached in Engl. Baptized 3 children. At night preached myself from Job 23:16.

Sund. 25. This forenoon Revd Ruthrauff preached in Germ. after which the Lord's Supper was administered in Germ. In the afternoon Revd Babb preached in Engl. after which the Lord's Supper was administered in Engl. At night Revd Babb preached again. During the whole of this day the ch. was crowded & the audience attentive.

Mond. 26. In the forenoon prepared my parochial report for Synod. In the afternoon went to Chambersburg to send my report to Synod by Revd Hoffman.

Tues. 27. Returned home after settling my accounts in Chambersburg. At night attended the bible-class.

Wed. 28. Engaged in packing my books till 12 o'clock. In the afternoon went to Mr. Unger's near Mercersburg.

Thurs. 29. This morning with Mr. Unger. He had the collecting of my salary for Mercersburg. Then went to the Gap and married John Keler to Miss Myring Johns. Then went to Henry Hickman's & baptized five of his children. Then returned home & preached in St. Thomas at candle lighting from Acts 20:17-21. Engl.

Frid. 30. To day at 10 a.m. preached my valedictory in St. Thomas from 2 Peter 3:18. Germ. In the afternoon settled with the church council &c. At candle lighting preached my valedictory in Engl. from 2 Peter 3:18. The church was crowded & the audience attentive & solemn.

Sat., Oct. 1. Went to Grossman's & preached from 1 John 1:9. Germ. preparatory to communion. All night at David Grossman's.

Sund. 2. Preached my valedictory in Germ. & Engl. at Grossman's from 2 Pet. 3:18. & after preaching administered the Lord's Supper in both languages. At candle lighting attended preaching in St. Thomas by Rev^d Mr. Babb.

Mond. 3. Visited some of my members in the country & in the village & made preparations to start for N. Carolina.

Tues. 4. Started for N. Carolina. Went to Chambersburg in Mr. Nead's dearburn. Then took the stage for Gettysburg — fare 1.75 — Extra 50 cts. All night at Mrs. Wampler's.

Wed. 5. Went to the country to Mr. Hoke's.

Thurs. 6. Returned to Gettysburg at 9 o'clock P.M. Started for Baltimore — fare 3.50 — Extra 1.00. Arrived in Balt. next morning at 8 o'clock. Stopped at Beltzhoover's Hotel.

Frid. 7. In Baltimore — Called on Revd Huntz & paid him some money for Luth. Obs. Soon became tired of the noise and bustle of the City. At 5 P.M. took the rail road Car for Washington city — fare 2.50 for Breakfast & dinner at Beltzhoover's 1.25. 2 trunks to rail road office 50 cts. Arrived in Washington at 8 P.M. — here all was noise & confusion. Seat in a hack to the hotel 25 cts. Supper at Gadsby's Hotel 50 cts. The coffee was too bitter to be drunk. Went on board the steam boat Sydney for Fredericksburg, at 9 o'clock, which started next morning at 4 o'clock.

Sat. 8. Arrived in Fredericksburg at 11 a.m. Breakfast 50 cts. Entered for Prince Edward fare 8.00. Dinner at Allsop's 50 cts. Lodging at Holliday's 75 cts.

Sund. 9. Break at Mill's 50 cts. Dinner at Cerub Court House 50 cts. Lodging Prince Edward 75 cts.

Mond. 10. Entered for Greensborough, N.C. fare 10.00 — breakfast at Charlotte Court House 50 cts. Dinner Halifax Court House 50 cts. Lodging in Milton 75 cts.

Tues. 11. Breakfast at Greves' 50 cts. Dinner Greensborough 50 cts. Entered here for Salem — fare 2.00. Lodging in Salem 50 cts.

Wed. 12. Hired a vehicle to father's 50 cts. Arrived at home to day at 11 a.m.

Thurs. 13. Went to St. Thomas' & Mr. Beckerdite's.

Frid. 14. Returned home.

Sat. 15. At home.

Sund. 16. Preached for Revd Shuls, Moravian, from 2 Cor. 5:17.

Mond. 17. Went to H. Thomas' & H. Beckerdite's.

Tues. 18. Went to Salem in the mail hack with Dr. Hazelius who happened to be on his way to Salem. Enjoyed myself very much in his company. Stopped at tavern.

Wed. 19. Returned home. Expense $2.25.

Thurs. 20. At home.

Frid. 21. Preached at Opossum-town from 2 Peter 3:18. The day was windy & cold & the congregation small.

Sat. 22. At home.

Sund. 23. Preached at Ripple's church from Ex. 20:8. The day was pleasant & the congregation large.

Mond. 24. Went to Rev. Miller's, to Mr. Thomas', & H. Beckerdite's.

Tues. 25. Returned home to father's. had the company of Dr. Hazelius this afternoon. At night took the stage for Lexington.

Wed. 26. Took the stage for Salisbury.

Rowan County, N. C.
July 21st 1838
Diary No. 7.

Wed. 11. At home.

Thurs. 12. Went to Salisbury to see how the printer was getting along with the Minutes of Synod.

Frid. 13. Took some thread and lining to Eliz. Brown for a quilt, then went to Salisbury to correct some proof sheets of the Minutes.

Sat. 14. At home.

Sund. 15. Preached at Union from John 5:40. After preaching, attended to Bible class.

Mond. 16. At home. Rev. Arey was with me to day.

Tues. 17. Went to Salisbury to see about the Minutes of Synod.

Wed. 18. At home.

Thurs. 19. Called to see Jacob Brown.

Frid. 20. At home.

Sat. 21. Went to Salisbury — in the evening returned home.

Sund. 22. Preached in Salisbury from Ps. 42:6. — baptized one infant. In the afternoon preached at St. Paul's ch. from the same text. After preaching returned home.

Mond. 23. Went to Salisbury & had settlement with my congregation. In the afternoon, distributed the Minutes of Synod. Returned home in the evening.

Tues. 24. Planted some potatoes. In the afternoon assisted Mrs. Arey in hanging a fishing sein.

Wed. 25. Engaged in fishing.

Thurs. 26. At home.

Frid. 27. Called to see Mr. Trexler.

Sat. 28. Went to Salisbury. In the afternoon returned home.

Sund. 29. Preached to day for Rev. Arey at Leonard's Ch. Baptized one infant. In the evening, went to father's.

Mond. 30. At father's.

Tues. 31. Returned home.

Wed., August 1. At home till the afternoon, then went to mill.

Thurs. 2. At home.

Frid. 3. At home.

Sat. 4. At home.

Sund. 5. This was my regular day at Union, but Rev. Arey, being present, preached in my place. Baptized Rev. Arey child in connection with two others.

Mond. 6. At home.

Tues. 7. Wrote letters to Dr Hazelius & br. Lewis. In the afternoon went to Salisbury.

Wed. 8. Called to see Christian Bringle & widow Barringer.

Thurs. 9. Engaged in fishing for trout in company with Milas Arey.

Frid. 10. Call to see Jacob Thomas.

Sat. 11. Preached at St. Paul's ch. from Mark 6:12. and settled with the congregation.

Sund. 12. Preached at St. Paul's ch. from Gen. 28:17. & baptized one infant. In the afternoon preached in Salisbury from the same text, baptized one child.

Mond. 13. Tues. 14. At home.

Wed. 15. Went to Griffin's mill in company with Mr. Arey. All night at Griffin's.

Thurs. 16. Returned home.

Frid. 17. Sat. 18. At home.

Sund. 19. Preached at Union from Luk. 17:32. Baptized one infant. After preaching attended to the Bible Class. In the afternoon had prayermeeting at Mr. Arey's — lectured from Gen. 28:17.

Mond. 20. Went to Mr. D. Barringer's Esqr. fishing.

Tues. 21. Went to Salisbury in company with Mrs. Arey.

Wed. 22. At home.

Thurs. 23. Went to the river fishing.

Frid. 24. At home.

Sat. 25. Went to see Charles Earnhart about buying his place. In the afternoon at home.

Sund. 26. Preached in Salisbury from Luk. 17:5. Took dinner with Moses L. Brown. In the afternoon Preached at St. Paul's ch. from the same text. At candle lighting had prayermeeting at Henry Hill's, sen. lectured from Phil. 3:20.21. All night at Mr. Hill's.

Mond. 27. Returned home by way of Salisbury.

Tues. 28. Went to Charles Earnhart's & to Salisbury. In the evening returned home.

Wed. 29. Thurs. 30. Frid. 31. At home.

Sat., Sept. 1. Attended a meeting of the Union Temperance Society at Union Ch. & addressed the meeting from Col. 2:16.17. Three of the Council joined the Society.

Sund. 2. Preached at Union from Luk. 16:8. latter clause. In the afternoon had prayermeeting at Jacob Brown's, lectured from Gen. 15:11. Staid all night at Mr. Brown's.

Mond. 3. Returned home.

Tues. 4. Attended to the funeral of Robert Wood in Salisbury. preached from Gen. 49:18.

Wed. 5. Went to see Jacob Walton to engage some corn. Returned home by Mr. Danl Swink's.

Thurs. 6. Started for Bear-creek ch. — Took dinner with Rev. B. Arey. Attended at Mr. Pool's sale awhile, & called to see Mr. S. Bayam, who was sick. All night with Mr. D. Barringer.

Frid. 7. Went to Bear-creek, preached from Gen. 49:18. Took dinner with Mr. Moos Esqr. Attended at the church at candle lighting and lectured from Gen. 28:17. All night at Col. Bernhart's.

Sat. 8. Preached at the church again from Luk. 17:5. Germ. In the afternoon returned home.

Sund. 9. Preached at St. Paul's ch. from Luk. 7:50. Preached in Salisbury in the afternoon from Prov. 29:1. After preaching returned home.

Mond. 10. Tues. 11. At home.

Wed. 12. At home.

Thurs. 13. Went to Jacob Thomas' & bought a gallon of honey & settled with Rachel for weaving.

Frid. 14. At home. Rev. Arey was with me to day.

Sat. 15. Went to father's.

Sund. 16. Exchanged pulpits to with Rev. Arey. — preached for him at Leonard's ch. from Ps. 90:12. the funeral of Mr. Hedrick. All night at Mr. A. Sink's.

Mond. 17. Returned home.

Tues. 18. Attended to the funeral of David Stork in Salisbury. Preached from Ps. 90:12. Returned home in the evening.

Wed. 19. Thurs. 20. At home.

Frid. 21. At home.

Sat. 22. Preached at St. Paul's ch. from 1 Cor. 5:7.8. preparatory to the Lord's Supper. In the afternoon had prayermeeting at George Randleman's, lectured from Math. 6:33. All night here.

Sund. 23. Preached at St. Paul's from Numb. 10:29. & administered the Lord's Supper. After preaching returned home.

Mond. 24. Went to Jacob Walton's to get some corn. Called to see Mr. Trexler at his mill.

Tues. 25. At home.

Wed. 26. Went to see Jacob Brown & Mrs. Barringer.

Thurs. 27. Took some corn to mill, the balance of the day at home.

Frid. 28. To day a 3-days meeting commenced in Salisbury. Rev. Strobel preached for me. all night B. Fraley's.

Sat. 29. Rev. Strobel preached for me. Elected & inaugurated a church council. Baptized an infant. In the evening returned home.

Sund. 30. Returned to Salisbury. Rev. Strobel preached — confirmed one person, then administered the Holy Supper. In the afternoon preached from Mark 10:46-52. All night at B. Fraley's.

Mond., Oct. 1. Attended a Temperance meeting with Rev. Strobel at Henry Lentz's & formed a Society. In the evening returned here.

Tues. 2. Called to see Jacob Brown & in company with him, George Miller. — Called on my way home to see Mrs. Barringer.

Wed. 3. At home.

Thurs. 4. At home.

Frid. 5. Met Mr. Trexler & Mrs. Barringer, to restore peace between them, they having been at variance. At night had prayermeeting at Mr. Heilig's, lectured from Math. 6:33.

Sat. 6. Preached at Union from Rom. 12:2. first clause, preparatory to communion. Confirmed one person, Mr. Wade. At night had prayermeeting at Mr. Trexler's — lectured from Ps. 58:11.

Sund. 7. Preached at Union church from Isa. 25:6-8. & administered the Lord's Supper. Baptized one infant. At night had prayermeeting at Widow John Pealer's — lectured from Prov. 3:6.

Mond. 8. Tues. 9. At home.

Wed. 10. Went to Salisbury.

Thurs. 11. Frid. 12. At home.

Sat. 13. Attended a Temperance Meeting at Jacob Moyer's.

Sund. 14. Preached at St. Paul's ch. from Acts 16:16-34.

Mond. 15. Attended a Temperance Meeting at Mr. Kimbrel's, spoke from Eph. 5:18.

Tues. 16. Attended the funeral of Abel Troutman at the Stone ch. preached from Heb. 4:9. Rev. Stork staid with me to night.

Wed. 17. Thurs. 18. At home.

Frid. 19. Went to Salisbury.

Sat. 20. Went to David Wise's & had my horse shod. In the evening went to William Smith's, sen.

Sund. 21. Went to Salisbury. Rev. T. Stork preached for me. Confirmed Mr. C. Fisher. In the afternoon had meeting at William Smith's, sen. Rev. Stork officiated for me. All night there.

Mond. 22. Accompanied Rev. Stork to Salisbury. In the evening returned home.

Tues. 23. Went to Henry Lentz's & bought some corn.

Wed. 24. Attended to the funeral of B. F. Fraley's child in Salisbury. Preached from 2 Cor. 4:17.

Thurs. 25. Went to H. Lentz's after corn.

Frid. 26. At home quite indisposed.

Sat. 27. Had made an appointment for settlement with the congregation at Union to day, but was not able to attend in consequence of indisposition.

Sund. 28. Preached at Union ch. from 1 Thes. 2:11.12. & read part of the Discipline to the congregation.

Mond. 29. Commenced school.

Tues. 30. Wed. 31. In school.

Thurs. Nov. 1. Dug potatoes.

Frid. 2. Cut fire wood and made a hog pen.

Sat. 3. Went to Salisbury.

Sund. 4. Started for St. Paul's ch., but did not get to the church in consequence of the rain.

Mond. 5. Tues. 6. Wed. 7. In school.

Thurs. 8. Frid. 9. In school.

Sat. 10. Went to Salisbury & at night attended a prayermeeting at Mr. Vogler's. Rev. Stork lectured to the people. All night at Mr. Vogler's.

Sund. 11. This was my regular day for preaching at Salisbury, but Rev. Stork being present preached in my stead. In the afternoon returned home.

Mond. 12. Attended to the funeral of Jacob Weant at his residence — preached from Math. 5:8.

Tues. 13. Wed. 14. In school.

Thurs. 15. Frid. 16. In school.

Sat. 17. At home.

Sund. 18. Went to Union ch. this being my regular day to preach there, but the day being very inclement the congregation did not assemble. Returned home without preaching.

Mond. 19. Tues. 20. Wed. 21. Thurs. 22. In school.

Frid. 23. In school.

Sat. 24. Preached at St. Paul's ch. from Math 8:1-4. This was a day appointed for settlement.

Sund. 25. Preached at St. Paul's ch. from John 14:15.

Mond. 26. Tues. 27. Wed. 28. Thurs. 29. Frid. 30. In school.

Sat. Dec. 1. Went to Salisbury.

Sund. 2. Preached in Salisbury from Luk. 13:24. To day resigned the charge of the congregation. In the evening had prayermeeting at P. Arey's — lectured from John 14:15.

Mond. 3. Tues. 4. Wed. 5. Thurs. 6. Frid. 7. In school.

Sat. 8. At home. Made some preparations for Sunday.

Sund. 9. Preached at Union ch. from Micah 6:8. After sermon attended to the bible class. In the afternoon called at Allen Brown's to see his wife who was very sick. At night had prayermeeting at H. Trexler's. Revd Arey lectured for me.

Mond. 10. In school.

Tues. 11. Attended to the funeral of Elizabeth Brown, wife of Allen at Union ch. Preached from Ps. 90:12.

Wed. 12. Thurs. 13. Frid. 14. In school.

Sat. 15. Went to Salisbury.

Sund. 16. Preached at St. Paul's church from Josh. 24:15. In the afternoon married Alexander Brown to Miss Elizabeth Walton, at James Brown's.

Mond. 17. Tues. 18. Wed. 19. Thurs. 20. Frid. 21. In school.

Sat. 22. Went to Salisbury — in the afternoon preached at Wm. Smith's, sen. from 1 Tim. 4:7. latter clause.

Sund. 23. Preached at Union ch. from Gen. 3:13. latter clause. Attended also to the funeral of Henry Agner's child. This was an excessively cold day.

Mond. 24. At home.

Tues. 25. At home.

Wed. 26. Attended to butchering our hogs.

Thurs. 27. Salted away meat, &c.

Frid. 28. Had logs cut & hauled for a kitchen.

Sat. 29. Mended my shoes.

Sun. 30. Was to have assisted Revd Strobel at a 2-days meeting, but the inclemency of the weather prevented me from attending.

Mond. 31. In school.

Tues., Jan, 1, 1839. Went to Salisbury.
Wed. 2. Thurs. 3. In school.
Frid. 4. In school.
Sat. 5. Preached at Wm. Smith's from Rev. 2:4. Baptized 1 infant.
Sund. 6. Preached at St. Paul's ch. from 1 Tim. 4:7.
Mond. 7. Tues. 8. Wed. 9. Thurs. 10. Frid. 11. In school.
Sat. 12. At home.
Sund. 13. Preached at Union from Josh. 7:12. Baptized 1 infant. At night had prayermeeting at Mrs. Barringer's
    — lectured from 1 Tim. 4:7.
Mond. 14. Tues. 15. Wed. 16. Thurs. 17. Frid. 18. In school.
Sat. 19. Preached at Wm. Smith's from John 21:17. latter clause.
Sund. 20. Preached at St. Paul's church from 1 John 3:2. Suffered to day with cold.
Mond. 21. Attended to the funeral of Dan[1] Hottinger's wife at Union ch. — preached from Amos 4:12.
Tues. 22. Wed. 23. Thurs. 24. Frid. 25. In school.
Sat. 26. Started to St. Stephen's ch. all night at David Linn's.
Sund. 27. Preached at St. Stephen's ch. from 1 Tim 4:7. After preaching returned home.
Mond. 28. Tues. 29. Wed. 30. Thurs. 31. In school.

Frid., Feb. 1. In school till the afternoon, then went David Barringer's, whose wife was sick.
Sat. 2. Went to Salisbury.
Sund. 3. Preached at Union from Mark 6:12. After preaching went to David Barringer's. Returned home at
    night.
Mond. 4. Tues. 5. Wed. 6. Thurs. 7. In school.
Frid. 8. To day closed my school. In the afternoon called to David Barringer's family.
Sat. 9. Preached at Wm. Smith's, sen. from 1 Cor. 13:1-13.
Sund. 10. Preached at St. Paul's ch. from 1 Cor. 13:1-13. After preaching returned home. Had a son born this
    evening at about 7 o'clock.
Mond. 11. At home till afternoon. Then went to ask some hands to raise a kitchen.
Tues. 12. At home. had a kitchen raised. At night went to Jacob Brown's & married John L. Randleman to
    Nancy Brown.
Wed. 13. At home.
Thurs. 14. Went to Salisbury.
Frid. 15. Sat. 16. At home.
Sund. 17. Preached at Union from Isa. 48:18.
Mond. 18. Tues. 19. At home.
Wed. 20. Called on H. Trexler to haul me some wood.
Thurs. 21. At home.
Frid. 22. Had some wood hauled to day. In the afternoon went to H. Trexler's mill & ground my ax.
Sat. 23. Preached Wm. Smith's, sen. from Isa. 55:6.7.
Sund. 24. Preached at St. Paul's ch. from Isa. 55:6.7. Baptized 2 children.
Mond. 25. Went to Salisbury — got wet.
Tues. 26. Attended to the funeral of old Mr. Folk at his house. Gave a short address from Amos 4:12.
Wed. 27. At home — covered the kitchen.
Thurs. 28. At home.

Frid., March 1. Went to Salisbury & to Henry Hill's, sen. to engage some sweet potatoes to plant.

Sat. 2. Attended a Meeting of the Union Temperance Society at Union ch.

Sund. 3. Preached at Union ch. from Ps. 27:4. Baptized one infant.

Mond. 4. At home.

Tues. 5. Went to Salisbury & at night had prayermeeting at B. Fraley's, — lectured from Is. 48:18.

Wed. 6. Returned home.

Thurs. 7. At home. Made a cutting room.

Frid. 8. Attended Dan⁻ Swink's sale.

Sat. 9. Attended St. Matthew's ch. & preached from Is. 55:6.7. German.

Sund. 10. Preached at St. Paul's ch. from Prov. 1:24-26. Baptized one infant.

Mond. 11. Went to Salisbury.

Tues. 12. Wed. 13. Thurs. 14. Frid. 15. At home.

Sat. 16. Preached at Wm. Smith's, sen. from Phil. 3:20.21.

Sund. 17. Preached at Union from Hos. 13:9. At night had prayermeeting at Peter Arey's, lectured from Math. 12:41.

Mond. 18. At home.

Tues. 19. Went to Salisbury.

Wed. 20. At home.

Thurs. 21. Went to Salisbury.

Frid. 22. At home.

Sat. 23. Had an appointment for to day at John May's to preach German, but the rainy weather prevented me from attending.

Sund. 24. Preached at St. Paul's ch. from Ex. 33:14. Took dinner at Moses Brown's & then returned home.

Mond. 25. Went to Henry Hill's for sweet potatoe plantings. A very cold day.

Tues. 26. Went to Salisbury.

Wed. 27. Attended to the funeral of Andrew Holdshouser's child at Union ch. preached from John 3:36.

Thurs. 28. Planted sweet potatoes.

Frid. 29. Went to St. Stephen's ch. to attend a protracted meeting. Preached from John 3:16. Germ. Attended a prayermeeting at night in the church — lectured from Is. 48:18. All night at Mr. Peck's, sen.

Sat. 30. Preached at the church from John 14:15. Germ. Attended a prayermeeting at night in the church. All night at Mr. Nussman's.

Sund. 31. Preached in the afternoon in the ch. from John 5:40. At night attended a prayermeeting at Dewalt Lentz's — lectured from Math. 12:41. All night at Mrs. Kimbrel's.

Mond., April 1. Attended a Temperance Meeting at Dewalt Lentz's. In the afternoon returned home.

Tues. 2. Went to Salisbury.

Wed. 3. Went for Dr. Bell, to see P. Arey.

Thurs. 4. At home.

Frid. 5. At home.

Sat. 6. Preached at Union preparatory to communion from Math. 26:41. Confirmed one person & received another by certificate. Baptized 5 children.

Sund. 7. Preached at Union from Is. 27:13. & administered the Lord's Supper. At night had prayermeeting at H. Trexler's & lectured from Prov. 1:23.

Mond. 8. At home.

Tues. 9. Called at John Kesler's to look at his place. Called at Ad. Casper's to see his wife who was sick. At night had prayermeeting in Salisbury at B. Fraley's — lectured from 1 Tim. 4:7.

Wed. 10. Returned home. Called at Union ch. to see the church land surveyed.

Thurs. 11. At home & planted corn.

Frid. 12. Had an appointment to day at Wm. Smith's, sen. but could not cross the creek.

Sat. 13. Preached at St. Paul's ch. from Rom. 12:2. preparatory to communion. After preaching returned home.

Sund. 14. Preached at St. Paul's ch. from John 3:14.15. & administered the Lord's Supper. At night had prayermeeting at Adam Casper's — lectured from Math. 5:6. to a full house. All night here.

Mond. 15. Returned home by way of Salisbury.

Tues. 16. At home, making preparations to go to Synod.

Wed. 17. Started for Synod as far as Father's — all night here.

Thurs. 18. Went to Greensborough.

Frid. 19. Arrived at Rev. Artz's about 12 M. In the afternoon went to preaching. All night at Rev. Artz's.

Sat. 20. Attended at the church — at 2 p.m. the Synod was organized. All night at Mr. Edwin Holt's.

Sund. 21. At the church. In the afternoon preached a missionary sermon from Ps. 116:12.13. All night at Mr. E. Holt's.

Mond. 22. In Synod. All night at Mr. Michael Holt's.

Tues. 23. In synod. All night at Mr. Whitesel's.

Wed. 24. Started for home as far as Mr. Brummel's. All night here.

Thurs. 25. Arrived at home by way of Father's.

Frid. 26. At home.

Sat. 27. In the afternoon, went to a Temperance Meeting at Mr. Allen Brown's.

Sund. 28. Had prayermeeting in the afternoon at Abram Arey's — lectured from Gal. 6:14.

Mond. 29. Went to Salisbury.

Tues. 30. Wed., May 1. At home.

Thurs. 2. Frid. 3. At home.

Sat. 4. Preached at Wm. Smith's, sen. from John 8:36.

Sund. 5. Preached at Union ch. from Is. 3:10.††. Baptized one infant. In the afternoon preached at Jacob Walton's from Job. 23:16. the funeral of Mrs. W., who had died a short time previous. Baptized also Mr. W.'s infant child.

Mond. 6. At home.

Tues. 7. Went to Salisbury.

Wed. 8. At home, Mrs. R. Being sick.

Thurs. 9. }
Frid. 10. } At home, replanting corn.

Sat. 11. Went to Salisbury & in the afternoon attended a prayermeeting at Mr. Bischeron's — Rev. J. D. Scheck lectured to the people.

Sund. 12. Preached at St. Paul's ch. from Gen. 3:13. after preaching returned home.

Mond. 13. }
Tues. 14. } At home, making preparations to the General Synod.
Wed. 15. }

Thurs. 16. Started for Pennsylvania as far as Salisbury. All night at Mr. Heilig's.

Frid. 17. Took a seat in the Raleigh Stage. Arrived in Baltimore on Mond. morning the 20th for breakfast. Staid here two days.

Wed. 22. Started for Gettysburg and arrived there the same evening. Staid in Gettysburg and vicinity 2 days.

Frid. evening 24. Started for Chambersburg and arrived there next morning at the break of day. Remained 2 days.

Sund. 26. Preached for Rev. Hoffman twice; in the morning from Is. 25:6-8. at night from Prov. 29:1.

Mond. 27. Went to St. Thomas, where I was once stationed — met with many warm friends.

Tues. 28. Went to M'Connellsburg.

Wed. 29. Preached at night in the Luth. ch. in M'Connellsburg from 1 Pet. 4:18. Baptized at Mr. Flore's one child.

Thurs. 30. Returned to St. Thomas.

Frid. 31. Went to Chambersburg in company with Rev. Sahm.

Sat., June 1. In Chambersburg.

Sund. 2. Went to St. Thomas in company with Rev. Sahm, & preached from Math. 11:28. Germ. In the afternoon Engl. from 2 Cor. 5:17. After preaching returned to Chambersburg.

Mond. 3. The General Synod commenced its business, & closed its sessions on Wednesday evening the 5th.

Thurs. 6. Started on my return home. Took stage for Baltimore in company with Dr. Hazelius & arrived there next morning at 1 o'clock.

Frid. 7. Took steam boat at 5 o'clock p.m. for Norfolk & arrived there next morning at 7 o'clock. Started immediately on the Rail Road & at Gary's at 2 p.m. Obliged to remain at Gary's till next morning.

Sund. 9. Started for Henderson, Raleigh, &c. & arrived at home safely on Tues. evening the 11th.

Wed. 12. Thurs. 13. Frid. 14. Sat. 15. At home.

Sund. 16. Preached at Union church from John 7:37. Baptized 2 children.*

Mond. 17. Went to Salisbury. At home the balance of the week, engaged part of the time in writing the Minutes of Synod.

Sund. 23. Preached at St. Paul's ch. from Eph 6:18. Took dinner at Moses Brown's, sen.

Mond. 24.
Tues. 25.
Wed. 26. } At home — finished preparing the Minutes of Synod for the press.
Thurs. 27.

Frid. 28. Went to Salisbury, to employ the printer to print the Minutes of our Synod.

Sat. 29. Went to Father's.

Sund. 30. Assisted Rev. Crim at Opossumtown — preached from 1 Pet. 4:18.

* Attended also to day to the funeral of old Mrs. Eller, preached from Rev. 14:13. in German.

Mond. July 1. Returned home.

Tues. 2. At home.

Wed. 3. Went to Salisbury.

Thurs. 4. Went to Salisbury.

Frid. 5. }
Sat. 6. } At home, making some preparations for Sunday.

Sund. 7. Preached at Union church from Jer. 5:26. first clause. In the afternoon preached at St. Matthew's ch. from Prov. 29:1.

Mond. 8. At home.

Tues. 9. Preached at Adam Casper's (whose wife was very sick) from Ps. 138:6. In the afternoon returned home by way of Salisbury.

Wed. 10. At home.

Thurs. 11. Went to Alex.ʳ Brown's with Mrs. R. to a quilting.

Frid. 12. Attended to the funeral of Mrs. Adam Casper, at the Stone Church. (Ger. Ref.ᵈ) preached from Ps. 90:12.

Sat. 13. Went to Salisbury.

Sund. 14. This was my regular day to preach at St. Paul's ch. but did not attend in consequence of rain.

Mond. 15. Tues. 16. At home.

Wed. 17. Went to Salisbury.

Thurs. 18. At home.

Frid. 19. To day commenced a protracted Meeting at Union church. Rev. Crim preached the first sermon. At night had a prayermeeting at Christian Bringle's — Rev. Strobel & Crim lectured.

Sat. 20. Rev. Strobel & Arey preached. At night had prayermeetings at Jacob Brown's & Widow Jesse Walton's.

Sund. 21. Rev. Strobel & Arey preached. At night had prayermeeting at Henry Trexler's.

Mond. 22. Had a Temperance meeting at the church. Rev. Strobel delivered an address.

Tues. 23. Went to Salisbury.

Wed. 24. Went to John Kesler's to look at his place.

Thurs. 25. Went to Rev. Strobel's in company with Rev. Arey to attend a protracted meeting at Coldwater.

Frid. 26. Preached at Coldwater from 1 Thes. 2:11.12. At night preached in the Presbyterian ch. in Concord from Luk. 13:24. All night at Mr. Abram Arey's.

Sat. 27. Preached at Coldwater from Ex. 33:14. In the evening at Genl. Barringer's from Phil. 3:20.21. All night at Mr. Barringer's.

Sund. 28. Preached at Coldwater from 1 John 3:2. At night attended a prayermeeting in the church. Gave a short lecture to the people. All night at Widow Urey's.

Mond. 29. Returned home.

Tues. 30. Went to Salisbury.

Wed. 31. Preached at St. Paul's ch. from 1 Thes. 2:11.12. Baptized 2 children.

Thurs., Aug. 1. In the afternoon went to the river fishing.

Frid. 2. Preached at Kencade's school house from Rev. 2:4.5.

Sat. 3. Commenced catechization at Union ch.

Sund. 4. Preached at Union ch. from Ex. 14:15. In the afternoon at St. Mathew's ch. from Phil. 3:20.21.

Mond. 5. At home.

Tues. 6. Sent for to see Cruso Brown who was very sick.

Wed. 7. Called to see Cruso Brown.

Thurs. 8. Had straw & corn hauled till 12 o'clock. In the afternoon went to Salisbury to attend the elections — voted to day for the first time — voted for Charles Fisher for Congress & for free schools.

Frid. 9. At home.

Sat. 10. Had catechization at Union church.

Sund. 11. Preached at St. Paul's ch. from Is. 48:18. Made a beginning towards organizing a congregational Missionary and Education Society. On my way home called by to see Cruso Brown.

Mond. 12. At home.

Tues. 13. Went to David Barringer's.

Wed. 14. At home.

Thurs. 15. At home till 12 o'clock. Then went to Salisbury.

Frid. 16. At home.

Sat. 17. Had catechization at Union.

Sund. 18. Attended to the funeral of Cruso Brown at Union ch. — preached from Math. 22:5. Commenced the formation of a Missionary & Education Society.

Mond. 19. Called to see Caleb Peeler, to get him to haul straw. In the afternoon assisted Mr. Peeler in hauling a load of straw.

Tues. 20. At home.

Wed. 21. Went to Salisbury.

Thurs. 22. Daubed the spring house till 12 o'clock. Then went to Widow Cawble's, & in the evening married Moses Trexler to Margaret Cawble. All night at Mr. Trexler's.

Frid. 23. At Mr. Trexler's to dinner.

Sat. 24. Preached at St. Paul's ch. from Acts 20:17-21. Baptized one infant.

Sund. 25. Preached at St. Paul's ch. from Micah 6:8. Completed the organization of a Missionary & Education Society.

Mond. 26. Went to Salisbury.

Tues. 27. At home.

Wed. 28. Shelled corn, stripped fodder & went to mill.

Thurs. 29. At home.

Frid. 30. Had catechization at Union.

Sat. 31. At home.

Sund., Sept. 1. Preached at Union ch. from 1 Tim. 6:10. Completed the organization of a Missionary and Education Society.

Mond. 2. Tues. 3. At home.

Wed. 4. Had catechization at Union.

Thurs. 5. Started to St. Enoch's ch. to attend a protracted meeting. All night at Robert Linn's.

Frid. 6. Went to St. Enoch's church, preached from Rev. 2:4.5. At night had a prayermeeting at Mr. Oehler's, lectured from 1 Tim. 4:7. All night here.

Sat. 7. Preached at St. Enoch's from Math. 11:28. German. At night lectured in the church from Mark 10:46-52. All night at Mr. Overcash's.

Sund. 8. Preached in the afternoon from 1 Pet. 4:18. At night attended prayermeeting in the ch. Rev. Scheck lectured. All night at Mr. Rose's, Esqr.

Mond. 9. Attended a special Meeting of the Synodical Missionary & Education Society at St. Enoch's. Preached with reference to the Missionary & Ed. subject from Acts 26:17.18. Took dinner with Mr. Rose, & then returned home.

Tues. 10. Started to Orange County to attend a protracted meeting at St. Paul's ch. All night at Father's.

Wed. 11. Had my mare shod at Jonathon Beard's. Took dinner at Brummel's, paid 50 cts. All night at Jamestown, paid $1.25.

Thurs. 12. Arrived at Rev. Artz's. All night here.

Frid. 13. Attended at St. Paul's ch. Rev. Strobel preached. Cong^{n} small. All night at Rev. Artz's.

Sat. 14. Preached at St. Paul's ch. from Josh. 24:18. At night attended a prayermeeting in the ch. Rev. S. lectured. All night at M. Holt's, Esqr.

Sund. 15. Preached a Dedication sermon from Gen. 28:17. Aided in the administration of the Lord's Supper. Attended a prayermeeting at night in the ch. lectured from 2 Cor. 5:17. All night at Mr. M. Holt's, Esqr.

Mond. 16. Started for home. Took dinner at McGibbony's. In the afternoon preached at a stand in the neighborhood from 2 Cor. 5:17. All night at McGibbony's.

Tues. 17. Went to Father's. All night here.

Wed. 18. Reached home.

Thurs. 19. Went to Salisbury.

Frid. 20. Had catechization at Union.

Sat. 21. Attended a meeting of the Union Temperance Society at Union.

Sund. 22. Preached at St. Paul's ch. from John 14:22. In the afternoon Rev. B. Arey preached for me at Union Ch.

Mond. 23. At home.

Tues. 24. Went to Salisbury.

Wed. 25. At home.

Thurs. 26. Went to Father's to attend a protracted meeting at Hopewell Church.

Frid. 27. Attended at Hopewell Ch. followed Rev. Crim with an exhortation.

Sat. 28. At Hopewell ch. preached from Jer. 5:26. At night attended a prayermeeting at H. Thomas'.

Sund. 29. At Hopewell — preached from Math. 22:5. Consecrated the elements for communion & then aided in the administration of the L's Supper. At night attended a prayermeeting at H. Thomas'.

Mond. 30. Returned home.

Tues. Oct. 1. Went to Salisbury.

Wed. 2. Went to Mr. Johnson's with sister Salome, then to J. Hartman's to buy hay, but obtained none. In the afternoon went to Jac. Brown's & bought 1 cwt. of flour.

Thurs. 3. At home till evening, then went to Jacob Brown's for flour.

Frid. 4. Had catechization at Union.

Sat. 5. Had preaching at Union preparatory to communion, preached from Ps. 51:2. Baptized one child.

Sund. 6. Preached at Union ch. from James 1:12. then administered the Lord's Supper. At night had prayermeeting at the Widow John Pealer's — lectured from Math. 6:33.

Mond. 7. Went to Father's — took sister Salome home.

Tues. 8. Returned home. Mrs. R. sick in bed.

Wed. 9. Went to Salisbury.

Thurs. 10. At home.

Frid. 11. Had catechization at Union.

Sat. 12. Preached at St. Paul's church from Ps. 51:2. preparatory to the Lord's Supper.

Sund. 13. Preached at St. Paul's ch. from Math. 22:5. then administered the Lord's Supper.

Mond. 14. Went to Salisbury.

Tues. 15. At home, digging potatoes, &c.

Wed. 16. At home till 12 o'clock, then went to Mr. Glover's for a pair of shoes.

Thurs. 17. Went to Salisbury — bought a few shoemaker's tools.

Frid. 18. Had catechization at Union, in the afternoon went to Alex^r Brown's sale & bought some wheat & a hog.

Sat. 19. Attended to the getting wheat, &c. home.

Sund. 20. Preached at Union from Prov. 23:26. Baptized two chil^n.

Mond. 21. At home.

Tues. 22. Went to Charles Eller's & bought a stack of hay.

Wed. 23. Went to Salisbury.

Thurs. 24. At home.

Frid. 25. Had catechization at Union ch.

Sat. 26. Preached at Geo. Garner's from Ps. 116:12-14. in German and administered the Lord's Supper to old Mrs. Garner.

Sund. 27. Preached at St. Paul's ch. from Prov. 23:26. Baptized 1 child.

Mond. 28. Went to Father's in company with br. Lewis.

Tues. 29. Returned home.

Wed. 30. Went to Salisbury.

Thurs. 31. At home cutting fire-wood.

Frid. Nov. 1. Had catechization at Union ch.

Sat. 2. At home.

Sund. 3. Preached at Union ch. from Mark 1:40-45. Baptized one infant.

Mond. 4. At home till 12 o'clock, then went to Alex. Brown's & settled with him.

Tues. 5. At home. Rev. Crim was with me to day.

Wed. 6. Went to Salisbury & attended a Temperance Convention.

Thurs. 7. At home.

Frid. 8. This was my day to attend catechization ar Union ch. but did not attend.

Sat. 9. At home, storing away potatoes.

Sund. 10. Preached at St. Paul's ch. from Rev. 3:20.

Mond. 11. Called to see Thomas Earnheart to engage a meat stand.

Tues. 12. Went gunning some but with little success.

Wed. 13. Went gunning in company with Milas Arey.

Thurs. 14. Went to Salisbury.

Frid. 15. Went to Union ch. to attend catechization, but for the want of sufficient previous notice, the catechumens did not attend.

Sat. 16. This was the day appointed for settlement & election of Church Council at Union ch. but as the attendance of the members was small, the election was deferred.

Sund. 17. Preached at Union ch. from John 14:15. then held an election for Church Council & took the vote of the congregation in relation to the building of a School-house.

Mond. 18. Went to Father's.

Tues. 19. Hired my boy, Dan, to father for one year for $20. & then returned home.

Wed. 20. Went to Jacob Brown's to engage his waggon & team to haul hay & wood.

Thurs. 21. At home cutting fire-wood.

Frid. 22. Had catechization at Union ch.

Sat. 23. At home - received a load of hay & in the evening hauled some wood.

Sund. 24. This was my day to preach at St. Paul's ch. but the day being very inclement, did not attend.

Mond. 25. Went to Salisbury.

Tues. 26. At home.

Wed. 27. Attended to the funeral of old Mrs. Lemly at St. Matthew's Ch. preached from Amos 4:12.

Thurs. 28. Attend Mr. Cornup's sale.

Frid. 29. Had appointed catechization at Union, but the day being very inclement did not attend.

Sat. 30. At home.

Sund. Dec. 1. Preached at Union from Prov. 23:15. Then installed a part of the Church Council & held the first quarterly meeting of the Missionary & Education Society.

Mond. 2. Assisted in setting up a coal kiln at P. Arey's.

Tues. 3. At home.

Wed. 4. At home — had a few hands to assist in cutting fire wood.

Thurs. 5. Went to Salisbury to aid Rev. Scheck in a protracted meeting — preached in the afternoon from 2 Cor. 5:17. Lectured at night at Mr. Heilig's from Prov. 23:26. All night at Rev. S's.

Frid. 6. Preached in the afternoon from Math. 22:5. & then returned home.

Sat. 7. Returned to Salisbury — at night lectured at Mr. Culberhouse's from Mar. 1:40-45. All night here.

Sund. 8. Preached at St. Paul's ch. from Jam. 1:12. Baptized one inf.

Mond. 9. At home made preparations to butcher.

Tues. 10. Had Amos Eller to help me butcher.

Wed. 11. At home.

Thurs. 12. Attended the burial of Wilie Cawble's child.

Frid. 13. Had catechization at Union ch.

Sat. 14. Attended a Temperance Meeting at Jacob Brown's — lectured from 1 Thes. 5:6. latter clause — the day being inclement, the attendance was small.

Sund. 15. Preached at Union from Math. 18:20. Installed 2 of the Church Council, they having been prevent from attending 2 weeks before.

Mond. 16. At home, prepared troughs to feed the cows.

Tues. 17. At home.

Wed. 18. Went to Salisbury.

Thurs. 19. At home.

Frid. 20. Wrote a letter to Dr. Hazelius & in the afternoon called to see G. H. Brown at his father's.

Sat. 21. At home — snowed all day.

Sund. 22. This was my day to preach at St. Paul's ch. but the day being very inclement, did not attend.

Mond. 23. At home.

Tues. 24. Went to Salisbury.

Wed. 25. Preached at the widow Dan^1 Agner's, German & English from Isa. 9:6. — a good attendance.

Thurs. 26. At home.

Frid. 27. Sat. 28. At home.

Sund. 29. Preached at St. Mathew's ch. from Prov 23:26. Weather very cold.

Mond. 30. Tues. 31. At home.

Jan. Wed. 1. Thurs. 2. Frid. 3. At home.

Sat. 4. At home till afternoon, then went to P. Arey's.

Sund. 5. Was to have exchanged Pulpits to day with Rev. Scheck, but was prevented in consequence of the inclemency of the weather & bodily indisposition. Preached at Union from Ex. 23:2.

Mond. 6. At home.

Tues. 7. Shelled corn & went to mill.

Wed. 8. At home.

Thurs. 9. At home till 12 o'clock then went to David Wise's & had my mare shod.

Frid. 10. Attended to the funeral of Jacob Weaver at St. Paul's ch. preached the funeral at his house from Mark 13:37.

Sat. 11. At home.

Sund. 12. Preached at St. Paul's ch. from Math. 18:20.

Mond. 13. Went to mill & to Jacob Thomas' for honey.

Tues. 14. Went to Salisbury.

Wed. 15. At home till the afternoon, then went to mill.

Thurs. 16. Went to the sale at Andrew Holshouser's.

Frid. 17. Had catechization at Union, & in the afternoon, attended at the funeral of Jacob Thomas' wife.

Sat. 18. At home.

Sund. 19. Preached at Union from Gen. 3:19. the funeral of Cornelius Lineberger's child.

Mond. 20. Went to Salisbury.

Tues. 21. Wed. 22. At home.

Thurs. 23. At home till afternoon, then went to Widow Jno. Peeler's & married Mr. Adam Casper to Miss Sophia Peeler. Then went to Jacob Thomas' & staid over night there.

Frid. 24. Returned home.

Sat. 25. At home. In the afternoon the Council of Union Church met at my house.

Sund. 26. Preached at St. Paul's ch. from Jer. 5:26. first clause.

Mond. 27. Went to Salisbury — settled with B. Fraley.

Tues. 28. At home — wrote some for P. Arey & tried to shoot some ducks.

Wed. 29. Thurs. 30. At home.

Frid. 31. Had catechization at Union.

Sat., Feb. 1. At home.

Sund. 2. This was my regular day to preach at Union, but the weather being very inclement, the congregation was very small. — had some devotional exercises & then dismissed.

Mond. 3. Attended at the funeral of Mrs. Butner.

Tues. 4. At home.

Wed. 5. Had Amos Eller to help me cut fire-wood.

Thurs. 6. At home — this evening Adam came over for us, sister Christena being very sick.

Frid. 7. Went to father's.

Sat. 8. Went to Hugh Beckerdite's & in the evening returned to father's.

Sund. 9. At father's.

Mond. 10. Started for home. all night at Mrs. Moyer's, the creek being too full to cross.

Tues. 11. Returned home by way of Butner's Bridge.

Wed. 12. Went to Salisbury.

Thurs. 13. At home — shot a duck.

Frid. 14. Had catechization at Union.

Sat. 15. Went to Jacob Brown's to engage his waggon to haul wood.

Sund. 16. Preached at Union, the funeral of Wilie Cawble's child, from Eccl. 11:9. Baptized an infant.

Mond. 17. Tues. 18. At home, engaged in hauling wood, &c.

Wed. 19. At home mending shoes.

Thurs. 20. At home mending shoes, till 12 o'clock, then went to mill.

Frid. 21. Went to Salisbury.

Sat. 22. At home.

Sund. 23. Preached at St. Paul's ch. from Eccl. 11:9. All night at G. Garner's.

Mond. 24. Returned home.

Tues. 25. Wed. 26. At home making shoes.

Thurs. 27. Went to Salisbury.

Frid. 28. Had catechization at Union.

Sat. 29. At home.

Sund. March 1. Preached at Union from Acts 17:11.12. At night had prayermeeting at Jacob Walton's, lectured from Math. 12:22-32.

Mond. 2. Tues. 3. Wed. 4. At home.

Thurs. 5. Attended the sale at widow Butner's, & at night married Richard Julin to Miss Sophia Creason at P. Hartman's. All night with Wm. Chambers at the white house.

Frid. 6. Returned home, & in the afternoon went to D. Barringer's in company with Mrs. R.

Sat. 7. Accompanied D. Barringer & others who went to the river fishing, but caught nothing. In the evening returned home.

Sund. 8. Preached at St. Paul's ch. from Acts 17:11.12.

Mond. 9. Went to John Arey's to meet Mrs. R. & help her home.

Tues. 10. Went to mill.

Wed. 11. Went to Salisbury.

Thurs. 12. At home. mended shoes & cleaned the spring.

Frid. 13. Had catechization at Union ch.

Sat. 14. Preached at Linn's school house from Act. 26:17.18. & assisted in organizing a Sunday School. Took dinner at D. Linn's. In the afternoon went in company with S. Linn to Robert Linn's.

Sund. 15. Preached at Savitze's Church from Prov. 23:26. German & English from the same text. In the evening came to Salisbury — afflicted with the ear-ache — at candle lighting, attended preaching in the Methodist ch. All night at M. L. Brown's.

Mond. 16. Returned home. In the afternoon called to see John Arey & paid him for corn bought of him & bought 5 bush. wheat. Suffered with ear-ache.

Tues. 17. Wed. 18. Thurs. 19. At home — suffered with ear-ache.

Frid. 20. At home.

Sat. 21. Preached for Rev. Arey at St. Mathew's ch. from Act. 26:17.18. In the evening went to H. Trexler's to bring Mrs. R. home, who had been there quilting.

[Sunday, March 22, 1840 through Saturday, November 20, 1841 missing from original diaries.]

Rowan County, N. C.
November 25, 1841
Diary No. 9

Sund. 21. Preached at St. Mathew's ch. from Mal. 3:7.
Mond. 22. Went by way of Caleb Peeler's to Mrs. Arey's to measure out wheat, &c. All night here.
Tues. 23. Returned home by way of Salisbury.
Wed. 24. Sowed wheat & took Paul Goodman's Plow & gears home.
Thurs. 25. Went to Sam¹ Linn's to borrow a shovel & fork. In the afternoon at home.
Frid. 26. Went to Henry Hill's & brought home a guinea shoat.
Sat. 27. Preached at St. Stephen's ch. from Mal. 3:7.
Sund. 28. This was my day at Union ch. but the day being very inclement, the congregation did not assemble. All night Mrs. Arey's.
Mond. 29. Called to see H. Trexler & engaged to have a load hauled. Called also to see Tobias Brown & John Arey.
Tues. 30. At home.

Wed. Dec. 1. Went to Jacob Miller's to engage a meat stand.
Thurs. 2. At home.
Frid. 3. At home.
Sat. 4. Collected a few hands & repaired my kitchen.
Sund. 5. Preached at St. Paul's ch. from Eph. 4:1. Took dinner at Mʳ H. Hill's. All night at Mʳ Moses Brown's sen.
Mond. 6. Went to Salisbury. All night at Mrs. Arey's
Tues. 7. Returned home.
Wed. 8. Went to see Mr. Bullin about corn. Returned home by way of Mrs. Arey's.
Thurs. 9. Frid. 10. At home.
Sat. 11. Assisted in raising David Camel's house.
Sund. 12. Preached at St. Stephen's Ch. from Neh. 7:2. (latter clause) Baptized one infant. In the afternoon had catechization.
Mond. 13. Attended to the funeral of Moses Brown, sen, at his house. Preached from Neh. 7:2. (latter clause).
Tues. 14. Attended the sale of Moses Cawble's property. In the evening went to John Cornup's to engage the making of shoes.
Wed. 15. Went to P. Barrier's for iron, shovels, &c. which he had brought out from Salisbury for me.
Thurs. 16. Attended the sale of D. R. Linn's property — bought a horse for $30.50.
Frid. 17. Brought my horse home.
Sat. 18. Preached at St. Paul's ch. from Math. 22:35-40. A very cold day.
Sund. 19. Preached at St. Mathew's ch. from Math. 22:35-40. Bapᵈ one infant. In the afternoon preached at Sam¹ Linn's from Math. 22:35-40. Baptized the widow Moses Cawble's child.
Mond. 20. Went to Jacob Miller's for a meat stand.
Tues. 21. Butchered my hogs.
Wed. 22. Went to Frayley's store for salt & salted away my meat.
Thurs. 23. At home.
Frid. 24. Went to Chaˢ Eller's & sold some hay, &c. belonging to the Estate of P. Arey, decᵈ.
Sat. 25. Preached at St. Stephen's ch. from Math. 1:21. A very cold day. In the afternoon preached the funeral of Martin Hoffner at his late residence from Math. 25:13. in German.
Sund. 26. Preached at Union from Eph. 4:1. All night at Mrs. Arey's.
Mond. 27. Went to Salisbury. Returned to Mrs. Arey's.
Tues. 28. Returned home, Mrs. A. being with us.
Wed. 29. At home.
Thurs. 30. Accompanied Mrs. Arey to David Barringer's.
Frid. 31. Went to Mr. Paulus to the Blacksmith Shop.

Sat., Jan. 1, 1842. Preached at St. Mathew's ch. from Gal. 5:1.

Sund. 2. Preached at St. Paul's ch. from Gal 5:1. Very indisposed in consequence of a severe cold.

Mond. 3. At home.

Tues. 4. Went for a load of pine.

Wed. 5. Went to Mrs. Arey's & brought Lewis home.

Thurs. 6. Went to Mr. Stokes' & in the evening married Mr. John Ingram to Miss Jane Stokes. All night here.

Frid. 7. Returned home.

Sat. 8. Went to Danl Hoffman's to attend to the funeral of his child, but the coffin not being ready in time, returned home again.

Sund. 9. This was my day at St. Stephen's Church. Revd Macken of the Methodist Church, being present, preached to the congregation.

Mond. 10. Went to Mr. Powlus' after corn.

Tues. 11. Wed. 12. Thurs. 13. Frid. 14. At home, Mrs. R. being at Tobias Brown's.

Sat. 15. Preached at St. Paul's ch. from Math. 7:21. Went to Mrs. Arey's. All night here.

Sund. 16. Preached at St. Mathew's ch. from Math. 7:21. Baptized one infant.

Mond. 17. At home.

Tues. 18. Went to the Post Office in the morning. In afternoon at home. At night attended a debating society at Linn's Schoolhouse.

Wed. 19. Thurs. 20. At home.

Frid. 21. Went to D. Barringer's Esqr. to attend an arbitration. Henry Harkey & Jacob Powlus vs. John Bullen.

Sat. 22. Preached at St. Stephen's ch. from Math. 7:21. German.

Sund. 23. Preached at Union from Phil. 3:20.21. Baptized two children. All night at D. Barringer's.

Mond. 24. Returned home.

Tues. 25. Went with Milas Arey to John Knup's. In the afternoon at home.

Wed. 26. Went to Mr. Powlus' & had my horse, Jack, shod.

Thurs. 27. Attended the sale of the property of D. R. Linn, dec^{d}. Bot 50 bushs. corn.

Frid. 28. Attended to the getting of my corn home.

Sat. 29. Went to Mr. May's for a small bedstead.

Sund. 30. Preached at St. Paul's ch. from Math. 2:1-12.

Mond. 31. At home.

Tues. Feb. 1. Wed. 2. At home.

Thurs. 3. At home. Transcribed Saml Linn's Sale list.

Frid. 4. Went by way of John Knup's to Mrs. Arey's.

Sat. 5. Preached at St. Mathew's ch. from Math. 2:1-12. In the afternoon attended a meeting at Union to consult about repairing the Grave Yard. All night at Mrs. Arey's.

Sund. 6. To day Revd P. Kistler preached for me at Union. Revds. B. Arey & P. Kistler with me to night.

Mond. 7. Went to Salisbury & made a report of 2nd Sale to Court. All night at John Randleman's.

Tues. 8. Married Mr. John Yost to Miss Sarah Safret.

Wed. 9. At home.

Thurs. 10. Went to Salisbury.

Frid. 11. At home.

Sat. 12. This was my day to preach at St. Paul's ch. but the inclemency of the weather prevented me from attending.

Sund. 13. Had an appointment to day at St. Stephen's ch. but the morning being very rainy did not attend. In the afternoon attended preaching at Noah Knup's by Revd Stoner (Baptist).

Mond. 14. Tues. 15. At home.

Wed. 16. Started to father's as far as William Smith's, Senr.

Thurs. 17. Went to father's.

Frid. 18. At father's.

Sat. 19. Returned home as far as Caleb Peeler's.

Sund. 20. Preached at St. Mathew's ch. from Amos 4:12. the funeral of Mrs. Stoner.

Mond. 21. Tues. 22. At home.

Wed. 23. Went to Mr. Linn's & made a bed cord. Called also to see Noah Knup.

Thurs. 24. In the morning, went to Paul Goodman's for some beef. The balance of the day at home.

Frid. 25. At home till in the afternoon, then went to David Fraley's Store.

Sat. 26. Preached at St. Stephen's ch. from Math. 2:1-12. After preaching had catechization. Took dinner with Dewald Harkey.

Sund. 27. Preached at St. Paul's ch. from Josh. 23:8. Congregation large. All night with M. S. Brown.

Mond. 28. Went to Salisbury.

Tues., March 1. At home. Commenced sowing oats. At night attended the Debating Society.

Wed. 2. At home. A wet day.

Thurs. 3. In the morning went to Fraley's Store. Balance of the day at home.

Frid. 4. At home. Engaged in making a plow stock.

Sat. 5. Preached at St. Mathew's ch. from Eph. 5:14.

Sund. 6. Preached at Union from Josh. 23:8. Baptized four children. All night at Tobias Brown's.

Mond. 7. Went to Mrs. Arey's. In the afternoon returned home.

Tues. 8. Attended the sale of the property of Moses Brown, dec^d.

Wed. 9. At home.

Thurs. 10. Went to Fraley's store to the Post Office. The balance of the day at home.

Frid. 11. Took Jane Arey to David Barringer's. In the afternoon at home.

Sat. 12. Preached at St. Paul's ch. from Acts 16:13-34. Baptized one infant.

Sund. 13. Preached at St. Stephen's ch. from Josh 23:8.

Mond. 14. Went to Salisbury in company with Milas Arey. All night at Mrs. Arey's.

Tues. 15. Returned home.

Wed. 16. Plowed & hauled some chip manure on clover lot.

Thurs. 17. Attended sale at Michael Heilig's.

Frid. 18. Plowed till 12 o'clock, then went to blacksmith's shop.

Sat. 19. Went to blacksmith's shop in the morning. In the evening went to David Barringer's.

Sund. 20. Preached at St. Mathew's ch. from Luke 15:11-32. Baptized 2 children.

Mond. 21. At home till afternoon, then went to Post Office.

Tues. 22. Went to Salisbury. All night at Mrs. Arey's.

Wed. 23. Returned home. In the evening sowed some flax seed.

Thurs. 24. At home. Made a pair bar posts & half soled Mrs. Arey's shoes.

Frid. 25. Attended to the funeral of Mr. Pasinger at Union ch. Preached from 2 Cor. 5:1. Was prevented from filling my appointment to day at St. Stephen's ch. in consequence of the funeral. Mrs. Arey called to see us this evening.

Sat. 26. At home — planted sweet potatoes, &c.

Sund. 27. Preached at St. Paul's ch. from Luke 16:19-31.

Mond. 28. Preached at Linn's School house from Micah 6:8. Organized the Sunday School.

Tues. 29. At home.

Wed. 30. At home, laying off corn ground.

Thurs. 31. Laid off corn ground till 12 o'clock, then went to Mr. Linn's for seed corn.

Frid. Apr. 1. At home, crossing off corn ground.

Sat. 2. Preached at St. Mathew's ch. from Luke 16:19-31. Br. Adam & C. Peeler called to see me this evening.

Sund. 3. Preached at Union from 1 Peter 5:5. (latter clause). Baptized 5 children. In the afternoon had prayermeeting at Mrs. Arey's, lectured from Micah 6:8. All night here.

Mond. 4. Returned home.

Tues. 5. Attended to the funeral of John Cawble's wife at Union, preached from Math. 5:6.

Wed. 6. Went to father's in company with C. Peeler & Lady.

Thurs. 7. At father's till evening. Then went to Martin Rothrock's & married Jacob Brown to Miss Eliza Rothrock.

Frid. 8. Returned home.

Sat. 9. Preached at St. Stephen's ch. from 1 Thes. 2:11.12. preparatory to communion. — Baptized 2 children.

Sund. 10. Preached at Stephen's ch. from John 7:37. Baptized 3 adults, confirmed 20, & administered the Lord's Supper.

Mond. 11. Called to see Saml Linn on business.

Tues. 12. At home.

Wed. 13. Went to Mrs. Arey's & brought Lewis Hazelius home.

Thurs. 14. Went to Henry Miller's Esqr & married Peter L. Barringer to Miss Rose Ann Miller.

Frid. 15. At home.

Sat. 16. Preached at St. Mathew's ch. from Prov. 28:13. preparatory to communion. Baptized 2 children.

Sund. 17. Had an appointment to day at St. Mathew's Ch. for communion, but the day being very rainy did not attend.

Mond. 18. Went to Mr. Paulus' to the blacksmith's shop.

Tues. 19. At home till evening, then went to the Post Office.

Wed. 20. Went to John Cawble's & brought a grind-stone home.

Thurs. 21. At home.

Frid. 22. Preached at St. Stephen's ch. from 1 Sam. 12:23.24.

Sat. 23. Preached at St. Paul's ch. from Prov. 28:13. preparatory to communion. Baptized 3 children. In the afternoon had prayermeeting at Widow Weaver's, lectured from Math. 5:6. Administered to her the Lord's Supper, she not being able to attend at the Church in consequence of bodily affliction. All night at M. S. Brown's.

Sund. 24. Preached at St. Paul's ch. from 1 Sam. 12:23.24. & administered the Lord's Supper. In the afternoon went to William Walton's & married Asa Ribelin to Miss Susan C. Walton. All night at Mrs. Arey's.

Mond. 25. Returned home & in the afternoon went back to Mrs. Arey's.

Tues. 26. Went to Iredell in company with Milas Arey. All night at B. Arey's.

Wed. 27. At B. Arey's till evening then went to Chas Barringer's.

Thurs. 28. Returned home.

Frid. 29. At home till afternoon then went to Tobias Brown's.

Sat. 30. Preached at Union ch. from Prov. 28:13. preparatory to communion. Baptized 7 children, confirmed 2 persons. In the evening had prayer-meeting at the widow John Pealer's. All night at Mrs. Arey's.

Sund. May 1. Preached at Union from 1 Sam. 12:23.24. & administered the Lord's Supper. All night at David Barringer's.

Mond. 2. Went to Salisbury, in the afternoon returned home by way of Mr. Barringer's.

Tues. 3. In the morning went to the Post Office. The balance of the day at home.

Wed. 4. Went to Salisbury.

Thurs. 5. At home till afternoon, then went to the Post Office.

Frid. 6. Went to Elias Earnheart's & paid him some money.

Sat. 7. Went to St. Paul's church, but being indisposed with a cold had short religious services and dismissed the congregation. Bap^{d} one infant.

Sund. 8. Went to St. Stephen's ch. but being indisposed with a cold, Rev. MacMackin of the Methodist ch. preached for me. Baptized one infant.

Mond. 9. At home till afternoon, then went to the Post Office.

Tues. 10. Wed. 11. Thurs. 12. At home engaged in transcribing the Minutes of Synod.

Frid. 13. At home till afternoon, then went to Mr. Powlus' to the blacksmith's shop.

Sat. 14. At home, hoed corn.

Sund. 15. Had a communion meeting at St. Mathew's church — Mr. George Brown, student from Lexington Seminary, preached for me, after which administered the Lord's Supper. In the afternoon called to see Abram Arey, Sen. (he being sick) whilst Mr. Brown filled an appointment for me at Union church. All night at Caleb Pealer's.

Mond. 16. Went to Mrs. Arey's — went gunning awhile. In the afternoon called to see Abram Arey again & returned home.

Tues. 17. Went to the Post Office. The balance of the day at home.

Wed. 18. At home till afternoon, then called to see Mr. Linn on business.

Thurs. 19. Went to Salisbury. All night at Mr. Arey's.

Frid. 20. Went to Salisbury — in the evening returned home.

Sat. 21. Preached at St. Stephen's ch. from Prov. 28:13.

Sund. 22. This was my regular day at St. Paul's ch. Mr. Brown, student from the Lexington Seminary, preached for me. Had an election for Church Council, & a quarterly meeting of the Missionary & Education Society.

Mond. 23. At home. This evening Mr. Geo. Brown called to see me.

Tues. 24. Wed. 25. At home.

Thurs. 26. Started to Father's as far as Mrs. Arey's.

Frid. 27. Went to father's in company with Milas Arey.

Sat. 28. Attended the sale of Zerker's land. In the evening baptized 3 children at father's.

Sund. 29. Preached at Opposumtown from Joshua 23:8.

Mond. 30. Returned home as far as Mrs. Arey's.

Tues. 31. Returned home.

Wed. June 1. At home till afternoon, then went to the Post Office.

Thurs. 2. Went to Mrs. Arey's to engage hands to mow grass.

Frid. 3. At home.

Sat. 4. Preached at St. Mathew's ch. from Math. 6:33. Baptized 3 children. In the afternoon had prayermeeting a Abram Hill's, lectured from Math. 7:7. Baptized Hill's child. All night at Caleb Peeler's.

Sund. 5. Preached at Union from 1 Tim. 6:17-19. on the subject of the Centenary. Baptized 1 child.

Mond. 6. Commenced mowing grass.

Tues. 7. Worked in the meadow.

Wed. 8. At home — a rainy day.

Thurs. 9. In the morning went to Mr. Linn's — balance of day in the meadow.

Frid. 10. To day I got the balance of my hay away.

Sat. 11. Preached at St. Paul's ch. from Math. 7:7.

Sund. 12. Preached at St. Stephen's ch. from 1 Tim. 6:17-19. on the subject of the Centenary. Baptized one infant.

Mond. 13. Tues. 14. Plowed corn.

Wed. 15. Plowed corn till dinner. In the afternoon went to Mr. Linn's & to Mr. Powlus' to the shop.

Thurs. 16. Plowed corn.

Frid. 17. Sat. 18. At home.

Sund. 19. Preached at St. Mathew's ch. from 1 Tim. 6:17-19. on the subject of the Centenary. In the afternoon preached at Union from Luke 16:19-32. All night at David Barringer's.

Mond. 20. Returned home. In the afternoon had some hands to cradle wheat.

Tues. 21. Cut the balance of my wheat. In the afternoon went to Mrs. Arey's.

Wed. 22. Returned home by way of D. Kern's shop & Elias Earnheart's.

Thurs. 23. At home till afternoon then went to the Post Office. In the evening went to S. Ribelin's & baptized his child which was very sick.

Frid. 24. At home — had a great deal of rain.

Sat. 25. Preached at St. Stephen's ch. from Acts 16:16-34.

Sund. 26. Preached at St. Paul's ch. from 1 Tim. 6:17-19. on the subject of the Centenary.

Mond. 27. At home — hauled in my wheat.

Tues. 28. Attended to the funeral of Eliza Brown, wife of Jacob Brown, Jr. at Union ch. Preached from 2 Cor. 4:17. All night at Mrs. Arey's.

Wed. 29. Returned home by way of David Barringer's.

Thurs. 30. In the morning took Dawalt Lentz's scythe & cradle home. In the afternoon bound oats.

Frid. July 1. At home.

Sat. 2. At home — was prevented from preaching at St. Mathew's ch. in consequence of rain.

Sund. 3. Preached at Union from John 4:14. Collected some subscribers for the Luth. Observer. All night at Mrs. Arey's.

Mond. 4. Went to Salisbury.

Tues. 5. Went by way of Mrs. Arey's to Salisbury.

Wed. 6. At home till evening then went to Post Office.

Thurs. 7. Went to John Hartman's Dept. Shff. but did not find him at home. At night went to Mr. Linn's & staid all night.

Frid. 8. At home.

Sat. 9. Had an appointment at St. Paul's ch. but did not get there in time in consequence of the rain. All night at Dawalt Lentz's.

Sund. 10. Preached at St. Stephen's ch. from John 4:14. In the afternoon preached at Lentz's School house from Ps. 34:11. After preaching returned home.

Mond. 11. At home.

Tues. 12. Went to John Trexler's & staid all night.

Wed. 13. Returned home.

Thurs. 14. In the afternoon went to Peter Lentz's & married Mr. John Powless to Miss Amey Lentz.

Frid. 15. Attended to the funeral of Sophia Hartman's child at John Hartman's. Preached from 1 Sam. 12:23. (latter clause). All night at Mrs. Arey's.

Sat. 16. Went to the Tax-paying at widow Miller's.

Sund. 17. Preached at St. Mathew's ch. from Neh. 7:2. In the afternoon Rev. B. Arey preached at Union ch. All night at Mrs. Arey's.

Mond. 18. Went to John Kerns & engaged a plow.

Tues. 19. Returned home.

Wed. 20. At home.

Thurs. 21. In the afternoon assisted Mrs. Linn in winnowing her wheat.

Frid. 22. Preached at St. Stephen's ch. from Josh. 7:12. This evening br. Adam called to see me.

Sat. 23. Went to the tax paying & called to see sister Salome, she being sick at Widow Pealer's.

Sund. 24. Preached at St. Paul's ch. from John 4:14. & installed the Church Council.

Mond. 25. Attended to the funeral of Louisa Pealer at Union ch. Preached from John 9:4.

Tues. 26. Called to see D. Barringer & Alex. Holshouser.

Wed. 27. Went to Salisbury — from Salisbury to Mrs. Arey's to assist in boiling apple-butter.

Thurs. 28. In the afternoon returned home.

Frid. 29. Went to Mrs. Arey's to bring Mrs. R. & the children home.

Sat. 30. Went to Mr. Powless' & had a horse shod.

Sund. 31. Went in company with B. Arey to Bear creek ch. Preached from Acts 24:25.

Mond. Aug. 1. In the afternoon went in company with Rev. B. Arey to Mrs. Arey's.

Tues. 2. Went to Salisbury.

Wed. 3. At home.

Thurs. 4. Went to Salisbury.

Frid. 5. At home.

Sat. 6. Preached at St. Mathew's ch. from Josh. 7:12.

Sund. 7. Preached at Union from 1 John 5:21.

Mond. 8. Tues. 9. At home.

Wed. 10. Attended to the funeral of Mrs. Wise at Union. Preached from Math. 11:28.

Thurs. 11. Frid. 12. At home.

Sat. 13. Preached at St. Paul's ch. from Col. 1:28.

Sund. 14. Preached at St. Stephen's ch. from 1 John 5:21. Bapt^d 1 infant.

Mond. 15. Went to Iredell co. — all night at B. Arey's.

Tues. 16. Went to Statesville. All night at Henry Lentz's.

Wed. 17. Returned to Mrs. Arey's.

Thurs. 18. Returned home by way of Caleb Pealer's & David Barringer's. Reached home in the afternoon. This evening between sun set & dark, Milas Luther died very suddenly, without any previous sickness.

Frid. 19. On the evening of this day, Milas Luther was buried at Union church. All night at Mrs. Arey's.

Sat. 20. Attended a meeting of the Council of Union church. All night at Mr. S. Linn's.

Sund. 21. Preached at St. Mathew's ch. from Math. 4:19. In the afternoon Preached at Union ch. in German from John 3:3. All night at Mrs. Arey's.

Mond. 22. Went to Salisbury.

Tues. 23. Returned home.

Wed. 24. At home.

Thurs. 25. At home till afternoon then went to the Post Office.

Frid. 26. Preached at St. Stephen's ch. from Math. 4:19.

Sat. 27. Attended to the funeral of Danl Frick's child at the Lower Stone Church. Preached from Heb. 4:9.

Sund. 28. Preached at St. Paul's ch. from Math. 5:8. funeral of Mr. Lee's child. In the afternoon went to Union. Revd Scheck preached the funeral of Milas Luther. All night at Mrs. Arey's.

Mond. 29. Returned home by way of David Barringer's.

Tues. 30. Wed. 31. At home.

Thurs. Sept. 1. At home.

Frid. 2. Went to Caleb Pealer's & Mrs. Arey's.

Sat. 3. Preached at St. Mathew's Ch. from Gal. 6:14. All night at Caleb Pealer's.

Sund. 4. Preached at Union ch. from Eccl. 11:9. Baptized 2 inf^{ts}. All night at Mrs. Arey's.

Mond. 5. Returned home.

Tues. 6. Wed. 7. Thurs. 8. At home. Made my hay.

Frid. 9. At home.

Sat. 10. Attended the funeral of Mrs. Ketchey (widow) at Union Church. Preached from Heb. 4:9.

Sund. 11. Preached at St. Stephen's ch. from Eccl. 11:9. Baptized 1 infant.

Mond. 12. Went to Salisbury.

Tues. 13. Went to Salisbury, having been summoned to attend as a witness in Court.

Wed. 14. Called to see Mr. Brady, he being very sick, & also at the Post Office.

Thurs. 15. At home till afternoon, then called to see Mr. Brady.

Frid. 16. Started to Davie County. All night at Jesse Johnson's.

Sat. 17. Went to St. Mathew's ch. in Davie Co. & preached from Josh. 23:8. All night at David Dawalt's.

Sund. 18. Preached at the church from 1 Sam. 12:23.24. in Engl. & from Math. 11:28. in German. All night at Solomon Sifford's.

Mond. 19. Returned home.

Tues. 20. At home.

Wed. 21. At home.

Thurs. 22. Preached at St. Paul's ch. from Math. 26:41. All night at H. Hill's, Senr.

Frid. 23. Went Luther's Chapel to attend the meeting of Synod & continued in attendance till Tuesday afternoon following, then returned home.

Wed. 28. Thurs. 29. Frid. 30. At home, gathering corn.

Sat. Oct. 1. Preached at Union ch. from John 3:1-12. All night at Tobias Brown's. To day baptized 3 inf^{ts} and conf^d 2 persons.

Sund. 2. Preached at Union from Ex. 14:15. & administered the Lord's Supper. All night at Mrs. Arey's.

Mond. 3. Attended to the burial service of Mrs. Johnson at Union ch. All night at Mrs. Arey's.

Tues. 4. Went to Father's.

Wed. 5. At Father's till 12 o'clock then went to Lexington. All night at Mrs. Rounsaville's.

Thurs. 6. Called to see Lawyer Shober on business. After the calling of Court, returned home.

Frid. 7. This morning received word of the serious illness of mother. Made arrangements as speedily as possible & went to Father's.

Sat. 8. At Father's.

Sund. 9. At Father's. This evening took the ague.

Mond. 10. Returned home. as far as Mrs. Arey's. A very inclement day. Felt very much indisposed.

Tues. 11. Returned home, Mrs. R. staying at her mother's. All night at Mr. Linn's.

Wed. 12. Thurs. 13. At home, sick.

Frid. 14. Called to see Simeon Heilig's wife, she being very sick. All night Mrs. Arey's.

Sat. 15. At Mrs. Arey's, sick. This was my day at St. Mathew's ch. preparatory to communion, but could not attend. Rev. B. Arey attended the meeting for me.

Sund. 16. Returned home.

Mond. 17. Tues. 18. Wed. 19. At home, improving in health.

Thurs. 20. Attended the funeral of Jacob Miller, dec^d at his house – preached from Neh. 7:2. In the evening called to see Mr. Burrage. All night at Mrs. Miller's.

Frid. 21. Returned home by way of Mr. Powlus'. This evening had the ague again.

Sat. 22. Preached at St. Paul's ch. from 2 Peter 3:18. preparatory to communion. At night had prayermeeting at Mrs. Hill. All night at Geo. Garner's.

Sund. 23. Preached at St. Paul's from Math. 25:1-13. & administered the Lord's Supper. Baptized one infant. In the afternoon preached the funeral of Mr. Josey's daughter, dec^d at his house from Amos 4:12. Afterwards returned home.

Mond. 24. Went to Conrad Eller's on business. All night at Mrs. Arey's.

Tues. 25. Returned home.

Wed. 26. At home till 12 o'clock then went to Salisbury. All night at Jeremiah Brown's.

Thurs. 27. Returned home.

Frid. 28. Went to Mrs. Arey's, it being hiring day.

Sat. 29. Went to Sandy Creek ch. & preached from Ex. 14:15. All night at Mr. Swicegood's.

Sund. 30. Preached again at the church from Prov. 3:6. In the evening went to Father's.

Mond. 31. Started for home as far as Peter Owens'.

Tues. Nov. 1. Returned home.

Wed. 2. At home.

Thurs. 3. Attended the sale of John Miller, dec^d.

Frid. 4. Went to Mr. Powlus' to see about a pickling stand.

Sat. 5. At home.

Sund. 6. Preached at Union ch. from John 5:40. In the afternoon attended to the funeral of Mrs. Bringle, dec^d —preached from Math. 25:13. All night at Mrs. Arey's.

Mond. 7. At Mrs. Arey's. A very inclement day.

Tues. 8. Returned home.

Wed. 9. Called to see Rev. H. Graeber.

Thurs. 10. Went to Salisbury. All night at Wm. Smith's, Sen.

Frid. 11. Went to Father's.

Sat. 12. Sund. 13. At Father's.

Mond. 14. Attended Court in Lexington & qualified on the will of Saml Zerker, dec^d. All night at Caleb Pealer's.

Tues. 15. Returned home.

Wed. 16. Commenced school.

Thurs. 17. Frid. 18. In school.

Sat. 19. At home.

Sund. 20. At home — indisposed.

Mond. 21. In school.

Tues. 22. Went to D. Barringer's & baptized his 3 children.

Wed. 23. In school.

Thurs. 24. At home, indisposed.

Frid. 25. In school.

Sat. 26. At home.

Sund. 27. At home, indisposed.

Mond. 28. In school.

Tues. 29. In school.

Wed. 30. Went to widow Jacob Miller's in company with D. Fraley & laid off her dower in provision for one year. All night at Conrad Miller's.

Thurs. Dec. 1. Returned home.
Frid. 2. In school.
Sat. 3. Went to Mr. Linn's.
Sund. 4. At Union ch. Messrs. Linn & Brown preached for me.
Mond. 5. In school.

> From this time up until New Year's Day no regular diary
> kept. Was Most of the time unable to attend to business
> of any kind in consequence of sickness.

Sund. Jan. 1. At home & under the operation of medicine.
Mond. 2 to Frid. 6. At home taking medicine.
Sat. 7. Started to Father's as far as Mrs. Arey's.
Mond. 9. Arrived at Father's.
Tues. 10. At father's attending his sale.
Wed. 11. To day sold the property of Saml Zerker, dec^{d}.
Thurs. 12. Married br. Adam to Miss Elizabeth Whitlow.
Frid. 13. Returned home as far as Mrs. Arey's.
Sat. 14. Reached home.
Sund. 15. At home, Mr. Linn filling an appointment at St. Mathew's ch.
Mond. 16. Went to Salisbury.
Tues. 17. At Mrs. Arey's, she having hands to roll logs.
Wed. 18. Returned home by way of Salisbury.
Thurs. 19. Attended the sale of Jacob Miller, dec^{d}.
Frid. 20. Went to Chas Waller's.
Sat. 21. Returned home.
Sund. 22. Attended to the funeral of Andrew Eller's Mother-in-law, at Union, preached from Heb. 9:27.
Mond. 23. to Frid. 27. Took a jaunt to Iredell & during the trip bargained for land.
Sat. 28. At home.
Sund. 29. Preached a funeral at Jacob Earnheart's from Heb. 4:9. In the afternoon had prayermeeting at Mr. John Peck's.
Mond. 30. Went back to Iredell to dissolve my land bargain, sundry reasons me therunto moving, but did not succeed.
Tues. 31. In Iredell. All night at Chas Barringer's.

Wed. Feb. 1. Returned home.

Thurs. 2. Frid. 3. At home.

Sat. 4. At home.

Sund. 5. Preached at Union from Math. 18:20. All night at Tobias Brown's.

Mond. 6. In Salisbury at Court. All night at Mrs. Arey's.

Tues. 7. Returned home by way of Salisbury.

Wed. 8. Thurs. 9. At home.

Frid. 10. Went to Salisbury. In the evening call to see Mrs. Hill. All night at G. Garner's.

Sat. 11. Returned home.

Sund. 12. Preached at St. Stephen's ch. from Math. 18:20. − had the Ague to day very hard. All night at Mrs. Arey's.

Mond. 13. Went to Lexington to Court.

Tues. 14. Returned to Mrs. Arey's.

Wed. 15. At Mrs. Arey's sick.

Thurs. 16. Returned home.

Frid. 17. Called to see Mr. Peck.

Sat. 18. At home. Br. Lewis with me to night.

Sund. 19. Attended preaching at St. Mathew's ch. Mr. Linn preached.

Mond. 20. Went to Iredell. All night at C. Barringer's.

Tues. 21. Went to Statesville. All night at B. Arey's.

Wed. 22. Returned to Statesville. Closed the bargain with Mr. W. F. Steele.

Thurs. 23. Returned home. To night br. Lewis was with me again.

Frid. 24. At home.

Sat. 25. Preached at St. Stephen's ch. from Rev. 2:4.5.

Sund. 26. Preached at St. Paul's ch. from Hebr. 9:27. (fun[1]) In the afternoon had prayermeeting at Mrs. Hill's, lectured from Math. 5:6. All night at Mr. H. Hill's.

Mond. 27. Returned home.

Tues. 28. Went to D. Barringer's.

Wed. March 1. At home.

Thurs. 2. Went to James Goodman's & preached the funeral of his child from Heb. 9:27.

Frid. 3. At home.

Sat. 4. Went to the Post Office & to Mr. Powlus' in search of seed oats.

Sund. 5. Went to Union church but the day being very inclement the congregation did not assemble.

Mond. 6. At home.

Tues. 7. Assisted John Knup in raising a stable.

Wed. 8. At home.

Thurs. 9. At home.

Frid. 10. Went to Christian Kesler's & baptized Lony Kesler's child.

Sat. 11. Preached at St. Paul's ch. from Math. 8:1-4.

Sund. 12. Preached the funeral of Christena Kesler's child at Union ch. from Rev. 14:13.

Mond. 13. Went to Widow Miller's to assist in laying off her year's support.

Tues. 14. At home.

Wed. 15. Preached the funeral of the Widow Hill at St. Paul's ch. from Rev. 14:13. All night at Hill's, Sen̲ᵣ.

Thurs. 16. At Mr. Hill's, the day being very inclement.

Frid. 17. Returned home.

Sat. 18. At home.

Sund. 19. Preached at Union ch. from Rev. 2:4.5.

Mond. 20. Went to Salisbury. Staid all night at Mr. Culberhouse's.

Tues. 21. In Salisbury till 12 o'clock, then returned home.

Wed. 22. Thurs. 23. At home.

Frid. 24. Attended to the funeral of the Widow John Peeler at Union ch. Preached from Phil. 1:21. All night at Mrs. Arey's.

Sat. 25. Was sent for this morning to Mrs. Barringer's to see David Barringer's child, it being very sick. Felt much indisposed to day from cold. All night at Mrs. Arey's.

Sund. 26. Preached the funeral of Mr. Thomas Rimert's wife at St. Paul's ch. from Phil. 1:21. Baptized 1 inf̲ᵗ.

Mond. 27. Tues. 28. Wed. 29. Thurs. 30. Frid. 31. At home. Mrs. R. absent to Iredell.

Sat. April 1. In the morning went to the Post Office — the balance of the day at home.

Sund. 2. Preached at Union ch. from Jam. 1:5. Baptized 1 inf^t. All night at Tobias Brown's.

Mond. 3. Went to Lexington to Court. All night at Mr. Andrew Sink's.

Tues. 4. At Lexington till afternoon then returned home as far as Mrs. Arey's.

Wed. 5. Returned home.

Thurs. 6. At home — had the ague.

Frid. 7. At home.

Sat. 8. Preached at St. Paul's ch. from Jam. 1:5.

Sund. 9. Preached at St. Stephen's ch. from Jam. 1:5. Baptized 2 children. In the afternoon had the Ague.

Mond. 10. Went to the river for fish — all night at Mr. Kirk's.

Tues. 11. Returned home.

Wed. 12. At home — had the ague.

Thurs. 13. At home till afternoon then went to the Post Office.

Frid. 14. Went to Jacob Miller's to the singing.

Sat. 15. At home — had the ague.

Sund. 16. Preached at Union from Micah 6:8. After preaching attended to burial service of Mrs. Agner.

Mond. 17. Went to Salisbury.

Tues. 18. At home — had the ague.

Wed. 19. At home till afternoon, then went to Mr. Linn's on business.

Thurs. 20. At home till afternoon then went to see the Gold Mine.

Frid. 21. At home — had the ague.

Sat. 22. Preached at St. Stephen's ch. from Ps. 138:6.

Sund. 23. Preached at St. Paul's ch. from Micah 6:8. Baptized 2 children.

Mond. 24. At home. Sheared the sheep.

Tues. 25. Went to the Post Office & to the blacksmith's shop.

Wed. 26. At home.

Thurs. 27. Started to Synod. All night at Mr. Thompson's.

Frid. 28. Sat. 29. At Synod.

Sund. 30. At Mr. Swicegood's, the day being too inclement to turn out.

Mond. May 1. At Synod till 12 o'clock, then started home as far as Salisbury. All night at Mr. Vogler's.

Tues. 2. Attended Court till afternoon, then returned home.

Wed. 3. Attended to the funeral of Mrs. Henry Brown at the Stone house, preached from Math. 5:8. All night at Widow Brown's.

Thurs. 4. Frid. 5. Went to Salisbury.

Sat. 6. Preached at Union from Rom. 8:32. Baptized 5 children & confirmed one person. In the evening had prayermeeting at Mr. Tobias Brown's, lectured from John 14:22.

Sund. 7. Preached at Union ch. from Math. 22:5. & administered the Lord's Supper. All night at Mrs. Arey's.

Mond. 8. Went to Father's.

Tues. 9. At Father's.

Wed. 10. Returned home as far as Mrs. Arey's. Called in Lexington to attend to some Court business.

Thurs. 11. Returned home. In the afternoon went to the Widow Barrier's in Cabarrus and married Mr. Caleb Heilig to Miss Mary Barrier. All night here.

Frid. 12. Returned home.

Sat. 13. Preached at St. Stephen's ch. from John 14:22. preparatory to communion. Baptized 2 inf.ts.

Sund. 14. To day Mr. J. Linn preached preached [written twice] for me. Administered the L's S.r.

Mond. 15. Went to Iredell — all night at Cha.s Barringer's.

Tues. 16. Went to Statesville — all night at Alfred Patterson's.

Wed. 17. Returned home.

Thurs. 18. Attended to the funeral of Peter Hartman's son at Union ch. — preached from Is. 55:6.

Frid. 19. At home till afternoon then went to the blacksmith shop.

Sat. 20. Preached at St. Mathew's ch. from Is. 55:6. Baptized 3 infants.

Sund. 21. Preached at Union ch. the funeral of Mrs. Henry Agner, dec.d from Ps. 90:12. In the afternoon preached the funeral of Capt. J. Hartman, dec.d at his late residence from John 9:4. All night David Barringer's.

Mond. 22. Returned home.

Tues. 23. Attended Mr. Fite's sale.

Wed. 24. At home.

Thurs. 25. Went to Salisbury — at night married Mr. Franklin Smith to Miss Mary Ann Fisher.

Frid. 26. Preached at St. Stephen's church from Phil. 3:20.21.

Sat. 27. Preached at St. Paul's ch. from Rom. 12:2. preparatory to communion. Baptized one adult & one infant. In the afternoon had prayermeeting at Mrs. Weaver's, lectured from Phil. 3:20.21. & administered the Lord's Supper to her. All night at Geo. Garner's.

Sund. 28. Preached at St. Paul's ch. from Luk. 14:22. & administered the Lord's Supper.

Mond. 29. Went to Jacob Trexler's for a cradling scythe, & to Mr. Powlus' to have cradle screws cut.

Tues. 30. Went to Jacob Earnheart's & married Mr. Stephen Kirk to Miss Mary Earnheart.

Wed. 31. At home till evening then went to Mrs. Arey's.

Thurs. June 1. In the morning attended the Widow Peeler's Sale. In the afternoon went to Rev. George Boger's and married Mr. Daniel Techour to Miss Leah Boger.

Frid. 2. Returned home.

Sat. 3. At home.

Sund. 4. Preached the funeral of Mrs. Johnson, dec[d] at Union ch. from Mal. 3:17. Baptized one infant. In the afternoon preached at St. Mathew's ch. from Rom. 12:2. Baptized four infants. After preaching returned home.

Mond. 5. Attended preaching at the Lower Stone church.

Tues. 6. Wed. 7. Thurs. 8. Frid. 9. At home making hay.

Sat. 10. Preached at St. Paul's ch. from 2 Cor. 5:17. Took dinner with Mr. H. Hill, Sen.

Sund. 11. Preached the funeral of John Peck, sen. Dec[d] at St. Stephen's ch. from Mal. 3:17. Took dinner with Mr. Sol. Neusman.

Mond. 12. Attended to the funeral of Mrs. Hoffman at St. Mathew's church — preached from John 14:6.

Tues. 13. Went to Salisbury.

Wed. 14. At home. In the afternoon plowed corn.

Thurs. 15. Plowed corn till 12 o'clock, then went to Mr. Linn's on business.

Frid. 16. At home till 12 o'clock then helped Mr. Peeler haul hay.

Sat. 17. Preached at St. Mathew's ch. from 2 Cor. 5:17. Baptized one infant.

Sund. 18. Preached at Union ch. from Acts 8:39. Baptized one infant.

Mond. 19. Went to the Post office.

Tues. 20. Wed. 21. Thurs. 22. At home.

Frid. 23. Went to Mrs. Arey's.

Sat. 24. At home.

Sund. 25. Preached at St. Paul's ch. from Mal. 3:17. the funeral of Daniel Weaver's son. Baptized one infant. In the afternoon went to Moses Lemly's & baptized his child, it being very sick. All night here.

Mond. 26. Returned home.

Tues. 27. Went to Salisbury.

Wed. 28. Helped Mrs. Peeler haul her hay.

Thurs. 29. At home. Hauled in some wheat.

Frid. 30. At home.

Sat. July 1. Had catechization at Union ch.

Sund. [2]. Preached at Union ch. from Hos. 6:4. In the afternoon preached at St. Mathew's ch. from 1 Pet. 4:18. All night at David Barringer's.

Mond. 3. Returned home. Father called to see me.

Tues. 4. At home.

Wed. 5. Attended to the funeral of Stufle Bayam's child at St. Mathew's ch. — preached from Math. 5:8.

Thurs. 6. Attended the tax paying at D. Kern's on business.

Frid. 7. Attended the tax paying at Peter Lentz's on business.

Sat. 8. Preached at St. Paul's ch. from Acts 8:39. After preaching had catechization.

Sund. 9. Preached at St. Stephen's ch. from Josh. 24:15. Baptized one infant. In the afternoon preached German from the same text.

Mond. 10. Went to father's.

Tues. 11. Went to H. Beckerdite's.

Wed. 12. Went to Salem.

Thurs. 13. Returned home as far as Mrs. Arey's.

Frid. 14. Returned home.

Sat. 15. Had catechizing at Union ch. In the afternoon attended to the funeral of Charles Eller at Union — preached from Gen. 3:19.*

Sund. 16. Preached at Union from John 14:15. In the afternoon preached at St. Mathew's ch. from Gen. 3:19. the funeral of Tice Bayam's child.

Mond. 17. Went to Salisbury. All night at Mrs. Arey's.

Tues. 18. Returned home.

Wed. 19. Thurs. 20. Frid. 21. At home.

Sat. 22. Preached at John May's from Josh. 24:15. German.

Sund. 23. Preached at St. Paul's ch. from Josh. 24:15.

Mond. 24. Went to the gold mine.

Tues. 25. Wed. 26. Thurs. 27. At home.

Frid. 28. Commenced a Protracted Meeting to day at St. Stephen's ch. Preached from Acts 13:26.

Sat. 29. Sund. 30. In attendance at the Meeting. Rev.^{ds} Graeber & Scheck being with me.

Mond. 31. Went to John Lineberger's & engaged a waggon. All David Barringer's.

* Baptized the deceased Eller's child to day.

Tues. Aug. 1. Returned home.

Wed. 2. Attended to the fun[l] of Col. Lell at Tice Barringer's — preached from Heb. 4:9. German.*

Thurs. 3. Went to Salisbury.

Frid. 4. At home.

Sat. 5. Had catechization at Union ch.

Sund. 6. Preached at Union ch. from Mark 10:46-52. In the afternoon preached at St. Mathew's ch. from Acts 13:26. and installed the Church Council.

Mond. 7. Went to Salisbury.

Tues. 8. Called to see Pleasant May's wife, she being very sick. In the evening married John Smithdeal to Margaret Pealer. All night at Mr. Pealer's.

Wed. 9. Went to Salisbury.

Thurs. 10. In the afternoon to Salisbury. All night at Wm. Smith's.

Frid. 11. Returned home.

Sat. 12. Attended to the funeral of Mich[l] Heilig's child at St. Paul's ch. — preached from Numb. 23:10.

Sund. 13. Preached at St. Stephen's ch. from Phil 1:21. (fun[l]) To day Br. Lewis & family were with me.

Mond. 14. Went with Br. Lewis as far as Mrs. Arey's.

Tues. 15. Went to Lexington.

Wed. 16. Had a trial in court about Zerker's will.

Thurs. 17. In the evening returned back to Mrs. Arey's.

Frid. 18. Returned home.

Sat. 19. Had catechization at Union ch. In the afternoon went to Salisbury in company with Milas Arey. All night at Mrs. Arey's.

Sund. 20. This was my day to preach at Union & St. Mathew's ch[s] but the day being inclement did not attend.

Mond. 21. At home.

Tues. 22. Went to Mrs. Barringer's & married Milas Arey to Sophia Hartman. All night at Mrs. Arey's.

Wed. 23. At Mrs. Arey's. Commenced settlement with the heirs of Peter Arey's Estate.

Thurs. 24. Finished the settlement & returned home.

Frid. 25. Went to Dewalt Harkey's & backed out from a trade for my plantation.

Sat. 26. Preached at St. Stephen's ch. from 1 Pet. 4:18. & after preaching had catechization.

Sund. 27. Attended to the funeral of Moses Pealer at St. Mathew's ch. — preached from Job 14:14. In consequence of the funeral, disappointed my congregation at St. Paul's ch.

Mond. 28. At home till 12 o'clock then went to D. Barringer's on business.

Tues. 29. Attended the sale of J. Peck, dec[d]. Sold my plantation to D. Harkey.

Wed. 30. At John Trexler's boiling apple butter.

Thurs. 31. Married Marg. Newman to Mr. Jack Garner.

* Baptized to day 7 children.

Frid. Sept 1. At home.

Sat. 2. Had catechization at Union.

Sund. 3. Preached at Union ch. from Gen. 6:22. Baptized one infant.

Mond. 4. Attended to the funeral of Mr. Hahnberger's child at Organ ch. preached from Math. 5:8.

Tues. 5. Attended to the funeral of John Kern's child at his house, preached from Math. 25:13. All night at D. Barringer's.

Wed. 6. Returned home, & bought my plantation back.

Thurs. 7. At home.

Frid. 8. Went to Mr. Paulus' — in the afternoon at home.

Sat. 9. Preached at St. Paul's ch. from Gen 6:22.

Sund. 10. Preached at St. Stephen's from Gen. 6:22. Baptized one inf^t & held an election for Church Council. After preaching had catechization. In the evening called to see Saml Ribelin.

Mond. 11. Attended to the funeral of Mr. Fullenwider's child at Saml Linn's. Preached from Math. 25:13.

Tues. 12. Went to Lexington.

Wed. 13. Attended the burial of Revd H. Graeber at Organ ch.

Thurs. 14. Had catechization at Union ch.

Frid. 15. Commenced a Protracted Meeting at Union ch. Was disappointed in getting help — preach^d from Prov. 23:26. All night at Tobias Brown's.

Sat. 16. Preached at Union from Acts 17:11.12. Baptized one infant. At night had prayermeeting at Tobias Brown's, lectured from Heb. 2:3. All night here.

Sund. 17. Preached at Union ch. from 1 Tim. 6:12. Baptized one infant. In the afternoon preached again from Prov. 29:1. After preaching returned home.

Rowan County, N. C.
September 28th 1843
Diary No. 10

Mond. 18. Went to Salisbury — all night at Mrs. Arey's.

Tues. 19. Attended to the funeral of Andrew Brown at Union ch. Preached from Numb. 23:10.

Wed. 20. Went to Mr. Paulus' in the morning to the Shop. In the afternoon at home.

Thurs. 21. Attended to the funeral of old Mrs. Starnes at St. Mathew's ch. — preached from Job 19:25.

Frid. 22. Preached at Organ ch. from Prov. 3:6. Baptized one infant.

Sat. 23. Preached at St. Stephen's ch. from Is. 48:18. Afterwards had catechization.

Sund. 24. Preached at St. Paul's ch. from Is. 48:18. Baptized one infant. After preaching had catechization. All night at Geo. Randleman's.

Mond. 25. Returned home by way of Salisbury.

Tues. 26. At home till afternoon, then went to Mr. Linn's.

Wed. 27. Went to Mr. Lineberrier's & Rusher's on business, & to Mrs. A's. to see D. Barringer, he being sick. To night Br. L. was with me.

Thurs. 28. Called at Mr. S. Linn's, his wife being sick. In the afternoon went to the Post Office.

Frid. 29. At home.

Sat. 30. Had catechization at Union.

Sund. Oct. 1. Attended to the funeral of Christian Kesler at Union ch. Preached from Gen. 5:24.

Mond. 2. Went to Lexington.

Tues. 3. Wed. 4. Thurs. 5. In Lexington.

Frid. 6. Returned in the afternoon to Mrs. Arey's.

Sat. 7. Preached at St. Paul's ch. from Rev. 3:20.

Sund. 8. Preached at St. Stephen's ch. from Acts 24:25. After preaching had catechization.

Mond. 9. Had some hands to rebuild my corn cribs. In the evening went to David Barringer's.

Tues. 10. Called to see Jacob Holshouser, sen^r & And. Troutman on business.

Wed. 11. At home till evening, then went to Mr. Linn's to help chuck corn.

Thurs. 12. Preached at Organ ch. from Acts 20:17-21.

Frid. 13. Attended to the funeral of Geo. Lyerly's child at Union ch. Preached from Mark 10:14-16. After preaching had catechization.

Sat. 14. Preached at Union ch. from 2 Cor. 5:7.8. preparatory to communion. Baptized three adults & confirmed 18 persons. All night at Mrs. Arey's.

Sund. 15. Preached at Union ch. from John 3:14.15. & administered the Lord's Supper. In the afternoon attended to the funeral of Danl Swink. Preached from John 9:4.

Mond. 16. Went to D. Barringer's & in the afternoon to Union ch. having forgotten my hymn book & Liturgy the previous day.

Tues. 17. Attended to the burial of Charles Wise's child at Union ch. in the forenoon, & in the afternoon attended to the funeral of Peter Miller's child at Organ ch. Preached from Amos 4:12.

Wed. 18. In the morning turned out for some hands & in the afternoon chucked my corn.

Thurs. 19. At home till 12 o'clock, then went to Alex^r Holshouser's & helped chuck his corn.

Frid. 20. At home.

Sat. 21. Preached at St. Paul's ch. from 2 Cor. 5:7.8. preparatory to communion. Baptized 4 adults and 1 infant, & confirmed 9 persons.

Sund. 22. Preached at St. Paul's ch. from Ps. 119:63. & administered the Lord's Supper.

Mond. 23. Went to Salisbury.

Tues. 24. At home till afternoon then went to D. Barringer's.

Wed. 25. Returned home, & in the afternoon went to Mr. Paulus' to the Shop.

Thurs. 26. At home.

Frid. 27. Preached at Organ ch. from 2 Cor. 5:17.

Sat. 28. Preached at Organ ch. from 2 Cor. 5:17. Germ. Baptized 2 infants & attended to the service preparatory to communion.

Sund. 29. To day Rev. Scheck preached Rev. Graeber's funeral, followed after & preached from Ex. 33:14. & assisted in the administration of the Lord's Supper.

Mond. 30. Went to the Post Office & in the afternoon to the gold mine.

Tues. 31. Attended to the funeral of John Josey's son at Organ ch. preached the fun^l at Mr. Josey's from Luk. 12:37.

Wed. Nov. 1. Went to Mr. Rusher's & John Linebarrier's.

Thurs. 2. Attended to the funeral of Mathias Barrier's child at St. Stephen's ch. — preached from Luk. 12:37.

Frid. 3. Went to the Post Office & the Tan-Yard, & in the evening to D. Barringer's.

Sat. 4. Preached at St. Mathew's ch. from Luk. 12:37. In the afternoon attended to the funeral of Peter Cawble's child at Union ch. Preached from Luk. 12:37.

Sund. 5. Preached at Union ch. from John 14:6. the funeral of Charles Wise's child.

Mond. 6. Went to Frederick Fesperman's to see his son, he being very sick — administered to him the Lord's Supper. In the evening went to D. Barringer's.

Tues. 7. Attended to the funeral of D. Barringer's child at Union ch. — preached from Math. 5:8.

Wed. 8. Attended to the funeral of Joseph Miller's child at the Lower Stone ch. — preached from Math. 19:14.

Thurs. 9. Went to Salisbury.

Frid. 10. Preached at St. John's ch. from Josh. 23:8. Took dinner with Danl D. Ridenhour.

Sat. 11. Preached at St. Stephen's ch. from 2 Cor. 5:7.8. preparatory to communion. Baptized 2 children. All night at Mr. John Lentz's.

Sund. 12. Preached at St. Stephen's ch. from Is. 25:6.7.8. Confirmed 19 persons & baptized 2 adults & administered the Lord's Supper.

Mond. 13. Went to Salisbury. All night at Mrs. Arey's.

Tues. 14. Attended to the burial service of Saml Peeler's child at Union ch. In the afternoon started for Lexington. All night at Jacob Sink's.

Wed. 15. Went to Lexington & settled with Absalom Williams Adm^{r} of Saml Zerker, dec^{d}. All night at Mrs. Rounsaville's.

Thurs. 16. Returned home as far as Mrs. Arey's.

Frid. 17. Returned home.

Sat. 18. Preached at St. Mathew's ch. from 1 Saml 12:23.24. & administered the Lord's Supper. Baptized one infant.

Sund. 19. Went to Union ch. but was unable to preach in consequence of a severe cold.

Mond. 20. Went to Mrs. Kesler's & to Mrs. Arey's.

Tues. 21. Returned home.

Wed. 22. Went to Salisbury.

Thurs. 23. At home.

Frid. 24. Preached at Organ ch. from Job. 14:14. in Germ. the funeral of Mr. Reimert. Baptized one inf^{t}.

Sat. 25. Attended to the funeral of John Josey's child at Organ ch. — preached from Job 14:14. at Mrs Josey's house. Baptized also his child.

Sund. 26. Preached at St. Paul's ch. from Jam. 1:25. All night at Mr. Garner's.

Mond. 27. Went to Salisbury.

Tues. 28. Went in the morning to John Cawble's & baptized his child, it being very sick — then went Mrs. Arey's & returned home by way of C. Kesler's sale.

Wed. 29. Attended to the funeral of Peter Earnheart at Union ch. Preached from Amos 4:12.

Thurs. 30. Went to Jacob Lyerly's & married Mr. Danl Brown to Miss Polly Lyerly.

Frid., Decem. 1. Was to have attended to the funeral of John Cawble's child, but the day being very inclement did not attend.

Sat. 2. At home till afternoon then went to the Post Office.

Sund. 3. Attended to the funeral Saml Peeler's child at Union. Preached to day the funeral of three of Mr. Peeler's children & of John Cawble's child from Job 23:16. Held an election to day for Church Council.

Mond. 4. Attended to the funeral of Dr. Kelley's child at St. Stephen's ch. — preached from Rev. 14:13. In the afternoon went to Mrs. Graeber's.

Tues. 5. Attended the sale of Rev. Graeber's property. In the afternoon went to Leonard Klutts' & married Laurence Misenheimer to Christena L. Klutts.

Wed. 6. Attended to the funeral of Andrew Earnheart's wife at the Lower Stone church. — preached from Luk. 12:37.

Thurs. 7. At home.

Frid. 8. Went to Mr. Linn's & engaged him to haul a load of pine.

Sat. 9. Attended to the funeral of Danl Hoffman's child at St. Mathew's ch. — preached from Phil. 3:20.21.

Sund. 10. Preached at St. Stephen's ch. from Acts 16:30.31. & Installed H. J. Barringer as Elder.

Mond. 11. Attended to the funeral of Jeremiah Brown at Union ch. preached from Rev. 14:13. All night at Jacob Brown's, he being very sick.

Tues. 12. Returned home by way of Joseph Williams'.

Wed. 13. Attended to the funeral of Moses Eagle's child at St. Stephen's ch. — preached from Math. 19:14.

Thurs. 14. Attended to the funeral of Jacob Brown, Sen. at Union church. — preached from Ps. 58:11. In the evening called to see Mrs. Kesler, she being sick, & Abram Arey, he being sick. All night at Mr. Arey's.

Frid. 15. Preached at Organ Ch. from Phil. 3:20.21. Baptized one inf^t.

Sat. 16. Attended to the funeral of Polly Miller at St. Stephen's ch. — preached from Ps. 58:11.

Sund. 17. Preached at Union from Acts 16:16-34. An inclement day. All night at Mrs. Arey's.

Mond. 18. Called to see Mrs. Kesler. She died while there. Returned home by way of Abram Arey's.

Tues. 19. Attended to the funeral of Mrs. Kesler at Union. — preached from Ps. 138:6. A very rainy day.

Wed. 20. Attended to the funeral of Mrs. Adam Trexler at Union church — preached from John 3:36.

Thurs. 21. Went to Gold mine for nails — balance of day at home.

Frid. 22. Went to Jacob Walton's to preach a funeral, but rain, sickness, &c. prevented neighbors from attending. All night at Mrs. Arey's.

Sat. 23. Preached at St. Mathew's ch. from Ps. 73:1. the funeral of Moses Lemly's child.

Sund. 24. Preached at St. Paul's ch. from Acts 16:30.31.

Mond. 25. Preached at Organ ch. from Math 1:21. Baptized five inf^ts. In the afternoon attended to the funeral of Mr. Linn's colored woman — preached to the colored people from Amos 4:12.

Tues. 26. Attended to the funeral of Saml Barrier's child at Lower Stone ch. preached from Hebr. 9:27.

Wed. 27. Thurs. 28. At home.

Frid. 29. Went to Salisbury to aid Revd Scheck in a Protracted Meeting. Preached from Ps. 73:1. All night at Mr. Vogler's.

Sat. 30. Preached from Jam. 1:25. In the evening lectured at Mr. Culberhouse's.

Sund. 31. Preached from Math. 22:5. In the evening lectured at Mr. Fraley's. At night at Mr. Culberhouse's.

Mond. Jan. 1, 1844. In Salisbury.

Tues. 2. At home.

Wed. 3. Attended to the funeral of Abram Arey at Union — preached from Heb. 6:12.

Thurs. 4. Went to Jacob Lyerly's & married Adam Trexler, jr. to Miss Margaret Lyerly.

Frid. 5. Went to Alex. Miller's for a Guinea Pig.

Sat. 6. Preached at St. Mathew's ch. from Heb. 6:12.

Sund. 7. Preached at Union ch. from Math 20:1-16. & installed the Church Council. In the afternoon preached at Jacob Walton's from Math. 18:14. the funeral of Mr. Walton's child. All night at Mrs. Arey's.

Mond. 8. Went to Iredell Co. in company with D. Klutts Esqr. All night at Chas Barringer's.

Tues. 9. Rode over & looked at my Iredell land. All night at Mr. H. Lentz's.

Wed. 10. In the afternoon went to Statesville. All night at B. Arey's.

Thurs. 11. Returned home.

Frid. 12. At home — a very inclement day.

Sat. 13. Attended to the funeral of Widow Barrier's child (Tobias) at Lower Stone church — preached the funeral at the residence from Heb. 6:12.

Sund. 14. To day Revd J. Mackin preached for me at St. Stephen's ch. Baptized 2 children (Twins).

Mond. 15. Went to D. Klutts' & sold him my land in Iredell county.

Tues. 16. Went to Mr. Paulus' & engaged some horse shoes. In the afternoon, myself & Mr. Linn staked off the line dividing our lands.

Wed. 17. At home.

Thurs. 18. Went to Mr. Castor's & married George Basinger to Miss Anna Ghentz. In the afternoon attended to the funeral of John Plott, dec^d at Organ ch. — Preached from Phil. 1:21.

Frid. 19. At home.

Sat. 20. Preached at St. Mathew's ch. from Rev. 14:13. the funeral of Mrs. Bullen.

Sund. 21. Preached at Union from Math 8:5-13. In the afternoon attended to the burial of Mrs. Bayam at St. Mathew's ch. All night at Mr. Hoffman's.

Mond. 22. Called to see Isaac Agner, he being very sick. In the afternoon called to see Peter Barrier.

Tues. 23. Went to the Post Office & to Jacob Holshouser's, sen. & paid him some Money. In the afternoon went to Mr. Yost's.

Wed. 24. Attended to the funeral of old Mrs. Randleman, dec^d at St. Paul's ch. Preached from Is. 3:10.

Thurs. 25. At home.

Frid. 26. Preached at Organ ch. from Math. 20:1-16. Baptized one inf^t.

Sat. 27. Attended to the funeral of Mr. Speck's child at Organ ch. preached from Gen. 3:19.

Sund. 28. Preached at St. Paul's ch. from Math. 20:1-16. In the aftenoon attended to the funeral of Jacob Brown's child at the Stone House — preached from Luk. 12:37. All night at Widow Brown's.

Mond. 29. Returned home.

Tues. 30. Went to S. Ribelin's to have my saw filed.

Wed. 31. Assisted Mr. Linn in making his settlement of David Linn's Estate.

Thurs. Feb. 1. At home.

Frid. 2. At home.

Sat. 3. Preached at St. Mathew's ch. from Math. 20:1-16.

Sund. 4. This was my day at St. Stephen's ch. but the day being very inclement, did not turn out.

Mond. 5. Went to Salisbury. All night at Mrs. Arey's.

Tues. 6. Returned home by way of Salisbury. Chas Barringer staid with me to night.

Wed. 7. At home.

Thurs. 8. Frid. 9. At home.

Sat. 10. Attended to the funeral of Mrs. Rauch at St. Mathew's ch. preached from John 3:36.

Sund. 11. Attended to the funeral of Alex^r Holshouser's daughter at the Lower Stone Church. Preached the funeral at the house at 8. o'clock A.M. from Job 23:16. at 12 M. preached at Organ Church from Ps. 90:12. the funeral of Mrs. Eagle & Alex^r Eagle.

Mond. 12. Attended to the funeral of Mrs. David Knup at the Lower Stone Church — preached the funeral at the house from Numb. 23:10.

Tues. 13. Went to Father's.

Wed. 14. Returned home as far as Mrs. Arey's.

Thurs. 15. Attended Mrs. Barringer's Sale. In the afternoon returned home.

Frid. 16. At home till afternoon then called to see Alex^r Holshouser, he being sick — & to the Post Office.

Sat. 17. Preached at St. Stephen's ch. from Math. 20:1-16.

Sund. 18. Preached at Union from Ps. 39:1. All night at D. Barringer's.

Mond. 19. Returned home. In the afternoon called to see Mr. Peeler & Alex^r Holshouser.

Tues. 20. Went to Jacob Walton's & attended to the funeral of his little daughter — preached from Amos 4:12. All night here.

Wed. 21. Returned home by way of Salisbury.

Thurs. 22. Went to Mrs. Brown's & Married Mr. Henry Barringer to Miss Maria Brown. All night here.

Frid. 23. Returned home by way of Mrs. Arey's.

Sat. 24. Preached at St. Paul's ch. from Luk. 13:24.

Sund. 25. Preached at Organ ch. from Luk. 13:24. Germ. — baptized one infant. In the afternoon preached at John Smith's from Math. 7:7. Germ. All night at Philip Eddleman's.

Mond. 26. Returned home.

Tues. 27. Went to Jno. Randleman's to Widow R's. Sale.

Wed. 28. At home.

Thurs. 29. Attended the widow Redwine's Sale.

Frid. March 1. At home.

Sat. 2. Preached at St. Mathew's ch. from Numb. 23:10. fun[l].*

Sund. 3. Preached at St. Stephen's ch. from Math. 8:5-13. Bapt[d] one inft.

Mond. 4. Went to John Fesperman's & preached the funeral of his daughter from Luk. 12:37. Germ. In the afternoon attended the funeral of Geo. Kesler at Union – preached from John 9:4. All night at Mrs. Arey's.

Tues. 5. Attended Jacob Brown's Sale.

Wed. 6. Went to Mr. Paulus' & paid off a Note of hand.

Thurs. 7. Attended to the funeral of Widow Heilig at Organ ch. Preached from John 9:4.

Frid. 8. At home.

Sat. 9. Preached at St. Paul's ch. from Math. 8:5-13. Took dinner at John Fisher's.

Sund. 10. Attended to the funeral of Peter Miller's child at Organ ch. – preached from 1 Pet. 4:18. Baptized 2 children. In the evening went to David Barringer's, he having a sick child.

Mond. 11. Attended to the funeral of John Kern's child – preached the funeral at J. Kern's from Ps. 90:12. & buried the child at Peter Kern's. All night at Mrs. Arey's.

Tues. 12. Returned home, & in the afternoon went to the Gold Mine in company with S. Linn.

Wed. 13. At home.

Thurs. 14. Attended to the funeral of Philip Lemly at St. Mathew's ch. – preached from Ps. 90:12. A very inclement day.

Frid. 15. At home till 12 o'clock – in the afternoon went to D. Klutts' Sale.

Sat. 16. This was my day at St. Stephen's ch., but the day being very rainy did not attend.

Sund. 17. Preached at Union from Luk. 16:19-32. All night at Tobias Brown's.

Mond. 18. Went to Salisbury. All night at Mrs. Arey's.

Tues. 19. Went to Salisbury. In the afternoon returned home.

Wed. 20. Went to Salisbury. All night at B. Fraley's.

Thurs. 21. Returned home by way of Mrs. Arey's.

Frid. 22. In the afternoon went to Organ ch. to meet the Church Council – a majority however did not attend.

Sat. 23. This was my day at St. Paul's ch. but the day being somewhat unfavorable did not attend.

Sund. 24. Preached at Organ ch. from Mark 10:46-52. Baptized 3 children & installed 2 Elders & 1 Deacon.

Mond. 25. Went in company with Milas Arey to the fishery.

Tues. 26. At the fishery.

Wed. 27. Returned home.

Thurs. 28. Went with Mr. Paulus to show him a piece of Land.

Frid. 29. Attended to the funeral of Moses Barringer's child at Organ ch. – preached from 2 Sam. 12:23.

Sat. 30. Attended to the funeral of Esrom Weaver's wife at the Lower Stone ch. – preached from Luk. 12:37. German.

Sund. 31. Preached the funeral of Henry Holshouser's child at Linn's School House from Luk. 12:37. Baptized also Mr. Holshouser's Child.

* Bapt[d] one inf[t].

Mond. Apr. 1. Went to Mr. Paulus' & had my horse shod, & to the Gold Mine.

Tues. 2. Attended to the funeral of George Hoffner at St. Mathew's church — preached from Math. 5:8.

Wed. 3. Went to Salisbury.

Thurs. 4. Went to Lexington. All night at Michael Sink's.

Frid. 5. Called to see Mr. Mendenhall in the morning & then returned home.

Sat. 6. Preached at St. Stephen's Church from Ps. 51:2. preparatory to communion.+

Sund. 7. + Preached at St. Stephen's ch. from Luk. 14:22. & administered the Lord's Supper.

Mond. 8. Attended singing at Mr. Sam¹ Linn's.

Tues. 9. Wed. 10. At home.

Thurs. 11. Frid. 12. At home.

Sat. 13. Attended to the funeral of Paul Klutts' child at the Lower Stone Church — preached from Heb. 4:9. German.

Sund. 14. Preached at Organ ch. from John 20:19-31. German. Baptized five children.

Mond. 15. At home — sheared the sheep.

Tues. 16. Went in the morning to Andrew Troutman's & paid him some money. The balance of the day at home.

Wed. 17. Attended to the funeral of old Mrs. Reimert at Organ church — preached from Math. 10:32.

Thurs. 18. Frid. 19. At home.

Sat. 20. Went to Union ch. this being the day for preparatory service, but the inclemency of the weather prevented the congregation from assembling. All night at Mrs. Arey's.

Sund. 21. Preached at Union from John 4:14. & administered the Lord's Supper & baptized one infant.

Mond. 22. Called to see Isaac Eller, he being very sick. All night at Tobias Brown's.

Tues. 23. Returned home by way of Salisbury.

Wed. 24. Called in company with B. Arey to see Wm. Paulus. In the afternoon called & paid off Andrew Troutman.

Thurs. 25. At home.

Frid. 26. At home till afternoon, then went to Post office & to John Trexler's.

Sat. 27. Preached at Organ Ch. from Prov. 28:13. preparatory to communion & baptized one infant. All night at Philip Eddleman's.

Sund. 28. To day Mr. J. Linn preached for me at Organ ch. Confirmed one person & administered the Lord's Supper. All night at P. A. Seaford's.

Mond. 29. Attended to the fun¹ of Mrs. Smith at Organ church — preached from Is. 3:10. Germ.

Tues. 30. At home.

\+ At candlelighting, had prayermeeting at Dr. Kelly's at the Gold Mine — lectured from Ex. 23:2. All night here.

\+ Baptized 2 chil. on Saturday & one on Sunday.

Wed. May 1. Attended to the funeral of Eliza Hill at St. Mathew's ch. — preached from Is. 3:10.

Thurs. 2. Went to Jacob Lyerly's & Married Mr. Moses Klutts to Miss Leah Lyerly. In the afternoon went to Concord to attend the meeting of Synod. All night at Mr. Waggoner's.

Frid. 3. In Synod. Staid during the Meeting of Synod at Alf. Brown's.

Sat. 4. In Synod — preached to day from Prov. 23:26.

Sund. 5. Attended preaching in the Luther. Church — preached at night from Acts 24:25.

Mond. 6. In Synod — preached at 2 o'clock from Math. 20:6.

Tues. 7. Returned home.

Wed. 8. Went to Salisbury. All night at B. Fraley's.

Thurs. 9. Returned home.

Frid. 10. At home.

Sat. 11. Had catechization at Organ ch.

Sund. 12. Preached at Organ ch. from Jam. 1:25. Engl. & from Rev. 2:10. Germ. (fun[1])

Mond. 13. Went to the gold mine to hear Col. Hoke's speech.

Tues. 14. Went to widow Hoffner's & married John Bullen to Tena Hoffner.

Wed. 15. At home.

Thurs. 16. At home till afternoon then went to Samuel Linn's.

Frid. 17. At home.

Sat. 18. Went to Salisbury.

Sund. 19. Preached at St. Stephen's ch. from Jam. 1:12.

Mond. 20. Went to Tobias Brown's.

Tues. 21. Wed. 22. At home.

Thurs. 23. At home till afternoon, then went to Dr. Kelly's & in the evening married Mr. Goodman Spencer to Miss Elis. Gadlin.

Frid. 24. At home.

Sat. 25. Had catechization at Organ church.

Sund. 26. Preached at Organ ch. from John 14:23-31. German & English from the same text. In the afternoon attended to the fun[1] of widow Klutts' child at Lower Stone ch. — preached from Rev. 2:10. Baptized to day at Organ ch. 3 children.

Mond. 27. Had meeting to day at Sam[1] Linn's — lectured from John 3:16-21.

Tues. 28. At home.

Wed. 29. Thurs. 30. Mr. Linn had his Land surveyed for the purpose of partition — went along around part of the time.

Frid. 31. Went in company with Mrs. R. to Salisbury.

Sat. June 1. Preached at St. Stephen's ch. from Rev. 2:10.

Sund. 2. Preached at Union from Deut. 6:3. Baptized 5 children.

Mond. 3. Commenced hay making.

Tues. 4. At work in the meadow.

Wed. 5. At home — a cloudy day.

Thurs. 6. Attended to the funeral of Mr. Smithdeal's child — preached at the house from Math. 19:14. In the afternoon finished hauling hay.

Frid. 7. In the morning went to the Post Office, the balance of the day at home.

Sat. 8. Had catechization at Organ Church.

Sund. 9. In the morning married Alexander Corl to Mary Klutts. Preached at Organ Church from Acts 9:36-42. Baptized 2 infants.

Mond. 10. Went to D. Barringer's & paid him $101.00 on my note. In the afternoon called to see Widow Miller, she being sick.

Tues. 11. Went to the post office in the morning, the balance of the day at home.

Wed. 12. Thurs. 13. At home.

Frid. 14. Called to see Widow Holshouser & Joseph Linn.

Sat. 15. Had catechization at Linn's School House.

Sund. 16. Preached at St. Stephen's Church from Deut. 6:3. Baptized 1 inft. Took dinner with Daywald Harkey. Afterward's called to see old Mrs. Earnheart.

Mond. 17. Went to Mr. Paulus' & had my horses shod.

Tues. 18. Went to Salisbury.

Wed. 19. Went to Tobias Brown's.

Thurs. 20. Called to see J. Rusher & J. Linebarrier in relation to my waggon. Was sent for to see Mr. John May, sen. who was very sick & at his request wrote his will.

Frid. 21. At home till 12 o'clock then called to see old Mrs. Earnheart & administered to her the Lord's Supper, she being very old & infirm.

Sat. 22. Had catechization at Organ ch.

Sund. 23. Preached at Organ ch. from Ruth 1:16. Baptized   . In the afternoon preached at Michael Heilig's from Rev. 14:13. the funeral of an aged colored person.

Mond. 24. Took Phebe Brown home, she having assisted Mrs. R. in making some dresses.

Tues. 25. Wed. 26. No distinct recollection of those days.

Thurs. 27. Had catechization at Linn's School House. Called to see Asa Miller's family. In the afternoon called to see Saml Bayam, he being very sick. Baptized his child & administered to him the L's Supp^{r}.

Frid. 28. Attended a Protracted Meeting at St. Mathew's Church. Preached from Jam. 1:12. & from Ruth 1:16.

Sat. 29. Sund. 30. In attendance at the Meeting.

Mond. July 1. Tues. 2. No distinct recollection of those days.

Wed. 3. Went to the carding Machine, & called to see Rev. Geo. Brown at his mother's.

Thurs. 4. Attended the 4th of July celebration at the Gold Mine.

Frid. 5. At home — hauled in oats.

Sat. 6. Had catechization at Linn's School House. In the evening called to see Rev. J. Linn, he being sick.

Sund. 7. Preached at St. Stephen's ch. from Prov. 29:1. Baptized one infant. Took sick to day in the ch. Had an appointment to day at Chas Cruse's but did not attend in consequence of indisposition. All night at Mrs. Peck's.

Mond. 8. Returned home — was taken down with the Billious Fever — in the hands of the Doctors & confined to home till the 22nd of the month.

Mond. 22. Rode to Mr. Fraley's with my family.

Tues. 23. Returned home — not very well in the evening.

Wed. 24. At home. From this time up to Aug. 12th confined almost exclusively to home with the Fever & Ague.

Mond. Aug. 12. Started to Father's — all night at Mrs. Arey's.

Tues. 13. Went to Father's.

Wed. 14. At Father's, it being a damp, inclement day.

Thurs. 15. Called to see some of my relations. Baptized to day H. Thomas' child. All night at H. Beckerdite's.

Frid. 16. Went to Salem. Returned to Father's. Baptized to day H. Beckerdite's child.

Sat. 17. Sund. 18. Attended preaching at the Moravian Church in the neighborhood of Father's.

Mond. 19. Returned home.

Tues. 20. Went to Salisbury.

Wed. 21. Went to Tobias Brown's & returned his carriage.

Thurs. 22. At home.

Frid. 23. Went to James Klutts' to see Dr. Wahl & Mrs. Klutts, they being sick.

Sat. 24. Attended Church settlement at Organ Ch.

Sund. 25. Preached at Organ church from Mark 1:40-45. in German.

Mond. 26. Tues. 27. Wed. 28. At home — Made my hay.

Thurs. 29. At home till afternoon & the Ague. In the evening went to John Arey's & staid all night.

Frid. 30. In the morning called at Mr. Rusher's to see about my waggon — then attended preaching at Union church. In the evening returned home.

Sat. 31. In attendance at the meeting at Union church.

Sund. Sept. 1. Mond. 2. In attendance at the Meeting.

Tues. 3. Started back to Union ch. in search of my saddlebags, went as far as Michael Peeler's & there had to go to bed in consequence of the Ague. In the evening returned home.

Wed. 4. Went to L. Barringer's for my saddlebags, he having found them. On my return home stopped at Leonard Klutts' & went to bed several hours with the Ague. Afterwards returned home.

Thurs. 5. Went to Peter Lentz's to have some clothes cut.

Frid. 6. Went to Jacob Trexler's in the afternoon for some brandy for medicinal purposes.

Sat. 7. Had catechization at Organ church.

Sund. 8. Preached at Organ church from Gal. 6:14. Baptd 1 infant. Took dinner at John Miller's.

Sund. 15. Preached at St. Stephen's ch. from Acts 16:30. No regular account kept of the preceding week.

Thurs. 19. Married Ambrose Lentz to Polly Caroline Dry. All night at Mr. Dry's.

Frid. 20. Returned home.

Sat. 21. Had catechization at Organ church.

Sund. 22. Started to Organ ch. to fill my appointment, but took sick on the road & stopped at Mr. Holshouser's. In the evening returned home. Confined to the house by sickness till October 2nd.

Oct. 3. Went with my family to Iredell County.

Tues. 8. Returned home quite indisposed.

Wed. 9. Thurs. 10. At home confined to bed.

Frid. 11. In the morning went to Mr. S. Linn's.

Sat. 12. From this time up to Thurs. 17. at home & in feeble health.

Frid. 18. At home.

Sat. 19. Went to St. Stephen's ch. & attended to the services preparatory to communion. Bapt^d to day 2 infants.

Sund. 20. Rev. B. Arey preached for me at St. Stephen's ch. Assisted in the administration of the Lord's Supper. In the afternoon went to Daywalt Miller's & married Harris M. Ridenhour to Levina Miller.

Mond. 21. Went to Mr. Fraley's to the Post Office.

Tues. 22. At home.

Wed. 23. Went to Mr. Rusher's & had my horse shod.

Thurs. 24. Went to Mr. Goodman's tanyard & D. Barringer's.

Frid. 25. Went to D. Barringer's but did not find him at home. In the afternoon went to the Gold-Mine.

Sat. 26. At home till afternoon then went to D. Barringer's but did not find him at home.

Sund. 27. Preached at Organ ch. from Gen. 6:22. Bap^t 1 inf^t. Took dinner at Danl Miller's.

Mond. 28. Went to see D. Barringer on business. Returned home by way of the Post office. In the afternoon went to Mr. Troutman's & Mr. Paulus' on business.

Tues. 29. Went & settled with D. Barringer — paid him $60.00 & some cents.

Wed. 30. In the morning called to see Mr. Troutman & Mr. Paulus on business. In the afternoon went to Peter Trexler's & baptized his child, it being very sick.

Thurs. 31. Attended to the funeral of Mrs. Arey, dec^d, widow of Abram Arey, dec^d, at Union ch. — preached from Math. 25:10. All night at her late residence.

Frid. Nov. 1. Assisted the Executors in looking over the papers, &c. In the afternoon returned home.

Sat. 2. Attended to the funeral of Widow Hoffner, dec^d, at the Lower Stone ch. – preached the funeral at her late residence from Math. 25:10.

Sund. 3. Preached at St. Stephen's ch. from 1 Tim. 6:12. first clause. Took dinner at Dr. Kelly's.

Mond. 4. Went to Salisbury, it being election day for President. In the afternoon went in with P. A. Seaford to look at a Tract of Land belonging to the Estate of Rev. H. Graeber, dec^d. All night at Mr. Seaford's.

Tues. 5. Returned to Salisbury & in the evening returned home.

Wed. 6. In the morning went to Mr. Goodman's & got leather for a bridle & martingal. In the afternoon worked on my bridle.

Thurs. 7. Finished my bridle & martingal.

Frid. 8. To day commenced a protracted Meeting at Organ ch. Rev. Plassman preached to day in German. Baptized 1 child.

Sat. 9. At Organ ch. – Preaching by Rev^{ds} Linn & Anthony. Confirmed 1 person & baptized 1 child.

Sund. 10. At Organ Ch. Preaching by Rev. Anthony. Installed 2 deacons, baptized 1 child & administered the Lord's Supper.

Mond. 11. Went to Lexington. All night at Michael Sink's.

Tues. 12. Returned home as far as Tobias Brown's.

Wed. 13. Returned home by way of Mr. Rusher's & brought my waggon home.

Thurs. 14. At home.

Frid. 15. Went to the Post office.

Sat. 16. Went to Jacob Walton's & preached the funeral of Mrs. Lewis Jacobs & her infant child.

Sund. 17. Preached at St. Stephen's ch. from 1 Sam. 12:23.24. Took dinner at Mr. S. Neusman's.

Mond. 18. At home.

Tues. 19. Attended to the funeral of Adam Trexler's daughter at Union ch. – preached from Job 14:14. Took dinner with Peter Trexler.

Wed. 20. At home.

Thurs. 21. Attended to the funeral of Mrs. Louisa Pless at Organ ch. – preached from Gen. 5:24. including the funeral of John Barringer's child. All night at John Barringer's.

Frid. 22. Returned home – got very wet with rainy._

Sat. 23. Had catechization at Organ ch. In the afternoon called to see Elihu Holshouser's daughter, she being very sick.

Sund. 24. Preached at Organ ch. from John 9:4. in German, the funeral of Mrs. Reimert, dec^d.

Mond. 25. Tues. 26. At home.

Wed. 27. In the afternoon went to Tobias Brown's.

Thurs. 28. Attended the Sale of Abram Arey, Dec^d & bought Eliza. In the evening went to George Heilig's & married Mr. John H. Miller to Camilla C. Heilig. All night here.

Frid. 29. Returned to the sale. All night at Mrs. Arey's.

Sat. 30. Had catechization at Organ Church.

Sund. Dec. 1. Preached at St. Stephen's ch. from Ruth 1:16. Took dinner at Mr. Harkey's. In the afternoon preached at David Knup's from Job 14:14. the funeral of his child, dec^{d}.

Mond. 2. Went to Mr. Fraley's & distributed the Minutes.

Tues. 3. At home — a rainy day.

Wed. 4. Had catechization at Organ Church.

Thurs. 5. Met the council at Organ ch. to inspect the repairs of the organ. In the afternoon called to see Mr. Josy, a sick man & administered to him the Lord's Supper.

Frid. 6. Went to Rusher's, Linebarrier's, & John Arey's & made some settlements.

Sat. 7. Had catechization at Organ ch.

Sund. 8. Preached at Organ church. from Josh. 23:8. Took dinner at Saml Ribelin's. Bapt^{d} 1 inf^{t}.

Mond. 9. Tues. 10. At home.

Wed. 11. Had catechization at Organ ch. Albert Arey with us to night.

Thurs. 12. At home.

Frid. 13. In the morning went to the Gold Mine.

Sat. 14. Catechization at Organ ch.

Sund. 15. Preached at St. Stephen's ch. from Rom. 14:17.18. Took dinner at Daywalt Harkey's.

Mond. 16. Went to Salisbury in company with John Lentz to purchase a stove for St. Stephen's ch., but found none to suit.

Tues. 17. At home.

Wed. 18. Catechization at Organ ch.

Thurs. 19. Frid. 20. At home.

Sat. 21. Catechization at Organ ch.

Sund. 22. Preached at Organ ch. from Rom. 14:17.18.

Mond. 23. At home.

Tues. 24. Went to Philip Yost's & married Mr. John Bostian to Polly Eliza Yost. All night here.

Wed. 25. Preached at Organ church from Luk. 7:16. Bapt^{d} 1 inf^{t}. To day commenced a 5 days Meeting.

Thurs. 26. Preaching to day by Rev. Joseph A. Linn. Confirmed to day 53 persons & bapt^{d} 1 inf^{t}. All night at Ambrose Eddleman's.

Frid. 27. Sermon by br. Linn — preached also from Acts 26:17.18. All night at P. A. Seaford's Esqr.

Sat. 28. Sermon by Bro^{s}. Linn and Anthony. Confirmed 1 person and bapt^{d} 1 inf^{t}.

Sund. 29. Sermon by Br. Anthony. Administered the Lord's Supper. Very large attendance.

Mond. 30. At home, mended shoes.

Tues. 31. In the afternoon went to Salisbury. All night at B. Fraley's.

Rowan County, N. C.
January 16th 1845
Diary No. 11

Wed., Jan. 1. In Salisbury. In the evening returned home.

Thurs. 2. At home.

Frid. 3. Went to Union ch. to a protracted meeting. All night at Mrs. Arey's.

Sat. 4. Preached at Union from 1 Thes. 5:6. In the evening, returned home.

Sund. 5. Preached at St. Stephen's ch. from 1 Thes. 5:6. Indisposed with cold. Took dinner at Daywald Harkey's.

Mond. 6. Tues. 7. Wed. 8. At home.

Thurs. 9. Attended to the funeral of John Barringer at Organ ch. — preached from Neh. 7:2. In the afternoon called to see Sam[l] Seaford, he being sick.

Frid. 10. At home.

Sat. 11. Had catechization at Organ ch. Called to see Sam[l] Seaford. At night had prayermeeting at John Foutz's, lectured from Mark 1:40-45. All night here.

Sund. 12. In the morning, married Michael Goodman to Sarah Foutz — preached at Organ ch. from Math. 11:28. German. Took a chill to day.

Mond. 13. At home.

Tues. 14. Went to Salisbury to settle with M. L. Brown, late Treasurer of Seminary Fund. Had the Ague very hard — all night at M. L. Brown's.

Wed. 15. Returned home.

Thurs. 16. At home — had the Ague.

Frid. 17. At home — hauled rails.

Sat. 18. At home — not very well.

Sund. 19. This was my day at St. Stephen's ch. but the day being very inclement, did not turn out.

Mond. 20. At home and made a riding bridle.

Tues. 21. Laid fence warm in the forenoon — in the afternoon went to Geo. Miller's to see his son, John, he being very sick. All night here.

Wed. 22. Returned home. In the afternoon laid fence warm.

Thurs. 23. At home. In the afternoon hauled rails.

Frid. 24. At home till 12 o'clock. In the afternoon went to the Gold Mine.

Sat. 25. Had catechization at Organ church. All night at Peter Miller's.

Sund. 26. Preached at Organ ch. from 1 Thes. 5:6. Engl. Took dinner at Charles Barringer's.

Mond. 27. At home till 12 M. In the afternoon took some turkeys to the Gold Mine.

Tues. 28. Wed. 29. At home.

Thurs. 30. Went to Peter Berger's and married Henry L. Brown to Magdalene Berger.

Frid. 31. At home.

Sat. Feb. 1. In the morning had catechization at my house — the balance of the day at home.

Sund. 2. Preached at St. Stephen's ch. from 2 Kings 5:1-14. Took dinner at Daywalt Harkey's.

Mond. 3. At home.

Tues. 4. Went to Salisbury — all night at Wm. Smith's.

Wed. 5. Returned home.

Thurs. 6. Went to Mr. Goodman's to purchase a dog. In the afternoon went to Mr. Alex. Holshouser's to engage his waggon to haul rails, &c.

Frid. 7. In the morning went to the School house & settled my school bill. In the afternoon went to Mr. Linn's.

Sat. 8. Attended to the funeral of Nicholas Ludwig's child at St. Stephen's ch. — preached from Math. 5:8. All night at Mrs. Graeber's.

Sund. 9. Preached at Organ ch. from Prov. 13:6. on the evils of drunkenness. Baptized one inf^t. Attended also to the funeral of Widow Reimert. — preached from Math. 5:6.

Mond. 10. At home till 12 M. In the afternoon went to Wm. Paulus' and settled my smith bill. Also called to see Mrs. Linn (widow) on business.

Tues. 11. Went to Salisbury.

Wed. 12. Went to St. Stephen's ch. and assisted in setting up the stove. In the evening went to Mr. John Trexler's and staid the night.

Thurs. 13. Returned home. In the evening went to Mr. Asa Miller's and married Mr. David Knup to Miss Philpena Miller.

Frid. 14. Attended to the funeral of Mr. Hollman, an English miner, at St. Stephen's ch. — preached from Phil. 3:20.21.

Sat. 15. At home. In the morning had catechization at my house.

Sund. 16. Preached at St. Stephen's ch. from Hos. 6:4. Took dinner at Widow Harkey's.+ Bap^t 1 inf^t.

Mond. 17. At home. Had Messrs. Trexlers making barn doors.

Tues. 18. In the morning went to Mr. Paulus' to engage door hinges. The balance of the day at home.

Wed. 19. At home till 12 o'clock. In the afternoon went to Mr. Fraley's, to William's infare.

Thurs. 20. Went to Salisbury in company with H. Beckerdite, he having staid with me the night previous.

Frid. 21. Went to Mr. Geo. Troutman's and preached from Ps. 116:12-14. Germ. All night here.

Sat. 22. Had catechization at Organ ch.

Sund. 23. Preached at Organ ch. from John 3:14.15. Germ. Took dinner at Jacob Miller's.

Mond. 24. Went to Daniel Miller's to mill. All night here.

Tues. 25. Paid the Seminary money of Synod over to D. Miller, the Treasurer & took his bond. Returned home by way of John Barringer's Sale.

Wed. 26. In the afternoon was sent for to Frederic Fesperman's to see his sick son. Had a prayermeeting this evening at Mr. F's & lectured from Acts 20:21. All night here.

Thurs. 27. Returned home.

Frid. 28. At home.

+ Attended to the fun^l of J. Udy's child. Preached from Heb. 4:8.

Sat. March 1. Attended to the funeral of Henry Klutts' wife at the Lower Stone Church. Preached from Phil. 1:21. Germ. At night had prayermeeting at Mr. M. Barrier's Esqr., lectured from Phil. 3:20.21. All night here.

Sund. 2. Preached at St. Stephen's ch. from Acts 20:17-21. Took at Doctor Kelly's. In the afternoon had catechization at my house.

Mond. 3. Attended to the funeral of John Fesperman at St. Paul's ch. – preached from Phil. 1:21. Took dinner at Mr. Geo. Garner's.

Tues. 4. Attended Geo. Hoffman's Sale.

Wed. 5. In the morning went to Jacob Holshouser's, jr. on business – balance of day at home.

Thurs. 6. At home.

Frid. 7. At home.

Sat. 8. Had catechization at Organ church. In the afternoon called at Danl Miller's, his family being sick.

Sund. 9. Attended to the funeral of John Miller, son of George, at Organ ch., it being my regular day for Organ ch. – preached from Mal. 3:17. Bapt^d 1 inf^t. Called to see Danl Miller's family.

Mond. 10. At home till afternoon, then went to the Post office.

Tues. 11. Called to see D. Miller's sick family, & engaged some hands to roll logs & raise a kitchen.

Wed. 12. At home – had a rolling & raising.

Thurs. 13. At home till afternoon, then called to see Danl Miller's sick family.

Frid. 14. At home.

Sat. 15. At home till 12 o'clock, then went to John Melchior's & at night had prayermeeting, lectured in Germ. from Math. 11:28. Rev'd Harter followed in Engl.

Sund. 16. Called to see Mrs. N. Ludwig, who appeared to labor partial mental derangement. Attended to the burial service of David Culp's child at St. Stephen's ch. Preached at the ch. from Luk. 13:24. Baptized one inf^t. Took dinner at Solomon Neusman's. In the afternoon had catechization at my house.

Mond. 17. Went to Salisbury.

Tues. 18. Attended to the funeral of Joseph Miller's wife, dec^d at the Lower St. ch. Preached from Phil. 3:20.21. Called in the afternoon to see old Mrs. Ribelin, she being sick.

Wed. 19. Attended to the funeral of Miss Sybilla Miller at Organ ch. – preached from 2 Tim. 4:7.8.

Thurs. 20. At home.

Frid. 21. Preached at Organ ch. from John 14:22. Took dinner with Col. Holshouser.

Sat. 22. Went to Luther's ch. to attend a 2 days meeting. – preached from 1 Pet. 4:18. At candlelighting preached again from Phil. 3:20.21. All night at Daywald Lentz's.

Sund. 23. Preached from 2 Cor. 5:17. In the evening returned home.

Mond. 24. At home.

Tues. 25. Went to the Post office. The balance of the day at home.

Wed. 26. In the afternoon went to the Widow Harkey's and in the evening married William McDaniel to Miss Susanne Harkey. All here.

Thurs. 27. Returned home. In the afternoon went to Mr. Fraley's & to Wm. Paulus' & paid Mr. Paulus some money.

Frid. 28. Went to Salisbury to attend a Protracted meeting. – preached from Phil. 3:20.21. In the afternoon preached again from 2 Cor. 5:17. All night at Moses L. Brown's.

Sat. 29. In Salisbury. At candlelighting preached from Math. 11:28. All night at B. F. Fraley's.

Sund. 30. In the afternoon preached from Ex. 33:14. In the evening returned home. In the night went to Saml Ribelin's, he being very sick, & died next morning at 4 o'clock A.M.

Mond. 31. Attended to the fun^l of Geo. Troutman's at the house and buried him at Organ ch. – preached from Amos 4:12. German.

Tues. April 1. Attended to the fun[l] of Sam[l] Ribelin. — preached at the house from Ps. 58:11. & buried him at the Lower Stone ch.

Wed. 2. At home till afternoon, then went to Mr. Linn's on business.

Thurs. 3. Attended to the funeral of William Seaford, 80 yrs old, at Organ ch. — preached from Rev. 14:13. Germ. Took dinner at John Seaford's. In afternoon went to Dan[l] Dry's & married Henry M. Isahower to Catherine Dry. All night here.

Frid. 4. Returned home.

Sat. 5. At home till afternoon, then went to John Lentz's & at night had prayermeeting — lectured from Rev. 3:20. All night here.

Sund. 6. Preached at St. Stephen's ch. from Josh. 24:15. Baptized one infant. Took dinner at Mr. Tobias Klutts'. In the afternoon had catechization at my house.

Mond. 7. Attended to the funeral of Mrs. Henry Beaver at the Lower Stone ch. Preached at Mr. B. Brady's where she died from 2 Kings 20:1. Germ.

Tues. 8. Attended to the funeral of Catherine Overcash at Organ ch. — preached from Ps. 90:12. Germ.

Wed. 9. At home. To day brother Adam called to see me.

Thurs. 10. Went to Salisbury. Mrs. R. accompanied me.

Frid. 11. At home.

Sat. 12. Had catechization at Organ ch. In the afternoon had prayermeeting at P. A. Seaford's, lectured from Rev. 3:20. All night here.

Sund. 13. In the morning called to see two aged members of the church, Mr. & Mrs. Ghents and had prayer with them. Preached at Organ ch. from Jos. 24:15. Germ. & baptized 2 infants. In the afternoon had catechization at my house.

Mond. 14. Went to Tobias Brown's & Mr. Rusher's and had my horses shod.

Tues. 15. Attended to the funeral of Mr. Henry Beaver at the Lower Stone ch. — preached from Math. 25:10. Germ. In the afternoon called to see some sick persons.

Wed. 16. At home.

Thurs. 17. Went to the Post Office — balance of the day at home.

Frid. 18. Called to see Daywald Miller, he being sick. Baptized his child. Had catechization at Organ ch. Rev[d] Harter with me over night.

Sat. 19. Preached at St. Stephen's ch. from John 14:22. — preparatory.

Sund. 20. Preached at St. Stephen's ch. from John 7:37. & administered the Lord's Supper.

Mond. 21. Tues. 22. At home.

Wed. 23. Went to Mr. D. Fraley's to witness the marriage of Rev. John Lantz and Miss Nancy Fraley. Married by Rev. Crooks.

Thurs. 24. At home.

Frid. 25. Had catechization at Organ ch. Took dinner at widow Barrier's. In the afternoon had preaching at old Mr. Ghentz's. Preached from John 7:37. Germ. & administered the Lord's Supper to 3 aged persons. All night at Mr. Dan[l] Eddleman's.

Sat. 26. Preached at Organ ch. from 2 Peter 3:18. preparatory to communion. Confirmed 15 persons & baptized 2 adults.

Sund. 27. Preached at Organ ch. from Ps. 116:12-14. After an intermission, administered the Lord's Supper to a large congregation.

Mond. 28. Started for Synod as far as Lexington.

Tues. 29. Went to Father's & took dinner — all night at Mr. Hugh Beckerdite's.

Wed. 30. Went as far as Mr. McGibbony's.

Thurs. May 1. Went to Rev. Artz's.

Frid. 2. At St. Paul's ch. Synod commenced its business. All night at Mr. Mich^l Shaffner's.

Sat. 3. At Synod. All night at Rev. Artz's.

Sund. 4. At St. Paul's Church. All night at Mr. Carigen's.

Mond. 5. At Synod. All night at E. Holt's Esqr.

Tues. 6. Returned home as far as Mr. McGibbony's.

Wed. 7. Came as far as Mr. And. Sink's.

Thurs. 8. Arrived at home.

Frid. 9. Attended to the funeral of Mr. Michael Heilig at Organ Church. – preached from Is. 3:10.11.

Sat. 10. Attended to the funeral of Jacob Holshouser, sen. at the Lower Stone ch. – preached from Ps. 4:3. In the evening went to Frederick Stirewalt's.

Sund. 11. In the morning married Mr. John Smith to Catharine Stirewalt. Preached at Organ ch. from Josh. 24:15. Bapt^d 2 inf^{ts}.

Mond. 12. At home till evening, then went to Jacob Trexler's & staid over night.

Tues. 13. Returned home.

Wed. 14. Went to Danl Miller's to mill.

Thurs. 15. Attended to the funeral of Moses Cruse at Organ ch. – preached from Prov. 28:26. All night Moses Barringer's.

Frid. 16. Returned home.

Sat. 17. At home.

Sund. 18. Preached at St. Stephen's ch. from Jam. 1:25. Took dinner at Laurence Lingle's. In the afternoon preached at Paul Beaver's school house from Rev. 3:20. In the evening married Mr. Adam Cruse to Miss Catherine Troutman.

Mond. 19. At home.

Tues. 20. Went by request to David Barringer's to aid in the settlement between the Treasurer & Council of Union Church, but D. B., one of the Council having gone from home, nothing was done. In the afternoon at home.

Wed. 21. At home.

Thurs. 22. Went to Salisbury & made arrangements to have the Minutes of Synod printed.

Frid. 23. At home.

Sat. 24. At home, preparing for Sunday.

Sund. 25. Preached at Organ ch. from 1 Thes. 2:11.12. Germ. Took dinner at Mr. Philip Eddleman's. In the afternoon preached at Mr. Frederick Stirewalt's from 1 Thes. 2:11.12. Engl. All night at John Eagle's.

Mond. 26. Returned home by way of Sybilla Miller's sale.

Tues. 27. At home till afternoon, then went to Mr. Cress' and married Joseph Miller to Nuly Cress. All night at John Cruse's. Mrs. Cruse being sick.

Wed. 28. Returned home.

Thurs. 29. Frid. 30. Attended the sale of Saml Ribelin's, dec^d property.

Sat. 31. Commenced a course of catechetical instruction at St. Stephen's ch. All night at Danl Miller's.

Sund. June 1. Preached in Concord, from 1 Thes. 2:11.12. Having exchanged pulpits to day with Rev. Harter. All night at John Cruse's, Mrs. Cruse being very sick.

Mond. 2. Attended the burial of Mrs. Regina Peeler at the Lower St. ch. took dinner with Col. Holshouser.

Tues. 3. Went to Salisbury.

Wed. 4. Attended to the funeral of Sophia, wife of John Cruse, at Organ ch. — preached from John 9:4.

Thurs. 5. Frid. 6. At home, hay making.

Sat. 7. At home, making preparations for Sunday.

Sund. 8. Preached at Organ ch. from 1 Chron. 4:9.10. Baptized one inf^t. In the afternoon preached at Laurence Lingle's from John 3:16. Germ.

Mond. 9. At home.

Tues. 10. Went to the Gold Mine on business.

Wed. 11. Took a load of hay to the Gold Mine.

Thurs. 12. At home till 12 o'clock, then went to Mr. Geo. Seaford's and married Mr. Henry Kluts to Miss Susan Seaford.

Frid. 13. Attended to the funeral of Anna Louisa Ketner at Organ ch. — preached from 2 Cor. 5:17. Germ.

Sat. 14. Had catechization at St. Stephen's ch.

Sund. 15. Preached at St. Stephen's ch. from 1 Chron. 4:9.10. In the afternoon preached at Paul Beaver's School house from Luk. 13:24. Germ.

Mond. 16. At home.

Tues. 17. Took a load of hay to the Gold Mine.

Wed. 18. At home. helped some in hauling in wheat.

Thurs. 19. Went to Salisbury. All night at widow Sarah Brown's.

Frid. 20. Returned home in the morning — balance of day at home.

Sat. 21. At home till afternoon, then went to Danl Miller's, Mrs. being with me. All night here.

Sund. 22. Preached at St. John's ch. from 1 Thes. 2:11.12. Germ. Revd Scheck preached for me at Organ ch. having exchanged pulpits to day.

Mond. 23. Went to Mr. Powlus' & had shoes nailed on my horse. In the afternoon went to Mr. J. Randleman's. All night here.

Tues. 24. Attended to the funeral of Charles Safret at Organ ch. Preached from Heb. 4:9. Germ.

Wed. 25. Went to Meisenheimer's Mill on the river. All night at Mr. Bringle's.

Thurs. 26. Returned home. In the evening went to Tobias Brown's.

Frid. 27. Returned home, and started for Lincolnton as far as widow Rose's.

Sat. 28. Went to Lincolnton. All night with br. Lewis.

Sund. 29. At br. Lewis' — preached in the afternoon from 2 Cor. 5:17. & at night from Prov. 29:1.

Mond. 30. Started home. All night at Mr. John Thomas'.

Tues. July 1. Went as far as Charles Barringer's. All night here.

Wed. 2. Returned home.

Thurs. 3. In the afternoon went to Tobias Brown's & returned his carriage.

Frid. 4. At home.

Sat. 5. Went to Daywald Beaver's in the morning & preached the funeral of his deceased child at his house from Heb. 4:9. Germ. Then went to St. Stephen's ch. & had catechization. Took dinner at Mr. Honeycut's. In the afternoon went to Mr. J. Melchior's to see Rev. Harter, he being sick. All night at Mr. Honeycut's.

Sund. 6. Preached at St. Stephen's ch. from John 7:37. Germ. Took dinner at Daywald Harkey's. In the afternoon attended preaching at Col. Alex. Holshouser's by Rev. John Lantz.

Mond. 7. Went to the Post office — the balance of the day at home.

Tues. 8. Wed. 9. At Mr. Holshouser's clerking sale.

Thurs. 10. Went to Mr. Holshouser's in the forenoon, the balance of the day at home.

Frid. 11. Went to Mr. Stirewalt's to the Carding Machine.

Sat. 12. At home.

Sund. 13. Preached at Organ ch. from Prov. 29:1. Germ. Baptized one infant. In the afternoon preached at Paul Cruse's from Mal. 3:7. Germ. Then returned home.

Mond. 14. At home.

Tues. 15. Went to the Gold Mine & to Dan'l Stikeleather's.

Wed. 16. At home.

Thurs. 17. At home.

Frid. 18. Had catechization at St. Stephen's Church.

Sat. 19. Attended to the funeral of two of Peter Trexler's children at the Lower Stone Church — preached from Amos 4:12. Returned home by way of the Muster & paid my tax & made my return of taxables.

Sund. 20. Preached at St. Stephen's ch. from 1 Tim. 4:7. Baptized 2 infants. Took dinner at Dr. Kelly's.

Mond. 21. Went to Mr. Fraley's to hear the candidates (Barringer & Fisher) speak.

Tues. 22. Went to Mr. Rusher's & my horses shod.

Wed. 23. Went to the river-mill. All night here.

Thurs. 24. In the afternoon, returned home.

Frid. 25. At home, Mrs. Rothrock being sick.

Sat. 26. Preached the funeral of George Hcilig, dec[d] at his late residence from Math. 26:41. Then went to a protracted meeting at St. Mathew's ch. — preached from Luk. 13:24.

Sund. 27. At St. Mathew's ch. and assisted in the ordination of Rev. J. A. Linn.

Mond. 28. Tues. 29. Wed. 30. At home.

Thurs. 31. Had catechization at St. Stephen's ch.

Frid. Aug. 1. In the afternoon went to the Camp Meeting at the Hatter Shop. After preaching returned home.

Sat. 2. At the Camp Meeting.

Sund. 3. Preached at St. Stephen's ch. from John 5:40. In the afternoon attended preaching at the Gold Mine by Rev. Plassman.

Mond. 4. In the afternoon went to the Gold Mine for nails.

Tues. 5. Went to Mr. Geo. Smith's in the Jersey Settlement, & married Mr. John Hartman to Miss Nancy Ann Smith. All night here.

Wed. 6. Returned home.

Thurs. 7. Called to see Peter Miller & then attended the election at Fraley's Store.

Frid. 8. Went to Salisbury.

Sat. 9. Started to St. Enoch's church. All night at Peter Kesler's.

Sund. 10. Preached at St. Enoch's ch. from Prov. 3:6. Eng$^{\underline{1}}$. After an intermission, preached from John 3:37. German. All night at Mr. File's.

Mond. 11. Returned home.

Tues. 12. In the afternoon went to Jacob Thomas' & married Mr. Levi Thomas to Miss Susan Walton. All night at Tobias Brown's.

Wed. 13. Returned home.

Thurs. 14. At home.

Frid. 15. At home till afternoon then went to the Post Office.

Sat. 16. Had catechization at St. Stephen's ch. This evening Caleb Peeler & wife called to see us.

Sund. 17. Preached at St. Stephen's ch. from Prov. 3:6. Took dinner at Paul Beaver's. In the afternoon preached at Beaver's School house from Math. 25:1-13.

Mond. 18. To day C. Peeler & wife started home with mother, she being very sick. Accompanied them part of the to Salisbury. The balance of the day at home.

Tues. 19. Wed. 20. At home.

Thurs. 21. At home.

Frid. 22. In the morning went in company with Mrs. R. to the Gold Mine. In the afternoon received the mournful intelligence of the death of my mother. Started to father's as far as Tobias Brown's.

Sat. 23. Went to father's & attended the burial of Mother at the Moravian Church in the neighborhood. The funeral was preached by Rev. Mr. Sensamon. All night at M. Beckerdite's.

Sund. 24. Preached at Rev. Sensamon's Church from Prov. 3:6. Called in the afternoon to see Martin Riple, he being in feeble health. All night at father's.

Mond. 25. At father's.

Tues. 26. Returned home.

Wed. 27. At home.

Thurs. 28. Started for Catawba County. All night at Alex. Brown's

Frid. 29. Reached Catawba. All night at Dan$^{\underline{1}}$ Smoyers'.

Sat. 30. At St. Paul's ch. — preached in the afternoon from 1 Tim. 4:7. All night at Mr. Lutz's, jr.

Sund. 31. Preached at St. Paul's ch. in the afternoon from Prov. 3:6. At night attended preaching in Newton by Rev. Linn. All night at Mr. Elias Bost's.

Mond. Sept. 1. Started for home as far as Revd Arey's.

Tues. 2. Reached home.

Wed. 3. At home.

Thurs. 4. Had catechization at St. Stephen's church.

Frid. 5. Went to Concord to assist Revd Harter in a Protracted Meeting. Preached in the afternoon from 1 Tim. 4:7. All night at Genl Means.

Sat. 6. Preached in the forenoon from Prov. 3:6. & at night from 1 Pet. 4:18. All night at Mr. Cook's Esqr.

Sund. 7. Preached in the forenoon from 1 Chron. 4:9.10. & at night from Mark 10:46-52. All night at Mr. Winecoff's Esqr.

Mond. 8. Returned home. Took dinner at Mr. Henry Blackwelder's.

Tues. 9. Went to Misenhimer's Mill. All night at Mr. Bringle's.

Wed. 10. Returned home.

Thurs. 11. Went to Salisbury.

Frid. 12. Sat. 13. At home.

Sund. 14. Preached at Organ ch. from Ex. 23:2. & in the afternoon at Linn's School house from Eccl. 12:13. to the colored people.

Mond. 15. Went to Salisbury in company with Mrs. R.

Tues. 16. Went to Salisbury.

Wed. 17. At home.

Thurs. 18. At home.

Frid. 19. At home till afternoon then called to see George Miller, he being sick.

Sat. 20. Had catechization at St. Stephen's ch.

Sund. 21. Preached at St. Stephen's ch. from Is. 35:8-10. An inclement day.

Mond. 22. Tues. 23. At home.

Wed. 24. Called to see several sick families in the bounds of St. Stephen's ch.

Thurs. 25. At home.

Frid. 26. At home, chucking corn.

Sat. 27. Went to Organ ch. for the purpose of holding Church Settlement.

Sund. 28. Preached at Organ ch. from Prov. 14:34.+ In the afternoon called to see Peter Trexler, he being very sick.

Mond. 29. Called to see Peter Trexler & George Miller & his son, Henry.

Tues. 30. At home till 12 o'clock, then went to the Gold Mine & preached the funeral of Mrs. Cameron from John 9:4.

+ Baptized to day 2 infants.

Wed. Oct. 1. At home. Commenced sowing wheat. In the afternoon went to Mrs. Ribelin's to shucking.

Thurs. 2. Attended to the funerals of Geo. Miller & his son, Henry at Organ ch., they having died within 7 hours of each other — preached from Ps. 50:15.

Frid. 3. At home.

Sat. 4. Had an appointment to day at St. Stephen's ch. for catechization, but did not reach there in consequence of rain.

Sund. 5. This my regular day at St. Stephen's ch. but did not get there — was sent for early this morning to go to Mrs. Arey's, my Mother-in-law's, she being very sick. Reached there between 10 & 11 o'clock - about 12 o'clock she died. In the evening returned home.

Mond. 6. Attended to the burial of Mrs. Arey, at Union ch. Sermon by Revd J. B. Anthony. All night at the old homestead.

Tues. 7. Went to Salisbury and entered with Milas Arey as Special Administrator on the Estate of Mrs. Arey, to serve until the following Court. All night at the old homestead place.

Wed. 8. Returned home.

Thurs. 9. At home, sick, in bed the greater part of the day.

Frid. 10. At home, not very well. A very rainy day.

Sat. 11. At home — a rainy day.

Sund. 12. Preached at Organ Church from Math. 12:41.42. German. Baptized one child. In the afternoon preached the funeral of Mrs. Barringer's negro girl at the house, from Phil. 1:21. In the evening returned home.

Mond. 13. At home till 12 o'clock. In the afternoon went to the Gold Mine.

Tues. 14. At home till 12 o'clock. In the afternoon went to the Post Office.

Wed. 15. At home.

Thurs. 16. At home.

Frid. 17. Had catechization at St. Stephen's ch.

Sat. 18. Had preaching to day at St. Stephen's ch. preparatory to communion. Revd Harter preached. At night had prayermeeting in the Church — lecture by Mr. Criminger, a layman. All night at Henry Lentz's.

Sund. 19. At St. Stephen's Ch, baptized 3 adults & confirmed 24 persons — preaching by Revd Harter — then administered the Lord's Supper. In the afternoon went to the Lower Stone Church and attended to the burial service of David Troutman's wife.

Mond. 20. At home.

Tues. 21. In the forenoon went to the Tanyard (Mr. Goodman's) & to the Post Office. In the afternoon went to the Gold Mine.

Wed. 22. Took some Turnips and Sweet Potatoes to the Gold Mine.

Thurs. 23. At home.

Frid. 24. Commenced a three days Meeting to day at Organ ch. Revd J. B. Anthony preached for me.

Sat. 25. Preached to day, after br. Anthony, from 2 Cor. 13:5. preparatory to communion. Baptized one infant.

Sund. 26. Preached from John 3:14.15. and administered the Lord's Supper to a large congregation.

Mond. 27. Went to the late residence of Mrs. Arey, dec^d.

Tues. 28. Wed. 29. Attended the sale of Mrs. Arey's property.

Thurs. 30. Returned home.

Frid. 31. Attended to the funeral of Old Mr. Ghents, dec^d at Organ ch. In the afternoon called at Saml Barrier's and baptized his child, it being sick.

Sat. Nov. 1. At home till afternoon then went to W. T. Miller's & had prayermeeting — lectured from the parable of the 10 virgins. All night here.

Sund. 2. Preached at St. Stephen's ch. from Ps. 7:9. Took dinner with Mr. Nussman. In the afternoon preached at David Troutman's the funeral of his deceased wife from Luk. 12:37. Germ.

Mond. 3. Went to Salisbury. All night at Milas Arey's. Made out my report to Court as Special Administrator of Phebe Arey, Dec^d.

Tues. 4. Returned home by way of Salisbury.

Wed. 5. At home.

Thurs. 6. Frid. 7. Sat. 8. At home.

Sund. 9. Preached at Organ ch. from Jerm. 6:16. In the afternoon went to Mr. Paul Nussman's & married Mr. Peter Earnheart to Miss Catherine Nussman — then returned home.

Mond. 10. Went to the Gold Mine & brought Dr. Kelly to see Mrs. R. she being very indisposed.

Tues. 11. Attended to the funeral of Andrew Eller at Union ch. — preached from Amos 4:12.

Wed. 12. At home.

Thurs. 13. Went to Salisbury.

Frid. 14. At home — Mrs. R. being very sick.

Sat. 15. Assisted Revd Anthony at a meeting at Union ch. — preached from Mark 10:46-52.

Sund. 16. Filled Revd Linn's appointment at Luther's ch. — preached from Mark 10:46-52. Baptized one infant.

Mond. 17. At home.

Tues. 18. Took Mrs. R. to Dr Kelly's on a visit.

Wed. 19. In the forenoon went to the Piny woods for a load of pine. In the afternoon at home.

Thurs. 20. Went to the Gold Mine & brought Mrs. R. home.

Frid. 21. Went to Salisbury to assist Revd Anthony at a meeting. — preached at 11 o'clock from Prov. 3:6. at 3 o'clock from Mark 1:40-45. At night from 1 Pet. 4:18. All night at Col. J. Brown's.

Sat. 22. Preached at 10 a.m. from Acts 20:17-21. In the afternoon returned home. Father called to see me.

Sund. 23. Preached at Organ ch. from 1 Pet. 4:18. Germ. Bapt^d 1 infant. In the afternoon attended to the funeral of David Earnheart's child at the Lower Stone ch. — preached from Luk. 12:37.

Mond. 24. At home butchering hogs.

Tues. 25. Attended to the funeral of Michael Eller at Union ch. — preached from Luk. 12:37.

Wed. 26. Attended to the funeral of Mrs. Ketchy at Organ ch. — preached the funeral at the house from Ps. 90:12. Germ. Took dinner at Moses Barringer's.

Thurs. 27. Attended to the funeral of Danl Cawble's daughter at Fullenwider's ch. — preached from Luk. 12:37.

Frid. 28. Preached at St. Mathew's ch. from Prov. 3:6.

Sat. 29. Went to St. Paul's ch. to fill an appointment for Rev. J. A. Linn, but owing to a misunderstanding as to the day, the congregation did not assemble.

Sund. 30. Preached at Organ ch. from Prov. 3:6. Germ. Baptized one infant. In the afternoon attended to the funeral of old Mr. Ketchey at Organ ch. — preached from Math. 5:8. Germ. Took dinner at John Seaford's.

Mond. Dec. 1. Attended to the funeral of old Mr. Adam Casper at the Lower St. ch. — preached from Luk. 13:24. Germ.

Tues. 2. At home.

Wed. 3. In the afternoon called to see Andr. Troutman.

Thurs. 4. At home. A very inclement day.

Frid. 5. Went to the late residence of Jacob Earnheart, dec^d to preach his funeral, but the inclemency of the weather prevented the people from attending.

Sat. 6. At home till afternoon, then went to Daywald Harkey's. & at night had prayermeeting at Henry Lentz's — lectured from 2 Kings 5:1-14. All night at Mr. Harkey's.

Sund. 7. Preached at St. Stephen's ch. from Prov. 14:34. Baptized one infant.

Mond. 8. At home.

Tues. 9. Went to the Sale of Mrs. Arey, dec^d. In the evening returned home.

Wed. 10. Went to D. Barringer's to meet the Legatees to settle some business.

Thurs. 11. Went to Mr. Goodman's, to John Knup's, & returned home by Mr. Fraley's.

Frid. 12. Went to Tobias Brown's.

Sat. 13. In the morning took some corn to Mr. Lewis Peeler's — the balance of the day at home.

Sund. 14. This was my regular day at Organ ch. but the day being very inclement did not attend.

Mond. 15. At home — a very inclement day.

Tues. 16. Wed. 17. At home.

Thurs. 18. In the afternoon called to see Revd J. A. Linn.

Frid. 19. In the forenoon went to the Gold Mine.

Sat. 20. Went to Salisbury & brought Jane Arey out to spend Christmas with us. A very cold inclement day. Broke the shaft of my carryall & got my horse crippled. Borrowed Mr. Henry Brown's horse & buggie to return home — reached home at 9 o'clock p.m.

Sund. 21. Preached at St. Stephen's ch. from Luk. 18:1-8. Elected H. Peck Esqr, Elder in place of H. J. Barringer, resigned.

Mond. 22. Returned Mr. Brown's horse & buggie.

Tues. 23. Called to see And. Troutman.

Wed. 24. At home.

Thurs. 25. Christmas day. At home.

Frid. 26. Sat. 27. At home.

Sund. 28. Preached at Organ ch. from Acts 16:16:34. Baptized one infant. Took dinner at John Miller's.

Mond. 29. Tues. 30. At home.

Wed. 31. Took Jane Arey to Mr. Tobias Brown's.

Thurs. Jan. 1, 1846. Went to Salisbury. In the evening returned home, Revd Arey being with me.

Frid. 2. Attended to the funeral of John Bostian's infant child at Organ ch. — preached from Math. 19:14.

Sat. 3. At home.

Sund. 4. Preached at St. Stephen's church from Rom. 13:11. Installed Mr. H. Peck, Esqr. as an Elder.

Mond. 5. Went to Salisbury. In the evening returned home, & brought my crippled horse home.

Tues. 6. A very inclement day. In the afternoon went to Mr. John Melchor's & married Geo. W. Barringer to Miss Caroline Melchor. Returned home after night.

Wed. 7. At home.

Thurs. 8. In the afternoon went to George Seaford's & married Mr. Guy Hill to Miss Anna Seaford. Returned home after night.

Frid. 9. At home.

Sat. 10. Went to St. Stephen's ch. Revd Daniel Scherer preached.

Sund. 11. This was my regular day at Organ ch. Revd Daniel Scherer preached in Germ. and Engl.

Mond. 12. Called in company with Mrs. R. to see Revd Linn and Lady.

Tues. 13. Called at the School House 12 o'clock & settled my school bill with Mr. Murdock (Teacher).

Wed. 14. At home till afternoon, then went to the Post office.

Thurs. 15. Went to Jacob Holshouser's awhile in the forenoon to the chopping, in the afternoon at home.

Frid. 16. At home, mending shoes.

Sat. 17. At home.

Sund. 18. Preached at St. Stephen's ch. from Math. 4:1-11. Was sent for Mrs. R. being very sick.

Mond. 19. Tues. 20. Wed. 21. At home.

Thurs. 22. At home.

Frid. 23. Attended preaching at Gold Hill by Revd D. Scherer. Revd Fink with me to night.

Sat. 24. At home.

Sund. 25. Preached at Organ ch. from Math. 5:1-12. Baptized one infant. Took dinner at Moses Barringer's.

Mond. 26. Went to Jacob Trexler's, Mrs. Trexler being sick.

Tues. 27. At home.

Wed. 28. Attended to the funeral of Mrs. Josey (Widow) at Organ ch. Preached the funeral of her at the house from Rev. 14:13.

Thurs. 29. Called to Mrs. Trexler, she being still sick.

Frid. 30. Went to Mr. Rusher's in the forenoon to settle some accounts, but found him not at home. In the afternoon at home.

Sat. 31. In the forenoon went to the Piny-woods for some pine. In the afternoon at home.

CARL A. RUDISILL LIBRARY
LENOIR-RHYNE COLLEGE

Sund. Feb. 1. Preached at St. Stephen's ch. from Deut. 11:16. took dinner at Mr. Mackins'.

Mond. 2. Went to Salisbury, it being Court time.

Tues. 3. At home.

Wed. 4. Attended to the funeral of Sophia Klutts (daughter of Leonard Klutts) at the Lower Stone ch. Preached from 2 Cor. 4:17.

Thurs. 5. Frid. 6. At home.

Sat. 7. At home.

Sund. 8. Preached at Organ ch. from Dan. 6:10. Baptized one infant.

Mond. 9. At home, mending shoes.

Tues. 10. Wed. 11. At home.

Thurs. 12. In the forenoon called to see Mrs. James Klutts, she being sick — in the afternoon went to Mr. John Eagle's & married Mr. Charles Bostian to Miss Sena Eagle. In the evening returned home.

Frid. 13. Sat. 14. At home.

Sund. 15. Preached at St. Stephen's ch. from Acts 10:38. Baptized one infant. Took dinner at Mr. Sol^{n} Nussman's.

Mond. 16. Attended the burial of Sophia, wife of Milas Arey at Union ch. Sermon by Rev. J. B. Anthony.

Tues. 17. Wed. 18. At home.

Thurs. 19. Frid. 20. Sat. 21. At home.

Sund. 22. Preached at Organ ch. from Acts 10:38. Germ. Baptized one infant. In the afternoon attended to the funeral of Mrs. John Harkey at the Lower Stone ch. — preached from Prov. 3:6.

Mond. 23. At home.

Tues. 24. Went to Salisbury.

Wed. 25. Engaged some hands to roll logs.

Thurs. 26. In the forenoon went to the Post Office, & to Mr. Jacob Trexler's, he being very sick. In the afternoon at home, rolling logs.

Frid. 27. At home. Worked on the new ground.

Sat. 28. Attended to the funeral of Jacob Trexler, sen. at the Lower Stone ch. — preached the funeral at the house of the deceased from Math. 10:32. In the afternoon went to Organ ch. & attended to the burial service of Valentine Reimer, dec^{d}.

Sund. March 1. Preached at St. Stephen's ch. from Math. 10:32.33. Baptized one infant. A very inclement day.

Mond. 2. At home. A very snowy day.

Tues. 3. At home.

Wed. 4. Went to the Gold Mine & had shoes put on my horse.

Thurs. 5. At home.

Frid. 6. Called to see Jacob Trexler, jr., he being sick.

Sat. 7. At home till afternoon, then called to see Jacob Trexler again.

Sund. 8. Preached at Organ ch. from Luk. 15:11-32. In the morning before public worship, attended to the burial service of John Josey's infant child. In the afternoon attended to the funeral of Mary Ann Smith at St. Paul's ch. — preached from Rev. 14:13. After preaching returned home.

Mond. 9. Attended to the funeral of Eli Shuping at Lower Stone ch. — preached from John 14:6. In the afternoon called at Elihu Holshouser's, his family being sick.

Tues. 10. Attended to the funeral of Mr. Castor's son at Organ church. — preached from Is. 55:6.

Wed. 11. Went to Salisbury, Mrs. R. being with me.

Thurs. 12. In the afternoon went to Dan¹ Kirk's in Stanly county, & at night married Simon P. Eddleman to Miss Eve Kirk. All night at Mr. Pennington's. A very inclement day.

Frid. 13. Returned home.

Sat. 14. In the morning went to Mr. John Goodman's, one of his sons being buried to day.

Sund. 15. Preached at St. Stephen's ch. from Luk. 15:11-32.

Mond. 16. Went to Salisbury — Court week.

Tues. 17. In the forenoon went to Adam Casper's late residence for straw. In the afternoon at home — sowed flax, &c.

Wed. 18. At home.

Thurs. 19. Went to D. Barringer's & Milas Arey's.

Frid. 20. Went to Salisbury in company with Milas Arey.

Sat. 21. At home.

Sund. 22. Preached at Organ ch. from Eccl. 11:9. The funeral of Valentine Reimer, who had died some weeks previous. Baptized two infants. Married Wilie Knup to Elizabeth Arey in the church in the presence of the congregation. In the afternoon had prayermeeting at Mr. James Klutts', his wife being sick, lectured from Math. 5:6.

Mond. 23. At home.

Tues. 24. Attended to the funeral of Mrs. Troutman at St. Stephen's church. — preached from Rev. 14:13.

Wed. 25. At home, breaking flax.

Thurs. 26. Attended to the funeral of Mrs. Henry Miller's at Fullenwider's church. — preached from Prov. 23:26.

Frid. 27. Went to Paul Seaford's Esq. & attended the closing of his school. All night here. My family with me.

Sat. 28. Went to St. Paul's ch. to assist Rev. Linn at a communion meeting. Preached from Josh. 23:8. the funeral of Eliz. Ann Hill. At night had prayermeeting at George Garner's, lectured from 2 Kings 5:1-14. All night here.

Sund. 29. Preached at St. Paul's ch. from Luk. 15:11-32. & assisted in the administration of the Lord's Supper. In the afternoon returned home.

Mond. 30. Tues. 31. At home.

Wed. April 1. Called to see Rev. Linn & Lady, Mrs. R. being with me.

Thurs. 2. At home, a very inclement day.

Frid. 3. Went in the morning to Mr. Powlass' & made some settlements. In the afternoon at home.

Sat. 4. At St. Stephen's ch. — had service preparatory to communion. Rev. Linn preached for me — baptized one infant. Took dinner at M. Barrier's Esq[r] At night had prayermeeting at the Church. Lectured from Prov. 23:26. Baptized William J. McDaniel. All night at Widow Peck's.

Sund. 5. At St. Stephen's ch. Rev. Linn preached — baptized four infants & administered the Lord's Supper.

Mond. 6. Went to Dan[l] Miller's to mill.

Tues. 7. At home — plowed my potatoe ground.

Wed. 8. Went to widow P. Cawble's in the forenoon & preached the funeral of her child from Am. 4:12. Very rainy. In the afternoon went to the Post office.

Thurs. 9. In the forenoon went to Wilie Knup's to rent him some land. In the afternoon at home making potatoe-hills.

Frid. 10. At home till 12 o'clock. In the afternoon went to the Gold Mine.

Sat. 11. At home.

Sund. 12. This was my regular day for German preaching at Organ ch., but Rev[d] Lepperd being present, preached in English to the congregation. Took dinner at Joseph Miller's. bapt[d] 1 inf[t].

Mond. 13. At home till afternoon, then went in company with Mrs. R. to Milas Arey's.

Tues. 14. Went to Salisbury. In the afternoon went to widow Sarah Brown's & married John J. Miller to Mary Ann Brown.

Wed. 15. At Jacob Trexler's, dec[d] & clerked sale for Administrators.

Thurs. 16. Attended to the funeral of Polly C. Lentz, wife of Ambrose Lentz, at St. Stephen's ch. — preached from John 9:4. Took dinner at Moses Eagle's.

Frid. 17. Attended to the funeral of Peter Cawble at Fullenwider's ch. — preached from 1 Peter 4:18. This evening Rev[d] J. F. W. Lepperd called to see me.

Sat. 18. At home. Rev[d] Lepperd with me.

Sund. 19. This my day at St. Stephen's ch. Rev[d] Lepperd preached for me. Dinner at Dr. Kelly's.

Mond. 20. Went to Mr. Pennington's on the river for fish.

Tues. 21. Went to the Gold Mine — engaged Isaac Earnheart to build a chimney.

Wed. 22. At home.

Thurs. 23. In the forenoon took Phebe Cunningham home, she having been with us for several days sewing.

Frid. 24. Went to Col. Holshouser's & clerk the sale of a little property of Jacob Holshouser, dec[d].

Sat. 25. Preached at Organ ch. from Ps. 116:12-14. Germ. Preparatory to communion. After an intermission, attended to the preparatory service in English. Afterwards attended to the funeral of Mrs. Ketner — preached from John 9:4. Germ. All night at Daniel Eddleman's. Baptized 5 inf[ts] to day.

Sund. 26. Preached at Organ ch. from 1 Sam. 12:23.24. After an intermission administered the Lord's Supper — All night at George Randleman's.

Mond. 27. Attended to the funer[l] of John Fisher at St. Paul's ch. — preached the funeral at the residence of the deceased from Neh. 7:2. latter clause. In the afternoon returned home.

Tues. 28. At home.

Wed. 29. Went with my family to Milas Arey's.

Thurs. 30. Returned home & in the afternoon went back to Milas Arey's.

Frid. May 1. Went to Union ch. To day commenced..

Sat. 2. Sund. 3. Mond. 4. Tues. 5. At Union ch. On Tues. night the ministerium met at D. Barringer's & continued its session till 2 o'clock A.M.

Wed. 6. Called (having staid at Sam[l] Peeler's) to see Jacob Thomas & George Peeler, & in the afternoon returned home.

Thurs. 7. At home — sheared the sheep.

Frid. 8. At home.

Sat. 9. At home till afternoon, then went with Mrs. R. to Moses Barringer's & staid all night.

Sund. 10. Preached at Organ ch. from 1 John 5:21. Baptized 2 infants. Took dinner at Simeon Miller's.

Mond. 11. Started for Giles County, Virginia to attend the Synod of South Western Virginia & arrived at the place on the following Friday. — Sat. & Sunday in attendance & on Mond. till 12 o'clock. In the afternoon started for home, & arrived at home on Saturday 23rd.

Sund. 24. At Organ ch. Rev. Arey preached for me. Took dinner at Dan[l] Miller's.

Mond. 25. In the morning called to see Peter Earnheart, he being sick.

Tues. 26. Went to Salisbury.

Wed. 27. At home.

Thurs. 28. Preached the funeral of Peter Earnheart, dec[d] at his residence from John 9:4. In the afternoon aided in laying off Mrs. Trexler's year's provisions.

Frid. 29. Went to Mr. Linn's mill.

Sat. 30. Had catechization at Organ ch. In the afternoon had prayermeeting at Geo. Bost's. Lectured from John 7:37. Germ. and administered the Lord's Supper to Mr. Bost, he being aged & infirm. All night at Col. Lentz's.

Sund. 31. Preached at St. Stephen's ch. from Ex. 20:8. Baptized 1 infant.

Mond. June 1. Went to Milas Arey's.

Tues. 2. Went to Salisbury to General Muster.

Wed. 3. Thurs. 4. At home making hay.

Frid. 5. Went to Post Office & to Henry Knup's.

Diary No. 12
June 1846

Sat. 6. Went to Mr. Barrier's Esqr Settled with Seminary Treasurer. At night had prayermeeting – Lectured from Gal. 5:1.

Sund. 7. Preached at St. Stephen's ch. from Ex. 33:14.

Mond. 8. Tues. 9. Wed. 10. At home.

Thurs. 11. Went to Widow Brown's (Jeremiah's) & married Edward Baim to Margaret Brown.

Frid. 12. Attended to the funeral of James Klutts' wife at Organ ch. – preached from Job 14:14.

Sat. 13. Had catechization at Organ ch.

Sund. 14. Preached at Organ ch. from Ps. 119:63. Baptized 2 inf^{ts}. In the afternoon attended to the funeral of Wm. Bost's child. – preached from Phil. 1:21. Germ.

Mond. 15. Tues. 16. At home.

Wed. 17. In the afternoon went to procure hands to harvest.

Thurs. 18. Frid. 19. At home.

Sat. 20. At to the funeral of George Seaford's wife at Organ ch. – preached from Math. 5:6. In the evening to Widow Peck's & staid all night.

Sund. 21. Preached at St. Stephen's ch. from Math. 12:41.42. Baptized 2 inf^{ts}. Took dinner at Mr. Nussman's.

Mond. 22. At home.

Tues. 23. Wed. 24. At home – (hay making.)

Thurs. 25. In the afternoon went to Widow Geo. Miller's & married Moses Trexler to Widow Miller.

Frid. 26. Sat. 27. At home – hauling Wheat.

Sund. 28. Preached at Organ ch. from Luk. 16:19-31. Took dinner at Jacob Miller's.

Mond. 29. At home.

Tues. 30. Went to Gold Mine & had my horses shod.

Wed. July 1. In the afternoon went to Geo. Klutts' to have boots repaired.

Thurs. 2. Frid. 3. At home.

Sat. 4. Went to Gold Mine.

Sund. 5. Preached at St. Stephen's ch. from Danl 6:10.

Mond. 6. Tues. 7. Wed. 8. Thurs. 9. Frid. 10. At home, gathering in my oats.

Sat. 11. Had catechization at Organ ch. All night at widow Geo. Heilig's.

Sund. 12. Preached at Organ ch. from Luk. 15:11-24. Baptized 1 inf^t. In the afternoon had prayermeeting at Philip Eddleman's — lectured from Ps. 50:15. Germ. All night here.

Mond. 13. Returned home.

Tues. 14. At home.

Wed. 15. Went to Danl Miller's to mill.

Thurs. 16. Frid. 17. At home.

Sat. 18. Went to the tax-paying at Widow Miller's.

Sund. 19. To day Rev. Fink preached for me at St. Stephen's ch. & in the afternoon at Paul Beaver's School house.

Mond. 20. Took Lewis to Dr. Cunningham's to School. In the afternoon at home.

Tues. 21. Went to Post office.

Wed. 22. Went to Gold Mine. In the afternoon took sick with bilious fever.

Thurs. 23. Frid. 24. Sat. 25. Sund. 26. At home sick.

Mond. 27. At home — able to be up some.

Tues. 28. Wed. 29. At home.

Thurs. 30. Went to J. Holshouser's & had wind mill hopper repaired.

Frid. July 31. Sat. Aug. 1. At home.

Sund. 2. Preached at St. Stephen's ch. from Prov. 13:6. Took dinner at Mr. Spencer's. In the afternoon preached at Linn's School house from Mark 6:12. to the colored people.

Mond. 3. Went to Salisbury.

Tues. 4.* Wed. 5. At home.

Thurs. 6. At home till afternoon, then went to Mr. Fraley's to the election.

Frid. 7. At home.

Sat. 8. Had catechization at Organ ch.

Sund. 9. Preached at Organ ch. from Ps. 7:9. Baptized   infants. In the afternoon preached in the grove near the church the funeral of 2 colored persons who had died sometime before from Amos 4:12.

Mond. 10. Attended the sale of Jacob Thomas, dec^{d}.

Tues. 11. Went to Blacksmith's Shop.

Wed. 12. Thurs. 13. At home.

Frid. 14. In the afternoon went to Post Office.

Sat. 15. Went to John Lentz's to attend to the funeral of Ambrose Lentz's child, but was too indisposed to officiate.

Sund. 16. Was unable to preach to day in consequence of sickness. Returned home early in the morning.

Mond. 17. Went to Tobias Brown's in Iredell County.

Tues. 18. At Mr. Brown's.

Wed. 19. Went by way of Rev. B. Arey's to Daywald Harkey's.

Thurs. 20. Went to C. Barringer's.

Frid. 21. Returned home.

Sat. 22. Had catechization at Organ ch.

Sund. 23. Preached at Organ ch. from Rom. 8:9. Germ. Baptized 4 infants. Took dinner at John Seaford's.

Mond. 24. Attended to the fun^{l} of Moses Lyerly's child at the Lower Stone ch. − preached from Math. 19:14.

Tues. 25. At home, cleaning up wheat.

Wed. 26. Started to father's as far as Milas Arey's.

Thurs. 27. Went to father's.

Frid. 28. Went to Salem. In the evening returned to Hugh Beckerdite's.

Sat. 29. In the morning went to Salem. In the afternoon returned to father's.

Sund. 30. Preached at the school house near Father's from Ps. 116:12-14. it being the anniversary of Sunday School here.

Mond. 31. Returned home as far as Milas Arey's.

* To day married Jacob Stirewalt to Mary K. Shaver.

Tues. Sept. 1. Returned home.

Wed. 2. Went to the Post office — balance of the day at home.

Thurs. 3. Attended to the fun¹ of Henry Stirewalt's son at the church near Widow Graeber's. — preached from Job. 14:14. Germ. Took dinner at Mrs. Graeber's.

Frid. 4. At home.

Sat. 5. Went to Gold Mine — balance of the day at home.

Sund. 6. Preached at St. Stephen's ch. from Jam. 1:5. Baptᵈ 1 infᵗ.

Mond. 7. Visited some sick neighbors.

Tues. 8. At home.

Wed. 9. Went to the Post office.

Thurs. 10. At home.

Frid. 11. At home, till afternoon, then went to Gold Mine.

Sat. 12. Had catechization at Organ ch. Took dinner at Mr. Moses Barringer's. In the afternoon went with Mrs. R. to John Eagle's & staid all night. Very unwell.

Sund. 13. Preached at Organ ch. from Is. 35:8-10. Bapt. 2 infᵗˢ.

Mond. 14. Went to Salisbury.

Tues. 15. At home.

Wed. 16. At home till afternoon then went to Gold Mine on business.

Thurs. 17. Went to Salisbury.

Frid. 18. Commenced a 3 days meeting at St. Stephen's ch. Revᵈ Harter preached — confirmed one person.

Sat. 19. At St. Stephen's ch. Revds. Harter & Linn preached — All night at W. T. Miller's. Confirmed to day one person and bapt. 2 infants.

Sund. 20. At St. Stephen's ch. All night at Mr. John Lentz's at Gold Hill.

Mond. 21. Returned home & in afternoon went to Rivermill.

Tues. 22. Returned home.

Wed. 23. Went to post office, &c.

Thurs. 24. Went to Mr. Linn's to the wedding of Moses Goodman & Clarrissa Heilig.

Frid. 25. Had catechization at Organ ch.

Sat. 26. Had preparatory service at Organ ch. Revds. Linn & Anthony preached. Baptized one infᵗ. All night at Michael Bostian's.

Sund. 27. Had communion at Organ ch. Rev. Anthony preached. Baptized one inft. All night at Caleb Heilig's.

Mond. 28. Returned home. In the afternoon went to Jacob Miller's for a keg of vinegar.

Tues. 29. At home.

Wed. 30. Went to Salisbury.

Thurs. Oct. 1. Went to Philip Cruse's and married Dan[l] Klutts to Catherine Cruse. In the evening went to Concord to a three days meeting. All night at Mr. Waggoner's.

Frid. 2. Preached from Jam. 1:25. All night at Mr. Cook's Esq[r].

Sat. 3. Preached in the afternoon from Luk. 15:11-24. At night had prayermeeting at Mr. Leip's — lectured from 2 Kings 5:1-14. All night here.

Sund. 4. Preached from Ex. 33:14. All night at Mr. Brown's.

Mond. 5. Returned home. Took dinner at Caleb Heilig's.

Tues. 6. Attended the funeral of Peter Culp at St. Stephen's ch. — preached from Is. 3:10.

Wed. 7. Went to Jacob Holshouser's in the morning & borrowed some tools to put a lock on the house door. In the afternoon went to Mr. Paulus' to Smithshop.

Thurs. 8. Hauled some manure & went to Moses Trexler's for some plank. In the afternoon at home.

Frid. 9. Went in company with Rev. Harter to Luther's ch. to attend a three days meeting, but as the congregation did not assemble had no preaching — all night at Conrad Miller's.

Sat. 10. At Luther's Church. In the evening returned home.

Sund. 11. At Luther's ch. — preached from Josh. 23:8. & aided in the administration of the Lord's Supper. In the evening returned home.

Mond. 12. Called in the evening to see Rev. Linn, he being sick. In the afternoon went to the Gold Mine.

Tues. 13. Went to Alex[r] Miller's Sale. In the afternoon aided Col. Holshouser in shucking corn.

Wed. 14. At home, received a load of corn.

Thurs. 15. Went to C. Barringer's in Iredell County.

Frid. 16. Went to Tobias Brown's.

Sat. 17. Preached at St. Michael's ch. from Josh. 23:8. & in the afternoon from Ex. 23:2. At night attended a prayermeeting at Henry Ostwalt's — lectured from 2 Kings 5:1-14. All night at Mr. John Thomas'.

Sund. 18. Preached at St. Michael's ch. from Luk. 15:11-24. All night at Mr. Jacob Thomas'.

Mond. 19. Returned to B. Arey's. & in the afternoon went to Statesville. All night at Michael Reckart's.

Tues. 20. Returned to C. Barringer's.

Wed. 21. Came to Milas Arey's.

Thurs. 22. Returned home.

Frid. 23. At home. Bought Milas Arey's Iredell land.

Sat. 24. Had catechization at Organ ch. In the evening called to see old Mrs. Barbara Holshouser.

Sund. 25. Preached at Organ ch. from Luk 2:41-52. In the afternoon attended to the funeral of old Mrs. Lyerly at Lower Stone ch. — preached from Deut. 11:16.

Mond. 26. At home till 12 o'clock then went to Caleb Heilig's & brought my horse home.

Tues. 27. Went to Widow Eddleman's & married Wilson A. Lentz to Polly Eddleman.

Wed. 28. Went to Iredell & rented my plantation to Abner Seats. All night at Chas. Barringer's.

Thurs. 29. Returned home.

Frid. 30. Went to And[r] Troutman's & the Gold Mine.

Sat. 31. At home.

Sund. Nov. 1. Preached at St. Stephen's ch. from Gen. 5:24. Took dinner at Mr. McMacken's. In the afternoon preached the fun[1] of Sophia Troutman at David Troutman's from Joh. 9:4. Germ.

Mond. 2. At home.

Tues. 3. Went to Salisbury.

Wed. 4. Thurs. 5. At home.

Frid. 6. Went to Salisbury.

Sat. 7. Had catechization at Organ ch.

Sund. 8. Preached at Organ ch. from Math. 12:22-37. Baptized one infant. Took dinner at Mr. John Miller's.

Mond. 9. Went to John Arey's & paid over him some money.

Tues. 10. Attended Rev. John McMacken's Sale.

Wed. 11. Thurs. 12. At home.

Frid. 13. In the forenoon took some turkeys to Gold Mine & in the afternoon went to Dr. Cunningham's.

Sat. 14. Attended Laurence Porter's Sale.

Sund. 15. Preached Ambrose Lentz's child's funeral at St. Stephen's ch. from Job 14:14.

Mond. 16. Attended to the funeral of Edmond Culp at St. Stephen's ch. — preached from Ps. 58:11.

Tues. 17. Went to the weaver's. (Christena Kesler's.)

Wed. 18. In the afternoon went to Gold Mine & had horse shod.

Thurs. 19. At home.

Frid. 20. Attended Caleb Knup's Sale.

Sat. 21. Had catechization at Organ ch.

Sund. 22. Preached at Organ ch. from John 14:6. Germ. & installed Church Council.

Mond. 23. At home till afternoon then went to weaver's (D. Knup's).

Tues. 24. Attended to the funeral of John Setzer at Organ ch. — preached from 2 Tim. 4:7.8. Took dinner at Frederic Holshouser's.

Wed. 25. At home.

Thurs. 26. Frid. 27. At home.

Sat. 28. At home.

Sund. 29. Attended at Organ ch. to reconcile some difficulties between several of the members.

Mond. 30. Went to Dan[l] Miller's mill.

Tues. Dec. 1. Attended to the funeral of Henry Barringer at Organ ch. — preached from Mark 13:32-37.

Wed. 2. At home.

Thurs. 3. At home — butchered hogs.

Frid. 4. Attended to the funeral of John Peck, jr. at St. Stephen's ch. — preached from Acts 13:36.

Sat. 5. At home till afternoon then went to Mr. Linn's.

Sund. 6. Preached at St. Stephen's ch. from Math. 12:22-37. Held an election for deacons.

Mond. 7. At home, till afternoon then went to the Post office.

Tues. 8. In the afternoon went the Gold Mine.

Wed. 9. Went to Salisbury.

Thurs. 10. Frid. 11. At home.

Sat. 12. Had catechization at Organ Church.

Sund. 13. Preached at Organ ch. from Math. 9:1-17. Baptized one infant. Took dinner at Jacob Miller's.

Mond. 14. At home.

Tues. 15. Went to Gold Hill.

Wed. 16. Thurs. 17. At home.

Frid. 18. Went to see Henry Hahnberger, he having died of Hydrophobia.

Sat. 19. Attended to the funeral of H. Hahnberger at Organ ch. — preached from Is. 55:6. Baptized Mr. H's child.

Sund. 20. Preached at St. Stephen's ch. from Acts 16:17. Installed Mr. S. Nussman as Deacon.

Mond. 21. Went to the weaver's (Christena Kesler).

Tues. 22. Wed. 23. Thurs. 24. At home.

Frid. 25. Preached at Linn's School house for the negroes from Math. 11:28.

Sat. 26. Had catechization at Organ ch.

Sund. 27. Preached at Organ ch. from Math. 22:1-14. Took dinner at Jacob Miller's.

Mond. 28. At home.

Tues. 29. At home, hauling rails.

Wed. 30. In the afternoon went to Salisbury, & at night married Rev. W. G. Harter to Miss Margaret V. Nuttall, returned home after supper.

Thurs. 31. Went to Milas Arey's.

Frid. Jan. 1, 1847. Went to Salisbury.

Sat. 2. At home.

Sund. 3. Preached at St. Stephen's ch. from 2 Chron. 7:14. Baptized one infant.

Mond. 4. At home till afternoon, then went to Post office.

Tues. 5. At home.

Wed. 6. Called to see Rev. Linn.

Thurs. 7. At home. Rev. J. B. Anthony & family called to see us.

Frid. 8. At home till afternoon, then went to Gold Mine.

Sat. 9. At home.

Sund. 10. Preached at Organ ch. from Math. 10:32.33. the funeral of Elizabeth Rimer. In the afternoon attended to the funeral of Mrs. Philip File at Lower Stone ch. Preached from Luk. 13:24. Germ.

Mond. 11. At home till afternoon, then went to Gold Mine.

Tues. 12. At home till afternoon, then went to Post office.

Wed. 13. Had a daughter born this morning at 4 o'clock.

Thurs. 14. Frid. 15. At home.

Sat. 16. Had catechization at Organ ch.

Sund. 17. Preached at St. Stephen's ch. from Josh. 7:12. Took dinner at Dr. Kelly's.

Mond. 18. At home.

Tues. 19. At home, till afternoon, then went to Gold Mine.

Wed. 20. At home.

Thurs. 21. At home till afternoon, then went to Post office, Dr. Cunningham's, & Rev. Lants'.

Frid. 22. In the afternoon went to Wilie Knup's & Gold Mine.

Sat. 23. Went to Salisbury.

Sund. 24. Preached at Organ ch. from 1 Kings 18:21-40. Baptized one infant. Dinner at D. Miller's.

Mond. 25. At home till 12 o'clock, then went to Post office.

Tues. 26. Wed. 27. At home.

Thurs. 28. At home — hauling wood.

Frid. 29. At home.

Sat. 30. Had catechization at Organ ch. In the afternoon attended to the funeral of John Klutts at Lower Stone Church. Preached from Rev. 14:13. Germ.

Sund. 31. Attended preaching at Linn's School house by Rev. J. A. Linn.

Mond. Feb. 1. Went to Salisbury.

Tues. 2. Returned to Salisbury.

Wed. 3. Attended to the funeral of Mrs. David Holshouser at Organ ch. — preached from Ps. 90:12.

Thurs. 4. Went to Salisbury.

Frid. 5. At home.

Sat. 6. Had catechization at Organ ch.

Sund. 7. Preached at St. Stephen's ch. from 1 Kings 19:13. Baptized 1 infant. In the afternoon called at Tobias Klutts' & baptized his child.

Mond. 8. Went to D. Miller's to mill.

Tues. 9. Returned home.

Wed. 10. Thurs. 11. At home.

Frid. 12. Went to D. Miller's to mill.

Sat. 13. Returned home by way of the Gold Mine.

Sund. 14. Preached at Organ ch. from Jam. 1:12. Baptized 2 infants. Took dinner at Mrs. Heilig's.

Mond. 15. Went to Laurence Lingle's.

Tues. 16. Assisted Widow Peeler at her chopping.

Wed. 17. Went to Salisbury.

Thurs. 18. At home.

Frid. 19. Went to Geo. Klutts' to the tanyard.

Sat. 20. Had catechization at Organ Church.

Sund. 21. Preached at St. Stephen's ch. from Ps. 1:1-6. Baptized one infant. Took dinner at Solomon Nussman's. In the afternoon attended to the funeral of John Troutman's son at his house — preached from Amos 4:12. Germ.

Mond. 22. Took some wheat to Milas Arey's.

Tues. 23. Attended to the funeral of Moses Josey's child at Organ ch. — preached from Math. 5:8.

Wed. 24. Attended to the funeral of Jacob Smith at Organ ch. — preached from 2 Cor. 5:17. Germ.

Thurs. 25. Went to Widow J. Trexler's & married Mr. Moses Lingle to Miss Louisa Trexler. In the evening went to Paul Cruse's, to see Susanna Bame, she being sick. Had a prayermeeting, lectured from Math. 11:28. Germ. All night here.

Frid. 26. Returned home.

Sat. 27. At home.

Sund. 28. Preached at Organ ch. from Jer. 6:16. Germ. Baptized one infant. In the afternoon had prayermeeting at Paul Cruse's, lectured from Rev. 3:20. Germ. & administered the Lord's Supper to Susanna Bame, she being sick.

Mond. March 1. At home.

Tues. 2. At home.

Wed. 3. At home till afternoon then went to Post Office.

Thurs. 4. At home.

Frid. 5. Attended the closing of P. A. Seaford's School & gave an address on the occasion. Took dinner at Mr. John Eagle's & staid over night at P. A. Seaford's.

Sat. 6. Had catechization at Organ ch.

Sund. 7. Preached at St. Stephen's ch. Took dinner at John Lentz's.

Mond. 8. At home.

Tues. 9. Assisted Dr. Cunningham in rolling his house.

Wed. 10. Attended to the funeral of Susanna Bame at Paul Cruse's — Preached from Joh. 9:4. Germ.

Thurs. 11. Frid. 12. At home.

Sat. 13. In the morning went to Moses Goodman's for a shoat.

Sund. 14. Preached at St. Mathew's ch. from 1 Kings 19:13. having exchanged pulpits to day with Rev. J. A. Linn.

Mond. 15. At home.

Tues. 16. Went to Salisbury.

Wed. 17. In the afternoon went to Laurence Lingle's. Mr. T. Brown & Lady with us to night.

Thurs. 18. In the morning went to the Post Office. The balance of the day at home.

Frid. 19. At home — sowing oats.

Sat. 20. Had catechization at Organ ch. Attended also to the funeral of Mr. Geo. Hartzel, preached from John 9:4. Took dinner at Joseph Miller's & called to see Mr. J. Goodman, he being sick.

Sund. 21. This was my day at St. Stephen's ch. but did not attend being indisposed & the day very inclement. In the evening called to see Mr. Goodman.

Mond. 22. Went for fish. All night at Mrs. Kirk's.

Tues. 23. Returned home.

Wed. 24. Attended to the funeral of John Goodman at Fullenwider's ch. — preached from John 9:4.

Thurs. 25. At home — plowing.

Frid. 26. At home.

Sat. 27. At home.

Sund. 28. This was my day at Organ ch. but being quite indisposed with cold & Rev. Anthony being present, he preached for me. Had our daughter, Charlotte Lucetta Jane baptized to day by br. Anthony.

Mond. 29. Went to Jacob Earnheart's, sen. & did some writing for him.

Tues. 30. Plowed till dinner, in the afternoon went to D. Miller's to mill.

Wed. 31. Returned home.

Thurs. Apr. 1. At home — ploughing.

Frid. 2. Went to Salisbury.

Sat. 3. Had catechization at Organ ch.

Sund. 4. Preached at St. Stephen's ch. from Luke 16:19-31. In the afternoon attended to the funeral of widow Barrier at Lower Stone ch. — preached from 1 Thes. 5:6.

Mond. 5. Attended to the funeral of Widow Geo. Goodman at Phanuel's Church. Preached from Mal. 3:17.

Tues. 6. At home.

Wed. 7. At home.

Thurs. 8. Went to Salisbury.

Frid. 9. Went to Gold Mine & had horse shod.

Sat. 10. Had catechization at Organ ch.

Sund. 11. Preached at Organ ch. from Deut. 6:3. Germ. Baptized 2 children.

Mond. 12. Went to Jacob Holshouser's, his son Tobias being sick.

Tues. 13. Attended to the funeral of Mrs. Jacob Pool — preached the funeral at the house from Heb. 4:9.

Wed. 14. Bought a Buggy. In afternoon went to Gold Mine & horse shod. In the evening went to Mr. Holshouser's.

Thurs. 15. At home.

Frid. 16. Attended to the fun[1] of Tobias Holshouser at Lower St. ch. — preached from Job 14:1.2.

Sat. 17. Preached at St. Stephen's ch. from Ps. 51:2. preparatory to communion. Baptized 3 infants.

Sund. 18. Preached at St. Stephen's ch. from Lam. 4:2. & administered the Lord's Supper.

Mond. 19. Called to see Col. Holshouser & went to Salisbury.

Tues. 20. Called to see Col. Holshouser & went to Post Office.

Wed. 21. Thurs. 22. Frid. 23. Called each day to see Col. Holshouser. The balance of the time at home preparing for Synod.

Sat. 24. Had catechization at Organ Church. Attended also to the funeral of John Garner. Preached from John 14:6.

Sund. 25. Preached at Organ ch. from Acts 17:11-22. Took dinner at Mr. John Cress'.

Mond. 26. At home.

Tues. 27. Went to Organ ch. the members having met to build a stand. Went also to Jacob Yost's & married George Troutman to Miss Sophia C. Yost.

Wed. 28. At home.

Thurs. 29. At Organ ch. Rev. J. A. Linn preached. Confirmed 48 persons & bapt[d] 1 adult.

Frid. 30. Synod met at Organ ch. — preached the opening sermon from 1 Thes. 2:11.12.

Sat. May 1 — to Tues. 4. in synod.
Wed. 5. Went to Gold Mine.
Thurs. 6. Went to Salisbury.
Frid. 7. Sat. 8. At home.
Sund. 9. Preached at Organ ch. from Mal. 3-7. Took dinner at Paul Miller's.
Mond. 10. At home.
Tues. 11. Went to Widow Kistler's & married David Holshouser to widow Sally Kistler.
Wed. 12. Went to Gold Hill in the morning.
Thurs. 13. Went to Mr. Linn's.
Frid. 14. Went to Mr. Holshouser's to mill.
Sat. 15. At home.
Sund. 16. Preached at St. Stephen's ch. from Prov. 14:34. and in the afternoon at Gold Hill from Rev. 2:4.5.
Mond. 17. Went to Iredell to Chas Barringer's.
Tues. 18. At Chas Barringer's, it being a very rainy day.
Wed. 19. Returned home.
Thurs. 20. Attended to the funeral of Mrs. Lydia Sides, wife of Nelson Sides, at Organ church. — preached from Phil. 1:21. Germ.
Frid. 21. At home till evening, then went to Gold Hill and brought Lewis home from school.
Sat. 22. At home.
Sund. 23. Preached at Organ ch. from 1 Tim. 4:7. Germ. In the afternoon preached at old Mr. Bost's from Mark 6:12. Germ. & administered the L's Supper to Mr. Bost.
Mond. 24. Took Lewis to Gold Mine to school.
Tues. 25. At home till afternoon then went to Henry Earnheart's & attended to the fun^l of Christopher Earnheart. — preached from Heb. 4:9.
Wed. 26. Thurs. 27. At home.
Frid. 28. Went in company with Revd Linn to Davidson to attend a 2 days meeting at Pilgrim's ch. All night at Michael Sink's.
Sat. 29. Preached at Pilgrim's ch. from Prov. 3:6. All night at Father's.
Sund. 30. Preached at Pilgrim's from Luk. 15:11-24. All night at Andrew Sink's.
Mond. 31. Returned home by way of Salisbury.

Tues. June 1. In the morning went to Gold Hill. In the afternoon went to Danl Miller's to mill.

Wed. 2. Returned home by way of Gold Hill.

Thurs. 3. Went to Post Office, &c.

Frid. 4. At home till evening then went & brought Lewis home from Gold Hill.

Sat. 5. In the afternoon took some chickens to Gold Hill.

Sund. 6. Preached at St. Stephen's church from 2 Pet. 3:18. Baptized 3 infants. In the afternoon preached at Gold Hill from Luk. 15:11-24.

Mond. 7. Went to Gold Hill & Mr. Powlass' &c & engaged hands to mow grass.

Tues. 8. Went to Milas Arey's & in the evening to Solomon Peeler's to M. Arey's wedding.

Wed. 9. In the afternoon went to B. Arey's in Iredell.

Thurs. 10. Went to Mr. John Thomas' to attend the wedding of D. Setzer & Fanny Thomas. All night at Tobias Brown's.

Frid. 11. Went to Mr. Setzer's & took dinner. In the afternoon returned to Charles Barringer's.

Sat. 12. Returned home.

Sund. 13. Preached at Organ ch. from Heb. 2:3. In the afternoon preached at Alex^{r} Holshouser's from Math. 11:28.

Mond. 14. Tues. 15. Wed. 16. Thurs. 17. At home hay making.

Frid. 18. In the afternoon went to post office and Gol[d] Hill.

Sat. 19. At home.

Sund. 20. Preached at St. Stephen's ch. from Gal. 6:14. Had an appointment for the afternoon at Gold Hill but did not preach in consequence of rain.

Mond. 21. In the afternoon called to see Mr. Luky at Gold Hill, he being afflicted.

Tues. 22. Called to see Ambrose Eddleman he being sick.

Wed. 23. Returned home.

Thurs. 24. Went to Charles Barringer's & married Mr. John Lowder to Miss Sarah L. Barringer.

Frid. 25. Attended to the fun^{l} of Mrs. David Casper at the Lower Stone ch. Preached from Is. 3:10.

Sat. 26. At home.

Sund. 27. Preached at Organ ch. from Eccl. 11:9. fun^{l}. In the afternoon attended to the funeral of old Mrs. Ribelin at the Lower St. ch. Preached from Eccl. 9:10.

Mond. 28. Took Lewis to Gold Hill to School — the balance of the day at home.

Tues. 29. Attended to the funeral of Ambrose Eddleman at Organ ch. — preached from Num. 23:10.

Wed. 30. Went to see Mr. Moses Bost, he being sick.

Thurs. July 1. At home.

Frid. 2. At home till evening then went to Gold Hill & brought Lewis home.

Sat. 3. At home till afternoon then went to John Miller's and Post office.

Sund. 4. Preached at St. Stephen's ch. from Jerm. 5:26. Baptized 2 infants. In the afternoon, preached at Gold Hill from Ps. 7:9.

Mond. 5. In the morning took Lewis to Gold Hill to School, the balance of the day at home.

Tues. 6. Wed. 7. At home.

Thurs. 8. Went to Post office — balance of day at home.

Frid. 9. At home till evening, then went to Gold Hill & brought Lewis home.

Sat. 10. At home.

Sund. 11. Preached at Organ ch. from Acts 20:17-21. German. Baptized 3 infants. Took dinner with Capt. J. Miller.

Mond. 12. At home.

Tues. 13. At Goodman's Sale.

Wed. 14. At home hauling oats.

Thurs. 15. Went to Salisbury.

Frid. 16. Had catechization at St. Stephen's church.

Sat. 17. Went to tax-paying.

Sund. 18. Preached at St. Stephen's ch. from 2 Tim. 4:7.8. In the afternoon at Gold Hill from 2 Kings 5:1-14.

Mond. 19. Went to Iredell. All night at Capt. A. Miller's.

Tues. 20. Returned home as far as Danl Lyerly's.

Wed. 21. Returned home.

Thurs. 22. At home.

Frid. 23. Went to Gold Hill.

Sat. 24. Went to Gold Hill for a load of plank.

Sat. [sic] 25. Preached at Organ ch. from Acts 16:16-34. Baptized one infant. In the afternoon called to see Moses Bost.

Mond. 26. At home.

Tues. 27. Went to Danl Miller's to mill.

Wed. 28. Returned home. In the afternoon went to Peter Trexler's & baptized his child, it being very sick. Mr. Beckerdite with me to night.

Thurs. 29. Went to hear Mr. Henry Goodman preach.

Frid. 30. At home.

Sat. 31. Had catechization at St. Stephen's ch.

Sund. Aug. 1. This my regular day at St. Stephen's ch. but in consequence of incessant rain did not attend.

Mond. 2. Went to Salisbury.

Tues. 3. Brought a sack of salt from Mr. Holshouser's.

Wed. 4. In the morning went to Gold Hill. In the afternoon called to see David Barringer, he being sick.

Thurs. 5. Went to D. Fraley's to the election. In the afternoon at home.

Frid. 6. Went to a Protracted Meeting at St. Enoch's ch. All night at Francis Overcash's.

Sat. 7. At St. Enoch's ch. preached from Luk. 16:19-31. In the evening had prayer meeting at Dan[l] Techour's, lectured from Mark 1:40-45. All night here.

Sund. 8. At St. Enoch's ch. preached from Luk. 15:11-24. All night at Allen Rose's.

Mond. 9. Returned home.

Tues. 10. Went to Salisbury.

Wed. 11. At home.

Thurs. 12. Had catechization at St. Stephen's ch.

Frid. 13. Went to Union ch. to attend a protracted meeting. All night at Sam[l] Peeler's.

Sat. 14. At Union ch. − preached from Acts 16:16-34. All night at Milas Arey's.

Sund. 15. Preached at Union ch. from Luk. 15:11-24. In the evening returned home.

Mond. 16. Returned to Union & preached from Josh. 23:8. & aided in the administration of the Lord's Supper.

Tues. 17. In the forenoon went Dr. Cunningham's School house to hear chanting geographical instruction.

Wed. 18. At home till afternoon then went to Gold Hill to see Dr. Kelly, Lucetta being sick.

Thurs. 19. At home.

Frid. 20. Had catechization at St. Stephen's church.

Sat. 21. Went to Organ ch. & had church settlement.

Sund. 22. Preached at Organ ch. from Math. 4:19. Germ. Baptized one inf[t]. Dinner at D. Lentz's.

Mond. 23. Went to Gold Hill to the Store.

Tues. 24. Attended the Sale of Barbara Holshouser, dec[d].

Wed. 25. Went to Post office.

Thurs. 26. At home.

Frid. 27. Attended a meeting on the subject of public schools.

Sat. 28. Went to several of the neighbors on the subject of common schools, & to Gold Hill for some tobacco.

Sund. 29. Was to have attended a meeting at Hopewell, but was prevented, having been summoned to go to Troy as a witness in court.

Mond. 30. Went to Troy.

Tues. 31. At Troy till afternoon, then started for home as far as Widow Harris'.

Wed. Sept. 1. Returned home.
Thurs. 2. Hauled some hay, then went br. Adam to Gold Hill.
Frid. 3. At home till afternoon then went to Post Office & Mrs. Goodman's.
Sat. 4. Went to Salisbury in company with Mr. Coffman, a student from Lexington Seminary.
Sund. 5. Preached at St. Stephen's ch. from Gen. 6:22. Baptized one infant. In afternoon preached from Ex. 23:2. at Gold Hill.
Mond. 6. Went to B. Braddy's & baptized his child, it being very sick. Called to see several other sick persons in the neighborhood.
Tues. 7. Attended to the funeral of Mr. Braddy's child at Lower St. ch. In the evening went to Mr. Linn's.
Wed. 8. At home till afternoon then took some flour to Gold Hill.
Thurs. 9. At home — had the company of Revd Linn & Lady, Mr. Shuler, Revd Coffman & others.
Frid. 10. In the morning went to Milas Arey's. In the afternoon attended to the funeral of Rachel Cawble (widow) at Fullenwider's ch. — preached from Am. 4:12.
Sat. 11. At home till afternoon then went to Widow George Heilig's & staid all night.
Sund. 12. Preached at Organ ch. from John 7:37.
Mond. 13. At home till afternoon then went to Post office.
Tues. 14. In the morning went to Gold Hill to see Dr. Kelly. The balance of day at home.
Wed. 15. At home.
Thurs. 16. Went with Mrs. R. to Salisbury.
Frid. 17. Assisted Revd Linn at St. Mathew's ch. — preached from Luk. 16:19-31.
Sat. 18. Went to St. Stephen's ch. (catechization).
Sund. 19. Preached at St. Stephen's ch. from Micah 6:8. In the afternoon at Gold Hill from Math. 20:6. Baptized at St. Stephen's 2 infants.
Mond. 20. At home — hauling manure.
Tues. 21. Went to Paul Cruse's.
Wed. 22. At home — hauling manure preparatory to sowing wheat.

Diary No. 13
Sept., 1847

Thurs. 23. Went to Mrs. Peck's & married Mr. Edmond Honeycut to Miss Caroline Peck. All night here.
Frid. 24. Returned home — had horse shod at Gold Hill.
Sat. 25. In the evening went to Peter Miller's & staid all night.
Sund. 26. Preached at Organ ch. from Math. 6:1-15. Took dinner at Peter Miller's.
Mond. 27. At home hauling manure.
Tues. 28. Went to Salisbury.
Wed. 29. Went to Danl Miller's to mill. All night here.
Thurs. 30. Returned home.

Frid. Oct. 1. Had catechization at St. Stephen's ch.

Sat. 2. Had services to day at St. Stephen's ch. preparatory to communion. Rev. Anthony preached. Baptized 1 inf.^{t}, one adult & confirmed six persons. All night at Mr. Barrier's Esqr.

Sund. 3. At St. Stephen's ch. Revd Anthony preached. Administered the Lord's Supper.

Mond. 4. Attended to the funeral of Jesse Kesler at St. Mathew's ch. — preached from Math. 5:6.

Tues. 5. Went to Salisbury & attended the meeting of the Board of Superintendants of Common Schools.

Wed. 6. Went to see Dr. Kelly to get some medicine for the children.

Thurs. 7. At home.

Frid. 8. Went to Gold Hill & sold some veal — also to see Dr. Kelly concerning the children. This evening took chill.

Sat. 9. Went to Organ ch. & had service preparatory to communion. Revd Harter preached. Baptized one infant.

Sund. 10. At Organ ch. Revd Harter preached. Administered the Lord's Supper.

Mond. 11. Met the Board of Superintendants in Salisbury. In the afternoon went to Iredell.

Tues. 12. In Iredell.

Wed. 13. Returned home.

Thurs. 14. Attended to the funeral of Moses Beaver's child at the Lower Stone ch. — preached from Math. 5:8. Germ.

Frid. 15. Attended old Mr. Peeler's sale.

Sat. 16. At home till evening, then went to Wiley Knup's.

Sund. 17. Preached at St. Stephen's ch. from Neh. 6:3. In the afternoon at Gold Hill from Ex. 20:15.

Mond. 18. At home till evening, then went to Col. Holshouser's to shucking.

Tues. 19. Wed. 20. At Mr. Goodman's clerking sale.

Thurs. 21. Went to Mr. Miller's Esqr in Stanly county & married Mr. Ambrose Lentz to Rebecca E. Miller. After supper returned home.

Frid. 22. At home till afternoon then went to Mrs. Ribelin's to shucking.

Sat. 23. At home — had shucking this afternoon.

Sund. 24. Preached at Organ ch. from Gal. 5:1. German.

Mond. 25. Went to Gold Hill in aforenoon. Balance of day at home.

Tues. 26. Went to Jacob Earnheart's & married Wiley Kirk to Susan Earnheart.

Wed. 27. At home till afternoon then went to Widow Peeler's to shucking.

Thurs. 28. At home. Revd Harter and Lady with us to night.

Frid. 29. Attended to the funeral of William Holshouser's child at Lower St. ch. — preached from Math. 5:8.

Sat. 30. At home till evening, then went with Mrs. R. to Dr. Kelly's.

Sund. 31. Went to Bear Creek ch. & preached from John 9:4. In the afternoon married Dr. J. T. Cunningham to Miss Margaret A. Bernhardt at Col. Bernhardt's.

Mond. Nov. 1. Went with Mrs. R. to Salisbury.

Tues. 2. At home till afternoon then went to Jacob Miller's for some seed wheat.

Wed. 3. Went to Salisbury, & in the evening to Milas Arey's & made some settlement with him. All night here.

Thurs. 4. Returned home, & in the evening went to Henry Troutman's & married Thomas Reimer to Sally Icehour.

Frid. 5. Took some sweet potatoes to Gold Hill.

Sat. 6. Went to Salisbury, & brought my carriage home.

Sund. 7. Preached at St. Stephen's ch. from 1 Thes. 5:6. In the afternoon attended to the funeral of John Cruse at Organ ch. preached from 1 Thes. 5:6.

Mond. 8. At home — had workmen this week to work on my house.

Tues. 9. Took the negros corn to Gold Hill.

Wed. 10. At home till afternoon, then called to see old Mrs. Holshouser, she being very sick.

Thurs. 11. At home, till afternoon then went to Mr. Fraley's to shucking.

Frid. 12. At home till 12 o'clock then took my family to see Gold Hill.

Sat. 13. Took Mr. J. Lentz & son home as far as Gold Hill.

Sund. 14. Preached at Organ ch. from Neh. 6:3. In the afternoon attended to the funeral of Mrs. Hannah Holshouser at Lower St. ch. Preached from Ps. 42:6.

Mond. 15. Went to Salisbury.

Tues. 16. At home till afternoon, then called to see Col. Holshouser, he being sick.

Wed. 17. Went to John Miller's in company with Mrs. R. and Phebe Brown on a visit.

Thurs. 18. At home.

Frid. 19. At home.

Sat. 20. Attended to the burial of William Miller at Lower Stone ch. — preached at the house from Math. 10:32.33.

Sund. 21. Preached at St. Stephen's ch. from Rom. 12:2. Had an appointment in the afternoon at Gold Hill. Revd Bradly being present, preached.

Mond. 22. Took Mrs. R. to Salisbury to be privately examined by the Judge, it being court time. All night at Milas Arey's.

Tues. 23. Returned home by way of D. Barringer's.

Wed. 24. Went to Salisbury.

Thurs. 25. Frid. 26. At home.

Sat. 27. Attended to the funeral of Henry Earnheart, Sen. at his residence. — preached from Math. 10:32.33.

Sund. 28. Preached at Organ ch. from 1 Kings 19:13. Baptized 3 infants.

Mond. 29. Made arrangements for butchering.

Tues. 30. At home — butchering.

Wed. Dec. 1. At home. Salted my pork.

Thurs. 2. Went to Stephen Kirk's & in the evening married Mr. Eli Lentz to Miss Elizabeth Kirk. All night here.

Frid. 3. Returned home.

Sat. 4. Attended to the fun^l of Mrs. Penninger at Lower St. ch. — preached at the house from Math. 10:32.33. Germ.

Sund. 5. Preached at St. Stephen's ch. from Luk. 13:24. In the afternoon preached at Gold Hill from Ps. 39:1.

Mond. 6. Attended to the fun^l of Lewis Peeler at Lower St. ch. — preached from Rev. 14:13. Germ.

Tues. 7. Went to Paul Cruse's & had my horse shod.

Wed. 8. At home.

Thurs. 9. Went to Gold Hill to get some medicine for Mrs. R. & Lucetta.

Frid. 10. Went to Capt. Miller's to aid in locating the School house for that district.

Sat. 11. In the morning went to Capt. Miller's. In the afternoon at home.

Sund. 12. Preached at Organ ch. from Ps. 7:10. Germ. Bapt^d 2 children. In the afternoon called to see Henry Peck Esqr, he being deranged. Mr. Peck & Tobias Klutts all night with me.

Mond. 13. Went by way of widow Peck's to Paul Stirewalt's.

Tues. 14. Attended John Cruse's Sale. All night at Dr. Kelly's.

Wed. 15. Returned home. Mr. John H. Coffman with me to night.

Thurs. 16. Called over to Mr. Linn's — the balance of the day at home.

Frid. 17. Attended the Sale of Mrs. Holshouser, dec^d.

Sat. 18. Went to Gold Hill & brought Mrs. R. & the children home from Dr. Kelly's.

Sund. 19. Preached at St. Stephen's, from John 14:15. In the afternoon preached at Gold Hill from Acts 24:25.

Mond. 20. Went to Salisbury.

Tues. 21. At home.

Wed. 22. At home.

Thurs. 23. Went to Gold Hill to have some shoes mended.

Frid. 24. In the evening went to Gold Hill after some shoes.

Sat. 25. Attended Revd Linn's preaching at the School house.

Sund. 26. In the morning preach^d the fun^l of Jacob Mowry's Son at the house from Am. 4:12. Buried him at Organ ch. Preached at Organ ch. from John 5:40. Baptized 1 infant. Took dinner at Jacob Miller's.

Mond. 27. In the morning went to Mr. Brady's with Milas Arey. In the afternoon called to see Revd Linn.

Tues. 28. Went to Wilie Knup's for some pine.

Wed. 29. Had John Miller to assist me in killing a Beef. In the afternoon took half of it to Gold Hill.

Thurs. 30. At home.

Frid. 31. Attended to the fun^l of Jacob Randleman's child at St. Stephen's church. — preached from 1 Pet. 5:7.

Sat. Jan. 1, 1848. Went to Salisbury.
Sund. 2. Preached at St. Stephen's ch. from Rom. 13:11. and in the afternoon at Gold Hill from 2 Cor. 5:17.
Mond. 3. Went to Iredell. All night at Cha⁵ Barringer's.
Tues. 4. In Iredell. All night at Cha⁵ Barringer's.
Wed. 5. Returned home.
Thurs. 6. At home till afternoon, then went to Gold Hill.
Frid. 7. At home.
Sat. 8. Went to Gold Hill to see Dr. Kelly, Mrs. R. being indisposed.
Sund. 9. Preached at Organ ch. from Josh. 7-12. Baptized one infant.
Mond. 10. Took Lewis to Gold Hill to go to school.
Tues. 11. At home till afternoon, then went to Col. Holshouser's & settled my smithing account & went to Post Office.
Wed. 12. At home. Gave an ad interim license to John H. Coffman.
Thurs. 13. Attended to the fun¹ of Guy Hill at St. Paul's ch. – preached from John 9:4.
Frid. 14. In the afternoon went to Gold Hill & distributed some Tracts among some of the Miners. Returned home in the evening, quite indisposed. Mr. J. Trexler & family with us to night.
Sat. 15. At home indisposed.
Sund. 16. Preached at St. Stephen's ch. from Math. 8:18-22. In the afternoon at Gold Hill from Phil. 3:20.21.
Mond. 17. In the morning took Lewis to Gold Hill to School. In the afternoon went to Post Office.
Tues. 18. At home.
Wed. 19. Went to widow Miller's (of Wm.) & married Edmond Fesperman to Margaret D. Miller. Baptᵈ also Mrs. Miller's son.
Thurs. 20. Went to Gold Hill & brought Dr. Kelly, Mrs. R. being quite indisposed.
Frid. 21. Took Mrs. R. & baby to Gold Hill. In the afternoon cleaned some oats.
Sat. 22. Went to Gold Hill – in the afternoon, returned home.
Sund. 23. Preached at Organ ch. from John 14:22. Germ. Took dinner at John Seaford's.
Mond. 24. In the morning went to Post Office. In the afternoon went to Gold Hill. All night at Dr. Kelly's.
Tues. 25. In the morning returned home, & then went to Milas Arey's & paid him some money. All night here.
Wed. 26. Returned home. Milas Arey came with me.
Thurs. 27. Hunted some for Partriges. In the afternoon went to Gold Hill.
Frid. 28. Hunted some for Partriges. In the evening went to Gold Hill – all night at John Lentz's.
Sat. 29. Returned home.
Sund. 30. Preached at Gold Hill from Luk. 12:13-21. Brought Mrs. R. home.
Mond. 31. In the afternoon went to Jacob Miller's for some Honey.

Tues. Feb. 1. At home.
Wed. 2. Took Lewis H. to Gold Hill to School.
Thurs. 3. Frid. 4. Sat. 5. At home.
Sund. 6. Preached at St. Stephen's ch. from Acts 26:17.18. And in the afternoon at Gold Hill from Luk. 2:41-52.
Mond. 7. Took Lewis to Gold Hill to school.
Tues. 8. In the afternoon went to the Post office.
Wed. 9. At home — hunted Rabbits in company with David Miller — caught eight.
Thurs. 10. Went to Salisbury.
Frid. 11. Went to Mr. Linn's on business.
Sat. 12. Attended to the letting out of the District School House. In the evening went to the Post office.
Sund. 13. Preached at Organ ch. from Mark 16:15. Baptized four infants. Organized the congregational Miss. and Ed. Society. Took dinner at John Miller's.
Mond. 14. Took Lewis to Gold Hill to School. In the evening went to Post office.
Tues. 15. At home hauling rails & wood.
Wed. 16. Went to Geo. Bost's and wrote his will. in the evening called by Geo. Klutts' & got a collar for my horse.
Thurs. 17. Frid. 18. At home — hauling rails, &c.
Sat. 19. At home till evening, then went to Danl Miller's & brought Mrs. R. home.
Sund. 20. Preached at St. Stephen's ch. from Mark 16:15. Organized the congregational Miss. and Ed. Society. In the afternoon preached at Gold Hill from Gal. 5:1.
Mond. 21. Took Lewis to Gold Hill to School. In the afternoon went to the Post Office.
Tues. 22. Went to Christian Bringle's & attended to the funeral of his wife. — preached from Phil. 1:21. All night here.
Wed. 23. Returned home before day, & then went to widow George Heilig's to raising.
Thurs. 24. At home.
Frid. 25. At home till afternoon, then went to Gold Hill & brought Lewis home.
Sat. 26. Went to Salisbury.
Sund. 27. Preached at Organ ch. from John 8:36. Baptized 3 infants. In the afternoon had prayermeeting at Mr. Curf's, he being sick, lectured from Math. 11:28. Germ. and administered the Lord's Supper, Returned home.
Mond. 28. Went to Troy to Court as witness.
Tues. 29. Returned as far as Mrs. Kirk's.

Wed. March 1. Returned home.

Thurs. 2. At home.

Frid. 3. Went to Gold Hill & brought Lewis home.

Sat. 4. At home.

Sund. 5. Preached at St. Stephen's ch. from Prov. 28:13. Baptized one infant. In the afternoon preached at Gold Hill from Prov. 13:6. on the subject of drunkeness.

Mond. 6. At home.

Tues. 7. Went to Dan¹ Miller's to mill.

Wed. 8. Returned home, & in the aftenoon went to Moses Goodman's to Barn-raising.

Thurs. 9. At Moses Goodman's raising barn.

Frid. 10. At home till afternoon, then went to Gold Hill & Lewis home. P. A. Seaford, Esq. with me to night.

Sat. 11. Helped to raise our district School house.

Sund. 12. Preached at Organ ch. from Math. 9:12. Germ. Baptized one infant. Took dinner at Jacob Miller's.

Mond. 13. Went to Mr. Linn's & helped to raise his Sawmill.

Tues. 14. Went to Gold Hill & Post office.

Wed. 15. Thurs. 16. Frid. 17. At home.

Sat. 18. Br. Lewis with us. Went Mathias Barringer's & preachᵈ old Mrs. Sell's fun¹ from Rev. 14:13. All night at Mr. James Honeycutt's.

Sund. 19. Preached at St. Stephen's ch. from Math. 9:12. Installed Dan¹ Miller and David Earnheart as Elders. In the afternoon, preached at Gold Hill from 1 Thes. 2:11.12.

Mond. 20. Went in company with Br. Lewis to Salisbury.

Tues. 21. To day Br. Lewis returned home.

Wed. 22. In the afternoon went to Gold Hill.

Thurs. 23. Went to Mr. Fouts' & married Jesse Barrier to Elizabeth C. Fouts.

Frid. 24. Attended to the funeral of Mr. Korf at Organ ch. – preached from Ps. 50:15. Germ. Was sent for in the evening to David Brown's, his wife being very sick. Went to Mr. Brown's & baptized their child. All night at Moses Barringer's.

Sat. 25. Returned home by way of Gold Hill.

Sund. 26. Attended to the fun¹ of Mrs. David Brown at Organ ch. – preached from Prov. 3:6. Baptized 2 infᵗˢ & held an election for to Elders.

Mond. 27. Went to Gold Hill.

Tues. 28. At home plowing.

Wed. 29. At home.

Thurs. 30. Attended Lewis Peeler's Sale.

Frid. 31. At home. Plowing in the afternoon.

Sat. Apr. 1. At home.

Sund. 2. Preached at St. Stephen's ch. from Hos. 2:17. In the afternoon from Luk. 16:19-31.

Mond. 3. At home, planting corn.

Tues. 4. Wed. 5. At home.

Thurs. 6. Went in company with br. Lewis to Henry Klutts' & married Geo. E. Bost to Caroline Klutts.

Frid. 7. Went to Gold Hill & to Mr. John Lentz's.

Sat. 8. At home.

Sund. 9. This was my day to preach at Organ ch. but the day being very rainy, did not attend.

Mond. 10. Went to Gold Hill.

Tues. 11. At home. Had some hogs spayed by Mr. John Lentz. Dr. Kelly & family with us to night.

Wed. 12. Went to Salisbury.

Thurs. 13. At home.

Frid. 14. At home.

Sat. 15. Preached at St. Stephen's ch. preparatory to communion from 1 John 1:9. Baptized one infant & one adult, & held a meeting of the congregational Miss. and Ed. Society. All night at Wilie Knup's.

Sund. 16. Preached at St. Stephen's ch. from Deut. 32:46.47. and administered the Lord's Supper. In the afternoon preached at Gold Hill from Ps. 1:1-6.

Mond. 17. Went to Post Office.

Tues. 18. Went to Gold Hill.

Wed. 19. At home.

Thurs. 20. At home burning off a small newground.

Frid. 21. In the afternoon went to Post Office & Gold Hill. In the evening attended to by request a prayermeeting at Dr. Cunningham's, lectured from Ps. 1:1-6.

Sat. 22. Preached at Organ ch. from Math. 10:32.33. preparatory to communion. Baptized 8 infants & installed P. A. Seaford and Chas. Fisher as Elders of the Church. All night at Paul Cruse's.

Sund. 23. Preached at Organ ch. from Deut. 6:3. & administered the Lord's Supper.

Mond. 24. Preached the fun[l] of John Hays dec[d] at Jacob Austin's in Stanly County, from Ps. 50:15.

Tues. 25. At home till afternoon then went to Post Office.

Wed. 26. Thurs. 27. At the Widow Miller's assisting in raising a Barn.

Frid. 28. In the morning went to Gold Hill. In the afternoon to Eliza Linn's & rented her house for br. Lewis.

Sat. 29. Assisted br. Lewis in moving to Mrs. Linn's house.

Sund. 30. Attended a communion meeting at the Lower Stone ch.

Mond. May 1. At home.

Tues. 2. Started to Synod. All night at Charles Barringer's.

Wed. 3. In Iredell. All night at Daywald Harkey's.

Thurs. 4. Went to Newton in Catawba county. All night at Mr. Bost's Esqr.

Frid. 5. To day Synod met in St. Paul's Church. — preached the opening sermon from Acts 20:17-21. Synod adjourned to hold the balance of its sessions in Newton.

Sat. 6. Sund. 7. Mond. 8. Tues. 9. In attendance at Synod. Preached on Sat. night in the Court House from Luk. 16:19-31.

Wed. 10. Started for home as far as Charles Barringer's.

Thurs. 11. Returned home.

Frid. 12. Sat. 13. At home.

Sund. 14. Preached at Organ ch. from Ps. 1:1-6. Germ. Baptized 2 inf^{ts}. Took dinner at John Miller's.

Mond. 15. In the forenoon sheared the sheep. In the afternoon went to Gold Hill.

Tues. 16. At home.

Wed. 17. In the afternoon took some chicken's to Gold Hill & went to Post office.

Thurs. 18. At home.

Frid. 19. Went to Milas Arey's & Rev. Anthony's.

Sat. 20. At home.

Sund. 21. Preached at St. Stephen's ch. from Math. 13:24-30. In the afternoon preached at Gold Hill from Josh. 7:12.

Mond. 22. Went to Father's.

Tues. 23. Called to see H. Beckerdite & uncle Joseph Rothrock.

Wed. 24. Returned home.

Thurs. 25. At home.

Frid. 26. Went with Mrs. R. to Gold Hill.

Sat. 27. At home.

Sund. 28. Preached at Organ ch. from Acts 24:16. Took dinner at John Seaford's. P. A. Seaford & Lady with us to night.

Mond. 29. In the afternoon went with P. A. Seaford & Lady to John Trexler's.

Tues. 30. Went to Wilie Knup's & Gold Hill.

Wed. 31. Went in the morning to Gold Hill for a sack of salt. In the afternoon went to Moses Barringer's.

Thurs. June 1. Went to Salisbury.

Frid. 2. Returned Moses Barringer's mare.

Sat. 3. Went to Jacob Austin's in Stanly co. & preached from Luk. 13:24. Baptized 5 children. In the evening returned home.

Sund. 4. Preached at St. Stephen's ch. from Acts 24:16. In the afternoon at Gold Hill from Ex. 33:14.

Mond. 5. In the afternoon went to Gold Hill on business, & to Mr. Powlass' for a sythe.

Tues. 6. Wed. 7. At home making hay.

Thurs. 8. Went to Gold Hill on business, & to Moses Trexler's.

Frid. 9. Went to Berger's Stand above Salisbury to attend a three days meeting. — preached from Luk. 13:24. All night at Mr. John Berger's.

Sat. 10. Preached from Eccl. 9:10. All night at Mr. John Cress'.

Sund. 11. Preached from Josh. 7:12. An inclement day. In the afternoon returned home.

Mond. 12. At home.

Tues. 13. Wed. 14. At home making hay.

Thurs. 15. At the widow Peeler's mowing grass & raking hay.

Frid. 16. Called to see Rev. Linn, & in the afrernoon called to Moses Barringer.

Sat. 17. Took my family to M. Barrier's Esq. on a visit.

Sund. 18. Preached at St. Stephen's ch. from Eccl. 9:10. and at Gold Hill from Prov. 14:34. All night at Dr. Kelly's.

Mond. 19. Returned home.

Tues. 20. At home.

Wed. 21. At home, binding wheat till afternoon, then called to see Mrs. Peter Miller, she being sick.

Thurs. 22. Attended to the fun^l of Danl Waggoner's child at St. Stephen's ch. — preached from Is. 55:6.

Frid. 23. At home plowing corn.

Sat. 24. Commenced a course of Catechetical instruction at Organ ch. Dinner @ M. Barringer's.

Sund. 25. Preached at Organ ch. from Prov. 1:24-26. German & baptized 1 inft. Afternoon preached English from same text.

Mond. 26. Called to see B. Brady, he being badly hurt by fall from a horse. Called also to see John & Peter Miller's families, they being sick.

Tues. 27. Hauled in my wheat.

Wed. 28. Thurs. 29. At home — plowing corn.

Frid. 30. Plowed corn till dinner, then went to engage Wilie Knup to cradle Oats.

Sat. July 1. In the afternoon went with my family to Dan¹ Miller's in Cabarrus Co. & staid over night.

Sund. 2. Preached at St. Stephen's ch. from John 4:14. & in the afternoon at Gold Hill from Acts 10:38.

Mond. 3. Tues. 4. At home engaged about my oats.

Wed. 5. Went to Gold Hill and heard the candidates speak.

Thurs. 6. At home — hauling oats till 12 o'clock. In the afternoon it rained.

Frid. 7. Went to Peter Miller's, he & family being sick.

Sat. 8. Went to Tax-paying at widow Miller's.

Sund. 9. Preached at Organ ch. from Deut. 8:2. Baptized one infant. Took dinner at Widow Heilig's.

Mond. 10. Went to Iredell. All night at Chaˢ Barringer's.

Tues. 11. In Iredell attending to business.

Wed. 12. Returned home.

Thurs. 13. Went to Gold Hill.

Frid. 14. At home.

Sat. 15. Had catechization at Organ ch.

Sund. 16. Preached at St. Stephen's ch. from 2 King 7:3.4. In the afternoon at Gold Hill from Deut. 8:2.

Mond. 17. In the afternoon went to Mr. Powlass' & had mare shod.

Tues. 18. Wed. 19. At home.

Thurs. 20. Went to Mrs. Eliza Linn's (widow) & married her to Isaac Kessler. All night at Mr. Reid's.

Frid. 21. Returned home by way of Mr. Kessler's.

Sat. 22. Had had [repeated] catechization at Organ ch. All night at Mr. Philip Eddleman's.

Sund. 23. Preached at Organ ch. from John 3:16. Took dinner at Col. D. Lentz's.

Mond. 24. In the afternoon went to Gold Hill.

Tues. 25. At home.

Wed. 26. Went to Salisbury and heard the candidates for the office of governor speak.

Thurs. 27. At home cleaning up wheat.

Frid. 28. At home.

Sat. 29. Attended to the funeral of Polly Earnheart at Organ ch. — preached from Math. 25:13. Germ.

Sund. 30. Preached at Jacob Austin's in Stanly co. from Jam. 1:25. In the evening returned home.

Mond. 31. Went to Iredell co. All night at Chaˢ Barringer's.

Tues. Aug. 1. Sold my corn & wheat. All night at Alfred Patterson's.

Wed. 2. Went to Statesville & returned home as far as Peter Barrier's.

Thurs. 3. Returned home.

Frid. 4. Called to see Mr. Linn's family, Mrs. L. being sick.

Sat. 5. At home.

Sund. 6. Preached at St. Stephen's ch. from Prov. 1:23. In the afternoon at Gold Hill from Ex. 5:2.

Mond. 7. Took Lucetta to Gold Hill, she being sick.

Tues. 8. At home, making cider to boil apple butter.

Wed. 9. Went to Salisbury.

Thurs. 10. Went to John Lippard & married Moses Seaford to Sarah M. Lippard. In the afternoon to Mr. Uhrey's near Mt. Pleasant & married John D. Gadlin to Rebecca Barringer. All night here.

Frid. 11. Returned home — took dinner at Danl Miller's.

Sat. 12. Had catechization at Organ ch. All night at John Eagle's.

Sund. 13. Preached at Organ ch. from Ex. 5:2. Germ. In the afternoon Engl. from the same text & baptized three infants. Dinner at J. Miller's.

Mond. 14. Went to Gold Hill on business.

Tues. 15. In the afternoon went to Gold Hill & exchanged horses with Dr. Kelly.

Wed. 16. At home.

Thurs. 17. Started for Iredell as far as Christopher Lyerly's.

Frid. 18. Went to Chas Barringer's. Took very sick to day. All night at Mr. Barringer's.

Sat. 19. Went to B. Arey's. All night here & very sick.

Sund. 20. A very rainy day. In the evening returned to Mr. B's.

Mond. 21. Tues. 22. Wed. 23. At Mr. Barringer's & very sick.

Thurs. 24. Returned home, very sick.

Frid. 25. Sat. 26. Sund. 27. At home, sick.

Mond. 28. Started for Troy as far as Mr. Bell's.

Tues. 29. Went to Troy. (court)

Wed. 30. Returned to Gold Hill.

Thurs. 31. Returned home and back to Gold Hill.

Frid. Sept. 1. Returned home.

Sat. 2. At home, indisposed.

Sund. 3. Went to St. Stephen's ch. but was too indisposed to preach. Baptized 2 inf.[ds].

Mond. 4. At home.

Tues. 5. Took my family to Gold Hill to see an animal exhibition.

Wed. 6. At home.

Thurs. 7. Frid. 8. Made arrangements for hay making the following week.

Sat. 9. Had catechization at Organ church.

Sund. 10. Preached at Organ ch. from Prov. 1:23. Baptized one infant. Took dinner at Jacob Miller's.

Mond. 11. Tues. 12. At home making hay.

Wed. 13. Went to Paul Cruse's to have horses shod but found him not at home.

Thurs. 14. Went to Gold Hill — in the afternoon to John Trexler's.

Frid. 15. Called to see Mr. Jacob Holshouser, his family being sick.

Sat. 16. At home.

Sund. 17. Preached at St. Stephen's ch. from 2 Cor. 13:5. & at Gold Hill from Luk. 23:39-43.

Mond. 18. Started to Father's with my family. All night at Wm. Smith's, Sen.[r]

Tues. 19. Arrived at Father's.

Wed. 20. Went to Salem. All night at Father's.

Thurs. 21. Took Jane Arey back to Salem, she having come to the country with us the previous evening from School. All night H. Beckerdite's.

Frid. 22. In the afternoon went to Mr. Gobble's Esq.[r]

Sat. 23. Went to Sandy Creek ch. to assist Rev. Anthony at a 2 days meeting. — preached from 2 Cor. 13:5. All night at Mr. Thompson's.

Sund. 24. Preached at the ch. from 1 Thes. 2:11.12. All night at Mr. Thompson's.

Mond. 25. Returned home.

Tues. 26. Went to Gold Hill on business.

Wed. 27. At home, till evening then went to Gold Hill for pair pants.

Thurs. 28. Started to St. Michael's ch. in Iredell co. to a Camp Meeting. All night at Alex.[r] Brown's.

Frid. 29. Arrived at the Church. At night preached from Math. 12:41.42.

Sat. 30. At the meeting.

Sund. Oct. 1. Preached at 8 o'clock from 1 Kings 19:9.

Mond. 2. Preached at 8 o'clock from Josh 7:12. and at night from Mark 10:46-52.

Tues. 3. Meeting closed. All night at Tobias Brown's.

Wed. 4. Started home as far as Cha⁵ Barringer's.

Thurs. 5. Arrived at home.

Frid. 6. In the afternoon went to Gold Hill on business.

Sat. 7. Had catechization at Organ Church.

Sund. 8. Preached at Organ ch. from Eph. 5:14. Baptized one infant. Took dinner at Jacob Miller's.

Mond. 9. In the afternoon went to Gold Hill on business.

Tues. 10. Called to see Jacob Holshouser, he being sick, and to the Post Office.

Wed. 11. At home.

Thurs. 12. Attended to the funˡ of Elihu Holshouser's child at Organ ch. – preached from Gen. 3:19.

Frid. 13. At home.

Sat. 14. Preached at St. Stephen's ch. from Ps. 51:2. preparatory. All night at John Lentz's. Baptized 2 infants to day.

Sund. 15. Preached at St. Stephen's from John 7:37. Sacramental. Administered the Lord's Supper. In the afternoon at Gold Hill from Phil. 3:20.

Mond. 16. At home till afternoon, then went to shucking at John Miller's.

Tues. 17. At home till afternoon, then went to Alex. Holshouser's to shucking.

Wed. 18. Asked hands to shuck corn. In the afternoon shucked my corn.

Thurs. 19. Put my corn in the crib.

Frid. 20. Had catechization at Organ ch. All night at P. A. Seaford's Esqʳ.

Sat. 21. Preached at Organ ch. from Ps. 51:2. Germ. preparatory & Egl. from same text. Baptized 5 infts. All night at Danˡ Eddleman's.

Sund. 22. Revᵈ J. B. Anthony preached for me. Baptized one infᵗ. Administered the Lord's Supper. All night at John Miller's.

Mond. 23. Returned home & in the afternoon went to Gold Hill & to Paul Cruse's. All night here.

Tues. 24. Went to Jacob Hous', but did not find him at home.

Diary No. 14

Nov. 1848

Wed. 25. Went to Salisbury.

Thurs. 26. In the afternoon went to Chas. Barringer's & married Edward Moss to Christiana Barringer.

Frid. 27. Went to Davidson to attend a 3 days meetings at Hopewell ch. All night at Father's.

Sat. 28. At Hopewell ch. At night preached in the church from Josh. 7:12. All night at H. Beckerdite's.

Sund. 29. At the church.

Mond. 30. Returned home as far as Salisbury. All night at B. Fraley's.

Tues. 31. Returned home.

Wed. Nov. 1. Started to Jacob Hous' as far as Danl Miller's. Mr. Hous' not being at home, returned home.

Thurs. 2. At home digging potatoes till dinner. In the afternoon went to Dr. Cunningham's to shucking.

Frid. 3. Went to Gold Hill.

Sat. 4. Went to Salisbury.

Sund. 5. This was my day to preach at St. Stephen's ch. but being indisposed and the morning inclement did not attend. In the afternoon preached at Gold Hill from 1 Tim. 4:7. All night at Dr. Kelly's.

Mond. 6. Returned home.

Tues. 7. Went to Mr. Fraley's to Presidential election.

Wed. 8. At home.

Thurs. 9. Went to Jacob Hous. All night at Danl Eddleman's.

Frid. 10. Called in company with Danl Eddleman to see Revd Scheck. In the evening returned home.

Sat. 11. Attended to the fun^l of Jacob Stirewalt's wife at Phanuel's ch. — preached from Prov. 14:26. Then went to Organ ch. and had catechization.

Sund. 12. Preached at Organ ch. from Prov. 14:26. Germ.

Mond. 13. At home.

Tues. 14. Went to Jacob Hous'. All night here.

Wed. 15. Called at D. Miller's, John Richy's, & Mr. Faggart Esqr. All night at Laurence Lingle's.

Thurs. 16. Returned home.

Frid. 17. In the afternoon went to Gold Hill.

Sat. 18. Attended singing at Beaver's School House.

Sund. 19. Preached at St. Stephen's Church. from Math. 4:10. In the afternoon at Gold Hill from Ps. 19:7. Baptized one infant at St. Stephen's.

Mond. 20. Went to Salisbury — all night at D. A. Davis'.

Tues. 21. Returned home.

Wed. 22. At home.

Thurs. 23. Went to Salisbury.

Frid. 24. At home. Lawyer Mendenhall with me to night.

Sat. 25. Had catechization at Organ Church.

Sund. 26. Preached at Organ ch. from Eph. 6:4.

Mond. 27. In the afternoon went to Gold Hill.

Tues. 28. Met P. A. Seaford, Esq. above Organ ch. to locate a public school house. All night at P. A. Seaford's Esq.

Wed. 29. Returned home.

Thurs. 30. Went to Gold Hill. To night Rev. B. Arey & Revd J. A. Linn with me.

Frid. Dec. 1. At home.

Sat. 2. At home.

Sund. 3. Preached at St. Stephen's ch. from Math. 25:14-30. In the afternoon at Gold Hill from Math. 25:1-13. At night went to Geo. Culp's and Henry Dry to Mary Ann Culp. All night here.

Mond. 4. Went by way of M. Barrier's to G. Melchior's Esq. In the afternoon returned home by way of Mr. Nussman's.

Tues. 5. Went to Wilie Knup's and engaged some shingles. Returned home by way of Gold Hill.

Wed. 6. At home.

Thurs. 7. At home. To night received word of the death of Father.

Frid. 8. Went to Father's.

Sat. 9. Attended the burial of Father at the Moravian Church. Funeral preached by Revd Sensiman. United with the congregation in their Love-feast and communion. All night at C. Peeler's.

Sund. 10. Preached at the School house in the neighborhood from Math. 25:14-30. All night at H. Beckerdite's.

Mond. 11. Returned home.

Tues. 12. Wed. 13. Thurs. 14. At home.

Frid. 15. Went to Gold Hill, & at night to the debate.

Sat. 16. Went to D. Barringer's, Milas Arey's, &c.

Sund. 17. Preached at St. Stephen's ch. from Math. 11:28. Baptized one infant. In the afternoon at Gold Hill from Rev. 3:20.

Mond. 18. Went to J. Holshouser's and Post office.

Tues. 19. Went to chopping at J. Holshouser's, & bought black boy Henderson.

Wed. 20. Went to Salisbury.

Thurs. 21. Went to Gold Hill.

Frid. 22. At home. At night attending debating society.

Sat. 23. Had catechization at Organ ch. All night at Jacob Miller's.

Sund. 24. Preached at Organ ch. from Math. 1:21. German. All night at Joseph Miller's.

Mond. 25. Had a Temperance Meeting at Joseph Miller's.

Tues. 26. In the afternoon went to Abraham Shaver's & at night married Danl C. Kirk to Mary Shaver. All night here.

Wed. 27. Went to D. Barringer's on business. All night here.

Thurs. 28. Went to Jacky Garner's & married James Klutts to Matty Garner. After dinner returned home.

Frid. 29. Sat. 30. At home.

Sund. 31. Preached at Gold Hill from Rom. 13:11.

Mond. Jan. 1, 1849. Went to Salisbury. All night here.

Tues. 2. Preached the funeral of Christena Cawble, who had died sometime previous, at Mr. Butner's from John 9:4.

Wed. 3. Thurs. 4. At home.

Frid. 5. Attended to the fun[1] of Mrs. Peacock at St. Stephen's ch. − preached from John 9:4. Heard Rev. Cascadden at Gold Hill at night.

Sat. 6. At home.

Sund. 7. Preached at St. Stephen's ch. from Eph. 6:4. In the evening attended to the burial of John Richard's at St. Stephen's ch. who died from the effects of a shot in the head in an affray.

Mond. 8. Started for Caleb Peeler's. All night at Solomon Hinkle's. Had Jane along on her way to Salem.

Tues. 9. Arrived at C. Peeler's. − a very snowy day. Attended the sale of Father's property.

Wed. 10. Took Jane to Salem. Returned to C. Peeler's.

Thurs. 11. Started home as far as Mr. Nulison's. A very cold day.

Frid. 12. Returned home.

Sat. 13. Had catechization at Organ ch.

Sund. 14. Preached at Organ ch. from 1 Sam. 12:23.24.

Mond. 15. Went to Gold Hill.

Tues. 16. At home.

Wed. 17. Went to Post office.

Thurs. 18. Went to Laurence Lingle's to rail splitting.

Frid. 19. Sat. 20. At home mending shoes.

Sund. 21. Preached at St. Stephen's ch. from Eph. 5:18. on the subject of Temperance. In the afternoon at Gold Hill from 1 Sam. 12:23.24.

Mond. 22. At home.

Tues. 23. Went to Gold Hill & took dinner with the Mauneys, Bernhardts, & co.

Wed. 24. Butchered a Beef. − in the afternoon took one-half to Gold Hill.

Thurs. 25. Went to Moses Trexler's to chopping.

Frid. 26. Called to see Col. Holshouser, he being sick.

Sat. 27. Had catechization at Organ ch. − Preached the fun[1] also of John Yost's child from John 14:6.

Sund. 28. Preached at Organ ch. from Math. 25:14-30. Took dinner at Jacob Miller's.

Mond. 29. Went to Salisbury.

Tues. 30. Returned home.

Wed. 31. Attended to the burial of two of Henry Troutman's children at St. Stephen's ch.

Thurs., February 1, 1849. Hauled some logs to the saw mill.

Frid. 2. At home.

Sat. 3. Hauled logs to saw mill.

Sund. 4. Preached at St. Stephen's ch. from Josh. 24:15. & in the afternoon at Gold Hill from Math. 12:41.42.

Mond. 5. Went to Iredell — all night at Chas Barringer's.

Tues. 6. In Iredell — all night at Tobias Brown's.

Wed. 7. In Iredell — all night at Chas. Barringer's.

Thurs. 8. Returned home.

Frid. 9. At Simeon Lentz's part of day at chopping.

Sat. 10. Had catechization at Organ ch.

Sund. 11. Preached at Organ ch. from Rev. 2:4.5. Germ. Took dinner at John Seaford's.

Mond. 12. Went to Gold Hill.

Tues. 13. At home till afternoon, then went to Post office. In the evening went to Asa Miller's & married John Miller to Eliz. A. Air.

Wed. 14. Went to D. Barringer's and Milas Arey's. All night here.

Thurs. 15. Returned home.

Frid. 16. At home.

Sat. 17. Preached at Kendall's church from Eccl. 9:10. the fun[1] of 2 of James Crowel's children.

Sund. 18. Preached at St. Stephen's ch. from Is. 3:10.11. & in the afternoon at Gold Hill from Ps. 116:12-14.

Mond. 19. At home mending shoes.

Tues. 20. At Wilie Knup's helping in raising a barn.

Wed. 21. In the forenoon at Wilie Knup's — finished raising barn. In the afternoon went to Gold Hill on business.

Thurs. 22. Frid. 23. At home.

Sat. 24. Had catechization at Organ Church.

Sund. 25. Preached at Organ Church. from Ps. 19:7. & baptized three infants. Took dinner at Mrs. Heilig's.

Mond. 26. Attended the Sale of Moses Goodman's property.

Tues. 27. In the forenoon went to Gold Hill for nails. In the afternoon at home. Revd Crist with me.

Wed. 28. At home.

Thurs., March 1. In the afternoon went to John Trexler's & assisted in raising the frames of sheds around his barn.
Frid. 2. Went to Salisbury.
Sat. 3. At home.
Sund. 4. Preached at St. Stephen's from Luk. 7:16. & in the afternoon at Gold Hill from 1 Thes. 5:6.
Mond. 5. Tues. 6. Wed. 7. Thurs. 8. At home.
Frid. 9. Had catechization at Organ Church.
Sat. 10. Revd Crist preached for me to day at Organ ch. Baptized two infants. All night at Moses Barringer's.
Sund. 11. Revd Crist preached for me at Organ ch.
Mond. 12. Went to Gold Hill for nails.
Tues. 13. Wed. 14. Thurs. 15. At home.
Frid. 16. Sat. 17. At home.
Sund. 18. Preached at St. Stephen's ch. from Acts 13:36. Baptized one infant. In the afternoon from Gold Hill from Acts 26:17.18. Baptized one infant.
Mond. 19. Went to Salisbury to assist at a protracted meeting. In the afternoon preached from Eccl. 9:10. All night at B. Fraley's.
Tues. 20. Preached at night from Rev. 3:20. All night at M. L. Brown's.
Wed. 21. In Salisbury. All night at B. Fraley's.
Thurs. 22. Returned home. In the afternoon went to Gold Hill for nails.
Frid. 23. At home.
Sat. 24. Had catechization at Organ ch.
Sund. 25. Preached at Organ ch. from 2 Cor. 5:17. Germ. Bapt^d one infant. Took dinner at Jacob Miller's.
Mond. 26. In the forenoon went to Post office. In the afternoon at home.
Tues. 27. Attended to the fun^l of John Troutman at David Troutman's. — preached from John 9:4. German. In the afternoon employed masons to build a chimney.
Wed. 28. At home.
Thurs. 29. Went to J. Goodman's for Lime.
Frid. 30. At home.
Sat. 31. Had catechization at Organ ch.

Sund., Apr. 1. Preached at St. Stephen's ch. from 2 Cor. 5:17. & in the afternoon at Gold Hill from 1 Pet. 4:18.

Mond. 2. Tues. 3. Wed. 4. At home.

Thurs. 5. Went to Gold Hill.

Frid. 6. At home.

Sat. 7. Had catechization at Organ ch.

Sund. 8. Preached at Organ ch. from 1 Thes. 2:11.12. Took dinner at Mrs. Heilig's. Baptized to day 3 inf^{ts}.

Mond. 9. Went to Mr. Linn's.

Tues. 10. Wed. 11. Thurs. 12. About home.

Frid. 13. Commenced a three days meeting at St. Stephen's ch. Rev^{ds} Crist & Linn with me.

Sat. 14. At St. Stephen's ch. Baptized one inf^{t}. All night at Geo. Culp's.

Sund. 15. At St. Stephen's ch. Had the assistance of Revds. Rankin, Crist, & Linn. Administered the Lord's Supper. A very snowy day.

Mond. 16. Tues. 17. Wed. 18. Thurs. 19. About home.

Frid. 20. Commenced a three days meeting at Organ Church. — preached from Prov. 23:26. Confirmed 51 persons.

Sat. 21. Rev. Arey preached — Bapt. 1 infant. Had prayermeeting at night in the church, lectured from Ex. 14:15. All night at Moses Barringer's.

Sund. 22. Revd Arey preached. Administered the Lord's Supper.

Mond. 23. Went to Gold Hill.

Tues. 24. Went to Salisbury.

Wed. 25. At home.

Thurs. 26. Went with Rev. J. A. Linn to Luther's ch. to a Protracted meeting — Preached from Prov. 23:26. All night at Daywalt Lentz's.

Frid. 27. At Luther's ch. — preached from John 9:4. All night at Daywalt Lentz's.

Sat. 28. At Luther's ch. — Preached from Josh. 24:15.

Sund. 29. At Luther's ch. — In the evening returned home.

Mond. 30. In the forenoon went to Gold Hill. In the afternoon went to Allen Rose's.

Tues., May 1. Attended to some business & returned home as far as P. A. Seaford's, Esq.

Wed. 2. Returned home & then went to Gold Hill to return Dr. Kelly's horse.

Thurs. 3. Started to St. John's. ch. to Synod. All night at Danl Miller's.

Frid. 4. Went to St. John's ch. Synod met. Settled a difficulty between myself & Rev. Scheck, he retracted what he had said against me. In the evening went to St. Stephen's ch. Revd Crist preached. All night at Mrs. Peck's.

Sat. 5. At St. Johns's ch. — Synod in session. All night at Danl Miller's.

Sund. 6. At St. John's ch. All night at Col. Shimpock's.

Mond. 7. At St. John's ch. Synod in session. All night at Nelson Misenheimer's. Had intended to go to Mr. Melchor's Esqr. but could not cross the Creek.

Tues. 8. At St. John's ch. This evening Synod adjourned. All night at Danl Miller's.

Wed. 9. Returned home. Revd Arey with me.

Thurs. 10. Frid. 11. At home. A very rainy time. Revd Arey & T. Brown & family with me.

Sat. 12. Went to Gold Hill on business. M. Arey & family with me to night.

Sund. 13. Preached at Organ ch. from 1 Thes. 2:11.12. Germ. Took dinner at Moses Barringer's.

Mond. 14. Attended to the fun^l of Moses Josey's child at Organ church. — preached from Heb. 9:27. Took dinner at John Seaford's.

Tues. 15. At home — sheared the sheep.

Wed. 16. Thurs. 17. Frid. 18. At home.

Sat. 19. Preached at Kendall's ch. from Luk. 15:11-24. Took dinner at Green Burchhead's.

Sund. 20. This was my day at St. Stephen's ch. & Gold Hill, but was so indisposed with Diarrhea that I could turn out. A travelling agent of the Presbyterian church (Mr. Brown) filled my appointments.

Mond. 21. At home sick.

Tues. 22. Went to Mrs. Elizabeth Eddleman's. (widow of Ambrose Eddleman, dec^d) and married Jeremiah L. Graeber to Mrs. E. Eddleman. All night at Philip Eddleman's.

Wed. 23. Returned home. In the afternoon went to Gold Hill & had carriage repaired.

Thurs. 24. At home.

Frid. 25. Went to Salisbury.

Sat. 26. Attended to the fun^l Adam Trexler dec^d at Union ch. — preached from Eccl. 9:10.

Sund. 27. Preached at Organ ch. from Eph. 5:18. (Temperance)*

Mond. 28. Went to Gold Hill.

Tues. 29. At home — had hogs spayed.

Wed. 30. Went to Salisbury. All night at Milas Arey's.

Thurs. 31. Called in the morning to see Geo. Peeler. In the afternoon returned home by way of D. Barringer's.

* Baptized to day one inf't.

Frid. June 1. At home.

Sat. 2. Had catechization at St. Stephen's ch. Took dinner at Moses Eagle's. Called also to see Mr. Paul Nussman.

Sund. 3. Attended to the burial of Dr. Kelly's child at St. Stephen's ch. Preached at St. Stephen's from John 3:3. In the afternoon at Gold Hill from Josh. 24:15.

Mond. 4. In the morning went to the Post Office.

Tues. 5. In the forenoon went to Wilie Knup's on business. In the afternoon mowed the little meadow.

Wed. 6. At home. A very rainy day.

Thurs. 7. Started for St. Enoch's ch. All night at P. A. Seaford's.

Frid. 8. Went to St. Enoch's ch. in fulfilment of an appointment of Synod, to aid in the settlement of some congregational difficulties, but the Pastor & others appointed by Synod did not attend. Returned home as far as Jesse Barrier's.

Sat. 9. Returned home.

Sund. 10. Preached at Organ ch. from Ex. 20:8-11. Baptized two infants. In the afternoon preached again from Jam. 1:5.

Mond. 11. Tues. 12. Wed. 13. At home making hay.

Thurs. 14. Went to Salisbury to attend the Rail Road Convention.

Frid. 15. Assisted Mrs. Peeler in getting her hay away.

Sat. 16. Had catechization to day at St. Stephen's ch. At night had prayer meeting at the church – lectured from the first Psalm. All night at Peter Lentz's.

Sund. 17. Preached the funeral of three of Henry Troutman's children at St. Stephen's ch. they having died sometime before, from Ps. 90:12. Baptized one infant. In the afternoon at Gold Hill from Ex. 20:8-11. Took dinner at John Lentz's.

Mond. 18. Engaged hands for harvesting.

Tues. 19. At home harvesting.

Wed. 20. At home.

Thurs. 21. Attended to the fun[1] of Mr. Keijnick's child, at Organ ch. – preached from Math. 18:3.

Frid. 22. Sat. 23. At home.

Sund. 24. Preached at Organ ch. from Phil. 1:11. Germ. & Engl. from the same text. Baptized two infants. Took dinner at John Miller's.

Mond. 25. Went to Gold Hill. Dr. Cunningham & lady with us to night.

Tues. 26. At home. In the afternoon assisted Mrs. Peeler in her hay.

Wed. 27. Went with Milas Arey to Gold Hill.

Thurs. 28. Frid. 29. At home hauling Wheat.

Sat. 30. Had catechization at St. Stephen's ch. In the afternoon attended the election of School Committee at the School House.

Sund. July 1. Preached at St. Stephen's ch. from Job 1:21. the funeral of Dr. Kelly's deceased child. In the afternoon at Gold Hill from Is. 48:18.

Mond. 2. At home till afternoon then went to the Post office.

Tues. 3. Engaged hands to cradle oats.

Wed. 4. Went to Wilie Knup's & engaged him to cut oats.

Thurs. 5. At home — binding Oats.

Frid. 6. Finished my oats.

Sat. 7. Went to the tax-paying. All night at John Miller's.

Sund. 8. In the morning attended to the fun[l] of Geo. Earnheart's child at the Lower stone ch. — preached from Is. 55:6. Preached at Organ ch. at the regular hour from Is. 48:18.* After the usual intermission, held a meeting of the Miss. & Ed. society.

Mond. 9. Went to Iredell. All night at Cha[s] Barringer's.

Tues. 10. Went to Tobias Brown's for Lucetta. All night here.

Wed. 11. Returned to C. Barringer's.

Thurs. 12. Returned home.

Frid. 13. Had catechization at St. Stephen's ch. In the afternoon attended to the fun[l] of Wilson Honeycutt's child at St. Stephen's. — preached from Math. 18:3.

Sat. 14. Preached at Kendall's ch. from Prov. 29:1.

Sund. 15. Preached at St. Stephen's ch. from Is. 34:16. & in the afternoon at Gold Hill from Acts 16:16-34.

Mond. 16. Met the Grammar Class at the School house.

Tues. 17. Went to the sale of Adam Trexler dec[d] and clerked the same.

Wed. 18. Went to the School house & assisted in making benches for the same.

Thurs. 19. Went to P. A. Seaford's School house & had prayermeeting at 2 o'clock, lectured from Ps. 73:1.

Frid. 20. At home — a very rainy day & my children sick.

Sat. 21. Attended to the fun[l] of Mr. Troutman's child at St. Stephen's ch. — preached from Math. 5:8.

Sund. 22. Preached at Organ ch. from Is. 34:16.

Mond. 23. Tues. 24. Wed. 25. At home.

Thurs. 26. Went to Gold Hill.

Frid. 27. Met the Grammar Class at the School House.

Sat. 28. Started for Berger's Stand. All night at B. F. Fraley's.

Sund. 29. Preached at Berger's Stand from Prov. 29:1. In the afternoon at the same place from Ps. 73:1. All night at John Berger's.

Mond. 30. Returned home.

Tues. 31. Went to Mr. D. Fraley's, he being sick & at his request wrote his Will. In the afternoon went to Jacob Fisher's & married Jacob Lyerly, jr. to Anna Fisher. In the evening went to John Lippart's & married George A. Rusher to Louisa M. Lippard. All night at Jacob Miller's.

* Confirmed 3 persons to day.

Wed. Aug. 1. Returned home. In the afternoon went to Gold Hill.

Thurs. 2. Went to Mr. D. Fraley's To day Mr. Fraley died. Assisted in laying him out.

Frid. 3. Attended to the fun[l] of D. Fraley at the Lower St. ch. — preached from Mal. 3:16.17.

Sat. 4. Had catechization at St. Stephen's ch.

Sund. 5. Preached at St. Stephen's ch. from Ps. 73:1. Did not preach at Gold Hill in the afternoon in consequence of rain. In the evening went to Dan[l] Miller's & to M. Barrier's Esqr. All night here.

Mond. 6. Settled with the treas[r] of Seminary Fund & took the board the Treas[r] elect as per Resolution of Synod. Met the Grammar Class to day at the School House.

Tues. 7. Went to Salisbury.

Wed. 8. Stacked some straw, & in the afternoon assisted Mr. S. Lentz to roll some logs.

Thurs. 9. Went to Gold Hill.

Frid. 10. In the afternoon aided the widow Peeler to roll logs.

Sat. 11. Went to Seaford's School house & in the afternoon held a prayer meeting — lectured from Mark 1:40-45. Formed a Grammar class. All night at Geo. Randleman's.

Sund. 12. At Organ ch. Rev. Rankin preached for me. Baptized one infant. All night at Jacob Miller's.

Mond. 13. Met the Grammar Class at the School-house.

Tues. 14. Went to Gold Hill.

Wed. 15. At home.

Thurs. 16. Went to Mich[l] S. Brown's & married Geo. A. Brown to Maria S. Brown.

Frid. 17. Attended Grammar Class at Seaford's School house.

Sat. 18. Catechization at St. Stephen's ch.

Sund. 19. Preached at St. Stephen's ch. + from Hos. 13:9. In the afternoon at Gold Hill Job 14:14. fun[l].

Mond. 20. Attended the Grammar Class at our school house.

Tues. 21. At Mr. Linn's.

Wed. 22. In the evening went to John C. Bernhardt's Esq. & married Rev. J. A. Linn to Margaret A. Bernhardt. All night at G. M. Bernhardt's.

Thurs. 23. Attended the infare at Mr. Linn's.

Frid. 24. Met the Grammar Class at Seaford's School house. In the afternoon had prayermeeting — lectured from Rev. 3:20. All night at Henry Pless'.

Sat. 25. Attended to the fun[l] of David Holshouser's daughter at St. Paul's ch. — preached from Eccl. 9:10. All night Jacob Pless'.

Sund. 26. Preached at Organ ch. from Acts 26:17.18. Germ. Baptized one inf[t]. In the afternoon held a meeting of the Miss. & Ed. Society.

Mond. 27. At home.

Tues. 28. In the morning went to Gold Hill to the Post office.

Wed. 29. At home.

Thurs. 30. In the morning called to see Mr. Linn.

Frid. 31. Took Mrs. R. to quilting to Mrs. Heilig's. All night at John Miller's.

+ Baptized 1 inf[t] to day.

Sat., Sept. 1. Returned home.

Sund. 2. Had no regular appointment for to day. Attended a prayer meeting at St. Stephen's ch. — lectured from Luk. 18:9-14.

Mond. 3. At home.

Tues. 4. Went to Gold Hill, to Post office.

Wed. 5. In the afternoon went with Rev. B. Arey to George M. Bernhardt's on business.

Thurs. 6. At home.

Frid. 7. Went to George Klutts' for Leather.

Sat. 8. At home.

Sund. 9. Preached at Organ ch. from Math. 7:21. Baptized one infant. Preached in afternoon from Luk. 2:41-52. Took dinner at Jacob Miller's.

Mond. 10. Went to Gold Hill to Post office.

Tues. 11. Wed. 12. Thurs. 13. Frid. 14. At home — family not well.

Sat. 15. Had catechization at St. Stephen's ch.

Sund. 16. Preached at St. Stephen's ch. from Math. 6:10. & in the afternoon at Gold Hill from Math. 7:21.

Mond. 17. Met the Grammar Class at the School House.

Tues. 18. In the afternoon took my family to Gold Hill. All night at Doctor Kelly's.

Wed. 19. Returned home.

Thurs. 20. At home.

Frid. 21. Attended to the fun[l] of Philpena Holshouser, wife of Frederic Holshouser at the Lower Stone ch. — preached from Phil. 1:21.

Sat. 22. At home Mrs. R. being sick.

Sund. 23. This was my day at Organ ch. but did not attend, Mrs. R. being sick.

Mond. 24. Went to Bear-creek ch. to Camp Meeting. — preach[d] from Math. 7:21. Returned home.

Tues. 25. Went to Bear-creek — preached from 1 Thes. 2:11.12. In the evening returned home.

Wed. 26. Thurs. 27. Frid. 28. At home. Mrs. R. being sick.

Sat. 29. Went to Union ch. to Camp Meeting — Preached from Math. 11:28. Returned home in evening.

Sund. 30. In the afternoon returned to Union ch. — preached at night from 1 Pet. 4:18. All night on the ground.

Mond. Oct. 1. At the meeting till afternoon, then returned home.

Tues. 2. Went to Gold Hill to Post Office.

Wed. 3. Went to Post office.

Thurs. 4. Frid. 5. At home.

Sat. 6. Had catechization at St. Stephen's ch.

Sund. 7. Preached at St. Stephen's from Ps. 85:6. & in the afternoon at Gold Hill from Mal. 3:7.*

Mond. 8. Met the Grammar Class at the School house.

Tues. 9. Went to Post office & in the afternoon to shucking at Mr. Powlass'.

Wed. 10. In the afternoon went to Mrs. Heilig's to shucking.

Thurs. 11. In the afternoon went to Alex. Holshouser's to shucking.

Frid. 12. At home.

Sat. 13. In the afternoon went to Simeon Miller's to shucking.

Sund. 14. Preached at Organ ch. from John 5:40. Germ. Bapt^d one infant. Dinner at John Miller's.

Mond. 15. Raised potatoe house.

Tues. 16. Wed. 17. Clerked Sale at D. Fraley's, dec^d.

Thurs. 18. At Fraley's till afternoon settling business.

Frid. 19. Had appointed to commence a three days meeting to day at St. Stephen's ch. but the day being very inclement but few persons attended. Had a short prayermeeting and dismissed.

Sat. 20. Preached at St. Stephen's ch. from Josh. 23:8. Baptized six adults & confirmed 16 persons. Had night had prayermeeting at the church. All night at Mr. Nussman's.

Sund. 21. A very rainy day. Rev. G. Scherer preached — post-poned communion. At night had prayermeeting at the ch. All night at John Lentz's.

Mond. 22. Revd Scherer preached. In the afternoon returned home.

Tues. 23. Went to Iredell. All night at B. Arey's.

Wed. 24. In Iredell. All night at Chas Barringer's.

Thurs. 25. Returned home.

Frid. 26. Preached at Organ ch. from Ps. 85:6. Baptized one infant.

Sat. 27. Rev. G. Scherer preached. Baptized 2 infants. At night had prayer meeting in the ch. All night at Moses Barringer's.

Sund. 28. Rev. Scherer preached. Administered Lord's Supper. In afternoon returned home.

Mond. 29. Met the Grammar class at School house. In the afternoon engaged in raising a school.

Tues. 30. At Peter Trexler's — did some writing for him.

Wed. 31. Attended to the funeral of Margaret E. Overcash at Organ ch. — preached at from Eccl. 12:1.

* Bapt^d Mr. Hegler's 6 chil^n to day.

Thurs. Nov. 1. Went to Salisbury. Thence to P. A. Seaford's. All night here.

Frid. 2. Met the upper Grammar Class at the School house.

Sat. 3. At home — Shucked & put away my corn.

Sund. 4. Preached at St. Stephen's from Deut. 11:16. & administered the Lord's Supper. At night had prayermeeting at D. Lentz's, lectured from Phil. 3:20. Ret^d home.

Mond. 5. Started for Iredell as far as Dan^1 Lyerly's.

Tues. 6. Went to Iredell — all night at Rev. B. Arey's.

Wed. 7. Started home as far as widow Sarah Brown's.

Thurs. 8. Returned home.

Frid. 9. Met the upper Grammar class at P. A. Seaford's.

Sat. 10. Called at various places in neighborhood getting subscribers to school.

Sund. 11. Preached at Organ ch. from Mark 1:40-45. Baptized one inf^t.

Mond. 12. Met the grammar class at School house.

Tues. 13. Went to Gold Hill.

Wed. 14. Thurs. 15. At home.

Frid. 16. In the afternoon went to John Eagle's.

Sat. 17. Met the upper Grammar class. All night at D. Miller's.

Sund. 18. Preached at John Culp's from Math. 11:28. Germ. & Engl. from Mark 1:40-45. At night attended prayermeeting at St. Stephen's ch. Then returned home.

Mond. 19. Tues. 20. At school.

Wed. 21. At home sick.

Thurs. 22. Frid. 23. At school.

Sat. 24. Met the upper Gr. class.

Sund. 25. Preached at Organ ch. from Luk. 13:24. Germ. Held a meeting of Miss. & Ed. Society.

Mond. 26. Tues. 27. Wed. 28. At school.

Thurs. 29. In the afternoon went to Stephen Kirk's & married Peter E. Fouts to Miss Rebecca Kirk. Returned home.

Frid. 30. Met my upper Grammar class at Seaford's School house.

Sat. Dec. 1. At home.

Sund. 2. This my day at St. Stephen's ch. but the day being very inclement did not attend.

Mond. 3. In school, Rev. Scherer with me to night.

Tues. 4. Wed. 5. In school.

Thurs. 6. In school till 12 o'clock. At night attended preaching at Gold Hill by Rev. G. Scherer.

Frid. 7. In school till 12 o'clock. In the afernoon attended the sale of the old bridge plank.

Sat. 8. Met my upper Grammer class at Seaford's School house.

Sund. 9. Preached at Organ ch. from Luk. 23:39-43. Baptized one infant.

Mond. 10. Tues. 11. Wed. 12. In school.

Thurs. 13. Commenced a Protracted meeting at St. Stephen's ch. — the day being very inclement had a prayermeeting & dismissed. Took dinner at Mr. Nussman's.

Frid. 14. Preached at St. Stephen's from Luk. 23:39-43. At night had prayermeeting at Barrier's School house, lectured from Phil. 3:20. All night at Mr. Barrier's.

Sat. 15. Preached at St. Stephen's from Is. 44:23. At night had prayermeeting in the church, lectured from 2 Cor. 5:17. All night at Mrs. Peck's.

Sund. 16. Preached at St. Stephen's from Mat. 12:41.42. In the afternoon at Gold Hill from 2 Cor. 5:17. Then returned home.

Mond. 17. Attended to the fun[l] of Moses Trexler's wife at Organ ch. — preached from Numb. 23:10.

Tues. 18. In school. Wed. 19. In school.

Thurs. 20. In school till 12 o'clock. At night attended a prayermeeting in the School house at Lower St. ch. lectured from 2 Cor. 5:17. All night at Capt. Miller's.

Frid. 21. Met the upper Grammar class at P. A. Seaford's. All night at Mich[l] Bostian's.

Sat. 22. Met the Grammar class at the School house. Returned home in the evening.

Sund. 23. Preached at Organ ch. from 1 John 5:21. Baptized one inf[t]. Dinner at Jac. Miller's.

Mond. 24. At home till 12 o'clock, then went to Post Office (Gold Hill).

Tues. 25. Attended to the funeral of Sam[l] Berger at Lower St. ch. — preached from 2 Kings 20:1. Dinner at Mr. John Miller's.

Wed. 26. Went to Iredell. All night at Charles Barringer's.

Thurs. 27. In Iredell. All night at John Patterson's.

Frid. 28. In the afternoon went to John Berger's. All night here.

Sat. 29. Met the upper Grammar class. Returned home.

Sund. 30. Preached at Gold Hill from Acts 10:38. Attended prayer meeting at Simeon Lentz's.

Mond. 31. In school part of the day.

Tues. Jan. 1, 1850. Went to Salisbury.

Wed. 2. In school. At night had prayermeeting at the School house, lectured from Rev. 3:20.

Thurs. 3. Frid. 4. Sat. 5. At home. Had the Mumps.

Sund. 6. At home – indisposed.

Mond. 7. In the afternoon walked to the School house.

Tues. 8. Wed. 9. In school. Had prayermeeting at night at the School house, lectured from Mat. 8:12-22.

Thurs. 10. In school.

Frid. 11. Went to Gold Hill to P. Office.

Sat. 12. At home.

Sund. 13. Preached at Organ church from Math. 11:16-19. German. At night at prayermeeting at S. Lentz's.

Mond. 14. In school.

Tues. 15. Went to Gold Hill.

Wed. 16. At home. At night went to School-house to prayer meeting, but the evening being very inclement, but few persons attended.

Thurs. 17. Went to Gold Hill.

Frid. 18. At home.

Sat. 19. Went to Gold Hill & brought Mrs. R. home.

Sund. 20. Preached at St. Stephen's ch. from 2 Kings 7:3.4. Held a meeting of Missionary & Ed. Society. In the afternoon at Gold Hill from Mat. 8:28-34.

Mond. 21. In the afternoon went to Milas Arey's. All night here.

Tues. 22. Went to Salisbury – paid Boger and Wilson for Watch, Shoe Shop Acct, &c.

Wed. 23.+ Thurs. 24. Frid. 25. At home.

Sat. 26. Attended singing at Organ ch. All night at Moses Barringer's.

Sund. 27. Preached at Organ Church from Acts 4:33. Bapt^d one inf^t.

Mond. 28. Went by way of Paul Cruse's & Charles Fisher's to Geo. Klutts'. Had prayermeeting to night at Klutts' School house. Lectured from Eccl. 9:10. All night at Mr. Klutts'.

Tues. 29. Had some bridles cut out, & in afternoon returned home.

Wed. 30. At home. Had prayermeeting to night at School house, lectured from Eccl. 9:10.

Thurs. 31. Went by way of Gold Hill to see old Mr. Nussman. Took supper at Jacob Fisher's. At night attended prayermeeting at School house at Lower St. church, lectured from Mat. 25:1-13. All night at John Seaford's.

+ Prayermeeting to night @ School house, lectured from Math. 25:1-13.

Frid. Feb. 1. Met the upper Grammar class at P. A. Seaford's Esq. All night here.

Sat. 2. Met the Grammar Class at Seaford's School house. Returned home.

Sund. 3. Preached at St. Stephen's ch. from Acts 16:30.31. in the afternoon at Gold Hill from Gal. 6:14.

Mond. 4. Went to Salisbury.

Tues. 5. Wed. 6. At home. Made two bridles & martingale. Wed. night had prayermeeting at our School house, lectured from Is. 55:6.7.

Thurs. 7. At home till afternoon, then went to Gold Hill.

Frid. 8. Met the upper class at P. A. Seaford's. At night had prayermeeting at Pless' School house, lectured from Math. 25:1-13. All night at Henry Pless'.

Sat. 9. Met the Grammar class at the School house. In the afternoon preached at the School house No. 23 from Eccl. 9:10. All night at Dan[l] Eddleman's.

Sund. 10. Preached at Organ ch. from Hos. 6:4. Bapt. 2 infants. Dinner at Dan[l] Miller's.

Mond. 11. Attended to the fun[l] of Old Mrs. Barger at Lower St. ch. − preached from Ps. 73:24.

Tues. 12. Went to Gold Hill.

Wed. 13. At home − had prayermeeting this evening at our School house, lectured from Luk. 13:24.

Thurs. 14. Attended to the fun[l] of Mrs. Dan[l] Brown at Organ ch. − preached from Is. 3:10. In the afternoon Married Mr. Geo. A. Barger to Rebecca C. Fouts. All night at Geo. Randleman's.

Frid. 15. Met the Grammar class at P. A. Seaford's. At night had prayermeeting at the School house No. 23. lectured from Luk. 13:24. All night at Michael Bostian's.

Sat. 16. Met the Grammar class at the School house. In the evening returned home.

Sund. 17. Preached at St. Stephen's ch. from Hos. 6:4. & in the afternoon at Gold Hill from Neh. 6:3.

Mond. 18. Started for Iredell as far as C. Lyerly's.

Tues. 19. Went to Iredell. All night at David Kistler's.

Wed. 20. Returned to John Barger's.

Thurs. 21. Met the Grammar class at P. A. Seaford's. Had prayermeeting to night at Pless' School house, lectured from Math. 7:21. All night at Henry Pless'.

Frid. 22. Met the Grammar class at the School house. At night had prayermeeting at the School house No. 23. lectured from Rev. 2:4.5. All night at John Long's.

Sat. 23. Closed the Grammar class at the School house. Returned home in the afternoon.

Sund. 24. Preached at Organ ch. from Mark 16:15. Germ. After preaching held a short meeting of Miss. & Ed. Society. Took dinner at C. A. Heilig's.

Mond. 25. In the afternoon went to Gold Hill.

Tues. 26. Went to Widow Goodman's in Cabarrus & married Aaron Richie to Leah Goodman.

Wed. 27. At home.

Thurs. 28. In the afternoon went to Dan[l] Icehour's & married Michael A. Bostian to Rachel Icehour.

Frid. March 1. Attended to the fun[1] of Charles Barringer at Organ ch. — preached from Ps. 58:11. Took dinner at Jacob Miller's. Called & settled with John Trexler.

Sat. 2. At home till after dinner, then went to M. Barrier's School house. At night had prayermeeting here, lectured from Ps. 58:11. Took supper at Geo. Culp's. All night at M. Barrier's.

Sund. 3. Preached at St. Stephen's ch. from 2 Tim. 4:7.8. & in the afternoon at Gold Hill from Acts 24:16. Took dinner at John Lentz's.

Mond. 4. At home.

Tues. 5. Assisted Simeon Lentz in rolling logs.

Wed. 6. At home.

Thurs. 7. Went to St. John's ch. to attend a Protracted Meeting. At night preached from 1 Thes. 5:6. All night at D. D. Ridenhour's.

Frid. 8. Preached at night from Heb. 2:3. All night at Sandy Blackwelder's.

Sat. 9. Preached in the afternoon from 2 Cor. 5:17. Germ. All night at Mr. Fisher's.

Sund. 10. Preached in the forenoon from Prov. 29:1. All night at Dan[l] Miller's.

Mond. 11. In the afternoon returned home.

Tues. 12. Went back to St. John's ch. preached at night from Eccl. 9:10. All night at Mr. House's.

+Wed. 13. Returned home, Rev. Arey being in company.

Thurs. 14. Went to Gold Hill.

Frid. 15. Sat. 16. At home.

Sund. 17. Preached at St. Stephen's ch. from John 3:14.15. Took dinner at Dr. Kelly's. Very rainy afternoon.

Mond. 18. Went to Peter Troutman's to visit his mother, she being old and afflicted. Had meeting here. — preached from Math. 11:28. Germ.

Tues. 19. Attended the closing of our free School. Talked to the people from Prov. 22:6.

+Wed. 20. At home, till afternoon then went to S. Lentz' to shop.

Thurs. 21. Went to S. Lentz's and had Ben shod & a plow pointed.

Frid. 22. Attended to the fun[l] of Sally Weaver at Organ ch. — preached from Job 14:14. Germ.

Sat. 23. Attended a concert (singing & violins) at Organ church.

Sund. 24. Preached at Organ ch. from Josh. 24:15. Baptized two infants. Dinner at John Miller's.

Mond. 25. Tues. 26. At home.

Wed. 27. Went to Gold Hill to Post office. Sent per Post Master — Seven dollars to American Messenger, New York.

Thurs. 28. Attended to the fun[l] of Michael Bostian. — preached the funeral at the house from Math. 5:8. — buried him at Luther's Chapel.

Frid. 29. Sat. 30. At home.

Sund. 31. Had no appointment for to day. Spent the day at home.

+ Had prayermeeting to night at our School house — lectured from Phil. 3:20.21.

+ Lectured at School House from Ps. 138:6.

Mond. April 1. Went to D. Barringer's. In the afternoon returned home by way of Post Office.

Tues. 2. Wed. 3. Thurs. 4. Frid. 5. At home.

Sat. 6. Attended to the fun^l of Mrs. Henry Wilhelm at St. Mathew's Church. — preach^d from Phil. 3:20.21.

Sund. 7. Preached at St. Stephen's ch. from Is. 55:7. Bapt^d 2 infants. In the afternoon preached at Gold Hill from 2 Pet. 3:18. Dinner at Dr. Kelly's.

Mond. 8. Tues. 9. Wed. 10. At home.

Thurs. 11. At Simeon Lentz's, helping to make gate hinges.

Frid. 12. At home till afternoon, then went to Andr. Troutman's & paid off a note of hand.

Sat. 13. Attended to the funeral of Widow Eddleman at Organ ch. — preached from John 14:6.

Sund. 14. Preached at Organ ch. from Is. 55:7. Germ. Baptized one infant. Dinner at Moses Barringer's.

Mond. 15. Went to Salisbury.

Tues. 16. Went to Mr. Linn's & invited them to Charlotte's wedding. In the evening went to Gold Hill & heard Rev. Dervelle on the Bible cause. All night at Dr. Kelly's.

Wed. 17. A very inclement day. Returned home. In the afternoon married John Clarke to Charlotte Arey.

Thurs. 18. Frid. 19. At home.

Sat. 20. Preached at St. Stephen's ch. from Acts 4:33. preparatory to communion. Bapt^d one inf^t. Returned home.

Sund. 21. Preached at St. Stephen's from 2 Cor. 4:7. Baptized one inf^t & administered the Lord's Supper. In the afternoon preached at Gold Hill from 1 Pet. 4:18.

Mond. 22. Went by way of D. Barringer's to Saml Peeler's and collected of him a note of hand. In the evening went to Jacob File's. All night here.

Tues. 23. Examined in company with Alex^r Holshouser & Jacob File, Second Creek up to Cheraw Road.

Wed. 24. Continued the examination of the creek up to M. Barringer's Mill & districted to same to have it cleaned out.

Thurs. 25. Went to Gold Hill on business. In the afternoon went to Saml Beaver's and married Jacob Holshouser to Anna Beaver. Then went to Daniel Goodman's & married John E. Miller to Elizabeth Goodman. Returned home.

Frid. 26. At home.

Sat. 27. Preached at Organ ch. from John 3:16. preparatory to communion. Baptized 4 infants. All night at Jos. Miller's.

Sund. 28. Preached at Organ ch. from 1 Chron. 4:9.10. & administered the Lord's Supper. Dinner at Jacob Miller's. Returned home.

Mond. 29. Went to Post office — then at home.

Tues. 30. At home till dinner, then went to Jacob Holshouser's & helped him roll logs.

Wed. May 1. At home till 12 o'clock, then went to Peter Troutman's to see his mother, she being sick.
Thurs. 2. Went to St. Mathew's ch. to meeting of Synod. Returned home in the evening.
Frid. 3. At Synod — at home at night.
Sat. 4. At Synod — all night with family at Jacob File's Esqr.
Sund. 5. At St. Mathew's ch. — preached in the afternoon with reference to the Missionary & Education Society from Ps. 116:12.13. Rev. Coffman being indisposed & unable to preach as he had been appointed to do.
Mond. 6. At Synod. At night the Ministerium met at Mr. A. Hill's. All night here.
Tues. 7. Returned home.
Wed. 8. Went to Salisbury. Very rainy in the evening.
Thurs. 9. Frid. 10. At home, not very well.
Sat. 11. At home.
Sund. 12. Preached at Organ Church from Dan. 6:10. Baptized 2 inf'ts. Dinner at Danl Miller's.
Mond. 13. Went to Gold Hill.
Tues. 14. Attended to the burial of Mich^l Bostian, Sen. at Organ ch. The day being very rainy, did not preach the funeral.
Wed. 15. Went to David Lentz's.
Thurs. 16. At home — mended my shoes.
Frid. 17. In the afternoon went to John Miller's for molasses.
Sat. 18. At home.
Sund. 19. Preached at St. Stephen's ch. from 1 Pet. 1:12. & in the afternoon at Gold Hill from Col. 1:28. Took dinner at John Lentz's.
Mond. 20. Went to Salisbury.
Tues. 21. Wed. 22. At home making Shoes. Spent Wed. night Col. A. Holshouser's.
Thurs. 23. At home.
Frid. 24. Commenced catechization at Organ ch. Took dinner at Paul Cruse's. All night at Danl Miller's.
Sat. 25. Preached at St. John's ch. from Ex. 33:14. Returned home.
Sund. 26. Preached at Organ ch. from Math. 25:13. Germ. the funeral of Mich^l Bostian, Sen. Baptized one inf^t. In the afternoon Eng^l from Math. 4:1-11. Took dinner at John Miller's.
Mond. 27. Went to Salisbury.
Tues. 28. Went to Sale at Chas Barringer's, dec^d. Dinner at Simeon Miller's.
Wed. 29. Went to Gold Hill.
Thurs. 30. Attended to the fun^l of James F. Fraley at Lower St. ch. Preached from Mark 13:35-37. Mr. Fraley was drowned while bathing.
Frid. 31. At home.

Sat. June 1. At home.

Sund. 2. Preached at St. Stephen's ch. from 1 Cor. 9:24-27. In the afternoon attended to the funeral of Christena Troutman (widow) at Organ Church. — preached from Rev. 14:13. Took dinner at Laurence Lingle's.

Mond. 3. In the morning went to Post Office. Balance of day at home.

Tues. 4. Wed. 5. At home.

Thurs. 6. In the afternoon went to Daywalt Beaver's & married Moses A. Bost to Caroline Beaver. In the evening went to Gold Hill to Post office.

Frid. 7. Had catechization at Organ Church.

Sat. 8. Preached in the afternoon at Peter Miller's from Math. 5:8. the funeral of his deceased child.

Sund. 9. Preached at Organ ch. from Math. 20:6. In the afternoon held a Meeting of Miss. & Ed. Society.

Mond. 10. Tues. 11. At home — Made hay.

Wed. 12. Helped Mrs. Peeler in her meadow.

Thurs. 13. Married to day Andrew Berger to Sarah C. Lingle. In the afternoon helped Mrs. Peeler put her hay away.

Frid. 14. At home.

Sat. 15. Went to John Moose's & had prayermeeting at night, lectured from Mark 1:40-45. All night here. Took dinner to day at Laurence Lingle's.

Sund. 16. Preached at St. Stephen's ch. from Math. 20:6. Held a meeting of our Miss. & Ed. Society. In the afternoon preached at Gold Hill from Ps. 1:1-6.

Mond. 17. At home — Plowed corn till evening, then went to Gold Hill & attended a meeting of Bible Society.

Tues. 18. In the afternoon went to the Post office & to Dr. Cunningham's to see Mr. Moyer on the subject of making shoes.

Wed. 19. Thurs. 20. At home.

Frid. 21. Had catechization at Organ Church.

Sat. 22. In the afternoon went to Simeon Miller's & staid all night.

Sund. 23. Preached at Organ ch. from 1 Cor. 9:24-27. Installed John Trexler & John J. Miller as Deacons. In the afternoon held a meeting of Miss. & Ed. Society.

Mond. 24. Took Mrs. R. to Gold Hill to stay a few days.

Tues. 25. At home making shoes.

Wed. 26. In the afternoon brought Mrs. R. home.

Thurs. 27. Frid. 28. At home.

Sat. 29. Went to Iredell. Dinner at P. Berger's. All night at B. Arey's.

Sund. 30. Preached for Revd Arey at Shepherd's + Roads from 1 Cor. 9:24-27. Dinner at John Barringer's. All night at B. Arey's.

Mond. July 1. Returned home.

Tues. 2. At home.

Wed. 3.+ Thurs. 4. Frid. 5. At home.

Sat. 6. At home — Thrashed wheat.

Sund. 7. This my day at St. Stephen's — J. S. Heilig preached for me. Had no preaching in the afternoon at Gold Hill in consequence of rain.

Mond. 8. At home till afternoon, then went to Linn's Mill.

Tues. 9. Wed. 10. Thurs. 11. At home.

Frid. 12. Had catechization at Organ ch. Dinner at Moses Barringer's.

Sat. 13. In the morning went to Gold Hill. In the evening to John J. Miller's. All night here.

Sund. 14. Preached at Organ ch. from Mal. 3:7. Germ. & Engl. from same.

Mond. 15. At home. Plant^d potatoes (late).

Tues. 16. In the morning went to mill.

Wed. 17. Went to Gold Hill & had horses shod.

Thurs. 18. Frid. 19. At home.

Sat. 20. In the evening went to Wilie Knup's & staid all night.

Sund. 21. Preached at St. Stephen's from Josh. 24:15. In the afternoon Solomon Heilig preached at Gold Hill.

Mond. 22. Went to David Barringer's.

Tues. 23. Went to Salisbury. All night at Milas Arey's.

Wed. 24. In the afternoon visited Isaac Kesler's. All night at Milas Arey's.

Thurs. 25. Returned home.

Frid. 26. Had catechization at Organ Church.

Sat. 27. Went to the muster & paid my Tax. All night at Jacob Miller's.

Sund. 28. Preached at Organ ch. from Acts 17:11.12. Baptized 2 infants. In the afternoon preached from 2 Cor. 13:5.

Mond. 29. At home.

Tues. 30. Went Danl Miller's to mill.

Wed. 31. Returned home.

+ Funeral of Sol. Cruse, Organ ch. Text Prov. 27:1.

Thurs. Aug. 1. Started for Nazereth ch. in Forsythe co. All night at David Koons'. Milas & Jane Arey in company with us.

Frid. 2. Took dinner at C. Peeler's. All night in Salem. 1.25 bill.

Sat. 3. Went to Nazereth church. Preached from Mat. 7:21. to a small congregation. All night at Mr. Bidding's Esqr

Sund. 4. Preached again from 1 Thes. 2:11.12. Returned in the afternoon to Mr. H. Beckerdite's.

Mond. 5. Went D. Fishel's & to Waughtown to look-out a one horse Waggon. At night preached at Chestnut Grove School house from 1 Thes. 2:11.12. All night at C. Peeler's.

Tues. 6. Called to see Aunt Christena Ripple & D. Fishel. All night at C. Peeler's.

Wed. 7. Returned home.

Thurs. 8. At home.

Frid. 9. Had catechization at Organ ch.

Sat. 10. In the evening went to David Lentz's. All night here.

Sund. 11. Preached at Organ ch. from Gen. 28:17. Bapt^d 1 inf^t. In the afternoon preached from Prov. 23:26. Dinner at John Miller's.

Mond. 12. At home.

Tues. 13. Wed. 14. At home — making hay.

Thurs. 15. In the evening went to St. Stephen's ch. & commenced a Protracted Meeting. Lectured from John 14:22. All night at Mrs. Peck's.

Frid. 16. At the church. After preaching at night, returned home.

Sat. 17. At St. Stephen's Church. All night at Mrs. Peck's.

Sund. 18. At the Church. A very rainy day. All night at Dr. Kelly's.

Mond. 19. At the Church. Closed the meeting. Returned home.

Tues. 20. At home.

Wed. 21. Went to Gold Hill for some medicine, not being well.

Thurs. 22. Went to Leonard Klutts's & married Moses Trexler to Eve C. Klutts. Started in the evening for the Camp Meeting at St. Michael's Church, Iredell Co. All night at Thomas Lock's.

Frid. 23. Went to the meeting.

Sat. 24. Preached from Prov. 23:26.

Sund. 25. Preached from Deut. 11:16.

Mond. 26. At the meeting.

Tues. 27. Preached from Mark 1:40-45.

Wed. 28. Preached from 2 Cor. 5:17. To day the meeting closed. All night at B. Arey's.

Thurs. 29. Returned home.

Frid. 30. Went to Concord to Protracted Meeting. Preached at night from John 9:4. All night at Mr. Winecoff's Esq.

Sat. 31. Preached from Luk. 13:24. All night at John Bost's.

Sund. Sept. 1. Preached from 1 Thes. 2:11.12. All night at Albert Arey's.

Mond. 2. Preached from 2 Cor. 5:17. & from 1 Pet. 4:18.+

Tues. 3. Returned home.

Wed. 4. Went D. Barringer's on business.

Thurs. 5. Went to John Bost's & baptized his child, it being very sick — went also to Gold Hill to Post office.

Frid. 6. Had catechization at Organ Church.

Sat. 7. Attended to fun^l of Paul Beaver's child at Lower Stone Church. — preached from Ps. 90:12. Germ.

Sund. 8. Preached at Organ ch. from Josh. 24:15. Germ.+ Held a meeting of Miss. & Ed. Society.

Mond. 9. Called to see old Mr. Nussman. Also had horse shod at Gold Hill.

Tues. 10. At home.

Wed. 11. Attended to the fun^l of John Bost's child at Organ ch. — preached from Math. 5:8. Took dinner at John Seaford's.

Thurs. 12. Frid. 13. Sat. 14. At home.

Sund. 15. Preached at St. Stephen's ch. from Eph. 6:18. Baptized two infants.

Mond. 16. At home.

Tues. 17. Took some oats to Gold Hill.

Wed. 18. At home till afternoon, then went to Laurence Lingle's. All night here.

Thurs. 19. Had catechization at Organ Church.

Frid. 20. Commenced a Protracted Meeting at Organ Church. Revds. Scheck & Arey assisted. All night John Seaford's. Baptized to day one infant.

Sat. 21. Sund. 22. At the Church. All night at Moses Barringer's.

Mond. 23. Took sick in the Church. All night at Moses Barringer's.

Tues. 24. Returned home sick.

Wed. 25. Thurs. 26. Frid. 27. Sat. 28. At home sick.

Sund. 29. At home improving.

Mond. 30. Went to Gold Hill for wool rolls.

+　Baptized Rev. Harter's child.

+　Bapt. to day 3 inf^ts.

Tues. Oct. 1. At home.

Wed. 2. Went to Salisbury.

Thurs. 3. Went to Gold Hill and Mrs. Fraley's & settled Postage, & to Dr. Cunningham's & paid tuition.

Frid. 4. Went to D. Barringer's & Milas Arey's. All night @ latter place.

Sat. 5. Went to Union Church. A Protracted Meeting commenced here to day. Preached from Eccl. 9:10. In the evening returned home.

Sund. 6. Went to St. Stephen's. Revd Rankin preached for me. In the afternoon went John Earnheart's & married George Goodman to Catherine Hahnberger.

Mond. 7. At home.

Tues. 8. Attended to the funeral of Mrs. Pasinger at Organ ch. — preached from Phil. 3:20.21. Took dinner at Jacob Miller's.

Wed. 9. At home.

Thurs. 10. At home.

Frid. 11. Had catechization at Organ Church.

Sat. 12. Preached at Organ ch. from 1 John 1:9. preparatory to communion. Baptized 5 infants. Confirmed 1 person. In the afternoon held a meeting of the Missionary and Education Society. J. M. Graeber & L. C. Miller were taken up as beneficiaries. All night at N. Klutts'.

Sund. 13. Baptized 1 inf^t Preached from John 7:37. & administered the Lord's Supper. In the evening called by David Lentz's & baptized Danl Moyer's child.

Mond. 14. Went to Salisbury.

Tues. 15. Went to Gold Hill and brought Dr. Kelly to see Sophia Peeler, she being sick.

Wed. 16. Went to John Long's & married Augustus F. Graeber to Margaret A. Misenheimer. All night at Jerem. Graeber's.

Thurs. 17. Called at Mrs. Graeber's & took dinner. In the afternoon returned home.

Frid. 18. Sat. 19. Sund. 20. At home, sick.

Mond. 21. Went to Mrs. Fraley's to Post office.

Tues. 22. At home — had my corn shucked and cribbed.

Wed. 23. At home.

Thurs. 24. Went to Gold Hill. In the afternoon at home.

Frid. 25. This my day for catechization at Organ Church, but the morning being inclement, did not turn out.

Sat. 26. At home.

Sund. 27. Preached at Organ ch. from Lam. 4:2. Germ. Bapt. 1 inft.

Mond. 28. Tues. 29. At home.

Wed. 30. Went to blacksmith shop — to Mr. Link's at Gold Hill. At night had prayermeeting at School house, lectured from Eph. 6:18.

Thurs. 31. Went to J. A. Troutman's & married said Troutman to Amelia Parham.

Frid. Nov. 1. Attended to the fun[l] of Wm. Holshouser's child at Lower St. ch. — preached from Math. 19:14.

Sat. 2. Preached at St. Stephen's ch. from Luk. 16:8. preparatory to communion. Baptized 4 infants.

Sund. 3. Preached at St. Stephen's from Jer. 17:9. 2 Cor. 13:5. and administered the Lord's Supper.

Mond. 4. Attended to the fun[l] of Simeon Hoffner's step child at Tice Barringer's. — preached from Ps. 90:12. Baptized 5 infants here.

Tues. 5. Went to Salisbury.

Wed. 6. Went to Gold Hill.

Thurs. 7. Went to Mill to Mr. Linn's.

Frid. 8. Had catechization at Organ ch.

Sat. 9. In the morning went to mill, then to Gold Hill.

Sund. 10. Preached at Organ ch. from Eph. 6:18. Baptized five infants. Took dinner at Widow Miller's.

Mond. 11. Attended to the funeral of William Holshouser at Lower St. ch. — preached from Ps. 90:12. A very rainy day. Took dinner at John Miller's. In the afternoon started for Iredell as far as Salisbury. All night at Moses L. Brown's.

Tues. 12. Went to Iredell. All night at Rev. B. Arey's.

Wed. 13. In Iredell. Made arrangements to have corn hauled to Rowan, &c. All night again at Rev. B. Arey's.

Thurs. 14. Returned home.

Frid. 15. At home.

Sat. 16. Preached at Peter Troutman's from Math. 5:6. Germ. Baptized 4 infants & administered the Lord's Supper to old Mrs. Troutman, she being confined to her bed by sickness & the infirmities of old age.

Sund. 17. Preached at St. Stephen's ch. from Math. 18:20.

Mond. 18. In the forenoon went to Gold Hill. In the afternoon butchered two hogs.

Tues. 19. At home till afternoon, then went to the Post office.

Wed. 20. At home till evening — had an appointment this evening at school house for prayermeeting but the evening being rainy the people did not attend.

Thurs. 21. Went to Salisbury & had clothes cut out.

Frid. 22. Had catechization at Organ Church.

Sat. 23. At home.

Sund. 24. Preached at Organ ch. from Math. 18:20. After preaching, held a meeting of Missionary & Education Society. Dinner at John Miller's.

Mond. 25. In the morning went to Gold Hill. Afternoon at home.

Tues. 26. At home till afternoon, then went to Gold Hill — at night attended preaching by Rev. Piggers in Methodist ch. All night at Dr. Kelly's.

Wed. 27. Returned home. In the afternoon went to Sale of James Porter, dec[d]. At night had prayermeeting at School house, lectured from Math. 5:6. Went to see Sam[l] Powlass, he being afflicted with bleeding at nose. All night here.

Thurs. 28. At home.

Frid. 29. In the morning went to Gold Hill on business. (Sold corn to M. L. Holmes) Then went to St. Mathews to Protracted Meeting. Preached from Math. 5:6. All night at Moses Lemly's.

Sat. 30. Preached again from Phil. 3:20. Had a very sore throat. In the evening returned home.

Sund. Dec. 1. At home. Could not fill my appointment at St. Stephen's in consequence of bad cold & very sore throat.

Mond. 2. At home.

Tues. 3. At home. C. Peeler here to night.

Wed. 4. In the forenoon went to Gold Hill to blacksmith shop. Prayer Meet. to night @ sch. house. Lectured from Luk. 5:1-11.

Thurs. 5. At home. Rec^d load corn this evening from Iredell.

Frid. 6. Attended to the funeral of Widow Sarah Brown. — preached from Ps. 90:12. at the house. Buried her at Stone house. Very rainy afternoon.

Sat. 7. At home.

Sund. 8. Preached at Organ ch. from John 14:6. Held an election to day for Church Officers. Dinner at Danl Miller's.

Mond. 9. Went to Iredell. All night at Charles Barringer's.

Tues. 10. At my plantation, counting out Oats, &c. All night at C. Barringer's.

Wed. 11. Returned home. Had prayermeeting to night at School House — lectured from 1 Tim. 4:7.

Thurs. 12. Went to Wilie Knup's in forenoon to engage pine.

Frid. 13. Had catechization at Organ church.

Sat. 14. At home till 12 o'clock, then went to Dr. Cunningham's to barn raising.

Sund. 15. Attended to the fun^l of old Mrs. Culp at St. Stephen's ch. — preached from Prov. 3:6. Dinner at John Lentz's.

Mond. 16. At home.

Tues. 17. Went to Gold Hill.

Wed. 18. At home. At night had prayermeeting at School house. Lectured from Ps. 73:1.

Thurs. 19. Started to St. John's Church to Protracted Meeting. Dinner at Mr. Laurence Lingle's. All night at Danl Miller's. A very rainy day.

Frid. 20. Went to St. John's Church. Preached from Math. 4:19. Preached again at night from Luk. 15:11-24. All night at Jacob House's.

Sat. 21. Preached from Jer. 17:9. 2 Cor. 13:5. and at night from 1 King 19:13. All night at Mr. House's.

Sund. 22. Preached from Eph. 6:18. & at night from Josh. 7:12. All night at Danl Miller's.

Mond. 23. Returned home by way of Mr. Nussman's & Gold Hill.

Tues. 24. At home.

Wed. 25. Preached at School house from Math. 1:21. John Lentz & Lady, & J. S. Heilig & Lady with us to night.

Thurs. 26. At home.

Frid. 27. Had catechization at Organ ch. Dinner at Moses Barringer's.

Sat. 28. At home.

Sund. 29. Preached at Organ ch. from Rom. 13:14. Baptized one infant. Dinner at Jacob Miller's.

Mond. 30. Went to Gold Hill.

Tues. 31. In the afternoon went to Jacob Holshouser's & aided him in making out his Post office Return.

Wed. Jan. 1. Went to Salisbury. All night at David Barringer's.

Thurs. 2. Returned home. Commenced snowing in the afternoon.

Frid. 3. A very deep snow on the ground. In the afternoon went to Organ ch. & attended to the fun[1] of Mrs. Richie.

Sat. 4. At home.

Sund. 5. Preached at St. Stephen's ch. from Rom. 13:14. Congregation small, the day being inclement.

Mond. 6. Went to Gold Hill.

Tues. 7. At home.

Wed. 8. At home, butchered hogs. At night had prayermeeting at school house, lectured from parable of Prodigal Son.

Thurs. 9. At home.

Frid. 10. Had catechization at Organ ch.

Sat. 11. In the afternoon assisted Jacob Holshouser in laying the foundation for a kitchen.

Sund. 12. Preached at Organ ch. from Jer. 17:9. 2 Cor. 13:5. Baptized 3 infants. Dinner at David Lentz's.

Mond. 13. Went to Gold Hill.

Tues. 14. Attended to the funeral of Mathias Barringer at his residence.

Wed. 15. Assisted Jacob Holshouser in raising his kitchen.

Thurs. 16. Went to Gold Hill.

Frid. 17. Attended to the funeral of Sam[1] Powlass at Lower St. Church. — preached from Ps. 73:24. Dinner at Jacob Randleman's.

Sat. 18. At home till afternoon, then went Laurence Lingle's. All night here.

Sund. 19. Preached at St. Stephen's ch. Ps. 1:1-6. Very cold day.

Mond. 20. At home till afternoon, then went to mill (Mr. Linn's).

Tues. 21. Went to Klutts' Tan Yard.

Wed. 22. Thurs. 23. At home mending shoes.

Frid. 24. Had catechization at Organ Church. All night at Philip Eddleman's.

Sat. 25. Returned home. Called on the way to see David Brown, he being sick.

Sund. 26. Preached at Organ ch. from Prov. 14:26. Baptized two infants. Dinner at C. Heilig's.

Mond. 27. Took Catherine Bahn home to Gold Hill.

Tues. 28. Went to Gold Hill & heard P. S. White lecture on the subject of Temperance. Disappointed in expectation. All night at John Lentz's.

Wed. 29. Returned home, very cold.

Thurs. 30. In the afternoon went to mill (Mr. Linn's).

Frid. 31. At home.

Sat. Feb. 1. Went to Bostian's School House & preached (the last day of school) from Eccl. 12:1. Returned home after preaching.

Sund. 2. Preached at St. Stephen's ch. from Math. 5:20. Dinner at Dr. Kelly's. In the evening went to John Trexler's his wife being very sick. All night here — his wife died.

Mond. 3. Returned home.

Tues. 4. Attended to the funeral of Leah Trexler, wife of John, at the Lower St. ch. — preached from Ps. 34:19.

Wed. 5. In the afternoon went to Gold Hill to blacksmith shop. At night had prayermeeting at School house, lectured from 1 John 3:2.

Thurs. 6. Went to David Ketner's & married Elam A. Patterson to Barbara M. Ketner. All night at Michael Overcash's.

Frid. 7. Had catechization at Organ ch.

Sat. 8. At home.

Sund. 9. Preached at Organ ch. from Luk. 12:32. Baptized one infant. Dinner at John J. Miller's.

Mond. 10. Went to Gold Hill & had carriage mended.

Tues. 11. At home.

Wed. 12. At home. Had prayermeeting at School house — lectured from 1 Pet. 4:18. Milas Arey with us to night.

Thurs. 13. At home. Had company.

Frid. 14. Sat. 15. At home.

Sund. 16. Preached at St. Stephen's from 1 Pet. 2:15: setting forth objections to the Order of Sons of Temperance.

Mond. 17. Went to Iredell. All night at Charles Barringer's.

Tues. 18. Went to Statesville, then to John Clarke's. All night here.

Wed. 19. Bought Rose of J. Clarke. Took dinner at Tobias Brown's. In the afternoon went to B. Arey's. All night here.

Thurs. 20. Returned home. At night went to Asa Miller's & married Pinkney Summit to Barbara B. Miller.

Frid. 21. This the day for catechization at Organ ch. but the day being rainy did not attend. Called at David Holshouser's & settled weaving bill.

Sat. 22. Went to Widow Garner's & preached the funeral of her daughter, who died a few weeks before, from Heb. 4:9. Dinner at Mich[l] Bostian's.

Sund. 23. Preached at Organ ch. from Rom. 1:16. Baptized one infant. Held a meeting of Missionary & Education Society.

Mond. 24. At home.

Tues. 25. Attended to the funeral of John Lentz's child at St. Stephen's ch. Preached from Rev. 14:13.

Wed. 26. At home.

Thurs. 27. Went to Gold Hill to blacksmith shop.

Frid. 28. Had catechization at Organ ch. All night at J. Foutz's.

Sat. March 1. Returned home. In the afternoon attended the closing of our School.
Sund. 2. Preached at St. Stephen's ch. from Hab. 2:15.
Mond. 3. At home.
Tues. 4. Went to David Brown's School House & preached from Eccl. 9:10. being the last of school.
Wed. 5. In the morning went to the Post office.
Thurs. 6. At home, ingrafted some apple cions.
Frid. 7. This my day for catechization at Organ Church but did not attend, it being a very rainy day.
Sat. 8. Went to St. Stephen's Church in relation to building Pulpit.
Sund. 9. Preached at Organ Church from Acts 16:30.31. Germ. Dinner at Paul Miller's.
Mond. 10. Went to Salisbury.
Tues. 11. At home.
Wed. 12. At home. Tobias Brown called to see us this evening.
Thurs. 13. Went with Mr. Brown to Mr. Linn's Mill, he wished to see it.
Frid. 14. Had catechization at Organ church.
Sat. 15. At home.
Sund. 16. Preached at St. Stephen's ch. from Amos 4:12. Baptized one inf^t Dinner at John Lentz's.
Mond. 17. At home. Had Col. Holshouser & Rufus to assist in inclosing the yard around the house.
Tues. 18. At home — had hands & finished inclosing the yard.
Wed. 19. Thurs. 20. Frid. 21. At home.
Sat. 22. Had an appointment to day to address the people of Organ Church on the subject of the Order of Sons of Temperance. Started as far as John Miller's, but the day being very rainy, did not go to the church. All night at Mr. Miller's.
Sund. 23. Preached at Organ ch. from Hab. 2:15. on the evils of drunkeness. Confirmed Uriah M. Pless.
Mond. 24. Went to Gold Hill.
Tues. 25. At home. Had Danl Miller and Col. Holshouser to make boards.
Wed. 26. Thurs. 27. At home in my study.
Frid. 28. Had catechization at Organ ch.
Sat. 29. Addressed the congregation at Organ ch. in relation to the Order of Sons of Temperance, setting forth my objections to the order as an institution.
Sund. 30. Preached at Organ ch. from Eph. 5:18. German, on the subject of the evils of drunkeness & the blessings of sobriety.
Mond. 31. In the morning went to Jacob Holshouser's, & assisted him in making out his quarterly settlement as Post Master.

Tues. Apr. 1. In the evening went to John Trexler's & spent the night with him.

Wed. 2. In the afternoon returned home by way of Moses Trexler's & Mrs. Goodman's.

Thurs. 3. In the afternoon went to Gold Hill & Wilie Knup's.

Frid. 4. In the afternoon assisted Mrs. Peeler to roll logs.

Sund. 6. Preached at St. Stephen's ch. from Luk. 19:1-10. Dinner at Dr. Kelly's.

Mond. 7. At home.

Tues. 8. Wed. 9. Thurs. 10. At home.

Frid. 11. Had catechization at Organ ch.

Sat. 12. At home.

Sund. 13. Preached at Organ ch. from Luk. 19:1-10. Dinner at J. J. Miller's.

Mond. 14. Went to Gold Hill.

Tues. 15. Went in the afternoon to Danl Miller's.

Wed. 16. Returned home by way of Daywald Beaver's.

Thurs. 17. Frid. 18. At home.

Sat. 19. At home till evening, then went to Dr. Kelly's.

Sund. 20. Preached at St. Stephen's ch. from Ex. 23:2. Dinner at Dr. Kelly's.

Mond. 21. Went to D. Barringer's.

Tues. 22. Went to Salisbury.

Wed. 23. At home.

Thurs. 24. Went to widow Lentz's & married Paul Holshouser to Elenora Lentz. In the evening went to Milas Arey's.

Frid. 25. Attended to the funeral of William Smith, sen. Preached the funeral at the house of dec^{d} from Ps. 90:12. & buried him at Jacob Smith's burying ground. Dinner at D. Barringer's.

Sat. 26. Preached at Organ church from Ps. 50:14. preparatory to communion & confirmation. Confirmed 46 persons. At night had prayermeeting at Mr. Henry Klutts' — lectured from Rev. 3:20.

Sund. 27. Preaching at Organ ch. Mr. S. Heilig preached for me. Administered the Lord's Supper to a large number of communicants. Dinner at John Miller's.

Mond. 28. At home. S. Heilig & Lady with us to night.

Tues. 29. In the afternoon went to St. Stephen's to see how the workmen were getting on with the Pulpit.

Wed. 30. At home.

Thurs. May 1. Went to St. Stephen's ch. Synod commenced to day. At night returned home.

Frid. 2. At Synod — all night at George Culp's.

Sat. 3. At Synod — all night at Dr. Kelly's.

Sund. 4. At the church — all night at Geo. Culp's.

Mond. 5. At Synod. All night at Dr. Kelly's.

Tues. 6. At Synod till 12 o'clock. Synod then adjourned, Returned home. Rev. S. Scherer with me to night.

Wed. 7. At home. A bad cold.

Thurs. 8. At home till 12 o'clock. Revd Leppard with me this forenoon. In the afternoon went to Henry Klutts' and married Mathias M. Lentz to Caroline Klutts.

Frid. 9. At home — quite indisposed with bad cold.

Sat. 10. At home.

Sund. 11. Preached at Organ ch. from Math. 25:10. Baptized 2 infants. Dinner at Jacob Miller's.

Mond. 12. Went to Salisbury.

Tues. 13. In the afternoon went to Peter Miller's & engaged him to spay hogs.

Wed. 14. Had my hogs spayed.

Thurs. 15. Went to Gold Hill.

Frid. 16. At home.

Sat. 17. At home.

Sund. 18. This my regular day at St. Stephen's. Rev. J. S. Heilig preached for me. Dinner at Dr. Kelly's. In the afternoon preached at our School house from Eccl. 8:12.

Mond. 19. At home.

Tues. 20. Went to Salisbury. All night at Milas Arey's.

Wed. 21. Returned home by way of D. Barringer's, Esq.

Thurs. 22. Assisted Mrs. Peeler in raising barn sheds, &c.

Frid. 23. Went to Salisbury.

Sat. 24. At home.

Sund. 25. Preached at Organ ch. from Prov. 22:6. Held the annual Meeting of the Miss. & Ed. Society.

Mond. 26. At home.

Tues. 27. Went to Milas Arey's.

Wed. 28. At home.

Thurs. 29. Went to Salisbury.

Frid. 30. At home.

Sat. 31. In the afternoon went to M. Barrier's, Esq.

Sund. June 1. Preached at St. Stephen's from Mal. 3:16. Din^r at Dr. Kelly's. In the afternoon at the School house from Math. 11:28.

Mond. 2. Tues. 3. At home.

Wed. 4. In the afternoon went to Wilie Knup's to engage him to cut grass.

Thurs. 5. Went to Gold Hill.

Frid. 6. At home, hauled hay.

Sat. 7. Went to Mr. Chas Fisher's.

Sund. 8. Preached at Organ ch. from Mal. 3:16. Baptized two infants. Dinner at John Seaford's.

Mond. 9. Attended to the fun^l of Paul Nussman at St. Stephen's. — preached from Ps. 58:11.

Tues. 10. At home, making hay.

Wed. 11. At home.

Thurs. 12. Went to Wilie Knup's & Dr. Kelly's to engage hands to cradle wheat.

Frid. 13. At home, harvesting.

Sat. 14. At home, harvesting.

Sund. 15. Preached at St. Stephen's ch. from 1 Tim. 6:17-19. Held the annual meeting of Missionary & Education Society. Dinner at John Lentz's. In afternoon preached at School house from Prov. 29:1. Called in the evening to see John Hartman near Stokes Ferry, he being afflicted with dropsy. All night at Daywalt Lentz's.

Mond. 16. Returned home.

Tues. 17. In the afternoon went to mill.

Wed. 18. Thurs. 19. Helped widow Peeler make hay.

Frid. 20. Finished harvesting.

Sat. 21. At home — Milas Arey here to night.

Sund. 22. Preached at Organ ch. from Is. 55:6.7. Germ. Baptized one infant. In the afternoon Rev. S. Scherer preached in English.

Mond. 23. Went to Lexington.

Tues. 24. Returned home.

Wed. 25. At home.

Thurs. 26. At home.

Frid. 27. Went to Luther's church to attend a protracted meeting. The congregation being very small held a short prayermeeting. At night had prayermeeting at Mr. John Hartman's, lectured from Luk. 15:11-24. All night at Daywalt Lentz's.

Sat. 28. Preached at the church from Amos 4:12. In the afternoon called to see Mr. Hartman. Restored him to membership in the church by a of the Council, & then administered to him the Lord's Supper.

Sund. 29. Preached at the church from Acts 26:17.18. Returned home in the evening.

Mond. 30. In the forenoon went to Post Office, and assisted Post Master in making out his quarterly settlement.

Tues. July 1. At home, harvesting Oats.

Wed. 2. At home till afternoon, then went to Gold Hill.

Thurs. 3. At home.

Frid. July 4. Went to Charles Fisher's & then to Geo. Klutts' to Tan yard.

Sat. 5. Went to John Miller's to see the thresher start.

Sund. 6. Preached at St. Stephen's from Acts 17:30.31. Took dinner at D. Earnheart's — In the afternoon at School house from Matt. 4:10.

Mond. 7. Part of the day at Col. Holshouser's threshing wheat.

Tues. 8. At home threshing wheat.

Wed. 9. Went to Iredell. All night at Cha.ˢ Barringer's.

Thurs. 10. Attended to business & then returned home.

Frid. 11. Sat 12. At home.

Sund. 13. Preached at Organ ch. from Jer. 6:16. Baptized 4 chil. Dinner at Leonard Klutts'. In the afternoon at Peter Lentz's dec.ᵈ his funeral from Ecl. 9:10. Bapt.ᵈ one infant.

Mond. 14. At home cleaning wheat.

Tues. 15. In the afternoon went to John Trexler's & helped thresh wheat.

Wed. 16. At home cleaning wheat.

Thurs. 17. In the morning went to mill — in the afternoon to Gold Hill.

Frid. 18. At home.

Sat. 19. Had catechization at Luther's ch. In the afternoon preached from Math. 4:10. In the evening returned home.

Sund. 20. Preached at St. Stephen's ch. from John 3:36. & in the afternoon at the School house from Is. 48:18.

Mond. 21. At home.

Tues. 22. In the evening went to John Trexler's Esq. & spent the night with him.

Wed. 23. Returned home. In the evening went to John Miller's to see Andr. Barrier's wife, she having been badly hurt by the running away of a horse in the Buggie. — All night here.

Thurs 24. Took dinner at the widow Miller's, and in the evening returned home.

Frid. 25. In the afternoon went to John Miller's to see Mrs. Barrier.

Sat. 26. Went to tax-paying, All night at Dan.ᴸ Miller's.

Sund. 27. Preached at Organ ch. from Luk. 11:32. Bapt. 1 inf.ᵗ.

Mond. 28. At home.

Tues. 29. In the afternoon went to Gold Hill.

Wed. 30. Called to see Mrs. Barrier & went to Mr. Klutts' to tan-yard.

Thurs. 31. Went in afternoon to Stephan Kirk's & married Mr. Ellick M. Miller to Miss Edith Kirk. All night at Conrad Miller's.

Frid. Aug. 1. Returned home.

Sat. 2. Went to Gold Hill.

Sund. 3. Preached at St. Stephen's ch. from Luk. 11:32. Dinner at John Powlass'. In the afternoon at School house from Mal. 3:7. Germ. Baptized to day at St. Stephen's one inf^t.

Mond. 4. In the afternoon went to John Miller's to see Mrs. Barger.

Tues. 5. Went to Philip Earnheart's & married James Montgomery to Leah Earnheart.

Wed. 6. Went to Salisbury. Over night at Danl Peeler's.

Thurs. 7. Attended to the funeral of Jacob Trexler's child at Lower St. church. Preached from Math. 25:13.

Frid. 8. Went to mill & to David Holshouser's & had cutting box repaired.

Sat. 9. In the forenoon went to Gold Hill. In afternoon at home.

Sund. 10. Preached at Organ ch. from John 3:36. Germ. and Engl. from same text.

Mond. 11. Went to Salisbury.

Tues. 12. Wed. 13. At home.

Thurs 14. Went to Henry Troutman's & married Danl Brown to Leah Troutman.

Frid. 15. At home.

Sat. 16. Went to Luther's Church & had catechization & preached from Prov. 3:6.

Sund. 17. Preached at St. Stephen's ch. from Jam. 1:5. and in the afternoon at the School house from Acts 24:25.

Mond. 18. At home.

Tues. 19. Wed. 20. Thurs. 21. Frid. 22. At home.

Sat. 23. Attended church settlement at Organ Church.

Sund. 24. Preached at Organ ch. from Math. 20:1-16. Dinner at Simeon Miller's.

Mond. 25. In the afternoon went to Peter Trexler's.

Tues. 26. Attended & clerked the sale of Peter Lentz dec^d.

Wed. 27. In the forenoon went to Gold Hill to Shop.

Thurs. 28. At home building rock fence.

Frid. 29. Went awhile to Sale to Mr. Powlass'.

Sat. 30. Called to see Paul Heilig, & in afternoon went to Mathias Miller's. All night here.

Sund. 31. Preached at Dry's ch. from John 3:36. Germ. & from Josh. 23:8. Engl. All night at Danl Barrier's.

Mond. Sept. 1. Returned home.

Tues. 2. Made some arrangements for hay making. In afternoon butchered a beef.

Wed. 3. Thurs. 4. Frid. 5. At home haymaking.

Sat. 6. In the afternoon preached at Peter Troutman's from Ps. 50:15. Germ.

Sund. 7. Preached at St. Stephen's ch. from Ps. 51:2. In afternoon at schoolhouse from Rom. 1:16.

Mond. 8. Went to Andrew Troutman's & Gold Hill on business.

Tues. 9. Went to Andrew Troutman's & paid him some security money. In the afternoon started for Iredell as far as Danl Lyerly's.

Wed. 10. Went to Iredell. All night at B. Arey's.

Thurs. 11. In Iredell attending to business. All night at C. Barringer's.

Frid. 12. In Iredell. Started for home after night and reached home next morning for breakfast.

Sat. 13. At home.

Sund. 14. Preached at Organ ch. from Ps. 51:2. Baptized 2 infants. Din^r at Philip Eddleman's. In the afternoon had prayer meeting at Bostian's School house. All night at Augustus F. Graeber's.

Mond. 15. Returned home.

Tues. 16. At home, indisposed with Colic.

Wed. 17. Went to Gold Hill.

Thurs. 18. Frid. 19. Sat. 20. At home.

Sund. 21. Preached at St. Stephen's ch. from Danl 12:3. The congregational Miss. & Ed. Society held a meeting to day. In the afternoon preached at the School house from Math. 21:28-32.

Mond. 22. At home. To day Lucetta took sick.

Tues. 23. Wed. 24. Thurs. 25. At home Lucetta very sick.

Frid. 26. This morning awhile before 4 o'clock Lucetta died.

Sat. 27. Had Lucetta's funeral preached by Rev. Linn, then went with a few friends to Union Church Grave Yard & buried her. David Lentz & Lady with us to night.

Sund. 28. Had an appointment to day at Organ ch. but did not attend, my mind being desolate & not in a condition to preach.

Mond. 29. At home.

Tues. 30. Went to Salisbury.

Wed. Oct. 1. Assisted Jacob Holshouser in making out his quarterly settlement to the Post Office Department.

Thurs. 2. Went to Gold Hill.

Frid. 3. Attended to the fun[l] of Alex. Kesler's child at Union ch. preached from Ps. 90:12.

Sat. 4. At home.

Sund. 5. Preached at St. Stephen's from Ps. 136:23. & in the afternoon at the School house.

Mond. 6. Tues. 7. At home.

Wed. 8. Attended to the funeral of Mrs. Walton, widow of Jesse, at Union ch. preached from Math. 10:32.

Thurs. 9. At home.

Frid. 10. Went to Gold Hill to blacksmith shop.

Sat. 11. In the afternoon went to David Lentz's.

Sund. 12. Held a meeting to day of Miss. & Ed. Society of Organ ch. In the afternoon had prayermeeting in Germ. at Geo. Bost's.

Mond. 13. Went to Iredell — all night at Cha[s] Barringer's.

Tues. 14. In Iredell — All night at B. Arey's.

Wed. 15. In Iredell — all night at Thos. A. Patterson's.

Thurs. 16. In Iredell — all night at John Clark's.

Frid. 17. Preached at St. Michael's ch. from Ps. 51:2. At T. Brown's.

Sat. 18. Preached from Math. 10:32. All night at Jacob Thomas'.

Sund. 19. Preached from Jer. 17:9. 2 Cor. 13:5. All night at T. Brown's.

Mond. 20. Returned to B. Arey's.

Tues. 21. Returned home as far as Peter Berger's.

Wed. 22. Returned home.

Thurs. 23. At home.

Frid. 24. In the afternoon went to shop to Gold Hill.

Sat. 25. Had preparatory service at Organ ch. Rev. J. S. Heilig preached. Baptized two infants. In the afternoon went to Geo. Bost's & administered to him the communion, he being old & feeble. Baptized 1 infant. All night here.

Sund. 26. Rev. J. S. Heilig preached. Administered the Lord's Supper. All night at C. A. Heilig's Esq.

Mond. 27. Returned home.

Tues. 28. At home.

Wed. 29. In the morning went after Dr. Kelly for Sol. Peeler.

Thurs. 30. At home.

Frid. 31. Went to Peter Trexler's & made inventory of estate of Peter Lentz dec[d].

Sat. Nov. 1. Had preparatory service at St. Stephen's Church. Rev. Arey preached. All night at Mrs. Peck's. At night had prayer meeting at the ch. — lectured from Math, 21:28-38.

Sund. 2. Revd Arey preached again, afterward's administered the Lord's Supper. Dinner at John Lentz's.

Mond. 3. Went to Isaac Kesler's & attended to the funeral of Elizabeth Linn, preached from Am. 4:12.

Tues. 4. Went to Salisbury.

Wed. 5. Went to Philip Earnheart's, a jury having been summoned to decide as to his capacity to manage his own affairs.

Thurs. 6. Went to mill to D. Miller's. had a chill to day.

Frid. 7. Returned home, had another chill.

Sat. 8. Sund. 9. Mond. 10. In bed, very sick.

Tues. 11. Wed. 12. Confined to room.

Thurs. 13. Frid. 14. Able to be about.

Sat. 15. Went to school house to singing.

Sund. 16. Preached at St. Stephen's Church from Ex. 14:15.

Mond. 17. Went to Salisbury. All night at D. Barringer's.

Tues. 18. Attended to the funeral of Lewis Walton at his residence. Buried him at Peter Walton's.

Wed. 19. Thurs. 20. At home, Mr. and Mrs. Clark with us to night.

Frid. 21. In the afternoon went to Jacob Miller's.

Sat. 22. Preached at Union ch. from 2 Cor. 5:17. Dinner at D. Barringer's.

Sund. 23. Preached at Organ ch. from Ps. 136:23. Germ. Dinner at Danl Miller's. In the afternoon at the School house from 2 Cor. 5:15.

Mond. 24. In the afternoon went to Mr. Linn's, Mrs. Linn being very sick. All night here.

Tues. 25. To day Mrs. Linn died. In the afternoon returned home.

Wed. 26. At home.

Thurs. 27. Attended to the fun^l of Mrs. Linn at Organ ch. preached from 2 Tim. 1:12.

Frid. 28. At home.

Sat. 29. Was to have assisted Rev. J. S. Heilig to day at Luther's Church, but having a severe cold & sore throat did not attend.

Sund. 30. Went in the morning early to Widow Barringer's & married William A. Lentz to Lunda M. Barringer. Started for Luther's ch. as far as Gold Hill, but weather being very inclement went no further.

Mond. Dec. 1. At home.

Tues. 2. In the morning went to Gold Hill.

Wed. 3. At home. Butchered hogs.

Thurs. 4. Commenced a protracted meeting at St. Stephen's ch. preached from John 4:14. Dinner at Solomon Nussman's.

Frid. 5. Preached at St. Stephen's from Luk. 18:9-14. Dinner at John Lentz's Sen. At night had prayermeeting at the Church.

Sat. 6. Preached at St. Stephen's from Prov. 22:6. Dinner at Wm. Culp's. Baptized 3 children. Prayermeeting at night at the church.

Sund. 7. Confirmed 3 persons, preached from Neh. 2:17. Returned home.

Mond. 8. This morning Mrs. R. hurt herself badly by falling.

Tues. 9. Wed. 10. Thurs. 11. Frid. 12. Sat. 13. Confined to home.

Sund. 14. Preached at Organ ch. from 2 Kings 20:1. the fun[1] of Mrs. John Lingle who died some time before. In the afternoon at the School House from Luk. 18:9-14.

Mond. 15. At home.

Tues. 16. Went to Gold Hill.

Wed. 17. Thurs. 18. At home.

Frid. 19. At home.

Sat. 20. Went to Gold Hill & had horse shod & collected subscribers for Am. Messenger, Child's Paper, &c.

Sund. 21. Preached at St. Stephen's ch. from Is. 9:6. and in the afternoon at the School house from Math. 4:19.

Mond. 22. Went to John Trexler's and then to the widow Wm. Miller's to inquire into & settle some misunderstandings.

Tues. 23. Went to Gold Hill and collected subscribers to Am. Mes. & Child's Paper &c. At night attended a meeting of Gold Hill Bible Society. All night at Dr. Kelly's.

Wed. 24. Attended to the fun[1] of Widow Mowry's child at Organ Church. preached from Math. 19:14.

Thurs. 25. Called to see Jacob Miller, he being sick, commenced a protracted meeting to day at Organ Church —preached from Is. 9:6. At night had prayermeeting at Bostian's school house — lectured from Luk. 18:9-14. All night at Philip Eddleman's.

Frid. 26. At Organ ch. Rev. Lantz preached for me to day. In the afternoon called to see Jacob Miller — At night had prayermeeting at Klutts' School house, lectured from Math. 4:19. All night at Charles Fisher's.

Sat. 27. Preached at Organ ch. from John 5:40. Dinner at John Miller's. In the evening returned home.

Sund. 28. Went in the morning before day (having been sent for) to see Jacob Miller. Preached to day at Organ ch. from Math. 25:14-30. In the afternoon called to see Jacob Miller & then returned home.

Mond. 29. Wrote to Am. Tract Society & sent on money for Am. Messenger & Child's Paper. In the afternoon went to Jacob Miller's. All night here.

Tues. 30. At home.

Wed. 31. Assisted Mr. J. Holshouser in making out his quarterly settlement. In the afternoon called to see Jacob Miller.

Thurs. Jan. 1, 1852. At home.

Frid. 2. At home till afternoon then went to see Jacob Miller. All night here.

Sat. 3. Returned home. In the afternoon went to Paul Beaver's & had a coat cut for Lewis.

Sund. 4. Preached at St. Stephen's ch. from Heb. 6:12. Dinner at John Lentz's. In the afternoon at the School House from Math. 26:41.

Mond. 5. In the afternoon went to Gold Hill.

Tues. 6. In the afternoon went to see Jacob Miller.

Wed. 7. At home.

Thurs. 8. Frid. 9. No account kept.

Sat. 10. In the afternoon went to Frederick Stirewalt's & at night had prayermeeting at Bostian's School house — lectured from Math. 4:19. All night at Mich[l] Overcash's.

Sund. 11. Preached at Organ ch. from 1 Chron. 28:9. Germ. Baptized one inft. Dinner at John Miller's.

Mond. 12. Tues. 13. At home.

Wed. 14. Went by way of Caleb Heilig's to widow Safret's and married William Safret to Catherine Blackwelder — All night at Widow Fisher's.

Thurs. 15. Went to Salisbury.

Frid. 16. At home.

Sat. 17. At St. Stephen's Church. The congregation met to day, at the request of some disatisfied members, to decide the question whether there should be a change of preachers or not. The disatisfied lost it by a vote of more than 2 to 1.

Sund. 18. Preached at St. Stephen's ch. from 1 Chron. 28:9. Dinner at Mr. Laurence Lingle's.

Mond. 19. Tues. 20. At home.

Wed. 21. In the afternoon went to Gold Hill.

Thurs. 22. Frid. 23. At home.

Sat. 24. Went to Bostian's School house & preached from Math. 5:1-12. Dinner at Dan[l] Eddleman's. All night at John Eagle's.

Sund. 25. Preached at Organ ch. from 2 Tim. 3:15. All night at Peter Ketner's.

Mond. 26. Attended to the fun[l] of Mrs. Mich[l] Overcash — preached from Phil. 1:21. Called at Paul N. Heilig's & baptized his child it being sick.

Tues. 27. In the afternoon went to John Trexler's, he & mother being sick — all night here.

Wed. 28. In the afternoon went to Mr. Powlass', Jesse's wife being sick & went to Gold Hill.

Thurs. 29. Called to see Jacob Miller & John Trexler.

Frid. 30. In the afternoon went to John Bost's & baptized his child, it being very sick.

Sat. 31. Went to Gold Hill.

Sund. Feb. 1. Preached at St. Stephen's ch. from 2 Tim. 3:15. Baptized 3 children.

Mond. 2. Attended to the fun[l] of John Bost's child at Organ ch. preached from 2 Sam. 12:23. Dinner at John Seaford's.

Tues. 3. At home.

Wed. 4. Went to Widow Safret's and Geo. H. Ritchie to Eliza Safret.

Thurs. 5. In the went to Jacob Lyerla's & married Caleb Trexler to Elizabeth L. Lyerla. Afterwards attended to the fun[l] Mrs. Eleonor Fraley at Lower St. ch. preached from Eccl. 8:12.

Frid. 6. Went to Gold Hill.

Sat. 7. Went to Bostian's School House & preached from Ps. 116:12-24. All night at John Yost's.

Sund. 8. Preached at Organ Church from Math. 5:13-16. Bapt. 4 inf[ts].

Mond. 9. Went M. Barrier's Esq.

Tues. 10. Returned home.

Wed. 11. Went to look at Fraley's plantation.

Thurs. 12. Went to Gold Hill.

Frid. 13. Went to John and Jacob Miller's.

Sat. 14. In the afternoon went to William Culp's & staid over night.

Sund. 15. Preached at St. Stephen's ch. from Math. 5:13-16. Dinner at Dr. Kelly's. In the afternoon heard preaching by a Baptist preacher.

Mond. 16. Attended to the fun[l] of Mrs. Zaceriah Lyerla at Organ ch. preached from Is. 3:10. Dinner at Widow Miller's.

Tues. 17. At home.

Wed. 18. At home mending shoes.

Thurs. 19. Frid. 20. At home plowing.

Sat. 21. At home.

Sund. 22. Preached at Organ ch. from Ez. 33:11. Germ. Baptized one infant. Dinner at Joseph Miller's.

Mond. 23. Went to Rocky River Church in company with David Miller to get information in relation to the Academy taught there. Over night at John Bost's.

Tues. 24. Returned home.

Wed. 25. At home.

Thurs. 26. Frid. 27. Clerked sale at Fraley's.

Sat. 28. At Fraley's till 12 o'clock. In afternoon at home.

Sund. 29. Went to the new church near John Berger's & preached from Ex. 33:14. All night at John Berger's.

Mond. Mar. 1. Returned home.

Tues. 2. Wed. 3. At home.

Thurs. 4. Went with Rev. B. Arey to Mr. Geo. M. Bernhardt's.

Frid. 5. At home.

Sat. 6. Attended in the morning at 8 o'clock at Peter Peeler's & preached the fun[l]. of his son Moses dec[d] At 11 o'clock preached the fun[l] of George Brown decd. at his late residence.

Sund. 7. Preached at St. Stephen's ch. from John 3:16. Dinner at John Powlass'.

Mond. 8. Engaged in trying to make a School for Mr. Robison.

Tues. 9. In the afternoon called at Col. Holshouser's on the subject of the School.

Wed. 10. Called at various places soliciting scholars for the School. Called also at Col. D. Lentz's.

Thurs. 11. Went to Gold Hill.

Frid. 12. At home sowing clover seed.

Sat. 13. Preached in the afternoon at Bostian's School House from John 3:16. Dinner at Jer. Graeber's. All night at Jacob Bostian's.

Sund. 14. Preached at Organ ch. from Ps. 119:63. Baptized 1 inf[t]. After preaching held a meeting of the Miss. & Ed. Society.

Mond. 15. At home till 12 o'clock, then went to Dr. Cunningham's to see Mrs. Dan[l] Brown she being there sick.

Tues. 16. At home.

Wed. 17. At home.

Thurs. 18. Attended to the funl of Mrs. Dan[l] Brown at Organ Church preached from Ps. 73:24. Dinner at Moses Barringer's — assisted Mr. B. in making his quarterly statement with the Post Office Department. In the evening went to Philip Cruse's & married Dan[l] Fisher to Rose Ann Cruse — All night at Geo. Randleman's.

Frid. 19. Returned home by way of Salisbury.

Sat. 20. Commenced catechization at St. Stephen's Church.

Sund. 21. Preached at St. Stephen's ch. from John 4:34. In the afternoon at the School House from Acts 13:26.

Mond. 22. Tues. 23. At home.

Wed. 24. Went to Milas Arey's to engage some plank.

Thurs. 25. Went to John Barger's and married John S. Long to Esther Barger.

Frid. 26. At Mr. Barger's.

Sat. 27. Preached at Barger's ch. from Ps. 116:12-14. Returned home.

Sund. 28. Preached at Organ ch. from John 4:34.

Mond. 29. Tues. 30. At home.

Wed. 31. Assisted J. Holshouser in making his quarterly settlement with P. O. Dep[t].

Thur. April 1. Went to Lants' sale.

Frid. 2. At home.

Sat. 3. Had catechization at St. Stephen's ch.

Sund. 4. Preached at St. Stephen's ch. from Prov. 14:32. In the afternoon at the School House from Luk. 17:32.

Mond. 5. At home. Revd Efirt called to see me.

Tues. 6. At home, till 12 o'clock then went to Danl Icehower's to engage some furniture.

Wed. 7. Went to Jacob House's & married Eli A. Propst to Amelia A. House. All night at Danl Miller's.

Thurs. 8. Returned home.

Frid. 9. Attended singing at Low^r St. Church.

Sat. 10. In the forenoon went to Gold Hill.

Sund. 11. Preached at Organ ch. from Luk. 11:32. Germ.* Had an appointment at Bostian's School house for the afternoon, but the day being rainy, did not attend.

Mond. 12. Tues. 13. At home.

Wed. 14. Thurs. 15. At home.

Frid. 16. Had catechization at St. Stephen's ch.

Sat. 17. Preached at St. Stephen's ch. preparatory to communion from Prov. 23:26.

Sund. 18. Preached at St. Stephen's ch. from Math. 22:1-14. afterwards administered the sacrament of the Lord's Supper.

Mond. 19. Tues. 20. At home.

Wed. 21. Attended to the funeral of Peter Mowry at Lower St. ch. preached from Heb. 9:27.

Thurs. 22. Went Laurence Lingle's & married John Trexler Esq. to Anna Lingle.

Frid. 23. At home.

Sat. 24. Attended to the fun^l of Peter Trexler's wife at Lower St. ch. preached from Job 23:16. Afterwards preached at Organ ch. from 1 Cor. 11:28. preparatory to the Lord's Supper. In the afternoon held a meeting of the Gold Hill Bible Society. All night at John Miller's. Bapt^d to day 3 infants.

Sund. 25. Preached at Organ ch. from Luk. 14:22. & administered the Lord's Supper. Dinner at Jacob Miller's.

Mond. 26. At home.

Tues. 27. Attended to the fun^l of Alex. Cauble at Organ ch. preached from Gen. 3:19.

Wed. 28. Started for Synod as far as Caleb Peeler's.

Thurs. 29. Went as far as John Cobb's — all night here.

Frid. 30. Went to Frieden's ch. To day Synod commenced. All night at Lud. Summers' Esq.

* Baptized to day 4 inf^{ts}.

Sat. May 1. At Synod — preached to day from Luk. 11:32. All night at Ludwig Summers Esq.

Sund. 2. At the Church. All night at Jacob Foust's.

Mond. 3. At Synod. All night at Jacob Summers.

Tues. 4. At Synod. All night at Lud. Summers' Esq.

Wed. 5. Started for home — all night at Eli Harris'.

Thurs. 6. Reached home.

Frid. 7. At home — Not well.

Sat. 8. Went to Gold Hill — Not well.

Sund. 9. Preached at Organ ch. from Ps. 73:1. Had an appointment for the afternoon at Bostian's School House, but did not attend, being quite indisposed. Dinner at John Miller's.

Mond. 10. Tues. 11. At home.

Wed. 12. Went to widow Graeber's & married John Lippard to Louisa R. H. Graeber. Dinner to day at Mrs. Heilig's. All night at Aug. Graeber's.

Thurs. 13. Returned home.

Frid. 14. At home.

Sat. 15. Had catechization at St. Stephen's ch. All night at John Culp's.

Sund. 16. Preached at St. Stephen's ch. from Ps. 5:7. Baptized one infant. Dinner at Dr. Kelly's. In the afternoon preached at the School House from Acts 17:30.

Mond. 17. Went to Salisbury. All night at Wm. Smith's.

Tues. 18. Returned home.

Wed. 19. At home.

Thurs. 20. Went to widow Smith's & married Alexander Bostian to Mary E. Smith.

Frid. 21. At home.

Sat. 22. Commenced catechization at Organ Church. Dinner at Jesse Barger's. All night at P. A. Seaford's.

Sund. 23. In the morning married George M. Ketner to Margaret Seaford. Preached at Organ ch. from Acts 10:38. Germ. Dinner at John Foutz's.

Mond. 24. Went to mill & in the afternoon to Gold Hill and had horse shod.

Tues. 25. Attended to the fun[l] of David Lentz (son of Jacob) at Organ ch. preached from Job 14:14. Germ. Dinner at John Miller's. In the evening went to Mrs. Peacock's (widow) & married George Moyer to Mrs. Peack.

Wed. 26. In the afternoon went to David Barringer's — all night here.

Thurs. 27. Went to Salisbury — in the afternoon returned home.

Frid. 28. Went to Laurence Lingle's to barn covering. All night at Jacob Randleman's.

Sat. 29. Returned home. Messrs. Clarke & Brown & families called to see us from Iredell.

Sund. 30. To day held the annual meeting of the Missionary and Education Society of Organ ch. In the afternoon attended to the fun[l] of old Mrs. Troutman at the Lower Stone Church, preached from Job 14:14.

Mond. 31. At home.

Tues. June 1. At home.
Wed. 2. Went to mill.
Thurs. 3. Moved into my study.
Frid. 4. Engaged hands for haymaking.
Sat. 5. Had catechization at St. Stephen's ch. All night at David Culp's.
Sund. 6. Preached at St. Stephen's from Prov. 14:34. Dinner at Dr. Kelly's. In the afternoon preached at School House from Gal. 5:1.
Mond. 7. At home. Commenced mowing grass, but weather very unfavorable.
Tuesd. 8. In the afternoon went to Gold Hill.
Wed. 9. Went to Danl Isahower & settled for some furniture.
Thurs. 10. Frid. 11. At home.
Sat. 12. Had catechization at Organ ch.
Sund. 13. Revd J. S. Heilig preached for me at Organ ch. Baptized one infant. Dinner at Danl Eddleman's. In the afternoon preached at Bostian's School House from Ps. 1:1-6. Called to see John Smith, he being afflicted with palsy. All night at Danl Eddleman's.
Mond. 14. Returned home.
Tues. 15. In the afternoon went to mill.
Wed. 16. At home.
Thurs. 17. At home.
Frid. 18. Went to Salisbury & brought Buggy home.
Sat. 19. Had catechization at St. Stephen's ch. All night at Danl Miller's.
Sund. 20. Preached at St. Stephen's ch. from Math. 11:28.
Mond. 21. Looked out for hands to help harvest.
Tues. 22. Wed. 23. At home.
Thurs. 24. Went to Gold Hill.
Frid. 25. At home.
Sat. 26. Had catechization at Organ ch. All night at Jacob Fisher's.
Sund. 27. Preached at Organ ch.* from Luk. 18:9-14. In the afternoon at Bostian's School House from John 9:4. Germ. All night at Philip Eddleman's.
Mond. 28. Returned home.
Tues. 29. Wed. 30. At home.

* Baptized to day at Organ ch. one infant.

Thurs. July 1. At home.

Frid. 2. Aided Mr. Holshouser in making out his quarterly statement.

Sat. 3. Had catechization at St. Stephen's ch. Dinner at Mr. Hegler's. All at Peter Peck's.

Sund. 4. Preached at St. Stephen's ch. from John 5:39. & in the afternoon at our School House from same.

Mond. 5. Tues. 6. Wed. 7. At home.

Thurs. 8. Had wheat threshed.

Frid. 9. Helped thresh at Mrs. Peeler's.

Sat. 10. Had catechization at Organ ch. Dinner at Moses Barringer's.

Sund. 11. Preached at Organ ch. from Eccl. 9:10. Germ. Baptized 1 inf^t. Installed two Deacons. In the afternoon had Bible-Class. Dinner at Jacob Miller's.

Mond. 12. In afternoon went to Gold Hill.

Tues. 13. At home.

Wed. 14. Thurs. 15. Frid. 16. No account kept.

Sat. 17. Had catechization at St. Stephen's ch. Dinner at Sol. Nussman's. All night at M. Barrier's Esq.

Sund. 18. Preached at St. Stephen's ch. from 1 Chron. 28:9. Baptized one inf^t.

Mond. 19. Tues. 20. At home. Wife sick.

Wed. 21. In the afternoon went to Concord to attend Convention. All night at Mr. Alfred Brown's.

Thurs. 22. In Concord. Preached from John 5:39. All night at Mrs. Arey's.

Frid. 23. In Concord. Reached home late at night.

Sat. 24. Attended to the funeral of Col. A. Holshouser at Lower St. Church — preached from Josh. 23:8. In the afternoon attended Tax-paying.

Sund. 25. Preached at Organ ch. from 1 Chron. 28:9. Baptized one infant. Held meeting of Miss. & Ed. Society. Revd Artz with me to night.

Mond. 26. At home.

Tues. 27. Went to Mich^l L. Brown's & married Peter A. Fisher to Elizabeth C. Brown.

Wed. 28. Thurs. 29. At home.

Frid. 30. Had catechization at Organ ch.

Sat. 31. Had catechization at St. Steven's ch.

Sund. Aug. 1. Revd J. S. Heilig preached for me at St. Stephen's ch. — Bible class.

Mond. 2. Went to Salisbury.

Tues. 3. Attended to the funeral of Melchor Troutman at Organ ch. preached from Is. 3:10.

Wed. 4. At home.

Thurs. 5. Went to Gold Hill to election.

Frid. 6. At home.

Sat. 7. Had catechization at Organ ch. All night at Chas Fisher's.

Sund. 8. Preached at Organ ch. from Prov. 1:24.25.26. Bible class after preaching. In the afternoon preached the funeral of John Josey dec^d at his residence from Math. 25:10

Mond. 9. At home.

Tues. 10. In the afternoon went to Gold Hill to blacksmith-shop.

Wed. 11. Attended to the fun^l of Andr. Berger's child at Lower St. ch. preached from Math. 2:18. Returned home by way of David Lentz's.

Thurs. 12. Frid. 13. At home.

Sat. 14. Had catechization at St. Stephen's ch. All night at George Culp's.

Sund. 15. Preached at St. Stephen's from Prov. 1:24.25.26. Bapt. one infant. Bible class after preaching. In the afternoon attended preaching in the Methodist church on Gold Hill.

Mond. 16. At home.

Tues. 17. At home.

Wed. 18. Went after a load of shingles.

Thurs. 19. In the afternoon went to Mrs. Heilig's & married Reuben Y. Holmes to R. S. Caroline Heilig. Revd Artz & daughter came to my house this evening.

Frid. 20. Sat. 21. At home. Saturday was my day for catechization at Organ ch. but the day being very rainy did not attend.

Sund. 22. To day Revd Artz preached at Organ ch. in Engl. Followed in Germ. from 2 Cor. 5:17. All night at Jacob Miller's.

Mond. 23. Returned home. In the afternoon went to Gold Hill.

Tues. 24. Wed. 25. At home.

Thurs. 26. Went to Mr. Weaver's & married Alexander Yost to Elizabeth S. Weaver. All night at Henry J. Barringer's.

Frid. 27. Went to Chas Barringer's.

Sat. 28. Had an appointment at St. Michael's ch. but the rain & high waters prevented the congregation from assembling. All night at Tobias Brown's.

Sund. 29. Preached at St. Michael's from Prov. 1:24-26. In the afternoon preached at the widow King's from Math. 25:10. All night at Chas Barringer's.

Mond. 30. Returned home.

Tues. 31. At home. Adam with me to night.

Wed. Sept. 1. Thurs. 2. At home.

Frid. 3. At home.

Sat. 4. Had catechization at St. Stephen's ch.

Sund. 5. Preached at St. Stephen's ch. from Phil. 3:20. Bible class after preaching.

Mond. 6. Went to Post Office and in the afternoon to Gold Hill.

Tues. 7. Wed. 8. Thurs. 9. Frid. 10. At home.

Sat. 11. Had catechization at Organ ch.

Sund. 12. Preached at Organ ch. from Acts 17:30.31. Baptized one inft. Bible class after preaching. Dinner at John Miller's.

Mond. 13. Tues. 14. Wed. 15. At home.

Thurs. 16. Frid. 17. At home.

Sat. 18. Had catechization at St. Stephen's ch. − Dinner at Mrs. Peck's. All night at Solomon Nussman's.

Sund. 19. Preached at St. Stephen's ch. from Ps. 40:1-3. Baptized one inf^t. Miss. & Ed. Society met. Dinner at Dr. Kelly's.

Mond. 20. Went to Salisbury.

Tues. 21. Went to Salisbury.

Wed. 22. Went to Gold Hill & brought Dr. Kelly out wife being sick.

Thurs. 23. At home.

Frid. 24. This my day for catechization at Organ ch. but did not attend, family being sick.

Sat. 25. Went to Danl Miller's (creek) on business.

Sund. 26. To day Revd Artz preached for me at Organ ch. − Afterwards preached the funeral of Martha Klutts, wife of James from Numb. 23:10. Dinner at John Miller's.

Mond. 27. Tues. 28. At home.

Wed. 29. Went to Danl Isahower's on business.

Thurs. 30. Attended to the fun^l of Mrs. Danl Peeler at Lower St. ch. preached from Ps. 4:3. Dinner at John Knup's. All night at Robard's Tavern, Salisbury.

Frid. Oct. 1. Went to Jacob Goodman's & preached from Luk. 13:24. Baptized his child. All night here.

Sat. 2. Went to Shepherd's + Roads to assist Revd^d Arey at a communion meeting. Commenced preaching but got very sick. Sick in the afternoon. All night at Mrs. McNeely's.

Sund. 3. Preached for Rev. Arey from Ps. 40:1-3. & in afternoon from Ps. 116:12. Dinner at Mrs. McNeely's — All night at Alexander Brown's.

Mond. 4. Started for home — got very sick on the way — All night at Robard's, Salisbury.

Tues. 5. Returned home.

Wed. 6. At home.

Thurs. 7. Assisted J. Holshouser in his quarterly settlement.

Frid. 8. Went to St. Enoch's ch. All night at Fran. Overcash's.

Sat. 9. Preached at St. Enoch's ch. from Rev. 3:20. All night at D. M. Isenhower's.

Sund. 10. Preached again from Ps. 40:1-3. Assisted in communion. All night at widow Beaver's.

Mond. 11. Returned home.

Tues. 12. Attended to the funeral of Barbara M. Patterson at Organ ch. Preached from Eccl. 9:10.

Wed. 13. In the afternoon aided in laying off one year's provision for Widow Holshouser (of Alex^r.)

Thurs. 14. In afternoon went to School house to election of committee.

Frid. 15. Had catechization at St. Stephen's ch.

Sat. 16. Preached at St. Stephen's from Rev. 3:20. preparatory to communion. Baptized 1 inft.

Sund. 17. Revd Arey preached for me — Administered the Lord's Supper. Dinner at Dr. Kelly's.

Mond. 18. Tues. 19. At home.

Wed. 20. At home. Danl Miller with me to day.

Thurs. 21. Attended the sale at Col. Holshouser's, dec^d.

Frid. 22. Had catechization at Organ ch.

Sat. 23. Had preparatory service at Organ ch. Revd Heilig with me. Preached Germ. from Luk. 5:32. Baptized four infants.

Diary No. 16

Sund. 24. At Organ church. Rev. Heilig preached. Afterwards administered the Lord's Supper.

Mond. 25. Went to Gold Hill & had horse shod.

Tues. 26. Went to G. M. Bernhardt's on business.

Wed. 27. Called to see Philip Eddleman, he being sick. Administered to him the Lord's Supper. All night here.

Thurs. 28. Called to see John Smith, an aged member of the church, he being sorely afflicted with Palsy. Went to Danl Beaver's & married Mr. Beaver to Anna C. Rimer. All night at Thos Atwell's.

Frid. 29. Went to Tobias Brown's. All night at John Clarke's.

Sat. 30. Preached at St. Michael's ch. from Rev. 3:20. preparatory to communion. All night at Tobias Brown's.

Sund. 31. Preached at St. Michael's from 1 Thes. 2:11.12. Then assisted Revd Arey in the administration of the Eucharist. All night at Revd B. Arey's.

Mond., Nov. 1. Attended to some settlements. In the afternoon started home as far a Peter Berger's. All night here.

Tues. 2. Attended the Presidential election in Salisbury. Went & spent the night with D. Barringer.

Wed. 3. Returned home.

Thurs. 4. In the afternoon went to Gold Hill on business.

Frid. 5. Went to see John Smith & administered to him the Lord's Supper. Called also to see Philip Eddleman & then returned home.

Sat. 6. Had catechization at St. Stephen's church.

Sund. 7. A very inclement morning. The congregation being small did not preach but went over the Bible Lesson.

Mond. 8. At home.

Tues. 9. In the afternoon went to John Lentz's & had horse shod.

Wed. 10. Attended to the fun^{l} of Moses Klutts' child at Lower St. ch. − preached from Ps. 34:19.

Thurs. 11. Went to Widow Fisher's & married William A. Houck to Catherine L. Fisher. All night here.

Frid. 12. Returned home.

Sat. 13. Had catechization at Organ ch. All night at C. A. Heilig's Esq.

Sund. 14. Preached at Organ ch. from Ps. 40:1-3. Baptized 2 inf^{ts}. In the afternoon called to see old Mrs. Josey, (aged & frail) & administered to her the Lord's Sup^{r}.

Mond. 15. At home.

Tues. 16. Went to Post office.

Wed. 17. At home.

Thurs. 18. Started for Iredell as far as Alexander Brown's.

Frid. 19. Went to St. Michael's ch. and preached from 1 Thes. 5:6. Dinner at Andr. Barringer's. All night at Daywald Harkey's.

Sat. 20. Preached at St. Paul's ch. from Math. 10:32.33. preparatory to communion. All night at Henry Lentz's.

Sund. 21. Preached at St. Paul's ch. from Ex. 33:14. & administered the Lord's Supper being assisted by Rev. B. Arey. All night at Rev. Arey's.

Mond. 22. A very rainy day. Returned home as far as Mich^{l} Brown's. All night here.

Tues. 23. Returned home.

Wed. 24. Went with wife to Gold Hill.

Thurs. 25. Went to Gold Hill to Blacksmith Shop.

Frid. 26. Called to see Mrs. Peck, she being sick.

Sat. 27. Had catechization at Organ ch. Dinner at M. Barringer's.

Sund. 28. Preached at Organ ch. the fun^{l} of Mrs. Jacob Cruse, from Ps. 34:19. Germ. Dinner at Jacob Miller's. Bap^{d} 1 inf^{t}.

Mond. 29. Tues. 30. At home.

Wed., Dec. 1. In the evening went to P. N. Heilig's & brought wife home.

Thurs. 2. Attended a meeting of the Board of Directors of the contemplated school at Organ ch. Dinner at Mrs. Heilig's.

Frid. 3. Had appointed a Protracted meeting to commence to day at St. Stephen's ch., but the day being very rainy did not get to the ch.

Sat. 4. Preached at St. Stephen's ch. from 1 Thes. 5:6. All night at M. Barrier's Esq.

Sund. 5. Preached at St. Stephen's from Luk. 15:11-24. Called to see Mrs. Peck.

Mond. 6. At home.

Tues. 7. Went to Post office.

Wed. 8. At home.

Thurs. 9. A very rainy day. Went to William Bost's and married Jesse Beaver to Catherine L. Bost.

Frid. 10. Went to Salisbury.

Sat. 11. Had catechization at Organ ch. Took dinner with old Mrs. Barringer (Widow).

Sund. 12. Preached at Organ ch. from Luk. 19:31. Dinner at John Miller's.

Mond. 13. At home, butchered hogs.

Tues. 14. At home.

Wed. 15. In the afternoon went to Gold Hill.

Thurs. 16. Went to Elihu Holshouser's & married Charles Lyerly to Sarah Holshouser. Then went to Jacob Bostian's & married George Smith to Margaret A. Bostian. All night here.

Frid. 17. Returned home.

Sat. 18. Had catechization at St. Stephen's ch.

Sund. 19. Preached at St. Stephen's ch. from Math. 12:22-42. Dinner at Dr. Kelly's.

Mond. 20. In the afternoon went to Mr. Linn's mill.

Tues. 21. At home. Married to day Milas Shuping to Mary Cauble. In the evening went to Jacob Holshouser's & staid all night.

Wed. 22. Thurs. 23. At home.

Frid. 24. Went to Gold Hill. In the afternoon went to Jacob Fisher's, Mrs. Fisher & son Lauson being sick.

Sat. 25. Had catechization at Organ ch. In the afternoon called at David Lentz's & Jacob Fisher's to see the sick.

Sund. 26. Preached at Organ ch. from Math. 1:21. Held a meeting of the Miss. & Ed. Society.

Mond. 27. Attended to the fun[1] of Mrs. Christena, wife of Jacob Fisher. Preached the fun[1] at Mr. Fisher's from Math. 5:6. Buried her at Lower St. Church.

Tues. 28. Went to Milas Arey's.

Wed. 29. Went to Casper Holshouser's & married Eli Seaford to Margaret Holshouser. All night here.

Thurs. 30. Returned home.

Frid. 31. Went to Gold on business.

Sat., Jan. 1. Had catechization at St. Stephen's ch.

Sund. 2. Preached at St. Stephen's ch. from Luk. 13:6-9. Dinner at Dr. Kelly's.

Mond. 3. At home.

Tues. 4. Aided Mr. Holshouser in making his quarterly settlement as Post Master. In the afternoon went to Mr. Moyer's for shoes. Bapt^d his child.

Wed. 5. Went to Geo. Goodman's in search of tallow for candles — & to J. Lentz's & had horse shod.

Thurs. 6. At home.

Frid. 7. Went to John Knup's for tallow.

Sat. 8. Had catechization at Organ ch.

Sund. 9. Preached at Organ ch. from Luk. 13:6-9. Germ. Baptized 2 children. Dinner at Mrs. Heilig's.

Mond. 10. In the afternoon went to Milas Arey's, all night here.

Tues. 11. Went to Salisbury.

Wed. 12. Went to David Holshouser's on business.

Thurs. 13. At home.

Frid. 14. Went to Gold Hill & to Wilie Knup's on business.

Sat. 15. Had catechization at St. Stephen's.

Sund. 16. Preached at St. Stephen's ch. from Math. 15:1-20. Baptized 2 inf^{ts}. Dinner at Dr. Kelly's.

Mond. 17. At home.

Tues. 18. Engaged some hands to chop wood.

Wed. 19. At home — had a chopping.

Thurs. 20. Went in the morning in company with D. Barringer to Gold Hill.

Frid. 21. Sat. 22. At home.

Sund. 23. Preached at Organ ch. from Math. 15:1-20. Installed 2 elders & 2 deacons.

Mond. 24. Tues. 25. At home.

Wed. 26. Went to Mt. Pleasant to attend a meeting of the Board of Directors of the School contemplated by the Synod of N. C., but a majority not being there no business was done. All night at Danl Miller's.

Thurs. 27. Returned home, calling at various places and settling accounts.

Frid. 28. Sat. 29. At home.

Sund. 30. Preached at our school house from 1 Cor. 13:1-13.

Mond. 31. In forenoon went to Gold Hill & Post Office.

Tues., February 1, 1853. At home, had hands hewing timber. Mr. John Clarke with us to night.

Wed. 2. In the morning went to Andr. Troutman's on business and to Gold Hill.

Thurs. 3. Frid. 4. Sat. 5. At home.

Sund. 6. Went to Salem ch. & preached from Luk. 13:6-9. A very rainy day. All night at Mr. Dan[l] Lyerly's.

Mond. 7. Returned home thro' Salisbury.

Tues. 8. In the afternoon went to Gold Hill.

Wed. 9. Thurs. 10. At home.

Frid. 11. At Widow Peeler's at chopping.

Sat. 12. Had catechization at Organ ch.

Sund. 13. Preached at Organ ch. from Luk. 13:6-9. Bapt[d] 1 inf[t].

Mond. 14. Tues. 15. At home, had hands hewing timber.

Wed. 16. In the morning went to Post Office.

Thurs. 17. Had Taylor shod at John Lentz's. Took Taylor to P. N. Heilig's. In the afternoon went to Mr. Linn's saw mill.

Frid. 18. Attended to the fun[l] of Mrs. Eli Klutts at Lower St. ch. Preached from Math. 24:44.

Sat. 19. This the day for catechization at St. Stephen's ch. but the day being very inclement did not attend.

Sund. 20. Preached at St. Stephen's ch. from Ps. 138:6.

Mond. 21. At home till afternoon then went to David Holshouser's for harrow.

Tues. 22. Went to Gold Hill.

Wed. 23. At home.

Thurs. 24. Frid. 25. At home.

Sat. 26. Had catechization at Organ church.

Sund. 27. Preached at Organ ch. from Jam. 1:25. Germ. Baptized two infants.

Mond. 28. At home.

Tues., March 1, 1853. Went to Gold Hill.

Wed. 2. At John Lentz's at Barn raising.

Thurs. 3. Frid. 4. At home.

Sat. 5. Had catechization at St. Stephen's ch. Dinner at Mr. Philip Hegler's. A very inclement day.

Sund. 6. Preached at St. Stephen's ch. from Eccl. 12:13.14. Baptized one infant.

Mond. 7. Went to Gold Hill to Blacksmith shop.

Tues. 8. Went to D. Barringer's.

Wed. 9. Thurs. 10. At home.

Frid. 11. At home.

Sat. 12. Had catechization at Organ ch. All night at Andrew Cruse's.

Sund. 13. Preached at Organ ch. from 1 Sam. 20:3. (latter clause). The funeral of Dan[l] Cruse, who was killed by the running away of his team of horses on the road to Fayetteville. Dinner at John Miller's.

Mond. 14. At home.

Tues. 15. Attended to the fun[l] of old Mrs. Josey at Organ ch. Preached from Math. 11:28.

Wed. 16. Went to Mt. Pleasant to attend the meeting of the Board of Directors. All night at Dan[l] Miller's.

Thurs. 17. Returned home. In the evening went to D. Barringer's. All night here.

Frid. 18. Returned home.

Sat. 19. Had catechization at St. Stephen's ch.

Sund. 20. Preached at St. Stephen's ch. from John 8:36. Baptized one infant.

Wed. 23. In the afternoon went to Widow Miller's to log rolling.

Thurs. 24. Went to Salisbury.

Frid. 25. Had catechization at Organ ch.

Sat. 26. Went to Union ch.

Sund. 27. Preached at Organ ch. from Ps. 138:6. Bapt. 5 inf[ts]. Dinner at Simeon Miller's.

Mond. 28. Went to Union ch. and preached from Ps. 40:1-3.

Tues. 29. Went to Gold Hill & Andrew Troutman's.

Wed. 30. Thurs. 31. At home.

Frid., April 1, 1853. At home.

Sat. 2. Had catechization at St. Stephen's ch. In the afternoon went William Culp's jr.in order to see about some shingles.

Sund. 3. Preached at St. Stephen's ch. from 2 Cor. 4:7. Dinner at Dr. Kelly's.

Mond. 4. In the afternoon went to J. Holshouser's & assisted him in making his quarterly settlement with Post Office Department.

Tues. 5. Wed. 6. At home.

Thurs. 7. Went to Washington Henly's & in the evening married Aaron W. Miller to Rachel L. Henly. All night at Peter Miller's.

Frid. 8. Returned home.

Sat. 9. Had catechization at Organ church.

Sund. 10. Preached at Organ ch. from Math. 12:41.42. Germ. Bapt^d 2 inf^{ts}. Dinner at Danl Miller's.

Mond. 11. Tues. 12. At home.

Wed. 13. Went to C. A. Heilig's Esqr. In the afternoon called to see Eve Ann Miller, she being sick.

Thurs. 14. Frid. 15. At home.

Sat. 16. Had an appointment for to day at St. Stephen's ch. for confirmation and preparatory service, but being indisposed, & the day very inclement, dispensed with service. All night at John Culp's.

Sund. 17. Much indisposed with cold. Preached from Jam. 1:25. Postponed communion. Dinner at Dr. Kelly's.

Mond. 18. At home, till afternoon, then went to Lower St. Church & attended to the fun^l of Regina Klutts. Preached from John 9:4.

Tues. 19. Went to Mt. Pleasant. All night at Col. Shimpock's.

Wed. 20. Attended a meeting of the Board of Directors of the contemplated school. A quorum not being present, no business was done. Returned home.

Thurs. 21. At home. In afternoon rolled logs.

Frid. 22. At home.

Sat. 23. Preached at Organ ch. from Ps. 50:14. preparatory to communion. Confirmed 61 persons. All night at Danl Eddleman's.

Sund. 24. Preached at Organ ch. from Jam. 1:25. & administered the Lord's Supper. Took dinner at Mrs. Heilig's.

Mond. 25. In the afternoon went to Gold Hill. Rev. Heilig & Lady with us to night.

Tues. 26. At home making some preparations to go to Synod.

Wed. 27. Started for Synod as far as Tobias Goodman's.

Thurs. 28. Dinner at T. Brown's. All night at Danl Smoyer's.

Frid. 29. Went to Newton. Synod commenced its sessions and continued till Wednesday evening May 4. Preached on Sunday morning from Jam. 1:25.

Thurs., May 5. Started for home. All night at Rev. B. Arey's.

Frid. 6. Reached home. Very sick all night.

Sat.. 7. Attended a meeting at Organ ch. on the subject of enlarging the church.

Sund. 8. This my day at Organ ch. but the day being inclement & health feeble, did not attend.

Mond. 9. At home till evening, then went to D. Barringer's.

Tues. 10. Attended to the funeral of Henry Holshouser dec^d at Lower St. ch. Preached from Amos 4:12. Dinner at Laurence Lingle's.

Wed. 11. Went to Salisbury. All night at B. F. Fraley's.

Thurs. 12. Returned home.

Frid. 13. At home.

Sat. 14. Preached at St. Stephen's ch. from Ps. 50:14. preparatory to communion. Confirmed 19 persons & baptized 1 adult. All night at G. M. Bernhardt's. Baptized also 2 infants.

Sund. 15. Preached from 1 Cor. 9:24-27. & then administered the Lord's Supper.

Mond. 16. At home.

Tues. 17. Went to Danl Miller's to mill.

Wed. 18. Returned home.

Thurs. 19. Frid. 20. Sat. 21. No account kept.

Sund. 22. Preached at Organ ch. from 1 Thes. 2:11.12. German. Baptized 2 inf^ts. Held a meeting of the Miss. & Ed. Society.

Mond. 23. Tues. 24. Wed. 25. No account kept.

Thurs. 26. Went to Moses Barringer's & married Osborne M. Klutts to Mary C. Barringer.

Frid. 27. Attended to the funeral of Solomon Klutts' child at Lower St. ch. Preached from Math. 19:14.

Sat. 28. In the afternoon went to Simeon Miller's & staid over night.

Sund. 29. Preached at Organ ch. from Ps. 133:1-3. Dinner at John Miller's.

Thurs. June 2. Went to Henry Klutts' & married George M. Fisher to Amy Klutts.

Frid. 3. At home.

Sat. 4. Went to Gold Hill and heard the congressional candidates.

Sund. 5. Preached at St. Stephen's ch. from Haggai 2:9. In the afternoon heard Revd Holtam at Gold Hill.

Mond. 6. Tues. 7. At home.

Wed. 8. Went to Mt. Pleasant & attended a meeting of the Board of Directors of W. C. M. Academy. All night at Laurence Lingle's.

Thurs. 9. At home.

Frid. 10. In the afternoon went to Henry Klutts'. All night here.

Sat. 11. Called to see John Smith which is afflicted with palsy. In the afternoon went to John Eagle's & met Henry Pless, his son-in-law V. Propst, & others & settled some misunderstandings between them. All night at Paul Miller's.

Sund. 12. Preached at Organ ch. from Hag. 2:9. Bapt^d 1 inft. Dinner at Joseph Miller's.

Mond. 13. Went in the evening to David Barringer's.

Tues. 14. Attended the burial of D. Barringer's child at Union ch. Dinner at Milas Arey's.

Wed. 15. Thurs. 16. Frid. 17. Sat. 18. At home.

Sund. 19. Preached at St. Stephen's ch. from Math. 6:10. Held a meeting of the Miss. & Ed. Society. In the afternoon attended a meeting of the Gold Bible Society.

Mond. 20. Went to Salisbury.

Tues. 21. At home.

Wed. 22. At night attended a meeting of Bible Society at Gold Hill.

Thurs. 23. Frid. 24. At home.

Sat. 25. Went to taxpaying at at Morgan's.

Sund. 26. Preached at Organ ch. from Rom. 10:1. Baptized four infants. Dinner at Moses Barringer's. In the afternoon met the Bible class. Stopped at Widow Miller's.

Mond. 27. Tues. 28. At home.

Wed. 29. Visited Frederic Yost, he being sick with consumption & administered to him the Lord's Supper. All night at _old_ Mr. Yost's.

Thurs. 30. Went to John Foutz's & married Joseph Beaver to Rachel M. Foutz.

Frid., July 1, 1853. At home.

Sat. 2. Went to taxpaying at Danl Klutts' in the Rocks.

Sund. 3. Preached at St. Stephen's ch. from Rom. 10:1. Had Bible Class before preaching. Dinner at Dr. Kelly's. Attended Bible Class in the afternoon at Gold Hill.

Mond. 4. Tues. 5. At home, had wheat threshed.

Wed. 6. Went to Gold Hill to Blacksmith's shop.

Thurs. 7. At home.

Frid. 8. At home.

Sat. 9. In the afternoon went to Peter Miller's & staid all night.

Sund. 10. Preached at Organ ch. after Bible class in the morning, from Prov. 14:32. Germ. Baptized three infants. In the afternoon preached Engl. from the same text. Dinner at John Miller's.

Mond. 11. Called to see sundry of the members of Organ ch.

Tues. 12. Attended to the funl. of John Lingle's daughter at Organ ch. — preached from Math. 5:8. Called to see several of the members of the church. All night at Danl Miller's.

Wed. 13. Attended to the funl. of Frederic Yost at Organ ch. — preached from Rev. 2:10. Visited some of the members. All night at Wm. Bost's.

Thurs. 14. Visited some & returned home.

Frid. 15. At home.

Sat. 16. In the afternoon went to Tobias Klutts' & staid all night.

Sund. 17. Preached at St. Stephen's ch. after Bible exercises in the morning, from Prov. 14:32. Dinner at Elias Link's. In the afternoon preached at Gold Hill from Luk. 13:24.

Mond. 18. In the evening went to Gold Hill on business.

Tues. 19. At home.

Wed. 20. At home.

Thurs. 21. In the afternoon attended to the funl. George Safret at Organ ch. — preached from Math. 25:13. In the afternoon went to Casper Holshouser's & married Jacob Klutts to Eliza M. Holshouser.

Frid. 22. At home.

Sat. 23. Went to Tax-paying. All night at Danl Miller's.

Sund. 24. Preached at Organ ch. from Ex. 23:2. In the afternoon held a meeting of the Miss. & Ed. Society.

Mond. 25. In the afternoon went to Gold Hill on business.

Tues. 26. Wed. 27. Thurs. 28. Visited some of the members of Organ Church.

Frid. 29. At home.

Sat. 30. In the afternoon went to singing at Lower St. ch. All night at Mr. Lingle's.

Sund. 31. Attended singing at Lower St. Church.

Mond. 1. Went to Salisbury.

Tues. 2. Wed. 3. At home.

Thurs. 4. Went to Gold Hill to

Frid. 5. Sat. 6. At home.

Sund. 7. Preached at St. Stephen's from Ps. 133:1-3. In the afternoon at Gold Hill from Luk. 13:6-9.

Mond. 8. At home.

Tues. 9. Went to Gold Hill & had likenesses (Daguerrotypes) taken.

Wed. 10. Went to Gold Hill to blacksmith's shop.

Thurs. 11. Frid. 12. At home.

Sat. 13. Attended a meeting of the congregation at Organ ch. on the subject of enlarging the church.

Sund. 14. Preached at Organ ch. from Mark 6:12. Baptized 2 infants.

Mond. 15. Tues. 16. Wed. 17. At home.

Thurs. 18. In the morning went to Gold Hill for nails. In the afternoon went to Mich[l] Peeler's and married John Lingle to Eve Ann Peeler. All night here.

Frid. 19. Returned home.

Sat. 20. At home.

Sund. 21. Preached at St. Stephen's from Prov. 14:34. In the afternoon at Gold Hill in the Meth. ch.

Mond. 22. At home.

Tues. 23. In the forenoon went to Gold Hill to Blacksmith shop.

Wed. 24. Went to John Trexler's Esq. & Mr. Linn's on business.

Thurs. 25. Started to St. Enoch's ch. All night at Allen Rose's.

Frid. 26. Preached at St. Enoch's ch. from Luk. 13:6-9. and in the afternoon from Mark 6:12. All night at Jacob Overcash's.

Sat. 27. Preached at St. Enoch's from Prov. 14:32. All night at Mich[l] Bostian's.

Sund. 28. Preached at Organ ch. from Gal. 5:1. Germ. Dinner at John Miller's.

Mond. 29. Tues. 30. At home.

Wed. 31. Attended to the funeral of Tobias Stirewalt at Organ ch. – preached from Eccl. 7:2. Germ.

Thurs. Sept. 1. Started to Davidson as far as Milas Arey's.

Frid. 2. Went to Caleb Peeler's.

Sat. 3. At Caleb Peeler's. A very rainy day.

Sund. 4. Preached at Hopewell from Rom. 10:1. Congregation small in consequence of rain. All night at H. Beckerdite's.

Mond. 5. Called to see, and spent the day with uncle Jos. Rothrock. All night at aunt Christena Ripple's. Met to day with uncle Peter Rothrock from Indiana.

Tues. 6. Went to Hezekiah Thomas'. All night here.

Wed. 7. Returned to Caleb Peeler's.

Thurs. 8. Started home as far as Isaac Kesler's. All night here.

Frid. 9. Returned home.

Sat. 10. At home.

Sund. 11. Preached at Organ ch. from Josh. 23:8. In the afternoon preached the fun[l] of Mrs. George Bost at the residence from Ps. 90:12. Germ.

Mond. 12. At home.

Tues. 13. Went to Gold Hill to shop.

Wed. 14. Went to Mt. Pleasant to meet Board of Directors.

Thurs. 15. Frid. 16. Sat. 17. At home.

Sund. 18. Preached at St. Stephen's from Ps. 61:2. Baptized 1 inf[t]. In the afternoon at Gold Hill from Josh. 23:8. Dinner at Mr. Love's.

Mond. 19. to Sat. 24. At home.

Sund. 25. Preached at Organ ch. from Ps. 61:2. Baptized 2 infants.

Mond. 26. At home.

Tues. 27. In the afternoon went to Paul Beaver's & baptized his child, it being very sick.

Thurs. 29. Attended to the funeral of Paul Beaver's child at L. St. church. — preached the funeral at the house from Math. 19:14. Germ. In the afternoon went to Martin Leppard's & married Jacob Klutts to Catharine L. Leppard. All night at John Seaford's.

Frid. 30. Attended to the fun[l] of Widow Boger at Organ ch. — preached from Rev. 14:13.

Sat., Oct. 1. Went to Mathias Barringer's old residence & preached the funeral of old Mrs. Hegler from Heb. 4:9. Baptised 3 chil^n

Sund. 2. Preached at St. Stephen's from Ps. 5:7. & in the afternoon at Gold Hill from 1 Cor. 9:24-27.

Mond. 3. At home.

Tues. 4. Attended to the funeral of Leonard Klutts at L. St. church. – preached from Rev. 2:10. Dinner at John Miller's.

Wed. 5. Went to Danl Frick's & Peter Miller's.

Thurs. 6. Had Peter Miller to spay some hogs.

Frid. 7. Went to Salisbury.

Sat. 8. Attended to the funeral of Dawalt Ketner at Organ ch. – preached from Mar. 13:34.35.

Sund. 9. Preached at Organ ch. from Mark 1:40-45. Germ. and Engl. from same. Baptized one inf^t.

Mond. 10. At home.

Tues. 11. Attended to the funeral of Andrew Berger's child at L. St. ch. – preached from Gen. 3:19.

Wed. 12. In the afternoon to Gold Hill to Shoe Shop.

Thurs. 13. In the evening went to Gold Hill after my boots.

Frid. 14. At home.

Sat. 15. Preached at St. Stephen's ch. from Prov. 28:13. preparatory to communion. Baptized 2 chil^n. Confirmed one person. In the afternoon attended to the fun^l of George Bost at Organ ch. – preached from Neh. 7:2.

Sund. 16. Preached at St. Stephen's ch. from 1 Thes. 2:11.12. and administered the Lord's Supper. At night preached at Gold Hill from Luk. 11:32. After preaching returned home.

Mond. 17. Went to George Bost's dec^d and read his Will to the heirs.

Tues. 18. At home. Had shucking.

Wed. 19. Attended to the fun^l of Paul Striker at Organ ch. – preached from Phil. 1:21. Germ. Dinner at Jacob Miller's.

Thurs. 20. Attended to the funeral of Mrs. John Rimer at Organ ch. – preached from Heb. 4:9. In the afternoon went to Martin Leppard's & married Archibald M. A. Klutts to Clarissa M. Leppard. All night at Jacob Pless's.

Frid. 21. Had an appointment for to day at Widow Yost's, but the day being very inclement, did not attend. Returned home in the afternoon.

Sat. 22. Preached at Organ ch. from 1 Cor. 5:7-8. preparatory to communion. Bapt^d 2 inf^{ts}.

Sund. 23. Preached at Organ ch. from John 19:30. Took a chill & was unable to hold communion. In the evening returned home.

Mond. 24. At home, the week out.

Sund. 30. Went to St. Stephen's ch. but not being able to preach, had bible exercises & dismissed. In the afternoon gave a short lecture at Gold Hill from Mark 10:46-52.

Mond. 31. Went to Salisbury.

Tues., Nov. 1. At home.

Wed. 2. Thurs. 3. Frid. 4. Made some preparation to go to S. C. Synod.

Sat. 5. In the evening went to John Miller's & staid all night.

Sund. 6. Held communion at Organ ch. All night at Moses Barringer's.

Mond. 7. Mr. Barringer took me to Concord in his Buggy. In the afternoon went to Charlotte by stage — all night here.

Tues. 8. Took Rail Road for Columbia, S. C. Was met here by Revd J. B. Anthony who took me in his Buggy 16 miles to his residence. Remained here, sharing the hospitalities of his house till Thurs. 10.

Thurs. 10. Started after dinner in company with Rev. A. for the seat of Synod. All night at Parson Wonnamaker's.

Frid. 11. Went to the place of meeting of Synod. All night at Mr. Barber's. Synod met in Mathew's ch., Orangeburg District, S. C.

Sat. 12. At Synod. All night again at Mr. Barber's.

Sund. 13. Succeeded Dr. Bachman & preached from 1 Thes. 2:11.12. All night at Mr. Bookhardt's.

Mond. 14. At Synod. All night at Revd Dufford's.

Tues. 15. At Synod. All night in company with Dr. Bachman at Mrs. Bookhardt's, an aged Widow Lady.

Wed. 16. At Synod. This evening Synod adjourned, after a very harmonious meeting. All night at Mr. Keller's.

Thurs. 17. Parted to day with Rev. J. B. Anthony at Louisville. At this point took Rail Road for Columbia. All night in Columbia at Mr. H. Muller's.

Frid. 18. Took Rail Road for Charlotte, & at Charlotte took stage for Concord. Reached Concord same evening at 9 P.M. All night at Mr. Foard's Tavern.

Sat. 19. Returned home in Buggy (son Lewis having met me in Concord) and found all well.

Sund. 20. Preached at Organ ch. from John 3:16. Baptized one infant. Dinner a Jacob Miller's.

Mond. 21. In the afternoon went to Post office. Mr. Tobias Brown with us to night.

Tues. 22. Started for Iredell. All night at Alex^r Brown's.

Wed. 23. Reached Iredell. All night at Tobias Brown's.

Thurs. 24. Married Dr. Littleton W. Coleman to Jane Arey at Mr. John Clarks's. All night here.

Frid. 25. Started home as far as John Berger's.

Sat. 26. Reached home.

Sund. 27. Preached at St. Stephen's ch. from Col. 1:28. Baptized one infant. In the afternoon preached at Gold Hill from Prov. 29:1.

Mond. 28. At home.

Dec. 1. Went to Widow Misenheimer's and married Moses Safret to said Widow Christena L. Misenheimer. In the afternoon went to David Bostian's & married Joseph A. Patterson to Margaret L. Bostian. All night at P. A. Seaford's.

Dec. 2. Clerked the sale of Dawalt Ketner, dec^d. In the evening returned home.

Sat. 3. At home.

Sund. 4. Preached at St. Stephen's ch. from 1 Pet. 4:18. The fun^l of David Troutman's daughter, dec^d.

Mond. 5. Tues. 6. Wed. 7. Thurs. 8. Frid. 9. At home.

Sat. 10. Attended to the fun^l of Barbara Klutts dec^d at Organ ch. — preached from Job 14:14.

Sund. 11. Preached at Organ ch. from Math. 25:1-13. Germ. Dinner at John Miller's.

Mond. 12. At home. Slaughtered hogs to day.

Tues. 13. Attended to the funeral of Eve, widow of Peter Peeler, at Lower St. ch. — preached from 2 Tim. 4:7.8. Dinner at C. Heilig's Esqr.

Wed. 14. At home.

Thurs. 15. Preached at St. Stephen's ch. from 1 Tim. 6:6. Returned home after preaching.

Frid. 16. Preached at St. Stephen's ch. from Math. 4:16. on the subject of the Reformation. All night at Jacob Isahour's. Baptized on infant.

Sat. 17. Preached at St. Stephen's from Hab. 2:15. on the subject of drunkeness & its remedy. All night at G. M. Bernhardt's.

Sund. 18. Preached at St. Stephen's ch. from Ex. 20:8. on the subject of Sabbath Sanctification. At night preached at Gold Hill from Hab. 2:15. on the subject of drunkeness & its remedy. All night at Dr. Kelly's.

Mond. 19. Returned home.

Tues. 20. Wed. 21. At home.

Thurs. 22. Commenced a protracted meeting at Organ Church — preached from Math. 4:16. on the subject of the Reformation. In the evening went to Mr. Geo. Klutts' & married John D. Miller to Eve Elizabeth Klutts. All night at Col. L. Klutts'.

Frid. 23. Preached at Organ ch. from Ex. 20:8. on the subject of Sabbath Sanctification. All night at Mr. John Miller's.

Sat. 24. Preached at Organ church. from Hab. 2:15. on the subject of drunkeness & its remedy. All night at Mrs. Heilig's.

Sund. 25. Preached at Organ ch. from Mal. 3:17. the funeral of Mrs. Eddleman dec^d. Dinner at John Miller's. Bapt^d 2 inf^ts.

Mond. 26. Preached at Zacheriah Lyerla's from Phil. 3:20. the fun^l of his deceased child.

Tues. 27. In the evening went to D. Barringer's & staid over night.

Wed. 28. Returned home. In the afternoon collected a few subscribers for the Luth. Obs.

Thurs. 29. Went to Post Office & sent off money & new subscribers to Luth. Obs.

Frid. 30. At home.

Sat. 31. In the afternoon went to John Seaford's to see Eli Seaford's sick child, which died before getting there.

Sund., Jan. 1, 1854. Had an appointment to day at St. Stephen's ch. also in the afternoon to attend to the fun[1] of Cha[s] Klutts dec[d] at Lower St. Church, but the day being very inclement, & being indisposed with cold, did not leave home.

Mond. 2. Had an appointment to attend to the funeral of Eli Seaford's deceased child, but being indisposed with cold did not leave home.

Tues. 3. Wed. 4. Thurs. 5. Frid. 6. At home.

Sat. 7. In the afternoon went into the neighborhood & attended to some business.

Sund. 8. Had an appointment to day at Organ ch. but in consequence of the deep fall of snow did not attend.

Mond. 9. Tues. 10. Wed. 11. At home.

Thurs. 12. At home.

Frid. 13. In the afternoon went to Gold Hill.

Sat. 14. At home.

Sund. 15. Went to St. Stephen's. Rev[d] Groseclose preached for me.

Mond. 16. Started to Bethany ch. to take Lewis H. to school. All night at Rev[d] Arey's.

Tues. 17. Went to Bethany ch. & returned to Rev[d] Arey's.

Wed. 18. Returned as far as Salisbury. All night at Mr. G. Vogler's.

Thurs. 19. Returned home. All night at Mr. Lentz's.

Frid. 20. Sat. 21. At home.

Sund. 22. Preached at Organ ch. from 1 Tim. 6:6. Baptized one infant. All night at P. N. Heilig's.

Mond. 23. Returned home.

Tues. 24. Went to Gold Hill.

Wed. 25. Thurs. 26. Frid. 27. At home.

Sat. 28. Went to Gold Hill & had horse shod.

Sund. 29. Preached at St. Stephen's from Heb. 1:14. Dinner at Mr. Link's. In the afternoon preached at Gold Hill from Acts 16:16-34.

Mond. 30. At home.

Tues. 31. At Mr. J. Lentz's chopping.

Wed. Feb. 1. In forenoon went to mill. In afternoon started to see Lewis at Ebenezer Academy. All night at Dan[l] Lyerly's.

Thurs. 2. Went to Ebenezer. Dinner at Adam Eagle's. All night at H. R. Hall's, Esq.

Frid. 3. Started home. All night at Peter Berger's.

Sat. 4. Returned home.

Sund. 5. Preached at St. Stephen's from Josh. 24:15. Dinner at Dr. Kelly's. In the afternoon preached at Gold Hill from 2 Kings 5:1-14.

Mond. 6. In the afternoon took some flour to Gold Hill.

Tues. 7. In the forenoon took some wheat to mill.

Wed. 8. At home.

Thurs. 9. At home.

Frid. 10. Attended to the fun[l] of James Holshouser's child at Lower St. ch. — preached from Mark 13:37.

Sat. 11. At home till afternoon, then went to Dan[l] Miller's and staid all night.

Sund. 12. Preached at Organ ch. from Ps. 97:11. fun[l]. Dinner at Widow Miller's.

Mond. 13. In the afternoon went to mill & took some flour to Gold Hill.

Tues. 14. In the afternoon went to Daniel Miller's, Cabarrus co. All night here.

Wed. 15. Attended a meeting of the Board of Directors in Mt. Pleasant. Returned home in the evening.

Thurs. 16. Frid. 17. At home.

Sund. 19. Preached at St. Stephen's ch. from John 5:40. In afternoon at Gold Hill From Luk. 16:19-31. Dinner at Dr. Kelly's.

Mond. 20. Tues. 21. At home.

Wed. 22. In afternoon went to David Holshouser's for Plow stock.

Thurs. 23. Went to Elihu Holshouser's & married Jesse Miller to Margaret Holshouser.

Frid. 24. Went to Salisbury.

Sat. 25. In the afternoon went to Mr. Jacob Miller's & staid over night.

Sund. 26. This my day at Organ ch. but could not attend in consequence of high waters. Dinner at P. N. Heilig's, & in the afternoon returned home.

Mond. 27. At home.

Tues. 28. Went to Widow Klutts' & married Solomon Kluttz to Maria, widow of Dan[l] Cruse. All night at John Foutz's.

Wed. March 1. Went to Mt. Pleasant & attended a meeting of Board of Directors. Returned home. Rev^d
    Scherer with me to night.
Thurs. 2. Frid. 3. Sat. 4. At home.
Sund. 5. Preached at St. Stephen's ch. from Math. 25:14-30. In the afternoon at Gold Hill from Ps. 1:1-6.
    Dinner at Dr. Kelly's.
Mond. 6. In the evening went to D. Barringer's & staid all night.
Tues. 7. Returned home.
Wed. 8. Took Wilie Holshouser to Ebenezer Academy. Went as far as Adam Eagle's. All night here.
Thurs. 9. Went to Mr. Hall's. Saw Lewis, took dinner, & returned to Rev. B. Arey's.
Frid. 10. Returned to D. Holshouser's & staid all night.
Sat. 11. Returned home.
Sund. 12. Preached at Organ ch. from Rom. 12:2. Germ. Bapt^d 5 infants. Dinner at John Miller's.
Mond. 13. In the afternoon called to see Peter Berger at his son Andrew's.
Tues. 14. In the morning went to mill.
Wed. 15. Called to see D. Lentz. His family being sick.
Thurs. 16. At home.
Frid. 17. In the afternoon went to Gold Hill.
Sat. 18. At home.
Sund. 19. Preached at St. Stephen's ch. from Rom. 12:12. & at Gold Hill from 2 Cor. 5:17. Dinner at Dr.
    Kelly's.
Mond. 20. In the forenoon went to P. N. Heilig's to shop.
Sat. 25. Preached at Bostian's School House from Hab. 2:15. on the subject of drunkeness and its remedy. All
    night at Philip Eddleman's.
Sund. 26. Preached at Organ ch. from Heb. 1:14. In the afternoon at Widow Garner's from Eccl. 9:10. Fun^l.
    All night at Mich^l Bostian's.
Mond. 27. Returned home.
Tues. 28. In the afternoon went to Wilie Knup's & to Gold Hill.
Wed. 29. At home.
Thurs. 30. Started for Iredell co. to assist Revd Arey at a protracted meeting. All night at Widow Kistler's.
Frid. 31. Went to Shepherd's Cross Roads & preached from Ps. 133:1-3. All night at Chas Barringer's.

Sat. Apr 1. Preached at Cross Roads from Prov. 14:34. All night at Chas Barringer's.

Sund. 2. At Cross Roads. At night preached at C. Barringer's from Hab. 2:15. on the subject of drunkeness & its remedy.

Mond. 3. Preached at Cross Roads from Rom. 10:1+ and at night at John Goodman's from Math. 25:14-30. All night at Chas. Barringer's.

Tues. 4. Took Lewis H. back to Bethany to school. All night at Revd B. Arey's.

Wed. 5. Returned home.

Thurs. 6. Aided Mr. Holshouser in making his quarterly settlement.

Frid. 7. At home.

Sat. 8. In the afternoon went to John J. Miller's & staid all night.

Sund. 9. Preached at Organ ch. from Math. 25:14-30. Bapt. one infant. Dinner at Joseph Miller's.

Mond. 10. At home.

Tues. 11. Went to C. Heilig's mill.

Wed. 12. At home.

Thurs. 13. In afternoon went to John J. Miller's & married Henry G. Lentz to Elizabeth Hudgins. Returned to Widow Peeler's & married Milas A. Holshouser to Sophia L. Peeler.

Frid. 14. Heard Revd Butler preach at Lower St. Church.

Sat. 15. Had an appointment to day at St. Stephens ch. for preparatory service, but the day being rainy did not attend.

Sund. 16. Went to St. Stephen's ch. Had an appointment to day for communion, but the day being very inclement, postponed it. Revd Arey preached.

Mond. 17. Went to Milas Arey's.

Tues. 18. Returned home.

Wed. 19. Went to Gold Hill to blacksmith shop.

Thurs. 20. Went to C. Heilig's mill.

Frid. 21. Took some Pork to Gold Hill.

Sat. 22. Preached at Klutts' School House from Hab. 2:15. on the subject of Drunkeness & its Remedy.

Sund. 23. Preached at Organ ch. from Rom. 10:1. & English from Luk. 18:1-8. Bapt^d one infant.

Mond. 24. Called at Henry Miller's, his wife being sick.

Tues. 25. Went to Salisbury.

Wed. 26. Attended to the fun^l of Mrs. Elizabeth Caroline, wife of Moses Shuping at Phanuel's Church. — preached from Eccl. 12:13. Germ. Dinner at Mrs. Greaber's.

Thurs. 27. Went to John Reimer's & married Tobias Cruse to Miss Catherine L. Reimer. Returned to Mrs. Ribelin's & married Alexander M. Miller to Miss Clotilda Ribelin. All night at widow Sally Holshouser's.

Frid. 28. At home.

Sat. 29. Had prepory service at Organ ch. — preaching by Revs. Linn and Anthony. All night at Mr. Moses Barringer's.

Sund. 30. Revd J. B. Anthony preached. Administered the Lord's Supper, being assisted by Revds. Anthony, Linn and Butler.

+ Baptized Revd Arey's child.

Mond. May 1. At home. Rev. A. with us.

Tues. 2. Went to Salisbury.

Wed. 3. At home — had company.

Thurs. 4. In the morning went to Mr. Linn's & brought Rev. J. B. Anthony home. In the afternoon started for Synod. All night at Mr. John Moose's.

Frid. 5. Went to Bethel church to Synod. All night at Mr. M. Barrier's.

Sat. 6. At Synod. All night at Mr. Barrier's Esq.

Sund. 7. At Bethel ch. all night at widow Moose's.

Mond. 8. At Synod. All night at Wilson Barringer's.

Tues. 9. At Synod. All night John Moose's.

Wed. 10. At Synod. All night at John Melchior's.

Thurs. 11. At Synod till 12 o'clock. Synod adjourned. Returned home.

Frid. 12. In the morning went to Post office and smith shop.

Sat. 13. In the afternoon went to John Seaford's. All night here.

Sund. 14. Preached at Organ ch. from 2 Cor. 4:7. Dinner at John Miller's.

Mond. 15. At home.

Tues. 16. In the evening went to Gold Hill & attended the meeting of the Gold Hill Bible Society. All night at Dr. Kelly's.

Wed. 17. Aided Rev. Dervelle in collecting contributions to the Bible cause, & then returned home.

Thurs. 18. Attended to the funeral of Laurence Misenheimer's child at Organ ch. preached from Eccl. 12:13. Dinner at Paul Cruse's. All night at Mr. Mathias Miller's.

Frid. 19. Preached at Mt. Carmel ch. from 2 Cor. 5:17. Germ. & Engl. from Rom. 10:1. Dinner at Mr. John Dry's. All night at Mr. Mathias Miller's.

Sat. 20. Preached at St. Stephen's ch. from Prov. 23:26. preparatory to communion. Baptized 3 infants. Dinner at Mr. S. Nussman's. In the evening returned home.

Sund. 21. Preached at St. Stephen's ch. from Is. 25:6-8. Confirmed one person & administered the Lord's Supper.

Mond. 22. At home.

Tues. 23. Started for Concord as far as Henry Blackwelder's.

Wed. 24. Went to Concord & aided in the settlement of some church differences. All night at Mr. John Heilman's.

Thurs. 25. Returned home by way of Concord. Dinner at Mr. Henry Blackwelder's.

Frid. 26. At home.

Sat. 27. Commenced catechization at Organ ch. Dinner at Mr. John Miller's. All night at Mr. Henry Pless'.

Sund. 28. Attended to the burial of Mr. Solomon Ketchey's child. Preached at Organ ch. from Math. 20:6. Baptized three infants. In the afternoon had a meeting of the Miss. & Ed. Society. Dinner at Mr. John Miller's.

Mond. 29. Went to C. A. Heilig's mill, returned by way of Mr. Jacob Miller's for some Salt.

Tues. 30. Went to C. A. Heilig's mill & returned by way of Mr. John Miller's for some Molasses.

Wed. 31. Went to Mt. Pleasant to attend a meeting of the Board of Directors of W. C. M. Academy.

Thurs., June 1. Frid. 2. At home.

Sat. 3. Attended the fun[1] of Stephen Brady's son at Lower St. Church — preached from Math. 5:8.

Sund. 4. Preached at St. Stephen's ch. from Eph. 6:18. Dinner at John Powlass'. In the afternoon preached at Gold Hill from Is. 3:10.

Mond. 5. Went to Gold Hill to shop.

Tues. 6. At home.

Wed. 7. Went to Lower St. ch. to hear a temperance lecture. Took dinner at Jacob Randleman's.

Thurs. 8. Went to P. N. Heilig's to Blacksmith shop.

Frid. 9. Went to Post Office and shop in the morning. Balance of the day at home.

Sat. 10. Had catechization at Organ ch. Dinner at John Seaford's.

Sund. 11. Preached at Organ ch. from 1 Thes. 5:7. Germ. Dinner at Frederick Stirewald's. In the afternoon preached at Nelson Sides', the fun[1] of his deceased son, from John 9:4. Called to see John Smith, he being much afflicted & administered to him the Lord's Supper. All night at Jeremiah L. Graeber's.

Mond. 12. Returned home. In the afternoon engaged some hands to cut grass.

Tues. 13. Started to Ebenezer Academy. All night at Rev. Arey's.

Wed. 14. Went to H. R. Hall's Esq. at Ebenezer Academy. All night here.

Thurs. 15. Attended the public speaking of the students. In the afternoon started for home bringing Lewis H. along. All night at Adam Eagle's.

Frid. 16. Reached home.

Sat. 17. At home.

Sund. 18. Preached at St. Stephen's ch. from 1 Pet. 5:8. In the afternoon at Gold Hill from Math. 8:22. Dinner at Dr. Kelly's.

Mond. 19. Tried in the morning to engage hands to cradle wheat but failed.

Tues. 20. Wed. 21. Thurs. 22. Frid. 23. At home.

Sat. 24. Had catechization at Organ ch.

Sund. 25. Preached at Organ ch. from Prov. 3:6. the fun[1] of Elizabeth Josey dec[d]. Baptized one inf[t]. In the afternoon at Paul Cruse's from 2 Cor. 13:5. Germ. Dinner here. All night at Laurence Lingle's.

Mond. 26. In the morning returned home.

Tues. 27. At home.

Wed. 28. Went to Mt. Pleasant to attend a meeting of the Board of Directors of W. C. M. Academy.

Thurs. 29. At home.

Frid. 30. Went to Salisbury.

Sat., July 1. At home.

Sund. 2. Preached at St. Stephen's ch. from Acts 24:25. In the afternoon at Gold Hill from John 6:37.

Mond. 3. In the afternoon went to Dan[l] Miller's. All night here.

Tues. 4. Went to Mt. Pleasant & attended the laying of the corner stone of Western Carolina Male Academy. All night at Dan[l] Miller's.

Wed. 5. Returned home.

Thurs. 6. At home.

Frid. 7. Had catechization at Organ Church.

Sat. 8. Attended to the fun[l] of Bostian Lentz dec[d] at Union ch. — preached from Rev. 2:10.

Sund. 9. Preached at Organ ch. from 1 King 19:13. Dinner at Widow Miller's. Bapt[d] one infant.

Mond. 10. Tues. 11. Wed. 12. At home.

Thurs. 13. Frid. 14. At home.

Sat. 15. Had catechization at St. Stephen's ch. All night at S. Nussman's.

Sund. 16. Preached at St. Stephen's ch. from 1 Kings 19:13. Dinner at E. Link's. In the afternoon preached at Gold Hill from Luk. 15:11-24.

Mond. 17. Started to take son Lewis to Ebenezer Academy. All night at Mr. File's.

Tues. 18. Went to H. R. Hall's & returned to Mrs. Forsythe's. All night here.

Wed. 19. Returned home.

Thurs. 20. Frid. 21. Sat. 22. At home, sick.

Sund. 23. Went to Organ ch. & had bible class, baptized one infant, & then dismissed the congregation. Health feeble. Dinner at Dan[l] Miller's.

Mond. 24. Attended to the burial of John Yost dec[d] at Organ ch. Did not preach in consequence of feeble health. Baptized said Yost's infant child. Dinner at John Seaford's.

Tues. 25. At home.

Wed. 26. Went to Gold Hill In the forenoon. At night went to D. Barringer's Esq., his family being sick. All night here.

Thurs. 27. Returned home. In the afternoon went to D. Holshouser's on business.

Frid. 28. Went to Gold Hill & heard the candidates address the people. Replied to their grounds against a prohibitory liquor law.

Sat. 29. Attended our Tax paying at Widow Miller's. Replied again to the positions the candidates took against a Prohibitory Liquor Law. Suffered very much from sore throat. All night at John Miller's.

Sund. 30. Preached at Organ ch. from Luk. 13:24. Germ. In the afternoon preached the fun[l] of John Yost dec[d] from 2 Tim. 4:7.8. Suffered from sore throat.

Mond. 31. At home. Indisposed.

Tues. Aug. 1. Went to David Peelers' & married Peter Trexler Esq. to Sarah C. Peeler. Suffered intensely from sore throat.

Wed. 2. In the afternoon called with wife to see P. N. Heilig & family.

Thurs. 3. Frid. 4. At home.

Sat. 5. Had catechization at Stephen's ch.

Sund. 6. Went to St. Stephen's ch. and had bible class. Did not preach in consequence of sore throat and hoarseness. Dinner at N. Brown's.

Mond. 7. Went to Salisbury.

Tues. 8. At home.

Frid. 11. In the evening went to N. Brown's, Gold Hill. At night attended at the Methodist Camp Meeting. All night at Mr. N. Brown's.

Sat. 12. Had catechization at Organ ch. All night at Mr. Lingle's.

Sund. 13. Preached at Organ ch. from Josh. 7:12. Dinner at Peter Miller's. In the afternoon preached at Charles Lyerla's from Amos 4:12. the fun. of his deceased child. All night at Peter Miller's.

Mond. 14. Returned home.

Thurs. 17. Started to assist Rev. Crim at a Protracted Meeting at Bethel. All night at M. L. Brown's.

Frid. 18. Preached at Bethel from Am. 4:12. All night at J. C. Miller's.

Sat. 19. Preached at Bethel from 1 Thes. 5:6. & at night from Luk. 13:24. All night at J. C. Miller's.

Sund. 20. Preached at Bethel from Rom. 10:1. & at night from 2 Cor. 5:17. All night at Dan. Hoffman's.

Mond. 21. Returned home.

Tues. 22. Wed. 23. At home.

Thurs. 24. Started to assist Rev. J. S. Heilig at a Protracted Meeting at St. Enoch's ch. Dinner at Paul Miller's. All night at a Mr. Bostian's. Very sick this afternoon.

Frid. 25. Went to St. Enoch's ch. & preached from Prov. 14:32. Germ. All night at Capt. Isenhour's. Very sick again this afternoon.

Sat. 26. Being very sick, started for home. All night at John Seaford's.

Sund. 27. Reached home early in the morning.

Mond. 28. Tues. 29. Wed. 30. At home.

Thurs. 31. In the afternoon went to Gold Hill for nails.

Frid. Sept. 1. At home.

Sat. 2. Had catechization at St. Stephen's ch.

Sund. 3. Preached at St. Stephen's ch. from Josh. 7:12. & in the afternoon at Gold Hill from Ex. 23:2. Dinner at Widow Hegler's.

Mond. 4. Attended to 2 fun^ls at Organ ch., first the fun^l of Danl Eddleman's child, preached from Ps. 50:15. Secondly, the funeral of Margaret Fisher (widow) preached from 2 Tim. 1:12. Dinner at C. A. Heilig's.

Tues. 5. At home. At work in the meadow.

Wed. 6. Went to Mt. Pleasant to attend a meeting of the Board of Directors of W. C. M. Academy.

Thurs. 7. Frid. 8. At home.

Sat. 9. This the day for catechization at Organ ch. but the day being very rainy did not attend. All night at C. A. Heilig's.

Sund. 10. Preached at Organ ch. from John 5:40. Germ. & Engl. from Phil 2:4. on the subject of a Prohibitory Liquor Law. All night at Jacob Miller's.

Mond. 11. Returned home. In the afternoon went to mill.

Tues. 12. In the afternoon went to Philip Eddleman's.

Wed. 13. Attended to the fun^l of P. A. Seaford's child at Organ ch. preached from Job 1:21. Dinner at John Miller's.

Thurs. 14. In the forenoon went to Gold Hill. In the afternoon to Jacob Holshouser's.

Frid. 15. Had catechization at Organ ch.

Sat. 16. Had catechization at St. Stephen's ch. Dinner at Widow Peck's.

Sund. 17. Preached at St. Stephen's ch. from Math. 5:6. Baptized one infant. In the afternoon preached at Gold Hill from Math. 6:33. Dinner at Dr. Kelly's.

Mond. 18. Called to see Paul Miller, he bring afflicted, & at David Holshouser's & settled bill for tailoring.

Tues. 19. Went to Post Office & hunted up my hogs.

Wed. 20. At home.

Thurs. 21. At home.

Frid. 22. Went to Bear Creek ch. to Camp Meeting. Preached in the afternoon from Am. 4:12. & at night from Rev. 3:20. All night with Mr. Ridenhour on the Camp ground.

Sat. 23. Preached in the forenoon from Ex. 33:14. in the afternoon from Prov. 29:1. & at night from 1 Pet. 4:18. All night as before.

Sund. 24. Preached in the forenoon from Ps. 40:1-3. and administered the Lord's Supper. Preached in the afternoon from Rom. 10:1. & at night from Mark 1:40-45. All night as before.

Mond. 25. Held a prayermeeting at 8 o'clock a.m. & closed the meeting. Then returned home.

Tues. 26. Attended to the funeral of Mich^l Goodman's child at Organ ch. – preached from Job 14:1.2.

Wed. 27. In the afternoon went to D. Barringer's & staid all night.

Thurs. 28. Returned home.

Frid. 29. At home.

Sat. 30. Had catechization at St. Stephen's Church.

Sund. Sept. 1. Preached at St. Stephen's ch. from Ps. 50:15. the fun[l] of Peter Troutman's little daughter.

Mond. 2. At home. Tues. 3. At home.

Wed. 4. Attended to the fun[l] of Simeon Earnheart at Lower St. ch. — preached from Eccl. 12:1. In the afternoon attended to the fun[l] of Henry Peck Esq. at St. Stephen's ch. — preached from Rev. 2:10.

Thurs. 5. Assisted Mr. Holshouser in making out his quarterly settlement. In the afternoon went to Milas Arey's.

Frid. 6. Went to Salisbury.

Sat. 7. Had catechization at Organ ch.

Sund. 8. Preached at Organ ch. from Mic. 6:8. All night Mr. Laurence Lingle.

Mond. 9. Returned home.

Tues. 10. Went to C. A. Heilig's mill.

Wed. 11. Went to Smith Shop.

Thurs. 12. In the afternoon went to Paul Beaver's and married Reuben W. Bost & Catherine E. Beaver. Rev. Crim with me to night.

Diary No. 18
Oct. 1854

Frid. 13. Went to St. Stephen's ch. Revs. Crim & Linn preached. All night at home.

Sat. 14. At St. Stephen's ch. Revs. Crim & Linn preached. All night at Mr. S. Nussman's.

Sund. 15. At St. Stephen's ch. Administered the Lord's Supper. Revds. Crim and Linn preached. At night Rev. Crim preached at Gold Hill. All night at Dr. Kelly's.

Mond. 16. Returned home.

Tues. 17. Wed. 18. At home.

Thurs. 19. Had catechization at Organ Church.

Frid. 20. Preached at Organ ch. from Rev. 2:4.5.

Sat. 21. Preached at Organ ch. from 2 Cor. 13:5. In the afternoon from Mark 1:40-45. Held the usual preparatory service. At night at Moses Bost's.

Sund. 22. Rev. Harter preached, then administered the L. Supper. All at A. F. Graeber's.

Mond. 23. Attended to the burials of John Smith & John Louder's child. Preached Mr. Smith's fun[l] from Phil. 3:20. English and German.

Tues. 24. Called to see Sam[l] Linn, he being sick.

Wed. 25. At Mr. Linn's. To day Mr. Linn died.

Thurs. 26. Attended to the fun[l] of Sam[l] Linn at Organ ch. preached from Math. 10:32.

Frid. 27. Started for St. Enoch's ch. All night at Mr. Plaster's.

Sat. 28. Preached at St. Enoch's ch. from Hab. 2:15. on the subject of drunkeness. All night at Mr. D. Isenhower's.

Sund. 29. Rev. Harter preached, we then ordained Rev. John S. Heilig to the Gospel Ministry. All night at Allen Rose's.

Mond. 30. Returned home. Dinner at George Eagle's.

Tues. 31. At home.

Wed. Nov. 1. Attended to the funeral of Peter Cruse's child at Organ ch. – preached from Heb. 9:27.

Thurs. 2. At home.

Frid. 3. In the afternoon attended the letting out of the bridge across Second Creek.

Sat. 4. Had catechization at St. Stephen's church.

Sund. 5. Preached at St. Stephen's ch. from Eccl. 12:1. the fun[l] of Charles Barringer dec[d]. In the afternoon at Gold Hill from Rev. 2:4.5. Dinner at Dr. Kelly's.

Mond. 6. Went to Salisbury.

Tues. 7. At home – had company.

Wed. 8. At home.

Thurs. 9. In the afternoon went to A. F. Graeber's. All night here.

Frid. 10. Attended the sale of the property of John Yost dec[d]. All night at Dan[l] Eddleman's.

Sat. 11. Had catechization at Organ Church.

Sund. 12. Preached at Organ ch. from Heb. 2:3. German. Dinner at C. A. Heilig's Esq.

Mond. 13. In the morning went to Post Office & in afternoon to Gold Hill.

Tues. 14. At home.

Wed. 15. Thurs. 16. Frid. 17. At home.

Sat. 18. Had catechization at St. Stephen's ch. Dinner at Mrs. Hegler's. All night at Mrs. Peek's.

Sund. 19. Preached at St. Stephen's from Math. 11:28. In the afternoon at Gold Hill from Math. 4:19.

Mond. 20. Went to Salisbury.

Tues. 21. Wed. 22. At home.

Thurs. 23. Had catechization at Organ Church.

Frid. 24. Assisted Rev. J. A. Linn at St. Mathew's church – preached from Rev. 3:20. At night from Amos 4:12. All night at Mr. File's.

Sat. 25. Preached at St. Mathew's again from Romans 10:1. Returned home.

Sund. 26. Preached at Organ ch. from Gen. 45:28. the fun[l] of John Louder's child. Dinner at Dan[l] Miller's.

Mond. 27. Went to Post office, balance of day at home.

Tues. 28. Wed. 29. At home.

Thurs. 30. Preached at Organ ch. from Ps. 116:12-14. it being Thanksgiving day appointed by the Governor of the State. Dinner at John Miller's.

Frid. Dec. 1. At home.
Sat. 2. Had catechization at St. Stephen's ch.
Sund. 3. Preached at St. Stephen's ch. from Acts 7:9. In the afternoon at Gold Hill from Jam. 1:25. Dinner at Dr. Kelly's.
Mond. 4. At home.
Tues. 5. Started for Mt. Pleasant. All night at M. Barrier's Esq.
Wed. 6. Attended the meeting of the Board of Directors of W. C. M. Academy. All night at Dan$^{\underline{l}}$ Miller's.
Thurs. 7. Attended the Convention of delegates to District the congregations within the bounds of Synod, which met at Organ ch. All night at J. L. Graeber's.
Frid. 8. Attended the fun$^{\underline{l}}$ of Philip Eddleman at Organ ch. Preached from Heb. 4:9. Dinner at John Miller's.
Sat. 9. Had catechization at Organ ch.
Sund. 10. Preached at Organ ch from James 1:25. Dinner at Jacob Miller's.
Mond. 11. At home. Butchered.
Tues. 12. Started for Ebenezer Academy to bring Lewis home. All night at Peter Berger's.
Wed. 13. Went to H. R. Hall's Esq. at Ebenezer Bethany Church.
Thurs. 14. Attended the examination.
Frid. 15. Started for home. All night at John C. Miller's.
Sat. 16. Returned home.
Sund. 17. Preached at St. Stephen's ch. from Mark 6:12. In the afternoon at Gold Hill from Gal. 5:1.
Mond. 18. At home.
Tues. 19. Started for Mt. Pleasant. All night at Daniel Miller's.
Wed. 20. Attended the meeting of the Board of Directors of W. C. M. Academy at Mt. Pleasant. All night at M. Barrier's, Esq.
Thurs. 21. Returned home.
Frid. 22. At home.
Sat. 23. Preached at Organ ch. from Acts 9:36-42. preparatory to communion. Baptized one infant.
Sund. 24. Preached at Organ ch. from Luk. 11:32. All night at Mr. Laurence Lingle's.
Mond. 25. Administered the Lord's Supper at Organ ch.. Dinner at Mr. John Seaford's — all night at Mr. P. N. Heilig's.
Tues. 26. Assisted in letting out the rebuilding of the Bridge across Second Creek. Had company to night.
Wed. 27. At home.
Thurs. 28. Went in the afternoon to Rev. J. A. Linn's.
Frid. 29. At home.
Sat. 30. Preached at St. Stephen's ch. from Is. 55:7. preparatory to communion. Baptized one infant.
Sund. 31. Preached at St. Stephen's ch. from Acts 16:30.31. and administered the Lord's Supper.

Mond., Jan. 1, 1855. Went to Salisbury. All night at Milas Arey's.

Tues. 2. Went to D. Barringer's & staid all night.

Wed. 3. Returned home.

Thurs. 4. Went to Salisbury to the Rail Road Celebration. Saw Mr. Elliot make a Balloon ascension.

Frid. 5. In the afternoon went to John Trexler's to spend the night. At night attended a debate at the school house in the vicinity.

Sat. 6. Returned home. In the evening went to Jacob Miller's & staid all night.

Sund. 7. Preached at Organ ch. from Mark 1:15. German. Dinner at John Seaford's. The congregation held an election to day for a Pastor.

Mond. 8. Started to take Lewis back to Ebenezer Academy at Bethany Church, Iredell co. All night at Mr. Tobias File's.

Tues. 9. Went to Bethany, & returned as far as Mr. Eagle's.

Wed. 10. Went to Chas Barringer's and staid all night.

Thurs. 11. Returned home.

Frid. 12. At home.

Sat. 13. At home.

Sund. 14. Preached at Organ ch. from 1 Peter 5:8. Dinner at John Miller's.

Mond. 15. Went to mill to C. A. Heilig's.

Tues. 16. Went to Milas Arey's.

Wed. 17. Went with Milas Arey to P. N. Heilig's Shop.

Thurs. 18. Attended to the funeral of P. N. Heilig's child at Organ ch. – preached from Rev. 14:13. All night at P. N. Heilig's.

Frid. 19. Returned home.

Sat. 20. At home.

Sund. 21. Preached at St. Stephen's ch. from John 14:22. A very rainy day.

Mond. 22. Went to Post office & called at P. N. Heilig's & settled my blacksmithing account.

Tues. 23. At home.

Wed. 24. In the evening went to John Lentz's.

Thurs. 25. In the evening went to Widow Peeler's.

Frid. 26. In the evening went to Widow Ribelin's.

Sat. 27. Had catechization at Organ ch. All night at Moses Barringer's.

Sund. 28. Preached at Organ ch. from Mark 1:14.15. Dinner at Joseph Miller's – all night at Mrs. Heilig's.

Mond. 29. Returned home.

Tues. 30. Went to M. Barrier's Esq., wife being with me.

Wed. 31. Went to Mt. Pleasant to attend the meeting of the Board of Directors of W. C. M. Academy. Became acquainted with Rev. W. Gerhard, Professor elect. Returned to Mr. Barrier's & at night married Daniel M. Moose & Anna Louisa Barrier. All night here.

Thurs. Feb. 1. Returned home.

Frid. 2. At home.

Sat. 3. Went with wife by way of David Barringer's to Milas Arey's. P. N. Heilig & wife in company.

Sund. 4. Preached at Charles Earnheart's from John 9:4. the fun[l] of Sophia Thomas, who had died some time before. All night at Milas Arey's.

Mond. 5. Went with M. Arey to Salisbury, & wife returned home. Returned home with Rev. Linn in his buggy.

Tues. 6. Wed. 7. Thurs. 8. Frid. 9. At home.

Sat. 10. Had catechization at Organ Church. Dinner at John J. Miller's. All night at David Lentz's.

Sund. 11. Preached at Organ Church from 1 Tim. 4:7. Baptized 4 inf[ts] and installed church officers. Dinner at Dan[l] Miller's.

Mond. 12. Tues. 13. At home.

Wed. 14. Thurs. 15. At home.

Frid. 16. Went to Gold Hill. In the afternoon called to see Asa Miller & family, they being sick.

Sat. 17. Called to see Rev. J. A. Linn, & Rev. W. Gerhardt.

Sund. 18. Preached at St. Stephen's from Mark 1:14.15. Baptized one infant. In afternoon called to see Asa Miller and family.

Mond. 19. At home. Mr. Milas Arey with us.

Tues. 20. Went to Salisbury.

Wed. 21. At home.

Thurs. 22. Attended to the funeral of Margaret Solena Miller. Preached the fun[l] at Asa Miller's from Eccl. 9:10. Buried her at Lower St. Church. Rev. W. Gerhardt with us to night.

Frid. 23. At home. Rev. Gerhardt & Rev. J. S. Heilig with us.

Sat. 24. Had catechization at Organ Church. Mr. Milas Arey & family & Mrs. A. Redwine with us to night.

Sund. 25. Rev. Gerhardt preached for me to day at Organ ch. Dinner at John Miller's.

Mond. 26. Attended to the fun[l] of Peter Eagle at Organ ch. — preached from Matth. 25:13.

Tues. 27. Called to see Asa Miller & went to Gold Hill.

Wed. 28. At home.

Thurs. March 1. At home, mending shoes.

Frid. 2. Attended to the fun[1] of Mr. Asa Miller — preached the fun[1] at the house from Math. 25:13. Buried him at Lower St. ch.

Sat. 3. In the afternoon went to David Bostian's & staid all night.

Sund. 4. Baptized this morning Joseph A. Patterson's child. Preached at Bostian's School house from Math. 22:5. Dinner at Frederick Stirewald's. Baptized Mr. Rumple's child. Returned home.

Mond. 5. In the afternoon went to P. N. Heilig's shop.

Tues. 6. At home. The old mare sick all day & died at night.

Wed. 7. Went to Mt. Pleasant to attend a meeting of the Board of Directors of W. C. M. Academy. All night at Dan[l] Miller's.

Thurs. 8. Returned home.

Frid. 9. At home.

Sat. 10. Had catechization at Organ ch.

Sund. 11. Preached at Organ ch. from 1 Timothy 6:6. Baptized two infants. Dinner at Wm. Bost's.

Mond. 12. Went to Ebenezer Academy in Iredell County. All night at H. R. Hall's.

Tues. 13. Returned home. Rev. Swicegood & Lady with us to night.

Wed. 14. At home.

Thurs. 15. In the afternoon went to the Post office.

Frid. 16. Went to Concord to attend a Protracted Meeting — All night at R. Winecoff's.

Sat. 17. Preached from Prov. 14:34. All night at R. Winecoff's.

Sund. 18. Preached at night from Math. 25:10. Inclement weather.

Mond. 19. Returned home.

Tues. 20. At home.

Wed. 21. In the evening went to D. Barringer's Esq. & staid all night.

Thurs. 22. Returned home.

Frid. 23. At home.

Sat. 24. Had catechization at Organ Church.

Sund. 25. Preached at Organ ch. from 1 Cor. 4:2. Dinner at C. A. Heilig's Esq.

Mond. 26. Tues. 27. Wed. 28. Thurs. 29. Frid. 30. At home.

Sat. 31. Attended a congregational meeting at Organ ch.

Sund. Apr. 1. Preached my valedictory at St. Stephen's ch. from 2 Peter 3:18. Bapt. one infant.

Mond. 2. Went to D. Barringer's mill.

Tues. 3. Went to Gold Hill and sold some flour.

Wed. 4. Thurs. 5. Frid. 6. At home.

Sat. 7. Had catechization at Organ Church.

Sund. 8. Preached at Organ Church from Gal. 6:7. Dinner at Mrs. Heilig's.

Mond. 9. Went to mill & then to Gold Hill & sold some flour.

Tues. 10. At home.

Wed. 11. Attended to the funeral of Catharine Barringer, widow of John P. Barringer, at Union ch. — preached from 2 Tim. 1:12. All night at Milas Arey's.

Thurs. 12. Returned home.

Frid. 13. At home.

Sat. 14. Attended a congregational meeting at Organ Church. All night at P. A. Seaford's.

Sund. 15. Went in the morning to widow Smith's & married Charles S. Patterson to Rose Anna Smith. Preached at Bostian's School house from John 3:36. Dinner at J. L. Graeber's. Returned home.

Mond. 16. In the afternoon went to Stephen Brady's.

Tues. 17. At home.

Wed. 18. Attended a meeting of the Board of Directors at Mt. Pleasant.

Thurs. 19. At home. Caleb Peeler with us to night.

Frid. 20. At home.

Sat. 21. At Organ ch. Rev. D. I. Dreher preached for me. Baptized 3 infants. confirmed 53 persons. Lewis H. at home. Dinner at John Miller's.

Sund. 22. At Organ church. Rev. D. I. Dreher preached for me. Administered the Lord's Supper. Dinner at John Miller's.

Mond. 23. Went to Salisbury.

Tues. 24. At home.

Wed. 25. Thurs. 26. Frid. 27. No account.

Sat. 28. Went to St. Paul's ch. and preached from Ps. 40:1-3. & in the afternoon from John 3:36.

Sund. 29. Preached at Organ ch. from John 7:37. German. In the afternoon from 2 Tim. 1:12. the fun[l] of John Josey dec[d].

Mond. 30. At home.

Tues. May 1. Went to widow Seaford's & married Mr. Moses Bostian & Miss Temperance L. Seaford.

Wed. 2. In the morning called to see Mrs. Jacob Miller, she being very sick. In the afternoon started for Synod as far as Milas Arey's.

Thurs. 3. Went to Caleb Pealer's.

Frid. 4. Went to Fredericktown, the place of meeting of Synod. Preached the opening sermon from Ex. 33:14. All night at Peter Sink's.

Sat. 5. At Synod. All night at John Beckerdite's.

Sund. 6. At church. All night at Philip Sink's.

Mond. 7. At Synod. All night at Mr. Bodenhamer's.

Tues. 8. At Synod. All night at Philip Sink's.

Wed. 9. This afternoon Synod adjourned. Supper with Martin Rothrock. All night at Hugh Beckerdite's.

Thurs. 10. Dinner at Caleb Pealer's. Returned home as far as Milas Arey.

Frid. 11. Returned home. In the afternoon went to see Mrs. Miller, wife of Jacob, she being very sick.

Sat. 12. At home.

Sund. 13. Went to Organ ch. & had bible class. Rev. Butler preached a funeral. Baptized 3 infants. In the afternoon attended to the fun[l] of James Montgomery's child at Lower St. ch. Preached from Math. 5:8. Dinner at C. A. Heilig's. Called to see Mrs. Miller.

Mond. 14. Called in the afternoon to see Mrs. Miller.

Tues. 15. Went to Salisbury.

Wed. 16. Called in the afternoon to see Mrs. Miller.

Thurs. 17. Attended a congregational meeting of Organ Church congregation. Called also to see Mrs. Miller.

Frid. 18. At home.

Sat. 19. Called in the afternoon to see Mrs. Miller.

Sund. 20. Had an appointment for to day at Bostian's School House, but did not attend in consequence of indisposition. Called in the afternoon to see Mrs. Miller, but found her a corpse.

Mond. 21. Attended to funeral of Mrs. Miller at Organ ch. — preached from Ps. 40:4.

Tues. 22. At home.

Wed. 23. Started for Mt. Pleasant — all night at Mr. Dan[l] Miller's.

Thurs. 24. Attended the inauguration of Rev. W. Gerhardt, as principal of W. C. M. Academy. Attended also the meeting of the Board of Directors.

Frid. 25. Sat. 26. At home.

Sund. 27. Preached at Organ ch. from Mark 16:15.* In the afternoon held the Annual Meeting of the Miss. & Ed. Society. All night at Moses Barringer's. Still quite indisposed.

Mond. 28. Returned home. In the afternoon went to Union ch. & attended to the funeral of Dan[l] Boger's daughter — preached from Eccl. 12:1. All night at Milas Arey's.

Tues. 29. Went to Salisbury.

Wed. 30. Thurs. 31. At home.

* Baptized one infant.

Frid. June 1. At home.

Sat. 2. Had an appointment to day at Union ch. preparatory to communion. Was relieved from preaching by a Methodist preacher (Anderson) who was present.* Dinner at Geo. Lyerly's.

Sund. 3. Preached at Union ch. from Jam. 1:25. & administered the Lord's Supper. All night at Milas Arey's.

Mond. 4. Returned home by way of David Barringer's, Esq. & Bapt^d 1 inf^t.

Tues. 5. Went to Elihu Holshouser's, his wife being sick.

Wed. 6. Started for Ebenezer Academy to bring Lewis home. All night at Rev. B. Arey's.

Thurs. 7. Went to Ebenezer Academy. All night at H. R. Hall's.

Frid. 8. Returned home.

Sat. 9. At home.

Sund. 10. Attended to the fun^l of Polly Holshouser, wife of Elihu, at Organ ch. — preached from 1 Sam. 2:30. Dinner at John Miller's. Bapt^d 1 inf^t.

Mond. 11. Rode out in the morning to procure some hands to mow grass, but obtained but one.

Tues. 12. At home, haymaking.

Wed. 13. Attended to the fun^l of Elenora, wife of Paul Holshouser, at Organ ch. — preached from Ps. 73:24. Dinner at Paul Miller's.

Thurs. 14. At home, haymaking.

Frid. 15. Attended to the fun^l of John Bostian's child at Organ ch. — preached from Math. 5:4. Dinner at John Seaford's.

Sat. 16. Went to John Eagle's in the afternoon & staid all night.

Sund. 17. Preached at Mrs. Yost's (widow of John Yost) from Eccl. 12:1. the fun^l of her deceased child. In the afternoon returned home.

Mond. 18. Engaged some hands to cradle wheat.

Tues. 19. Went to Gold Hill.

Wed. 20. Went to Mill.

Thurs. 21. Frid. 22. Sat. 23. At home.

Sund. 24. In the morning went to Col. D. Lentz's & married Rufus Miller & Elizabeth C. Moyer. To day Rev. Savage addressed the congregation of Organ ch. on the subject of Sunday Schools. Dinner at Mrs. Heilig's. Baptized one infant.

Mond. 25. Went to mill.

Tues. 26. Wed. 27. At home.

Thurs. 28. Frid. 29. At home.

Sat. 30. In the afternoon preach^d at Nancy Waller's, the fun^l of John Waller dec^d from Eccl. 9:5.

* Bapt^d 2 inf^{ts} + Bapt^d 1 inf^t.

Sund. July 1. Preached at St. Peter's ch. from 1 Tim. 6:12. Dinner at Henry Miller's.

Mond. 2. Went to blacksmith shop and to Post office.

Tues. 3. At home.

Wed. 4. Attended in the forenoon to the funeral of Eli Seaford's child at Organ ch. Preached from Math. 11:28. In the afternoon to the fun[l] of John J. Miller's child at same place — preached from Eccl. 9:5. A very rainy day.

Thurs. 5. Frid. 6. Sat. 7. At home. commenced building a Dry-house. Dr. Kelly & family with us.

Sund. 8. Preached at Organ ch. from Eccl. 11:9. the fun[l] of Frank Yost's wife. Baptized 1 inf[t]. Dinner at John Seaford's.

Mond. 9. Tues. 10. Wed. 11. Thurs. 12. Frid. 13. No account kept.

Sat. 14. Went to John S. Long's — all night here.

Sund. 15. Preached at Bostian's School house from Math. 7:13.14. Dinner at A. F. Graeber's. Returned home.

Mond. 16. Tues. 17. Wed. 18. Thurs. 19. At home, threshed my wheat.

Frid. 20. Went to Mt. Pleasant.

Sat. 21. At home.

Sund. 22. To day Rev. Bernheim preached for me at Organ ch. Dinner at C. A. Heilig's. All night at Jacob Miller's.

Mond. 23. Returned home.

Tues. 24. Wed. 25. Thurs. 26. Frid. 27. At home.

Sat. 28. Attended to the funeral of Henry Troutman's wife. Preached the fun[l] at the house from Heb. 4:9. & buried her at Organ ch. In the afternoon attended the Taxpaying.

Sund. 29. Commenced a Special Conference at Organ ch. Revds. Linn & Hall preached. All night at Paul Miller's.

Mond. 30. At Organ ch.

Tues. 31. Called to see Mrs. Overcash. All night at Daniel Miller's.

Wed., Aug. 1. Attended a meeting of the Board of Directors at Mt. Pleasant. Returned home.

Thurs. 2. In afternoon went to Gold Hill to election.

Frid. 3. Sat. 4. At home.

Sund. 5. Preached at St. Peter's ch. from 1 Cor. 9:24.

Mond. 6. Tues. 7. At home.

Wed. 8. Went to Salisbury.

Thurs. 9. Started for Surry co. All night at Milas Arey's.

Frid. 10. Went as far as Mocksville, Milas Arey being in company.

Sat. 11. Went to Rockford.

Sund. 12. Preached in Rockford from Luk. 13:24. Dinner at Mr. Hamlin's Esq. Staid two nights at Mark York's.

Mond. 13. Went to Dobson. Took lodgings at Mr. Dobbin's.

Tues. 14. Started for home at 11 o'clock. All night at Hinton Comer's.

Wed. 15. Reached Milas Arey's.

Thurs. 16. Reached home. In the afternoon went to Gold Hill & engaged some Flour.

Frid. 17. Went to Gold Hill & delivered Flour.

Sat. 18. Went to John Hileman's.

Sund. 19. Preached at German Reformed Church (formerly cold Water) in vicinity of Concord from 1 Cor. 9:24-27. Dinner at Henry Long's. Returned home.

Mond. 20. Went to Salisbury.

Tues. 21. Wed. 22. Thurs. 23. At home.

Sat. 25. Attended church settlement at Organ Church.

Sund. 26. Preached at Organ ch. from Ps. 51:2. Baptized 2 inf[ts].

Mond. 27. Went to Salisbury.

Tues. 28. Attended to the fun[l] of David Brown at Organ ch. preached from Eccl. 9:10. Dinner at John J. Miller's.

Wed. 29. Thurs. 30. Frid. 31. At home.

Sat. Sept. 1. Preached at St. Peter's ch. from Luk. 13:24.

Sund. 2. Preached at St. Peter's ch. from Rev. 3:20.

Mond. 3. At home.

Tues. 4. Assisted Rev. Linn in repairing his barn.

Wed. 5. At home.

Thurs. 6. Went to Michael L. Brown's & married David Fisher to Mary A. L. Brown.

Frid. 7. At home.

Sat. 8. In the afternoon went with family to J. J. Miller's & staid all night.

Sund. 9. Preached at Organ ch. from James 1:22. Baptized one infant. Held a meeting of Miss. & Ed. Society. Dinner at Widow Miller's.

Mond. 10. Went to mill.

Tues. 11. At home.

Wed. 12. At home.

Thurs. 13. In the afternoon went to David Roseman's & staid all night.

Frid. 14. Attended to the funeral of Polly Caroline Overcash at Organ ch. − preached from Ps. 2:12. (latter clause). Dinner at Paul Ribelin's.

Sat. 15. Went to George Ketner's & staid over night.

Sund. 16. Preached the fun[l] of David Shuping's child at Bostian's School House from Am. 4:12. Dinner at Dan[l] Eddleman's. Returned home.

Mond. 17. Attended to the fun[l] Mary Ann Bostian, an orphan child, at Organ ch. − Preached from Phil. 3:20. Dinner at John Seaford's.

Tues. 18. Attended to the funeral of John W. Earnheart at Lower St. ch. Preached from Eccl. 12:1. Dinner at J. J. Miller's. All night at Dan[l] Miller's, Sen.

Wed. 19. Attended the examination at Mt. Pleasant. Over night at Col. Shimpock's.

Thurs. 20. Went to Widow Leppard's & married David A. Bost and Sophia L. Leppard. Returned home.

Frid. 21. At home.

Sat. 22. In the afternoon preached at John Brady's, the fun[l] of his deceased child from Am. 4:12.

Sund. 23. Preached at Organ ch. from Ps. 1:1-6. & in the afternoon German from John 14:6.

Mond. 24. At home.

Tues. 25. At home.

Wed. 26. In the morning went to Gold Hill on business.

Thurs. 27. In the afternoon went to George Culp's and married L. Calvin Miller and Lovina Culp. Returned home.

Frid. 28. Attended Special Conference at St. Stephen's ch. All night at home.

Sat. 29. At St. Stephen's ch. Preached from Am. 4:12. All night at home.

Sund. 30. Attended to the fun[l] of Valentine Pence at Lower St. ch. Preached from Is. 55:6. Dinner Mrs. Heilig's.

Mond., Oct. 1. Went to Tan Yard, & in the afternoon to Joel Jackson's.

Tues. 2. Went to Salisbury.

Wed. 3. In afternoon went to Gold Hill to have clock repaired.

Thurs. 4. In afternoon went to Gold Hill on business.

Frid. 5. Sat. 6. At home.

Sund. 7. Preached at St. Peter's ch. from Luk. 13:6-9.

Mond. 8. Tues. 9. At home.

Wed. 10. Went to Henry Seaford's & baptized his child, it being very sick.

Thurs. 11. Frid. 12. Sat. 13. At home.

Sund. 14. Preached at Organ ch. from Luk. 13:6-9. Germ. & Engl. from same. Baptized one infant.

Mond. 15. At home till afternoon then went to John Lentz's to shucking.

Tues. 16. Went to Mt. Pleasant. all night at Mr. Danl Miller's.

Wed. 17. Returned home.

Thurs. 18. Frid. 19. At home.

Sat. 20. Attended to fun^{l} of Henry Seaford's child at Organ ch. Preached from Math. 19:14. All night at P. A. Seaford's.

Sund. 21. Preached at Bostian's School House from Luk. 15:11-39. Dinner A. F. Graeber's. Returned home.

Mond. 22. Went to Gold Hill.

Tues. 23. At home.

Wed. 24. Went to John Lentz's & to post office.

Thurs. 25. Went to Mt. Pleasant to attend meeting of Board of Directors. All night at D. Miller's.

Frid. 26. Returned home.

Sat. 27. Had preparatory service at Organ ch. – preached from Ex. 14:15. Baptized four infants. All night at Moses Barringer's.

Sund. 28. Preached at Organ ch. from Ps. 73:1. & administered the Lord's Supper. Returned home.

Mond. 29. Attended to the fun^{l} of John T. Lentz's child at Organ ch. – preached from Rev. 14:13. To day sent Lewis to Mt. Pleasant to school.

Tues. 30. In the forenoon went to Gold Hill. In the afternoon went to Catharine Kesler's (widow of Alexander) & married Benjamin F. Walton to Widow Catharine Kesler. All night at Milas Arey's.

Wed. 31. Returned home.

Thurs. Nov. 1. Went to Shoemaker & to C. A. Heilig's & made my tax return.

Frid. 2. At home.

Sat. 3. Went to Post office and to sale (Holshouser's) and bought some corn.

Sund. 4. Preached at St. Peter's ch. from Acts 10:38. Baptized one infant.

Mond. 5. In the morning rode out & borrowed some money from Milas Arey. In the afternoon went to Abram Hill's & settled a note for Milas Arey. All night at M. Arey's.

Tues. 6. Returned home. In the afternoon brought some corn home.

Wed. 7. In the forenoon brought home balance of corn.

Thurs. 8. At home.

Frid. 9. In afternoon went to Gold Hill.

Sat. 10. At home indisposed.

Sund. 11. This the regular day for Organ ch. but did not attend in consequence of indisposition.

Mond. 12. Tues. 13. At home.

Wed. 14. In afternoon went to Tanyard.

Thurs. 15. In afternoon went to Widow Holshouser's.

Frid. 16. In afternoon went to David Holshouser's.

Sat. 17. Went to P. A. Seaford's & staid all night. Dinner at Mrs. Heilig's.

Sund. 18. Preached at Bostian's Sch. House from Math. 5:13-16. Dinner at J. L. Graeber's. All night at Dan[1] Eddleman's.

Mond. 19. Returned home. Dinner at John Miller's.

Tues. 20. At home.

Wed. 21. In afternoon went to Gold Hill, & in the evening to D. Barringer's & staid all night.

Thurs. 22. Returned home.

Frid. 23. At home.

Sat. 24. Attended to the fun[1] of Charles Bostian's child at Organ ch. – preached from Math. 2:18. All night at Mr. Laurence Lingle's.

Sund. 25. Preached at Organ ch. from Acts 26:17.18. Dinner at C. A. Heilig's.

Mond. 26. At home.

Tues. 27. Attended to the fun[1] of Zacheriah Lyerly's child at Organ ch. – preached from Ps. 2:12.

Wed. 28. Attended to the fun[1] of Henry A. Miller's child at St. Peter's ch. – preached from Heb. 4:9.

Thurs. 29. Went to Salisbury. Rev. Kistler (Paul) with me to night.

Frid. 30. Went to Gold Hill.

Sat. Dec. 1. At home. Rev. D. Dervelle, Bible Agent, with me.

Sund. 2. Preached at St. Peter's ch. from John 5:39.

Mond. 3. Started for Mt. Pleasant. All night at M. Barrier's.

Tues. 4. Went to Mt. Pleasant. All night at Prof. Gerhardt's.

Wed. 5. Returned home. Dinner at J. H. Miller's.

Thurs. 6. Went to hear Rev. D. Dervelle at St. Peter's ch. Dinner at Rev. J. A. Linn's.

Frid. 7. At home. Rev. Dervelle & Mrs. S. Heilig with us.

Sat. 8. Went to Salisbury.

Sund. 9. At home, a very inclement day.

Mond. 10. At home.

Tues. 11. Attended to the fun[l] of Mrs. Sam[l] Beaver at Lower St. ch. — preached from Ps. 4:3. Dinner at Mr. Beaver's.

Wed. 12. Went to D. Holshouser's & to John Miller's.

Thurs. 13. In the evening went to Stephen Brady's & married Dan[l] Troutman & Catharine Brady.

Frid. 14. At home.

Sat. 15. Went to Milas Arey's. At night had prayermeeting at his house — lectured from Ps. 73:1. All night here.

Sund. 16. Went to a stand in the neighborhood, expecting to hear preaching, but as the preacher did not attend, preached myself to the people assembled, from Luk. 13:5. Dinner at George Peeler's. All night at Milas Arey's.

Mond. 17. Returned home.

Tues. 18. At home.

Wed. 19. At home, slaughtered my hogs.

Thurs. 20. At home.

Frid. 21. In the afternoon went to Mt. Pleasant to bring Lewis home for Christmas. All night at Prof. Gerhardt's.

Sat. 22. Returned home.

Sund. 23. Preached at Organ ch. from Jer. 3:22. Bap[d] 5 infants. Dinner at Jacob Miller's.

Mond. 24. At home.

Tues. 25. Had an appointment to day at Organ ch. but did not attend in consequence of the inclemency of the weather.

Wed. 26. Thurs. 27. Frid. 28. At home.

Sat. 29. At home, a very inclement day.

Sund. 30. Preached at Luther's Chapel from John 5:39. Dinner at Rineholt Ketchey's. All night at Joseph Miller's.

Mond. 31. Returned home. In the afternoon went to Gold Hill.

Tues., Jan. 1, 1856. Went to Salisbury.

Wed. 2. Went to Mt. Pleasant & attended a meeting of the Board of Directors. All night at Col. Shimpock's.

Thurs. 3. Went to Mich.^{l} Overcash's & married Jeremiah Beaver & Mary Ann C. Overcash. In the afternoon returned home.

Frid. 4. Went to Gold Hill.

Sat. 5. At home, a very snowy day. Continued at home in consequence of inclement weather (snow) until the 21st then started to Mt. Pleasant as far as Paul Cruse's, the weather being very cold. All night at Mr. Cruse's.

Tues. 22. Went to Mt. Pleasant & attended to the fun^{l} of Mrs. Christena, wife of Dr. Haines. Preached from 2 Tim. 1:12. All night at Mr. Danl Miller's.

Wed. 23. Returned home.

Thurs. 24. Went to Simeon Miller's & married Richard C. Brown & Mary C. Miller.

Continued at home till Feb. 1, then went to Salisbury.

Feb. 2. 3. & 4. At home.

Tues. 5. Went to Salisbury. In the evening went to D. Barringer's & staid over night.

Wed. 6. Returned home.

Thurs. 7. Frid. 8. Sat. 9. At home.

Sund. 10. Preached at Organ ch. from 2 Pet. 1:5-8. Dinner at Dan'l Miller's.

No account kept to 17th.

Sund. 17. In afternoon went to St. Peter's ch. & heard Rev. Linn preach.

Sund. 24. Preached at Organ ch. from Luk. 11:1-13. Baptized 3 infants. Dinner at C. A. Heilig's.

Mond. 25. At home. Lewis at home.

Tues. 26. Went to Gold Hill

Wed. 27. Thurs. 28. Frid. 29. At home.

Sat. March 1. In the evening went to H. A. Miller's & staid over night.

Sund. 2. Preached at St. Peter's ch. from Mark 1:15. Baptized one inf[t]

Mond. 3. Went to Salisbury & to Mr. Bradshaw's. All night at Milas Arey's.

Tues. 4. Returned home. In the afternoon went to Gold Hill.

Wed. 5. Went to Henry Klutts' & married Moses A. Fesperman & Mary Klutts.

Thurs. 6. Frid. 7. At home.

Sat. 8. At home.

Sund. 9. Preached at Organ ch. from 1 Tim. 1:15. Bapt[d] 2 inf[ts]. Dinner at John Seaford's.

Mond. 10. Tues. 11. Wed. 12. At home.

Thurs. 13. Went to David Barrier's & married John J. Barringer & Mary L. Barrier. All night here. A very snowy day.

Frid. 14. Returned home by way of Mt. Pleasant.

Sat. 15. At home.

Sund. 16. Had no appointment for to day. Went to Lower St. Ch. and heard Rev. Butler preach. Dinner at Mrs. Heilig's.

Mond. 17. In the morning went to Rev. Linn's. In the evening went with wife to D. Barringer's & staid over night.

Tues. 18. Returned home.

Wed. 19. Went to Mt. Pleasant. All night at Col. Shimpock's.

Thurs. 20. Dinner at Dan[l] Miller's. In the afternoon went to George Leppard's & married William Beaver & Crissa E. Leppard. Then went to Henry Klutts' & married John P. Eagle and Leah Klutts. Then returned home.

Frid. 21. Good Frid. Preached at our public school house from John 1:29. Dinner at Widow Holshouser's.

Sat. 22. At home.

Sund. 23. Preached at Organ ch. from Col. 3:1. Baptized one infant. Dinner at J. J. Miller's.

Mond. 24. In the morning went to Paul Beaver's and baptized his child. Then went to St. Peter's ch. & heard Rev. Linn preach. Dinner at John Lents's.

Tues. 25. Went to Salisbury.

Wed. 26. In the morning attended to some business in the neighborhood. In the afternoon ingrafted some apple cions.

Thurs. 27. Attend to the funeral of Paul Beaver's child at Lower St. Ch. Preached from Heb. 4:9.

Frid. 28. At home, quite indisposed with cold.

Sat. 29. Went to St. Paul's ch. to a special Conference meeting. Quite unwell with bath cold — did not preach. All night at George Randleman's.

Sund. 30. At St. Paul's ch. Rev. Linn preached. Aided in the administration of the Lord's Supper. Dinner at Mich[l] Heilig's. Returned home in the evening.

Mond. 31. In the afternoon went to Gold Hill. Mr. Caleb Lentz with us to night.

Tues. Apr. 1. Went to Post Office.

Wed. 2. Assisted Mr. Holshouser in making his quarterly settlement.

Thurs. 3. Went to Mr. Link's shop & had plows made & repaired.

Frid. 4. Went to St. Paul's ch. & attended to the funerals of Moses A. Brown & Mrs. Wilson Fisher. preached from Mat. 10:32.

Sat. 5. At home grafting apple cions. In the afternoon went to school house to election of committee men.

Sund. 6. Attended to the funeral of Jacob Bostian at Organ ch. preached from 1 Cor. 10:31. In the afternoon preached at St. Peter's ch. from same text.

Mond. 7. Went to blacksmith shop & to post office.

Tues. 8. Went with Wife to Gold Hill.

Wed. 9. Went to Jacob Miller's for some seed corn.

Thurs. 10. At home. Mr. Tobias Brown & wife with us to night.

Frid. 11. Mr. Brown & wife, & John Clarke & wife with us.

Sat. 12. At home.

Sund. 13. Preached at Organ church from 1 Thes. 2:11.12. Germ. In the afternoon preached from Danl 6:10. Baptized 4 infants.

Mond. 14. Started for Mt. Pleasant, all night at Danl Miller's.

Tues. 15. Went to Mt. Pleasant & attended the examination. All night at Col. Shimpock's.

Wed. 16. Attend a meeting of the Board of Directors & examination. All night at Col. Shimpock's.

Thurs. 17. Returned home.

Frid. 18. At home.

Sat. 19. Assisted Rev. Linn at St. Stephen's ch. — preached from Prov. 3:6.

Sund. 20. Preached at St. Stephen's ch. from 1 Thes. 2:11.12. Assisted in the administration of the Lord's Supper.

Mond. 21. Tues. 22. At home.

Wed. 23. Went to Post Office.

Thurs. 24. Frid. 25. At home.

Sat. 26. Preached at Organ ch. from John 4:14. preparatory to communion. Baptized 4 infants. All night at Henry Klutts'.

Sund. 27. At Organ ch. Prof. Gerhardt preached for me. Administered the Lord's Supper.

Mond. 28. At home.

Thurs. May 1. Started for Synod. Dinner at Paul Miller's. All night at Allen Rose's.

Frid. 2. Went to St. Enoch's ch. the place of meeting of Synod. Preached the Synodical sermon from 1 Cor. 4:2. All night at Allen Rose's.

Sat. 3. At Synod till afternoon, then went to David Barrier's. All night here.

Sund. 4. Attended to the fun[l] of Mrs. Catharine, wife of Henry Probst at St. John's ch. — preached from Math. 10:32. All night at Dan[l] Isenhower's.

Mond. 5. At Synod. All night at Mich[l] Overcash's.

Tues. 6. At Synod. Preach[d] fun[l] of Mrs. G. W. Smith from Math. 10:32. All night at Mich[l] Overcash's.

Wed. 7. At Synod. Adjourned this afternoon. All night at Robert Linn's.

Thurs. 8. Dinner at Paul Misenheimer's. In the afternoon went to Mrs. Maria S. Brown's (widow of George) and married Paul Misenheimer and Maria S. Brown. Returned home. Rev. Officer with me.

Frid. 9. At home.

Sat. 10. Went with Rev. Officer to Rev. J. A. Linn's. Dinner here. In the evening went to Paul Miller's.

Sund. 11. Rev. Officer preached for me at Organ ch. Dinner at John Miller's. Preached in the afternoon at St. Peter's ch. from Math. 25:10.

Mond. 12. Tues. 13. At home.

Wed. 14. In the afternoon went to see Mr. Foutz.

Thurs. 15. In the afternoon went to Mrs. Mary M. Barringer's (widow of Charles) & married Elihu Holshouser & Mary M. Barringer. Prof. Gerhardt with me.

Frid. 16. In the afternoon went to mill.

Sat. 17. At home.

Sund. 18. Attended the communion meeting at Lower St. ch.

Mond. 19. Attended the funeral of Amelia Ann, wife of David Casper at Organ ch. — preached from Math. 25:13. Dinner at Paul Miller's.

Tues. 20. Went to Salisbury.

Wed. 21. Started for Mt. Pleasant as far as Dan[l] Miller's.

Thurs. 22. Took Lewis to school at Mt. Pleasant & attended the meeting of the Board of Directors. Returned home in evening.

Frid. 23. In the afternoon went to mill.

Sat. 24. Commenced catechization at Organ ch.

Sund. 25. Preached at Organ ch. from 1 Chron. 4:9.10. Dinner at Simeon Miller's.

Mond. 26. Attended to the fun[l] of Wilie Holshouser at Organ ch. — preached from 2 Chron. 34:1-3.

Tues. 27. Went to Salisbury.

Wed. 28. In the forenoon went to Peter Miller's & brought Cultivator home.

Thurs. 29. At home.

Frid. 30. In the afternoon went with wife to Mrs. Ribelin's.

Sat. 31. In the evening went to Elias Beaver's. All night here.

Sund. June 1. In the morning married Joseph Cruse and Rachel Beaver. Then went to Luther's Chapel & preached from 2 Cor. 5:17. German, and Engl. from same in afternoon. All night at Mr. Smith's.

Mond. 2. Returned home.

Tues. 3. Attended to the fun⁻ of Susanna Rimer at Organ ch. − preached from Ps. 58:11.

Wed. 4. Attended to the fun⁻ of Arabella F. infant daughter of Henry A. & Ann Walton at Union ch. − preached from Ps. 58:11. Dinner at Milas Arey's.

Thurs. 5. In the morning went to Gold Hill.

Frid. 6. At home.

Sat. 7. Had catechization at Organ ch. − In the afternoon went to John Berger's. All night here.

Sund. 8. Preached at Salem from Luk. 15:11-24. Baptized one infant. Dinner at Chaˢ Miller's. All night here.

Mond. 9. Returned home.

Tues. 10. Wed. 11. At home.

Thurs. 12. In the afternoon went to Laurence Lingel's and married George A. Miller and Louisa Lingel. All night here.

Frid. 13. Attended to the fun⁻ of Joseph A. Patterson's child at Organ ch. − preached from 2 Cor. 5:1. Dinner at Paul Miller's. Baptized Mr. Patterson's child.

Sat. 14. Started for Luther's Chap⁻ as far as Rinhold Ketchey's.

Sund. 15. Preached at Luther's Chap⁻ from Prov. 29:1. Baptᵈ 1 infᵗ. Dinner at Henry Miller's Esq. Returned home.

Mond. 16. Tues. 17. At home.

Wed. 18. Attended to the fun⁻ of John Basinger's child at Organ ch. − preached the funeral at the house from Eccl. 9:10.

Thurs. 19. Went to Mr. Foutz's and married Henry M. Beaver and Susanna Foutz.

Frid. 20. Went to Gold Hill to blacksmith shop.

Sat. 21. Had catechization at Organ ch.

Sund. 22. Revᵈ Prof. Gerhardt being incidentally present, preached for me at Organ ch. Baptized 1 infant. Dinner at Moses Barringer's.

Mond. 23. Tues. 24. Wed. 25. At home.

Thurs. 26. Frid. 27. At home.

Sat. 28. Attended Special Conference at St. Peter's ch.

Sund. 29. At St. Peter's ch. Baptized one infant.

Mond. 30. In the evening went to P. A. Seaford's Esq. All night here.

Tues., July 1. Attended to the fun[l] of Geo. M. Ketner's child at Organ ch. — preached from Eccl. 12:7.

Wed. 2. In the afternoon went to P. M. Heilig's.

Thurs. 3. In the morning assisted Mr. Holshouser in making his quarterly settlement. In the afternoon went to Gold Hill.

Frid. 4. Went to Mt. Zion & attended to the funeral of Philip Correll's child. — preached from Eccl. 9:10. Dinner at Robert Linn's.

Sat. 5. Preached at Union ch. the fun[l] of Mrs. Blackwell dec[d] from Acts 9:6. Dinner at John Ketchey's. All night at Eli Bost's. Baptized at Union to day three infants.

Sund. 6. Preached at Luther's Chapel from Luk. 15:11-24. Baptized 1 infant. All night at John Smith's.

Mond. 7. Attended to the fun[l] of George A. Eagle's child at Organ ch. — preached from Rev. 14:13. Dinner at Moses Barringer's.

Tues. 8. Wed. 9. At home.

Thurs. 10. In the forenoon went to Gold Hill, & in the afternoon to C. A. Heilig's mill.

Frid. 11. At home.

Sat. 12. Had catechization at Organ Church.

Sund. 13. Had preaching at Organ ch. Prof. Gerhardt preached German for me in the morning. In the afternoon preached Engl. from Acts 9:5. the funeral of two of Mr. Rumple's children. Dinner at John Miller's.

Mond. 14. At home.

Tues. 15. In the forenoon took some flour to Gold Hill. In the afternoon went with wife to George Bernhardt's. All night here.

Wed. 16. Went to Mt. Pleasant to attend a meeting of the Board of Directors. All night at Dan[l] Miller's.

Thurs. 17. Dinner at Moses Barringer's. Then went to Michael Heilig's & married Milas Rusher & Mary Ann M. Heilig. Returned home.

Frid. 18. At home.

Sat. 19. Preached in the afternoon at Jacob Stirewald's, the fun[l] of 2 of his children dec[d] from Ps. 90:12. All night at Michael Litaker's.

Sund. 20. Preached at Luther's Chapel from Acts 9:5. Engl. In the afternoon from Math. 11:28. Germ. All night at Valentine Probst's, Sen.

Mond. 21. Went to Mt. Pleasant & then returned home.

Tues. 22. Went to Rev. Linn's on business, & in the afternoon to Gold Hill.

Wed. 23. Went to John Miller's on business.

Thurs. 24. In the morning went Linn's mill & horse shod. Then at home. Rev. Lane with me.

Frid. 25. Had catechization at Organ ch.

Sat. 26. Attended Taxpaying at Widow Miller's.

Sund. 27. Preached at Organ ch. from Eccl. 11:9. the fun[l] of Osborne Klutts' child dec[d] Baptized one inf[t] Dinner at Henry Miller's. In the afternoon preached at St. Peter's ch. from Luk. 15:11-24.

Mond. 28. Tues. 29. At home.

Wed. 30. At home, threshing wheat.

Thurs. 31. Went to George Troutman's & married Mr. Jeremiah Basinger & Miss Margaret Troutman.

Frid. Aug. 1. Went to Mt. Pleasant & attended a meeting of the Board of Directors of W. C. M. A. All night at Dan[l] Miller's.

Sat. 2. Dinner at Paul Cruse's. All night at John S. Long's.

Sund. 3. Preached at Luther's Chapel from Math. 12:41. Baptized 1 inf[t]. Dinner at Robert Linn's. Returned home.

Mond. 4. At John Lentz's threshing wheat.

Tues. 5. Went to Dan[l] Peeler's & married John W. Fisher & Christena L. Hartman. All night here.

Wed. 6. Went to Salisbury.

Thurs. 7. In the afternoon went to Gold Hill to the election.

Frid. 8. At home.

Sat. 9. Had catechization at Organ ch.

Sund. 10. Preached at Organ ch. from Ps. 136:23. Dinner at John Trexler's Esq. In the afternoon preached at St. Peter's ch. from Rev. 2:10.

Mond. 11. In the afternoon went to Gold Hill to blacksmith shop.

Tues. 12. At home.

Wed. 13. In afternoon went shop at Gold Hill.

Thurs. 14. Attended to the fun[l] of Elizabeth, wife of Mich[l] L. Brown at St. Paul's ch. — preached the funeral at the house from Ps. 40:4.

Frid. 15. In the afternoon went to Gold Hill to shop.

Sat. 16. Went to Augustus Petree's. All night here.

Sund. 17. Preached at Luther's Chapel from Rom. 10:1. Dinner at Dan[l] Eddleman's. All night at Cha[s] A. G. Miller's.

Mond. 18. Returned home.

Tues. 19. In the forenoon went to Rev. Linn's shop & had horse shod.

Wed. 20. At home. Rev. Artz with me.

Thurs. 21. At home. Milas Arey & wife with us.

Frid. 22. In the afternoon went to Gold Hill & sold some flour.

Sat. 23. Had catechization at Organ ch.

Sund. 24. In the morning attended to the fun[l] of Susanna, wife of Henry Klutts, at the Lower St. Ch. — preached from Math. 5:6. Then went to Organ ch. & preached from Prov. 3:9.10. Baptized 2 inf[ts]. Dinner at John Miller's.

Mond. 25. Attended to the fun[l] of Moses Trexler's child at Lower St. ch. — preached from Mark 1:15. Dinner at C. A. Heilig's.

Tues. 26. Attended to the fun[l] of Henry L. Brown's child at St. Paul's ch. — preached from James 4:14. Dinner at Solomon's Brown's.

Wed. 27. Thurs. 28. Frid. 29. At home.

Sat. 30. Attended a Methodist Camp meeting at Liberty.

Sund. 31. Preached at Organ ch. from Jam. 4:14. Dinner at Joseph Miller's.

Mond., Sept. 1. At home.

Tues. 2. Called in the evening to see John Foutz. All night here.

Wed. 3. Called to see old Mrs. Cruse. Returned home.

Thurs. 4. Went to John Trexler's and married George W. Misenheimer & Susanna Ketner.

Frid. 5. Went to Gold Hill & in the evening to P. N. Heilig's. Milas Arey & Mr. McBride with us to night.

Sat. 6. Went to W. Litaker's & staid over night.

Sund. 7. Preached at Luther's Chapel from Math. 25:1-13. Engl. & from Math. 25:10. Germ. All night at Widow Bostian's.

Mond. 8. Returned home.

Tues. 9. Assisted Rev. Linn in raising a frame stable till after dinner. In the afternoon at home, sick.

Wed. 10. In the afternoon went to George Culp's & married John Eddleman & Mary C. Culp.

Thurs. 11. Frid. 12. Sat. 13. Sund. 14. Mond. 15. At home, sick.

Tues. 16. Started for Mt. Pleasant. Dinner at Mrs. Heilig's. All night at Dan¹ Miller's.

Wed. 17. Went to Mt. Pleasant. Dinner at Prof. Gerhardt's. All night at Col. Shimpock's.

Thurs. 18. Returned home.

Frid. 19. Started for St. Enoch's ch. All night at W. Miller's.

Sat. 20. Went to St. E's ch. & preached from Phil. 6:6. All night at Mr. Plaster's.

Sund. 21. Preached at St. Enoch's from Ps. 133:1-3. All night at Henry Miller's.

Mond. 22. Returned home. Baptized to day David Bost's child.

Tues. 23. In the afternoon went to Milas Arey's.

Wed. 24. Returned home by way of Salisbury.

Thurs. 25. Attended to the fun¹ of Martin L. Walton at Union ch. − preached from 1 Sam. 2:30. All night at D. Barringer's.

Frid. 26. Returned home.

Sat. 27. Had catechization at Organ ch. All night at Paul Miller's.

Sund. 28. Preached at Organ ch. from Acts 16:16-34. Baptized 2 infants. Dinner at Jacob Miller's.

Mond. 29. At home.

Tues. 30. At home.

Wed. Oct. 1. At home.

Thurs. 2. Attended to the fun[l] of Charles Fisher's child at Organ ch. Included in one the fun[l] of Solomon Fisher's child which had died some time before. Preached from Ps. 46:1. In the evening went to John Lentz's to shucking.

Frid. 3. At home.

Sat. 4. Attended to the fun[l] of Martha, wife of Joseph Barringer at Organ ch. — preached from Ps. 61:2. Dinner at Moses Barringer's. All night at George Eagle's.

Sund. 5. Preached at Luther's Chap[l] from Eph. 6:18. Dinner at John Smith's. Returned home.

Mond. 6. Went to the sale of Moses Earnheart & to David Barringer's.

Tues. 7. In the afternoon went to Gold Hill.

Wed. 8. Went to Salisbury.

Thurs. 9. Went to Peter Ketner's & married Alexander Leip & Elizabeth L. Ketner. Then went to Reubin Shive's & married Peter A. Bostian & Barbara C. Shive. All night here.

Frid. 10. Returned home. Called at Moses Barringer's & made out his quarterly settlement.

Sat. 11. Had catechization at Organ Church.

Sund. 12. Preached at Organ ch. from Acts 17:30. Baptized one inf[t], & in the afternoon at St. Peter's ch. from Eph. 6:18. Baptized one infant.

Mond. 13. Called to see C. A. Heilig & family, they being sick.

Tues. 14. Wed. 15. Thurs. 16. At home.

Frid. 17. In the afternoon went to Tobias Cruse's & baptized his two children, one of them being very sick. All night at John Smith's.

Sat. 18. Went to Luther's Chap[l] & had service preparatory to communion. Rev. J. S. Heilig preached for me. Baptized one infant. All night at Robert Linn's.

Sund. 19. At Luther's Chapel. Confirmed one person. Rev. Heilig preached in the morning. Administered the Lord's Supper. In the afternoon preached the funeral of Eli Bostian's deceased child from Jam. 4:14. All night at Rinehold Ketchey's.

Mond. 20. Returned home.

Tues. 21. At home.

Wed. 22. Went to Widow Graeber's & married Michael Goodman & Sarah A. Graeber. All night at Daniel Miller's.

Thurs. 23. Went to Mt. Pleasant to attend a meeting of the Board of Directors. In the afternoon went to widow Shaver's & married Jacob Probst & Rebecca Shaver. Then went to Widow Lentz's & married Monroe Troutman & Margaret A. Lentz. Returned home.

Frid. 24. Commenced a 3 days meeting at Organ Church. Rev. Dreher preached. Dinner at J. J. Miller's. Returned home.

Sat. 25. At Organ Church. Rev[ds] Dreher and Lentz preached. All night at Laurence Lingle's.

Sund. 26. Rev. Lentz preached. Administered the Lord's Supper. All night at Moses Klutts'.

Mond. 27. Attended to the fun[l] of Peter Cruse's Child — preached at the house from Heb. 9:27. & buried at Organ Church.

Tues. 28. Went to Salisbury with Lewis to examining Committee. Called on the way home to see widow Brown, she being at the time afflicted with cancer.

Wed. 29. Went to Mt. Pleasant to attend a meeting of the Board of Directors. All night at Col. Shimpock's.

Thurs. 30. Went to Concord to attend a Protracted Meeting. Preached at Candle lighting from Rom. 10:1. All night at Ransom Winecoff's.

Frid. 31. Preached in the morning from Heb. 1:14. & in the afternoon from Jam. 1:25. Supper at Rev. Dreher's. All night at Ransom Winecoff's.

Sat. Nov. 1. Preached in the morning from Acts 7:9. Dinner at Jacob Winecoff's. In the evening went to John Sloops & staid all night.

Sund. 2. Preached at Luther's Chapel from Jam. 1:25. Baptized one infant. Dinner at P. A. Seaford's. Returned home.

Mond. 3. In the morning went to the school house, it being the day for the commencement of school. In the afternoon had shucking.

Tues. 4. In the afternoon went to Gold Hill to Presidential election.

Wed. 5. At the school house part of the day — then at home.

Thurs. 6. In the afternoon went to Tanyard & to Peter Trexler's.

Frid. 7. At home.

Sat. 8. Had catechization at Organ church.

Sund. 9. Prof. Gerhardt preached for me to day at Organ ch. Dinner at Henry Miller's. In the afternoon preached at St. Peter's ch. from Jam. 1:25.

Mond. 10. Tues. 11. Wed. 12. Thurs. 13. In school.

Frid. 14. In school.

Sat. 15. Started for Luther's Chapel. All night at Henry Pless'.

Sund. 16. Preached at Luther's Chapel from Heb. 1:14. Baptized 2 infants. Returned home after preaching.

Mond. 17. Tues. 18. Wed. 19. Thurs. 20. In school.

Frid. 21. In school.

Sat. 22. Had catechization at Organ Church.

Sund. 23. Attended to the funeral of Elizabeth, wife of Philip Cruse at Organ ch. — preached from 1 Thes. 4:14. A very inclement day.

Mond. 24. In school. In the evening went to Paul N. Heilig's, his child being very sick. Returned home after night, Milas and Benjamin Arey & Elizabeth Barringer having called to see us.

Tues. 25. At home.

Wed. 26. Went to John Leppard's and married Peter A. Brown & Eliza. S. Leppard.

Thurs. 27. At home till 11 a. m. then went to Rev. Linn's on business. In the afternoon at home.

Frid. 28. Attended to the fun[l] of P. N. Heilig's child. Preached the funeral at the house from Ps. 46:1. and buried at Organ ch. All night at A. F. Graeber's.

Sat. 29. Went to Luther's Chap[l] to attend Special Conference. All night at Robert Linn's.

Sund. 30. At Luther's Chap[l] All night at C. A. Heilig's.

Mond., Dec. 1. Returned home. In school. Had my hogs slaughtered to day.

Tues. 2. Wed. 3. In school.

Thurs. 4. Attended to the fun[1] of Mrs. Susanna Seaford at Organ ch. — preached from Ps. 46:1. Dinner at John Seaford's.

Frid. 5. In school.

Sat. 6. Started for Luther's Chapel. All night at Rinehold Ketchey's.

Sund. 7. Preached at Luther's Chapel from Ps. 46:1. the funeral of Moses Beaver's deceased child. Baptized one infant. Returned home & married Moses Linn & Elizabeth Wormington at my house. Dr. Coleman & wife with us.

Mond. 8. In school.

Tues. 9. Attended to the fun[1] of Jesse Beaver's child at Organ Church — preached from Ps. 90:10.

Wed. 10. In school.

Thurs. 11. In school till 12 o'clock, then went to Milas Arey's & staid over night.

Frid. 12. Preached at Levi Thomas' from Ps. 46:1. the fun[1] of his deceased child.

Sat. 13. Had catechization at Organ church.

Sund. 14. At home, the day being very inclement.

Mond. 15. In school till 12 o'clock. Rev. Anthony with us.

Tues. 16. Attended to the fun[1] of Conrad Casper at Lower St. ch. — preached from Prov. 16:31.

Wed. 17. Thurs. 18. In school.

Frid. 19. Attended preaching at St. Peter's ch. by Rev. J. B. Anthony. All night at D. Barringer's.

Sat. 20. Attended preaching at St. Peter's ch. by Rev. J. B. Anthony.

Sund. 21. Attended preaching at St. Peter's ch. by Rev. J. B. Anthony.

Mond. 22. Attended to the funeral Clementine Harkey at Organ ch. — preached from Is. 57:15. "Eternity".

Tues. 23. Wed. 24. In school.

Thurs. 25. Went to Organ ch. this being the day for paying salary, &c. but no one attended. In the afternoon at Widow Peeler's & Mr. Holshouser's.

Frid. 26. Attended a meeting of the Board of Directors of W. C. M. A. at Organ Church.

Sat. 27. Had catechization at Organ ch.

Sund. 28. Preached at Organ ch. from Gal. 3:1. Baptized one infant. Dinner at Peter Miller's. Called to see Mrs. Brown, she being afflicted with cancer.

Mond. 29. In school.

Tues. 30. At home.

Wed. 31. In the afternoon called to see J. J. Miller, he being sick.

Thurs. Jan. 1, 1857. Went to Salisbury.

Frid. 2. At home.

Sat. 3. Started for Luther's Chapel. All night at Henry Miller's.

Sund. 4. Preached my valedictory at Luther's Chapel from 2 Pet. 3:18. Diner at Rinehold Ketchey's. Called at Widow Garner's, her daughter being sick. Returned home.

Mond. 5. Tues. 6. Wed. 7. Thurs. 8. In school.

Frid. 9. Went to Gold Hill.

Sat. 10. Had catechization at Organ ch. Dinner at John Bost's.

Sund. 11. Attended to the funeral of Sally Garner Organ ch. — preached from Gal. 6:9. Attended also to the burial service of Jane, a colored woman of Mrs. Sally Heilig's.

Mond. 12. Tues. 13. In school.

Wed. 14. Thurs. 15. In school.

Frid. 16. Went to D. Barringer's, his least child being very sick. All night here. During the night Mr. B's child died.

Sat. 17. Returned home.

Sund. 18. Went to St. Peter's ch. to attend to the fun[1] of Mr. B's child, but the day being very inclement, they did not bury.

Mond. 19. Attended to the burial of Mr. D. Barringer's child at St. Peter's ch.

Tues. 20. Went to Mr. Linn's to attend sale, but the day being very inclement, the sale was postponed.

Wed. 21. Thurs. 22. At home.

Frid. 23. Called to see John J. Miller, he being very sick. Then went to Paul Cruse's & staid all night.

Sat. 24. Attended to the fun[1] of Catherine Cruse, in the 89th year of her age at Organ ch. Preached from Micah 2:10. Returned home by way of David Holshouser's, he and his wife being very sick.

Sund. 25. Preached at Organ ch. from Math. 7:21. Dinner at C. A. Heilig's.

Mond. 26. At home.

Tues. 27. Called to see J. J. Miller & David Holshouser.

Wed. 28. Thurs. 29. At Linn's sale.

Frid. 30. At home.

Sat. 31. Attended to the fun[1] of John J. Miller at Organ ch. — preached from Neh, 7:2.

Sund., Feb. 1. Preached at St. Peter's ch. from Micah 2:10. the funeral of David & Mary Barringer's child, which had died a few weeks before.

Mond. 2. Attended to the fun¹ of Polly Brown at Union ch. — preached from Ps. 40:4. All night at Milas Arey's.

Tues. 3. Went to Salisbury.

Wed. 4. Thurs. 5. In school.

Frid. 6. In school.

Sat. 7. Had catechization at Organ church.

Sund. 8. Preached at Organ ch. from 2 Cor. 5:1. the funeral of Elizabeth Troutman dec^d. Baptized 2 infants.

Mond. 9. In school.

Tues. 10. Attended to the fun¹ of Alexander, son of John Trexler, at St. Peter's church. — preached from 1 Pet. 4:18.

Wed. 11. Thurs. 12. Frid. 13. In school.

Sat. 14. Went to P. N. Heilig's on business. In the afternoon went to Gold Hill.

Sund. 15. Preached at St. Peter's ch. from Math. 7:21. Dinner at David Barringer's.

Mond. 16. At home.

Tues. 17. In school.

Wed. 18. Went to Philip Safrets & married George V. Bost & Rosina C. Safret.

Thurs. 19. In the morning went to Jacob Fullenwider's & bought a horse. The balance of the day in school.

Frid. 20. Closed the school.

Sat. 21. Had catechization at Organ Church.

Sund. 22. Preached at Organ ch. from Luk. 18:13. Baptized two infants. Dinner at John Miller's.

Mond. 23. Went to Salisbury.

Tues. 24. At home.

Wed. 25. Went to Salisbury.

Thurs. 26. Went to Dan¹ Beaver's & married Andrew A. Bostian & Louisa Beaver.

Frid. 27. At home.

Sat. 28. Went to Gold Hill on business.

Sund. March 1. Preached at St. Peter's ch. the fun[ls] of two of John Trexler's children, from John 9:4. Dinner at John Trexler's Esq. In the afternoon heard Rev. J. M. Wagner preach.

Mond. 2. In the afternoon went to the Tan Yard on business.

Tues. 3. In the morning went to the Post Office. In the afternoon at home.

Wed. 4. Attended to the funeral of Elizabeth widow of Valentine Pence, at Lower St. ch. Preached from Math. 25:13.

Thurs. 5. Went to Cha[s] Fisher's & married John Klutts and Elizabeth C. Fisher. Returned home in the evening.

Frid. 6. Went to the infair at Dan[l] Miller's.

Sat. 7. Had catechization at Organ church.

Sund. 8. Preached at Organ ch. from John 8:36. Baptized 2 infants. Dinner at Laurence Lingel's.

Mond. 9. Tues. 10. At home.

Wed. 11. Attended to the fun[l] of Isaac Kesler — preached the funeral at the house of dec[d] from Gal. 6:9. & buried him at Union Ch. Dinner at David Barringer's.

Thurs. 12. Went to Gold Hill.

Frid. 13. In the forenoon went to Gold Hill on business.

Sat. 14. In the evening went to John Trexler's Esq. & staid all night.

Sund. 15. Preached at St. Peter's ch. from Gal. 3:1.

Mond. 16. Went to C. A. Heilig's for some bran. Balance of the week at home till Saturday.

Sat. 21. Had catechization at Organ ch.

Sund. 22. Preached at Organ ch. from Math. 26:69-75. Baptized one infant. Dinner at Sally Heilig's.

Mond. 23. In the afternoon went to Gold Hill.

Tues. 24. Wed. 25. At home.

Thurs. 26. Went to widow Josey's & married Joseph Basinger & Crissa F. Josey.

Frid. 27. Went to Mt. Carmel ch. to Special Conference. All night at Dan[l] Barrier's.

Sat. 28. At Mt. Carmel — preached from 1 Tim. 6:6. All night at Col. Shimpock's.

Sund. 29. Preached at Mt. Carmel from Rom. 10:1. Dinner at Mr. Mathias Miller's. All night at Dan[l] Miller's.

Mond. 30. Returned home.

Tues. 31. Went to D. Barringer's mill.

Wed., Apr. 1. Went to Widow Holshouser's to house covering.

Thurs. 2. Went to Gold Hill & had some Plows made.

Frid. 3. Went to Salisbury.

Sat. 4. Went to school house to election. Then went to Post Office & made out quarterly settlement.

Sund. 5. Preached at St. Peter's ch. from 1 Tim. 6:6.

Mond. 6. At home.

Tues. 7. Wed. 8. At home.

Thurs. 9. Went to Philip Safret's and married Jacob P. Goodman & Margaret Safret. Returned home.

Frid. 10. Went to Gold Hill.

Sat. 11. Had catechization at Organ church.

Sund. 12. Preached at Organ church. from Mark 10:46-52. Baptized one inf^t. Dinner at Jacob Miller's.

Mond. 13. Went to Rev. J. A. Linn's, he being sick — went also to John Lentz's.

Tues. 14. Went to Mt. Pleasant to meeting of Board of Directors. Dinner at Col. Shimpock's. Supper at M. Barrier's. All night with Prof. Gerhardt.

Wed. 15. Returned home.

Thurs. 16. At home.

Frid. 17. At home.

Sat. 18. A very inclement day. Had services to day at St. Peter's ch. preparatory to communion. Rev. C. Lentz preached for me.

Sund. 19. Preached at St. Peter's ch. from 1 Cor. 15:58. The day being very inclement, postponed communion.

Mond. 20. Attended to the fun[l] of Eliza Kesler at the house, — preached from 2 Cor. 5:1.

Diary No. 22
Dec. 1858.

Sund. Dec. 5. Preached at St. Peter's ch. from Josh. 7:12.
Mond. 6. At home.
Tues. 7. Went to Gold Hill.
Wed. 8. At home.
Thurs. 9. At home, butchered winter hogs.
Frid. 10. In the afternoon went to Gold Hill for plank.
Sat. 11. Had catechization at Organ ch.
Sund. 12. This the regular day for preaching at Organ ch. Rev. D. H. Bittle preached. Dinner at Laurence Lingel's.
Mond. 13. In the afternoon went to Dan[l] Miller's and staid all night.
Tues. 14. Went to Mt. Pleasant. In the afternoon returned home.
Wed. 15. At home.
Thurs. 16. Went to Jacob Miller's.
Frid. 17. Went to Salisbury.
Sat. 18. At home till afternoon then went to P. N. Heilig's.
Sund. 19. Preached at St. Peter's ch. from Ex. 14:15.
Mond. 20. At home.
Tues. 21. In the afternoon went to P. N. Heilig's to see his mother, she being sick at his house.
Wed. 22. Thurs. 23. At home.
Frid. 24. Had catechization at Organ ch. Attended also to the fun[l] of Cath. L. Rimer, preached from Is. 3:10.
Sat. 25. Christmas Day. Had preaching appointed for this day at Organ Church. Baptized one infant. Took dinner at Wilson Lentz's & baptized his child. Returned home.
Sund. 26. Preached at Organ ch. from Rom. 13:11. the fun[l] of the Widow Josey's daughter. Dinner at P. N. Heilig's.
Mond. 27. At home. The Rev[ds] Bittle and Linn called to see me.
Tues. 28. At home.
Wed. 29. At home.
Thurs. 30. In the afternoon went to the school house.
Frid. 31. At home, a very rainy day.

Sat. 1. At home. The morning of this day was very rainy.

Sund. 2. Preached at St. Peter's ch. from Is. 9:6. In the afternoon married Henry Troutman & Rachel Casper at my house.

Mond. 3. Assisted Mr. Holshouser in his quarterly settlement.

Tues. 4. Went to Mt. Pleasant.

Wed. 5. At home.

Thurs. 6. Went to Mrs. Eagle's & married John A. Barrier & Sophia L. Lentz.

Frid. 7. Went to Salisbury & thence to Iredell. All night at Daywalt Harkey's.

Sat. 8. Preached at St. Paul's ch. from Luk. 18:18. Bapt^d one infant. Dinner at Dr. Kelly's. In the evening went to John Clarke's. All night here.

Sund. 9. Preached at St. Michael's ch. from Is. 9:6. All night at Tobias Brown's.

Mond. 10. Went to John Clarke's, he being very sick. All night here.

Tues. 11. Returned to Daywalt Harkey's. Dinner at Dr. Kelly's.

Wed. 12. Returned home by cars & stage. In the afternoon went to St. Matthews ch. & attended to the funeral of Otho Poole's child — preached from Ps. 2:12. In the evening went to Widow Asa Miller's & married Daniel Miller & Catherine Goodman.

Thurs. 13. Went to shop and had my horse shod.

Frid. 14. In school.

Sat. 15. At home.

Sund. 16. Preached at St. Peter's ch. from 1 Cor. 9:24-27.

Mond. 17. Went by way of D. Barringer's & M. Arey's to John Clarke's in Iredell co. All night here.

Tues. 18. Returned to B. Arey's.

Wed. 19. Returned home by way of M. Arey's. In the evening went to Mathias Lentz's & baptized his child, it being very sick. All night at Laurence Lingel's.

Thurs. 20. Went to Mr. Makin's Sale. In the afternoon attended to funeral of Henry Earnheart's son at St. Peter's ch. — preached from Ps. 2:12.

Frid. 21. Attended to the fun^l of Mathias Lentz's child at Lower St. ch. — preached at the house from Jam. 4:14. Dinner at Mrs. Mary Miller's.

Sat. 22. Had catechization at Organ ch. Was sent for to go to Iredell co., Mr. John Clarke having died. Returned home & started for Iredell as far as Mr. Andrew Shuping's, but the weather turning very cold, declined going any farther.

Sund. 23. Returned home. Dinner at Mr. George Eagle's.

Mond. 24. Tues. 25. At home.

Wed. 26. Went to Tobias Cruse's, his wife being sick.

Thurs. 27. Frid. 28.

Sat. 29. Had catechization at Organ ch. Dinner at Moses Barringer's.

Sund. 30. Preached at Organ ch. from Mal. 3:16. Dinner at Mrs. Heilig's.

Mond. 31. At home.

Tues. Feb. 1. Went to Andrew Berger's, his child being sick.

Wed. 2. At home.

Thurs. 3. Went to Mr. Clarke's in Iredell Co. Dinner at Mr. Sloop's on the road.

Frid. 4. At Mrs. Clarke's.

Sat. 5. Returned home. Dinner at Caleb Hampton's.

Sund. 6. Preached at St. Peter's ch. from John 14:6. In the afternoon went to Caleb Heilig's, he & family being sick. All night here.

Mond. 7. Returned home, and then went to Salisbury.

Tues. 8. Wed. 9. At home, very rainy days.

Thurs. 10. Went to C. A. Heilig's, & to Peter Miller's. Found Mr. Miller's daughter a corpse.

Frid. 11. Went to C. A. Heilig's, found Mr. Heilig a corpse.

Sat. 12. Attended to the fun[l] of Mary Ann, daughter of Peter Miller, at Organ ch. Preached from Eccl. 12:1. Dinner at John Seaford's.

Sund. 13. Attended to the funeral of C. A. Heilig at Organ ch. — preached from Ps. 73:26. & 91:9.10. Dinner at Andrew Cruse's. Went to Mt. Pleasant, son Lewis being sick. All night at L. G. Heilig's.

Mond. 14. Took Lewis home. Dinner at G. M. Bernhardt's.

Tues. 15. Started for Mt. Pleasant, to attend a meeting of the Board of Trustees of N. C. College. Called to see Paul Miller & wife, they being sick. Called also to see Widow (Caleb) Heilig & family they being sick. All night at Paul Cruse's.

Wed. 16. Went to Mt. Pleasant. Lodged with L. G. Heilig.

Thurs. 17. At Mt. Pleasant.

Frid. 18. Returned home in the afternoon.

Sat. 19. Went to Salisbury.

Sund. 20. Preached at St. Peter's ch. from 1 Thes. 5:6. Dinner at H. A. Miller's. In the afternoon called to see Paul Miller.

Mond. 21. At home.

Tues. 22. Went to Widow Troutman's & made a division of money with the Legatees of Andrew Troutman dec[d] Called also to see Simeon Miller, he being sick.

Wed. 23. Went to Geo. Peeler's & married Alexander Peeler & Sarah Ann E. Peeler. All night at Milas Arey's.

Thurs. 24. Returned home.

Frid. 25. Attended to the fun[l] of Paul Miller. Preached the fun[l] at the house from Job 1:21. and buried him at Organ ch. Dinner at P. N. Heilig's.

Sat. 26. Attended to the fun[l] of Moses Seaford. Preached the fun[l] at the house from Job 14:14. and buried him at Organ ch.

Sund. 27. Preached at Organ ch. from 1 Thes. 5:6. Returned home after preaching.

Mond. 28. At home.

Tues. March 1. Attended to the fun[1] of James House's child at Organ ch. — preached from Eccl. 9:5. Dinner at the widow Mary A. Heilig's.

Wed. 2. Went for a few hours to Fullenwider's Sale.

Thurs. 3. Frid. 4. At home.

Sat. 5. Had catechization at Organ church. Dinner at Mr. M. Barringer's.

Sund. 6. Preached at St. Peter's ch. from Dan. 12:3.

Mond. 7. In the afternoon went to post office & to P. N. Heilig's.

Tues. 8. Went to Widow Weaver's & married Paul Yost and Adaline Weaver.

Wed. 9. Went to Salisbury & took out Letters of Special Administration on the Estate of Paul Miller dec[d].

Thurs. 10. In the afternoon went to Widow Paul Miller's & to Gold Hill.

Frid. 11. At home.

Sat. 12. Had catechization at Organ Church. Dinner at Moses Barringer's.

Sund. 13. Preached at Organ ch. from Ez. 33:5. Dinner at John Seaford's. In the afternoon attended to the funeral of Simeon Peeler at Lower St. ch. Preached from Am. 4:12.

Mond. 14. Tues. 15. At home.

Wed. 16. Went to Mt. Pleasant to attend a meeting of the Board of Directors of N. C. College. All night at Dan[1] Miller's.

Thurs. 17. Returned home. Dinner at Mrs. Mary A. Heilig's.

Frid. 18. Sat. 19. At home.

Sund. 20. Preached at St. Peter's ch. from Ez. 33:5. In the evening called to see Jacob Holshouser, he being sick.

Mond. 21. Took Lewis to Milas Arey's, he intending to go with M. Arey to Iredell to John Clarke's sale.

Tues. 22. In the afternoon went to Geo. Bayam's & to Mr. Kratzer's to see about my waggon.

Wed. 23. Went to Widow Paul Miller's & to Robison Klutts' on business.

Thurs. 24. At home.

Frid. 25. Went to Jacob Holshouser's (of David) and sold the land of Matilda Beaver. Went in the afternoon to Gold Hill on business.

Sat. 26. Attended to the fun[1] of Moses Klutts at Lower St. ch. — preached from Ps. 37:34. In the afternoon had catechization at Organ ch.

Sund. 27. Preached at Organ ch. from Eph. 3:15. — the funeral of Sally Emaline Klutts. Baptized 2 infants. In the afternoon preached at the widow Thomas Goodman's, the fun[1] of Nancy Goodman from Ex. 33:14. All night at Paul Klutts'.

Mond. 28. Returned home by calling at sundry places to see the sick, &c.

Tues. 29. Had sale at Paul Miller's dec[d] as his Special Administrator.

Wed. 30. Thurs. 31. At home.

Frid. Apr. 1. Went to Jacob Holshouser's & made out his quarterly settlement.

Sat. 2. Had catechization appointed for to day at Organ ch., but the day being rainy, did not attend.

Sund. 3. This was my regular day at St. Peter's church., but the creek being past crossing, did not attend. Dinner at Rev. J. A. Linn's.

Mond. 4. In the afternoon went to Danl Eddleman's. All night here.

Tues. 5. Attended to the fun^l of Catherine, relict of John Smith, at Phanuel's ch. — preached from Math. 6:33. Dinner at A. F. Graeber's.

Wed. 6. Went to Daywald Lentz's & sold a Filly to Wilie Lentz. In the afternoon took some flour sacks to H. A. Miller's mill.

Thurs. 7. Went to Salisbury.

Frid. 8. At home.

Sat. 9. Had catechization at Organ ch. Dinner at Moses Barringer's.

Sund. 10. Preached at Organ ch. from Acts 4:13. Baptized one infant. In the afternoon preached at widow Garner's, the fun^l of Solomon Ketchey's wife, from Ex. 33:14. Bapt^d Mr. Ketchey' child & administered the Lord's Supper to Mrs. Garner.

Mond. 11. Went with wife to P. N. Heilig's & spent the day. In the evening went to John Fesperman's to see his daughter, she being very sick.

Tues. 12. Went to Salisbury. In the evening went to Mr. Hill's & married Saml M. Rymer & Sarah J. Hill. All night at John Fesperman's.

Wed. 13. Went to Mt. Pleasant to attend a meeting of the Board of Trustees of N. C. C. Dinner at M. Barrier's. Horse fed at Danl Miller's. Returned home.

Thurs. 14. Went to H. A. Miller's & to Gold Hill.

Frid. 15. At home.

Sat. 16. Preached at St. Peter's ch. from Ps. 51:17. preparatory to communion. Baptized one adult, one infant, & confirmed two persons, & installed church Council.

Sund. 17. Preached at St. Peter's ch. from Acts 18:21. & administered the Lord's Supper.

Mond. 18. At home.

Thurs. 21. Went to Michael Brown's & married Jacob Berger & Mary A. L. Fisher. In the evening married James W. Rymer & Lydia Ann Hill near J. L. Randleman's. All night at John Klutts'.

Frid. 22. Returned home by way of Salisbury.

Sat. 23. Had preparatory service at Organ ch. — preached from Ps. 51:17. Baptized 7 infants, one adult, & confirmed 42 persons. Returned home.

Sund. 24. At Organ, Rev. D. H. Bittle preached and aided in the administration of the Lord's Supper. Returned home.

Mond. 25. At home.

Tues. 26. Went to Mrs. Paul Miller's on business.

Wed. 27. Went by way of Salisbury to Concord to attend Synod. All night at Mrs. Brown's. Lodged at Mrs. Brown's every night. Dinner on Saturday at Albert Arey's & on Sunday at R. Winecoff's. Supper on Sunday at Mr. Blackwelder's and on Monday at Mr. Wallace's. Preached on Sunday morning in the Meth. ch. from Luk. 13:3.

Tues., May 3, 1859. Returned home by way of Salisbury.

Wed. 4. Went to Widow Miller's (of Paul) on business.

Thurs. 5. Went to Salisbury.

Frid. 6. Went to Gold Hill.

Sat. 7. At home.

Sund. 8. Preached at Organ ch. from Neh. 13:31. Baptized three infants. Dinner at Jacob Miller's.

Mond. 9. At home.

Tues. 10. Went to Mrs. Heilig's mill & put up advertisements.

Wed. 11. Went to J. H. Miller's Sale. All night at Dan$^{\underline{l}}$ Miller's.

Thurs. 12. Returned home. Called at D. Bost's & had horse shod. Called also at Eli Foutz's, his children being sick.

Frid. 13. Went to Salisbury.

Sat. 14. At home.

Sund. 15. Preached at St. Peter's ch. from 2 Cor. 4:7. Organized the Sunday School. In the afternoon Rev. Ziker, Sunday School Agent, preached.

Mond. 16. In the afternoon went & viewed C. A. Heilig's land.

Tues. 17. Aided in allotting Dower in Land to Mary A., widow of C. A. Heilig dec^{d}.

Wed. 18. Went to Mrs. Miller's, widow of Paul, simply to be present at her allotment of Dower in the Lands of Paul Miller, dec^{d}. Called also to the Miss. Browns (daughters of Jeremiah Brown, dec^{d}) and at James Holshouser's.

Thurs. 19. At home.

Frid. 20. Went to Gold Hill.

Sat. 21. Went to Mrs. Mary A. Heilig's & aided in laying off her Year's Provision.

Sund. 22. Preached at Organ ch. from 1 Sam. 12:23.24. In the afternoon attended to the fun^{l} of Mr. Penninger's child. — preached from [long empty space]. Dinner at Mr. Moses Barringer's.

Wed. 25. Attended & Clerked the Sale of the property of C. A. Heilig dec^{d}.

Thurs. 26. At C. A. Heilig's closing up the sale List, &c.

Frid. 27. Went to Salem ch. to attend Special Conference. All night at John Berger's.

Sat. 28. At Salem. Preached from 1 Sam. 12:23.24. In the afternoon held a session of Conference. All night at P. L. Barringer's.

Sund. 29. At Salem Church. Attended, in connection with Rev. B. C. Hall, to the ordination of Rev. Julian. Preached from 1 Thes. 2:11.12. In the afternoon preached again from Luk. 13:3. All night at John C. Miller's.

Mond. 30. Returned home.

Tues. 31. Sold the property at public auction of Clementine Brown, dec^{d}.

Wed. June 1. Sold the property at public auction of Paul Miller dec^d.

Thurs. 2. Went to P. Miller's late residence on business connected with his Estate.

Frid. 3. Attended and clerked the sale of Elizabeth Troutman, dec^d

Sat. 4. Went to Salisbury to attend a meeting of the Ex. Com. of the Synod^l Missionary Society. Accepted of H. L. Robards' note for Abram, the securities in which were, upon inquiry, considered good.

Sund. 5. Preached at St. Peter's ch. from 1 Sam. 12:23.24. Baptized 2 infants. Dinner at John Earnheart's. In the afternoon heard Rev. Wagner preach. Rev. W. spent the night with me.

Mond. 6. Went to Salisbury and brought Mrs. Charlotte Clarke out. Balance of the week at home.

Sund. 12. Preached at Organ ch. from Ps. 103:1-4. Baptized 2 infants. Dinner at Joseph Miller's.

Mond. 13. Tues. 14. Wed. 15. At home & quite indisposed.

Sund. 19. Preached at St. Peter's ch. from Math. 7:24-27.

Mond. 20. Went to Gold Hill.

Tues. 21. Went to Salisbury.

Wed. 22. Thurs. 23. At home.

Frid. 24. Went to Danl Bost's to Blacksmith Shop.

Sat. 25. At home.

Sund. 26. Preached at Organ ch. from Is. 35:8-10. Baptized 2 infants. Dinner at J. L. Graeber's. In the afternoon preached at Bostian's School House from Math. 7:24-27. All night at J. S. Long's.

Mond. 27. Returned home.

Tues. 28. At home. Hauled wheat.

Wed. 29. Went to John Miller's. Mrs. Miller being sick.

Thurs. 30. Went to Widow Paul Miller's on business. Called also to see Jesse Miller, he & family being sick.

Frid. July 1. Assisted Jacob Holshouser in making out his quarterly settlement.

Sat. 2. Attended to the fun^{l} of Osborn Klutts' child. − preached the fun^{l} at the house from Ps. 84:12. Buried at Organ ch. Dinner at Moses Barringer's.

Sund. 3. Preached at St. Peter's ch. from Gen. 6:9. Dinner at Rev. J. A. Linn's.

Mond. 4. Attended to the fun^{l} of David Holshouser at Organ ch. − preached from Job 14:10. Dinner at John Miller's.

Tues. 5. In the afternoon went to David Holshouser's and examined his papers, &c.

Wed. 6. Went to Gold Hill & had my horse shod. Rev. Bernheim and Prof. Grim with us to night.

Thurs. 7. Went to Elihu Holshouser's & married Henry M. Miller & Melinda Boogs. Called also to see some sick families.

Frid. 8. Went to Iredell. All night at C. Barringer's.

Sat. 9. Preached at St. Michael's ch. from Gen. 6:9. Baptized 3 infants. Dinner at Tobias Brown's. All night at Charlotte Clarke's.

Sund. 10. Preached at St. Michael's ch. from Ps. 73:26. & Ps. 91:9.10. the fun^{l} of John Clarke dec^{d}. Baptized one infant. All night at Chas Barringer's.

Mond. 11. Returned home. Dinner at Saml Seaford's.

Tues. 12. Called to see some sick families. − All night at John Seaford's.

Wed. 13. Attended to the fun^{l} of Widow Catherine Garner dec^{d}. Preached the fun^{l} at the house from Micah 2:10. Buried at Organ ch. Dinner at Moses Barringer's.

Thurs. 14. Frid. 15. At home.

Sat. 16. Called at Jesse Miller's & John Miller's visiting the sick.

Sund. 17. Preached at St. Peter's ch. at 10 o'clock from Ps. 37:34. the funeral of Wm. Goodman's child. At 12 o'clock preached the funeral of Jacob Lyerly's child. In the afternoon preached at Milly Waller's, the fun^{l} of her daughter Eve M. S. Waller & of Nancy Waller. Preached from Acts 17:30. Dinner to day at Andrew Berger's.

Mond. 18. Attended to the funeral of Elizabeth, wife of John Miller, at Organ ch. − preached from Ps. 88:18. Dinner at Paul Cruse's. In the afternoon went to Mt. Pleasant to attend a meeting of the Board of Trustees of N. C. College. All night at M. Barrier's.

Tues. 19. Returned home. Dinner at Daniel Miller's.

Wed. 20. Attended to the funeral of Valentine Propst's, jr. child at Organ ch. − preached from John 14:2. Dinner at M. Barringer's. In the evening went to Rev. Linn's & staid over night.

Thurs. 21. At home.

Frid. 22. Visited some sick persons.

Sat. 23. Went to Salisbury.

Sund. 24. Attended to the fun^{l} of Elizabeth, wife of George Richey, at Organ ch. Preached from Ps. 90:12. Baptized 2 infants & installed Church Council. Dinner at Mrs. Mary Miller's.

Mond. 25. Attended to the fun^{l} of Christena Seaford at Organ ch. − preached from Prov. 14:32.

Wed. 27. Went in the afternoon to Michael File's & married Paul Peeler & Mary C. Hartman.

Thurs. 28. Threshed wheat till dinner. In the afternoon went to Gold Hill to Tax-paying.

Frid. 29. Went to Bear Creek Church to Special Conference. Preached from Gen. 6:9. Dinner at John Moose's Esq. Returned home.

Sat. 30. Attended Tax-paying at Jesse Miller's.

Sund. 31. Went to Bear Creek ch. − preached from Math. 7:24-27. Dinner at John Melchor's. Returned home.

Mond. Aug. 1. Went to Salisbury to Court.

Tues. 2. Wed. 3. At home.

Thurs. 4. Went to C. Harkey's to the Election & to M. Barringer's on business.

Frid. 5. Went to Salisbury.

Sat. 6. In the morning went to David Holshouser's & took charge of his money & note as Administrator on his Estate.

Sund. 7. Preached at St. Peter's ch. from Math. 13:33. Dinner at John Trexler's. Heard Rev. Wagner in the afternoon.

Mond. 8. At home.

Tues. 9. Went to Aaron Miller's to engage him to survey the lands of Paul Miller dec^d, in the division among the heirs.

Wed. 10. Went to Widow Paul Miller's & in the afternoon to George Eagle's & married Allison Misenheimer & Sophia L. Eagle. Called at John Ketner's to see his sick child. Called also to see Peter Ketner who was much afflicted. All night here.

Thurs. 11. Attended to the fun^l of Solomon Ketchey's child at Organ Church. — preached from Rev. 14:13. Dinner at Moses Barringer's. In the afternoon attended to the fun^l of John Ketner's child at Organ ch. —preached from Ps. 37:34.

Frid. 12. Went to Danl Bost's to Blacksmith Shop.

Sat. 13. In the morning went to George Culp's to meet Nathaniel Barringer on business. Then went to Saml Troutman's & made final settlement with the heirs of Andrew Troutman dec^d

Sund. 14. Preached at Organ ch. from Gen. 6:9. Dinner at Widow Mary Miller's. In the afternoon attended to the funeral of John Bost at Organ church. — preached from Phil. 1:21. All night at Mrs. Mary Miller's.

Mond. 15. Returned home.

Tues. 16. Went to Salisbury.

Wed. 17. In the afternoon went to Gold Hill.

Thurs. 18. Went to Frederick Stirewalt's & baptized Jacob Stirewalt's child. Dinner here. In the afternoon called to see Peter Ketner, he being sick. Returned home.

Frid. 19. Sat. 20. At home.

Sund. 21. Preached at St. Peter's ch. from Math. 21:28. Then held a meeting of Missionary Society.

Mond. 22. In the morning Rev. Linn and myself staked off a line between our lands.

Tues. 23. Went to David Holshouser's & prepared for sale.

Wed. 24. Had sale at David Holshouser's.

Thurs. 25. At David Holshouser's winding up affairs.

Frid. 26. Sat. 27. At home.

Sund. 28. Preached at Organ ch. from Math. 21:28. Dinner at Elizabeth Miller's, widow of Paul.

Mond. 29. At home.

Tues. 30. In the afternoon engaged hands to mow grass.

Wed. 31. At home.

Thurs. Sept. 1. Started for St. Enoch's ch. to assist Rev. Heilig at a protracted meeting. On the way called to see Peter Ketner. All night at P. A. Seaford's Esq.

Frid. 2. Went to St. Enoch's ch. and preached from Gen. 6:9. & in the afternoon from Math. 21:28. All night at Dan$^{\underline{l}}$ Overcash's.

Sat. 3. Preached at St. Enoch's ch. from Math. 7:24-27. and in the afternoon from Luk. 18:13. At night had prayermeeting at Mr. Beaver's & administered the Lord's Supper to old Mrs. Beaver, she being very aged & sick. All night here.

Sund. 4. Preached at St. Enoch's ch. from Acts 18:21. In the afternoon assisted in the Administration of the Lord's Supper. At night preached at Jacob Overcash's from Math. 5:6. & administered the Lord's Supper to Mr. & Mrs. Overcash. Mrs. O. being palsied & Mr. O. having been detained from church during the day on her account. All night at Abram Overcash's.

Mond. 5. Returned home. Dinner at John Ketner's. Called to see Peter Ketner. Got very wet.

Tues. 6. Wed. 7. Thurs. 8. At home.

Frid. 9. After dinner went to the late residence of David Holshouser dec^{d} & rented out his plantation.

Sat. 10. Attended to the fun$^{\underline{l}}$ of Peter Ketner at Organ. — preached from Eccl. 9:10. Dinner at Moses Barringer's. In the afternoon Rev. J. H. Mengert preached in German. All night at Moses Barringer's.

Sund. 11. Rev. J. H. Mengert preached morning & afternoon. Returned home.

Mond. 12. Attended to the fun$^{\underline{l}}$ of John Lyerla's child at St. Peter's ch. — preached from Eccl. 9:10.

Tues. 13. Attended to the fun$^{\underline{l}}$ of Mrs. Elizabeth, wife of Valentine Propst, at Organ ch. — preached from Heb. 4:9. Dinner at Mrs. Mary A. Heilig's. Assisted in allotting her dower in land.

Wed. 14. Attended to the fun$^{\underline{l}}$ of Charles Beaver's child at Lower St. ch. — preached from Ps. 50:15.

Thurs. 15. At home.

Frid. 16. At home.

Sat. 17. Went to widow Heilig's (of C. A. H.) to lay off Year's Provision but did nothing as some of the other Commissioners were prevented by sickness from attending.

Sund. 18. Preached at St. Peter's ch. from Is. 32:11. Held a meeting of congregational Miss. Society.

Mond. 19. Called at the residence of the late David Holshouser on business. Went also to Solomon Brown's.

Tues. 20. Went to Mt. Pleasant on business.

Wed. 21. At home.

Thurs. 22. In the morning went to Gold Hill on business.

Frid. 23. Went to Mary A. Heilig's & laid off her Year's Provisions.

Sat. 24. At home.

Sund. 25. Preached at Organ ch. from Acts 28:15. Held a meeting of Missionary Society.

Mond. 26. Called to see Rev. J. H. Mengert at Rev. Linn's & paid him over some money his church.

Tues. 27. Went to widow Garner's & married Solomon Ketchey & Susanna Garner.

Wed. 28. Went to Steam Saw Mill & to Dan$^{\underline{l}}$ Fisher's & business.

Thurs. 29. Went to Eli Lentz's on business.

Frid. 30. In the afternoon went to Jacob Holshouser's & made out his quarterly settlement.

Sat., Oct. 1. Went to Salisbury.

Sund. 2. At St. Peter's ch. Rev. Wagner preached for me. Dinner at John Earnheart's.

Mond. 3. Went to Steam Saw Mill on business.

Tues. 4. Went to Danl Bost's & had horse shod. Then went to Danl Miller's & staid over night.

Wed. 5. Attended the meeting of the Board of Trustees of N. C. College. Dinner & supper at M. Barrier's, Esq. All night at Col. J. Shimpock's.

Thurs. 6. Returned home, & in the afternoon started for Iredell as far as Henry Pless'. All night here.

Frid. 7. Went to Tobias Brown's. All night here.

Sat. 8. Preached at St. Michael's ch. from Math. 21:28. preparatory to communion.

Sund. 9. Preached at St. Michael's ch. from Ps. 40:4. the funeral of Mrs. Charlotte Clark, confirmed one person, & administered the Lord's Supper to the congregation. — All night at Tobias Brown's.

Mond. 10. At Tobias Brown's & the late residence of Charlotte Clark, dec^{d}.

Tues. 11. Attended the sale of the property of Charlotte Clark, dec^{d}.

Wed. 12. Started for home. All night at Catharine Kistler's.

Thurs. 13. Returned home.

Frid. 14. Went to Gold Hill.

Sat. 15. Had service preparatory to communion at St. Peter's ch. Rev. J. S. Heilig preached. Baptized 2 inf^{ts}.

Sund. 16. Had communion at St. Peter's ch. Rev. Heilig preached.

Mond. 17. Went to Tobias Klutts' & divided some corn belonging to the Estate of David Holshouser.

Tues. 18. Went to Gold Hill.

Wed. 19. Went to Salisbury.

Thurs. 20. In the morning went to Gold Hill on business. In the evening went to Eli Bost's to meet Rev. A. Phillippi. All night here.

Frid. 21. Returned home, Rev. P. being with me.

Sat. 22. Had service at Organ ch. preparatory to communion. Revds. Phillippi & Bikle preached. Baptized 2 inf^{ts} All night at Henry Klutts'.

Sund. 23. Had communion at Organ ch. Revd Phillippi preached.

Mond. 24. Went to Dr. Coleman's. Charlotte Clark's child being sick.

Tues. 25. At Dr. Coleman's. To day Mrs. Clark's child died.

Wed. 26. At home.

Thurs. 27. Went to St. Michael's ch. in Iredell, & attended to the fun^{l} of Mr. and Mrs. Clark's child, - preached from Math. 5:8. Returned as far as Salisbury. All night at B. F. Fraley's.

Frid. 28. Returned home.

Sat. 29. At home. Very unwell with a severe cold.

Sund. 30. Went to Luther's Church to Conferential Meeting.

Mond. 31. At home. Had shucking in afternoon & at night.

Tues. Nov. 1. Went to Mrs. Mary Ann Redwine's & married John C. Miller & Mary Ann Redwine.

Wed. 2. Called to see Henry Miller he being sick.

Thurs. 3. Called to see Henry Miller & Elihu Holshouser. Sold some rent corn belonging to the Estate of David Holshouser dec^{d}.

Frid. 4. At home.

Sat. 5. Went to Gold Hill.

Sund. 6. Preached at St. Peter's ch. from Math. 4:1-11. Dinner at H. A. Miller's. — Called to see Elihu Holshouser.

Mond. 7. Tues. 8.+ Wed. 9. At home.

Thurs. 10. Went to Salisbury.

Frid. 11. At home.

Sat. 12. In the afternoon called to see Elihu Holshouser.

Sund. 13. At Organ ch. Rev. J. L. Smithdeal preached. Baptized 2 infants.

Mond. 14. At home.

Tues. 15. In the morning went to Gold Hill, then called at L. Lingel's for dinner. In the afternoon went to Philip Safret's & married Thomas Sapp and Sarah Safret. All night at Peter Cruse's.

Wed. 16. Returned home by way of Mr. Foutz's. Dinner here.

Thurs. 17. In the afternoon called to see Elihu Holshouser.

Frid. 18. At home.

Sat. 19. Attended to the fun[1] of Elihu Holshouser at Organ ch. — preached from 2 Tim. 4:7.8.

Sund. 20. Preached at St. Peter's ch. from Math. 25:1-13.

Mond. 21. At home.

Tues. 22. Called at P. N. Heilig's, his child being sick; called also at Jacob Miller's.

Wed. 23. At home.

Thurs. 24. This day was appointed by the Governor of the State as a day of thanksgiving. Preached at Organ ch. from 2 Kings 4:26. Dinner at Moses Barringer's.

Frid. 25. Went to Salisbury.

Sat. 26. Went to Mrs. Bost's, widow of John Bost & assisted in laying off her Year's Provisions.

Sund. 27. Preached at Organ ch. from Mark 1:40-45. Baptized Mrs. Rebecca, wife of Peter E. Foutz, & at the same time admitted her to full membership in the church by the Rite of Confirmation.

Mond. 28. In the morning went to Gold Hill on business.

Tues. 29. At home.

Wed. 30. Clerked the sale of the property of John Bost, dec^{d}.

+ Called to day see E. Holshouser & H. A. Miller.

Thurs. Dec. 1. Was sent for in the evening, to go to Moses Lingel's, his wife being in a gloomy state of mind. All night here.

Frid. 2. Returned home.

Sat. 3. At home.

Sund. 4. Preached at St. Peter's ch. from Math. 25:14-30. The day being inclement, the congregation was small.

Mond. 5. At home.

Tues. 6. Started to Mt. Pleasant. Dinner at Danl Bost's. Had my horse shod here. All night at Danl Miller's.

Wed. 7. Went to Mt. Pleasant, dinner at M. Barrier's, Esq. In the afternoon went to widow Paul Miller's & married Eli Holshouser & Laura C. Miller. Returned home.

Thurs. 8. Went to Jacob Holshouser's to Infair.

Frid. 9. In the afternoon went to Gold Hill.

Sat. 10. In the morning went to Post Office.

Sund. 11. At Organ Church. Rev. C. Lentz preached.

Mond. 12. Went to widow Paul Miller's & Eli Klutts' on business.

Tues. 13. Went to widow Holshouser's to aid in building a Wheat house.

Wed. 14. At home.

Thurs. 15. Attended to the fun^{l} of Mrs. Catherine, wife of Jacob Earnheart. Preached from Eccl. 9:10. Buried on the plantation. In the afternoon went to Henry Klutts' & married Danl W. Propst & Mary E. Klutts. All night here.

Frid. 16. Returned home. In the afternoon went to sale at Elihu Holshouser's, dec^{d}. Supper at P. N. Heilig's.

Sat. 17. At home.

Sund. 18. Preached at St. Peter's ch. from Rom. 14:17.18. Dinner at John Trexler's. Mr. Trexler had the misfortune to have his leg broken to day on his way home from church, by the falling off his horse.

Mond. 19. In the afternoon went to Gold Hill on business.

Tues. 20. Called to see Mr. John Trexler.

Wed. 21. Went to P. N. Heilig's & aided in rolling his carriage house.

Thurs. 22. In the afternoon went to Gold Hill on business.

Frid. 23. Sat. 24. At home.

Sund. 25. Preached at Organ ch. from Math. 1:21.

Mond. 26. At home. P. N. Heilig & family, & Dr. Coleman & family with us to day to dinner.

Tues. 27. In the afternoon went to widow Miller's (of Paul) on business. Called also to see widow Holshouser (of Elihu) she being sick.

Wed. 28. Went to Danl Bost's & married Tobias Miller & Jemima E. Bost. Called also at the widow Mary A. Heilig's. In the afternoon went to widow Miller's (of Paul) & sold some Rails, Corn, &c.

Thurs. 29. At home. Slaughtered Hogs. Also made out an Inventory for Jesse Miller, Administrator on the Estate of John Bost, dec^{d}

Frid. 30. At home. Salted down my Pork.

Sat. 31. Had intended to start to day for Bethel ch. above Salisbury, to preach there on the following day, but as it snowed incessantly thro' the day, until the snow acquired some depth, did not go. Went to the Post Office and mailed letters containing money, to T. Newton Kurtz for Almanacs, to The Child's Paper, & to Luth. Sunday School Herald.

Sund. Jan 1, 1860. At home, the day being cold and the ground covered with Snow.

Mond. 2. Went to Post Office & aided Mr. Holshouser in making his quarterly settlement.

Tues. 3. Went to Gold Hill & sent $104 to Rev. J. H. Mengert, Missionary in Wilmington. Dinner at R. J. Holmes'.

Wed. 4. At home. This evening Caleb Peeler & daughters called to see us.

Thurs. 5. At home.

Frid. 6. Sat. 7. At home.

Sund. 8. Preached at Organ ch. from Math. 25:14-30. Dinner at Jesse Miller's.

Mond. 9. Went to Salisbury.

Tues. 10. Called to see John Trexler, he being still confined to his bed by his broken leg.

Wed. 11. Thurs. 12. Engaged in hauling rock (corner) from P. N. Heilig's.

Frid. 13. Hauled one load rock in the morning. In the afternoon went to Mrs. S. Heilig's & borrowed some money to purchase State Bond.

Sat. 14. Went with son Lewis to Salisbury. Purchased a State Bond, & made a special deposit of my State Bonds in the Bank.

Sund. 15. Preached at St. Peter's ch. from Luk. 13:6-9. Baptized one infant.

Mond. 16. At home. Slaughtered the balance of winter hogs.

Tues. 17. Hauled rock.

Wed. 18. At home till after dinner, then went to Post Office.

Thurs. 19. Hauled rock.

Frid. 20. Hauled rock.

Sat. 21. Went to Organ ch. to meet the Councils of Organ & St. Peter's Churches, to deliberate on the subject of Salary, &c., for another year. The Councils agreed to raise my salary to $500.

Sund. 22. Preached at Organ ch. from Math. 4:19. Baptized one infant. Dinner at Moses Barringer's. In the afternoon attended to the funeral of George R. Randleman at St. Paul's ch. — preached from Jam. 4:14. All night at Alexander Fisher's.

Mond. 23. Returned home.

Tues. 24. Went to Gold Hill & to Steam Saw Mill & handed out a Bill for lumber for a house. Dinner at J. Moose's Esq.

Wed. 25. Went to Dan[l] Bost's to blacksmith shop. Called also at Mrs. Ribelin's & paid a note against the Estate of David Holshouser dec[d]. Called also at School house.

Thurs. 26. In the afternoon called at P. N. Heilig's & settled for corner rock.($10).

Frid. 27. Went to Luther's Chapel to attend a meeting of the Central Conference. Preached from Math. 21:28. All night at Mr. Petre's.

Sat. 28. At Luther's Chapel, baptized one infant. At night preached from Luk. 13:6-9. All night at Henry Miller's Esq.

Sund. 29. Preached at Luther's Ch[l] from Math. 25:14-30. Dinner at Mrs. Ketchey's. All night at P. A. Seaford's, Esq.

Mond. 30. Returned home.

Tues. 31. At home.

Wed. Feb. 1. At home.

Thurs. 2. Went to Gold Hill & to Jacob Holshouser's (of David) on business.

Frid. 3. Sat. 4. At home.

Sund. 5. Preached at St. Peter's ch. from Eph. 6:13-18. After preaching called to see John Trexler, Esq.

Mond. 6. At home, a very inclement day.

Tues. 7. Went to Salisbury to Court.

Wed. 8. Thurs. 9. Frid. 10. At home.

Sat. 11. Went to Bostian's School House & preached at 2 p. m. from Luk. 13:6-9. Dinner at George Ketner's. All night at A. F. Graeber's.

Sund. 12. Preached at Organ ch. from Eph. 6:13-18. Dinner at Mary A. Miller's.

Mond. 13. Tues. 14. No account kept.

Wed. 15. At home.

Thurs. 16. Was present a little at the division of the land of David Holshouser, dec^{d}.

Frid. 17. Sat. 18. At home.

Sund. 19. Preached at St. Peter's ch. from Acts 16:13-15.

Mond. 20. In the morning went to Gold Hill for some Plank.

Tues. 21. Started for Mt. Pleasant. Dinner at Jacob Cruse's. Called to see widow Goodman, who has been crippled & confined to her bed for many years. All night at Danl Miller's.

Wed. 22. At Mt. Pleasant. Attended a meeting of the Board of Directors of N. C. College. Dinner at Rev. J. B. Anthony's. All night at C. Melchor's, Esq.

Thurs. 23. Attended a meeting of the Board of Directors. Dinner at Danl Miller's. Returned home.

Frid. 24. Attended the closing exercises of Lewis' school.

Sat. 25. Attended to the fun^{l} of Joseph Alexander, son of Danl Frick, at Lower St. Church. Preached from Is. 3:10.

Sund. 26. Preached at Organ ch. from Acts 16:13-15. Baptized two infants. Dinner at Mrs. Sarah Heilig's.

Mond. 27. Called at the Miss' Browns & widow Paul C. Miller.

Tues. 28. Went to Moses Lingle's & Moses Lyerly's. Dinner at Mr. Lyerly's.

Wed. 29. Went to Elihu Holshouser's sale.

Thurs. March 1. Went to Allison Misenheimer's & married Alfred W. Rusher & Malissa C. Brown.

Frid. 2. Sat. 3. At home.

Sund. 4. Preached at St. Peter's ch. from Acts 24:25. Dinner at P. N. Heilig's.

Mond. 5. Tues. 6. Wed. 7. Thurs. 8. At home.

Frid. 9. In the afternoon went to Frederic Stirewalt's. All night here.

Sat. 10. Went to John S. Long's & remained till after dinner. In the afternoon preached at Bostian's School house from Acts 24:25. All night at David Bostian's.

Sund. 11. This was my day at Organ ch. Rev. D. H. Bittle preached. Baptized one infant. Dinner at John Miller's.

Mond. 12. In the morning went to P. N. Heilig's and aided in Settlement with L. C. Miller. Balance of day at home.

Tues. 13. Went in afternoon to A. F. Graeber's on business. All night here.

Wed. 14. Returned home in the afternoon, A. F. Graeber being in company.

Thurs. 15. At home. Had Mr. Graeber to assist in locating my house.

Frid. 16. Sat. 17. At home.

Sund. 18. Preached at St. Peter's ch. from Deut. 8:2. A very inclement day.

Mond. 19. Tues. 20. At home.

Wed. 21. At home.

Thurs. 22. Went to Gold Hill on business.

Frid. 23. Went to Gold Hill for lumber.

Sat. 24. At home.

Sund. 25. Preached at Organ ch. from Deut. 8:2. Baptized 2 infants. Dinner at John Seaford's.

Mond. 26. Went to Salisbury.

Tues. 27. Went to Mrs. Sallie Heilig's & paid up a note of hand.

Wed. 28. Went to Mt. Pleasant to attend a meeting of Board of Trustees of N. C. C. Dinner at Rev. J. B. Anthony's. In the afternoon went to George Eagle's & married Caleb A. Basinger & Catherine Ann Eagle. Returned home.

Thurs. 29. Frid. 30. Sat. 31. At home.

Sund. Apr. 1. Preached at St. Peter's ch. from Zech. 8:23.

Mond. 2. At home.

Tues. 3. Attended to the funeral of Anna Louisa Josey at Organ ch. – preached from Math. 11:28.

Wed. 4. At home.

Thurs. 5. Went to Steam Saw Mill.

Frid. 6. At home.

Sat. 7. Attended to the funeral of Leah C. Stricker. – preached the fun[1] at the house and buried at Organ ch. Returned home. In the evening went to Laurence Lingel's & staid over night.

Sund. 8. Preached at Organ ch. from Ps. 7:9. Baptized three infants. Dinner at Frederic Stirewald's. Here baptized Adam and Eve C. Stirewald's child. All night at George Smith's.

Mond. 9. Preached at Bostian's School House from 1 Pet. 4:18. Dinner at John S. Long's. Returned home.

Tues. 10. In the morning went to Gold Hill on business. In the afternoon at home. This afternoon A. F. Graeber & hands commenced getting Timber for my house.

Wed. 11. Went to Salisbury.

Thurs. 12. Went to Dan[l] Bost's, thence to Tobias Miller's & married Jacob W. Bost & Catharine Miller. Returned to Dan[l] Bost's to dinner.

Frid. 13. At home.

Sat. 14. At home.

Sund. 15. Preached at St. Peter's ch. from 1 Pet. 4:18. Baptized 2 inf[ts]. Dinner at Peter Trexler's. In the afternoon preached the widow John May's fun[l] at the house from Am. 4:12.

Mond. 16. At home.

Tues. 17. Went to Jesse Miller's & helped to move corn crib & roll logs.

Wed. 18. Thurs. 19. Frid. 20. At home.

Sat. 21. Had services at Organ ch. preparatory to communion. Rev. Artz preached. Baptized six infants. Returned home.

Sund. 22. Had communion at Organ Church. Rev. Artz preached. Rev. D. H. Bittle was also present & assisted in the communion services.

Mond. 23. At home.

Tues. 24. Went to Mrs. S. Heilig's to a stable raising.

Wed. 25. Attended to the fun[l] of Philip Earnheart at Lower St. ch. – preached from Amos 4:12. Dinner at Mrs. S. Heilig's. Returned home by way of Gold Hill.

Thurs. 26. At home.

Frid. 27. Attended a Special Conference at St. Peter's ch. Rev. Linn preached. Rev. Anthony with me over night.

Sat. 28. At St. Peter's ch. Rev. Linn preached. An inclement day.

Sund. 29. At St. Peter's ch. Rev. J. B. Anthony preached morning and afternoon. Administered the Lord's Supper.

Mond. 30. Attended to the fun[l] of Eli Klutts' child. Gave address with singing & prayer at the house. The child was buried at Lower St. ch. Went from Mr. Klutts' to Organ ch. & attended to the fun[l] of Charles Patterson's child. Preached from Mark 10:13-16.

Tues. May 1. At home.

Wed. 2. Started for Synod. All night at Robert Moore's.

Thurs. 3. Went to Sandy Creek ch., Davidson Co., to Synod, & continued in attendance at Synod until its adjournment on Monday evening following. Preached on Monday night from Luk. 13:24. Lodged during the sessions of Synod with J. H. Thompson, Esq.

Tues. 8. Returned home. Dinner at B. F. Fraley's.

Wed. 9. Thurs. 10. At home.

Frid. 11. Went to Salisbury.

Sat. 12. Commenced catechization at Organ ch.

Sund. 13. This was my regular day at Organ ch. The forenoon was very inclement. Had some religious exercises, & baptized one infant. Dinner at Moses Barringer's. In the afternoon preached at Bostian's Sch. House from Luk. 13:24. Called to see John S. Long, he being very sick. All night at Geo. M. Ketner's.

Mond. 14. Baptized Mr. Ketner's child. Called to see John S. Long. Dinner at P. A. Seaford's, Esq. Returned home by way of Geo. M. Bernhardt's.

Tues. 15. Attended to the fun[l] of John S. Long. Preached the fun[l] at the house from Ps. 37:34. & buried at the family burying ground. All night at D. Eddleman's.

Wed. 16. Returned home by way of Salisbury.

Thurs. 17. Went to Eli Seaford's & baptized his twin children, one of them being very sick.

Frid. 18.

Sat. 19. Went to Widow Wagner's (of Philip) & preached the fun[l] of Philip Wagner, who had died some time previous, from Eccl. 9:10.

Sund. 20. Preached at St. Peter's ch. from Luk. 13:24.

Mond. 21. In the afternoon went to Gold Hill on business.

Tues. 22. At home.

Wed. 23. At home.

Thurs. 24. To day married at my house Julius A. Coleman & Elizabeth A. Nichols. In the afternoon went to Widow Millers (of Paul) on business.

Frid. 25. Went to Gold Hill on business. Baptized also Reuben J. Holmes' child.

Sat. 26. Had catechization at Organ ch. Dinner at Moses Barringer's.

Sund. 27. Preached at Organ ch. from Prov. 23:26. Baptized two infants. Dinner at Mary A. Heilig's.

Mond. 28. Went with Lewis to Milas Arey's.

Tues. 29. Went to Salisbury. Lewis & Milas Arey went to Salem. Dinner at Peter Miller's. Settled with Sarah & Elizabeth Brown, Legatees of Clementine Brown, dec[d].

Wed. 30. At home.

Thurs. 31. Went to Mary A. Miller's & settled for hauling. Also to Dan[l] Bost's & horse shod.

Frid. June 1. At home.

Sat. 2. At home.

Sund. 3. Preached at St. Peter's ch. from Prov. 1:24-26. Baptized one infant. Dinner at H. A. Miller's. In the afternoon went to Cunningham's Stand and heard Rev. Shaver preach.

Mond. 4. Went to Salisbury to court.

Tues. 5. Wed. 6. Thurs. 7. Frid. 8. At home.

Sat. 9. Had catechization at Organ ch. Dinner at M. Barringer's.

Sund. 10. Preached at Organ ch. from Prov. 1:24-26. Baptized one infant. Dinner at J. L. Graeber's. In the afternoon preached at Bostian's Sch. House from Luk. 18:13. All at Jacob Pless'.

Mond. 11. Returned home. Dinner at Jacob Miller's.

Tues. 12. Wed. 13. At home.

Thurs. 14. In the evening went to Dan[l] Miller's on business.

Frid. 15. Returned home by way of the Steam Saw Mill & settled my bill for Lumber. Dinner at Col. Bernhardt's.

Diary No. 24
January 1862

Wed. Jan. 1. A very pleasant day. Went to Salisbury.

Thurs. 2. Went to Mr. Holshouser's & made out his Quarterly Settlement as Post Master. In the afternoon went to Gold Hill.

Frid. 3. Went to Jacob Mesimer's & to Nancy Arey's to attend to some business connected to some rent corn belonging to Eliz. Barringer's. All night at Mrs. Arey's.

Sat. 4. Made arrangements to have said cribbed and returned home. Wrote a letter to Lewis, then went to Gold Hill.

Sund. 5. Preached at St. Peter's ch. from Luk. 13:6-9. A very sleety inclement day. — Few hearers.

Mond. 6. Went to Salisbury.

Tues. 7. Went to Gold Hill.

Wed. 8. In the forenoon went to Widow Paul Miller's on business.

Thurs. 9. Went to sale at Sol. Peeler's. In the evening went to Gold Hill.

Frid. 10. Attended to the fun[l] of Andrew Berger's child at Lower St. ch. — preached from Gen. 15:1. Dinner at Widow Mary Miller's.

Sat. 11. Went to Salisbury.

Sund. 12. Preached at Organ ch. from Acts 16:13-15. Baptized one infant. Dinner at Jacob Trexler's.

Mond. 13. In the forenoon went to Gold Hill. In the afternoon at Mr. Holshouser's. Making out some Post Office accounts.

Tues. 14. At home fixing Mr. H's Post Office accounts.

Wed. 15. At home.

Thurs. 16. Went to P. N. Heilig's on business. In the afternoon went with Mr. H. Partridge hunting.

Frid. 17. In the forenoon went to Gold Hill. In the afternoon at home.

Sat. 18. Went to Gold Hill to attend the Sale of the property of D. Lisk, dec[d] In the afternoon called at Daniel Miller's (of Asa) his wife being sick.

Sund. 19. Preached at St. Peter's ch. from Jer. 17:9. 2 Cor. 13:5. Confirmed Amelia Waller. Dinner at H. A. Miller's.

Mond. 20. Went to Peter Trexler's.

Tues. 21. Went to Salisbury.

Wed. 22. At home.

Thurs. 23. Went early in the morning to David A. Bost's, he being very sick & wrote his Will. Returned home by way of Gold Hill.

Frid. 24. At home. A very inclement day.

Sat. 25. Went to Post Office.

Sund. 26. Preached at Organ ch. from Heb. 3:2. Baptized one inf[t]. Dinner at Joseph Miller's. Called to see D. A. Bost, he being still very sick.

Mond. 27. Went to Nancy Arey's on business.

Tues. 28. Called at Post Office and & signed Jacob Holshouser's Bond, as security, to the P. O. Department. Then went to Gold Hill.

Wed. 29. Attended to the funeral of David A. Bost at Organ church. Preached from Eph. 4:1. Dinner at D. A. Bost's. Returned home by way of Jacob Holshouser's (of David).

Thurs. 30. At home. Had Eli Klutts to make a box for Lewis' trunk.

Frid. 31. Went to Gold Hill.

Sat. Feb. 1. Called to see Widow John Trexler.

Sund. 2. Preached at St. Peter's ch. from Heb. 3:2. Baptized one inf^t. In the evening called to see Danl Miller's (of Asa) family, his wife being sick.

Mond. 3. Went to Salisbury to Court & administered on Matilda Beaver's Estate.

Tues. 4. Took a box, containing Lewis' Trunk & uniform, to Salisbury & put in the Express office to go to Manassas Junction.

Wed. 5. In the afternoon went to Salisbury & made settlement of Matilda Beaver's Estate as guardian.

Thurs. 6. In the afternoon went to Daywalt Beaver's, & married David Earnheart & Eve L. Beaver.

Frid. 7. Went to Widow David Bost's to meet Jess Beaver to look over some of David Bost's papers.

Sat. 8. In the afternoon went to Gold Hill.

Sund. 9. Preached at Organ ch. from 1 Cor. 4:2. Baptized one infant. Dinner at Laurence Lingel's.

Mond. 10. Attended to the funeral of John Klutts at Organ ch. − preached from 1 Cor. 7:29. Dinner at Jacob Miller's.

Tues. 11. At home.

Wed. 12. At home till after dinner. Then went and notified Paul Holshouser to attend settlement of D. Holshouser's Estate.

Thurs. 13. Called to see Jacob Holshouser (of David) & Lauson Fisher on business. Returned by way of Gold Hill.

Frid. 14. Had settlement with the heirs of David Holshouser, dec^d.

Sat. 15. Went to Widow Geo. A. Miller's & assisted in laying off her year's Provision.

Sund. 16. Preached at St. Peter's ch. from Rev. 2:4.5.

Mond. 17. Tues. 18. At home mending shoes.

Wed. 19. Went in forenoon to Aaron Lentz's on business.

Thurs. 20. Went to widow John Trexler's and assisted in laying off her dower in land & year's provision.

Frid. 21. At home.

Sat. 22. Attended muster at Jesse Miller's.

Sund. 23. Preached at Organ ch. from 1 Thes. 5:17. Baptized one inf^t.

Mond. 24. Clerked the sale of the property of George A. Miller, dec^d.

Tues. 25. Went to Salisbury.

Wed. 26. At home. Serg^t John P. M. Barringer, Com. G. 6th. Regt. N. C. State Troops called to see us and spent the night with us.

Thurs. 27. Clerked the Sale of the property of John Trexler, dec^d.

Frid. 28. This day was set apart by Pres. Davis as a day of humiliation & prayer − preached at Organ ch. from Job. 2:10. Dinner at M. Barringer's.

Sat. March 1. In the afternoon went to Gold Hill.

Sund. 2. Preached at St. Peter's ch. from 1 Thes. 5:17. Dinner at Moses Linn's.

Mond. 3. Went to Widow Jno. Trexler's.

Tues. 4. Clerked the sale of Eli Klutts' property. Special Sale.

Wed. 5. Mended shoes till dinner. In afternoon helped Milas A. Holshouser lay the foundation of his house.

Thurs. 6. In forenoon went with Calvin Brady to Danl Miller's to reconcile Brady & his wife. In the afternoon helped M. A. Holshouser at his house raising.

Frid. 7. Attended the closing exercises of Mr. Hardester's school.

Sat. 8. In afternoon went to Gold Hill.

Sund. 9. Preached at Organ ch. from Gal. 6:7. Dinner at John Seaford's.

Mond. 10. Went to Danl Bost's to blacksmith shop.

Tues. 11. Butchered beef. In afternoon went to St. Mathew's ch. and attended to the funeral of Charles Dry. Preached from Luk. 12:37.

Wed. 12. Engaged hands to roll Study.

Thurs. 13. Commenced rolling Study, but had to stop in consequence of rain.

Frid. 14. Went to Sandy Pool's for wheels to roll study.

Sat. 15. Went to Salisbury.

Sund. 16. Preached at St. Peter's from 1 Chron. 28:9.

Mond. 17. Engaged hands to roll study.

Tues. 18. Rolled Study, quite unwell.

Wed. 19. At home & quite unwell.

Thurs. 20. Frid. 21. Sat. 22. At home and indisposed.

Sund. 23. Preached at Organ ch. from Ps. 46:1.

Mond. 24. Went to Salisbury.

Tues. 25. Went to John Moose's on business.

Wed. 26. At home, an inclement day.

Thurs. 27. In afternoon went to mill.

Frid. 28. Went to Luther's ch. to Special Conference.

Sat. 29. Went to mill.

Sund. 30. At Conference.

Mond. 31. In afternoon made out Quarterly Settlement for Mr. Holshouser.

Tues. Apr. 1. Went to Salisbury.

Wed. 2. Went to blacksmith shop — also to Danl Miller's & Mt. Pleasant on business.

Thurs. 3. Frid. 4. Sat. 5. At home.

Sund. 6. Preached at St. Peter's ch. from Josh. 23:8.

Mond. 7. Tues. 8. At home.

Wed. 9. Thurs. 10. At home mending shoes.

Frid. 11. At home.

Sat. 12. Went to P. N. Heilig's to Tax Listing.

Sund. 13. Preached at Organ ch. from John 3:2. Dinner at Dr. Coleman's.

Mond. 14. Attended to the funeral of Simeon Seaford at Organ ch. Preached from Heb. 11:16. Dinner at Sally Heilig's.

Tues. 15. Went to Salisbury.

Wed. 16. Went to Jacob Pless' to Tan Yard.

Thurs. 17. Went to P. N. Heilig's to assist him in his settlement of the Estate of John H. Miller, dec^{d}

Frid. 18. In the forenoon went to Gold Hill.

Sat. 19. Preached at St. Peter's church. from John 14:15. preparatory to communion.

Sund. 20. Preached at St. Peter's ch. from Acts 4:13. and administered the Lord's Supper.

Mond. 21. Went to Post Office.

Tues. 22. At home & nailed on garden poles.

Wed. 23. Went to Post Office.

Thurs. 24. In the afternoon went to Gold Hill.

Sat. 26. Went to St. John's ch. to assist Rev. Anthony at a Communion meeting. — All night at Jacob House's.

Sund. 27. Preached at St. John's ch. from Math. 22: 1-14. Dinner at Danl Miller's.

Mond. 28. In the afternoon went to P. N. Heilig's on business.

Tues. 29. In forenoon went to Gold Hill. Afternoon at home.

Wed. 30. Went to Salisbury to have the members of Synod taken to the country.

Thurs. May 1. Went to Organ ch. Synod met to day. Returned home.

Frid. 2. At Organ ch. Returned home.

Sat. 3. At Organ ch. All night at Laurence Lingel's. Baptized 5 inf^{ts} to day.

Sund. 4. At Organ ch. Returned home.

Mond. 5. At Organ ch. All night at Moses Barringer's.

Tues. 6. At Organ ch. till 12 o'clock. In afternoon returned home.

Wed. 7. Went to Salisbury.

Thurs. 8. Prepared for the press the Minutes of Synodical Missionary Society & took them to Rev. Linn's.

Frid. 9. Went to Andr. Berger's for Salt, & in the evening went to mill.

Sat. 10. At home.

Sund. 11. Preached at Organ ch. from 2 Cor. 4:7. Baptized 1 inf^{t} Dinner at Jacob Miller's.

Mond. 12. At home, sheared the sheep.

Tues. 13. In the afternoon helped Milas A. Holshouser lay the foundation of his barn.

Wed. 14. Helped M. A. H. raise his barn.

Thurs. 15. Went to Salisbury to attend a convention for the formation of a Southern Genl Synod.

Frid. 16. Attended to the fun^{l} of Martin Lyerly at Organ ch. — preached from Heb. 4:7.

Sat. 17. At the Convention in Salisbury.

Sund. 18. Rev. Linn preached for me at St. Peter's church. Dinner at Rev. J. A. Linn's.

Sund. 25. Preached at Organ ch. from 2 Cor. 4:7.

Sund. June 1. Preached at St. Peter's ch. from 1 John 2:1.2. Dinner at Dr. Coleman's. In the afternoon to widow Cunningham's & heard Rev. Wood preach.

Mond. 2. Attended to the fun[l] of James House's child at Organ ch. — preached from Gen. 15:1. In the afternoon went to Salisbury & took the cars for Richmond to see Lewis.

Tues. 3. Arrived in Richmond in the evening. Stopped at the Spottswood House.

Wed. 4. Breakfast & dinner at the Park House. In the afternoon found Lewis 1½ miles from Richmond sick. Spent the night with him.

Thurs. 5. Spent the greater part of the day with Lewis.

Frid. 6. In the morning went into Richmond & drew 2 months pay for Lewis, bought a valise, some onions & bread for him and returned to his camp. In the afternoon went to Richmond to take the cars next morning for home. At the Spottswood house.

Sat. 7. Started for home & reached Salisbury on the following morning.

Sund. 8. In the morning arrived in Salisbury. Breakfast at B. F. Fraley's. Hired conveyance to Organ ch. & preached from Mark 16:15. & held a meeting of Miss'y. Society. Dinner at Mrs. Mary A. Heilig's.

Mond. 9. At home & unwell.

Tues. 10. In the afternoon went to Jacob Lyerly's, Sen. on business. In the evening went to Andrew Berger's, his wife being sick. All night here.

Wed. 11. Attended to the fun[l] of Sandy Stirewald's child. — preached the fun[l] at the house and buried at Organ Church.

Thurs. 12. Attended to the funeral of Sarah C. Berger, wife of Andrew Berger, at Lower St. ch. — preached from Rev. 2:10. Dinner at G. M. Bernhardt's. Then went to Mr. Bost's & had horse shod.

Frid. 13. Sat. 14. At home, hay making.

Sund. 15. This my day at St. Peter's ch. but was too unwell with cold to preach, but held a meeting of Missionary Society. Dinner at Mrs. Anna Trexler's.

Mond. 16. Called to see Jesse Beaver, he being sick. In afternoon went to Gold Hill.

Tues. 17. In the afternoon went to P. N. Heilig's & Rev. Linn's on business.

Wed. 18. Thurs. 19. At home.

Frid. 20. Went to Mr. Bost's to have old Safety shod. Dinner at Joseph Miller's. In afternoon went to Gold Hill.

Sat. 21. At home.

Sund. 22. Preached at Organ ch. from Is. 12:3. Dinner at Eli Klutts'.

Tues. 24. Attended to the fun[l] of William Bost. — preached from Gen. 42:36.

Frid. 27. Hauled in oats.

Sat. 28. At St. Peter's ch. Special Conference in session.

Sund. 29. At St. Peter's ch.

Mond. 30. Went to Salisbury.

Tues. July 1. At home till afternoon, then went to mill.

Wed. 2. At home.

Thurs. 3. In afternoon went to mill.

Frid. 4. Went to Henry Miller's for a pig.

Sat. 5. At home.

Sund. 6. Preached at St. Peter's ch. the funeral of Eli Earnheart, a volunteer, who died in Hospital in Petersburg.

Mond. 7. At home.

Tues. 8. Went to enrollment of Conscripts.

Wed. 9. At home.

Thurs. 10. At home. Calvin L. Miller, a wounded soldier with us.

Frid. 11. Went to Dan$^{\underline{l}}$ Bost's to Blacksmith shop.

Sat. 12. At home.

Sund. 13. Preached at Organ ch. from Prov. 22:2. Baptized 2 infants. Dinner at Dan$^{\underline{l}}$ Eddleman's. In afternoon preached at Bostian's School house from Mal. 3:16. Baptized Dan$^{\underline{l}}$ S. Sides' child. Returned home.

Mond. 14. In forenoon went to Eli Klutts' on business. In afternoon went to Gold Hill.

Tues. 15. Went to Salisbury.

Wed. 16. Went to Mt. Pleasant to attend a meeting of Board of College. Dinner at John Lentz's. Returned home.

Thurs. 17. At home.

Frid. 18. At home.

Sat. 19. In afternoon went to mill.

Sund. 20. Preached at St. Peter's ch. from Gen. 22:1.2. Dinner at Calvin Earnheart's.

Mond. 21. At home.

Tues. 22. Attended to the fun$^{\underline{l}}$ of Jeremiah Basinger's child at Organ ch. – preached from Ps. 34:17.

Wed. 23. Went to Gold Hill, & in afternoon called to see Mrs. Bost, widow of Wm. Bost, dec$^{\underline{d}}$.

Thurs. 24. In afternoon went to Dan$^{\underline{l}}$ Miller's after a shoat. All night here.

Frid. 25. Returned home.

Sat. 26. Preached at Pless' School house from Rev. 14:13. the fun$^{\underline{l}}$ of Alexander Blackwelder, who fell in battle May 31, 1862. on the plains of the Chickahominy, Va.

Sund. 27. Preached at Organ ch. from Gen. 5:24. the fun$^{\underline{l}}$ of Jacob Alex$^{\underline{r}}$ Eddleman, who also fell in battle May 31, 1862, on the Chickahominy, Va. Baptized 3 infants. Dinner at Sallie Heilig's.

Mond. 28. At home.

Tues. 29. At home.

Wed. 30. At home.

Thurs. 31. Went to Mrs. Nancy Arey's & to Salisbury.

Frid. Aug. 1. At home.

Sat. 2. Went to Mr. Pless' to Tan Yard.

Sund. 3. Preached at St. Peter's ch. from Luk. 12:32. Dinner at H. A. Miller's. In afternoon went to Moses Lyerly's to see old Mrs. Trexler, she being sick.

Mond. 4. At home till dinner threshing wheat & oats. In the afternoon helped to thresh at Mrs. Holshouser's.

Tues. 5. Went to Salisbury to court & administered on the Estate of Wm. Bost, dec^d. Entered also as Guardian for three of the minor heirs of Milas Arey, dec^d.

Wed. 6. Went to Widow Miller's & made partial settlement with the heirs of Paul Miller, dec^d.

Thurs. 7. Went to Gold Hill in the morning to election. In the afternoon started for Salem as far as Nancy Arey's. All night here.

Frid. 8. Went to Caleb Peeler's.

Sat. 9. Went to Salem to carding machine. Dinner at H. Thomas' in Winston. Returned to C. Peeler's.

Sund. 10. Preached at Hopewell from Gen. 5:24. the funerals of Solomon Zimmerman & his son, Julius. Dinner at H. Beckerdite's. All night at C. Peeler's.

Mond. 11. Returned home.

Tues. 12. At home.

Sund. 17. This my day at St. Peter's ch. Rev. Goodman from Iredell preached for me. Dinner at John Earnheart's.

Frid. 22. Went to Sale at D. A. Bost's, dec^d

Sund. 24. This my day at Organ ch. but the day being very inclement the congregation was very small. Had some religious exercises & dismissed. Called by Eli Holshouser's in the morning & baptized his child.

Mond. 25. Went to Mrs. Bost's (of William) & made preparations for sale.

Tues. 26. Had sale of the property of Wm. Bost, dec^d.

Wed. 27. Went to Mrs. Bost's to attend to delivery of property, &c.

Thurs. 28. Went to Martin Lyerly's & assisted in laying off a year's provision for Mrs. Lyerly. Attended sale also.

Frid. 29. Assisted Mrs. Sally Holshouser in her hay.

Sat. 30. Went to Mrs. Nancy Arey's & rented out some of the land of the minor heirs.

Sund. 31. Attended Sunday School at St. Peter's ch.

Mond. Sept. 1. Went to Salisbury.

Tues. 2. In afternoon went to Gold Hill to blacksmith Shop.

Wed. 3. In the morning went to Jacob Lyerly's, Sen. & paid him some money for Danl Miller.

Thurs. 4. Went to Gold Hill for Salt. In afternoon went to Joseph Miller's for some Brandy.

Frid. 5. Assisted Mrs. Susan Peeler in her hay.

Sat. 6. Went to Salisbury.

Sund. 7. Preached at St. Peter's ch. from Heb. 10:25. Baptized one infant.

Mond. 8. Tues. 9. Wed. 10. At home.

Thurs. 11. Attended to the fun^{l} of James C. Roseman's child, preached the fun^{l} at the house from Math. 5:8. and buried at Lower St. Church.

Frid. 12. Sat. 13. At home.

Sund. 14. Preached at Organ ch. from Heb. 10:25. Baptized 2 inf^{ts}. Dinner at Moses Barringer's.

Mond. 15. Went to Salisbury.

Tues. 16. Wed. 17. At home.

Thurs. 18. Had religious service at St. Peter's ch., the day having been set apart by President Davis as a day of Thanksgiving for victories achieved. In the afternoon went to Widow H. G. Lentz's on business.

Frid. 19. Called at Jesse Miller's on business.

Sat. 20. Attended to the fun^{l} of Alexander Casper at St. Mathew's ch. — preached from Gen. 15:1.

Sund. 21. Preached at St. Peter's ch. from Acts 16:30.31. Bap^{t} 1 inf^{t}.

Mond. 22. At home till afternoon, then went to Gold Hill.

Tues. 23. Went to Salisbury & at night started for Richmond.

Wed. 24. Reached Richmond in the evening & took lodging at the Park House.

Thurs. 25. In Richmond. Found Capt. Beard's company & staid with it till next day. Heard to day that Lewis suffered from the explosion of a shell in the battle of Sharpsburg. Preached at night for Capt. Beard's company & other soldier's.

Frid. 26. Took the train at 3 o'clock, P.M. for Gordonsville in company with Dr. Gibson & Col. Wallace. Reached Gordonsville about midnight & staid with the soldiers until day.

Sat. 27. Took the train for Staunton. Breakfast in Charlottesville. Arrived in Staunton late in the afternoon & here found Lewis.

Sund. 28. In Staunton. Attended Sunday School & preaching in the Lutheran church. At night preached in the Luth. ch. from Luk. 13:3. Lodged at the Virginia Hotel.

Mond. 29. Returned to Richmond bringing Lewis with me. Lodged at the Park House.

Tues. 30. Lewis reported at the Moore Hospital & filed his application for a furlough. Started for home at 3 P.M., leaving Lewis in Richmond.

Wed. Oct. 1. Arrived in Salisbury in the evening. All night at Mr. Fraley's.

Thurs. 2. Returned home.

Frid. 3. Attended Sale at the Miss. Brown's.

Sat. 4. Went to Widow Martin Lyerly's & brought blacksmith tools home.

Sund. 5. At St. Peter's ch. Rev. J. B. Anthony preached.

Mond. 6. Went to Post Office & made Mr. Holshouser's Quarterly Settlement.

Tues. 7. In the evening went to Mr. Danl Miller's on business. All night here.

Wed. 8. Returned home.

Thurs. 9. At home.

Sund. 12. Preached at Organ ch. from John 19:25-27. Bapt^d 1 inf^t.

Mond. 13. Went to J. Pless' Tan Yard.

Tues. 14. At home.

Wed. 15. At home.

Thurs. 16. Went to barn raising at Henry Peeler's.

Frid. 17. At home.

Sat. 18. Had preparatory service at St. Peter's ch. – preached from John 19:25-27. Bapt^d 2 inf^{ts}.

Sund. 19. Preached at St. Peter's from Is. 25:6-8. Administered the Lord's Supper. Dinner at H. A. Miller's. In the evening called to see & baptized Adam Goodman, he being sick.

Mond. 20. At home.

Tues. 21. At home. In the evening went to shucking to Mr. Linn's.

Wed. 22. Engaged hands to roll corn crib. At night went to shucking to Sally Holshouser's. At the close of shucking, C. M. Holshouser was brought home from Richmond a corpse.

Thurs. 23. Attended to the fun^l of C. M. Holshouser at Lower St. church. – preached from Gen. 42:36. Dinner at Mary A. Heilig's. At night went to shucking at Jesse Miller's.

Frid. 24. Rolled up corn crib.

Sat. 25. Had preparatory service at Organ ch., preached from John 15:5. In the afternoon attended to the fun^l of Eli Miller's child at Lower St. ch. – preached from Math. 5:4.

Sund. 26. Went to Organ ch. but had no service, the day being very inclement.

Mond. 27. Attended to the fun^l of Adam Goodman. – preached at the house from Amos 4:12. & buried at Union ch.

Tues. 28. At home. At night went to J. Holshouser's to shucking.

Wed. 29. At home.

Thurs. 30. Went to Widow Bost's & sold some corn & rented out some land. All night here.

Frid. 31. Attended to measuring corn. In the evening returned home.

Sat. Nov. 1. Went to D. Barringer's on business.

Sund. 2. Preached at St. Peter's ch. from John 1:29.

Mond. 3. Went to Salisbury to court.

Tues. 4. Wed. 5. At home.

Thurs. 6. Attended to the fun[l] of Widow Goodman, relict of Thomas Goodman Sen. Preached at the house from Prov. 16:31. Dinner at Cha[s] Fisher's.

Frid. 7. Went to Salisbury & to Enoch Phillips' to attend settlement of Estate of John Castor, dec[d] as agent for Henry M. Castor.

Sat. 8. At home, very unwell.

Sund. 9. Went to Organ ch. and administered the Lord's Supper. Very unwell.

Mond. 10. Went to mill and to Fred Waller's to have shoes made.

Tues. 11. At home, butchered beef.

Wed. 12. Attended to the fun[l] of Alex. M. Miller's child. at Lower St. ch. — preached from Amos 4:12. Dinner at Mary A. Miller's.

Thurs. 13. At home.

Frid. 14. Went to Gold Hill & to Dr. Coleman's. Indisposed.

Sat. 15. At home sick with Jaundice.

Sund. 16. to Sat. 22. inclusive at home and indisposed.

Sund. 23. Preached at Organ ch. from Heb. 11:16. The fun[l] of Henry Miller, who fell in the battle Sharpsburg, Md. Dinner at Dr. Coleman's.

Mond. 24. Took Lewis to Salisbury to return to his Regiment. Parted with him at the Town Creek.

Tues. 25. Wed. 26. At home.

Thurs. 27. At home, cut out & closed a pair of shoes.

Frid. 28. Went to St. John's ch. to Special Conference. All night at Dan[l] Miller's.

Sat. 29. At Conference. All night at John Lentz's.

Sund. 30. At Conference. Dinner at Dan[l] Miller's. Returned home in evening.

Mond. Dec. 1. Tues. 2. Wed. 3. Thurs. 4. At home making shoes.

Frid. 5. Went to post office.

Sat. 6. Started to Jerusalem ch. in Davie co. All night at Mathias Miller's.

Sund. 7. The day being very inclement (cold), & there being no stove in the church, preached at the dwelling of Rev. Bessants, Baptist Minister, dwelling from Mark 1:40-45. Dinner at Math. Miller's. All night at John C. Miller's.

Mond. 8. Returned home.

Tues. 9. Butchered 2 hogs.

Wed. 10. Went to Gold Hill & Post Office.

Thurs. 11. Cut out & closed a pair of shoes for wife.

Frid. 12. At home till dinner, then went Cleodora Earnhardt's, she having received the intelligence of her husband's death, C. M. Earnheart.

Sat. 13. Went to Chas. Bostian's late residence & preached his fun[1] from Acts. 13:36. Returned home after preaching. Baptized to day Mr. Bostian's child.

Sund. 14. Preached at Organ ch. from Is. 41:10. the funeral of Henry A. Seaford, who died in camp near Petersburg. Baptized 4 infants.

Mond. 15. Made shoes till dinner, then helped to cover Milas A. Holshouser's house.

Tues. 16. Helped cover Milas A. Holshouser's house.

Wed. 17. At home making shoes.

Thurs. 18. At home making shoes.

Frid. 19. Went to David Bostian's & preached the fun[1] of John M. Bostian, Soldier, who died at Charlottesville, Va. Preached from Job 1:21. Dinner here. Returned home.

Sat. 20. Attended the enrollment of conscripts up to 40 years.

Sund. 21. Preached at St. Peter's ch. from Heb. 10:24.

Mond. 22. At home.

Tues. 23. Went to blacksmith Shop at P. N. Heilig's to repair little wagon.

Wed. 24. At home.

Thurs. 25. Christmas Day. Went to Joseph A. Patterson's & preached his funeral from Ps. 144:15. Mr. Patterson was wounded in the battle of Sharpsburg, Md. and returned home & died.

Frid. 26. Sat. 27. At home.

Sund. 28. Preached at Organ ch. from Prov. 14:32. Bapt[d] [space] infants. Dinner at John Seaford's.

Mond. 29. At home, butchered hogs.

Tues. 30. Wed. 31. At home.

Thurs. Jan. 1, 1863. Went to Salisbury.

Frid. 2. Sat. 3. At home.

Sund. 4. Preached at St. Peter's ch. from Jer. 28:16.

Mond. 5. Tues. 6. At home.

Wed. 7. Went to Mich^l Goodman's for crocks.

Thurs. 8. At home.

Frid. 9. In the afternoon went to Gold Hill.

Sat. 10. Started for Salisbury, as far as Solomon Brown's, but the day being very inclement returned home. Dinner here.

Sund. 11. Preached at Organ ch. from Prov. 4:18. Dinner at Joseph Miller's.

Mond. 12. At home.

Tues. 13. Went to Salisbury.

Wed. 14. At home.

Thurs. 15. Went to Otho Pool's for wagon, he having repaired it, & returned home by way of Mrs. Arey's. At Mrs. A's attended to the burial service for a colored boy.

Frid. 16. Went to Danl Miller's on business. In afternoon went to Gold Hill.

Sat. 17. Went to Salisbury.

Sund. 18. Preached at St. Peter's ch. from Ps. 40:1-3. Dinner at Moses Linn's.

Mond. 19. In the afternoon went to Gold Hill.

Tues. 20. Went in forenoon to Mrs. John Trexler's & to Andrew Berger's on business.

Sund. 25. Preached at Organ ch. from Ps. 97:11. the fun^l of Eli Seaford, who fell in the battle of Fredericksburg.

Mond. 26. Went to Salisbury in order to visit the army on the Rappahannock.

Tues. 27. Took the cars at 3 o'clock A.M. & reached Raleigh the same evening. Started immediately for Weldon.

Wed. 28. Reached Richmond in the evening after dark.

Thurs. 29. Took the cars early in the morning for Hamilton's Crossing. Returned from Hamilton's Crossing to Guinea's Station at 3 P.M. Started thro' snow & mud in search of 5th Reg^t Reached 5th Reg^t after dark & staid over night on the camp.

Frid. 30. Started in search of 6th and 57th Reg^{ts}. Reached 6th Reg^t at dusk, & staid over night with Lewis in Officer's Tent.

Sat. 31. Visited 57th Reg^t, & at night went to Mr. Turner's in the vicinity & staid over night.

Sund. Feb. 1. With the soldiers. Had intended to preach, but the inclemency of the weather prevented. All night at Mr. Turner's.

Mond. 2. Started back to 4th and 5th Reg^{ts} Preached at night to the soldiers from Mark 1:40-45. Staid over night with Capt. Jones, Q.M. of 5th Regiment.

Tues. 3. Went to Guinea's Station, & by the aid of Eli Klutts & others exhumed Calvin M. Earnheart, put the body in a coffin & box preparatory to his removal home. All night at Col. White's.

Wed. 4. Took the cars for Hamilton's Crossing, thence went to Rowan Artillery in search of Steph. Brady. Returned on foot to Col. White's. All night here.

Thurs. 5. Took the cars at 2 P.M. for Richmond. All night at Am. Hotel.

Frid. 6. Went to Winder Hospital to see John R. Miller. Then went to Oakwood Cemetery in search of the grave of Abram Earnheart. Failed to have the grave identified with sufficient certainty to have the body exhumed & removed home. In the evening took the cars for Petersburg. All night at Jarrat's Hotel.

Sat. 7. Had the body of Eli Earnheart exhumed & boxed & carried to depot. Took the cars in the evening for Weldon & Raleigh.

Sund. 8. Arrived in Raleigh this morning after day light & remained here till the following morning.

Mond. 9. Took the cars for Salisbury, & reached Salisbury at night. All night at B. F. Fraley's.

Tues. 10. Had the bodies of Calvin & Eli Earnheart hauled to Calvin's late residence & then returned home.

Wed. 11. Attended to the burial of Calvin & Eli Earnheart at St. Peter's Church.

Thurs. 12. Went to Laurence Lingel's.

Frid. 13. At home.

Sat. 14. In the afternoon went & helped cut firewood for Sallie Holshouser.

Sund. 15. Preached at St. Peter's ch. from Acts 13:36. the fun^l C. W. Earnheart. Indisposed with bad cold.

Mond. 16. Went to Salisbury.

Tues. 17. At home.

Wed. 18. At home.

Thurs. 19. Went to Mr. Moyer's to have Collar mended.

Frid. 20. Took sick to day and was confined to the house till March 5.

Thurs., March 5. Went to Goodman's Tan Yard for Leather.

Frid. 6. Took Leather to Mr. Moyer's to have shoes made.

Sat. 7. Mended shoes till dinner. In afternoon went to Mr. Heilig's & had horse shod.

Sund. 8. Preached at Organ ch. from Luk. 13:24. Baptized 3 infants. Dinner at Mary A. Heilig's.

Mond. 9. Tues. 10. At home.

Wed. 11. Went to Salisbury.

Thurs. 12. Called at Mr. L. Lingel's on business. Balance of day at home.

Frid. 13. Took a box to Dr. Coleman's to take to Salisbury for Lewis. Balance of day at home.

Sat. 14. Went to Mr. Moyer's for a pr. of shoes. Also called by Elizabeth Klutts' to get Tobias' age.

Sund. 15. Preached at St. Peter's ch. from 1 Cor. 9:24-27. the fun^l of Tobias Klutts, who fell in the battle of Fredericksburg.

Mond. 16. In the morning went to blacksmith shop and to Post Office.

Tues. 17. At home.

Sund. 22. Preached at Organ ch. from 2 Cor. 12:9. Dinner at John Seaford's.

Monday 23. Went to Geo. Smith's & to Geo. Peeler's on business. Dinner at Nancy Arey's.

Frid. 27. Went to Mt. Carmel ch. to attend Special Conference — preached from 1 Cor. 9:24-27. All night at Abram Dry's.

Sat. 28. At Conference. All night at M. Barrier's, Esq.

Diary No. 27.
April 1865.

Sund. 30. This was the time for the meeting of Special Conference, but owing to the disturbed state of the country, did not attend. Preached at St. Peter's church from 1 Sam. 2:30. Confirmed 2 persons.

Sund. May 7. This was the time for the meeting of Synod, but owing to the disturbed state of the country, did not attend. Preached at St. Peter's church from Micah 6:8. Confirmed one person.
Sund. 14. Preached at Organ ch. from Rom. 13:14.
Sat. 20. Preached at St. Peter's from Rom. 13:14. preparatory to communion.
Sund. 21. In the morning married Samuel Snider & Ann Layton. Then went to St. Peter's ch. and preached from 1 Cor. 11:26. and administered the Lord's Supper. Baptized one infant.
Sat. 27. A very inclement day. Went to Organ church and had short services preparatory to communion.
Sund. 28. At Organ church. confirmed 2 persons. Preached from Deut. 11:16. and administered the Lord's Supper.
Mond. 29. Went to Salisbury and took amnesty oath.
Tues. 30. Wed. 31. At home.

Thurs. June 1. Went to widow Shuping's and married Peter A. Ritchey to Elizabeth C. Shuping (widow).
Frid. 2. Went to mill.
Sat. 3. At home.
Sund. 4. Preached at St. Peter's ch. from Acts 11:26. Dinner at Dr. Coleman's. In the afternoon preached the fun[l] of Adam Trexler dec[d] at his late residence from 2 Tim. 1:12.
Mond. 5. to Frid. 9. At & about house.
Sat. 10. Went to Salisbury.
Sund. 11. Preached at Organ ch. from Acts 11:26. Baptized one infant. Dinner at Jacob Miller's.
Mond. 12. At home. Commenced hay making. At & about home the the [repeated] balance of the week.
Sund. 18. Preached at St. Peter's ch. from Rom. 10:1. In the afternoon went to Dan[l] Eddleman's. All night here.
Mond. 19. Attended to the funl. of Geo. H. Eagle's child. Preached at the house from -------- and buried at Organ ch.
Wed. 21. This morning son Lewis returned from captivity on Johnson's Island, Ohio.
Sund. 25. Attended to the fun[l] of Sam[l] Troutman at Lower St. Church. preached from Ex. 33:14. In the afternoon went to F. A. Stirewalt's & preached the fun[l] of his child from Ex. 33:14.

Sund. July 2. Preached at St. Peter's ch. from Is. 32:11. Dinner at Moses Linn's.

July 28. Went to St. Mathew's ch. to attend Special conference, but the people & ministers not attending, returned home. Baptized one infant.

Sund. 30. Heard Revd Butler preach at Organ ch.

Sund. Aug. 20. Preached at St. Peter's ch. from Math. 6:33. the funeral of John Waller, decd.

Sund. Aug. 27. To day Revd Aldrich preached for me at Organ ch. Tendered to the council my resignation of the pastoral charge of the congregation. Baptized 1 infant.

Aug. 31. Went to Cleodora Earnheart's & married James P. Earnheart to Sophia C. Trexler.

Sund. Sept. 10. Preached at Organ ch. from 2 Cor. 5:1. and the funeral of Ambrose Cruse, who died a prisoner of war.

Sund. 17. Preached at St. Peter's ch. from 1 Pet. 5:4. Dinner at Mrs. Anna Trexler's.

Sund. 24. Preached at Organ ch. from Matth. 7:24-27. Baptized 2 infants.

Thurs. 28. Attended to the funl. of Caleb Eller at Union ch., preached from Matth. 25:13.

Sund. Oct. 1. Preached at St. Peter's from 2 Cor. 13:2. Baptized 1 infant.

Sund. 8. Preached at Organ ch. from Luk. 16:19-31. Dinner at Mrs. M. A. Heilig's.

Sund. 15. Preached the funeral of Moses A. Goodman at St. Peter's ch. from Deut. 32:6. Dinner at H. A. Miller's.

Sat. 21. Had preparatory Service at Organ ch. Revd Artz preached. Baptized 1 infant-1 adult and confirmed 3 persons.

Sund. 22. Had communion at Organ ch. Revd Artz preached.

Thurs. 26. Went to Andrew Cruse's and married John Fisher and Leah Cruse.

Frid. 27. Went to St. Peter's church. Special conference met. Revd Kimball preached.

Sat. 28. At St. Peter's ch. Revd Groseclose preached.

Sund. 29. At St. Peter's ch. Revd Aldrich preached in the morning and Revd Artz in the afternoon. Had communion to day.

Wed. Nov. 1. Went to Mt. Pleasant to attend meeting of Board of Trustees of College.

Thurs. 2. Attended the funeral of Sophia M. Brown at St. Paul's ch. Preached from 2 Cor. 5:1.

Sund. 5. Preached at St. Peter's ch. from Prov. 28:13. Dinner at Dr. Coleman's.

Mond. 6. Went to Salisbury.

Sund. 12. Preached at Organ ch. from --------. In the afternoon went to Widow Harkey's and married Crawford Holshouser and Elizabeth Harkey.

Wed. 15. Started to Charlotte to attend Protracted Meeting. Dinner at B. F. Fraley's. All night in Concord with Revd Dreher.

Thurs. 11. In the evening went in company with Revd Dreher to Charlotte. Stopped at Duls'.

Sat. 18. Preached from 2 Cor. 5:17. in the afternoon and at night from Mark 1:40-45.

Sund. 19. Preached from Heb. 1:14. and aided in the administration of the Lord's Supper.

Mond. 20. Returned home.

Tues. 21. Went to Mrs. Heilig's sale.

Frid. 24. Went to James Kirk's sale.

Sund. 26. Preached at Organ ch. from James 1:25. Dinner at Jacob Miller's.

Thurs. 30. Attended Abraham Earnheart's sale.

Sund. Dec. 3. Preached at St. Peter's ch. from Jam. 1:25.

Sund. 24. This was my day to preach my Valedictory at Organ ch. but the day being very inclement, did not turn out.

Thurs. 28. Attended to the funeral of James C. Roseman's child. Preached the fun[1] at the house & buried at Lower Stone Church.

Sund. Jan. 7. Preached at St. Peter's ch. from Rom. 12:2.

Sund. 21. Preached at St. Peter's ch. from 1 Pet. 4:18.

Sat. 27. Started for St. John's ch. All night at Dan[1] Miller's.

Sund. 28. Preached at St. John's ch. from John 3:2. Dinner at Paul Miller's. In the afternoon preached at Fink's School House from 1 Pet. 4:18. All night at Rev. Cone's.

Mond. 29. Returned home.

Tues. 30. Went to Mrs. Ribelin's & married Calvin L. Brown to Mititia Ribelin.

Wed. 31. Went to Mrs. Brown's & married Richard L. Brown & Nancy E. Agner.

Sund. Feb. 4. Preached at St. Peter's ch. from John 3:2. Dinner at David Barringer's. All night at Nancy Arey's.

Mond. 5. Went to Salisbury to court.

Tues. 6. Went to Sol. Nussman's to have axes repaired.

Wed. 7. At home.

Thurs. 8. Went by way of Mrs. Ribelin's to Moses Barringer's.

Frid. 9. Went to Salisbury.

Sat. 10. At home.

Sund. 11. Went to Organ ch. & conducted the devotions of the congregation by singing, prayer and reading the Sermon on the Mount.

Mond. 12. Tues. 13. At home.

Wed. 14. Went to Jacob Holshouser's & married John V. Fisher & Catharine L. Holshouser.

Thurs. 15. Frid. 16. At home.

Sat. 17. In the morning went to Gold Hill & engaged to sell a veal.

Sund. 18. Went to Bear Creek ch. & preached from John 3:2. A very rainy day. All night at Phil. Ridenhour's, Esq.

Mond. 19. Returned home.

Tues. 20. Attended to the fun[1] of John Basinger. Preached the fun[1] at the house from 2 King 20:1. and buried at Organ ch.

Wed. 21. Attended to the fun[1] of Alexander M. Miller at Lower St. ch. Preached from Ps. 87:3.

Thurs. 22. Frid. 23. At home.

Sat. 24. At home.

Sund. 25. Went to St. John's ch. and preached from Math. 20:6. Dinner at Widow Cress'. In the afternoon preached at Leppard's School House from Rom. 12:2. Returned home.

Mond. 26. Went to Redwine & Co.'s Tanyard.

Tues. 27. Went to Barn Raising at Crawford A. Miller's.

Wed. 28. Clerked Sale of the property of Sam[1] Troutman, dec[d].

Thurs. March 1. At home.
Frid. 2. Went to mill.
Sat. 3. Went to St. Peter's ch. to commence a course of catechization.
Sund. 4. Preached at St. Peter's ch. from Rom. 1:16.
Mond. 5. At home.
Tues. 6. Went to Salisbury.
Wed. 7., Thurs. 8., Frid. 9. At home.
Sat. 10. Went to Log Rolling at Joseph Eagle's.
Sund. 11. At home till 12 o'clock, then went to School House to hear Rev. Cone preach.
Mond. 12. Went to Moses Trexler's to blacksmith shop.
Tues. 13., Wed. 14., Thurs. 15., Frid. 16. At home.
Sat. 17. Had catechization at St. Peter's ch.
Sund. 18. Preached at St. Peter's ch. from Numb. 14:24. Dinner at David Barringer's.
Mond. 19., Tues. 20., Wed. 21. At home.
Thurs. 22. At home. At night married Henry H. Clark & Camilla Fesperman.
Frid. 23. Went to Salisbury.
Sat. 24. Went to Gold Hill & Moses Trexler's shop.
Sund. 25. Went to St. Peter's ch. & heard Rev. Henkel preach.
Mond. 26. Went to Gold Hill. In the afternoon to John Lingel's to get shoe patterns.
Tues. 27. At home.
Wed. 28. Went to Widow John Seaford's & married Dr. James P. Porter & Lovinia B. Seaford.
Thurs. 29. At home. Married to day Solomon Wotzman & Harriet E. Pool.
Frid. 30. At home.
Sat. 31. Had catechization at St. Peter's ch.

Sund. April 1. Preached at St. Peter's ch. from Col. 3:1. Had dinner at H. A. Miller's.
Mond. 2. In the afternoon attended to the burial of Dave Heilig's (colored) child at the African grave yard near the School house.
Tues. 3. Went to Salisbury.
Wed. 4. In the afternoon attended to the funeral Philip Cruse at Organ ch. – preached from Joh. 14:27.
Sund. 8. At home, a very inclement day.
Mond. 9. Went to Redwine's Tan Yard. The balance of the week principally about home.
Sat. 14. Had preparatory service at St. Peter's Church, preached from Ps. 50:14. Baptized one infant, one adult & confirmed one person.
Sund. 15. Preached at St. Peter's Church from Josh. 23:8. & administered the Lord's Supper. Baptized to day one infant, four adults, and confirmed seven persons.
Mond. 16. to Frid. 20. Principally about home.
Sat. 21. In the afternoon had preaching at the Widow Jacob Lyerly's, Sen. for the especial benefit of Mrs. Lyerly, she being old & afflicted. Preached from Math. 11:28.
Sund. 22. Attended preaching at St. Peter's ch. by Revds. Conder & Henkel.
Mond. 23. to Frid. 27. At and about home.
Sat. 28. Went to St. John's ch. to Special conference. – All night at John Lentz's.
Sund. 29. Preached at St. John's ch. from Math. 11:28. & aided in the administration of the Lord's Supper. In the evening returned home.
Mond. 30. At home.

Tues. May 1. At home.

Wed. 2. Started to Synod at Trinity Church. All night at Allen Rose's.

Thurs. 3. Arrived at Synod, & continued at Synod until the following Sunday afternoon.

Sund. 6. Started in afternoon for home. All night at Michael Bostian's.

Mond. 7. Returned home by way of Salisbury. At & about home the balance of the week & week following.

Sund. 20. Preached at St. Peter's ch. from Math. 6:33. Dinner at H. A. Miller's. In afternoon called to see Mrs. Lyerly, widow of Jacob Lyerly, Sen., she being severely afflicted. + At and about home the following week.

Sund. 27. Went to Sunday School at St. Peter's ch. In afternoon heard Rev. Fox preach.

+ Thurs. 24. Married Lewis M. Brady & Philpena E. Morgan.

+ Mond. 21. Went Frederick Stirewalt's & baptized 2 inf^{ts} & 1 adult

Aug 1869

Sund. 8. Preached at Luckey's Stand from Matth. 20:6. & assisted in the administration of the Eucharist. All night at Mr. Tobias File's.

Mond. 9. Returned to J. C. Miller's to dinner & in the afternoon returned home.

Tues. 10. Went to Gold Hill to Post Office and had my horse shod.

Wed. 11. Went to Nancy Arey's on business.

Thurs. 12. At home. Married to day Mr. J. M. Cross & Miss Rachel C. Earnheart.

Frid. 13. At home. To day Lewis moved.

Sat. 14. Went to J. C. Miller's.

Sund. 15. Preached at Salem ch. from. Jerm. 17:9. 2 Cor. 13:5. Dinner at C. R. Miller's. Preached in the afternoon at Oak Forest from Luk. 13:24. All night at Caleb Bernhardt's.

Mond. 16. Called to see Mrs. Bogle & Mr. R. J. Klutts, they being sick. Dinner at J. C. Miller's. In afternoon returned home.

Tues. 17. Went Andrew Berger's on business. In the afternoon went to Gold Hill to Store & Post Office.

Wed. 18. Went to Bethel ch. & attended to the funeral of R. J. Klutts — preached from Ps. 40:4. All night at J. C. Miller's.

Thurs. 19. Returned home.

Frid. 20. Went with wife to D. Barringer's.

Sat. 21. Went to J. C. Miller's.

Sund. 22. Preached at Bethel ch. from Jerm. 17:9. 2 Cor. 13:5. In the afternoon went to see Mrs. Danl Hoffman, she being sick.

Mond. 23. Attended a congregational meeting of Bethel ch. at brickyard in relation to making brick for a new Church. In afternoon returned home.

Tues. 24. Went to mill &c.

Wed. 25. In afternoon went to John C. Miller's.

Thurs. 26. Went to Salem ch. to attend an adjourned meeting of Synod. All night at John Berger's.

Frid. 27. Sat. 28. At synod. Lodged at John Berger's.

Sund. 29. At Synod. Assisted in the ordination of P. M. Bikle. — The Lord's Supper was administered by Ministers of Synod. Returned to J. C. Miller's.

Mond. 30. Returned home.

Tues. 31. Went to Gold Hill to Post Office.

Wed. Sept. 1. In afternoon went to mill.

Thurs. 2. Went to Rymer Mine to see the Shoemaker, but did not find him at home.

Frid. 3. At home.

Sat. 4. Went to J. C. Miller's.

Sund. 5. Preached at Salem from Numb. 10:29. Dinner at Alex. Brown's. In afternoon preached at Pinkney Earnheart's from Luk. 13:24. All night at Alexander Brown's.

Mond. 6. Returned to J. C. Miller's. Dinner at Daniel Lyerly's.

Tues. 7. Returned home.

Wed. 8. Went to mill.

Thurs. 9. At home till dinner. In afternoon took wife to Henry Harkey's to have Erysipilas cured.

Frid. 10. Went to Salisbury for corn.

Sat. 11. Took wife & Emma to see Lewis. All night at J. C. Miller's.

Sund. 12. Preached at Bethel from Prov. 3:6. the fun^l of Henry Cress dec^d. In afternoon called to see Danl Hoffman's family, they being sick. All night at J. C. Miller's.

Mond. 13. Returned home. Dinner at P. N. Heilig's.

Tues. 14. Went to mill & to Gold Hill to Post Office.

Wed. 15. At home.

Thurs. 16. At home till evening, then went with wife to David Barringer's & staid over night.

Frid. 17. Returned home.

Sat. 18. Started for Salem ch. All night at John Lingel's.

Sund. 19. Preached at Salem ch. from Prov. 23:17.18. Dinner at M. A. Bost's. In afternoon preached at Oak Forest School House from 1 Thes. 5:6. All night at C. R. Miller's.

Mond. 20. Returned home.

Tues. 21. Went to mill & to Gold Hill to Post Office.

Wed. 22. At home till afternoon, then went with wife to Dr. Coleman's on an hour's visit. Moses A. Goodman & wife from Illinois with us to night.

Thurs. 23. At home. In the evening took Mrs. Goodman & child in buggy to Mr. Wilie Lentz's.

Frid. 24. Went to son Lewis' — In afternoon went to Danl Hoffman's, his daughter being very sick. All night at J. C. Miller's.

Sat. 25. At Lewis'.— All night here.

Sund. 26. Attended to the funeral of Mary Jane Hoffman. Preached at the house from Ps. 90:12. & buried at Bethel ch. The day being very inclement did not preach at the church. All night at J. C. Miller's.

Mond. 27. Intended to go to Salem but the river being too full to cross, returned home.

Tues. 28. Started for Salem as far as Caleb Peeler's. All night here.

Wed. 29. Went to Salem to carding machine. Dinner at H. K. Thomas'. Returned to Caleb Peeler's.

Thurs. 30. Went back to Salem & attended a large Sunday School celebration. Dinner at E. A. Vogler's. Returned to Caleb Peeler's.

Frid. Oct. 1. Returned home.

Sat. 2. Started for Salem ch. All night at Sam¹ Seaford's.

Sund. 3. A very inclement day. Went to the church & had short religious exercises. All night at John Berger's.

Mond. 4. Returned home.

Tues. 5. Went in morning to David Barringer's on business. In afternoon at home.

Wed. 6. Went to Gold Hill to Post Office & had Horse shod.

Thurs. 7. At home till 12 o'clock. In afternoon called to see Rev. Cone on church business.

Frid. 8. Went with wife to Gold Hill to see Julia Moyle, she being on the eve. of going to Kansas.

Sat. 9. Went to Lewis'. All night here.

Sund. 10. Breakfast at J. C. Miller's. Preached at Bethel ch. from Numb. 10:29. Preached in afternoon at Col. D. Lentz's from Luk. 13:24. All night here.

Mond. 11. Returned to J. C. Miller's. In afternoon went to Salisbury. All night at Sheriff Walton's.

Tues. 12. Went to Lexington. In afternoon returned to J. C. Miller's.

Wed. 13. Returned home.

Thurs. 14. In the morning went to mill. In afternoon went to Gold Hill to Post Office & bought some guano.

Frid. 15. Started to Salem ch. A very inclement day. Dinner at Zachariah Lyerly's. All night at M. A. Bost's.

Sat. 16. Preached at Salem ch. from Ps. 34:19. the funeral of Mrs. Bogle who had died some weeks before. Afterwards held Preparatory Service. All night at Jesse Lyerly's.

Sund. 17. Preached at Salem ch. from Is. 25:6-8. & administered the Lord's Supper. All night at Lewis'.

Mond. 18. Breakfast at J. C. Miller's. Returned home.

Tues. 19. Went to Gold Hill to Post Office & to shoemaker.

Wed. 20. At home till dinner time. In afternoon went to mill and slaughtered hog.

Thurs. 21. At home till 12 o'clock, then went to widow Daywalt Lentz's to lay off Year's Provision.

Frid. 22. Went to John C. Miller's. Supper here & lodging at Lewis'.

Sat. 23. Had preparatory Service at Bethel ch. – preached from Rom. 12:1. Rev. G. D. Bernheim with me to night at J. C. Miller's.

Sund. 24. Rev. G. D. B. preached, after which administered the communion. After intermission Rev. J. H. Fesperman preached.

Mond. 25. Returned home.

Tues. 26. In forenoon went to Gold Hill to Post Office. In afternoon at home.

Wed. 27. At home. Moses A. Goodman with us to night.

Thurs. 28. Started for St. Michael's ch. Iredell Co., to attend Special conference. All night Mrs. Catharine Kistler's.

Frid. 29. Went to Special conference. All night at Phebe Brown's.

Sat. 30. At conference. Preached from Prov. 3:9.10. All night at Phebe Brown's.

Sund. 31. At St. Michael's ch. Aided in the Administration of the Lord's Supper. All night at Lansing White's.

Mond. Nov. 1. Started for home. Dinner at Jacob Goodman's. All night at John Harkey's.

Tues. 2. Returned home.

Wed. 3. Attended to the funeral of Peter L. Barringer at Union ch. — preached from 2 Cor. 5:1.

Thurs. 4. Went to Post Office & H. A. Miller's. Dinner here. In afternoon called to see John Miller he being in declining health.

Frid. 5. At home.

Sat. 6. Started for Salem ch. Wife with me. All night at Lewis'.

Sund. 7. Preached at Salem ch. from 2 Cor. 4:7. Dinner at Alexander Brown's. Baptized at Salem 1 inf^t In afternoon preached at Pinkney Earnheart's from 1 Thes. 5:6. All night at Alex^r Brown's. Baptized at P. Earnheart's 2 in^fts.

Mond. 8. Called at Catharine Kistler's. Dinner here. In afternoon went to J. C. Miller's. All night here.

Tues. 9. Returned home.

Wed. 10. Went for a load of pine.

Thurs. 11. At home. Inclement day.

Frid. 12. At home.

Sat. 13. Went to Lewis'. Very inclement day. Supper at J. C. Miller's. All night at Lewis'.

Sund. 14. Preached at Bethel ch. from 2 Cor. 4:7. All night at J. C. Miller's.

Mond. 15. Returned home.

Tues. 16. Went to Gold Hill to Post Office & to the Tailor.

Wed. 17. At home. Halfsoled Boots.

Thurs. 18. Went to Col. D. Lentz's and married Jesse A. Cozort & Mary J. Lentz. All night here.

Frid. 19. Went to infare at Mr. Cozort's. In afternoon went to Michael Shuping's & staid over night.

Sat. 20. Went to Lewis' & staid over night.

Sund. 21. Preached at Salem ch. from Prov. 14:34. After preaching went to Mr. Elliot's & married J. F. Watts & Martha Ann Sheets. All night with wife at Caleb Bernhardt's.

Mond. 22. Went to Salisbury. All night at Lewis'.

Tues. 23. Returned home. A very inclement day.

Wed. 24. At home. Slaughtered a Beef.

Thurs. 25. At home. Butchered 2 Hogs.

Frid. 26. In afternoon went to Nancy Arey's & staid over night.

Sat. 27. Had catechization at Bethel ch. in the afternoon. Dinner at Lewis'. All night at Calvin Hoffman's.

Sund. 28. Preached at Bethel ch. from Prov. 29:1. In the afternoon preached at Graeber Miller's from Math. 11:28. & baptized Mr. Miller's child. All night here.

Mond. 29. Returned home. Dinner at David Barringer's.

Tues. 30. At home.

Wed. Dec. 1. Went by way of Lewis' to John Eagle's. All night here.

Thurs. 2. Went to Mrs. Riles' & married John Eagle & Amanda J. Riles. Called in evening to see Dan[l] Hoffman. All night at son Lewis'.

Frid. 3. Went to Charles Barringer's. All night here.

Sat. 4. Preached at Mrs. Kistler's Stand from Matth. 25:1-13. Baptized 1 inf[t] Dinner at Jacob Goodman's. All night at Mrs. Kistler's.

Sund. 5. Preached at Salem ch. from Matth. 25:1-13. All night at Lewis'.

Mond. 6. Returned home.

Tues. 7. Went with wife to David Barringer's. All night here.

Wed. 8. Returned home in evening.

Thurs. 9. Attended to the funeral of Mrs. John Brady. Preached the fun[l] at the house from Amos 4:12. & buried on the premises. In afternoon went to Gold Hill.

Frid. 10. Started for Bethel ch. Dinner at Zechariah Lyerly's. All night at P. N. Heilig's.

Sat. 11. Had catechization at Bethel ch. at 2 p.m. Dinner at John C. Miller's. All at Andrew Shuping's.

Sund. 12. Preached at Bethel ch. from Matth. 25:1-13. Dinner at John C. Miller's. All night at Lewis'.

Mond. 13. Breakfast at J. C. Miller's. Returned home.

Tues. 14. At home.

Wed. 15. At home. Very inclement day.

Thurs. 16. Started for Salem ch. All night at Lewis'.

Frid. 17. Went to Salem ch. and preached from Prov. 14:32. All night at C. R. Miller's.

Sat. 18. An inclement morning. Preached at Salem ch. from Gen. 6:9. All night at Pleasant Wise's.

Sund. 19. Preached at Salem ch. the fun[l] of George Ruffty from 1 Chron. 28:9. All night at Jesse Lyerly's.

Mond. 20. Dinner at J. C. Miller's. In afternoon went to Salisbury. All night at Lewis'.

Tues. 21. Started for Davidson Co. All night at Dan[l] Kennerly's.

Wed. 22. Went to B. B. Young's in Davidson & married Jacob A. Berger & Elizabeth C. Young. Was water bound at the river. All night at Burell Young's.

Thurs. 23. The river still impassable. Dinner at Robert Moore's. All night at B. B. Young's.

Frid. 24. Had an appointment to day at Bethel ch. but could not cross the river in time. Crossed the river late in the evening. All night at Lewis'.

Sat. 25. A very inclement day. Could have no preaching.

Sund. 26. Prof. L. A. Bikle preached to day at Bethel ch. All night at Eli Propst's.

Mond. 27. A very inclement day. Could have no preaching. All night at J. C. Miller's.

Tues. 28. Returned home.

Wed. 29. At home till evening, then went to the Grave Yard for colored persons & buried a colored woman.

Thurs. 30. Attended the burial of John Miller at Organ ch. Attended to the burial service. Rev. Cone preached the fun[l]. Dinner at Dr. Coleman's.

Frid. 31. Went to Henry Brown's. All night here.

Sat. Jan 1, 1870. Preached at Mrs. C. Kistler's from Deut. 5:3. All night at John Berger's.

Sund. 2. Preached at Salem ch. from Deut. 5:3. A cold day. All night at Saml Seaford's.

Mond. 3. Returned home. Dinner at Mr. Ritz's, Salisbury.

Tues. 4. In forenoon went to Henry Harkey's & D. Barringer's on business. In afternoon at home. Rev. Cone with me to night.

Wed. 5. At home.

Thurs. 6. At home.

Frid. 7. Started for Bethel church. All night at Danl Hoffman's.

Sat. 8. Dinner at Lewis'. In afternoon had catechization at Bethel ch. All night at John Cawble's.

Sund. 9. Preached at Bethel ch. from Deut. 5:3. Dinner at Lewis'. All night at Washington Thomason's.

Mond. 10. Went to Alexander Brown's & took dinner. In afternoon went with Mr. Brown in his buggy to Phebe Brown's. All night here.

Tues. 11. At Mrs. Brown's making, at his request, Some inquiry into her temporal affairs. All night here.

Wed. 12. Mrs. Brown brought me in her buggy to Alex^r Brown's. All night here.

Thurs. 13. Went to John Smithdeal's. All night here.

Frid. 14. Went to Catherine Walton's to dinner. In the afternoon went to Eli Powlass'. All night here.

Sat. 15. Went to John Carson's and took dinner. In afternoon went to Mr. Robison's & staid all night.

Sund. 16. Preached at Salem ch. from Eph. 6:18. Baptized one infant. Dinner at Lewis'. Preached at night in Salisbury from Math. 11:28. All night at P. N. Heilig's.

Mond. 17. Returned home.

Tues. 18. At home.

Wed. 19. At home. Had some friends to share with us in a turkey dinner.

Thurs. 20. Went to Gold Hill to Post Office & settled up accounts.

Frid. 21. Started for Bethel church. All night at Leonard Krider's, he being very sick at the time.

Sat. 22. Dinner at John C. Miller's. In the afternoon had catechization at Bethel ch. Returned to J. C. Miller's & staid over night.

Sund. 23. Preached at Bethel ch. from Eph. 6:18. Baptized one infant. All night at Danl Hoffman's.

Mond. 24. Returned home.

Tues. 25. Went with wife to Charles Fisher's to have some weaving done. All night at Paul Cruse's.

Wed. 26. Returned home by way of sale at John Miller's dec^d. Dinner at Dr. Coleman's.

Thurs. 27. Started to Central Conference at Bethel church. All night at Widow Brown's (of Moses L.).

Frid. 28. Went to Bethel church. All night at son Lewis'. Supper at G. H. Miller's.

Sat. 29. At Bethel church. All night at Crawford Peeler's.

Sund. 30. At Bethel church. Supper at Alexander Lentz's. All night at H. G. Miller's.

Mond. 31. Returned home.

Tues. Feb 1. At home.

Wed. 2. Went to Blacksmith Shop at Paul Cruse's, & C. Melchor's Tanyard. All night at Dan$^{\underline{l}}$ Miller's.

Thurs. 3. Returned home. Dinner at Rev. W. H. Cone's.

Frid. 4. At home.

Sat. 5. Started for Salem ch. All night at Moses A. Bost's.

Sund. 6. Preached at Salem ch. from Luk. 18:18. All night at John Berger's.

Mond. 7. Returned home.

Tues. 8. Went with wife to Dr. Coleman's.

Wed. 9. At home.

Thurs. 10. Went to Post Office at Gold Hill & to the store & purchased some clover Seed.

Frid. 11. Started for Bethel Church. All night at Nancy Arey's.

Sat. 12. Had catechization in the afternoon at Bethel Church. All night at Lewis'.

Sund. 13. Preached at Bethel Church from Heb. 3:2. All night at John Fisher's.

Mond. 14. Returned home.

Tues. 15. Went to Gold Hill in the afternoon on business.

Wed. 16. Went with wife in the afternoon to Dr. Coleman's.

Thurs. 17. At home.

Frid. 18. At home. Inclement day.

Sat. 19. Started for Salem Church. All night at John Lingel's.

Sund. 20. A very inclement day, did not go to the church. In afternoon went to Lewis' & staid all night. Baptized to day Mr. Lingel's child.

Mond. 21. Returned home. A very cold day.

Tues. 22. Went to Mt. Pleasant. All night at Col. Shimpock's.

Wed. 23. Attended a meeting of the Board of Trustees of N. C. College. Dinner at Phebe Brown's. All night at Dan$^{\underline{l}}$ Miller's.

Thurs. 24. Returned home.

Frid. 25. Started for Bethel Church. All night at Dan$^{\underline{l}}$ Hoffman's.

Sat. 26. Had catechization at Bethel Ch. in the afternoon. All night at Joseph Swink's.

Sund. 27. Preached at Bethel ch. from Numb. 14:24. Dinner at Alex$^{\underline{r}}$ Lentz's. In afternoon went to hear Rev. Merkeson (Methodist) preach. All night at Lewis'.

Mond. 28. Returned home.

Tues. March 1. Went in forenoon to Gold Hill.

Wed. 2. Went with wife to David Barringer's. Dinner here. In afternoon went to Jacob Grufey's. All night here.

Thurs. 3. Returned home. In the evening married Adam Holshouser & Lydia Goodman.

Frid. 4. At home.

Sat. 5. Started for Salem church. All night at Daniel Lyerly's.

Sund. 6. Preached at Salem church from Numb. 14:24. Baptized one inf^t. All night at Jesse Lyerly's.

Mond. 7. Returned home.

Tues. 8. In forenoon went to mill. In afternoon at home.

Wed. 9. In forenoon went to mill. In afternoon at home.

Thurs. 10. In forenoon went to Gold Hill. In afternoon at home.

Frid. 11. Went to Lewis'. Took him some flour, 2 pigs, &c. All night here.

Sat. 12. In the afternoon had catechization at Bethel ch. All night at Lewis'.

Sund. 13. Preached at Bethel ch. from Josh. 24:15. All night at H. G. Miller's.

Mond. 14. Returned home.

Tues. 15. At home.

Wed. 16. Went to Charles Fisher's & to Paul Cruse's on business.

Thurs. 17. At home — very cold day.

Frid. 18. At home — made out Guardian Returns.

Sat. 19. Started for Salem ch. All night at John Berger's.

Sund. 20. Preached at Salem ch. from Josh. 24:15. All night at Saml Seaford's.

Mond. 21. Returned home. Made my Guardian Returns.

Tues. 22. In the forenoon went to Gold Hill. In afternoon went to mill.

Wed. 23. In forenoon mended harness. In afternoon went to mill.

Thurs. 24. Took wife to H. A. Miller's to dinner. In afternoon went to Widow Andrew Holshouser's and married Osborn M. Holshouser & Martha C. Klutts. Called by Moses Linn's for wife & returned home.

Frid. 25. Started for Bethel ch. All night at J. C. Miller's.

Sat. 26. At Lewis'. A very rainy day. All night here.

Sund. 27. Preached at Bethel Ch. from 1 Tim. 6:6. All night at John Cauble's.

Mond. 28. Returned home by way of Lewis'.

Tues. 29. Went to Salisbury and bought some corn.

Wed. 30. In forenoon went to Dr. Coleman's. In afternoon at home.

Thurs. 31. At home.

Frid. April 1. Started for Salem Church. Dinner at Dr. Coleman's. All night at Henry Miller's.

Sat. 2. Had catechization at Salem ch. All night at C. R. Miller's.

Sund. 3. Preached at Salem from 1 Tim. 6:6. Had prayermeeting in the afternoon at James D. Smith's. All night here.

Mond. 4. Returned home.

Tues. 5. Went in the afternoon to Mt. Pleasant. All night at Phebe Brown's.

Wed. 6. Attended a meeting of the Board of Trustees of N. C. College. All night at Dan$^{\underline{l}}$ Miller's.

Thurs. 7. Returned home. Dinner at Mary A. Heilig's.

Frid. 8. Started for Bethel Church. All night at Alexander Shoaf's.

Sat. 9. In the afternoon had catechization at Bethel Church. All night at Joseph Fisher's.

Sund. 10. Preached at Bethel Church from Jam. 1:25. All night at Lewis'.

Mond. 11. Returned home.

Tues. 12. Went awhile in forenoon to Solomon Peeler's log rolling. In afternoon at home.

Wed. 13. Went in forenoon to Rev. W. H. Cone's on business. In the afternoon went to Gold Hill.

Thurs. 14. Started for Salem Church. All night at M. A. Bost's.

Frid. 15. Had preaching at Salem ch. in forenoon & at night. Rev. Cone preached. All night at John Berger's.

Sat. 16. Had preaching during the day & at night. Rev. Cone preached. Held services preparatory to communion. All night at S. B. Colly's.

Sund. 17. Rev. Cone preached again at Salem ch. Administered the Lord's Supper. Preached at night in Salisbury from Jer. 17:9. 2 Cor. 13:5. All night at P. N. Heilig's.

Mond. 18. Returned home.

Tues. 19. In afternoon went with wife to Dr. Coleman's.

Wed. 20. Wemt in forenoon to Gold Hill, & in afternoon to D. Barringer's.

Thurs. 21. At home. Had log rolling.

Frid. 22. Started for Bethel Church. All night at John Eagle's.

Sat. 23. At Bethel ch. Rev. Bolles preached. Baptized 2 infants & held preparatory service. Dinner at J. C. Miller's. All night at Lewis'.

Sund. 24. Rev. Bolles preached. Administered the Lord's Supper. Dinner at Alex$^{\underline{r}}$ Lentz's. All night at Lewis'.

Mond. 25. Returned home.

Tues. 26. Started for Mt. Pleasant. All night at Dan$^{\underline{l}}$ Miller's.

Wed. 27. Went to Mt. Pleasant. Dinner at Col. Shimpock's. Supper at Rev. Dreher's. All night at Phebe Brown's.

Thurs. 28. Returned home. Dinner at Dr. Coleman's.

Frid. 29. Started for Salem Church. All night at Joseph Colly's.

Sat. 30. Had catechization at Salem ch. All night at Charles Beaver's.

Sund. May 1. Preached at Salem ch. from Luk. 16:19-31. Dinner at Mrs. Kistler's. In the afternoon preached at Mrs. Kistler's from Luk. 16:19-31. All night here.

Mond. 2. Called at John Smithdeal's. Dinner here. In the afternoon called at Mrs. Catharine Walton's. All night at John Lyerly's.

Tues. 3. Returned home by way of Lewis'.

Wed. 4. Went to Nussman's mill.

Thurs. 5. Went to Paul Shaver's to make return of Tax.

Frid. 6. Started for Bethel Church. All night at Mr. Rainy's.

Sat. 7. Had catechization at Bethel Ch. Attended singing in the afternoon at Bethel ch. All night at John C. Miller's.

Sund. 8. Preached at Bethel Ch. from Luk. 16:19-31. After an intermission preached the funeral of Crissa Ann Sewell, aged some 3 years, from 1 Chron. 28:9. All night at W. A. Lentz's.

Mond. 9. Returned home.

Tues. 10. At home.

Wed. 11. Went with wife to Dr. Coleman's.

Thurs. 12. At home shearing sheep till afternoon, then went to Gold Hill on business.

Frid. 13. Started for Salem Church. All night at James M. Colly's.

Sat. 14. Had catechization at Salem Ch. All night at J. L. Cress'.

Sund. 15. Preached at Salem Ch. from Prov. 3:6. After intermission preached from Matth. 11:29.30. Dinner at M. A. Bost's. Went to Salisbury & heard Rev. Neifer from Richmond, Va. All night at P. N. Heilig's.

Mond. 16. Returned home.

Tues. 17. At home & quite unwell.

Wed. 18. Went to Gold Hill on business. In the afternoon at home.

Thurs. 19. Went with wife to Lewis'. All night here.

Frid. 20. Attended the closing exercises of Franklin Academy. All night in the Academy.

Sat. 21. Breakfast at H. G. Miller's. Went to Sandy Creek Church in Davidson Co. & preached from Jerm. 17:9. 2 Cor. 13:5. All night at Henry Sink's.

Sund. 22. Preached at Sandy Creek from Heb. 1:14. & aided in administration of the Lord's Supper. All night at J. H. Thompson's.

Mond. 23. Returned home.

Tues. 24. At home.

Wed. 25. Went to Mt. Pleasant to attend a meeting of the Board of College Trustees. All night at Col. Shimpock's.

Thurs. 26. Returned home. Dinner at Rev. W. H. Cone's.

Frid. 27. At home.

Sat. 28. Went to Salisbury. All night at W. A. Walton's, She'ff.

Sund. 29. Preached in Salisbury at 10 o'clock from Gen. 45:28. & at night from Luk. 16:19-31. All night at P. N. Heilig's.

Mond. 30. Returned home & took dinner, then returned to Salisbury & took the train for Gibsonville. All night at Company Shops.

Tues. 31. Returned by Rail Road to Gibsonville. Breakfast at Rev. C. H. Bernheim's then went with Rev. Bernheim to L. W. Summers'. Found Mr. Summers in very feeble health. All night here.

Wed. June 1. At Mr. Summers by his bedside. All night here.

Thurs. 2. At Mr. Summers' till after dinner, then went to Lucy Summers & Brothers. All night here.

Frid. 3. Went to Gibsonville to Rev. Bernheim's. All night here.

Sat. 4. Took the Train for Salisbury. Then went to Salem Ch. & had catechization. Dinner at Moses Trexler's. All night at Jesse Lyerly's.

Sund. 5. Preached at Salem ch. from Gen. 45:28. In the afternoon preached at Kistler's Stand from Prov. 3:6. Dinner at Mrs. Kistler's & staid over night at Alex. Brown's.

Mond. 6. Returned home.

Tues. 7. At home.

Wed. 8. At home.

Thurs. 9. In afternoon went to Gold Hill on business.

Frid. 10. Started for Bethel church. All night at Lewis'.

Sat. 11. Had catechization at Bethel ch. In the afternoon had a conversational conference with several members of the church. All night at Lewis'.

Sund. 12. Preached at Bethel ch. from Gen. 45:28. All night at J. C. Miller's.

Mond. 13. Returned home.

Tues. 14. At home.

Wed. 15. In forenoon went to Gold Hill on business.

Thurs. 16. At home.

Frid. 17. Started for Salem Church. All night at John Lingel's.

Sat. 18. Had catechization at Salem Ch. All night at John Berger's.

Sund. 19. Preached at Salem ch. from 1 Pet. 5:4. After an intermission preached again from Gal. 4:5. All night at Joseph Beaver's.

Mond. 20. Returned home.

Tues. 21. At home.

Wed. 22. Went in the morning to engage hands to bind wheat. Balance of the day in the harvest field.

Thurs. 23. In the morning went to mill, balance of the day at home.

Frid. 24. Started for Bethel Church. Dinner at W. A. Lentz's. In afternoon heard candidates speak at Franklin Academy. All night at Col. D. Lentz's.

Sat. 25. Had catechization at Bethel ch. All night at Andrew Shuping's.

Sund. 26. Preached at Bethel Church from Eph. 6:1-4. All night at John C. Miller's. Baptized one infant to day.

Mond. 27. Returned home. Dinner at Dr. Coleman's.

Tues. 28. Went H. G. Miller's at Frank[n] Academy. All night here.

Wed. 29. Went to Franklin Church & saw W. L. Kistler & Lucy Foster married by Rev. Pharr. Dinner at H. G. Miller's. All night at Jesse W. Miller's.

Thurs. 30. Called & took dinner at C. R. Miller's. All night at Mr. Horton's.

Frid. July 1. Called & took dinner Caleb J. Bernhardt's. Called in afternoon to see old Mrs. Louder. All night at Richard Graham's.

Sat. 2. Had catechization at Salem ch. All night at Mr. Colly's, Sen.

Sund. 3. Preached at Salem Church from Eph. 6:1-4. Dinner at Mrs. Kistler's. Preached in afternoon at Kistler's Stand from Mark 1:40-45. All night at Mrs. C. Kistler's.

Mond. 4. Returned home.

Tues. 5. At home.

Wed. 6. Went to Mt. Pleasant to the meeting of Board of Col. Trustees. Dinner at Col. Shimpock's. All night at Danl Miller's.

Thurs. 7. Returned home.

Frid. 8. At home till evening then went to Dr. Coleman's & brought wife home.

Sat. 9. Went to Bethel Church & had catechization in the afternoon. All night at Leonard Krider's.

Sund. 10. Preached at Bethel ch. from Gen. 6:9. Dinner at Crawford Lentz's. Preached here in the afternoon from Mark 1:40-45. All night at J. C. Miller's.

Mond. 11. Returned home.

Tues. 12. In the morning went to Gold Hill, balance of day at home.

Wed. 13. At home.

Thurs. 14. At home till afternoon, then went to Gold Hill to the Store and bought some sugar.

Frid. 15. Took Lewis home. Dinner here. Then went to Eli Powlass' & staid over night.

Sat. 16. Had catechization at Salem ch. Dinner at Mrs. Ruffty's. All night at Jesse Lyerly's.

Sund. 17. Preached at Salem ch. from Acts 16:30.31. After an intermission preached from 2 Tim. 4:7.8. the fun^{l} of Mr. Campbell dec^{d}. All night at Saml Seaford's.

Mond. 18. Returned home. Dinner at Peter Trexler's. To day Emma Peters left.

Tues. 19. In the afternoon went to H. A. Miller's & bought some corn & carried it to Lentz's mill. Mr. Miller being thronged.

Wed. 20. At home till afternoon, then went to mill.

Thurs. 21. Went to Gold Hill & heard candidates speak.

Frid. 22. In the morning went to mill. Balance of day at home.

Sat. 23. Went to Bethel ch. & had catechization. Dinner at Lewis'. All night at Abner Hall's.

Sund. 24. Preached at Bethel from Ps. 116:12-14. Dinner at Lewis'. Returned home in afternoon.

Mond. 25. In the morning went to mill. Balance of day at home.

Tues. 26. Went to Gold Hill and had Buggy repaired. In afternoon engaged hands to mow grass.

Wed. 27. Went with wife to Calvin Brown's.

Thurs. 28. Went to Union ch. to Special Conference. Dinner at George Lyerly's. Returned home.

Frid. 29. Went to Union ch. to conference. Preached from Luk. 16:19-31. Returned home.

Sat. 30. Went with wife to Union ch. Preached from Prov. 3:9.10. All night at Nancy Arey's.

Sund. 31. At Union ch. Returned home in evening.

Mond. Aug. 1. At home till afternoon, then went to H. A. Miller's mill & also to Dr. Coleman's and purchased some bacon.

Tues. 2. In the morning went to mill. In the afternoon went to Mt. Pleasant to attend meeting of the Board of Trustees of N. C. College. All night at Phebe Brown's.

Wed. 3. In Mt. Pleasant till 12 o'clock. No quorum of Board of Trustees. Dinner at John Lentz's. In the afternoon returned home.

Thurs. 4. Went to Morgan's to election. Acted as Secretary of Registrar & tallied the votes given.

Frid. 5. Started for Salem ch. Called at Michael L. Brown's & baptized his child. Dinner here. All night at Moses A. Bost's.

Sat. 6. Had catechization at Salem ch. All night at John Berger's.

Sund. 7. Preached at Salem ch. from Math. 19:14. the fun[l] of Mr. Porter's child. In the afternoon preached at Kistler's stand from Math. 15:1-13. Dinner at Mrs. Kistler's. All night at Alex[r] Brown's.

Mond. 8. Returned home. Very unwell.

Tues. 9. Went to see about having wheat threshed.

Wed. 10. Attended to some business in the neighborhood.

Thurs. 11. In forenoon went to mill. In afternoon went to Dr. Coleman's on business.

Frid. 12. At home.

Sat. 13. Went to Bethel Church & had catechization in the afternoon. Dinner at Lewis'. All night at Ransom Jacobs'.

Sund. 14. Preached at Bethel ch. from Acts 24:25. Dinner at Lewis'. Returned home in afternoon.

Mond. 15. Tues. 16. At home & had wheat threshed.

Wed. 17. At Sol. Peeler's & Mrs. Overton's threshing wheat.

Thurs. 18. At home.

Frid. 19. Started for Salem Church. All night at Lewis'.

Sat. 20. Had catechization at Salem. Dinner at Mr. Menius'. All night at John Berger's.

Sund. 21. Preached at Salem ch. from Acts 24:25. In the afternoon preached at Monroe Barrier's from Rev. 14:13. the funeral of his deceased child. Dinner & all night here.

Mond. 22. Returned home. Very unwell.

Tues. 23. to Sund. 28. At home sick. Could not attend Synod in consequence of indisposed.

Mond. 29. Went to Morgan's to tax paying.

Tues. 30. Went to Milas Holshouser's & to Gold Hill.

Wed. 31. In the forenoon went to mill — In afternoon at home.

Thurs. Sep. 1. Halfsoled wife's shoes. In afternoon engaged hands to mow grass.

Frid. 2. Started for Salem church. All night at Lewis'.

Sat. 3. Had catechization at Salem ch. All night at C. R. Miller's.

Sund. 4. Preached at Salem ch. from Math. 4:1-11. In afternoon preached at Kistler's Stand from Ps. 73:1. Dinner at Mrs. Catharine Kistler's. All night at John Berger's.

Mond. 5. Returned home.

Tues. 6. In the morning went to Gold Hill. In afternoon worked in meadow.

Wed. 7. Thurs. 8. At home hauling hay.

Frid. 9. Went to Isaac Earnheart's on business for Solomon Peeler. Called by the Store at Gold Hill. In afternoon at home.

Sat. 10. Went to Bethel Church & in the afternoon had catechization. Dinner & all night at Lewis'.

Sund. 11. Preached at Bethel Church from Gen. 6:22. Dinner at Lewis'.

Mond. 12. Returned home.

Tues. 13. Went to mill at Nussman's.

Wed. 14. At home, hauled in hay.

Thurs. 15. At home.

Frid. 16. Started for Salem ch. All night at Lewis'.

Sat. 17. Went to Salem ch. and had catechization. Dinner at John Lingel's. All night here.

Sund. 18. Preached at Salem ch. from Gen. 6:22. Had to dispense with the afternoon service in consequence of the ague. All night at John Lingel's. Quite sick with ague.

Mond. 19. Returned home. In the evening went to Laurence Lingel's & staid all night.

Tues. 20. Returned home by way of Nussman's mill.

Wed. 21. Spent the forepart of the day with the Rail Road Surveyor's. In the afternoon at home.

Thurs. 22. Called in the morning to Mrs. Stephen Brady, she being sick. Then went to Gold Hill for two pigs. In the afternoon went to Dr. Coleman's to bring wife home.

Frid. 23. At home.

Sat. 24. Went to Bethel ch. & had catechization at 2 o'clock P.M. Dinner and all night at Lewis'.

Sund. 25. Preached at Bethel ch. from 1 Thes. 2:11.12. Baptized 2 infants. Dinner & all night at John C. Miller's.

Mond. 26. Returned home. Dinner at Dr. Coleman's.

Tues. 27. In the forenoon went to Gold Hill on business. In the afternoon went with wife to David Barringer's & staid all night.

Wed. 28. Went to Nancy Arey's on business. In afternoon returned home by way of D. Barringer's and brought wife home.

Thurs. 29. Went to D. Barringer's saw mill for some plank.

Frid. 30. Started for Salem ch. All night at Sam⊥ Seaford's.

Sat. Oct 1. Had catechization at Salem ch. Dinner and all night at D. Menis'.

Sund. 2. Preached at Salem ch. from Acts 20:17-21. Dinner and all night at M. A. Bost's. Had the ague.

Mond. 3. Returned home.

Tues. 4. At home. Quite sick with the ague.

Wed. 5. Went to Dr. Coleman's and got some medicine.

Thurs. 6. At home taking medicine.

Frid. 7. Went with wife to Lewis'. All night here. Dinner at Dr. Coleman's.

Sat. 8. In the afternoon had catechization at Bethel ch., also a meeting of business of Church Council. All night at Lewis'.

Sund. 9. Preached at Bethel ch. from Job 14:14. fun[1] of Cornelius Fesperman. All at J. C. Miller's.

Mond. 10. Returned home. Dinner at P. N. Heilig's.

Tues. 11. Wed. 12. At home.

Thurs. 13. Went to Mr. Nussman's to carding Machine.

Frid. 14. Started for Salem ch. All night at Joseph Colly's.

Sat. 15. Had preparatory services at Salem ch., preached from Ps. 51:17. All night at John Berger's.

Sund. 16. Preached at Salem ch. from John 7:37. Baptized one infant & administered the Lord's Supper. All night at Joseph Beaver's. Suffered very much during the night from Peritoneal Inflammation.

Mond. 17. Returned home. Quite unwell.

Tues. 18. Wed. 19. At home. Unwell.

Thurs. 20. Went to Gold Hill & brought wool rolls home.

Frid. 21. Went to Lewis' & staid all night.

Sat. 22. Had preparatory service at Bethel ch. Rev. Neifer from Salisbury preached. Dinner at Lewis'. All night at John Fisher's.

Sund. 23. Preached at Bethel ch. from John 7:37. Confirmed three persons & administered the Lord's Supper. All night at Lewis'.

Mond. 24. Returned home. Dinner at Dr. Coleman's. Had corn shucking to night.

Tues. 25. At home cribbing corn.

Wed. 26. In afternoon went to David Barringer's on business.

Thurs. 27. In the afternoon went to Elias Beaver's & staid over night.

Frid. 28. Attended the joint meeting of the Central & Western Conferences at Organ Ch. Returned home in the evening.

Sat. 29. At Organ ch. attending Conference. All night at Jacob Trexler's.

Sund. 30. At Organ ch. Returned home in the evening.

Mond. 31. Went to Salisbury. At night attended the Anniversary of the Reformation in the Lutheran Church. All night at B. F. Fraley's.

Tues. Nov. 1. Returned home.

Wed. 2. In the afternoon went with wife to Laurence Lingel's & staid all night.

Thurs. 3. Went to Widow Tobias Klutts' & married Caleb L. Nussman and Margaret C. F. Klutts. Returned home. At night married Henry Clay Loftin & Amy Ingram, a colored couple. Had the Ague this evening.

Frid. 4. Went to Lewis' & staid all night.

Sat. 5. Went to Saml Colly's. Had the Ague this afternoon. All night here.

Sund. 6. Preached a short sermon, my health being infirm, from Mark 10:46-56. Had an appointment for the afternoon at Jeremiah Barringer's, but my health being frail & the weather somewhat inclement, did not attend. Returned to Lewis'.

Mond. 7. Started for home, but took the Ague on the way & called in Michael L. Brown's & staid all night.

Tues. 8. Returned home.

Wed. 9. Went at dinner time to bring molasses home from Milas A. Holshouser's.

Thurs. 10. Attended the sale of the land of J. A. Linn dec^{d}.

Frid. 11. Went to Gold Hill to the shoemaker.

Sat. 12. Went to Lewis' & staid over night.

Sund. 13. Preached at Bethel ch. from Math. 4:16. on the subject of the Reformation by Luther. Dinner at H. G. Miller's. Went to Salisbury in the evening & heard Rev. J. G. Neiffer preach. Lodged with Rev. Neiffer.

Mond. 14. Breakfast at Col. P. N. Heilig's. Returned home.

Tues. 15. Went to Gold Hill to tailor & shoemaker.

Wed. 16. In the afternoon went to Gold Hill to the Tailorshop. In the evening married John Brady & Barbara Holshouser.

Thurs. 17. Went to Salisbury and attended the investigation of the charge of excessive use of liquor against Rev. W. Artz, which resulted in his acquittal. Dinner at Wm Crawford's & supper at B. F. Fraley's. Took the train in the night for Gibsonville. Reached Gibsonville next morning at 2½ o'clock.

Frid. 18. Breakfast at Rev. C. H. Bernheim's. Dinner at Mr. Right's. Then went to L. W. Summer's and staid all night.

Sat. 19. Went to Frieden's Church. All night at L. W. Summers'.

Sund. 20. Went to Frieden's Church. The new church was to have been dedicated to day, but the house not being completed, the dedication was postponed. All night at L. W. Summers'.

Mond. 21. Went to Frieden's Church & preached from John 7:37. All night at L. W. Summers'.

Tues. 22. Went to Frieden's Church & preached from Gen. 6:22. Then went to Rev. C. H. Bernheim's & took dinner. Took the Cars in the night & reached Salisbury next morning.

Wed. 23. Took breakfast at B. F. Fraley's. Returned home.

Thurs. 24. In the afternoon went to Gold Hill to shoemaker.

Frid. 25. At home.

Sat. 26. Went to Lewis' & staid all night.

Sund. 27. Preached at Bethel Ch. from Is. 32:11. Confirmed two persons. Dinner at Lewis'. In the afternoon called to see Mrs. Quilman, she being sick. All night at John Cawble's.

Mond. 28. Called in the morning to see Mrs. Quilman. Then returned home.

Tues. 29. In the forenoon went to Gold Hill to blacksmith shop.

Wed. 30. At home.

Thurs. Dec. 1. At home till afternoon then went to Dr. Coleman's & bought some pork.
Frid. 2. In the afternoon went to Nancy Arey's on business. All night here.
Sat. 3. Went to Mr. Freese's & staid over night.
Sund. 4. Preached at Salem ch. from Math. 4:16. on the subject of the Reformation. Dinner at Saml Seaford's. Returned home.
Mond. 5. Attended preaching at St. Peter's ch. Rev. C. H. Bernheim with me to night.
Tues. 6. Went to Salisbury.
Wed. 7. At home.
Thurs. 8. Went to Henry Peeler's hewing till 12 o'clock. In the afternoon at home making preparations for butchering.
Frid. 9. At home. Slaughtered 4 hogs.
Sat. 10. Started for Bethel ch. Dinner at Mr. Haines. Attached Lawyer to Mr. H's. buggy & took Mrs. H. & little son to Mr. Holtom's to see her sister. Attached Lawyer to Lewis' Buggy & went with Lewis to W. W. Miller's. All night here.
Sund. 11. Preached at Bethel from 1 Cor. 4:2. An inclement day. All night at Lewis'. Confirmed 1 person & installed Deacons.
Mond. 12. Returned home. Brought Mrs. Haines back from Mr. Holtom's. Dinner at Mr. Haines'.
Tues. 13. Went with wife to Mt. Pleasant. Dinner at Daniel Miller's. All night at Phebe Brown's.
Wed. 14. Attended meeting of Board of Trustees of N. C. College. Dinner at L. G. Heilig's. All night at Danl Miller's.
Thurs. 15. Returned home. Dinner at Paul Cruse's. Supper at Dr. Coleman's.
Frid. 16. Went to Franklin Academy. All night at J. C. Miller's.
Sat. 17. Went to Salem ch. and preached from 1 Cor. 4:2. All night at John Berger's.
Sund. 18. Preached at Salem from Josh. 23:8. Baptized one infant. All night at Lewis'.
Mond. 19. Returned home.
Tues. 20. Went to Gold Hill.
Wed. 21. At home.
Thurs. 22. Went to P. N. Heilig's plantation & married Richard C. Horton & M. P. Crowell. Also called at Dr. Coleman's.
Frid. 23. Started for Bethel Church. All night at John Fisher's. Very cold day.
Sat. 24. Had an appointment for this day at Bethel ch. but the day being very cold, but few persons attended. Had short religious exercises & dismissed. All night at Lewis'.
Sund. 25. Preached at Bethel ch. from Matth. 1:21. Installed Elders of the Church & then resigned the congregation. All night at Lewis'.
Mond. 26. In the afternoon went to Andrew Shuping's & staid over night.
Tues. 27. Went to Joseph Colly's & married Julius B. Sheets & Louisa H. Colly. After supper went to S. B. Colly's and staid over night.
Wed. 28. Returned to Joseph Colly's for breakfast. Afterwards returned home.
Thurs. 29. Went to Dr. Coleman's & bought some leather. Balance of the day at home.
Frid. 30. Went to Gold Hill to shoemaker.
Sat. 31. Started to Salem Church. All night at John Smithdeal's.

Sund. Jan. 1, 1871. Preached at Salem ch. from Acts 28:15. Dinner at Jesse Lyerly's. All night at Lewis'.

Mond. 2. Returned home.

Tues. 3. At home. Slaughtered two hogs. Also wrote Will for John Williams.

Wed. 4. Went to Mt. Pleasant by way of Paul Cruse's & C. Melchior's. Made partial payment on a note to Rev. Cone. All night at Col. Shimpock's.

Thurs. 5. Being associated with Col. Shimpock as a committee, settled with Mathias Barrier, Treasurer of Endowment Fund of N. C. College. Dinner at M. Barrier's. Returned home.

Frid. 6. Went with wife to Henry A. Miller's on a visit.

Sat. 7. Went to David Barringer's, his son Paul being sick. Called also at Henry Harkey's on business.

Sund. 8. At home, having no appointment.

Mond. 9. Called to see Paul Barringer. Called also at Henry Harkey's & H. A. Miller's on business.

Tues. 10. At home.

Wed. 11. At home.

Thurs. 12. Went to Bethel ch. and attended the funeral of Francis Victor Miller, preached from Micah 2:10. Dinner at John C. Miller's. All night at Nancy Arey's.

Frid. 13. Returned home.

Sat. 14. Started for Salem ch. All night at Moses A. Bost's.

Sund. 15. Very rainy in the morning. Preached at Salem ch. from Prov. 22:2. All night at John Berger's.

Mond. 16. Made my way leisurely towards Iredell Co. Dinner at John Harkey's. All night at W. L. Kistler's.

Tues. 17. Went to Alexander Brown's & staid over night.

Wed. 18. Dinner at Jacob Goodman's. All night at Charles Barringer's.

Thurs. 19. Called at Lansing White's. Went to Benjamin Arey's & staid over night.

Frid. 20. Went to Andrew Barringer's to dinner. All night at Robert Brown's.

Sat. 21. Dinner at Caleb Barrier's. Called also at Augustus Brown's. All night at Robert Brown's.

Sund. 22. Preached at St. Michael's ch. from Eph. 6:1-4. All night at Charles Barringer's.

Mond. 23. Returned home.

Tues. 24. At home.

Wed. 25. At home.

Thurs. 26. Started for Jerusalem in Davie Co. to attend Special Conference. A very inclement day. All night at Mathias Miller's.

Frid. 27. Went to Jerusalem ch. but the day being very inclement no congregation assembled. All night at M. Miller's.

Sat. 28. At Mr. Miller's. A very inclement day.

Sund. 29. Preached at Jerusalem from Math. 20:6. Dinner at Rev. Bressent's of the Baptist Church. All night at Mathias Miller's.

Mond. 30. Went with Mr. Miller to Mocksville to attend to some business connected with some church land on Dutchman's Creek. Dinner at Mr. Miller's. All night at Lewis'.

Tues. 31. Returned home.

Wed. Feb. 1. In the morning went to Mr. Holshouser's & in the afternoon went to Gold Hill.

Thurs. 2. In the morning went to Daniel Miller's & in afternoon to Gold Hill with wife.

Frid. 3. At home.

Sat. 4. Started for Salem ch. All night at Sam$^{\underline{l}}$ Seaford's.

Sund. 5. Preached at Salem ch. from Deut. 32:46.47. Baptized one infant. All night at John Lingel's.

Mond. 6. Returned home. An inclement day.

Tues. 7. Went with wife to see widow Klutts (of Leonard) she being sick.

Wed. 8. At home.

Thurs. 9. Started for St. Michael's ch. in Iredell Co. All night at John Harkey's.

Frid. 10. Dinner at Augustus Brown's. Crossed the Catawba River to Alexander Clark's. All night here.

Sat. 11. In the afternoon re-crossed the River. All night at Caleb Barrier's.

Sund. 12. Preached at St. Michael's ch. from Jam. 1:25. All night at Henry Cloninger's.

Mond. 13. An inclement day. Dinner at Alexander Brown's. All night at John Berger's.

Tues. 14. Dinner at R. J. Holmes in Salisbury. Baptized 2 of Mr. Holmes' children. In the afternoon returned home.

Wed. 15. At home.

Thurs. 16. Went to Dr. Coleman's to meet Rev. Neiffer. Went with Rev. Neiffer to Rev. Cone's. Dinner here. In afternoon returned home. Rev. Neiffer with me over night.

Frid. 17. Went to Gold Hill in the forenoon on business.

Sat. 18. Started for Salem ch. All night at Lewis'.

Sund. 19. Preached at Salem Ch. from Job 1:21. the funeral of the deceased child (9 yrs. old) of Monroe Barrier. Dinner at Joseph Colly's. All night at John C. Miller's.

Mond. 20. Returned home. Tom, the Barber treated me & Rev. Neiffer to a dinner of fish & crackers, seasoned with cheese.

Tues. 21. In the forenoon went to Gold Hill. In the afternoon went to Alexander Peeler's.

Wed. 22. At home.

Thurs. 23. At home till afternoon, then went with wife to Dr. Coleman's.

Frid. 24. Went with wife to Salisbury. At night attended lectures in the Luth. Church by Rev. J. G. Neiffer. All night at B. F. Fraley's.

Sat. 25. Went with wife to Lewis'. Dinner here. In afternoon returned to Salisbury. Preached at night from 1 Thes. 2:11.12. All night at B. F. Fraley's.

Sund. 26. Attended Rev. Neiffer's communion meeting. Assisted in the administration of the Lord's Supper. Supper at Sheriff Walton's. All night at B. F. Fraley's.

Mond. 27. Returned home. Dinner at Dr. Coleman's.

Tues. 28. At home.

Wed. March 1. At home.

Thurs. 2. Went with wife to David Barringer's.

Frid. 3. Assisted Henry Peeler Jr. in raising a stable.

Sat. 4. Very inclement till 12 o'clock. In the afternoon started for Salem ch. Supper at Mansion Hotel. Lodged with Rev. Neiffer. Sent my horse to P. N. Heilig's.

Sund. 5. Breakfast at P. N. Heilig's. Preached at Salem ch. from Acts 26:17.18. Dinner at William McNeely's. Supper at P. N. Heilig's. Attended Rev. Neiffer's preaching. Lodged with Rev. Neiffer.

Mond. 6. Breakfast at P. N. Heilig's. Returned home.

Tues. 7. Went to the sale of the property of Levi Thomas, dec$^{\underline{d}}$. Dinner at Nancy Arey's. Brought Bettie Thomas along home.

Wed. 8. Took wife to Dr. Coleman's. Then went to Rev. Cone's on business. Dinner at Dr. Coleman's.

Thurs. 9. Went to Salisbury. Supper at P. N. Heilig's. Attended the exhibition of Paradise Lost. Lodged with Rev. Neiffer.

Frid. 10. Breakfast at P. N. Heilig's. Dinner at Daniel Lyerly's. All night at John Smithdeal's.

Sat. 11. Went to Monroe Barrier's to dinner. In afternoon went to W. L. Kistler's & staid all night.

Sund. 12. Preached at Kistler's Stand. from Math. 10:32.33. Dinner here. In the afternoon went to Lewis' and staid all night.

Mond. 13. Returned home.

Tues. 14. Took wife to Dr. Coleman's. Dinner here. In the afternoon went with Rev. Neiffer to Dan$^{\underline{l}}$ Miller's & staid all night.

Wed. 15. Went to Mt. Pleasant to attend meeting of Board of Trustees N. C. College. Dinner at Col. Shimpock's. All night at Mrs. Phebe Brown's.

Thurs. 16. Returned home. Dinner at Dr. Coleman's.

Frid. 17. At home.

Sat. 18. Started for Salem ch. All night at C. R. Miller's.

Sund. 19. Attended to the funeral of Rose Sophia Miller, daughter of C. R. Miller, at Salem ch., preached from Ex. 33:14. After an intermission prea$^{\underline{d}}$ from Rev. 3:20. the funeral of Nancy Camel. Dinner at M. A. Bost's. All night at Lewis'.

Mond. 20. Returned home.

Tues. 21. At home.

Wed. 22. Went with wife to Gold Hill.

Thurs. 23. Went in the forenoon to Abram Lentz's & baptized his son, 9 yrs. old, he being sick.

Frid. 24. At home.

Sat. 25. Went with wife to Nancy Arey's. Dinner at Mr. Grupy's.

Sund. 26. Had an appointment for this at Union ch. to preach the funerals of Levi Thomas & wife, both deceased, but the day being very rainy did not attend. At Mrs. Arey's.

Mond. 27. Returned home. Dinner at David Barringer's.

Tues. 28. In the morning went to Mr. Holshouser's for Eve Ann Miller. Then went to Gold Hill.

Wed. 29. In forenoon repaired wife's shoes. In the evening went to Gold Hill to attend meeting of Bible Society. All night at E. Mauney's.

Thurs. 30. Returned home & then repaired my boots.

Frid. 31. At home.

Sat. April 1. Started for Salem Ch. All night at John Berger's.

Sund. 2. Preached at Salem Ch. from Is. 32:11. middle clause. Returned to John Berger's for dinner. In afternoon went to Capt. Jacob Fisher's & staid over night.

Mond. 3. Returned home. Dinner at Rev. Wm. Artz's. Called by Jesse Beaver's on business. Called also to see Alias Beaver, he being afflicted with paralysis of body.

Tues. 4. Went to Gold Hill. Balance of the day at home.

Wed. 5. At home. Lilly had her colt to day.

Thurs. 6. Went to Jacob Earnheart's & wrote several deeds for him.

Frid. 7. Went to Union Ch. & preached the funerals of Levi Thomas and wife from Prov. 3:6. Very indisposed & had to stop before finishing Sermon. Dinner at Rev. S. Scherer's. Returned home.

Sat. 8. At home.

Sund. 9. Preached at St. Peter's ch. from 1 Cor. 15:20. A good congregation.

Mond. 10. Preached at Amey Brown's from Matth. 11:28. Dinner at Adam Miller's.

Tues. 11. Went to Danl Miller's to Barn raising.

Wed. 12. Went to mill & to Gold Hill.

Thurs. 13. Started for Salem Church. All night at Lewis'.

Frid. 14. Had an appointment to day at 2 o'clock P. M. at Salem ch. to meet applicants for admission to church membership, but in consequence of incessant rain till 12 o'clock, did not attend. In the afternoon went to Jesse Lyerly's & staid all night.

Sat. 15. Had services at Salem ch. preparatory to communion. Rev. J. G. Neiffer preached. All night at Moses A. Bost's.

Sund. 16. Preached at Salem ch. from Acts 18:21. (middle clause). Baptized one adult & confirmed five persons. After an intermission administered the communion. Dinner at Saml Seaford's. Then went to Salisbury & heard Rev. Saml Pharr preach in the Lutheran Church. Left my horse at Col. P. N. Heilig's & lodged with Rev. Neiffer at Mich^{l} Brown's.

Mond. 17. Breakfast at Mich^{l} Brown's. Returned home.

Tues. 18. Went to Salisbury on business.

Wed. 19. Went to Gold Hill in the afternoon & bought some oats.

Thurs. 20. At home planting corn.

Frid. 21. At home. Sheared the Sheep.

Sat. 22. At home till afternoon, then went with wife to David Barringer's & staid over night.

Sund. 23. Preached at St. Peter's ch. from Gen. 6:22. Baptized one infant. Dinner at H. A. Miller's.

Mond. 24. Met Rev. J. G. Neiffer at Dr. Coleman's & took him in my Buggy to Mt. Pleasant. Dinner at G. M. Bernhardt's. All night at Phebe Brown's.

Tues. 25. In Mt. Pleasant. Listened to the deliberations of the Committee to settle a plan of Union between the N. C. and Tennessee Synods. Dinner at L. G. Heilig's. Supper & lodging at Phebe Brown's.

Wed. 26. In Mt. Pleasant. Dinner at Mrs. Dreher's. Supper at Col. Shimpock's. All night at Phebe Brown's.

Thurs. 27. Returned home.

Frid. 28. Went to Special Conference at St. Stephen's ch. Returned home in the evening.

Sat. 29. At Special Conference at St. Stephen's ch. Returned home.

Sund. 30. At Special Conference at St. Stephen's ch. Rev. Scherer with me to night.

Mond. May 1. Went with wife in afternoon to Caty Earnheart's to have cotton spun.

Tues. 2. In the morning went to Gold Hill & had horse shod. In afternoon went to Lewis'. Was overtaken by a heavy rain.

Wed. 3. Returned home. Dinner at Dr. Coleman's.

Thurs. 4. At home.

Frid. 5. At home.

Sat. 6. Started for Salem ch. Dinner at Michael Brown's. All night at John Berger's.

Sund. 7. Preached at Salem ch. from Ps. 40:1-3. Baptized one infant. Dinner at W. L. Kistler's. In the afternoon preached at Kistler's Stand from Ex. 14:15. All night at Mrs. Jacob Goodman's.

Mond. 8. Returned to Alexander Brown's & remained over night.

Tues. 9. Laid the corner stone of St. Luke's Ev. Luth. Church, being assisted by Revds. Aldrich and Neiffer. Dinner at Alexander Brown's. All night at Saml Seaford's.

Wed. 10. Returned home.

Thurs. 11. In forenoon went with wife to Dr. Coleman's. In afternoon at home.

Frid. 12. In forenoon went to Gold Hill on business. In afternoon at home.

Sat. 13. In the morning baptized & confirmed Leah Earnheart and Tiney Eliz. Kirk. Preached at St. Peter's ch. from Prov. 28:13. preparatory to communion.

Sund. 14. Preached at St. Peter's ch. from Is. 40:6-8. the funeral of Aaron Lefler. After an intermission administered the Lord's Supper.

Mond. 15. Went to Salisbury.

Tues. 16. Went to Gold Hill.

Wed. 17. At home.

Thurs. 18. At home till evening, then went to Jacob Holshouser's and married Moses G. Brady & Mary L. Holshouser.

Frid. 19. Went with wife to Franklin Academy to attend the closing exercises of the Session. Returned after night to Salisbury. All night at B. F. Fraley's.

Sat. 20. In the morning took the train for Gibsonville. All night at C. H. Bernheim's.

Sund. 21. Attended the dedication of Frieden's Church. Supper at Simeon Wagoner's. Took the train at 12 o'clock at night for Salisbury.

Mond. 22. Arrived in Salisbury in the morning. Breakfast at B. F. Fraley's. Returned home.

Tues. 23. Went to Gold Hill.

Wed. 24. Went to Mt. Pleasant. Dinner at Daniel Miller's. Supper at Col. Shimpock's. All night at Mrs. Phebe Brown's.

Thurs. 25. In Mt. Pleasant attending Commencement exercises of College. Dinner & supper at Col. Shimpock's. All night at Phebe Brown's.

Frid. 26. Returned home. Dinner at Rev. Cone's.

Sat. 27. In the afternoon went to Salisbury. All night at P. N. Heilig's.

Sund. 28. Attended the installation of Rev. J. G. Neiffer. Made a short address in the afternoon to the congregation on the subject of Baptism. Supper at Caleb T. Bernhardt's. All night at P. N. Heilig's.

Mond. 29. Quite indisposed-returned home.

Tues. 30. Wed. 31. At home.

Thurs. June 1. At home.

Frid. 2. Went with Lewis to Gold Hill, to John Earnheart's and to Henry Harkey's.

Sat. 3. Went to Lewis'.

Sund. 4. Preached at Salem Ch. from John 3:1-13. and in afternoon from Dan. 12:3. Dinner at Saml Seaford's. Returned to Lewis'.

Mond. 5. Returned home.

Tues. 6. Went to Gold Hill to Post Office. In afternoon took Alice Barringer's Valise home.

Wed. 7. Went to Salisbury for Cooking Stove.

Thurs. 8. Went to Salisbury on business.

Frid. 9. Went to Gold Hill in the morning. In the afternoon went to Mt. Pleasant. All night at Phebe Brown's.

Sat. 10. Returned home. Dinner at Dr. Coleman's. In the evening went with wife to David Barringer's.

Sund. 11. Preached at St. Peter's ch. from Luk. 16:19-31. Dinner at Z. Lyerly's. In afternoon Preached at widow Brown's from Rev. 3:20. Returned home.

Mond. 12. Went to Gold Hill to Post Office.

Tues. 13. In the afternoon engaged some hands to mow grass & went to mill.

Wed. 14. In the morning went to mill. Balance of day at home.

Thurs. 15. At home making hay.

Frid. 16. At home preparing for Sunday.

Sat. 17. Started for Salem ch. Dinner at Lewis'. All night at Pleas. Wise's.

Sund. 18. Met the Salem ch. Sunday School in the morning. Preached from Ps. 133:1-3. Dinner at D. M. Barrier's. Preached in afternoon at Kistler's Stand from 1 John 3:2. the funeral of Jacob C. Goodman dec^{d}. All night at Alexander Brown's. Had Lewis with me.

Mond. 19. Returned home. Dinner at Lewis'.

Tues. 20. Wed. 21. At home, haymaking.

Thurs. 22. Hauled hay till late in afternoon, then went to Post Office at Gold Hill.

Frid. 23. Engaged hands to mow grass.

Sat. 24. At home, − hauled in wheat.

Sund. 25. Met the Sunday School at St. Peter's ch. in the morning. Then preached from Ps. 133:1-3. Dinner at Anna Trexler's. Called in the afternoon at Moses Trexler's to see his afflicted daughter.

Mond. 26. In forenoon went to Gold Hill to Post Office. In the afternoon went to Mr. Burriss' to blacksmith shop.

Tues. 27. Went by Mr. Burriss' to Nancy Arey's.

Wed. 28. Thurs. 29. At home, hay making.

Frid. 30. Started for Salem Ch. All night at John C. Miller's.

Sat. July 1. Had catechization at Salem ch. All night at Jesse Lyerly's.

Sund. 2. Preached at Salem ch. from Prov. 29:1. In the afternoon attended Sunday School. Dinner at John Lingel's. Preached at night in Salisbury from 2 Cor. 5:17. All night with Rev. Neiffer.

Mond. 3. Breakfast at Mrs. Brown's. Returned home.

Tues. 4. Went to mill in the morning. In the afternoon helped to thresh wheat at Milas A. Holshouser's.

Wed. 5. Went to Salisbury.

Thurs. 6. In forenoon went to Gold Hill. In the afternoon went to Moses Trexler's to see his afflicted daughter.

Frid. 7. Went with wife to Dr. Coleman's.

Sat. 8. At home.

Sund. 9. In the morning met the Sund. School at St. Peter's ch. After an intermission preached from Gen. 28:17. Dinner at Chas Lyerly's. In the afternoon preached at widow Brown's from Luk. 13:24. Returned home.

Mond. 10. Went to Paul Beaver's to get some Brandy for wife to make Blackberry Cordial. In afternoon at home.

Tues. 11. Went to Gold Hill to Post Office, & to Dr. Coleman's to buy some Oats. In afternoon at home.

Wed. 12. In the morning went to mill. Then went with wife to Dr. Coleman's.

Thurs. 13. At home.

Frid. 14. Started for Salem ch. All night at Charles R. Miller's.

Sat. 15. Had catechization at Salem. All night at John Berger's.

Sund. 16. Attended Sunday School in the morning at Salem. Then preached from Gen. 28:17. Baptized 2 infants. Dinner at Mrs. Kistler's. In the afternoon preached at Kistler's Stand from Luk. 15:11-24. All night at Alexander Brown's.

Mond. 17. Returned home. Dinner at Mrs. Mich^l Brown's, Salisbury.

Tues. 18. Called to see Elias Beaver, he being much afflicted. Had religious exercises & administered to him the L's. Supper. Dinner here. Returned home.

Wed. 19. Thurs. 20. At home.

Frid. 21. Went by way of D. Barringer's to Salisbury. Supper at D. Barringer's.

Sat. 22. At home. Wife sick.

Sund. 23. Preached at St. Peter's ch. from Ps. 119:63.

Mond. 24. Attended fun^l of M. Trexler's daughter. Preached at house from 2 Tim. 1:12. Buried at Lower Stone Church.

Tues. 25. In afternoon went to Gold Hill to Post Office. In forenoon aided in laying of Corner Stone of Christiana Church.

Wed. 26. Attended the funeral of Danl Lyerly at Salem Ch. – preached from 2 Tim. 1:12. All night at M. A. Bost's.

Thurs. 27. Started for Central Conference at St. Michael's ch. Iredell Co. Rev. Neiffer in Buggy with me. All night at Alex. Brown's. Felt unwell this evening.

Frid. 28. Went to St. Michael's and attended Conference. All night at Robert Brown's. Quite unwell.

Sat. 29. Returned to the church. Had a severe chill. Went to Mr. Scroggs & procured a bed till chill wore off. In the afternoon started for home. All night at Alex. Brown's.

Sund. 30. Returned home.

Mond. 31. At home, quite sick.

Tues. Aug. 1. At home balance of the week & confined to my room.

Sund. 6. Mond. 7. At home & able to be up.

Tues. 8. to Sat. 12. At home.

Sund. 13. Preached at St. Peter's ch. from Matth. 25:1-13.

Mond. 14. At home till afternoon, then went to Mr. Holshouser's to get some information in relation to digging a well.

Tues. 15. In forenoon went to Gold Hill to get a well rope. Commenced digging well. In afternoon went with wife to Mt. Pleasant. All night at Phebe Brown's.

Wed. 16. In Mt. Pleasant till afternoon, then went to Danl Miller's & staid all night. Dinner to day at L. G. Heilig's.

Thurs. 17. Returned home. Called at Danl Goodman's & bought some crocks. Dinner at Charlie Fisher's.

Frid. 18. Started for Salem ch. All night at Lewis'.

Sat. 19. Had catechization at Salem ch. Dinner and all night at Danl Menis'.

Sund. 20. Preached at Salem ch. from Matth. 25:1-13. Dinner at D. Lentz's. Preached in the afternoon at Col. D. Lentz's from Rev. 2:4.5. Baptized Mr. Cosort's Child. All night at Lewis'.

Mond. 21. Breakfast at H. G. Miller's. Then returned home.

Tues. 22. Started for Synod. Went to Salisbury in M. A. Holshouser's wagon. Dinner at Mrs. Brown's. In the afternoon went to William Smith's, being accompanied by Rev. Neiffer, & confirmed Mr. Smith & administered to him the communion, he being very sick. Returned to Salisbury. All night with Rev. Neiffer at Mrs. Brown's.

Wed. 23. Took the train for Lexington, & then was carried to Pilgrim Church. Synod organized to day. Had lodgings assigned at Joseph Sink's & continued there during Synod.

Sund. 27. Was conveyed in the evening to Lexington. All night at Mr. Hege's.

Mond. 28. Took the train at 3 a.m. for Salisbury. Breakfast at National Hotel. Dinner R. J. Holmes'. In the evening returned home.

Tues. 29. At home.

Wed. 30. Went in forenoon to H. A. Miller's to ascertain the strength of St. Peter's Sunday School.

Thurs. 31. Went to Mr. Buress' & had horse shod.

Frid. Sept. 1. Started for Salem Church. All night at James Colly's.

Sat. 2. Had catechization at Salem. In the afternoon went to Mr. Carson's & preached from Rev. 2:4.5. All night here. Dinner to day at Eli Powlass'.

Sund. 3. Preached at Salem from Ps. 40:4. Buried Jacob Lyerly & baptized 2 infts. Dinner at John Harkey's. In the afternoon preached at Kistler's Stand from Acts 9:6. All night at Alexander Brown's.

Mond. 4. Returned home. Dinner at Mrs. Brown's, Salisbury.

Tues. 5. Wed. 6. Thurs. 7. At home.

Frid. 8. Went to Salisbury.

Sat. 9. Went to Dan[l] Miller's in Cabarrus Co. & borrowed fifty dollars.

Sund. 10. Preached at St. Peter's ch. from Acts. 9:6. Dinner at H. A. Miller's.

Mond. 11. At home, haymaking.

Tues. 12. Went in forenoon to Gold Hill to Smith Shop & Post Office.

Wed. 13. At home, haying.

Thurs. 14. At home. David Barringer & wife called to see us.

Frid. 15. Started for Salem ch. Dinner at Mrs. Brown's in Salisbury. All night at Lewis'.

Sat. 16. Went to Salem ch. & conducted the Sunday School celebration. All night at Legrand Elliot's.

Sund. 17. Preached at Salem ch. from James 1:5. Dinner at Sam[l] Seaford's. Preached at night in Luth. Church in Salisbury from Jam. 1:25. Supper at Sheriff Walton's. All night with Rev. Neiffer at Mrs. Brown's.

Mond. 18. Returned home.

Tues. 19. Went in afternoon to Caty Earnheart's after some thread and settled for spinning of same.

Wed. 20. Went in forenoon with wife to Gold Hill.

Thurs. 21. At home. Had well cleaned.

Frid. 22. At home.

Sat. 23. Went to Gold Hill on business. Called by Paul Beaver's & brought some Brandy home.

Sund. 24. Preached at St. Peter's ch. from James 1:5. & baptized one infant. Jacob Miller & wife dined with us to day.

Mond. 25. In afternoon went to Thomas Linn's on business. In the evening called to see Henry Harkey on business. All night at David Barringer's.

Tues. 26. Returned home in the morning. Haying some.

Wed. 27. Thurs. 28. At home.

Frid. 29. Started for Salem ch. All night at Lewis'.

Sat. 30. Had catechization at Salem. ch. All night at John Berger's.

Sund. Oct. 1. Preached at Salem ch. from Rom. 10:1. In afternoon preached at Kistler's Stand from Jam. 1:25. All night at Mrs. Kistler's.

Mond. 2. Went to Alex. Brown's to dinner. Called in afternoon in company with Alex. Brown to see widow Shoaf & family. All night at Mr. Brown's.

Tues. 3. Went to Charles Barringer's. All night here.

Wed. 4. Went to widow J. C. Goodman's & married Saml M. F. Martin & Altisa C. Goodman. All night at Mrs. Kistler's.

Thurs. 5. Returned home.

Frid. 6. Went to Gold Hill. In the afternoon took wife to Dr. Coleman's.

Sat. 7. Went in the morning & brought wife home. Lewis with us to night.

Sund. 8. Preached at St. Peter's ch. from 2 Tim. 1:13.

Mond. 9. Took Bettie Thomas to George Peeler's. All night at Nancy Arey's.

Tues. 10. Returned home by way of David Barringer's & Henry Harkey's. In the afternoon went to Gold Hill to Post Office.

Wed. 11. Thurs. 12. At home shucking corn.

Frid. 13. Started for Salem Church. Called at the Fair in Salisbury. All night at Saml Seaford's.

Sat. 14. Went early in the morning with Danl Seaford to the Water Station to meet Revs. Aldrich & Neiffer. Had preparatory service to day at Salem ch. Revds. Neiffer & Aldrich preached. All night at John Berger's.

Sund. 15. At Salem ch. Confirmed six persons. Rev. Aldrich preached an ordination sermon. Ordained J. H. Fesperman, W. R. Ketchie, & R. L. Brown. Administered also the Lord's Supper. Preached at night in Salisbury from Acts 9:6. All night at Paul N. Heilig's.

Mond. 16. Returned home. Dinner at Dr. Coleman's.

Tues. 17. Went to Gold Hill to Post Office.

Wed. 18. Went to Dr. Coleman's & brought Mrs. Coleman to eat an opossum dinner with us.

Thurs. 19. At home.

Frid. 20. Went to Gold Hill on business.

Sat. 21. Went to Organ ch. & preached from Acts 9:6. & held preparatory service. All night at Mary Heilig's.

Sund. 22. Preached at Organ ch. from James 1:25. consecrated the elements & assisted in the communion. All night at Rev. Cone's.

Mond. 23. Returned home.

Tues. 24. Went to Salisbury.

Wed. 25. Went to Gold Hill.

Thurs. 26. Started for Special Conference at Jerusalem ch. All night at Lewis'.

Frid. 27. Went to Jerusalem but had no preaching as preachers & people did not attend. All night at M. Miller's.

Sat. 28. Preached at Jerusalem from Acts 9:6. at 11 o'clock & at night from 2 Cor. 5:17. All night at Mathias Miller's.

Sund. 29. Preached at Jerusalem from James 1:25. & administered the Lord's Supper, being aided in the administration by Rev. Ketchie. Preached at night in Salisbury from Matth. 4:16. on the subject of the Reformation. All night at Sheriff Walton's.

Mond. 30. Dinner at B. F. Fraley's. In afternoon returned home.

Tues. 31. Went in forenoon to Gold Hill & in afternoon to Mr. Buress' & had horse shod.

Wed. Nov. 1. In the morning went to mill. Balance of day at home.

Thurs. 2. In the morning went to mill. In afternoon to Gold Hill.

Frid. 3. At home till afternoon, then went to Dr. Coleman's on business.

Sat. 4. Started for Salem ch. All night at Lewis'.

Sund. 5. Preached at Salem ch. from John 5:40. In the afternoon preached at St. Luke's ch. from Ex. 23:2. All night at John Berger's.

Mond. 6. Returned home, and in passing through Salisbury, attended to the fun[1] of John Casper.

Tues. 7. Went to Gold Hill to Post Office.

Wed. 8. Went to Salisbury.

Thurs. 9. At home.

Frid. 10. At home till evening, then went to Dr. Coleman's for some beef. Rev. Artz with us to night.

Sat. 11. Had preparatory service at St. Peter's ch. Rev. Artz preached.

Sund. 12. Had communion at St. Peter's ch. Revds. Artz & Cone preached.

Mond. 13. At home.

Tues. 14. Went in forenoon to Post Office at Gold Hill. Balance of day at home.

Wed. 15. Attended & clerked sale for P. N. Heilig.

Thurs. 16. Went to Mrs. Nancy Arey's. Returned home by way of Henry Harkey's & paid note for Lewis.

Frid. 17. Went to Caty Earnheart's for spun cotton. Also to Eli Holshouser's on business.

Sat. 18. Started for Salem ch. Dinner in Salisbury at Mrs. Brown's. At night attended the concert of the Tremain Brothers. All night with Rev. Neiffer at Mrs. Brown's.

Sund. 19. Preached at Salem Ch. from Neh. 10:39. Dinner at John Berger's. All night at Joseph Beaver's.

Mond. 20. Returned home. Dinner at Dr. Coleman's.

Tues. 21. Went to Gold Hill to Post Office.

Wed. 22. At home; had hands to hew timber for well frame.

Thurs. 23. Went to Nancy Arey's & to George Peeler's. All night at Mrs. Arey's.

Frid. 24. Returned home.

Sat. 25. In the morning went to Dr. Coleman's.

Sund. 26. Preached at St. Peter's ch. from Luk. 14:22. M. A. Holshouser & wife took dinner with us to day.

Mond. 27. Went to Salisbury.

Tues. 28. Went to Gold Hill, thence to Reuben Bost's & Jacob Trexler's. Dinner at R. Bost's.

Wed. 29. Went to widow Klutts' & to Moses Trexler's.

Thurs. 30. At home. Slaughtered my winter hogs. Snowed to day.

Frid. Dec. 1. At home.

Sat. 2. Started for Salem ch. All night at Lewis'.

Sund. 3. Preached at Salem ch. from Ps. 119:63. Had an appointment for this afternoon at St. Luke's ch. but the weather being inclement did not attend. Dinner at John Berger's. Spent the afternoon with Mr. Berger, he being in very feeble health. All night at M. A. Bost's.

Mond. 4. Returned home. Dinner at Sheriff Walton's.

Tues. 5. Went to Gold Hill to Post Office.

Wed. 6. At home.

Thurs. 7. Left home at 5 o'clock A.M. & rode 20 miles & attended to the burial of John Berger dec^d at Salem Ch. − preached from 1 John 3:2. All night at Mrs. Berger's.

Frid. 8. Returned home. Dinner at Mrs. Brown's in Salisbury.

Sat. 9. At home.

Sund. 10. Preached at St. Peter's ch. from Acts 16:13-15. Dinner at R. W. Lentz's.

Mond. 11. In the afternoon went to Gold Hill to Post Office.

Tues. 12. In the forenoon went to Mrs. Henry Harkey's & to Andrew Berger's on business. In afternoon went to widow Bost's, the weaver.

Wed. 13. At home.

Thurs. 14. In afternoon went to Gold Hill to the shoemaker to have boots repaired.

Frid. 15. In afternoon went to Gold Hill to the tailor.

Sat. 16. Started for Salem ch. All night at C. R. Miller's.

Sund. 17. Preached at Salem ch. from Acts 16:13-15. All night at Lewis'.

Mond. 18. Returned home by way of Mr. Burress' & had horse shod.

Tues. 19. Wed. 20. At home.

Thurs. 21. Went to Salisbury & attended in the Luth. Church the nuptial ceremonies by Rev. J. G. Neiffer of Mr. James H. Hodges & Miss Lizzie M. Ritz. Dinner at Mrs. Ritz's. All night at Lewis'.

Frid. 22. Returned home. Dinner at Mrs. Brown's in Salisbury.

Sat. 23. At home.

Sund. 24. Preached at St. Peter's ch. from John 9:4. the funeral of Henry Harkey dec^d.

Mond. 25. Went to R. W. Lentz's & assisted in the division of Rev. J. A. Linn's library.

Tues. 26. Went to widow Henry Harkey's & assisted in laying off a Year's Provision for said widow. In the afternoon called at David Barringer's on business. Caleb Peeler with us to night.

Wed. 27. Went to the sale of property of Henry Harkey dec^d.

Thurs. 28. At home.

Frid. 29. In the afternoon went to D. Barringer's on business.

Sat. 30. At home. Repaired a pr. shoes.

Sund. 31. Went to Organ Church & attended the dedication of the new Organ. Rev. Aldrich preached.

Mond. Jan 1, 1872. Went with wife to David Barringer's and spent the day.

Tues. 2. Wed. 3. Thurs. 4. At home.

Frid. 5. Went to Gold Hill to Post Office. Thence to Rev. Cone's and paid a note of hand. Dinner here.

Sat. 6. Started for Salem ch. Took Sammy to Salisbury & delivered him to Lewis to take home. All night at John Lingel's.

Sund. 7. Preached at Salem ch. from Luk. 2:41-52. In afternoon went to Adam Lentz's & married Daniel Harkey of Illinois and Harriet E. Lentz. All night at Col. David Lentz's.

Mond. 8. Returned home.

Tues. 9. Went to Gold Hill to Post Office.

Wed. 10. Thurs. 11. At home.

Frid. 12. Went by way of D. Barringer's to Nancy Arey's. All night here.

Sat. 13. Went to Salisbury & thence to Mrs. Cath. Kistler's. All night here.

Sund. 14. Preached at St. Luke's ch. from Acts 20:17-21. Dinner at Alex.ʳ Brown's. All night here.

Mond. 15. Dinner at Sam.ˡ Colly's. All night at John C. Miller's.

Tues. 16. Returned home.

Wed. 17. At home.

Thurs. 18. Went to Edmond Fesperman's to engage some rock cutting. Called at Mr. Frick's & had key mended. Dinner here. Supper at Dr. Coleman's.

Frid. 19. At home.

Sat. 20. Started for Salem ch. All night at Jesse Lyerly's.

Sund. 21. Preached at Salem ch. from Rom. 14:17.18. Went to Eli Powlass' & staid all night.

Mond. 22. Went to John Carson's & took dinner. In afternoon went to Jesse Powlass' & preached at night from Luk. 15:11-24. All night here.

Tues. 23. Went to Jackson Goodman's & took dinner. In afternoon went to Charles Barringer's & staid all night.

Wed. 24. Went to widow Jacob Goodman's & took dinner. In afternoon went to Alexander Brown's. All night here.

Thurs. 25. At Mr. Brown's. Married to day Jesse W. Miller & Laura M. Barrier. All night here.

Frid. 26. Sat. 27. At Mr. Brown's.

Sund. 28. Preached at St. Luke's ch. from Ps. 116:12-14. Dinner at John Harkey's. All night at Samuel Seaford's.

Mond. 29. Returned home.

Tues. 30. In afternoon went to Nancy Arey's. All night here.

Wed. 31. Returned home.

Thurs. Feb. 1. At home, mending shoes.

Frid. 2. Went to Salisbury to attend Special Conference, but had no quorum to transact business. Dinner and supper at B. F. Fraley's. Lodged with Rev. Neiffer.

Sat. 3. Breakfast at Mrs. Brown's. Dinner at Mr. Fraley's. In the afternoon went to M. A. Bost's & staid over night.

Sund. 4. Preached at Salem ch. from 1 Pet. 5:8.9. Dinner at Joseph Beaver's. Then returned home.

Mond. 5. At home.

Tues. 6. Went to Eli Klutts' sale.

Wed. 7. In afternoon went to Gold Hill to Smith Shop.

Thurs. 8. At home. Inclement day.

Frid. 9. At home.

Sat. 10. Started for St. Luke's ch. Dinner at Mrs. Brown's in Salisbury. Supper at Mrs. Brown's & lodged with Rev. Neiffer. At night went to hear the Swiss Bell Ringer's.

Sund. 11. Rev. Neiffer proposed an exchange of pulpits, & went & preached at St. Luke's ch. in my stead. Preached in Salisbury for Rev. Neiffer from Gen. 6:22. Dinner at Mrs. Ritz's. In afternoon attended Sunday School. Supper at B. F. Fraley's. At night Rev. J. G. Neiffer preached. Opened & closed service for him. Lodged with Rev. Neiffer.

Mond. 12. Returned home through Calabria. Was water bound at Mr. Hartman's mill & changed my course. Dinner at Mr. Grupy's.

Tues. 13. Went to Post Office at Gold Hill.

Wed. 14. Went to Calabria as far as Alfred Peeler's to engage a hand to work. Returned by way of Mr. Burress' & had horse shod.

Thurs. 15. Frid. 16. At home.

Sat. 17. Started for Salem ch. All night at Jacob Menis'.

Sund. 18. Preached at Salem from Acts 9:36-42. Dinner at Saml Seaford's. In afternoon returned to Salisbury. Left horse at Col. P. N. Heilig's. Conducted the opening & closing services in Lutheran Church. Rev. Mr. Moore addressed the people on the subject of Am. Tract Society. Rev. Neiffer indisposed & confined to his room. Lodged with him.

Mond. 19. Breakfast at Mrs. Brown's. Returned home. In the evening went to Michael Holshouser's & baptized his two children, one of them being very sick.

Tues. 20. In forenoon went to post office at Gold Hill. Afternoon at home.

Wed. 21. At home. Repaired my shoes.

Thurs. 22. In morning took wife to Dr. Coleman's to go to weaver. In afternoon at home.

Frid. 23. At home till afternoon, then went to Burress' shop & had shoe nailed on.

Sat. 24. Started for St. Luke's ch. All night at Alexander Brown's.

Sund. 25. Preached at St. Luke's ch. from Gen. 6:22. Dinner at Monroe Barrier's. All night at Widow John Berger's.

Mond. 26. Returned home.

Tues. 27. Went to Danl Miller's in Cabarrus Co. to solicit aid in paying for steps to St. Luke's ch. Was kindly received — took dinner here. Received a donation of $10 — returned home.

Wed. 28. Thurs. 29. At home.

Frid. March 1. At home.

Sat. 2. Had intended to start to day for Salem Church, but in consequence of a heavy snow storm, did not leave home. Had a deep snow to day.

Sund. 3. At home. Had an appointment for to day at Salem ch. but was kept at home by the snow.

Mond. 4. Tues. 5. At home.

Wed. 6. At home till afternoon, then went to mill.

Thurs. 7. In forenoon went to Mrs. Bost's to weaver's. In afternoon at home.

Frid. 8. Started for St. Luke's ch. Dinner at P. N. Heilig's in Salisbury. Lodged with Rev. Neiffer.

Sat. 9. Breakfast at P. N. Heilig's. Went to Mrs. Catharine Kistler's & staid over night. Dinner at Saml Colly's.

Sund. 10. Preached at St. Luke's ch. from Luk. 13:24. All night at M. A. Bost's.

Mond. 11. Returned home.

Tues. 12. At home.

Wed. 13. At home till afternoon, then went to Dr. Coleman's and brought wife home, she having gone there on a visit.

Thurs. 14. Went with wife to Gold Hill. Dinner at Mr. Coit's.

Frid. 15. In the morning went to Paul Beaver's & got some brandy. In afternoon went to M. A. Holshouser's on business.

Sat. 16. Went to Salisbury. Placed my horse at Mr. O'Neal's. All night at B. F. Fraley's.

Sund. 17. Preached to day in Salisbury for Mr. Neiffer from Luk. 13:24. & he went to Salem ch. & preached for me. Dinner at Mr. Fraley's. Supper at Dr. Sills. Lodged with Rev. Neiffer.

Mond. 18. Breakfast at Mrs. Brown's. Returned home.

Tues. 19. Went to Gold Hill to Post Office.

Wed. 20. Thurs. 21. At home.

Frid. 22. At home. Weather inclement with snow falling.

Sat. 23. Started for St. Luke's Church. All night at Mrs. John Berger's.

Sund. 24. Preached at St. Luke's Ch. from Prov. 1:24-26. Dinner at John Harkey's. All night at Joseph Beaver's.

Mond. 25. Started for Mt. Pleasant. Fell in company at Salisbury with Rev. Neiffer. Dinner at Moses Barringer's. All night at Danl Miller's. A very rainy day.

Tues. 26. Went to Mt. Pleasant. Stopped at Col. Shimpock's. Attended a conference to start a church paper. At night Rev. Neiffer preached. All night at Col. Shimpock's.

Wed. 27. Attended a meeting of the Board of Trustees of N. C. College. Dinner at Phebe Brown's. In the afternoon returned home.

Thurs. 28. In afternoon went to Salisbury. Lodged with Rev. Neiffer.

Frid. 29. This Good Friday. Preached in Salisbury from John 19:30. Staid at B. F. Fraley's.

Sat. 30. In Salisbury. Staid at Mr. Fraley's.

Sund. 31. Prof. Hubbert preached. Aided in the administration of the Lord's Supper. At Mr. Fraley's.

Mond. April 1. Returned home.

Tues. 2. In forenoon went to Gold Hill. In afternoon went to blacksmith Shop.

Wed. 3. Went to Tan Yard at Ed. Foil's.

Thurs. 4. Went in forenoon to Ribelin's School house to aid settlement between Isaac Earnheart Guard^n & his ward Mary A. Frick. In afternoon went to Jeremiah Graeber's. All night here.

Frid. 5. Attended to the funeral of Adam Cline at Ebenezer ch. — preached from John 9:4. Dinner at Danl Eddleman's. Returned home.

Sat. 6. Started for Salem Ch. All night at John Smithdeal's.

Sund. 7. Preached at Salem ch. from Ez. 33:5. Dinner at C. R. Miller's. All night at Wilson Lentz's. Baptized Mr. Lentz's grand-child, both parents being dead, & the child in feeble health.

Mond. 8. Returned home. Dinner at Mrs. Brown's in Salisbury.

Tues. 9. Went to post office at Gold Hill, in forenoon. In afternoon at home.

Wed. 10. Forenoon at home. In afternoon went to Ephriam Heilig's (Col^d) & engaged him to do some ditching.

Thurs. 11. At home.

Frid. 12. At home till 12 o'clock, then took wife to Dr. Coleman's, but they being absent, returned home.

Sat. 13. Started for St. Luke's ch. Dinner at Mrs. Brown's in Salisbury. All night at Alex^r Brown's.

Sund. 14. Preached at St. Luke's Ch. from Eph. 6:18. Dinner at John Harkey's. All night at Saml Seaford's.

Mond. 15. Returned home. Dinner at Mrs. Brown's, Salisbury.

Tues. 16. Went to Union Ch. to Special Conference. Returned home in afternoon.

Wed. 17. In afternoon went to Gold Hill to Post Office. Called also to see Wm. Paulass on business.

Thurs. 18. Started at 4 A.M. & went to Salem ch. & attended to the fun^l of Thomas F. Berger. Preached from Micah 2:10. All night at widow John Berger's.

Frid. 19. Went to Salisbury Post Office. Called on the way to see Mrs. Pleasant Wise, she being very sick. Read portions of scripture & had prayer. In the afternoon went to John Berger's & staid over night.

Sat. 20. Preached at Salem ch. from Deut. 11:16. Baptized one infant. Had preparatory service. Took dinner at Frank Robison's. Baptized also Mr. Robison's child. All night at Jesse Lyerly's.

Sund. 21. Preached at Salem ch. from 1 Cor. 5:7.8. After an intermission administered the Lord's Supper. All night at Joseph Colly's.

Mond. 22. Returned home. Called at Mr. Burress' shop & had horse shod.

Tues. 23. Went in forenoon to Gold Hill on business. In afternoon went to M. A. Holshouser's on business.

Wed. 24. Went in forenoon to R. W. Lentz's & exchanged seed corn. In afternoon at home.

Thurs. 25. Went in forenoon & made & made [repeated] Tax Return. In afternoon went to Salisbury. Left my horse with Mr. O'Neal. All night at Caleb Bernhardt's — Attended the marriage at night in the Luth. Church of David R. Julian & Bettie Culverhouse. They were married by Rev. Neiffer.

Frid. 26. Dinner to day at John Moose's. In afternoon went to Saml Seaford's & staid all night.

Sat. 27. Went to Alexander Brown's & took dinner. In the evening went to W. L. Kistler's & staid all night.

Sund. 28. Preached at St. Luke's ch. from Is. 32:11. Dinner at D. M. Barrier's. All night at John Lingel's.

Mond. 29. Returned home.

Tues. 30. Went to Jacob Miller's for buggy axles, he having brought them out from Salisbury for me, & then to Gold Hill. In afternoon at home.

Wed. May 1. At home. Had hay baled.

Thurs. 2. Went to Salisbury & exchanged buggy axles.

Frid. 3. In forenoon took buggy to Mr. Bunn's at Gold Hill to have new axles put in. In afternoon at home.

Sat. 4. Started for Salem ch. Dinner at Mrs. Brown's, Salisbury. All night at William Smith's.

Sund. 5. Preached at Salem Ch. from Matth. 6:33. Baptized one infant. Lectured in afternoon. All night at Andrew Shuping's.

Mond. 6. Attended to the funeral of Col. David Lentz at Bethel Ch. Preached from 1 John 3:2. Dinner at John C. Miller's. Returned home.

Tues. 7. Went in forenoon & brought Buggy home. Afternoon at home.

Wed. 8. At home.

Thurs. 9. Started with wife for St. Luke's ch. Dinner at John Lingel's. All night at Alexander Brown's.

Frid. 10. At St. Luke's ch. – Rev. C. H. Bernheim preached. All night at Catharine Kistler's.

Sat. 11. At St. Luke's ch. Rev. Bernheim preached in the morning. Confirmed one person & baptized one infant. Preached myself in afternoon from 2 Cor. 13:5. & held preparatory service. All night at Widow Jacob C. Goodman's.

Sund. 12. At St. Luke's Ch. Prof Hubbert preached the dedication sermon and Rev. J. G. Neiffer performed the dedication services. In afternoon Rev. C. H. Bernheim preached. Administered the Lord's Supper. All night at John Harkey's.

Mond. 13. Returned home. Dinner at Wm. Smith's. Supper at Dr. Coleman's.

Tues. 14. At home. Sheared the Sheep.

Wed. 15. At home.

Thurs. 16. In forenoon went to Thomas Lentz's to have shoes made for wife. Returned home by way of Gold Hill. In afternoon went to Mr. Burress' & had Lilly shod.

Frid. 17. At home. Rain to day.

Sat. 18. Started for Salem ch. All night at Osborn Graham's.

Sund. 19. Preached at Salem ch. from Ps. 7:9. Baptized one infant. Had lectures in afternoon. Dinner at Saml Seaford's. All night at B. F. Fraley's. Heard Rev. S. A. Repass preach to night in Luth. Ch.

Mond. 20. Returned home.

Tues. 21. In the morning took Lethia Swift to Dr. Coleman's. Then went with Dr. Coleman to Gold Hill.

Wed. 22. Went to mill in the afternoon.

Thurs. 23. In forenoon went to Thomas Lent's for a pair of shoes. In the afternoon went to mill.

Frid. 24. At home.

Sat. 25. Started for Salem ch. All night at Edmond Seaford's.

Sund. 26. Preached at Salem ch. from John 5:39. In afternoon lectured on the Commandments. All night at M. A. Bost's.

Mond. 27. Returned home.

Tues. 28. In afternoon went to Mt. Pleasant. All night at Col. Shimpock's.

Wed. 29. Attended meeting of Board of of N. C. College Trustees. Breakfast & dinner at Col. Shimpock's. Supper at Phebe Brown's. All night at Col. Shimpock's.

Thurs. 30. Attended commencement exercises in forenoon. In afternoon returned home.

Frid. 31. Engaged hands to mow grass.

Sat. June 1. Started for St. Luke's ch. Dinner at John Lingel's. All night at Henry Brown's.

Sund. 2. Preached at St. Luke's ch. from Ps. 7:9. All night at Alexander Brown's.

Mond. 3. Dinner at John Lingel's. Sup^r at C. T. Bernhardt's. Left my horse buggy with John Lingel. Took the cars at 9 P.M. for Lexington. All night at Lewis'.

Tues. 4. At Lewis'.

Wed. 5. Took the cars at 8½ A.M. for Gibsonville. Dinner at Lucy Summers'. In the afternoon Maj. A. Summers took me to widow Ludwig Summers'. All night here.

Thurs. 6. Went to W. N. Wright's. Dinner here & staid over night.

Frid. 7. Went to Simeon Wagoner's & took dinner. In the afternoon Simeon Wagoner sent me to John Wagoner's. All night here.

Sat. 8. John Wagoner took me to St. Paul's ch. Preached from Deut. 11:16. to 7 hearer's. All night at Mr. Ross'.

Sund. 9. Preached at St. Paul's church from Luk. 13:24. & after an intermission administered the Lord's Supper. John Wagoner took me back to his house, & after dinner took me to Gibsonville. Supper at Mr. Rankin's.

Mond. 10. Took the cars at 12 o'clock for Salisbury. Reached Salisbury at 4 A.M. Breakfast at Boyden Hotel. In afternoon returned home.

Tues. 11. In afternoon went to Gold Hill.

Wed. 12. In forenoon went to mill. In afternoon at home.

Thurs. 13. Frid. 14. At home.

Sat. 15. Started for St. Luke's ch. All night at Jesse W. Miller's.

Sund. 16. Went to St. Luke's ch. at 9 A.M. & organized a Sund. School. Preached at 11 A.M. from Prov. 3:17. After an intermission, lectured on the 3rd & 4th Commandments. All night at D. M. Barrier's.

Mond. 17. Returned home. Dinner at Mansion Hotel, Salisbury. Paid 50 cts.

Tues. 18. In afternoon went to Solomon Peeler's to engage a wheat cradler & binder.

Wed. 19. Thurs. 20. At home.

Frid. 21. In the afternoon went to Nancy Arey's & staid all night.

Sat. 22. Went to Salisbury in forenoon. Dinner at Caleb Bernhardt's. In afternoon went to Jacob Coon's and staid all night.

Sund. 23. Preached at Salem ch. from Prov. 3:17. After an intermission lectured on 5th and 6th commandments. Dinner at M. A. Bost's. In the evening went to Salisbury & heard Prof. Bikle preach at night. All night at P. N. Heilig's. Baptized to day one infant.

Mond. 24. Returned home.

Tues. 25. At home.

Wed. 26. At home. Sent Lewis with horse & buggy to Salisbury for Rev. P. A. Stroble, Ag^t of American Bible Society. Rev. Stroble with us to night.

Thurs. 27. In forenoon took Rev. Stroble to Gold Hill. In afternoon at home.

Frid. 28. Went to Eastern Conference at St. Matthew's Church and preached from Prov. 3:17. Returned home in the evening. Rev. Neiffer & delegate with us.

Sat. 29. At Conference. Returned home.

Sund. 30. At Conference. Preached in the afternoon from 2 Tim. 1:13.

Mond. July 1. Quite unwell with ague.

Tues. 2. Wed. 3. At home — indisposed.

Thurs. 4. Went in forenoon to engage hands to cradle Oats.

Frid. 5. In afternoon went with Lewis to Salisbury. Supper at Mrs. Brown's. Took the cars for Lexington. All night at Penny's Hotel.

Sat. 6. In Lexington till 5 o'clock, P. M. The object was to aid Lewis in buying a lot, but failed in the trade. Took the cars for Salisbury. Then started for St. Luke's ch. as far as Samuel Seaford's. All night here.

Sund. 7. Preached at St. Luke's ch. from Gen. 28:17. After an intermission lectured on 5 & 6th commandments. All night at Alexander Brown's.

Mond. 8. Returned home. Dinner at Mrs. Brown's with Rev. Neiffer.

Tues. 9. Called at Danl Miller's to see wheat threshers. Returned by way of Gold Hill.

Wed. 10. Thurs. 11. At home.

Frid. 12. At home. Threshed Wheat,

Sat. 13. Started for Salem ch. All night at widow John Berger's.

Sund. 14. Preached at Salem ch. from 2 Cor. 5:1. fun^{l} of Mrs. Henry Earnheart. After an intermission lectured on 7 & 8 command^{ts}. All night at Saml Colly's.

Mond. 15. Returned home. Dinner at Dr. Coleman's.

Tues. 16. Took wife in the morning to Jesse Miller's. Then went to Wilson Kesler's & refunded to him borrowed Money. In evening went & brought wife home.

Wed. 17. At home, — quite unwell.

Thurs. 18. At home, — quite unwell.

Frid. 19. Went to St. Paul's ch. to dedication meeting. All night at Alfred W. Rusher's.

Sat. 20. At St. Paul's ch. Read service for Rev. Neiffer. In the afternoon went to Salisbury. Returned to Allison Misenheimer's. All night here.

Sund. 21. At St. Paul's church. Dedicated the church. Rev. C. H. Bernheim preached. Preached in the afternoon from Neh. 10:39. All night at A. F. Graeber's.

Mond. 22. Returned home by way of Salisbury.

Tues. 23. At home.

Wed. 24. In forenoon went to Gold Hill. In afternoon at home.

Thurs. 25. At home.

Frid. 26. Took Joan and Sammy to Salisbury. Went with Lewis to John C. Miller's & staid over night.

Sat. 27. Brought Lewis back to Salisbury. Went to Jesse Lyerly's for dinner. In the afternoon went to Eli Powlass' & staid over night.

Sund. 28. Preached at Salem ch. from Heb. 10:24. Dinner at Saml Seaford's. All night at Wm. McNeely's.

Mond. 29. Returned home. Dinner at Dr. Coleman's.

Tues. 30. Wed. 31. At home.

Thurs. Aug. 1. Went in the forenoon to the election at Morgan's. In afternoon at home.

Frid. 2. In afternoon went to Mr. Wilie Lentz's & had horse shod.

Sat. 3. Started for St. Luke's ch. All night at Mrs. Cath. Kistler's.

Sund. 4. Preached at St. Luke's ch. from Ex. 20:15. After an intermission lectured on the last three commandments. All night at John Harkey's.

Mond. 5. Returned home.

Tues. 6. Wed. 7. At home.

Thurs. 8. Went in forenoon to Gold Hill. In afternoon at home.

Frid. 9. Went in afternoon to Adam Holshouser's to pay him for day's mowing.

Sat. 10. Started for Salem ch. All night at Mr. Frieze's.

Sund. 11. Preached at Salem ch. from John 4:14. Baptized two infants. Lectured in afternoon. All night at Moses Trexler's.

Mond. 12. Returned home.

Tues. 13. At home. Some relations from Iredell Co. called to see us.

Wed. 14. At home till afternoon, then took wife & Eliz. Barringer to Dr. Coleman's.

Thurs. 15. At home. Heavy rain to day.

Frid. 16. At home.

Sat. 17. Started for St. Luke's ch. Had Mrs. Eliz. Barringer in charge to take her home in Iredell Co. Dinner at Wm. Smith's. Left Mrs. Barringer at Mrs. C. Kistler's. All night at Alex. Brown's.

Sund. 18. Preached at St. Luke's ch. from 2 Tim. 1:13. Lectured in the afternoon. Dinner at Mrs. Goodman's. Took Mrs. Barringer home. All night here.

Mond. 19. Returned part of the way home. Brought Mrs. Kistler's to David Barringer's. All night here. Dinner at Sam$^{\underline{l}}$ Colly's.

Tues. 20. Returned home, then went to Gold Hill to the Tailor.

Wed. 21. Went to Organ ch. to Synod. Preached Synodical sermon from 2 Tim. 1:13. Organized Synod and & read Annual Report. All night at Paul Cruse's.

Thurs. 22. At Synod. All night at Elias Beaver's.

Frid. 23. At Synod. Quite unwell. All night at Moses Barringer's.

Sat. 24. At Synod. All night with wife at Laurence Lingel's.

Sund. 25. At Organ ch. Returned home.

Mond. 26. At Organ ch. Synod adjourned to day. Returned home.

Tues. 27. At home.

Wed. 28. Went with wife to Salisbury. All night at B. F. Fraley's.

Thurs. 29. Returned home. Dinner at Dr. Coleman's.

Frid. 30. In forenoon went to Gold Hill. In afternoon at home.

Sat. 31. Started for St. Luke's church. All night at Alexander Brown's.

Sund. Sep. 1. Preached at St. Luke's ch. from 1 Peter 4:18. After an intermission, lectured on doctrines of the Church. All night at D. M. Barrier's.

Mond. 2. Returned home.

Tues. 3. At home till evening, then went to mill.

Wed. 4. At home. Married to day Pleasant M. Brown & Maria C. Foster.

Thurs. 5. At home.

Frid. 6. Went with wife to Gold Hill. Dinner at Mrs. Coit's.

Sat. 7. Started for Salem ch. Dinner at P. N. Heilig's. All night at Danl Menis'.

Sund. 8. Preached at Salem ch. from Math. 22:1-14. Baptized one infant. Lectured in afternoon on doctrines of the church. All night at Joseph Beaver's.

Mond. 9. Returned home. Dinner at Dr. Coleman's.

Tues. 10. At home. Hauled hay.

Wed. 11. In the morning went to Gold Hill. In the afternoon started for Sunday School Convention at Luther's Chapel. All night at Mich^l Bostian's.

Thurs. 12. Went to Luther's Chapel & attended Convention. All night at Widow Henry Miller's.

Frid. 13. At Convention. After adjournment started for vicinity of St. Luke's ch. All night at Flin Bradshaw's.

Sat. 14. Went to Alex^r Brown's and took dinner. In the evening went to Mrs. Kistler's. & staid all night.

Sund. 15. Preached at St. Luke's ch. from Matth. 22:1-14. After an intermission lectured on Lord's Prayer. All night at Mrs. John Berger's.

Mond. 16. Returned home.

Tues. 17. Went to Gold Hill to Post Office, & to Paul Beaver's on business.

Wed. 18. Went to File's Tan Yard. In the evening to H. A. Miller's & borrowed some money for Lewis.

Thurs. 19. In the forenoon went to J. T. Lentz's to have shoes made for wife. In the afternoon went to Wilson Kesler's on business.

Frid. 20. Started for Salem ch. Dinner at Mansion Hotel, Salisbury. All night at Saml Seaford's.

Sat. 21. Attended Sunday School Celebration at Salem ch. Supper at Charles Beaver's. At night attended singing at the church. All night at M. A. Bost's.

Sund. 22. Preached at Salem ch. from Mal. 3:16. Baptized one infant. Dinner at John Lingel's. In the evening returned home.

Mond. 23. At home till afternoon, then called to engage Milas A. Holshouser to make & fix up a gate post.

Tues. 24. Went in forenoon to Mr. Burress' & had horse shod. In afternoon at home.

Wed. 25. Started for Conference at Frieden's ch., Guilford County. Supper at Mrs. Brown's, Salisbury. Took the cars at 9½ o'clock in company with Rev. Neiffer for Lexington. All night with Lewis.

Thurs. 26. Took the cars & arrived at Gibsonville at 12 M. Rev. Neiffer & myself walked to Lucy Summers'. Dinner and lodging here.

Frid. 27. Went to Frieden's ch. to Conference. Returned to Lucy Summers' & staid all night.

Sat. 28. At Conference. Preached from 2 Cor. 5:17. All night at the widow Ludwig Summers'.

Sund. 29. At Frieden's ch. Introduced the Gowns. Rev. Bowles preached an ordination sermon. After sermon, ordained Rev. E. P. Parker, being assisted by Rev^s. Bowles & Scherer. In afternoon went to Company Shops. Supper at Gideon Grieson's. At night read service & Rev. Neiffer preached. Took the cars at 12 o'clock for Salisbury.

Mond. 30. Arrived in Salisbury at 5 o'clock A.M. Breakfast at Mansion Hotel. Returned home.

Tues. Oct. 1. Took wife to Dr. Coleman's. Then went to H. A. Miller's on business. Dinner at Dr. Coleman's.

Wed. 2. Went to Gold Hill & bought some plow molds, then took them John Powlass' to have them made. In the afternoon took some leather to J. T. Lentz's to have some shoes made. Called at Mrs. Bost's to see her daughter Ellen, she being confined to her bed with a broken leg.

Thurs. 3. Went in forenoon by way of Mrs. Bost's to J. T. Lentz's. In afternoon went to D. Barringer's to see about getting a few plank for a wagon body.

Frid. 4. At home.

Sat. 5. Started for St. Luke's ch. Dinner at Mrs. Mich^{l} Brown's in Salisbury. In the afternoon attended at the burial of W. A. Walton, Sheriff of Rowan Co. All night at John Lingel's.

Sund. 6. Preached at St. Luke's ch. from Gal. 6:9. All night at Alex^{r} Brown's.

Mond. 7. Returned home. Dinner at Widow Walton's.

Tues. 8. Went to Burress' Shop & had buggy tire shrunk. Returned by way of Dr. Coleman's and brought wife home. Supper here.

Wed. 9. Went to John Powlass' shop for some plows & had steel put in an ax. Dinner here. Returned by way of J. T. Lentz's for some shoes.

Thurs. 10. Started with wife for the County Fair in Salisbury. All night at Dr. Coleman's.

Frid. 11. Took wife to the Fair. Returned home. Supper at Dr. Coleman's.

Sat. 12. Started for Salem ch. All night at Henry Miller's.

Sund. 13. Preached at Salem ch. from Math. 2:18. the funeral of H. Miller's deceased child. All night at M. A. Bost's.

Mond. 14. In the morning wrote Nancy Lyerly's will. Returned home. Rev. Neiffer with me.

Tues. 15. Started for Mt. Pleasant. All night at G. M. Bernhardt's.

Wed. 16. Took Rev. Neiffer in my buggy & went to Mt. Pleasant to attend the meeting of the College Trustees. Dinner at Col. Shimpock's. In the evening married Charles N. Simpson & Martha R. Brown. All night at Mrs. Brown's.

Thurs. 17. Returned home.

Frid. 18. Started for St. Luke's ch. All night at John Harkey's.

Sat. 19. Preached at St. Luke's ch. from Deut. 11:16. Preparatory to communion. All night at Jesse W. Miller's.

Sund. 20. Preached at St. Luke's ch. from 1 Cor. 5:7.8. Confirmed two persons, and after an intermission administered the Lord's Supper. All night at the widow Berger's.

Mond. 21. Returned home. Dinner at Dr. Coleman's.

Tues. 22. Took buggy to Gold Hill to have repaired. In the afternoon went to J. T. Lentz's for some shoes.

Wed. 23. Was sent for to Salem ch. to attend a funeral. All night at John Lingel's.

Thurs. 24. Attended to the fun^{l} of Mrs. Nancy Lyerly at Salem ch. preached from 1 Thes. 4:14. All night at M. A. Bost's.

Frid. 25. At Mr. Bost's till after, then went to Joseph Colly's and staid all night.

Sat. 26. Preached at Salem ch. from Acts 9:6. Baptized 4 infants & confirmed three persons. All night at Widow Berger's.

Sund. 27. Preached at Salem ch. from Josh. 23:8. & administered the Lord's Supper. All night at Saml Seaford's.

Mond. 28. Returned home.

Tues. 29. Went to Gold Hill to have pants cut & bring buggy home.

Wed. 30. At home. Mr. B. F. Fraley & wife with us to day.

Thurs. 31. Went to Daniel Miller's and borrowed some money for Lewis.

Frid. Nov. 1. Went to Dr. Coleman's for Beef, in afternoon at home.

Sat. 2. Started for St. Luke's church. All night at D. M. Barrier's.

Sund. 3. Preached at St. Luke's ch. from Numb. 10:29. Dinner at Mrs. Kistler's. All night at Alex Brown's.

Mond. 4. Returned to Salisbury. Supper at Widow Walton's. Left horse & buggy at P. N. Heilig's & took the cars for Lexington.

Tues. 5. In Lexington. In the evening returned to Salisbury & brought Sammy along. All night at B. F. Fraley's.

Wed. 6. Returned home.

Thurs. 7. Went to Gold Hill.

Frid. 8. At home. In the evening went to M. A. Holshouser's shucking.

Sat. 9. Started for Salem ch. All night at C. R. Miller's.

Sund. 10. Preached at Salem ch. from Phil. 2:5. Dinner at John Lingel's. All night at P. N. Heilig's. At night went to hear Rev. Neiffer preach.

Mond. 11. Returned home. Dinner at Dr. Coleman's.

Tues. 12. Went to J. T. Lentz's to have pr. shoes made. Called also at Mrs. Mary A. Heilig's to see George Heilig & M. Barrier, they being both sick. Dinner here.

Wed. 13. Thurs. 14. At home.

Frid. 15. Started with wife to Iredell. Sent horse home from Salisbury. All night at Mansion Hotel.

Sat. 16. Took the cars for Iredell. Breakfast & dinner at B. Arey's. In the evening went to Alanson White's & staid over night.

Sund. 17. Preached at Bethesda ch. from Ps. 116:12-14. the fun[l] of Elizabeth Barringer dec[d]. Dinner at A. White's. In the evening went to old Mr. White's & staid over night.

Mond. 18. Returned to A. White's & settled with the Legatees of Eliz. Barringer. In afternoon went to B. Arey's and staid over night.

Tues. 19. In afternoon returned home.

Wed. 20. Went to Elias Beaver's, he being much afflicted. Wrote his will & administered to him the Lord's Supper.

Thurs. 21. Went to Dan[l] Hoffman's and married A. R. Shoaf & Malinda C. Hoffman. All night here.

Frid. 22. Went to Salisbury and had horse shod. Then went to John C. Miller's & staid over night.

Sat. 23. Went to Jesse Lyerly's & staid over night.

Sund. 24. Went to Salem ch. but could not preach in consequence of severe cold. Read a chapter & had short devotional exercises. In afternoon buried Jacob Koon by reading burial service. All night at widow John Berger's.

Mond. 25. Went to Alex[r] Brown's to dinner. In afternoon went to Phebe Brown's in Iredell co. All night here.

Tues. 26. Crossed the river to Alex[r] Clark's & took dinner. In evening crossed back to Jane Hill's (widow) & staid over night.

Wed. 27. Went to Caleb Barrier's & took dinner. All night at Phebe Brown's.

Thurs. 28. Went to Augustus Brown's & took dinner. All night at Robert Brown's.

Frid. 29. Returned to Alexander Brown's & staid over night.

Sat. 30. Went to St. Luke's ch. it being the appointed day for setting up the stoves. All night at Catharine Kistler's.

Sund. Dec. 1. Preached at St. Luke's ch. from Rom. 10:1. All night at Saml Colly's.

Mond. 2. Returned home. Dinner at Dr. Coleman's.

Tues. 3. At home.

Wed. 4. In forenoon went to Gold Hill & in afternoon took some cotton to Jesse Miller's for Caty Earnheart to spin.

Thurs. 5. At home. Had winter hogs slaughtered.

Frid. 6. At home.

Sat. 7. Started for Salem ch. My horses being diseased, left my horse at home. Walked part of the way to Salisbury. From Salisbury rode on John Lyerly's wagon as far as Moses Trexler's. All night here.

Sund. 8. Moses Trexler furnished me a horse to ride to Salem ch. Preached at Salem ch. from Heb. 4:9. the fun^l of Jacob Koon dec^d. Went home with Jesse W. Miller in his buggy. All night here.

Mond. 9. Went in company with Alexander Brown to Phebe Brown's in Iredell Co. Made settlement between Phebe Brown & Caleb C. Barrier. All night at Mrs. Brown's.

Tues. 10. Returned to J. W. Miller's. All night here.

Wed. 11. In the afternoon went to Alexander Brown's & staid over night.

Thurs. 12. Called in afternoon at Catharine Kistler's & at W. L. Kistler's. All night at Alex^r Brown's.

Frid. 13. Called to see Mr. Wagoner. In afternoon went to St. Luke's ch. with Mr. Brown to adjust stove pipes. All night at J. W. Miller's.

Sat. 14. In afternoon went to W. L. Kistler's & staid all night.

Sund. 15. Preached at St. Luke's ch. from Prov. 29:1. Caleb Lentz brought me in his buggy near to Saml Seaford's. Dinner here. Daniel Seaford brought to the vicinity of Salisbury. Heard Rev. Dr. Pharr preach in the Lutheran Church. All night with Rev. J. G. Neiffer.

Mond. 16. Returned home in the mail hack & found all well.

Tues. 17. At home till afternoon, then went Dr. Coleman's and brought wife home.

Wed. 18. At home.

Thurs. 19. Started at 3 o'clock A.M. & went to Charles Reeves' and married Caleb Lentz and Maggie Reeves; then went to the residence of the late Col. D. Lentz and married David L. Elliott and Licetta J. Moyer. All night here. Very inclement weather.

Frid. 20. Went to Joicy Linn's & staid all night.

Sat. 21. Went to Salisbury, and in afternoon went to C. R. Miller's and staid over night.

Sund. 22. Attended to the funeral of C. R. Miller at Salem ch. – preached from Numb. 10:29. All night at Moses A. Bost's.

Mond. 23. Went to Salisbury and sent my horse home. All night with Rev. J. G. Neiffer.

Tues. 24. In Salisbury. Dinner with Saml E. Linton at Mr. Bell's. All night with Rev. Neiffer. At night witnessed the Christmas Tree in Luth. Church.

Wed. 25. In Salisbury. Dinner at David Julian's. All night B. F. Fraley's. Snowy weather.

Thurs. 26. Took the mail hack & returned home.

Frid. 27. At home.

Sat. 28. In forenoon went to Gold Hill for leather. In afternoon went to Paul Cruse's & staid over night.

Sund. 29. Attended to the funeral of Elias Beaver at Organ ch. Preached from 1 John 3:2. Returned home.

Mond. 30. At home mending shoes.

Tues. 31. At home.

Wed. Jan 1, 1873. Preached at Jesse Miller's the fun[1] of Peggy Earnheart, from Eccl. 9:10. Dinner at Jesse Miller's.

Thurs. 2. At home.

Frid. 3. Started for St. Luke's ch. All night at Zechariah Lyerly's.

Sat. 4. Went to John Harkey's & staid all night.

Sund. 5. Preached at St. Luke's ch. from Matth. 20:6. All night at Alexander Brown's.

Mond. 6. Called to see old Mr. Ray & wife, they being sick. All night at Mrs. John Berger's.

Tues. 7. Returned home.

Wed. 8. Slaughtered a Beef. In the evening went to Gold Hill & sold one quarter.

Thurs. 9. Went with wife to Dr. Coleman's & spent the day.

Frid. 10. Started for Salem ch. as far as Adam Miller's. All night here.

Sat. 11. Went to James Colly's & staid all night.

Sund. 12. Preached at Salem ch. from Eccl. 9:10. Dinner at Sam[l] Seaford's. All night at John Lingel's.

Mond. 13. Returned home.

Tues. 14. Went with wife to Jacob Grupy's & spent the day. Returned in evening.

Wed. 15. Went by way of Charles Fisher's & Foil's Tan Yard to Dan[l] Miller's. Paid a note of fifty dollars to Mr. Miller. All night here. Dinner to day at Charles Fisher's.

Thurs. 16. Returned home by way of Foil's Tan Yard.

Frid. 17. At home till afternoon, then went to David Eller's & staid over night.

Sat. 18. Went to Cath. Kistler's and staid over night. Dinner to day at Sam[l] Seaford's.

Sund. 19. Preached to day at St. Luke's from Jer. 17:9. 2 Cor. 13:5. Baptized one infant. Dinner at D. M. Barrier's. All night at John Smithdeal's.

Mond. 20. Dinner to day at John Lyerly's. In the afternoon came to Salisbury. All night with Rev. Neiffer at Mrs. Brown's.

Tues. 21. Returned home.

Wed. 22. In forenoon went to J. T. Lentz's to Shoemaker. In the afternoon at home.

Thurs. 23. At home. A very rainy day.

Frid. 24. Started for Newton and went as far as Salisbury. Sent my horse home. All night with Rev. Neiffer.

Sat. 25. Took the cars for Newton. Dinner at Robert Bost's. In the evening went to the country to Jacob Lutz's & staid all night.

Sund. 26. Returned to Newton & preached in forenoon from Jam. 1:25. Dinner at Rob. Bost's. Preached again at night from Jer. 17:9. 2 Cor. 13:5. All night at Robert Bost's.

Mond. 27. Returned to Salisbury. All night at Col. P. N. Heilig's.

Tues. 28. Returned home.

Wed. 29. Went to Caty Earnheart's at Jesse Miller's & settled for spinning. Dinner at Dr. Coleman's.

Thurs. 30. Called at Rev. Cone's, then went to J. T. Lentz's for a pair of Shoes.

Frid. 31. Started for St. Luke's ch. All night at Widow John Berger's.

Sat. Feb 1. Went to Alexander Brown's & staid over night. Dinner to day at Mr. Scott's.

Sund. 2. Preached at St. Luke's ch. from Neh. 10:39. latter clause. Dinner at John Harkey's. All night at M. A. Bost's.

Mond. 3. Called in the morning to see Sam[l] Seaford, he being unwell. Then returned home.

Tues. 4. At home.

Wed. 5. Went to D. Barringer's mill to engage some plank & oats.

Thurs. 6. At home. A very rainy day.

Frid. 7. In forenoon went to Gold Hill to Post Office. In afternoon at home.

Sat. 8. Started for Salem ch. All night at Joseph Beaver's.

Sund. 9. Attended to the fun[l] of Wilie Ruffty at Salem ch. — preached from Amos 4:12. All night at John C. Miller's.

Mond. 10. Started for Mt. Pleasant. Dinner at Moses Barringer's. All night at Dan[l] Miller's.

Tues. 11. Went to Mt. Pleasant & attended a meeting of Trustees of N. C. College. Dinner and lodging with Col. Shimpock.

Wed. 12. Returned home.

Thurs. 13. Went to Salisbury & in the Mayor's office married Moses Cress and Jane Graham. All night at Sam[l] Seaford's.

Frid. 14. Made my way into the neighborhood of St. Luke's church. Dinner at D. M. Barrier's. All night at W. L. Kistler's.

Sat. 15. A very rainy day. At Mr. Kistler's till afternoon then went to Alexander Brown's. Was sent for to go to Mrs. Jacob Goodman's to attend, on the following day, to the funeral of her daughter, Mrs. Altira C. Martin. All night at Mrs. Goodman's.

Sund. 16. A very rainy day. Preached the funeral of Mrs. Martin from Rev. 14:13. Could not bury the corpse, as the waters were too full to go to the Grave Yard. All night at Milton Cowan's.

Mond. 17. Returned in the morning to Mrs. Goodman's. Baptized Sam[l] M. Martin's child (infant) which was only one day old when the mother died. Went with funeral cortege to Back Creek Church (Presbyterian) & buried Mrs. Martin according to the burial service in the Book of Worship. Dinner at Alexander Brown's. All night at Sam[l] Colly's.

Tues. 18. Returned home.

Wed. 19. At home.

Thurs. 20. Frid. 21. At home.

Sat. 22. Started for Salem ch. All night at Mrs. Cha[s] R. Miller's.

Sund. 23. Preached at Salem ch. from Neh. 6:3. Dinner at John Lingel's. Then went to Salisbury & preached at night from Neh. 6:3. All night at B. F. Fraley's.

Mond. 24. Returned home.

Tues. 25. Wed. 26. At home.

Thurs. 27. At home.

Frid. 28. Started for St. Luke's ch. All night at Daniel Menius'.

Sat. Mar. 1. Went to Alex^r Brown's to dinner. In the evening went to Henry Brown's & staid all night.

Sund. 2. Preached at St. Luke's ch. from Matth. 4:1-11. Dinner at D. M. Barrier's. All night at John Lingel's.

Mond. 3. Returned home.

Tues. 4. At home. A very cold day.

Wed. 5. Went with wife in afternoon to David Barringer's & staid over night.

Thurs. 6. In afternoon returned home.

Frid. 7. At home.

Sat. 8. Started for Salem ch. All night at Legrand Elliott's.

Sund. 9. Preached at Salem ch. from Eccl. 12:1. the funeral of Moses Trexler's son, ag^d 15 yrs. Dinner at Saml Seaford's. Then went to Salisbury & heard Rev. Neiffer preach at night. All night at Mr. O'Neal's.

Mond. 10. Dinner at Mr. O'Neal's. In afternoon returned home.

Tues. 11. Wed. 12. Thurs. 13. At home.

Frid. 14. At home.

Sat. 15. Started for St. Luke's ch. All night at Alexander Brown's.

Sund. 16. Preached at St. Luke's ch. from Math. 15:21-28. Dinner at John Harkey's. All night at Mrs. John Berger's.

Mond. 17. Returned home.

Tues. 18. Went to John Powlass' and had 2 plows made.

Wed. 19. Thurs. 20. Frid. 21. At home. Had kitchen chimney rebuilt.

Sat. 22. Started for Salem ch. All night at M. A. Bost's.

Sund. 23. Preached at Salem ch. from Acts 16:16-34. Dinner and all night at John Lingel's.

Mond. 24. Returned home.

Tues. 25. Wed. 26. At home.

Thurs. 27. Started for Sandy Creek Church in Davidson Co. to attend the Eastern Conference. All night at Mrs. Thompson's.

Frid. 28. At Sandy Creek Church in attendance upon Conference. In the evening went over to Lexington & staid all night with Lewis.

Sat. 29. Returned to Sandy Creek ch. & preached from Rom. 10:1. All night at Rev. Bowles.

Sund. 30. Preached at Sandy Creek from Matth. 20:6. & assisted in the administration of the Lord's Supper. All night at Philip Sowers'.

Mond. 31. Returned home.

Tues. April 1. In afternoon went to Gold Hill to Post Office.

Wed. 2. At home. In the evening went with wife to Wilie Lentz's & sat till bed time.

Thurs. 3. In the afternoon went to Andrew Berger's for feathers.

Frid. 4. Went to M. A. Holshouser's & wrote bond, receipts &c.

Sat. 5. Started for St. Luke's ch. All night at Catharine Kistler's.

Sund. 6. Preached at St. Luke's ch. from Prov. 14:32. Dinner at Catharine Kistler's. Then went to Jackson Goodman's, his child being sick, & staid all night.

Mond. 7. Called at Rowan Mills & had some shoeing done. Viewed the operation of the Handle Factory. Dinner at Mrs. Jacob Goodman's. All night at Jesse W. Miller's.

Tues. 8. Called by W. L. Kistler's & went to Alexander Brown's. Over night here.

Wed. 9. In the afternoon went to Michael Goodman's & staid over night.

Thurs. 10. Returned to Alexander Brown's to dinner. In the afternoon went to W. L. Kistler's & staid over night.

Frid. 11. This being Good Friday preached at St. Luke's ch. from John 19:30. Had a meeting of Council after preaching & adjusted a misunderstanding between W. L. Kistler and Mr. Shuford. Over night at John Harkey's.

Sat. 12. Went to Salem ch. Rev. J. D. Bowles preached. Baptized 2 infants & held Preparatory Service. Dinner at M. A. Bost's. Overnight at Mrs. John Berger's.

Sund. 13. At Salem ch. Rev. Bowles preached. After an intermission had communion. Dinner at John Lingel's. Then went to Salisbury. At night read service in the Luth. ch. Rev. Bowles preached. All night at Mr. O'Neal's.

Mond. 14. Returned home. Dinner at Dr. Coleman's. Called to see R. W. Lentz, he being sick. Was sent for to Mr. Lentz's after night he having gotten worse. Staid till morning.

Tues. 15. Returned home in the morning. In the afternoon called back to Mr. Lentz's in time to see him die.

Wed. 16. Attended to the fun[1] of R. W. Lentz at Organ ch. — preached from Ex. 33:14.

Thurs. 17. In the afternoon took Mary Jane Arey to David Barringer's.

Frid. 18. Started for St. Luke's ch. Dinner at Mrs. Brown's in Salisbury. All night at D. M. Barrier's.

Sat. 19. Preached at St. Luke's ch. from Jam. 1:5. Confirmed 2 persons. Held Preparatory Service. All night at Alexander Brown's.

Sund. 20. Preached at St. Luke's ch. from Ps. 133:1-3. After an intermission administered the communion. Had a large congregation & solemn communion. All night at Moses A. Bost's.

Mond. 21. Returned home.

Tues. 22. Went with wife to Salisbury. Returned home in evening.

Wed. 23. At home.

Thurs. 24. Went in forenoon to Ribelin's School House & made return of Taxable property. In afternoon at home.

Frid. 25. Went in forenoon to Gold Hill to Post Office. In the afternoon started for Luther's Chapel. All night at Michael Bostian's.

Sat. 26. Went to Luther's Chapel & preached from 2 Cor. 5:17. All night at Mrs. Henry Miller's (widow).

Sund. 27. At Luther's Chapel. Preached from Prov. 3:6. Assisted in Confirmation & the Administration of the Communion. All night at Daniel Eddleman's.

Mond. 28. Returned home. A very rainy day.

Tues. 29. At home. Made arrangements to go to Synod.

Wed. 30. Went to St. Paul's Church to meeting of Synod. Synod was duly organized by the election of officers &c. Had lodging assigned at Widow Misenheimer's. All night here.

Thurs. May 1. In Synod. All night at Mrs. Misenheimer's.
Frid. 2. In Synod. All night at Mrs. Misenheimer's.
Sat. 3. In Synod. All night at Mr. Safret's.
Sund. 4. At St. Paul's church. Assisted in the Ordination of two candidates for the ministry. Consecrated the elements & assisted in the administration of the communion. All night at Mr. Allen Heilig's.
Mond. 5. To day Synod closed. Returned home.
Tues. 6. In forenoon went to Gold Hill to Post Office. In afternoon went with wife to Dr. Coleman's.
Wed. 7. At home, a rainy day.
Thurs. 8. Started with wife to Davidson Co. Supper at B. F. Fraley's. Left horse & buggy at Livery Stable in Salisbury, & at 9½ o'clock took the cars for Lexington. All night at Lewis'.
Frid. 9. Hired an ambulance and went to Caleb Peeler's. All night here.
Sat. 10. Caleb Peeler took us in his carriage to Friedberg Church (Moravian) to attend the Centennial celebration of the church. Partook with the congregation of their love feast. Concourse of people large & exercises interesting. Returned to C. Peeler's & staid all night.
Sund. 11. Went to Friedberg & was much pleased with the exercises. All night at C. Peeler's.
Mond. 12. Caleb Peeler took us in his carriage to Lexington. Dinner at Lewis'. In the evening took the cars for Salisbury. All night at B. F. Fraley's.
Tues. 13. Returned home. Dinner at Dr. Coleman's.
Wed. 14. At home.
Thurs. 15. Started for Phebe Brown's in Iredell Co. All night at Jesse W. Miller's. A rainy day.
Frid. 16. Went to Mrs. Brown's. All night here.
Sat. 17. Returned with Mrs. Brown's to Alexander Brown's. All night here.
Sund. 18. Preached at St. Luke's ch. from Numb. 14:24. In afternoon lectured on Book of Worship. All night at D. M. Barrier's.
Mond. 19. Returned home. Brought Mrs. Brown along home to spend a few days. Ed. Arey and wife with us to night.
Tues. 20. Wife & Mrs. Brown went to Dr. Coleman's. At home till evening then went to Dr. Coleman's to see wife & Mrs. Brown safe home.
Wed. 21. At home.
Thurs. 22. Took some flour to Caty Earnheart's & settled with her for spinning. Dinner at Dr. Coleman's. Spent part of afternoon at M. A. Holshouser's.
Frid. 23. At home.
Sat. 24. Started for Salem ch. All night at widow Jacob Koon.
Sund. 25. Preached at Salem ch. the fun[l] of Clementine Hunter dec[d]. Went to Jesse Lyerly's & staid all night.
Mond. 26. Returned home. Dinner at Dr. Coleman's.
Tues. 27. Went to Mt. Pleasant. Dinner at Charles Fisher's. Stopped with Col. Shimpock.
Wed. 28. In Mt. Pleasant. Attended meeting of Board of Trustees of N. C. College, &c.
Thurs. 29. Attended meeting of Board of Trustees. Commencement exercises, &c. In afternoon returned home.
Frid. 30. At home.
Sat. 31. Started for St. Luke's ch. Took Mrs. Phebe Brown to Alexan[r] Brown's. All night at W. L. Kistler's. Lewis with me to night.

Sund. June 1. Preached at St. Luke's ch. from Rev. 3:20. In afternoon lectured on the subject of Eucharist. All night at Mr. Beaver's.

Mond. 2. Went to third creek Station & took the cars for Statesville. Went to Clerk's Office & proved Mrs. Mary M. Miller's will. Dinner at Dr. Kelly's. In the evening went to the country to Andrew Barringer's & staid over night.

Tues. 3. Went to St. Michael's ch. as committee man to examine into irregularities there existing. Dinner at Mr. Troutman's. In the evening took the cars for Statesville. All night at Dr. Kelly's.

Wed. 4. Dinner to day at Mr. Palmer's. In the afternoon took the cars for Salisbury. Lewis met me at depot. Took a seat in buggy & returned home.

Thurs. 5. In the afternoon went to Gold Hill & married D. L. Parker & Ellen Jenkins.

Frid. 6. In forenoon took Mr. Lingel home in my buggy, his horse having died at David Brady's. In afternoon at home.

Sat. 7. Started for Salem church. All night at Joseph Colly's.

Sund. 8. Preached at Salem ch. from Matth. 7:24-27. In afternoon lectured of subject of Eucharist. Dinner & all night at Sam¹ Seaford's.

Mond. 9. Returned home.

Tues. 10. Went to Gold Hill in forenoon, in afternoon went to J. T. Lentz's to have shoes made.

Wed. 11. Took some flour to Gold Hill in forenoon — In afternoon went to mill.

Thurs. 12. Went in the morning to M. A. Holshouser's to engage mower. In afternoon at home.

Frid. 13. At home.

Sat. 14. Started for St. Luke's ch. A rainy afternoon. — All night at John Harkey's.

Sund. 15. Preached at St. Luke's ch. from Luk. 16:19-31. In afternoon lectured on subject of Baptism. All at D. M. Barrier's.

Mond. 16. Returned home. Brought Lewis & wife along from Salisbury.

Tues. 17. In forenoon took some flour to Gold Hill. In afternoon at home, rainy afternoon.

Wed. 18. Went to Salem ch. & attended the funeral of Sam¹ Colly's child, preached from Job 1:21. Dinner & all night at M. A. Bost's.

Thurs. 19. Returned home. In afternoon went to mill.

Frid. 20. In forenoon some flour to Gold Hill. In afternoon went to mill.

Sat. 21. Started for Salem ch. All night at Mr. Frieze's.

Sund. 22. At Salem ch. — Rev. Mr. Moore, Colporteus of Am. Tract Society, being present, preached. In afternoon he addressed the people on the subject of his agency. Dinner at John Lingel's. Went to Salisbury and read service for Rev. Neiffer. All night with Rev. Neiffer at Mrs. Brown's. Left my horse at P. N. Heilig's.

Mond. 23. Returned home.

Tues. 24. Took some Flour to Gold Hill in forenoon. In afternoon at home.

Wed. 25. Went to Burress' Shop and had horse shod. Dinner at Anna Trexler's.

Thurs. 26. Went with Lewis to Salisbury.

Frid. 27. Went to John Powlass' & had plows made. Returned home by way of John T. Lentz's.

Sat. 28. At home.

Sund. 29. This being the fifth sunday in the month, had no appointment. Was at home & spent the day in reading.

Mond. 30. At home, had some hand to mow grass.

Tues. July 1. to Frid. 4. At home making hay & gathering in wheat and oats.

Sat. 5. Started for St. Luke's ch. Dinner at Boyden House, Salisbury. All night at Mrs. Cath. Kistler's.

Sund. 6. Preached at St. Luke's ch. from Matth. 22:5. In afternoon lectured from Matth. 5:6. Dinner at John Harkey's. All night at Sam$^{\underline{l}}$ Colly's.

Mond. 7. Returned home.

Tues. 8. At home.

Wed. 9. In afternoon went with wife to Paul Cruse's and staid over night.

Thurs. 10. Went in forenoon to Daniel Miller's & borrowed $350 to pay on a lot in Lexington for Lewis. Returned to Mr. Cruse's for dinner. Went in afternoon with wife to Charles Fisher's & married Rev. Henry M. Brown & Lucetta J. Fisher. After supper returned home.

Frid. 11. At home.

Sat. 12. Started for Salem ch. All night at Otho Cawble's.

Sund. 13. Preached at Salem ch. from Heb. 2:3. In the afternoon lectured on the subject Naaman, the Leper. All night at John Lingel's. Lewis with me.

Mond. 14. Went to Salisbury early & took the cars for Lexington. Lewis with me. Lewis got dinner at his house for us. Supper at Mr. Heitman's. Lodged in Lewis' house.

Tues. 15. Returned home.

Wed. 16. At home. Mrs. Coit & Mrs. Boyden called to see us.

Thurs. 17. In the afternoon went to Mrs. Alias Beaver's (widow) & married Levi J. Hampton & Leah Beaver. Returned home in evening.

Frid. 18. In forenoon went to Steam mill at Gold Hill & had some corn ground. In afternoon at home.

Sat. 19. Started for St. Luke's church. All night at Alexander Brown's.

Sund. 20. Preached at St. Luke's ch. from Matth. 11:29.30. In afternoon lectured from 2 Kings 5:1-14. All night at widow John Berger's.

Mond. 21. Attended to the burial service of John Cress' child at Salem ch. Dinner at Sam$^{\underline{l}}$ Seaford's. In afternoon returned home.

Tues. 22. Wed. 23. Thurs. 24. At home.

Frid. 25. At home.

Sat. 26. Started for Salem ch. All night at Pleasant Wise's.

Sund. 27. Called to see Mrs. Cress. She being very sick. Preached at Salem ch. from Matth. 16:26. In afternoon lectured from Luk. 2:41-52. At night preached in Luth. Ch. in Salisbury, from Matth. 11:29.30. All night with Rev. Neiffer.

Mond. 28. Went to Lexington and paid for the Lot bought by Lewis & took Deed for the same. All night with Lewis.

Tues. 29. Returned to Salisbury & then home.

Wed. 30. At home.

Thurs. 31. Went to Gold Hill & paid my Tax. In the evening called at Mrs. Lentz's & Mr. Ritchey's & brought wife home.

Frid. Aug. 1. In forenoon went to Steam mill near Gold Hill. In afternoon at home.

Sat. 2. Started for St. Luke's ch. All night at old Mr. Freeze's.

Sund. 3. Preached the fun[1] of Mr. Freeze's daughter, Amanda, at the house from Matth. 5:8. Then went to St. Luke's ch. & and preached from Neh. 6:3. on Popular Amusements. In the afternoon lectured from Acts 19:21-41. All night at John Harkey's.

Mond. 4. Returned home. Dinner at Dr. Coleman's.

Tues. 5. In the afternoon went with wife to Dr. Coleman's, he being sick.

Wed. 6. Took wool to Gold Hill to carding machine.

Thurs. 7. Went to election at Morgan's. Called in awhile at a Baptist Meeting. Returned home by way of Gold Hill.

Frid. 8. Went to John Powlass' to Blacksmith Shop.

Sat. 9. Started for Salem ch. All night at Dan[l] Menius'.

Sund. 10. Preached at Salem ch. from John 3:14.15. In afternoon lectured from Act. 19:21-41. All night at Sam[l] Seaford's.

Mond. 11. Returned home. Called on the way to see Peter Trexler Sen., he being very sick.

Tues. 12. Went to Steam mill near Gold Hill.

Wed. 13. Went in afternoon to Mrs. Bost's to have some wool colored.

Thurs. 14. Went in the morning with M. A. Holshouser to Mrs. Lentz's, he being around to collect Toll Wheat. Balance of the day at home, not very well.

Frid. 15. Went to J. T. Lentz's to have some shoes made. Returned home by way of Gold Hill.

Sat. 16. Started for St. Luke's ch. All night at Jesse W. Miller's.

Sund. 17. Preached at St. Luke's ch. from 1 Sam. 12:23.24. Very unwell. Dinner at D. M. Barrier's. All night Sam[l] Colly's.

Mond. 18. Returned home. Dinner at Dr. Coleman's.

Tues. 19. At home.

Wed. 20. Went in forenoon to H. A. Miller's & took up note for Lewis & gave mine.

Thurs. 21. In the afternoon went to mill at Lentz's.

Frid. 22. In afternoon went to J. T. Lentz's for shoes. Called by Mrs. Bost's for some wool she colored for wife.

Sat. 23. Started for Salem ch. Dinner at Lewis' in Salisbury. All night Legrand Elliot's. Heard to day sentence of death passed upon John Allen Ketchy.

Sund. 24. Preached at Salem ch. from 1 Sam. 12:23.24. In afternoon went to Mathias Miller's & staid all night.

Mond. 25. Went with M. Miller to Mocksville & had Order recorded for the Sale of Dutchman Creek Church Land. Dinner at Mr. Booe's. Returned to J. C. Miller's & staid over night.

Tues. 26. Returned home. Heard to day Rev. Rumple preach J. T. Shaver's fun[l] in Salisbury. Wife met me in Salisbury. Made a Deed for house & lot in Lexington to Mr. Hardgrave.

Wed. 27. At home.

Thurs. 28. In afternoon went to Gold Hill to Shoemaker. Took also a bag of wool to Mauney's Store to be carded.

Frid. 29. Took Lewis to Salisbury. Dinner at Lewis'. Called to see prisoners in jail.

Sat. 30. Took wife to Dr. Coleman's on visit. Called at H. A. Miller's and paid note & interest ($381.97) money borrowed for Lewis to pay for house & lot in Lexington. Dinner here. Returned home by way of Dr. Coleman's.

Sund. 31. This being the 5th Sund. had no appointment. At home all day reading.

Mond. Sep. 1. Went to Dan[l] Miller's & paid notes ($500) money borrowed for Lewis to pay house & lot in Lexington. Dinner here. Returned home.

Tues. 2. Went to mill, also to Gold Hill for wool rolls.

Wed. 3. Went to widow Peter Trexler's & laid off year's provisions for widow & family. Dinner here.

Thurs. 4. In the morning took Alice Arey to Dr. Coleman's. In afternoon went to mill, also to Gold Hill to shoemaker.

Frid. 5. At home till noon, then took Alice Arey to D. Barringer's.

Sat. 6. Started for St. Luke's ch. Dinner at Lewis' in Salisbury. All night at W. L. Kistler's.

Sund. 7. Preached at St. Luke's ch. from John 3:14.15. In afternoon lectured from Judg. 3:20. All night at Moses A. Bost's.

Mond. 8. Returned home. Dinner at Lewis' in Salisbury. Rainy day.

Tues. 9. At home till noon, then went to Dr. Coleman's, he being sick.

Wed. 10. At home till noon, then went to M. A. Holshouser's & engaged him to make my hay.

Thurs. 11. At home.

Frid. 12. Started for Sandy Creek ch. in Davidson Co. Dinner at Lewis' in Salisbury. Took Rev. Neiffer in my buggy & crossed the river to Rev. J. D. Bowles. All night here.

Sat. 13. Attended the Sunday School Celebration at Sandy Creek Church. Was much pleased with all the exercises. After an intermission, delivered an address to the S. School & large congregation of people. In afternoon returned to Salisbury. All night at Lewis'.

Sund. 14. This was my day to preach at Salem ch. Had made arrangements with Rev. Neiffer to exchange pulpits. Rev. N. preached for me at Salem ch. − Rev. Rude, being in Salisbury, preached morning & night. Dinner at Col. P. N. Heilig's. In the afternoon baptized Lewis' child at his residence. All night here.

Mond. 15. Went to Union ch. and preached the fun[l] of George M. Smith, who had died sometime before, from 1 John 3:2. Dinner at Geo. Lyerly's. Returned home.

Tues. 16. In the afternoon went with wife to Jacob Grupy's and staid all night.

Wed. 17. Attended the Sunday School Convention at Providence ch. All night at Nancy Arey's.

Thurs. 18. At the S. Sch. Convention till 12 M. Dinner at Mr. Pool's. In afternoon returned home.

Frid. 19. At home.

Sat. 20. Started for St. Luke's church. Dinner at Lewis' in Salisbury. All night at Alexander Brown's.

Sund. 21. Preached at St. Luke's ch. from Prov. 14:34. After an intermission lectured from Mark 10:46-56. Called on the way in the afternoon to hear a colored man preach. No instruction in his sermon. All night at John Harkey's.

Mond. 22. Returned home. Dinner at Lewis' in Salisbury.

Tues. 23. Went to mill, & to Gold Hill to shop (Bunn's) & to get wool rolls.

Wed. 24. Went to Union church to Special Conference. All night at Henry Barringer's.

Thurs. 25. At Conference till afternoon, when Conference adjourned. Returned home.

Frid. 26. At home till 12 M. then started for Luther's Chapel. All night Michael Bostian's.

Sat. 27. Attended Sunday School celebration at Luther's Chapel & made a short address. Staid over night at Capt. Jacob Fisher's.

Sund. 28. Preached at Salem ch. from Luk. 11:32. In afternoon lectured from Mark 10:46-52. All night at John Lingel's.

Mond. 29. Returned home.

Tues. 30. Went to Steam Mill near Gold Hill. In afternoon called to see M. A. Holshouser on business.

Wed. Oct. 1. Went to Salisbury & bought 53 bush. corn. Took sick in afternoon & sick all night.

Thurs. 2. Went in the morning and engaged M. A. Holshouser to haul a load of corn from Salisbury. Unwell all day.

Frid. 3. At home.

Sat. 4. Started for St. Luke's ch. Dinner at Lewis'. All night at John Harkey's.

Sund. 5. Preached at St. Luke's ch. from Ps. 133:1-3. All night at Alex. Brown's.

Mond. 6. Returned home. Dinner at Lewis' in Salisbury.

Tues. 7. Went to mill & sawmill.

Wed. 8. Went with wife to Salisbury to the Fair. All night at Lewis'.

Thurs. 9. At the Fair till 12 M. then returned home.

Frid. 10. Went in forenoon to Sol^n Eagle's for Crout Stand. In afternoon went to M. A. Holshouser's & settled with him. Then went to saw mill.

Sat. 11. Started for Salem ch. Dinner at Lewis' in Salisbury. All night at Edmond Seaford's.

Sund. 12. Preached at Salem ch. from Math. 19:14. the fun^l of John Cress's child. In the afternoon lectured from Col. 1:28. All night at Mrs. Sarah Miller, widow of C. R. Miller.

Mond. 13. Returned home. Dinner at Lewis'. Rev. J. G. Neiffer with me.

Tues. 14. Started for Mt. Pleasant. Took Rev. Neiffer as far as Rev. Cone's. Dinner here. In afternoon went as far as Danl Miller's & staid all night.

Wed. 15. Went to Mt. Pleasant and attended meeting of the Board of Trustees of N. C. College. Dinner at Col. Shimpock's. All night at Paul Cruse's.

Thurs. 16. Went to Salisbury to attend court, having been summoned as witness by Mrs. Smithdeal in the case of John Smithdeal against his wife. Dinner & supper at Lewis'. Lodged with Rev. Neiffer at Mrs. Brown's.

Frid. 17. Breakfast at Mrs. Brown's. Started for St. Luke's ch. Dinner at Mr. Scott's. All night at W. L. Kistler's.

Sat. 18. Preached at St. Luke's ch. from Ps. 51:2. preparatory to communion. Baptized one infant. All night at J. W. Miller's.

Sund. 19. Preached at St. Luke's ch. from Josh. 23:8. After an intermission administered the Lord's Supper. The afternoon & evening was rainy & cold. All night at Newberry Hall's.

Mond. 20. Returned home. Dinner at Lewis' at Salisbury.

Tues. 21. At home.

Wed. 22. Wed to Salisbury, having been summoned to attend Court as witness in behalf of Polly Smithdeal in the case of John Smithdeal against his wife for divorce. Dinner with Rev. Neiffer at Mrs. Brown's. Supper at Lewis' in Salisbury. Attend lectures in Luth. Church. Lodged with Rev. Neiffer.

Thurs. 23. Breakfast at Lewis'. Attended to the funeral Mrs. Cath. C. Coon at Salem ch. Preached the funeral at the house from 2 Tim. 4:7.8. Dinner at Jacob Menius'. All night at Joseph Beaver's.

Frid. 24. Dinner at Frank Robison's. All night at Henry Miller's.

Sat. 25. Preached at Salem ch. from Ps. 51:2. preparatory to communion. All night at Mrs. John Berger's.

Sund. 26. Preached at Salem ch. from Is. 53:5. last clause. After an intermission administered the communion. All night at M. A. Bost's.

Mond. 27. Returned home.

Tues. 28. At home till evening, then went to M. A. Holshouser's to shucking.

Wed. 29. At home.

Thurs. 30. Went with wife to Organ church to the burial of P. N. Heilig's little daughter. Rev. Neiffer performed the burial service.

Frid. 31. In afternoon went to Gold Hill to shoe maker. At night went to Solomon Peeler's to shucking.

Sat. Nov. 1. Started for St. Luke's ch. All night at Monroe Barrier's.

Sund. 2. Preached at St. Luke's ch. from 1 Tim. 6:6. Dinner at John Harkey's. All night at Saml Seaford's.

Mond. 3. Returned home. Dinner at Lewis'. Brought Lewis' wife & children along home.

Tues. 4. At home. Rev. Wetmore called and took dinner.

Wed. 5. In afternoon went to Gold Hill to Post Office.

Thurs. 6. At home.

Frid. 7. At home till afternoon then went to mill. A rainy day.

Sat. 8. Started for Salem ch. All night at Jesse Lyerly's.

Sund. 9. Preached at Salem ch. from Matth. 25:14-30. Dinner at John Lingel's. Then went to Salisbury. Read service in the Luth. Church. Rev. P. A. Strobel preached. All night at Lewis'.

Mond. 10. Returned home.

Tues. 11. Took wife & Lewis' family to Mr. Grupy's. Dinner here.

Wed. 12. In forenoon took dress pattern to Mr. Grupy's. In afternoon went to Gold Hill to post office & shoe maker's.

Thurs. 13. In the morning took horse to Mr. Grupy's for wife & Lewis' family to come home. In afternoon at home.

Frid. 14. At home.

Sat. 15. Started for St. Luke's ch. All night at Mrs. Cath. Kistler's.

Sund. 16. Preached at St. Luke's ch. from Matth. 25:14-30. All night at D. M. Barrier's. Baptized to day one infant.

Mond. 17. A very rainy day till in the afternoon. Staid at Mr. Barrier's till 3 P.M. then started for home as far as John Rusher's. All night here.

Tues. 18. Returned home.

Wed. 19. Went to Gold Hill to shoe maker's.

Thurs. 20. Frid. 21. Went to Gold Hill on business.

Sat. 22. Started for Salem ch. Took Lewis' family to Salisbury. All night at John Lingle's.

Sund. 23. Preachhed at Salem ch. from Matth. 22:5. Dinner at Chas. Beaver's. All night at M. A. Bost's.

Mond. 24. Returned home.

Tues. 25. At home.

Wed. 26. In forenoon went to John Earnheart's to have some clothes cut & made. Went also to Andrew Berger's for feathers. In afternoon went to mill & to Gold Hill.

Thurs. 27. Went with wife & girls to David Barringer's for broom straw.

Frid. 28. Went in forenoon to Dr. Coleman's & to M. A. Holshouser's to arrange for slaughtering hogs.

Sat. 29. At home. D. Barringer & wife with us to night.

Sund. 30. At home.

Mond. Dec. 1. At home. Slaughtered winter hogs to day.

Tues. 2. Started for Mt. Pleasant to attend meeting of Board of Trustees of N. C. College. Dinner at Laurence Lingel's. All night at Daniel Miller's.

Wed. 3. Went to Mt. Pleasant. No meeting of the Board for want of a Quorum. Dinner at Rev. D. M. Henkel's. Returned home as far as Paul Cruse's. All night here.

Thurs. 4. Returned home. In afternoon went to John Earnheart's & settled for hauling pine.

Frid. 5. Took wife to Gold Hill to see Mrs. Coit, also Mrs. Boyden, she being sick. A rainy afternoon.

Sat. 6. Started for St. Luke's ch. Dinner at Lewis'. All night at John Harkey's.

Sund. 7. Preached at St. Luke's ch. from Luke 18:13. All night at Saml Colly's.

Mond. 8. Went to Salisbury & staid over night at Lewis'.

Tues. 9. Took the cars for Gibsonville. Dinner at Mr. Smith's. All night at Simeon Wagoner's.

Wed. 10. Went to Special Conference at Frieden's Church, to investigate charges preferred by Rev. P. A. Strobel against Rev. G. D. Bernheim. Upon the petition of Rev. Bernheim and his Church Council, after a lengthy colloquium, the investigation was postponed to next meeting of Synod. Supper at Rev. S. Scherer's. Took the cars at 11½ o'clock for Salisbury.

Thurs. 11. Breakfast at Lewis' and then returned home.

Frid. 12. In afternoon went to Gold Hill to Post Office; called also to see Mrs. Boyden, she being sick. Had prayer by her bedside.

Sat. 13. Started for Salem ch. All night at Saml Seaford's.

Sund. 14. Preached at Salem ch. from Hosea 14:1.2. All night at Alex. Brown's.

Mond. 15. Went to Phebe Brown's in Iredell co. All night here.

Tues. 16. Wed. 17. At Phebe Brown's.

Thurs. 18. Went to Statesville & got a certified copy of Tobias Brown's Will for Phebe Brown. Dinner at Dr. Kelly's. All night at Mrs. Brown's.

Frid. 19. Returned to Mrs. Jacob C. Goodman's & staid over night. Dinner to day at Cicero Moore's.

Sat. 20. Went to Alex. Brown's and staid over night.

Sund. 21. Preached at St. Luke's ch. from Matth. 1:21. Baptized one infant. All night at M. A. Bost's.

Mond. 22. Returned home.

Tues. 23. Went to Gold Hill to Post Office. Settled an account at Mauney's Store.

Wed. 24. At home.

Thurs. 25. Christmas day. At home, had some neighbors & friends to dinner to day.

Frid. 26. At home.

Sat. 27. An inclement day. Attended to the funeral of Mrs. Boyden, widow of Dr. Boyden. Attended to the funeral services at Gold Hill & buried at Organ church. Then went to Salisbury & staid all night at Lewis'.

Sund. 28. Went to Salem ch. & preached from Is. 9:6. Dinner at Calvin Cress'. Returned to Salisbury & staid over night at Mr. O'Neal's. At night heard Rev. P. A. Strobel preach in Luth. ch.

Mond. 29. In Salisbury. Dinner at B. F. Fraley's. All night at Mr. O'Neal's.

Tues. 30. In Salisbury. Met in committee to settle a money difficulty between Rev. N. Aldrich & the congregation in Salisbury. All night at Mr. O'Neal's.

Wed. 31. Returned home.

Thurs. Jan. 1. 1874. Called in the morning to see Polly Canup, widow of Dr. John Canup, she being very old & infirm. Returned home and then went to M. A. Holshouser's to dinner & spent the afternoon. Called at Solomon Peeler's and sat till bed time.

Frid. 2. In forenoon went to Mrs. Bost's to weaver's. In afternoon at home.

Sat. 3. Started for St. Luke's ch. Dinner at Lewis' in Salisbury. All night at D. M. Barrier's.

Sund. 4. Preached at St. Luke's ch. from 2 Kings 5:1-14. Dinner & over night at Mr. Freeze's.

Mond. 5. Returned home.

Tues. 6. Wed. 7. At home.

Thurs. 8. In forenoon went to Dr. Coleman's, in afternoon went to Gold Hill.

Frid. 9. At home.

Sat. 10. Started for Salem ch. Dinner at Lewis' in Salisbury. All night at Thomas Safret's.

Sund. 11. Attended to the fun[l] of Philip Freeze at Salem ch. — preached from 1 Thes. 5:6. Dinner at John Lingel's. All night at Lewis' in Salisbury. At night heard Rev. Strobel preach in Luth. Church.

Mond. 12. Returned home. Brought Sammy with me.

Tues. 13. At home. A very inclement day.

Wed. 14. Went to Dr. Coleman's & to Gold Hill.

Thurs. 15. At home, a very cold day.

Frid. 16. Started for St. Luke's ch. Called by Mich[l] Holshouser's and gave to the widow Klutts a German Almanac. All night at David Eller's. A very cold day.

Sat. 17. Went to W. L. Kistler's and staid over night. A cold day.

Sund. 18. Preached at St. Luke's ch. from Mark 10:47. All night at Alex[r] Brown's.

Mond. 19. Returned home. Brought Mrs. Phebe Brown with me in Mr. Alex. Brown's buggy.

Tues. 20. Took wife & Mrs. Brown to M. A. Holshouser's. Dinner here.

Wed. 21. Went with wife & Mrs. Brown to Mary A. Heilig's. Dinner here. Returned home in evening. Mrs. Brown remained at Mrs. Heilig's.

Thurs. 22. At home.

Frid. 23. Took Phebe Brown to Salisbury. Went by Union Church & attended to the funeral of John Shuman, preached from 1 Thes. 5:6. All night at Lewis' in Salisbury.

Sat. 24. Went to James Colly's and staid all night.

Sund. 25. Preached at Salem ch. from Mark. 10:47. All night at widow John Berger's. Baptized on inf[t] to day.

Mond. 26. Returned home.

Tues. 27. Wed. 28. At home.

Thurs. 29. In afternoon went to Sol[n] Peeler's to raising of wheat house.

Frid. 30. Went with wife to Gold Hill to sale of Mrs. Boyden dec[d]. Dinner at Mr. Coit's.

Sat. 31. Started for St. Luke's ch. All night at Alexander Brown's.

Sund. Feb. 1. Preached at St. Luke's ch. from Luke 18:18. Dinner & all night at Mrs. C. Kistler's.

Mond. 2. A very inclement day. Went to Jesse Miller's to dinner. In the evening went to Alexander Brown's & staid all night.

Tues. 3. Went to W. L. Kistler's to settle some misunderstanding between W. L. Kistler of the one part and Alex^r Brown & P. M. Brown of the other part. Had the parties together but failed in settling. Dinner at Alex^r Brown's. In the afternoon started for Luther's Chapel to Special meeting of Synod. All night at Rev. Kimball's.

Wed. 4. Attended Special meeting of Synod to elect officers. All night at Mich^l Bostian's.

Thurs. 5. Returned home.

Frid. 6. At home.

Sat. 7. Started for Salem ch. All night at M. A. Bost's.

Sund. 8. Preached at Salem ch. from 1 Kings 5:12. After preaching went to Salisbury. Stopped at Mr. O'Neil's. Was to have preached in the Luth. church. Commenced service but had to dismiss on account of smoke in the church. Supper at O'Neil's. Lodged with Rev. Neiffer.

Mond. 9. Breakfast at O'Neil's. Returned home.

Tues. 10. In forenoon went to Mrs. Bost's to weavers. In afternoon went to Barringer's & engaged some Oats.

Wed. 11. Went to D. Barringer's for Oats. In the evening called at Solomon Peeler's on business.

Thurs. 12. Went to hatter shop for Oats. In the evening went over to Solomon Peeler's to do some writing between him & Catharine Lentz.

Frid. 13. Started before day for Salem ch. & attended to the funeral of Margaret Alice, the daughter of Saml Elliot, whose death was occasioned by the burning of her clothes at the school house. Preached from 1 Sam. 20:3. Dinner at Saml Seaford's. All night with Rev. Neiffer in Salisbury.

Sat. 14. Breakfast at Lewis'. Went to John Harkey's & staid all night.

Sund. 15. Preached at St. Luke's ch. from Prov. 22:2. Dinner at John Harkey's. All night at John Lingel's.

Mond. 16. Returned home.

Tues. 17. Went to Dr. Coleman's and to H. A. Miller's. Dinner at Mr. Miller's.

Wed. 18. Attended to the burial of James Honeycutt Sen. at St. Stephen's ch. The weather being very inclement & some of the family indisposed, did not preach a funeral. Dinner at Solomon Nussman's.

Thurs. 19. At home. In the evening went to Solomon Peeler's & rented him a field for corn.

Frid. 20. At home.

Sat. 21. Started for Salem ch. Dinner at Lewis' in Salisbury. All night at Pleasant Wise's.

Sund. 22. Called in the morning at Widow John Berger's to see the sick. Had religious exercises & then went to Salem ch. and preached from 2 Cor. 9:6.7. on the subject of giving. Dinner at Mr. Goodman's. Then went to Salisbury & preached in the Luth. Church from 2 Kings 5:12. Lodged with Rev. Neiffer.

Mond. 23. Breakfast at Lewis'. Returned home. Dinner at Dr. Coleman's.

Tues. 24. Attended the burial of Augustus Heilig at Organ ch. Service by Rev. Strobel. Dinner at Mary A. Heilig's.

Wed. 25. At home. A very inclement day.

Thurs. 26. In afternoon called to see Solomon Peeler, he being sick. Called also at H. A. Miller's & Andrew Berger's.

Frid. 27. Started for St. Luke's ch. Took Sammy home. All night at Lewis'.

Sat. 28. Went to D. M. Barrier's & staid over night.

Sund. March 1. Preached at St. Luke's ch. from 2 Cor. 9:6.7. on benevolence. Dinner at D. M. Barrier's. Returned to Salisbury. Lodged with Rev. Neiffer.

Mond. 2. Breakfast at Lewis'. Returned home. Mrs. Ann Arey & son with us to night.

Tues. 3. Carried bouquet to Dr. Coleman's. Went to Moses Linn's & engaged Crawford Holshouser to work. Called also to see Solomon Peeler.

Wed. 4. In forenoon went to Gold Hill & bought Straw Cutter. Called at night to see Solomon Peeler.

Thurs. 5. In forenoon went to mill, also to David Barringer's to settle account. In afternoon at home.

Frid. 6. At home.

Sat. 7. Started for Salem ch. Dinner at Lewis'. All night at Saml Seaford's.

Sund. 8. Preached at Salem ch. from John 8:36. Dinner at John Lingel's. Returned to Salisbury. Heard Rev. Neiffer preach. All night with Rev. Neiffer.

Mond. 9. Breakfast at Lewis'. Returned home.

Tues. 10. Went to Mr. Foil's Tan Yard.

Wed. 11. Called at Mr. Lentz's, then went to Gold Hill. In the evening went to Jesse Miller's and brought wife home from quilting.

Thurs. 12. At home.

Frid. 13. Started for St. Luke's ch. Supper with Lewis in Salisbury. Lodged with Rev. Neiffer.

Sat. 14. Breakfast with Lewis. Dinner at Saml Seaford's. All night at W. L. Kistler's.

Sund. 15. Preached at St. Luke's ch. from Acts 17:11.12. Dinner at Alex^{r} Brown's. All night at Pleasant M. Brown's.

Mond. 16. Met with W. L. Kistler vs. Alex. Brown & P. M. Brown at St. Luke's ch. to settle a difficulty between them, but failed so to do. Dinner at M. A. Bost's. Supper at Lewis' in Salisbury. Lodged with Rev. Neiffer.

Tues. 17. Breakfast at Lewis'. Returned home.

Wed. 18. Went with wife & Emma to Mrs. Bost's to Weaver. In afternoon went to Gold Hill.

Thurs. 19. At home.

Frid. 20. Went with wife to Dr. Coleman's then took some cotton to Caty Earnheart's to have spun. Dinner at Dr. Coleman's. In afternoon called with wife & Mrs. Coleman at H. A. Miller's.

Sat. 21. Started for Salem ch. Dinner at Lewis' in Salisbury. All night at Danl Menis'.

Sund. 22. Preached at Salem ch. from 1 Cor. 9:24-27. Dinner at Lewis'. Attended preaching at night in the Luth. ch. Read service for Rev. Neiffer. All night at Phebe Brown's.

Mond. 23. Returned home.

Tues. 24. Called to see Rev. Artz. In the evening brought wife home from Dr. Coleman's.

Wed. 25. Started for Eastern Conference at Pilgrim Church, Davidson Co. All night at Lewis' in Salisbury.

Thurs. 26. Took the cars at 11 o'clock for Lexington. Was taken to Joseph Zink's & staid all night.

Frid. 27. Met the members of Conference at Pilgrim ch. & transacted our Conferential business. All night at Joseph Zink's.

Sat. 28. At Pilgrim ch. — preaching by several of the ministers. All night at William Zink's.

Sund. 29. Preached at Pilgrim ch. from Jam. 1:25., consecrated the elements for communion & aided in the Administration of the same. Preaching in afternoon by one of the ministers. In the evening returned to Salisbury. At night heard Rev. Scherer preach in Luth. Church. Lodged with Rev. Neiffer.

Mond. 30. Administered on the estate of Milas Arey Jr., dec^{d}. Returned home.

Tues. 31. In forenoon went Gold Hill. In afternoon called at John Earnheart's & Doctor Coleman's on business.

Wed. Apr. 1. An inclement day. At home till afternoon, then went to Laurence Lingel's & staid over night.

Thurs. 2. Returned home. In afternoon went with wife to Dr. Coleman's & bought beehive & bees home. Supper here.

Frid. 3. Started for St. Luke's ch. At night heard Rev. Neiffer preach in Luth. Church. All night at Phebe Brown's.

Sat. 4. Went to Alexander Brown's & staid all night.

Sund. 5. Easter Sunday. Preached at St. Luke's ch. from 1 Cor. 15:20. Had a meeting of Church Council after services to adjust misunderstandings between W. L. Kistler vs. Alexander & P. M. Brown, which resulted in the suspension of W. L. Kistler. All night at M. A. Bost's.

Mond. 6. Returned home. Brought Mr. James Dennison from Salisbury to transfer a swarm of bees.

Tues. 7. Took Mr. Dennison part of the way back to Salisbury. In the afternoon went to John Earnheart's to have a coat made. Went also to Gold Hill to post office.

Wed. 8. Called to see Danl Basinger, he being sick. In afternoon at home. Rev. Cone took dinner with us to day.

Thurs. 9. Went in the afternoon to Danl C. Basinger's, he being sick & baptized & confirmed him & received him as a member of St. Peter's church.

Frid. 10. At home.

Sat. 11. Started for Salem ch. Dinner at Lewis' in Salisbury. All night at Widow John Berger's.

Sund. 12. Preached at Salem ch. from 1 Cor. 15:58. & organized S. School. Dinner at Calvin Cress'. All night at John Lingel's.

Mond. 13. Returned home. Dinner at Phebe Brown's.

Tues. 14. Returned to Salisbury to attend Court as a witness. Supper at Lewis'. Lodged with Rev. Neiffer.

Wed. 15. Thurs. 16. In Salisbury.

Frid. 17. Started in afternoon for St. Luke's church. All night at D. M. Barrier's.

Sat. 18. Preached at St. Luke's ch. from Ez. 33:5. preparatory to communion. Baptized one infant. Dinner at D. M. Barrier's. All night at Jos. Beaver's.

Sund. 19. Had communion appointed for St. Luke's ch. The day being very rainey, postponed 4 weeks. Preached however from Rev. 2:4.5. Dinner at John Harkey's. All night at M. A. Bost's.

Mond. 20. Returned home. Dinner at Phebe Brown's in Salisbury.

Tues. 21. In forenoon went with wife to Mrs. Bost's to weaver's. In afternoon at home.

Wed. 22. At home.

Thurs. 23. In the afternoon went to Salisbury. Lodged with Rev. Neiffer.

Frid. 24. In Salisbury — Attended Court as a witness State vs. Chancy Young. All night at Lewis'.

Sat. 25. Went to Salem ch. & preached from Ez. 33:5. preparatory to communion. All night at Saml Elliott's. Baptized to day three of Mr. Elliott's children.

Sund. 26. Preached at Salem ch. from 1 Thes. 2:11.12. Confirmed 2 persons & administered the communion. Dinner at M. A. Bost's. All night at Lewis' in Salisbury.

Mond. 27. Started for Wilmington to Synod. Went as far as Company Shops. All night at Hotel.

Tues. 28. Took the Cars for Wilmington. Dinner in Raleigh. Arrived in Wilmington & was assigned lodging at Mr. L. Voller's.

Wed. 29. Preached in Luth. Church from 1 Thes. 2:11.12. Synodical. Organized Synod & was re-elected President. Synod in session till Tues. May 5. 2 o'clock, P.M.

Wed. May 6. Started for home.

Thurs. 7. Arrived in Salisbury at 4 o'clock A.M. joined in hiring a hack & returned home. In afternoon went to Col. Slough's and brought wife home.+

Frid. 8. Called at middle of day at M. A. Holshouser's & settled with him. Balance of day at home.

Sat. 9. Started for Salem ch. Dinner at Phebe Brown's at Salisbury. All night at Mrs. Sarah Miller's.

Sund. 10. Preached at Salem ch. from Ps. 63:8. Baptized 2 infants. All night at John Lingel's.

Mond. 11. Returned home.

Tues. 12. Took flour to Caty Earnheart's for spinning. Called also with wife at Dr. Coleman's. Dinner here.

Wed. 13. Sheared the sheep. In afternoon went to Gold Hill & had buggy repaired.

Thurs. 14. Ascension Day. In the morning took family to Col. Slough's to have Photographs taken, but the artist being absent, returned home. Balance of the day at home.

Frid. 15. Started for St. Luke's ch. All night at Lewis' in Salisbury. Supper at Phebe Brown's.

Sat. 16. Went to J. W. Miller's and staid all night. Dinner to day at Mr. Freeze's.

Sund. 17. Preached to day at St. Luke's ch. from John 3:16. & after intermission administered the Lord's Supper. Dinner at John Harkey's. All night at Saml Colly's.

Mond. 18. Returned home. Dinner at Lewis'. Baptized R. J. Holmes' child at his house.

Tues. 19. Took wife & Emma to Col. Slough's & had pictures taken. Dinner at Dr. Coleman's.

Wed. 20. Went in forenoon to Gold Hill. In afternoon went to J. T. Lentz's to have shoes repaired & new ones made.

Thurs. 21. At home.

Frid. 22. At home.

Sat. 23. Started for Salem ch. All night at Jesse Lyerly's.

Sund. 24. Preached at Salem ch. from Matth. 12:41.42. In afternoon lectured on commandments. Dinner at Danl Seaford's. At night heard Rev. Neiffer preach in Salisbury. All night at Phebe Brown's.

Mond. 25. Returned home. Brought Eve Ann Miller Zechariah Lyerly's to M. A. Holshouser's. Dinner at Dr. Coleman's. In afternoon started for Mt. Pleasant to attend College Commencement. All night at Danl Miller's.

Tues. 26. Went to Mt. Pleasant. Stopped at Col. Shimpock's. Dinner and lodging here.

Wed. 27. In Mt. Pleasant. Dinner at Rufus Barrier's. All night at Jonas Cook's.

Thurs. 28. Returned home.

Frid. 29. At home.

Sat. 30. Went to Salisbury & brought Lewis' family out.

Sund. 31. This being the fifth Sunday, had no appointment. Went to St. Peter's ch. & heard Adolphus Linn preach.

+ Married to night at my house Mr. Geo. A. Canup & Mary C. Morgan.

Mond. June 1. At home. Quite unwell.

Tues. 2. Went with wife, Lewis & family to M. A. Holshouser's & spent the day.

Wed. 3. At home.

Thurs. 4. Went in afternoon to engage hands to mow grass. Went also to H. A. Miller's & brought wife & Lewis' family home.

Frid. 5. Went in forenoon to J. T. Lentz's on business. In afternoon at home. Refreshing rain this afternoon.

Sat. 6. Started for St. Luke's ch. Dinner Phebe Brown's in Salisbury. All night at D. M. Barrier's.

Sund. 7. Preached at St. Luke's ch. from Matth. 12:41.42. After an Intermission Rev. Ketchie addressed the congregation. Dinner at John Harkey's. Returned to Salisbury. At night heard Rev. Prof. Bikle preach in the Luth. Church. All night at Mrs. Phebe Brown's.

Mond. 8. Returned home. Dinner at Dr. Coleman's.

Tues. 9. to Frid. 12. At home, engaged in hay making.

Sat. 13. Started for Salem ch. All night at Widow John Berger's.

Sund. 14. To day Calvin Seaford preached for me at 10 o'clock, A.M. After an intermission lectured to the congregation on Commandments. Dinner at M. A. Bost's. Returned to Salisbury. At Rev. Bikle preach. All night at Phebe Brown's.

Mond. 15. Called in company with others to see John Allen Ketchy, a condemned prisoner. Returned home.

Tues. 16. Went to Gold Hill to Post Office.

Wed. 17. At home. Slaughtered veal this evening.

Thurs. 18. In the morning took quarter Veal to Dr. Coleman's. Balance of day at home.

Frid. 19. Started for St. Luke's ch. Supper at Phebe Brown's. All night at Lewis'.

Sat. 20. Went to Alexander Brown's & staid over night. Dinner to day at John Lingel's.

Sund. 21. At St. Luke's ch. Prof. Bikle preached morning & afternoon. Dinner at John Lingel's. Returned to Salisbury. All night at Lewis'.

Mond. 22. Called to see John Allen Ketchy. Returned home. Dinner at Dr. Coleman's.

Tues. 23. Wed. 24. Thurs. 25. At home.

Frid. 26.

Sat. 27. Started for Salem ch. All night at Lewis' in Salisbury. Wife with me.

Sund. 28. Took Rev. Plyler in my buggy to Salem ch. & had him to preach for me morning & afternoon. Dinner at Sam⁻ Seaford's. Returned to Salisbury. All night at Phebe Brown's.

Mond. 29. Returned home. Dinner at Mr. Haynes. Baptized Mr. & Mrs. Simpson's child at Phebe Brown's.

Tues. 30. At home & helped to haul wheat till dinner. Was sent for late in evening to go to Salisbury & marry George Achenbach & Melinda F. Walton. Married them in the Lutheran church. All night at Lorenzo Walton's.

Wed. July 1. Went to Alexander Brown's. All night here.

Thurs. 2. Attended to the funeral of Pleasant Brown's child at St. Luke's ch. Preached from Matth. 2:18. All night at Pleasant Brown's.

Frid. 3. Dinner to day at Henry Brown's. In afternoon called to see Mrs. C. Kistler. In evening went to J. W. Miller's & staid all night.

Sat. 4. Went to Thomas Goodman's & took dinner. In afternoon went to W. L. Kistler's & staid over night.

Sund. 5. Preached at St. Luke's ch. from Hosea 14:1.2. After intermission lectured on commandments. Dinner & all night at D. M. Barrier's.

Mond. 6. Returned home.

Tues. 7. At home till 12 M. In afternoon went to Caty Earnheart's & settled for spinning. Called also at Dr. Coleman's.

Wed. 8. Thurs. 9. Frid. 10. At home.

Sat. 11. Started for Salem ch. All night at Jacob Klutts'.

Sund. 12. Preached at Salem ch. from Zech. 8:23. In afternoon lectured on Apos. Creed. Dinner & all night at Saml Seaford's.

Mond. 13. Returned home. Dinner at David Eller's.

Tues. 14. Went in forenoon to Gold Hill to Post Office. Afternoon at home.

Wed. 15. Went in afternoon with wife to David Barringer's & spent the night.

Thurs. 16. Returned home.

Frid. 17. Went in afternoon to Nancy Arey's & staid all night.

Sat. 18. Started for St. Luke's ch. Dinner at Phebe Brown's in Salisbury. All night at John Harkey's.

Sund. 19. Preached at St. Luke's ch. from Zech. 8:23. Lectured in the afternoon from on the Apostle's Creed. Dinner & all night at Alexander Brown's.

Mond. 20. Returned home. Dinner at Phebe Brown's in Salisbury.

Tues. 21. At home.

Wed. 22. Called at Dr. Coleman's. Dinner here.

Thurs. 23. Attended to the funeral of Elizabeth R., wife of Alfred Miller at Lower St. Church. Preached from Prov. 23:26. Dinner at Mrs. Mary A. Heilig's.

[Pages for July 24 through Aug. 7 are missing]

Sat. 8. Started for Salem ch. Dinner at Phebe Brown's in Salisbury. All night at Widow C. R. Miller's.

Sund. 9. Preached at Salem ch. from Prov. 23:26. & baptized one infant. After intermission lectured on subject of Baptism. Dinner at John Lingel's. All night at Phebe Brown's in Salisbury. At night heard Rev. Neiffer preach in Luth. Church.

Mond. 10. Returned home. Rev. Neiffer with me.

Tues. 11. At home till evening, then went to Dr. Coleman's & brought buggy home, having sent Rev. Neiffer thither.

Wed. 12. Went to Dr. Coleman's & took Rev. Neiffer to Rev. Cone's. Dinner at Dr. Coleman's. Brought wife home.

Thurs. 13. At home.

Frid. 14. In afternoon started for St. Luke's ch. All night at Zechariah Lyerly's.

Sat. 15. Dinner at Phebe Brown's, Salisbury. All night at Pleasant M. Brown's.

Sund. 16. Preached at St. Luke's ch. from Ps. 37:34. In afternoon lectured on subject of Lord's Supper. Dinner at John Harkey's. All night at M. A. Bost's.

Mond. 17. Returned home. Dinner at Phebe Brown's, Salisbury.

Tues. 18. Started for Salem ch. to attend Rowan County Sund. School Convention. Dinner at Dr. Coleman's. All night at Phebe Brown's, Salisbury.

Wed. 19. At Salem ch. attending Sund. School Convention. All night at Pleasant Wise's.

Thurs. 20. At Convention. All night at Jacob Klutts'.

Frid. 21. Went to Mathias Miller's in Davie County. All night here.

Sat. 22. Attended & conducted the laying of the Corner Stone of Cherry Hill Church. Dinner at Mathias Miller's. All night at Rev. H. M. Brown's.

Sund. 23. Preached at Salem ch. from Ps. 37:34. Baptized one inf^{t}. Dinner at M. A. Bost's. All night at Phebe Brown's, Salisbury. Heard Rev. Neiffer in Luth. church.

Mond. 24. Returned home. Dinner at Dr. Coleman's.

Tues. 25. In forenoon went to Gold Hill to Post Office. In afternoon went to Jacob Lyerly's & brought buggy shafts home.

Wed. 26. Took buggy to John Powlass' to have shafts ironed. In afternoon at home.

Thurs. 27. At home.

Frid. 28. Went to Special Conference at Christiana Church. In the evening returned home.

Sat. 29. Returned to Special Conference. Wife with me. All night at Adam Miller's.

Sund. 30. At Christiana Church. Dedicated the Church & preached from Ps. 133:1-3. In afternoon went with wife to Salisbury. Attended service at night in Luth. Church. All night at Phebe Brown's.

Mond. 31. Returned home.

Tues. Sept. 1. At home till afternoon, then went to mill.

Wed. 2. At home. At night married Mr. Thomas H. Kirk & Miss Eliza Jane Ludwick.

Thurs. 3. At home till afternoon, then went with wife to Dr. Coleman's, and spent afternoon.

Frid. 4. Started for St. Luke's ch. Dinner at Phebe Brown's, Salisbury. All at Mr. Freeze's.

Sat. 5. Had a meeting of consultation by Council & Rev. Kimball & Capt. J. Fisher relative to W. L. Kistler's suspension. Council restored him. Dinner at W. L. Kistler's. All night at Widow Jacob Goodman's.

Sund. 6. Preached at St. Luke's ch. from Hos. 14:1.2. After intermission lectured on mode of worship. All night at D. M. Barrier's.

Mond. 7. Returned home.

Tues. 8. Wed. 9. At home.

Thurs. 10. In afternoon went to Gold Hill to Post Office & had horse shod.

Frid. 11. At home.

Sat. 12. Started for Salem ch. Dinner at Phebe Brown's, Salisbury. All night at Osborn Graham's.

Sund. 13. To day Calvin Seaford preached for me at Salem. In the afternoon lectured on mode of worship in Book of Worship. Dinner at M. A. Bost's. All night at Phebe Brown's, Salisbury. Attended Luth. Church at night.

Mond. 14. Returned home. Dinner at Dr. Coleman's.

Tues. 15. In afternoon called at Dr. Coleman's on business.

Wed. 16. Went with wife to Mr. Coit's at Gold Hill & spent the day.

Thurs. 17. At home.

Frid. 18. Started for St. Enoch's Church. Dinner at Widow Rineholt Ketchie's. All night at Allen Rose's.

Sat. 19. At St. Enoch's ch. Preached from Jam. 1:25. Supper at John Icehour's. All night at Rev. Julian's.

Sund. 20. At St. Enoch's ch. Preached in forenoon in the woods from Luk. 13:24. Rev. Strobel in the mean time preached in the church. In afternoon dedicated the church & then preached from 2 Tim. 1:13. All night at Mr. Plaster's.

Mond. 21. Returned home. Dinner at Dr. Coleman's.

Tues. 22. Wed. 23. At home.

Thurs. 24. Went to Salisbury. At night aided in the marriage of Thomas J. Bashford & Lucy A. Krimminger by Rev. Neiffer in Luth. Church. All night at Phebe Brown's.

Frid. 25. Returned home. Dinner at Dr. Coleman's.

Sat. 26. Started for Bethel ch. Dinner at Phebe Brown's. All night at John C. Miller's.

Sund. 27. In forenoon attended Sund. School at Franklin Academy. Dinner at Joicy Linn's. In afternoon preached at Bethel ch. from Neh. 6:3. All night at Phebe Brown's in Salisbury. At night attended preaching in Luth. ch.

Mond. 28. A very rainy day. Remained at Mrs. Brown's till Tuesday morning.

Tues. 29. Returned home.

Wed. 30. At home.

Thurs. Oct. 1. In afternoon went to Gold Hill to Post Office.

Frid. 2. Started for St. Luke's ch. Dinner at Dr. Coleman's. All night at Tobias Lyerly's.

Sat. 3. Went to Alexander Brown's & staid over night. Dinner to day at Phebe Brown's in Salisbury.

Sund. 4. Preached at St. Luke's ch. from Gen. 6:9. Dinner at D. M. Barrier's. All night at Phebe Brown's.

Mond. 5. Returned home. Brought Rev. Neiffer part of the way on his way to Mt. Pleasant.

Tues. 6. Started for Mt. Pleasant. Dinner at Rev. Cone's. Called by Chas. Fisher's & Foil's Tan Yard. All night at Dan$^{\underline{l}}$ Miller's.

Wed. 7. Went to Mt. Pleasant and attended meeting of Board of Trustees of N. C. College. Dinner & all night at Col. Shimpock's. Supper at Prof. L. A. Bikley's.

Thurs. 8. Returned home.

Frid. 9. Went with wife to Mr. Coit's on Gold Hill & brought some furniture home. Dinner here.

Sat. 10. Started for Salem ch. Dinner at Phebe Brown's. All night at Lagrange Elliott's.

Sund. 11. Preached at Salem ch. from Gen. 6:9. Dinner at Sam$^{\underline{l}}$ Seaford's. All night at John Lingel's.

Mond. 12. Returned home. Dinner at Dr. Coleman's. Rev. Neiffer with me to night.

Tues. 13. In the morning went to Dr. Coleman's & brought wife home. In afternoon went went to Powlass' Shop.

Wed. 14. Went to Carding Machine on the river. (Morgan & Mauney's)

Thurs. 15. Called at Andrew Berger's on business. Thence to Dan$^{\underline{l}}$ Basinger's to engage shoemaking.

Frid. 16. Started for St. Luke's ch. Rev. J. G. Neiffer having staid with me over night, took him to Salisbury in my buggy. Dinner at Phebe Brown's. All night at D. M. Barrier's.

Sat. 17. An inclement day. Preached at St. Luke's ch. from Phil. 2:5. preparatory. Dinner at Alex$^{\underline{r}}$ Brown's. All night at P. M. Brown's.

Sund. 18. Preached at St. Luke's ch. from 1 Pet. 5:4. After an intermission administered the Communion. Dinner at John Harkey's. All night at Sam$^{\underline{l}}$ Seaford's.

Mond. 19. Returned home. Dinner at Phebe Brown's in Salisbury.

Tues. 20. At home. Not very well.

Wed. 21. At home till afternoon, then went to Dan$^{\underline{l}}$ Basinger's to shoemaker.

Thurs. 22. Went to Salisbury. All night at Mrs. Phebe Brown's, Salisbury.

Frid. 23. In Salisbury, it being Court week. All night at Mrs. Brown's.

Sat. 24. Went to Salem ch. – preached from Phil. 2:5. & held service preparatory to communion. All night at Mrs. John Berger's.

Sund. 25. Preached at Salem ch. from Ps. 116:12-14. Confirmed five persons. After an intermission administered the Communion. Dinner at John Lingel's. All night at Mrs. Brown's, Salisbury.

Mond. 26. Returned home. Dinner at Dr. Coleman's.

Tues. 27. At home.

Wed. 28. Went with wife to Salisbury. Supper at Phebe Brown's. Lodged with Rev. Neiffer, Mrs. B. being crowded.

Thurs. 29. Attended the fair.

Frid. 30. Attended Court. All night at Mr. Grupy's.

Sat. 31. Attended Court in forenoon. In afternoon started for St. Luke's church. All night at D. M. Barrier's.

Sund. Nov. 1. Preached at St. Luke's ch. from Ps. 73:1. Dinner at John Harkey's. All night at Phebe Brown's, Salisbury.

Mond. 2. Had some Photographs taken for wife. In afternoon returned home.

Tues. 3. Started for Mt. Pleasant. All night at Daniel Miller's.

Wed. 4. In Mt. Pleasant. Attended meeting of Board of Trustees of N. C. College. All night at Col. Shimpock's.

Thurs. 5. Returned home.

Frid. 6. At home.

Sat. 7. Started for Salem ch. Dinner at Phebe Brown's, Salisbury. All night at M. A. Bost's.

Sund. 8. Preached at Salem ch. from Job 14:14. the funeral of the infant daughter dec^d. of the Widow Nancy Cauble. Baptized one inf^t. Dinner at John Lingel's. Returned to Salisbury. Went at night & heard Rev. Neiffer preach. All night with Rev. Neiffer.

Mond. 9. Breakfast & dinner at Mrs. Brown's. In afternoon returned home.

Tues. 10. In forenoon went to Gold Hill to Post Office. In afternoon went to Mrs. Bost's to weaver.

Wed. 11. Went to Dr. Coleman's with wife to house raising.

Thurs. 12. At home.

Frid. 13. Started for St. Luke's ch. All night at Phebe Brown's in Salisbury.

Sat. 14. Went to Monroe Berger's — all night here.

Sund. 15. Preached at St. Luke's ch. from Luk. 19:1-10. In the afternoon attended to the burial of Caleb Setzer at Ebenezer ch. (Methodist). Mr. S. died of wounds received in his own house from a robber whom Mrs. S. disarmed and killed. All night at D. M. Barrier's.

Mond. 16. Returned on the way home as far as Salisbury. All night at Mr. O'Neal's.

Tues. 17. Returned home.

Wed. 18. Thurs. 19. Frid. 20. At home.

Sat. 21. Started for Salem ch. — Dinner at Phebe Brown's, Salisbury. All night at Henry Goodman's.

Sund. 22. Preached at Salem ch. from Luk. 19:1-10. An inclement day. — Dinner & all night at John Lingel's.

Mond. 23. In the afternoon attended to the fun^l of Wisley Propst's child at Salem ch. Returned on the way home as far as Salisbury. All night at Phebe Brown's.

Tues. 24. Returned home.

Wed. 25. Went to D. Basinger's & had Boots repaired. Called also at Andr. Berger's & at Dr. Coleman's.

Thurs. 26. Started in afternoon for Eastern Conference. All night at David Eller's.

Frid. 27. Went to Bethel ch. to Conference. All night at John C. Miller's.

Sat. 28. At Conference. All night at Andr. Shuping's.

Sund. 29. At Bethel ch. — Preached in forenoon from Jam. 1:25. In afternoon preach^d again from 1 Thes. 2:11.12. Preached at night in Salisbury from Prov. 3:6. All night at Phebe Brown's.

Mond. 30. Returned home.

Tues. Dec. 1. Went to Salisbury on Church business. All night at Phebe Brown's.

Wed. 2. Returned home.

Thurs. 3. At home.

Frid. 4. Started for St. Luke's ch. All night at Phebe Brown's, Salisbury. At night attended lectures by Rev. Neiffer in Luth. ch.

Sat. 5. Went to Henry Brown's and staid over night. Called on the way to see Mrs. Cath. Kistler who had been sick.

Sund. 6. Preached at St. Luke's ch. from Acts 3:1-11. Dinner & all night at Alexander Brown's.

Mond. 7. In the afternoon went to John Goodman's & staid over night.

Tues. 8. Went to Eli Powlass' & staid over night.

Wed. 9. In afternoon went to Jesse Powlass' & staid over night.

Thurs. 10. In afternoon went to Jackson Goodman's & married Joseph T. Carson & Martha L. Quillman. All night at Eli Powlass'.

Frid. 11. Went to John Carson's to infair. All night at Jesse Powlass'.

Sat. 12. In afternoon went to Daniel Menis' & staid over night.

Sund. 13. Preached at Salem ch. from Acts 3:1-11. Baptized one infant. All night at M. A. Bost's.

Mond. 14. Returned home.

Tues. 15. Went with wife to D. Barringer's.

Wed. 16. Went to Salisbury & at night took the cars for Greensboro under summons to attend Court as witness. Stopped at Planter's Hotel.

Thurs. 17. In Greensboro. Case put off. Took the cars at 12 at night for Salisbury.

Frid. 18. Breakfast at Phebe Brown's. Then went to John Harkey's & staid all night.

Sat. 19. In afternoon went to J. W. Miller's & staid all night.

Sund. 20. Preached at St. Luke's ch. from Ps. 90:12. Dinner at D. M. Barrier's. All night at John Lingel's.

Mond. 21. Returned home.

Tues. 22. Went to John Fisher's to barn raising.

Wed. 23. Went to Gold Hill for leather. Called by Paul Beaver's for some brandy.

Thurs. 24. Went to Mich.[1] Isenhour's and married Nathan R. Morgan and Mary M. Isenhour. In afternoon went to Margaret A. Lentz's and married Frank Heilig, colored, and Julia Linn, colored. At night went to St. Peter's ch. to Christmas Tree.

Frid. 25. Christmas Day. At home.

Sat. 26. Started for Salem ch. — All night at Sam.[1] Colly's.

Sund. 27. Preached at Salem ch. from 2 Kings 4:26. All night at Sam.[1] Seaford's.

Mond. 28. Returned home. Dinner at Phebe Brown's, Salisbury.

Tues. 29. At home till afternoon, then went to Dr. Coleman's & brought wife home.

Wed. 30. Went to Gold Hill & had boots repaired.

Thurs. 31. At home.

Jan. 1. At home. A very inclement day.

Sat. 2. At home. Day inclement.

Sund. 3. Had reserved this day to attend a communion season in Salisbury, but was detained at home by inclement weather. Married this afternoon at my house, John W. Fisher (colored) and Anna Crowell (colored).

Mond. 4. At home. Had winter hogs slaughtered.

Tues. 5. Started in afternoon for Mt. Pleasant. All night at Danl Miller's.

Wed. 6. Went to Mt. Pleasant to attend meeting of Board of Trustees of College. A quorum not being present, no business was transacted. Read service in Luth. Church at night & heard J. B. Davis, D.D. preach. All night at Col. Shimpock's.

Thurs. 7. Went to John E. Miller's & married Eli Holshouser & Leah Wagoner. Then returned home.

Frid. 8. At home.

Sat. 9. Started for Salem ch. — Dinner at Phebe Brown's. All night at M. A. Bost's.

Sund. 10. Preached at Salem ch. from John 12:21. Dinner at John Lingel's. Returned to Salisbury & heard Rev. Neiffer preach in the Luth. Church. All night with Rev. Neiffer at Mr. Achenbach's.

Mond. 11. Breakfast at Phebe Brown's. Returned home.

Tues. 12. At home. A very inclement day.

Wed. 13. Went to Milas A. Holshouser's & to Dr. Coleman's.

Thurs. 14. At home.

Frid. 15. At home.

Sat. 16. Started for St. Luke's ch. All night at Alex^r Brown's.

Sund. 17. Preached at St. Luke's church from Heb. 1:14. Dinner & all night at John Harkey's.

Mond. 18. Returned home. Settled, in the office of Probate Judge, the Estate of Milas Arey, dec^d, & made Guardian Returns.

Tues. 19. At home till afternoon, then went to M. A. Holshouser's to engage him to slaughter a beef.

Wed. 20. At home. Slaughtered Beef.

Thurs. 21. In forenoon took a quarter of Beef to Dr. Coleman's. Was sent for to attend funeral of Jesse Lyerly. Started at 2½ O'clock and went to John Berger's 18 miles. All night here.

Frid. 22. Attended to the fun^l of Jesse Lyerly at Salem ch. — preached from Matth. 25:13. All night at widow John Berger's.

Sat. 23. Attended singing at Salem ch. All night at Saml Seaford's.

Sund. 24. Preached at Salem ch. from Matth. 5:6. All night at Phebe Brown's in Salisbury.

Mond. 25. Returned home.

Tues. 26. Went to Joseph Eagle's & had horse shod.

Wed. 27. At home.

Thurs. 28. At home.

Frid. 29. Went to Eastern Conference at St. Peter's Church. No quorum being present did not organize.

Sat. 30. At St. Peter's ch. Organized & proceeded to business. Revds. Neiffer & H. M. Brown with us to night.

Sund. 31. At St. Peter's ch. Preaching by several of the ministers.

Mond. Feb. 1. Went with wife to Dr. Coleman's & spent the day.

Tues. 2. Started for Mt. Pleasant to attend meeting of Board of Trustees of College. Dinner at Rev. Cone's. All night at Dan¹ Miller's.

Wed. 3. Went to Mt. Pleasant. Attended meeting of Board of Trustees. Dinner at Rev. Strobel's. All night at Col. J. Shimpock's.

Thurs. 4. Returned home. Dinner at Rev. Cone's. Mrs. Cone died early this morning.

Frid. 5. Went to Rev. Cone's to attend to the funeral of his wife, but the funeral was postponed to next day.

Sat. 6. Attended to the funeral of Mrs. Cone at Organ ch. — preached from Matth. 25:13. A large collection of people present. Returned to Rev. Cone's & staid over night.

Sund. 7. This was my regular day at St. Luke's ch., but was prevented from attending by the death of Mrs. Cone. In the afternoon returned home.

Mond. 8. Tues. 9. At home.

Wed. 10. Went to Gold Hill on business.

Thurs. 11. At home. Inclement day.

Frid. 12. Started for Salem ch. All night at Phebe Brown's, Salisbury.

Sat. 13. Went to widow Jesse Lyerly's and staid over.

Sund. 14. Preached at Salem ch. from Matth. 4:1-10. Returned to Salisbury. Read service at night in Luth. church. All night at Mrs. Brown's.

Mond. 15. Returned home. Unwell.

Tues. 16. Wed. 17. In bed sick.

Thurs. 18. At home, not well.

Frid. 19. Sat. 20. At home indisposed.

Sund. 21. This was my day for regular service at St. Luke's ch. but did not attend in consequence of indisposition & inclement weather.

Mond. 22. Tues. 23. At home.

Wed. 24. Went with wife to Daniel Miller's & spent the day. Day inclement.

Thurs. 25. At home, a rainy day.

Frid. 26. At home.

Sat. 27. Went to Salem ch. & in afternoon attended singing. All night at John Lingel's.

Sund. 28. Preached at Salem ch. from Luk. 11:14-26. Dinner at M. A. Bost's. All night at Phebe Brown's, Salisbury.

Mond. March 1. Returned home.

Tues. 2. Went to Salisbury. All night with Rev. Neiffer. Left my horse at Crawford's Livery Stable.

Wed. 3. Went to Greensboro' to attend Court as a witness, Summers vs. Wagoner. Stopped at Planter's Hotel.

Thurs. 4. Frid. 5. In Greensboro'.

Sat. 6. Took the cars this morning at one o'clock for Salisbury. Breakfast at Phebe Brown's. Started for St. Luke's ch. — All night at Pleasant Brown's.

Sund. 7. A very rainy day. Remained at Pleasant Brown's until following morning.

Mond. 8. Returned home. Dinner at Mrs. Phebe Brown's.

Tues. 9. Went in afternoon with wife to David Barringer's & staid over night.

Wed. 10. Returned home.

Thurs. 11. In forenoon went to Gold Hill. In afternoon took wife, Joan & Ellen Grupy to Dr. Coleman's.

Frid. 12. In forenoon went to Dr. Coleman's & brought wife & Joan home. Balance of the day at home.

Sat. 13. Started for Salem ch. — Dinner at Mrs. Phebe Brown's in Salisbury. All night at Joseph Beaver's.

Sund. 14. Preached at Salem ch. from Acts 4:33. Returned to Salisbury. At night attended preaching in Luth. by Rev. Neiffer. — All night at Mrs. Brown's.

Mond. 15. Returned home. Dinner at Dr. Coleman's.

Tues. 16. Wed. 17. Thurs. 18. At home.

Frid. 19. Went to Salisbury & made final settlement, as guardian) with A. B. Arey. All night at Mrs. Phebe Brown's.

Sat. 20. Went to Alexander Brown's & staid over night. A rainy day & waters full.

Sund. 21. Preached at St. Luke's ch. from Matth. 21:28. Dinner at Alexander Brown's. All night at Widow Miller's (of Charles R.)

Mond. 22. Returned home.

Tues. 23. Attended the closing exercises of Lewis' school.

Wed. 24. Thurs. 25. At home.

Frid. 26. Good Friday. In the forenoon went to Gold Hill to Post Office. In afternoon at home.

Sat. 27. Started for Salem ch. — Dinner at Phebe Brown's in Salisbury. All night at Sam[l] Seaford's.

Sund. 28. Preached at Salem ch. from Col 3:1. Baptized one infant. Dinner at John Lingel's. At night preached in the Luth. Church Salisbury from Prov. 29:1. Full house. All night at Mr. O'Neal's.

Mond. 29. In afternoon returned home.

Tues. 30. Wed. 31. At home.

Thurs. April 1. At home.

Frid. 2. Started for St. Luke's ch. as far as Salisbury. Mrs. Phebe Brown having purchased a house & lot of D. R. Julian, attended to getting a bond for title & otherwise closing the trade. All night at Mrs. Brown's.

Sat. 3. Went to John Harkey's and staid over night.

Sund. 4. Preached at St. Luke's ch. from Gen. 5:24. Dinner & all night at D. M. Barrier's.

Mond. 5. Returned home. Dinner at Mrs. Phebe Brown's.

Tues. 6. In forenoon went to Gold Hill. — In afternoon at home.

Wed. 7. At home.

Thurs. 8. In afternoon went to Dan$^{\underline{l}}$ Miller's & brought churns home.

Frid. 9. At home till dinner, then went to mill.

Sat. 10. Started for Salem ch. Dinner at Mrs. Phebe Brown's, Salisbury. All night at Otho Cauble's.

Sund. 11. Preached at Salem ch. from Dan. 6:10. Baptized one infant. All night at James Brown's.

Mond. 12. Returned home. Dinner at Mr. George Achenbach's, Salisbury. Baptized George H. Shaver's child at the house of Wm. Smith's widow.

Tues. 13. At home.

Wed. 14. At home till 12 o'clock, then went to Gold Hill.

Thurs. 15. At home.

Frid. 16. Went to Salem ch. & attended to the funeral of Mrs. John Berger. Preached from Is. 3:10. Dinner at Sam$^{\underline{l}}$ Colly's. All night at John Harkey's.

Sat. 17. Preached at St. Luke's ch. from Dan. 6:10. preparatory to communion. Dinner at Alexander Brown's. Then went with Monroe Berger to see Rev. Mr. Chandler, Presbyterian Minister, he being much afflicted with a very sore knee. All night at Monroe Berger's. The day cold & windy.

Sund. 18. Preached at St. Luke's ch. from Acts 20:17-21. & administered the communion. In the afternoon went to Ebenezer Methodist ch. & heard Rev. Triplett preach the funeral of Mr. Setzer, who came to his death at the hands of robbers. All night at D. M. Barrier's. A very cold day with high wind.

Mond. 19. Returned home. Dinner at Phebe Brown's, Salisbury.

Tues. 20. In forenoon went to Gold Hill. In afternoon at home.

Wed. 21. At home.

Thurs. 22. At home. A heavy frost this morning.

Frid. 23. Started for Salem ch. — Dinner at Mrs. Phebe Brown's. All night at John Lingel's.

Sat. 24. At Salem ch. Rev. R. L. Brown preached. Baptized 2 infants. Held preparatory service. All night at Calvin Cress'.

Sund. 25. At Salem ch. Rev. R. L. Brown preached. After an intermission administered the communion. Dinner at John Lingel's. At night attended the Luth. ch. in Salisbury. Read service for Rev. Neiffer. All night at Mrs. Phebe Brown's.

Mond. 26. Returned home.

Tues. 27. Started for synod at St. John's ch. All night at Daniel Miller's.

Wed. 28. Went to St. John's ch. Preached Synodical Sermon from Acts 20:17-21. As President organized Synod. Was re-elected President of Synod. All night at widow Cress'.

Thurs. 29. At St. John's ch. in Synod. All night at Rufus Ridenhour's.

Frid. 30. At St. John's ch. in Synod. All night at Col. Shimpock's.

Sat. May 1. At St. John's ch. Ordained to day Calvin W. Sifferd, being assisted by the other officers of Synod. All night at Danl Miller's.

Sund. 2. At St. John's ch. Assisted in the administration of the communion. All night at Mrs. Maria Miller's.

Mond. 3. At St. John's ch. Synod closed to day. Went to Mt. Pleasant & paid money over to L. G. Heilig, Treasurer of Synod, & took his bond. All night at Col. Shimpock's.

Tues. 4. Returned home.

Wed. 5. Went to Salisbury. All night at James Crawford's.

Thurs. 6. In Salisbury till 7 P.M. then took the cars for Charlotte. Stopped at Central Hotel.

Frid. 7. Breakfast at hotel. Walked three miles to Mr. Icehower's in the country. Dinner here. In afternoon returned with Mr. Icehower to Charlotte & compromised a money difficulty between Rev. N. Aldrich and Mr. Icehower. Supper at Robert Brown's. Took the cars at 9 P.M. & returned to Salisbury. Lodged with Rev. Neiffer.

Sat. 8. Breakfast at Mr. Achenbach's. Went to Salem ch. & had catechlzation. All night at Abner H. Gheen's.

Sund. 9. Preached at Salem ch. from John 3:16. After intermission lectured from Gal. 5:1. All night at M. A. Bost's.

Mond. 10. Returned home. Forwarded to day a letter of dismission to Rev. Aldrich.

Tues. 11. At home.

Wed. 12. In forenoon went to Dr. Coleman's & to Gold Hill. In afternoon at home.

Thurs. 13. At home.

Frid. 14. Started for St. Luke's ch. Dinner at Phebe Brown's in Salisbury. All night at Alexander Brown's.

Sat. 15. Dinner at Pleasant M. Brown's. In afternoon at catechization at St. Luke's ch. All night at Jesse W. Miller's.

Sund. 16. Preached at St. Luke's ch. from Is. 34:16. Baptized Pleasant M. Brown's child. Dinner at John Harkey's. All night at Saml Colly's.

Mond. 17. Returned home. Dinner at Jacob Grupy's.

Tues. 18. At home.

Wed. 19. In forenoon went to Dr. Coleman's & H. A. Miller's. In afternoon went to mill.

Thurs. 20. In forenoon went to blacksmith shop at Mr. Eagle's. In afternoon went to mill.

Frid. 21. Went to Salisbury. Dinner at Mrs. Phebe Brown's. In afternoon went to J. C. Miller's. All night here. At night attended the closing exercises of Franklin Academy.

Sat. 22. Called in the morning at Mrs. Joicy Linn's. Dinner at Andrew Shuping's. In afternoon had catechization at Salem ch. All night at Edmond Seaford's.

Sund. 23. Preached at Salem ch. from Is. 34:16. first clause. After intermission lectured from Heb. 11:13. last clause. All night at Saml Seaford's.

Mond. 24. Returned home. In afternoon started for Mt. Pleasant to College Commencement. Took Adolphus Linn along in my buggy. All night at G. M. Bernhardt's.

Tues. 25. Went to Mt. Pleasant. Stopped at Col. Shimpock's. Heard Rev. Turner address Literary Societies. In afternoon attended meeting of Board of Trustees. At night heard Prof. Ludwig address Alumni of College.

Wed. 26. Attended graduating exercises & Board of Trustees.

Thurs. 27. Returned home.

Frid. 28. Sat. 29. At home.

Sund. 30. Went Christiana Church and preached from Prov. 3:6. Baptized Rev. R. L. Brown's child. Assisted in the administration of the Eucharist. After an intermission preached again from Is. 34:16. Returned home.

Mond. 31. At home.

Tues. June 1. In the morning went to J. Eagle's Shop. Balance of day at home.

Wed. 2. Thurs. 3. At home.

Frid. 4. Started for St. Luke's ch. Dinner at Phebe Brown's, Salisbury. Joe Beaver with me as far as Salem ch. All night at Alexander Brown's.

Sat. 5. In the afternoon had catechization at St. Luke's ch. All night at Mrs. Jacob C. Goodman's.

Sund. 6. Preached at St. Luke's ch. from Jerem. 5:26. After an intermission lectured from 1 Tim. 4:7. All night at D. M. Barrier's.

Mond. 7. Returned home.

Tues. 8. Attended the burial of Tobias Peeler at Lower St. ch. Rev. Trexler officiated. Mr. Peeler came by his death by being thrown out of his buggy by the running away of a mule.

Wed. 9. At home. Worked in meadow.

Thurs. 10. At home.

Frid. 11. At home.

Sat. 12. Went to Salem ch. & had catechization at 2 o'clock P.M. Dinner at Mrs. Phebe Brown's. All night at Widow John Berger's.

Sund. 13. Preached at Salem ch. from Jer. 5:26. After intermission lectured from 1 Tim. 4:7. All at John Lingel's.

Mond. 14. Returned home. Dinner at Mrs. Phebe Brown's.

Tues. 15. At home.

Wed. 16. In forenoon went to mill. In afternoon took wife to Dr. Coleman's.

Thurs. 17. In forenoon went to mill. In afternoon at home.

Frid. 18. Went to Monroe Berger's, 30 miles, & staid all night. Dinner to day at Mrs. Phebe Brown's.

Sat. 19. Called in forenoon to see Rev. Mr. Chandler, Presbyterian, who had recently had a leg amputated. Returned to Mr. Berger's to dinner. In afternoon had catechization at St. Luke's ch. All night at Alex^r Brown's.

Sund. 20. At St. Luke's ch. Rev. Neiffer preached in morning & afternoon. Called in afternoon to see old Mrs. Ray, who is in feeble health & old. All night at Mrs. Brown's, Salisbury.

Mond. 21. Returned home.

Tues. 22. Wed. 23. At home.

Thurs. 24. Went to John Lingel's & married Calvin H. Bost & Laura R. Lingle. Then went to Matthias Miller's in Davie Co. and staid over night.

Frid. 25. Attended the Eastern Conference at the Church of the Reformation at Cherry Hill. All night at Mr. M. Miller's.

Sat. 26. Attended divine service at the Church. Rev. C. H. Bernheim & Rev. Kimball preached. All night at Mr. M. Miller's.

Sund. 27. Service at the Church. Revds. Kimball & Bernheim preached. Dedicated the Church under the name of The Church of the Reformation. In the afternoon aided in the administration of the Lord's Supper. All night at Cicero Foard's.

Mond. 28. Returned home. Dinner at Phebe Brown's.

Tues. 29. Went to mill.

Wed. 30. At home.

Thurs. July 1. In forenoon went to Jos. Eagle's & had horse shod. In the evening went to Sallie Holshouser's & brought wife home having been on a visit there.

Frid. 2. In the morning went to mill, balance of day at home. Very washing rain this evening.

Sat. 3. Started for St. Luke's ch. All night at John Harkey's. Dinner to day at Mrs. Brown's in Salisbury.

Sund. 4. Preached to day at St. Luke's ch. from Ruth 1:16.17. After intermission lectured on ten commandments. All night at D. M. Barrier's.

Mond. 5. Returned home. Dinner at Mr. Grupy's. Rev. Neiffer with me as far as Mrs. Lentz's.

Tues. 6. Went to Mt. Pleasant. Rev. Neiffer with me. All night at Col. Shimpock's.

Wed. 7. Attended meeting of the Board of Trustees of N. C. College. In afternoon went to Danl Miller's & staid all night.

Thurs. 8. Returned home.

Frid. 9. At home.

Sat. 10. Went to Salem ch. & had catechization at 2 o'clock P.M. All night at Legrand Elliott's.

Sund. 11. Preached at Salem ch. from Ruth 1:16.17. After intermission lectured on Ten Commandments. Dinner at John Rusher's. All night at P. N. Heilig's.

Mond. 12. Returned home.

Tues. 13. At home.

Wed. 14. Started in afternoon for Bear Creek Church. All night at Wilson Barringer's.

Thurs. 15. Went to Bear Creek Church & with Col. Shimpock investigated and adjusted an existing difficulty as per resolution of Synod. In afternoon returned home.

Frid. 16. At home.

Sat. 17. Started for St. Luke's ch. Lewis with me. Dinner at Phebe Brown's. All night at Alexander Brown's.

Sund. 18. Preached at St. Luke's ch. from Judges 6:24. After intermission lectured on Apostle's Creed. Over night at John Lingel's.

Mond. 19. Returned home.

Tues. 20. Went in the morning to Mr. Slough's to see thresher's. Balance of day at home & had wheat & oats threshed.

Wed. 21. At home.

Thurs. 22. In the morning went to Gold Hill, balance of day at home.

Frid. 23. At home.

Sat. 24. Went to Salem ch. and had catechization at 2 o'clock P.M. Over night at Daniel Menius'.

Sund. 25. Preached at Salem ch. from Judges 6:24. After an intermission lectured on the Apostle's Creed. Dinner at M. A. Bost's. Over night at Wesley Propst's.

Mond. 26. Returned home. Dinner at Dr. Coleman's. Took sick this evening.

Tues. 27. Wed. 28. Thurs. 29. At home sick.

Frid. 30. Sat. 31. At home sick.

Sund. Aug. 1. This was my regular day to preach at St. Luke's ch. but could not attend in consequence of indisposition.

Mond. 2. At home improving.

Tues. 3. Went to Jesse Miller's & heard the candidates for Convention speak.

Wed. 4. At home.

Thurs. 5. Went with Lewis to election at Morgan's. Returned home by way of Gold Hill.

Frid. 6. At home.

Sat. 7. Took Eve Ann Miller to Mr. John Lyerly's. All night here. Dinner to day at Phebe Brown's, Salisbury.

Sund. 8. Preached at Salem ch. from Luke 18:9-14. Dinner at Saml Seaford's. Called to see Mrs. John Rusher, she being very sick. All night at Mrs. Brown's in Salisbury. Heard Rev. Crawford preach.

Mond. 9. Started for home. Took very sick on the way. Called in staid over night at Michael Brown's.

Tues. 10. Returned home.

Wed. 11 to Tues. 17. At home on account of sickness.

Wed. 18. Thurs. 19. Frid. 20. At home.

Sat. 21. Went wife to Salisbury. All night at Phebe Brown's,

Sund. 22. This was my day at Salem ch., but did not attend on account of bad health & the inclement weather. Dr. J. B. Davis preached for me. All night at Mr. Grupy's.

Mond. 23. Went to Davidson Co. — Dinner at Mr. Lomax's. — All night at Caleb Peeler's.

Tues. 24. Spent the afternoon at Philip Weers'.

Wed. 25. Visited in company with C. Peeler some relatives.

Thurs. 26. Went with C. Peeler & wife to Winston. Dinner & supper at Calvin Miller's. All night at Saml Thomas'.

Frid. 27. Dinner at Calvin Miller's. In afternoon went to J. M. Stafford's & staid over night.

Sat. 28. In afternoon returned to Caleb Peeler's & staid over night.

Sund. 29. Preached at Friedberg, Moravian, from James 1:25. Dinner at Christian Spaugh's. Returned to C. Peeler's.

Mond. 30. Started for home. All night at Phebe Brown's in Salisbury.

Tues. 31. Returned home. Dinner at Dr. Coleman's.

Wed. Sep. 1. At home.

Thurs. 2. Went to Dr. Coleman's on business.

Frid. 3. Rode out to engage hands to mow grass.

Sat. 4. Started for St. Luke's ch. Dinner at Phebe Brown's. All night at J. W. Miller's.

Sund. 5. Preached at St. Luke's ch. from Mark. 14:15-21. Baptized one infant. Lectured in afternoon from Is. 3:10.11. All night at D. M. Barrier's.

Mond. 6. Returned home. Dinner at Phebe Brown's.

Tues. 7. At home.

Wed. 8. Went a little while to the sale of Mrs. Lentz's property.

Thurs. 9. At home.

Frid. 10. At home till afternoon then called old Mr. Powlass.

Sat. 11. Started for Salem ch. Dinner at Phebe Brown's. All night at Jacob Klutts'.

Sund. 12. Preached at Salem ch. from Luk. 7:11-18. Dinner at M. A. Bost's. All night at John Rusher's.

Mond. 13. Went to Mrs. Jesse Lyerly's & took dinner. In afternoon went to Eli Powlass's and staid over night.

Tues. 14. At Mr. Powlass's till afternoon, then went to John Carson's and staid over night.

Wed. 15. Went to Unity Presbyterian Church & attended Rowan County Sunday School Convention. Returned to Mr. Carson's & staid over night.

Thurs. 16. At the convention at Unity church. Called in afternoon to see Moses Trexler, he being sick. Then went to Jesse Powlass' & staid over night.

Frid. 17. Went to Eli Powlass' and spent the day. All night here.

Sat. 18. An inclement day. At Mr. Powlass' till afternoon, then went to Pleasant M. Brown's and staid over night.

Sund. 19. Preached at St. Luke's ch. from Acts 24:16. All night at Sam[l] Colly's.

Mond. 20. Returned home. Dinner at Phebe Brown's. Called by the rock quarry to see several negroes who had met with a serious accident by the unexpected discharge of a blast.

Tues. 21. Wed. 22. Thurs. 23. At home.

Frid. 24. Went to Salisbury. Supper at Phebe Brown's. All night with Rev. Neiffer.

Sat. 25. Breakfast at Mr. Achenbach's. Went to Moses Trexler's & preached the funeral of his deceased wife from Heb. 4:9. All night at Widow Jesse Lyerly's.

Sund. 26. Preached at Salem ch. from Acts 24:16. Dinner at John Lingel's. Then went to Salisbury. Read service in Luth. ch. at night. Rev. Hubbert preached. All night at Phebe Brown's.

Mond. 27. Returned home.

Tues. 28. Went with wife to Cha[s] Fisher's. After dinner went to Foil's Tan Yard. Then returned home by way of Paul Cruse's. Rev. Neiffer with us to night.

Wed. 29. Went with Rev. Neiffer to Mt. Pleasant on business. Returned home.

Thurs. 30. At home.

Frid. Oct. 1. Started for St. Luke's ch. All night at George Cauble's.

Sat. 2. Went Alex.ʳ Brown's. Rev. Neiffer with me. Dinner to day at Mr. Achenbach's.

Sund. 3. Rev. Neiffer preached for me to day. Returned to Salisbury. All night at Phebe Brown's.

Mond. 4. Returned home.

Tues. 5. In afternoon went to Daniel Miller's & staid over night.

Wed. 6. Went to Mt. Pleasant & attended meeting of the Board of Trustees Of N. C. College. Stopped at Col. Shimpock's.

Thurs. 7. Returned home.

Frid. 8. At home.

Sat. 9. Started for Salem ch. Dinner at Phebe Brown's. All night at Charles Beaver's.

Sund. 10. Preached at Salem ch. from Matth. 22:1-14. Dinner at M. A. Bost's. All night at Phebe Brown's.

Mond. 11. In Salisbury. All night at Mrs. Brown's.

Tues. 12. Started for S. C. Synod. Took the cars for Columbia. All night at National Hotel.

Wed. 13. Took the Greenville cars for Prosperity in Newberry County. Dinner & all night at Mr. Boozer's.

Thurs. 14. Went to St. Luke's church to Synod. Had home assigned with Rev. J. D. Bowles.

Frid. 15. At Synod. Preached to day from Prov. 3:6.

Sat. 16. At Synod.

Sund. 17. Participated with Synod and congregation in public worship. In the evening returned to Prosperity. All night at Mr. Boozer's.

Mond. 18. Took the cars for Greenville on my homeward return. All night & supper at Dr. Berry's.

Tues. 19. Took the cars at 1 o'clock A.M. on Air Line Road for Salisbury. Took Breakfast at Charlotte Junction, reached Salisbury at 8 o'clock A.M. Remained in Salisbury till night. At night married Mr. John F. Eagle & Miss Addie H. Miller. Returned home after night.

Wed. 20. Went to Dr. Coleman's in the morning and brought valise home.

Thurs. 21. At home.

Frid. 22. Went to Salisbury Fair. All night at John Rusher's.

Sat. 23. Attended to the funeral of Mrs. Joseph Beaver at Salem ch. – preached from Eccl. 9:10. After an intermission held service preparatory to communion. All night at Widow John Berger's.

Sund. 24. Preached at Salem ch. from Prov. 3:6. Confirmed four persons. After an intermission administered the Holy Lord's Supper. All night at Phebe Brown's.

Mond. 25. Returned home. Phebe Brown with me. Had corn shucking this evening.

Tues. 26. At home. Aided in surveying land.

Wed. 27. Thurs. 28. Frid. 29. At home.

Sat. 30. Went to Gold Hill on business. Called also at Paul Beaver's & bought a little brandy.

Sund. 31. Preached at St. Peter's ch. from Prov. 3:6. the funeral of Mrs. Elizabeth Klutts dec.ᵈ Baptized also Thomas, Lewis' third child. In the evening took Phebe Brown & Jane Coleman to Dr. Coleman's.

Mond. Nov. 1. At home.

Tues. 2. In afternoon helped Solomon Peeler crib corn.

Wed. 3. Went in the morning to Mrs. Lentz's & bought 52 Bush. Corn & brought it home. In afternoon at home.

Thurs. 4. At home.

Frid. 5. Started for St. Luke's ch. Dinner at Phebe Brown's. All night at D. M. Barrier's.

Sat. 6. Preached at St. Luke's ch. from Prov. 4:18. preparatory to communion. Dinner at Alex. Brown's. In afternoon called to see Mrs. Thomas Goodman who was sick. Returned to Mr. Brown's and staid all night.

Sund. 7. Preached at St. Luke's ch. from Neh. 13:31. & administered the Lord's Supper. In the afternoon went to Eli Powlass' to see Calvin Powlass, he being very sick. All night here.

Mond. 8. Returned home. Dinner at Mrs. Brown's.

Tues. 9. Went to Salisbury to attend a congregational meeting in Luth. Church. All night at Mr. O'Neal's.

Wed. 10. Returned home.

Thurs. 11. At home.

Frid. 12. In forenoon went to Gold Hill to post office. In afternoon at home.

Sat. 13. Started for Salem ch. Dinner at Phebe Brown's. All night at John Lingel's.

Sund. 14. Preached at Salem ch. from Prov. 4:18. Dinner at Saml Seaford's. At night preached in Salisbury from Prov. 4:18. All night at Phebe Brown's.

Mond. 15. Dinner to day at Mr. Linton's. Baptized Mr. Linton's child at his house. In afternoon returned home.

Tues. 16. In forenoon went to mill. In afternoon at home.

Wed. 17. At home.

Thurs. 18. In forenoon went to mill and also to John Earnheart's to have pants made. In afternoon went to Gold Hill. Supper at Dr. Shimpock's. At night preached in Luth. Ch. from Jam. 1:25. Returned home after preaching.

Frid. 19. At home.

Sat. 20. Started for St. Luke's ch. Dinner at Phebe Brown's. All night at D. M. Barrier's.

Sund. 21. Preached at St. Luke's ch. from 1 Cor. 9:24-27. All night at Saml Colly's.

Mond. 22. Returned home. Dinner at Phebe Brown's.

Tues. 23. Went to Gold Hill to Post Office in forenoon. In afternoon at home.

Wed. 24. At home.

Thurs. 25. In forenoon went to Gold Hill to attend convention of delegates to arrange certain pastorates. In afternoon at home.

Frid. 26. This is my birthday. Sixty-six years old. At home all day. A rainy inclement day.

Sat. 27. Started for Salem ch. Dinner at Phebe Brown's, Salisbury. All night at Hampton Gheen's.

Sund. 28. Preached at Salem ch. from 1 Cor. 9:24-27. Dinner at Saml Seaford's. Preached at night in Salisbury from 1 Cor. 9:24-27. All night at Mr. O'Neal's.

Mond. 29. Returned home.

Tues. 30. At home. Made preparations for slaughtering hogs.

Wed. Dec. 1. At home. Slaughtered hogs.

Thurs. 2. At home till afternoon, then went to Gold Hill. Preached in Luth. ch. from 1 Cor. 9:24-27. Supper at Dr. Shimpock's. Returned home after preaching.

Frid. 3. At home.

Sat. 4. Started for St. Luke's ch. Dinner at Phebe Brown's. All night at John Harkey's.

Sund. 5. An inclement day. Preached at St. Luke's ch. from James 1:5. Very small attendance. Dinner & all night at Pleasant M. Brown's.

Mond. 6. Returned as far as Salisbury. Stopped at Mr. O'Neal's & staid till next morning. At night attended a congregational meeting in Luth. Church. Upon the second balloting Dr. Dosh was unanimously elected.

Tues. 7. Returned home. Rainy day.

Wed. 8. At home.

Thurs. 9. In afternoon went to Mrs. Catharine Barringer's & at night married Charles A. Miller & Ellen E. A. Barringer. After supper returned home.

Frid. 10. In forenoon called to see Eli Miller, he being indisposed. In afternoon at home.

Sat. 11. Started for Salem ch. Dinner at Phebe Brown's. All night at M. A. Bost's.

Sund. 12. Preached at Salem ch. from Jam. 1:5. Dinner at John Lingel's. At night preached in Salisbury from Acts 24:16. All night at Mr. O'Neal's.

Mond. 13. Returned home.

Tues. 14. At home. In afternoon sent my wagon to Mt. Pleasant with some flour &c. for Lewis.

Wed. 15. Called in forenoon to see Eli Miller. In afternoon at home.

Thurs. 16. At home making a bridle.

Frid. 17. At home.

Sat. 18. A very cold day. Started for St. Luke's.

[The rest of this book is missing. The next one begins with 1876.]

Sat. Jan. 1. At home.

Sund. 2. Preached at St. Stephen's ch. from Prov. 3:6. Baptized one inf.[t] Returned home after preaching.

Mond. 3. Went to Salisbury. Dinner at Phebe Brown's. Returned home.

Wed. 4. At home till 12 o'clock, then went to Gold Hill to Post Office. Col. Shimpock with us to night.

Wed. 5. In forenoon went to mill. In afternoon at home.

Thurs. 6. Frid. 7. At home.

Sat. 8. In forenoon went to mill. In afternoon at home.

Sund. 9. Preached at Organ ch. from 1 Tim. 6:6. Congregation large. Dinner at Dr. Coleman's.

Mond. 10. In afternoon went to Gold Hill to Post Office.

Tues. 11. Wed. 12. At Milas A. Holshouser's at the rolling of old houses.

Thurs. 13. In afternoon went to Gold Hill to Post Office.

Frid. 14. At home mending shoes.

Sat. 15. Went to Sandy Misenheimer's in Stanly Co. All night here.

Sund. 16. Preached at Old Bethel ch. from 1 Cor. 9:24-27. Dinner at Philip Ridenhour's. At night preached at New Bethel ch. from Prov. 23:26. All night at Philip Ridenhower's.

Mond. 17. Returned home.

Tues. 18. Went with wife to Salisbury. All night at Phebe Brown's.

Wed. 19. Returned home. Dinner at Dr. Coleman's.

Thurs. 20. Went to Cotton Gin & Sawmill.

Frid. 21. In afternoon went to Lentz's mill & engaged some bran. Then took some milk to Dr. Coleman's.

Sat. 22. In forenoon went to mill. In afternoon at home.

Sund. 23. Preached at Organ ch. from Matth. 8:1-4. Dinner at Mrs. Mary A. Heilig's. In evening returned home.

Mond. 24. Went to Salisbury.

Tues. 25. At home. B. Arey with us.

Wed. 26. In forenoon went to mill. In afternoon at home. Mrs. Heilig and Mrs. Dreher with us to day. B. Arey & Jane Coleman with us to night.

Thurs. 27. At home.

Frid. 28. Went to Salisbury to meet the Eastern Conference. Returned home.

Sat. 29. Went to Mt. Pleasant to meet the Western Conference. Preached at night from 1 Cor. [9]:24-27. All night at Lewis'.

Sund. 30. In Mt. Pleasant. Dinner at Rev. J. B. Davis', D.D. All night at Maj. L. G. Heilig's.

Mond. 31. Returned home. Brought Sammy & Bettie along.

Tues. Feb. 1. Went to Mt. Pleasant to attend meeting of Board of Trustees of N. C. College. All night at Col. Shimpock's.

Wed. 2. Attended meeting of Board of Trustees of N. C. College. All night at Lewis'.

Thurs. 3. Returned home. Dinner at G. M. Bernhardt's. Brought Lottie Coleman along. A cold day.

Frid. 4. Sat. 5. At home.

Sund. 6. Preached at St. Stephen's ch. from Acts 24:16. An inclement day. Returned home.

Mond. 7. Started for Salem ch. to attend to the fun^{l} of Moses Trexler, dec^{d}. All night at Phebe Brown's.

Tues. 8. Went to Salem ch. & preached the fun^{l} of Moses Trexler dec^{d}. Dinner at Saml Seaford's. All night at John Lingel's.

Wed. 9. Returned home.

Thurs. 10. In morning went to Jacob Holshouser's to engage some Oats. In afternoon went to Dr. Coleman's & brought wife home.

Frid. 11. At home.

Sat. 12. Went to Gold Hill to Post Office.

Sund. 13. Preached at Organ ch. from Matth. 20:6. Dinner at Jesse Miller's. Returned home.

Mond. 14. Went to J. Powlass' & settled blacksmith account. Dinner here. Returned by way of Gold Hill & got mail matter.

Tues. 15. At home.

Wed. 16. In forenoon cleaned wheat & went to mill. In afternoon at home, had company, M. Shemwell & wife & Mrs. Grupy.

Thurs. 17. At home.

Frid. 18. In the morning went to mill. Balance of day at home, had company.

Sat. 19. Started for Bethel ch. Stanly Co. All night at Philip Ridenhower's.

Sund. 20. Preached at Bethel ch.(new) from Prov. 29:1. Baptized 2 infants. Returned home.

Mond. 21. At home. A very rainy day. Very unwell with severe cold.

Tues. 22. Called to see David Earnheart, he being very sick. Called also at the Post Office at Gold Hill.

Wed. 23. Went in forenoon to Eagle's Shop. In afternoon at home.

Thurs. 24. Went to Gold Hill to Post Office & to Bunn's Shop to have lock repaired. Called also to see David Earnheart.

Frid. 25. Went in afternoon to Eagle's shop & had horse shod.

Sat. 26. At home till evening, then went to mill. Rev. Cone with us to night.

Sund. 27. Preached at Organ ch. from Luk. 18:38. Baptized 3 inf^{ts}.

Mond. 28. In forenoon went to Gold Hill to Post Office. In afternoon at home.

Tues. 29. Went to Salisbury. Dinner at Mrs. Brown's. Supper at Dr. Coleman's.

Wed. March 1. In afternoon went to Gold Hill on business.

Thurs. 2. Frid. 3. Sat. 4. At home.

Sund. 5. Preached at St. Stephen's ch. from Matth. 4:1-11. Baptized one infant. Returned home.

Mond. 6. In forenoon went to Gold Hill to Blacksmith shop & to Post Office. In the afternoon went to Mich[1] Holshouser's & brought David Lyerly's trunk. After supper went to Dr. Coleman's, having been sent for. Returned home again.

Tues. 7. Went to Salisbury.

Wed. 8. In afternoon went with wife & some friends to see Gold Hill.

Thurs. 9. In the morning went to mill. In afternoon went to Dr. Coleman's, having been sent for. Returned in evening.

Frid. 10. At home. Rev. R. L. Brown's with us to day. Settled with him as Treasurer of Eastern Conference.

Sat. 11. At home.

Sund. 12. Preached at Organ ch. from Gal. 6:9. Dinner at Jacob Miller's.

Mond. 13. In forenoon went to Gold Hill to Post Office. In afternoon went to Salisbury. Took Phebe Brown home. All night here.

Tues. 14. Dinner at Phebe Brown's. In afternoon returned home.

Wed. 15. At home. Sowed clover seed and orchard grass seed.

Thurs. 16. Rainy till 12 o'clock. In afternoon went to Gold Hill to Post Office.

Frid. 17. Took some flour & lard to William Beaver's for Lewis.

Sat. 18. In the afternoon went to Solomon Richie's & staid all night.

Sund. 19. Preached Bethel ch. Stanly Co. from Gal. 6:9. Baptized one infant. Dinner at Isom Misenheimer's. Then returned home.

Mond. 20. In afternoon went to to Gold Hill to Post Office.

Tues. 21. Wed. 22. At home.

Thurs. 23. In afternoon went to Gold Hill to Post Office.

Frid. 24. At home.

Sat. 25. In afternoon went to Jesse Miller's on business.

Sund. 26. Preached at Organ ch. from Gen. 6:9. Baptized five infants. Dinner at Crawford A. Miller's. In the afternoon preached at Elm Grove School house from Matth. 11:28. Returned home.

Mond. 27. In afternoon went to Gold Hill to Post Office.

Tues. 28. Wed. 29. At home.

Thurs. 30. In afternoon went to Gold Hill to Post Office.

Frid. 31. At home.

Sat. Apr. 1. Preached at St. Stephen's ch. from Matth. 19:14. fun[1] & preparatory. Dinner at Solomon Nussman's. All night at Caleb L. Nussman's.

Sund. 2. Preached at St. Stephen's ch. from Numb. 10:29. & administered the Holy Supper. Returned home.

Mond. 3. In afternoon went to Gold Hill to Post Office.

Tues. 4. Went to Mt. Pleasant. All night at Lewis'.

Wed. 5. Attended a meeting of the Board of Trustees of N. C. College. Dinner at Alexander Foil's. All night at Col. Shimpock's.

Thurs. 6. Returned home.

Frid. 7. In afternoon went to Salisbury. All night at Phebe Brown's.

Sat. 8. Went to Davie County. All night at Mr. Cartner's.

Sund. 9. Went to St. Matthew's church. Dedicated the Church, being assisted by other ministers. In the afternoon preached from Matth. 11:28. Aided in the administration of the Holy Supper. Returned as far as Tobias File's & staid over night.

Mond. 10. Returned home. Dinner at Phebe Brown's.

Tues. 11. Took Sarah A. Flory to Salisbury. Dinner at Phebe Brown's.

Wed. 12. At home. Had piazza covered.

Thurs. 13. In the morning went to Dr. Coleman's for medicine. In afternoon went to Gold Hill to Post Office.

Frid. 14. Went to Union Church & assisted in laying the corner stone of a new church.

Sat. 15. Went to Bethel ch. in Stanly Co. & preached from Ps. 51:17. preparatory to communion. Baptized one infant. All at Clayborn Misenheimer's.

Sund. 16. Preached at Bethel ch. from 1 Cor. 15:20. Confirmed one person & administered the Lord's Supper. Returned home.

Mond. 17. Attended Sunday School celebration at St. Peter's ch.

Tues. 18. In forenoon went to Gold Hill to Post Office. In afternoon at home.

Wed. 19. At home.

Thurs. 20. Attended to the burial of Rev. Wm. Artz, at St. John's ch.

Frid. 21. In forenoon went to Gold Hill to Post Office.

Sat. 22. Had preparatory service at Organ ch. Rev. W. W. Cone preached. Baptized 1 inf[t] & confirmed 3 person's. Returned home.

Sund. 23. Had communion at Organ ch. Rev. Cone preached in forenoon. Dinner at Mrs. Barringer's. In afternoon Rev. F. W. Dosh, D.D. addressed the congregation & consecrated the elements, after which the communion was administered. Called in the afternoon at Jesse Miller's & administered the communion to Eve Ann Miller, she being sick.

Mond. 24. At home.

Tues. 25. Took family to Gold Hill and had Photographs taken.

Wed. 26. Returned tax in forenoon. In afternoon went to H. A. Miller's on business & had a severe chill & had to remain over night.

Thurs. 27. Returned home by way of Dr. Coleman's.

Frid. 28. At home.

Sat. 29. In the evening went to Gold Hill & at night preached in Luth. ch. from Gen. 6:9. All night at Dr. Shimpock's.

Sund. 30. Preached at St. Stephen's ch. from Gen. 6:9. Dinner at Dr. Shimpock's. In afternoon preached in Luth. ch. at Gold Hill from Matth. 21:28. Returned home.

Mond. May 1. Started for Synod. Went to Rev. Cone's & took dinner. Took a seat in Rev. Cone's buggy. Called by Mrs. Artz's & went to Rev. Kimball's & staid all night.

Tues. 2. Went to St. Enoch's ch. the seat of Synod. Preached the Synodical sermon from Matth. 21:28. read my report and organized Synod. Had lodgings assigned at Hampton Overcash's.

Wed. 3. Thurs. 4. In Synod.

Frid. 5. In Synod. All night at Mr. Plaster's.

Sat. 6. In Synod. Entered my protest against refunding money to Rev. J. S. Heilig.

Sund. 7. Attended preaching in St. Enoch's ch. Returned in the evening to Capt. Jacob Fisher's and staid over night.

Mond. 8. Returned home by way of Salisbury. Dinner at Phebe Brown's.

Tues. 9. At home.

Wed. 10. Bought & brought home 50 bush. corn from Mrs. Lentz's. In afternoon went to And^r Berger's on business.

Thurs. 11. Went with wife to Gold Hill and had her Photograph taken.

Frid. 12. In the morning went to Mrs. Cath. Earnheart's & drew up a lease for one acre of land for Henry Williams.

Sat. 13. Had catechization at Organ ch. Called to see Luther Miller's child, it being very sick. Called also to see Eve Ann Miller, she being much afflicted. Dinner at Danl Miller's.

Sund. 14. Preached at Organ ch. from Rev. 3:20. Baptized 1 infant. Dinner at Mrs. Cath. Barringer's. In afternoon went to Salisbury. At night attended preaching in Luth. Church. All night at Phebe Brown's.

Mond. 15. Returned home. Brought Lillian Brown along. Supper at Dr. Coleman's.

Tues. 16. At home, sheared the sheep.

Wed. 17. Attended to the funeral of Luther Miller's child at Organ ch.— preached from Matth. 5:8. Dinner at Mary A. Heilig's.

Thurs. 18. In forenoon went to Gold Hill to post office. In afternoon went to Jesse Miller's, to see Eva Ann Miller, she being sick.

Frid. 19. Went to Salisbury.

Sat. 20. In afternoon went to Tobias Plyler's in Stanly Co. & staid over night.

Sund. 21. Preached at Bethel ch. from Ps. 116:12-14. the funeral of Elizabeth Sides dec^d. After an intermission lectured on our mode of worship. Returned home.

Mond. 22. Went to Mt. Pleasant to College Commencement. All night at Lewis'.

Tues. 23. In Mt. Pleasant. Dinner & over night at Col. Shimpock's.

Wed. 24. In Mt. Pleasant. Dinner & over night at Col. Shimpock's.

Thurs. 25. Returned home.

Frid. 26. At home.

Sat. 27. Had catechization at Organ Church. Returned home.

Sund. 28. Preached at Organ ch. from Ps. 116:12-14. Baptized one infant. Dinner at Calvin Brown's. In afternoon preached at Elm Grove School House from Mark 10:46-52. Returned home.

Mond. 29. Went to J. Powlass' shop & to Gold Hill to Post Office.

Tues. 30. Went to J. Powlass' shop & had horses shod. Dinner here.

Wed. 31. Took horse to Mt. Pleasant for Lewis to come home. All night at Lewis'.

Thurs. Jun. 1. Attended to the fun[l] of Eve Ann Miller at Organ ch. — preached from Heb. 4:9.

Frid. 2. Went to Dan[l] Miller's & settled note of hand. Dinner here.

Sat. 3. At home.

Sund. 4. Preached at St. Stephen's ch. from Matth. 11:29.30. Inclement day.

Mond. 5. Attended to the funeral of Crawford Peeler's child at Lower Stone Church, — preached from Ps. 50:15.

Tues. 6. Went to Gold Hill to Post Office.

Wed. 7. Thurs. 8. Frid. 9. At home, hay making.

Sund. 10. Had catechization at Organ Church.

Sund. 11. Preached at Organ ch. from 1 Pet. 5:4. the funeral of Rev. William Artz, dec[d]. Baptized 2 infants. Dinner at Dan[l] Miller's. In the afternoon preached at Elm Grove School House from 2 Cor. 5:17.

Mond. 12. In forenoon went to Gold Hill to Post Office. In afternoon at home.

Tues. 13. At home.

Wed. 14. Went to Salisbury. Dinner at Phebe Brown's.

Thurs. 15. In forenoon went to Gold Hill to Post Office. In afternoon at home.

Frid. 16. At home.

Sat. 17. Went to Bethel ch. in Stanly Co. — had catechization appointed, but the day being very rainy no one attended. Staid over night at David Lyerly's.

Sund. 18. Preached at Bethel church from Luk. 16:19-31. Baptized one infant. In the afternoon went to Daniel Miller's, having received a message of his death. In the evening went to Col. Shimpock's & staid over night.

Mond. 19. Attended to the funeral of Dan[l] Miller at St. John's church — preached from 1 Thes. 4:14. Returned Mr. Miller's late residence & took dinner. Returned home in afternoon.

Tues. 20. Went to Gold Hill to Post Office in forenoon. In afternoon at home.

Wed. 21. After dinner went to mill.

Thurs. 22. In the morning went to mill. Balance of day at home.

Frid. 23. At home.

Sat. 24. Had catechization at Organ Church. Dinner at Andrew Cruse's. Called to see Mrs. Reuben Bost, she being very sick. All night at Paul Klutts'.

Sund. 25. Preached at Organ ch. from Luk. 14:22. Dinner at David L. Brown's. In the afternoon preached at Elm Grove School House from Luk. 13:24. Returned home.

Mond. 26. Attended to the funeral of Mrs. Reuben Bost — preached from Matth. 5:6. Dinner at Mary A. Heilig's.

Tues. 27. In forenoon went to Gold Hill to Post Office. In afternoon at home.

Wed. 28. In forenoon went to H. A. Miller's on business. In afternoon at home.

Thurs. 29. Attended to the funeral of Mrs. Solomon Fisher at Organ ch.— preached from Is. 40:6-8. Dinner Catharine Barringer's.

Frid. 30. Went to Salisbury. Dinner at Phebe Brown's. Was prevented by rain from getting home. All night at Alfred Trexler's.

Sat. July 1. Returned home to breakfast.

Sund. 2. Preached at St. Stephen's ch. from Luk. 14:22. After an intermission lectured on Book of Worship. Returned home.

Mond. 3. Went to Gold Hill to Post Office.

Tues. 4. At home. Rev. Dosh, D.D. with us over night.

Wed. 5. At home.

Thurs. 6. In forenoon went to Gold Hill to Post Office.

Frid. 7. At home. Had spring house repaired.

Sat. 8. Had catechization at Organ ch. Dinner & over night at Paul Cruse's.

Sund. 9. Preached at Organ ch. from Eph. 6:1-4. Dinner at Simeon Miller's. In the afternoon preached at Elm Grove School House from 1 Pet. 4:18. Returned home.

Mond. 10. Attended to the funeral of Reuben Bost's child at Organ ch. preached from 2 Sam. 12:23. Dinner at Cath. Barringer's.

Tues. 11. Wed 12. Thurs. 13. At home.

Frid. 14. In the forenoon attended to the funeral of Mrs. Jacob Berger at Organ ch. — preached from Job. 23:16. Dinner at Mrs. M. A. Heilig's. In the afternoon attended to the funeral of John A. W. Bost at Organ ch. — preached from Amos. 4:12. Returned home. Baptized also to day Jacob Berger's infant child.

Sat. 15. In the afternoon went Alexander Meisenheimer's & staid over night.

Sund. 16. Preached at Bethel ch. from Eph. 6:14. Baptized one infant. After intermission, lectured on Book of Worship. Returned home.

Mond. 17. In forenoon went to Gold Hill to Post Office.

Tues. 18. Wed. 19. Thurs. 20. At home.

Frid. 21. Went to Salisbury. Dinner at Mrs. Brown's.

Sat. 22. Had catechization at Organ Church.

Sund. 23. Preached at Organ ch. from 2 Tim. 1:13. Dinner at Boyden Miller's. In afternoon preached at Elm Grove School House from Acts 16:16-31.

Mond. 24. In afternoon went to Gold Hill to Post Office.

Tues. 25. In forenoon went to Gold Hill to Post Office.

Wed. 26. At home, wife still very indisposed.

Thurs. 27. Went to St. Stephen's ch. it being the day appointed to arbitrate Rev. Strobel's claim of salary.

Frid. 28. Went to St. Stephen's ch. to attend meeting of Western Conference. Returned home in evening. Wife sick.

Sat. 29. At St. Stephen's ch. Returned home in afternoon. In the evening attended to the burial of James Trexler's child at St. Peter's ch. Wife sick.

Sund. 30. At St. Stephen's ch.

Mond. 31. In afternoon went to Gold Hill to Post Office. Wife still sick.

Tues. Aug. 1. At home. Wife very sick.

Wed. 2. At home attending to wife.

Thurs. 3. At home. Wife very sick. Sent to Mt Pleasant for Lewis.

Frid. 4. Sent to Salisbury for Lee and for Dr. Whitehead. Wife very sick.

Sat. 5. Sund. 6. At home, wife sick.

Mond. 7. Tues. 8. Wed. 9. Thurs. 10. Frid. 11. At home.

Sat. 12. Wife convalescing. Had catechization at Organ ch.

Sund. 13. In the morning, on the way to Organ ch. married John W. Miller & Eve Ann Maria Reimer. Preached at Organ ch. from Numb. 10:29. Dinner at Joseph Miller's.

Mond. 14. Tues. 15. Wed. 16. At home.

Thurs. 17. In the afternoon went to H. M. Isenhour's & married James C. Sides & Martha J. Isenhour. Then went in company with Rev. Kimball to Philip Ridenhour's & staid over night.

Frid. 18. At Bethel church. Rev. Kimball preached morning & afternoon. Then returned home.

Sat. 19. Went to Bethel church. Rev. Kimball preached. All night at Sandy Misenheimer's.

Sund. 20. At Bethel ch. Rev. Kimball preached in forenoon & Rev. Anthony in afternoon. Returned home.

Mond. 21. Tues. 22. At home.

Wed. 23. Took Mrs. Phebe Brown to Salisbury. Returned to Shiloh church to Sund. School Convention. Returned home.

Thurs. 24. Frid. 25. At home.

Sat. 26. Had catechization at Organ ch.

Sund. 27. Preached at Organ ch. from Luk. 18:13. Dinner at Laurence Lingel's.

Mond. 28. Tues. 29. At home. Wed. 30. At home.

Thurs. 31. Went to Salisbury.

Frid. Sept. 1. Went to St. Paul's ch. to assist Rev. Kimball at a Protracted meeting, preached in forenoon from Matth. 11:28. Preached at night from Luk. 13:24. Over night at Allison Misenheimer's.

Sat. 2. Preached in forenoon from Gen. 6:22. & in afternoon from Ex. 33:14. Returned home.

Sund. 3. Preached at St. Stephen's ch. from 1 Tim. 6:6. Baptized one infant. Dinner at home. Returned to St. Paul's ch. Heard Rev. Petrea preach. All night at Allison Misenheimer's.

Mond. 4. Preached from Jer. 17:9. 2 Cor. 13:5. Returned home in the evening.

Tues. 5. Sent money to Cook & Lutz by Adolphus Linn. Went to steam mill, & to Post Office at Gold Hill & registered a letter with $65 to News Publishing Co. at Raleigh to pay for printing of Minutes. In afternoon went to Mt. Pleasant. All night at Lewis'.

Wed. 6. Attended meeting of the Board of Trustees of College. Dinner at Col. Shimpock's. All night at Lewis'.

Thurs. 7. Returned home.

Frid. 8. Engaged hands to mow grass and went to mill.

Sat. 9. Had catechization at Organ ch.

Sund. 10. Preached at Organ C. from Rom. 10:1. Dinner at Crawford Miller's. In the afternoon lectured at Elm Grove School House.

Mond. 11. Had hands to mow grass. Went to Gold Hill to Post Office, & called also to see Mr. Powlass at John Powlass', he being old & in feeble health.

Tues. 12. Wed. 13. Thurs. 14. Frid. 15. At home making hay. Weather very unfavorable.

Sat. 16. At home.

Sund. 17. Preached at Bethel ch. Stanly, from Rom. 10:1. the funeral Mr. Ewing's child, dec^{d} Dinner at Mr. Ewing's. Baptized to day one inf^{t}

Mond. 18. At home haying.

Tues. 19. Engaged hands to mow grass. Went to Gold Hill to Post Office.

Wed. 20. At home.

Thurs. 21. In forenoon went to Gold Hill to Post Office. Afternoon at home.

Frid. 22. In forenoon went to Gold Hill on business & to Post Office.

Sat. 23. Had catechization at Organ ch.

Sund. 24. Preached at Organ ch from 1 Thes. 2:11.12. Baptized one infant. Dinner at Danl Miller's. In afternoon preached at Elm Grove from Rev. 2:4.5.

Mond. 25. At home haying till evening, then went to Gold Hill to Post Office.

Tues. 26. Took wife to Salisbury.

Wed. 27. At home, hauled hay.

Thurs. 28. At home, finished haying.

Frid. 29. Went to Steam Mill & Post Office.

Sat. 30. At home.

Sund. Oct. 1. Preached at St. Stephen's ch. from Gen. 6:22. Returned home.

Mond. 2. In forenoon went to Joseph Eagle's. In afternoon to Gold Hill to Isaac Earnheart's & John Powlass'.

Tues. 3. In afternoon went to Mt. Pleasant. All night Lewis'.

Wed. 4. Attended meeting of Board of Trustees of N. C. College. Dinner & supper at Col. Shimpock's. All night at Lewis'.

Thurs. 5. Returned home. In afternoon took Dr. Dosh to Salisbury. All night at Phebe Brown's.

Frid. 6. Attended to some business for Phebe Brown. In afternoon returned home.

Sat. 7. Had catechization at Organ ch.

Sund. 8. Preached at Organ ch. from Prov. 29:1. Dinner at Mary A. Heilig's. In the afternoon preached at Elm Grove from Matth. 22:1-14.

Mond. 9. Went to Paul Beaver's in forenoon for some brandy distilled on shares. In afternoon at home.

Tues. 10. In forenoon went to Gold Hill to Post Office. In afternoon at home.

Wed. 11. Went to Salisbury to lecture for Dr. Dosh at night, but thro' misunderstanding the church was not opened. All night at Phebe Brown's.

Thurs. 12. Returned home. Shucked corn to night.

Frid. 13. In forenoon went to Gold Hill to Post Office. In afternoon at home.

Sat. 14. Went to Bethel ch. Stanly co. & preached from Jer. 17:9. 2 Cor. 13:5. preparatory to communion. All night at John A. Troutman's.

Sund. 15. Preached at Bethel ch. from 1 Thes. 2:11.12. Baptized two infants, confirmed 2 persons, & administered the Lord's Supper. Returned home.

Mond. 16. In afternoon went to Danl Frick's to engage him to repair clocks.

Tues. 17. Went to Steam mill, also to Gold Hill to Post Office.

Wed. 18. At home till dinner. In afternoon took Phebe Brown to Salisbury.

Thurs. 19. At home, had Mr. Frick to repair clock's.

Frid. 20. Had catechization at Organ church.

Sat. 21. Had preparatory services at Organ church, Rev. T. W. Dosh, D.D. preached. Baptized one infant & confirmed eight persons. Dinner at Mary A. Heilig's. Returned home.

Sund. 22. At Organ ch. Rev. Dosh, D.D. preached in interesting Reformation Sermon. After intermission had communion. Returned home.

Mond. 23. Went to Gold Hill to Post Office.

Tues. 24. Went in forenoon to Steam Mill.

Wed. 25. Went in forenoon to M. A. Holshouser's for some putty to put in a window light. Caleb Peeler with us to night.

Thurs. 26. At home.

Frid. 27. Went to St. John's church to Western Conference. Rev. Kimball, Pres^{t}, preached the opening sermon. All night at Lewis' in Mt. Pleasant.

Sat. 28. At Conference, Rev. Bikle, D.D. preached. All night at Col. Shimpock's.

Sund. 29. At St. John's ch. Dr. Davis preached a Reformation Sermon. Attended to opening services & assisted in the administration of the Lord's Supper. Returned home.

Mond. 30. In forenoon called by Rufus Beaver's & went to Gold Hill to Post Office. At night went to Sol. Peeler's to shucking.

Tues. 31. At home.

Wed. Nov. 1. Thurs. 2. At home.

Frid. 3. Went to Steam Mill & Post Office.

Sat. 4. Had preparatory service at St. Stephen's ch. — preached from Matth. 11:28. Baptized two infants & confirmed one person.

Sund. 5. At St. Stephen's ch. Rev. Davis, D.D. preached a Reformation Sermon. After intermission administered the communion being assisted by Dr. Davis & Prof. Hubbert. Returned home.

Mond. 6. Attended to the funeral of Mrs. Paul Holshouser at Organ ch. preached from Ps. 39:4.

Tues. 7. Went to Morgan's to election. In afternoon at home.

Wed. 8. At home.

Thurs. 9. Went to Barringer's mill.

Frid. 10. At home.

Sat. 11. Had catechization at Organ ch.

Sund. 12. Attended to the funeral of William Powlass dec[d] at Lower Stone Church — preached from Ps. 58:11. Dinner at Mary A. Heilig's.

Mond. 13. Went to Barringer's mill.

Tues. 14. Went to George Peeler's & to Mr. Shemwell's.

Wed. 15. Went to Salisbury.

Thurs. 16. At home.

Frid. 17. Went to Gold Hill to Post Office.

Sat. 18. Called at John Powlass'— Dinner here. Then went to Mr. Lefler's & staid over night.

Sund. 19. Preached at Bethel ch. Stanly Co. from Matth. 4:16. on the subject of the Reformation. Returned home.

Mond. 20. Went by Rufus Beaver's to Gold Hill to Post Office & had Lucy shod.

Tues. 21. Wed. 22. At home.

Thurs. 23. Attended to the fun[l] of D. L. Bost's child at Lower Stone Church — preached from 1 Thes. 4:14. Dinner at Boyden Miller's. Returned home by way of Post Office at Gold Hill.

Frid. 24. At home.

Sat. 25. Had catechization at Organ church.

Sund. 26. Preached at Organ ch. from John 5:40. This my birthday. Dinner at Laurence Lingel's.

Mond. 27. Went to Salisbury.

Tues. 28. At home till afternoon, then went to mill.

Wed. 29. Went to Mt. Pleasant to attend meeting of the Board of Trustees of N. C. College. Dinner at Lewis'. Supper at Col. J. Shimpock's. All night at Lewis'.

Thurs. 30. Went to Solomon Fisher's and married Luther C. Miller & Laura A. Bost. Infare supper at Daniel Miller's.

Frid. Dec. 1. In forenoon went to mill. In afternoon at home.

Sat. 2. At home.

Sund. 3. Preached at St. Stephen's ch. from Is. 35:8-10.

Mond. 4. In forenoon went to Gold Hill to shoemaker & Post Office. In afternoon went to M. A. Holshouser's on business.

Tues. 5. In the morning went to Mrs. Lentz's & paid note of hand. Balance of the day at home.

Wed. 6. Went to Salisbury & entered in as Guardian for Elizabeth Thomas. Dinner at Phebe Brown's.

Thurs. 7. In afternoon went to mill.

Frid. 8. Went by way of Gold Hill to Mary A. Heilig's to assist in dividing land between Albert & Adolphus Heilig. All night here.

Sat. 9. Had catechization at Organ ch.

Sund. 10. Preached at Organ ch. from Hosea 6:4.

Mond. 11. At home. To day Rev. R. L. Brown called, by request, & baptized my ward, Elizabeth Thomas.

Tues. 12. In afternoon went to Mt. Pleasant. All night at Lewis'.

Wed. 13. Attended meeting of Board of Trustees of N. C. College. Dinner and all night at Col. Shimpock's.

Thurs. 14. Returned home.

Frid. 15. Went in forenoon to Gold Hill to Post Office. In afternoon at home.

Sat. 16. In afternoon went to Caleb Moose's & staid all night.

Sund. 17. Preached at Bethel ch. Stanly Co. from Hosea 6:4. Returned home.

Mond. 18. Slaughtered my winter hogs.

Tues. 19. In forenoon went to Gold Hill to Post Office. Afternoon at home.

Wed. 20. At home.

Thurs. 21. In forenoon went to Gold Hill to Post Office. In the evening went to M. A. Holshouser's to engage him to take wife & Emma to Mt. Pleasant on following day. Supper here.

Frid. 22. At home. Sent wife & Emma to Mt. Pleasant.

Sat. 23. At home.

Sund. 24. Had an appointment at Organ church, but in consequence of a severe snow storm did not attend. At home.

Mond. 25. Christmas Day. Had and appointment for Elm Grove School House but did not attend on account of snow. Called to see M. A. Holshouser to make arrangements to bring Wife & Emma home.

Tues. 26. At home.

Wed. 27. At home. Wife & Emma returned.

Thurs. 28. Went to & settled with D. Brady. Balance of day at home.

Frid. 29. Called & settled with M. A. Holshouser. Called also at Dr. Coleman's.

Sat. 30. At home. At night attended the Christmas Tree exercises at St. Peter's ch.

Sund. 31. This being the fifth Sunday, had no appointment for the day. At home all day. Snow on the ground.

Mond. Jan. 1. At home. A severe snow storm to day.

Tues. 2. Wed. 3. Thurs. 4. Frid. 5. At home. Weather very inclement with deep snow on the ground.

Sat. 6. At home.

Sund. 7. Preached at St. Stephen's church from Rom. 10:1. Weather inclement.

Mond. 8. Went in the morning to O. W. Hampton's and baptized his two children. Returned by way of Post Office. In afternoon went to Gold Hill on business.

Tues. 9. Took Bettie Thomas to Mt. Pleasant to school. All night at Lewis'.

Wed. 10. Attended a meeting of the Board of Trustees of N. C. College. Dinner at Capt. A. Foil's. All night at Col. Shimpock's.

Thurs. 11. Returned home.

Frid. 12. Sat 13. At home.

Sund. 14. Preached at Organ ch. from Heb. 1:14. Baptized one infant. Dinner at Mary A. Heilig's.

Mond. 15. Went with Lottie Coleman to Salisbury in Lawson Trexler's wagon. Left Lottie at Mrs. Shuman's. Supper at Phebe Brown's. All night at Boyden House.

Tues. 16. Took Lottie Coleman to Statesville to school. Breakfast at St. Charles Hotel. Dinner at Lansing White's. Returned in afternoon to Salisbury. All night at Phebe Brown's.

Wed. 17. Returned home as far as Dr. Coleman's. Over night here.

Thurs. 18. Returned home. In afternoon went to Post Office.

Frid. 19. At home.

Sat. 20. Went to Sandy Misenheimer's in Stanly Co. & staid over night.

Sund. 21. Preached at Bethel ch. Stanly co. from Heb. 1:14. Returned home.

Mond. 22. Tues. 23. At home.

Wed. 24. Went to M. A. Holshouser's to have kitchen lock repaired. To day my Lamer horse get his leg broke by being kicked. Got M. A. Holshouser to kill him, & Mr. Brady to drag him away.

Thurs. 25. Got some cedar posts to fix up grape vine, & some timber to make some addition to barn.

Frid. 16. At home.

Sat. 27. Had catechization at Organ church.

Sund. 28. Preached at Organ ch. from 1 Cor. 9:24-27.

Mond. 29. In forenoon went to Gold Hill to Post Office. In afternoon at home.

Tues. 30. Wed. 31. At home.

Thurs. Feb. 1. At home. Fixed up grape vine.

Frid. 2. In forenoon went to Gold Hill to Post Office. In afternoon at home.

Sat. 3. Went to D. Barringer's mill.

Sund. 4. Preached at St. Stephen's ch. from Luk. 8:18. Returned home.

Mond. 5. Went to Gold Hill to Post Office, & to Joseph Beaver's to engage him to make boards.

Tues. 6. Wed. 7. At home.

Thurs. 8. In afternoon went to Post Office.

Frid. 9. Went to Salisbury.

Sat. 10. Had catechization at Organ ch.

Sund. 11. Preached at Organ ch. from Heb. 10:24. Returned home after preaching.

Mond. 12. Went to E. Foil's Tan Yard amd settled tanning, bought blind bridle, &c.

Tues. 13. Took M. A. Holshouser's board cleaver home, & then went to Gold Hill to Post Office.

Wed. 14. In the morning went to Mr. Holshouser's for 2 stick brooms. Balance of day at home.

Thurs. 15. Went to J. Powlass' & had shoeing done. In afternoon went to Nussman's Foundry & then returned home.

Frid. 16. Went by way of Gold Hill to Mrs. Bost's & brought carpet home.

Sat. 17. Went in afternoon to Claborn Misenheimer's & staid over night.

Sund. 18. Preached at Bethel ch. from Matth. 4:1-11. Returned home after preaching.

Mond. 19. Attended to the funeral Moses Bost's child at Organ ch.— preached the funeral at the house from Eph. 5:16.

Tues. 20. In afternoon went to Mt. Pleasant. All night at Lewis'.

Wed. 21. Attended the meeting of the Board of Trustees of N. C. College. Dinner at Col. J. Shimpock's. All night at Lewis'.

Thurs. 22. Returned home. In afternoon went to Gold Hill to Post Office.

Frid. 23. In afternoon went to H. A. Miller's & paid a note of hand.

Sat. 24. Had catechization at Organ ch.

Sund. 25. Preached at Organ ch. from Luk. 8:18. the funeral of Martin A. Weaver's infant son, dec[d]. Baptized on infant.

Mond. 26. Went to Barringer's mill.

Tues. 27. Went to Salisbury. Dinner at Mrs. Phebe Brown's.

Wed. 28. Attended to the funeral of Mrs. Polly Canup, relict of Dr. John Canup, at St. Matthew's ch. — preached from Eph. 5:16.

Thurs. March 1. Went to Gold hill to Post Office & to J. Powlass' shop. Sold Molly (mare) to day to George Bame for $100.

Frid. 2. At home.

Sat. 3. At home.

Sund. 4. Preached at St. Stephen's ch. from 1 Cor. 16:10. Dinner at John Powlass'.

Mond. Tues. 6. At home.

Wed. 7. Went wife to Salisbury. Dinner and over night at Phebe Brown's. In the evening heard Dr. Dosh lecture in Luth. Church.

Thurs. 8. Returned home.

Frid. 9. At home.

Sat. 10. Had catechization at Organ Church.

Sund. 11. Preached at Organ ch. from Acts 20:21. Dinner at Charlie Miller's.

Mond. 12. At home.

Tues. 13. Went to Barringer's Mill.

Wed. 14. Went to Powlass' shop & had horses shod. In afternoon at home. Dinner at Mr. P's.

Thurs. 15. At home till afternoon, then went to Gold Hill to Post Office.

Frid. 16. Went to Salisbury. Dinner at Phebe Brown's.

Sat. 17. At home. A very inclement day.

Sund. 18. Went to Bethel ch. Stanly county & preached from Acts 20:21. Baptized two infants. Returned home.

Mond. 19. Went to Gold Hill in afternoon to Post Office.

Tues. 20. In forenoon went to Dan[l] Miller's. Dinner here. In afternoon went to Joseph Eagle's on business.

Wed. 21. Went to Joseph Eagle's & brought some old irons home. Then went to Dr. Coleman's & brought bedstead home.

Thurs. 22. Went to Gold Hill to Post Office.

Frid. 23. At home.

Sat. 24. Had catechization at Organ ch.

Sund. 25. Preached at Organ ch. from Prov. 22:2. Baptized two infants. Dinner at Jacob Miller's.

Mond. 26. Went to Gold Hill to Post Office.

Tues. 27. At home.

Wed. 28. Went to Barringer's mill. In afternoon went to Gold Hill & brought plow, spinning wheel &c. home.

Thurs. 29. At home till dinner, then went to Mr. Blackwelder's in Stanly Co. & staid over night.

Frid. 30. Preached at Bethel ch. Stanly Co. from John 19:30. Good Friday. Dinner at D. W. Plyler's. Returned home.

Sat. 31. At home. Lewis & his children with us to night.

Sund. April 1. Easter Sunday. Preached at St. Stephen's ch. from Col. 3:1. Dinner at John Powlass'. Returned home. Rev. Cone & wife with us to night.

Mond. 2. Had an appointment for Elm Grove School House, but the forenoon being rainy, did not attend. In the afternoon went to Gold Hill to Post Office. Calvin Pool & wife with us to night.

Tues. 3. At home.

Wed. 4. At home.

Thurs. 5. Went to Salisbury. Dinner at Phebe Brown's.

Frid. 6. At home.

Sat. 7. Had catechization at Organ Church.

Sund. 8. This was my regular day to preach at Organ ch., but the day being very rainy, did not attend.

Mond. 9. At home. Weather inclement.

Tues. 10. In afternoon went to Mt. Pleasant. All night at Lewis'.

Wed. 11. Returned home. Brought Bettie and Carrie along. In afternoon went to M. A. Holshouser's & brought barrel of Sugar & Fish home.

Thurs. 12. Went to Charles Fisher's. Dinner here. In afternoon went to William Beaver's and married Luther W. S. Bost & Ella Maria Beaver. Returned home.

Frid. 13. At home, a very rainy & stormy day.

Sat. 14. Went to Bethel church in Stanly Co. & preached from Matth. 10:32.33. preparatory to communion. Over night at Philip Ridenhower's.

Sund. 15. Preached at Bethel Church from Zech. 8:23. After an intermission administered the Lord's Supper. Returned home.

Mond. 16. Went to H. A. Miller's on business, but did not find him at home. In afternoon went Gold Hill to Post Office.

Tues. 17. Took a stand of soap to Mt. Pleasant for Lewis.

Wed. 18. In forenoon went to H. A. Miller's and paid a note of hand. In afternoon at home planting corn. W. A. Lutz with us to night.

Thurs. 19. At home planting corn.

Frid. 20. At home in my study.

Sat. 21. Went to Organ ch. – had Mr. Lutz to preach for me. Baptized two infants and confirmed eighteen persons. Had preparatory service. Returned home.

Sund. 22. Went to Organ ch. Mr. F. P. Cook preached. After an intermission baptized one infant and administered the Lord's Supper. Returned home.

Mond. 23. Went to Salisbury & settled sundry store accounts.

Tues. 24. At home.

Wed. 25. Attended to the funeral of Sam[l] R. Starnes at St. Matthew's ch. – preached from 1 Sam. 20:3. concluding clause.

Thurs. 26. At home.

Frid. 27. Went to Salisbury & brought Phebe Brown along home.

Sat. 28. Preached at St. Stephen's ch. from Prov. 28:13. preparatory to communion. Baptized four infants. All night at Peter J. Lentz's.

Sund. 29. Preached at St. Stephen's ch. from Josh. 23:8. Received on member by letter. after an intermission, administered the Lord's Supper. Returned home.

Mond. 30. At home.

Tues. May 1. Went by way of Gold Hill to Foil's Tan Yard & to Charles Fisher's.

Wed. 2. to Sund. 6. At Synod at St. Peter's ch.

Mond. 7. Took Mrs. Phebe Brown to Salisbury. A very inclement day.

Tues. 8. Went to Gold Hill to Post Office, & the late residence of Jacob Earnheart, dec^d, to aid in looking over the papers of said deceased.

Wed. 9. Went to Mt. Pleasant to attend a meeting of the Board of Trustees of N. C. College. Dinner & over night at Col. Shimpock's. Supper at Lewis'.

Thurs. 10. Returned home. Called to see Crawford Goodman, he being very sick.

Frid. 11. Went to John T. Lentz's to have shoes made & repaired. In afternoon at home.

Sat. 12. At home.

Sund. 13. Preached at Organ church from Eph. 6:18. In the afternoon attended to the funeral of Crawford J. Goodman, preached from Eccl. 9:10. Dinner at Mary A. Heilig's.

Mond. 14. Went by way of Gold Hill to Mr. J. Powlass' & had Lucy shod.

Tues. 15. Went to Salisbury. Dinner at Phebe Brown's.

Wed. 16. Went to Mrs. Jacob Earnheart's and assisted in laying off her year's provision. In the afternoon at home.

Thurs. 17. Went to Victor T. Melchor's and married George W. Barringer & Mrs. Mary A. Smith. Returned home.

Frid. 18. Went to St. Stephen's & formed a class of catechumens.

Sat. 19. Went to Bethel Church Stanly Co. and formed a class of catechumens. All night at Mr. House's.

Sund. 20. Preached at Bethel ch. from Eph. 6:18. Dinner at David Lyerly's. Returned home.

Mond. 21. At home.

Tues. 22. At home, sheared the sheep.

Wed. 23. Went to Mt. Pleasant to attend the closing exercises of Female Seminary. Dinner at Lewis'. Supper & all night at Col. Shimpock's.

Thurs. 24. Returned home.

Frid. 25. Went to mill, D. Barringer's mill.

Sat. 26. Took Bettie Thomas to Salisbury & had inverted toe nail removed by Drs. Whitehead & Coleman.

Sund. 27. Preached at Organ ch. from Luk. 18:18. Baptized one infant. Dinner at Widow Moses Bostian's. In the afternoon preached the funerals of Catharine Bostian & her son Moses Bostian at Ebenezer Church from Ps. 116:12-14. Over night at J. L. Graber's.

Mond. 28. Returned home by way of C. A. Miller's, Eli Holshouser's & J. T. Lentz's.

Tues. 29. Went to Gold Hill to Post Office and then engaged some hands to mow grass.

Wed. 30. Attended to the funeral of Solomon Ritchie, dec^d at his late residence. Preached from John 9:4. Dinner here. Returned home.

Thurs. 31. Went to Mr. Powlass' shop & then to Jesse Miller's for rakes. Dinner here.

Frid. June 1. Had catechization at Bethel Ch. Stanly Co. Dinner at Marvel Ritchie's.

Sat. 2. Had catechization at St. Stephen's ch.

Sund. 3. Preached at St. Stephen's church from Eph. 6:18. Dinner at C. L. Nussman's. Baptized 2 inf^{ts}.

Mond. 4. Tues. 5. Wed. 6. At home, haying.

Thurs. 7. Went with wife & grandchild, Carrie, to Salisbury.

Frid. 8. Went to Barringer's mill.

Sat. 9. At home.

Sund. 10. Went to Organ ch., it being my regular day to preach, but the day being very inclement, very few persons attended. Had some very short services and dismissed. Returned home.

Mond. 11. Went to Gold Hill in forenoon to Post Office.

Tues. 12. Went in forenoon to Gold Hill to Post Office to send off a letter. In afternoon went to M. A. Holshouser's to consult Jacob Holshouser in relation to a letter of inquiry from Illinois concerning the Holshouser family.

Wed. 13. Thurs. 14. At home.

Frid. 15. Had catechization at St. Stephen's ch.

Sat. 16. Had catechization at Bethel ch. Stanly co. All night at Danl Plyler's, Sen.

Sund. 17. Preached at Bethel ch. Stanly co. from Matth. 22:5. the G. E. Plyler's child dec^d. Dinner at Philip Ridenour's. Returned home.

Mond. 18. Went to Mt. Pleasant to attend College Commencement & meeting of Board of Trustees.

Tues. 19. Wed. 20. In Mt. Pleasant.

Thurs. 21. Returned home.

Frid. 22. Attended to the funeral of Margaret C. Ritchie at Organ ch. Preached fun^l at the house from Matth. 22:5.

Sat. 23. At home.

Sund. 24. Preached at Organ ch. from 1 Cor. 16:10. Baptized one infant. Had an appointment for the afternoon to preach a funeral at Ebenezer church, but the weather indicated rain, therefore did not attend.

Mond. 25. Tues. 26. Wed. 27. Thurs. 28. At home.

Frid. 29. Had catechization at Bethel ch. Stanly.

Sat. 30. Had catechization at St. Stephen's ch.

Sund. July 1. Preached at St. Stephen's ch. from Luk. 16:1-12. Returned home.

Mond. 2. At home.

Tues. 3. At home harvesting oats.

Wed. 4. At home harvesting oats.

Thurs. 5. At home, bought & received sheaf Oats of Moses Frick.

Frid. 6. At home.

Sat. 7. Started for Salem ch. to preach for Rev. Stickley. Dinner at Phebe Brown's, Salisbury. Called in afternoon to see Saml Seaford, he being very sick. All night at John Lingel's.

Sund. 8. Called to see Saml Seaford. Went to Salem ch. & preached from Luk. 16:1-12. Dinner at Saml Colly's. Called again to see Saml Seaford. Returned to Salisbury and preached at night for Dr. Dosh in Luth. ch. from Luk. 16:1-12. All night at Phebe Brown's.

Mond. 9. Returned home. Dinner at John Miller's.

Tues. 10. At home.

Wed. 11. At home till 12 o'clock, then went to John Rusher's & staid over night.

Thurs. 12. Attended to the funeral of Samuel Seaford at Salem ch. — preached from Prov. 3:6. Dinner at John Lingel's. Returned home.

Frid. 13. At home & very unwell. Failed to meet the catechumen's at St. Stephen's ch.

Sat. 14. At home & unwell. Failed to meet catechumen's at Bethel ch.

Sund. 15. Preached at Bethel ch. Stanly co. from Luk. 16:1-12. Baptized one infant. Dinner at Sandy Misenheimer's'. Returned home.

Mond. 16. Tues. 17. At home.

Wed. 18. Went with wife to Dr. Coleman's. Called also to see Jacob Miller he being sick.

Thurs. 19. Went to Barringer's mill.

Frid. 20. At home till 9 o'clock, then went to Gold Hill to Post Office. In afternoon at home.

Sat. 21. At home, had company. Lewis and family also called & staid over night.

Sund. 22. Preached at Organ ch. from Luk. 16:1-12. Installed Church Council. Dinner at J. L. Graeber's. In afternoon preached the funeral of Andrew Bostian at Ebenezer ch. from Prov. 3:6. All night at Mrs. Danl Eddlemann (widow).

Mond. 23. Returned home by way of Salisbury. Dinner at Phebe Brown's.

Tues. 24. Wed. 25. At home, had wheat & oats threshed.

Thurs. 26. Started in afternoon for Special Conference at St. Enoch's Church. All night at Eli Leppard's.

Frid. 27. Went to St. Enoch's Church. Had lodgings assigned at Aaron Yost's. Preached at night from Luk. 16:1-12.

Sat. 28. At conference. Preached again at night from Luk. 13:3.

Sund. 29. Attended preaching at St. Enoch's ch. In afternoon returned home.

Mond. 30. Tues. 31. At home.

Wed. Aug. 1. Aided D. Brady in having his land surveyed. In afternoon went to Jacob Miller's to see his son Cornelius, he being sick.

Thurs. 2. Went to Gold Hill to Post Office.

Frid. 3. Had catechization at Bethel, Stanly co. Dinner at Isom Misenheimer's.

Sat. 4. Had catechization at St. Stephen's.

Sund. 5. Preached at St. Stephen's ch. from Matth. 21:18-32. Dinner at Dr. Shimpock's. In the afternoon preached at Gold Hill from Prov. 3:6. the funeral of Jacob Earnheart, dec^d.

Mond. 6. At home till afternoon making preparations to have chimneys repaired. In afternoon went to Jacob Miller's to see his son, Cornelius, he being sick.

Tues. 7. In afternoon took apples to Jacob Holshouser's to have distilled.

Wed. 8. At home, had Mr. McAllister to repair chimneys.

Thurs. 9. Frid. 10. At home, Mr. McAllister repairing chimneys.

Sat. 11. At home till dinner. In afternoon went to Gold Hill to Post Office & took Emma to see her brother.

Sund. 12. Preached at Organ ch. from Prov. 14:32. Confirmed William F. Goodman. Dinner at Laurence Lingel's. In afternoon preached at Elm Grove School House from Prov. 3:17.

Mond. 13. Attended to the funeral of Cornelius W. Miller at Organ ch.— preached from Job. 1:21. In afternoon went to Gold Hill & brought Emma home.

Tues. 14. At home.

Wed. 15. At home, Rev. Lentz with us to night.

Thurs. 16. Went to Mt. Pleasant to see Lewis to have him go to Bethel ch. for me.

Frid. 17. Went to Davidson. Dinner at Mr. Barnes'. All night at Caleb Peeler's.

Sat. 18. Preached at Hopewell from Prov. 3:6. All night at Caleb Peeler's.

Sund. 19. Preached at Hopewell from Matth. 21:28. Aided in the communion. All night at Caleb Peeler's.

Mond. 20. Returned home. Dinner at Phebe Brown's in Salisbury.

Tues. 21. In the morning went to Moses Linn's to engage him to work on my house.

Wed. 22. At home.

Thurs. 23. In forenoon went to Barringer's mill. In afternoon took a load of fruit to Jacob Holshouser's.

Frid. 24. In forenoon went to mill. In afternoon at home.

Sat. 25. In afternoon attended to the funeral of Patsy Baily at St. Peter's ch. Preached from 2 Sam. 12:23.

Sund. 26. Preached at Organ ch. the funeral of Sarah Goodman from Heb. 4:9. Baptized 2 infants. Installed G. A. Berger as deacon. Dinner at Calvin L. Brown's. In the afternoon preached at Elm Grove School House from Rev. 2:4.5.

Mond. 27. In afternoon went to Gold Hill to Post Office.

Tues. 28. Took wife to Dr. Coleman's. In the went & brought wife home.

Wed. 29. Went to H. A. Miller's & borrowed some money. Then went to John Lentz's for shoes. In afternoon at home.

Thurs. 30. Went to Elizabeth Isenhour's and married James Owens & Ellen M. Isenhour. Returned home by way of John Powlass' & the Post Office.

Frid. 31. Had catechization at Bethel ch.

Sat. Sept. 1. Had catechization at St. Stephen's ch.

Sund. 2. Preached at St. Stephen's ch. from Prov. 14:32. Baptized one infant & installed H. M. Isenhour as Deacon. Dinner at John Powlass'. Called to see Henry Troutman.

Mond. 3. Went to Salisbury. Dinner at Mrs. Brown's. Brought Mrs. Brown along home.

Tues. 4. Wed. 5. Thurs. 6. Frid. 7. At home.

Sat. 8. At home.

Sund. 9. Attended to the fun[l] of Catharine E. daughter of Reuben W. Bost, at Organ Church. — preached from Matth. 22:5. including the regular services of the day. Dinner at Daywalt Beaver's. In the afternoon preached at Elm Grove School House from Is. 55:6.

Mond. 18. Went to Andrew Cruse's to see Mrs. Cruse, she being sick.

Tue. 11. Took Phebe Brown to Salisbury.

Wed. 12. At home.

Thurs. 13. At home, helped to haul in hay.

Frid. 14. Had catechization at St. Stephen's ch. Called at Mr. Powlass' shop on my return.

Sat. 15. Had catechization at Bethel ch. in Stanly Co. All night at Alex[r] Palmer's.

Sund. 16. Preached at Bethel ch., Stanly, from Job 14:14. the funeral of M. M. Daniel's child dec[d]. Baptized one infant. Installed church Treasurer & one Elder. Dinner at Frank Ridenhour's.

Mond. 17. At home.

Tues. 18. Went to Salisbury & bought a Dixie Plow. Dinner at Phebe Brown's.

Wed. 19. Went to Barringer's Mill.

Thurs. 20. Frid. 21. At home.

Sat. 22. At home helping to haul hay.

Sund. 23. Preached at Organ Church from Jam. 1:5. Dinner at L. G. Holshouser's. In the afternoon preached at Elm Grove School House from Josh. 24:15. first clause. Baptized 1 inf[t].

Mond. 24. In afternoon went to Gold Hill to Post office.

Tue. 25. Wed. 26. At home.

Thurs. 27. At home.

Frid. 28. Went to Ebenezer ch. to attend Conference. Preached from 2 Cor. 5:17. All night at P. A. Seaford's.

Sat. 29. At Conference. All night at Geo. Ketner's.

Sund. 30. In the morning went to Elijah Ludwig's & then to Mt. Mitchell ch. (Methodist) & buried said Ludwig's child. Then went to Organ ch. & attended to the fun[l] of Sarah, wife of Andrew Cruse — preached from Job 14:14. Dinner at Mr. Cruse's.

Mond. Oct. 1. Tues. 2. At home cutting & hauling sorghum cane to M. A. Holshouser's.

Wed. 3. Went to Mt. Pleasant. Heard Dr. Davis preach the funeral of Mrs. C. Melchor. Returned home. Got very wet.

Thurs. 4. Attended to the funeral of Andrew Berger's child, Charlie, at Lower St. Church. Preached fun[l] at house from Mark 10:14. In afternoon baptized Wesley T. Propst's child, it being sick.

Frid. 5. Had catechization at Bethel ch., Stanly. Dinner at Victor Melchor's. In the afternoon had catechization at St. Stephen's ch.

Sat. 6. Preached at St. Stephen's ch. from Luk. 18:13. preparatory to communion. Baptized one infant & confirmed 4 persons.

Sund. 7. Preached at St. Stephen's ch. from Acts 18:21. & administered the Lord's Supper.

Mond. 8. Went to John T. Lentz's, shoemaker.

Tues. 9. At home. Had Uriah Miller to repair clocks.

Wed. 10. Went to Organ ch, and buried Col. P. N. Heilig's infant child. Then went to Salisbury to Phebe Brown's, & married John J. Quantz Catharine M. Heilig. Returned home after night.

Thurs. 11. Went to Mauney & Morgan's carding machine.

Frid. 12. At home.

Sat. 13. Went to Lentz's mill.

Sund. 14. Preached at Organ ch.from Act. 9:6. Baptized one infant. In the afternoon attended to the funeral of John Morgan's child at St. Peter's ch. — preached from 2 Kings 4:26.

Mond. 15. At home. Tues. 16. At home.

Wed. 17. In forenoon went to Lentz's mill. In afternoon at home.

Thurs. 18. At home.

Frid. 19. Went to Bethel ch. Stanly co. to meet catechumens, but the class failed to attend. Returned home.

Sat. 20. Preached at Bethel ch. from Acts 9:6. preparatory to communion. Returned home.

Sund. 21. Preached at Bethel ch. from Luk. 22:19.20. After an intermission, administered the communion. Returned home.

Mond. 22. At home.

Tues. 23. In afternoon went to Gold Hill to see about having shoes made.

Wed. 24. In forenoon took leather to Gold Hill to have shoes made.

Thurs. 25. Brought rent corn home from Solomon Peeler's. In afternoon at home.

Frid. 26. At home.

Sat. 27. Preached at Organ ch. from 1 Cor. 5:7.8. preparatory to communion. In the afternoon attended to the fun[l] of Adolphus Eugene, son of Eli Lentz.

Sund. 28. Preached at Organ ch. from Ps. 133:1-3. & after an intermission administered the Lord's Supper.

Mond. 29. Brought corn home from Moses Frick's.

Tues. 30. At home.

Wed. 31. In afternoon went to Gold Hill to Post Office.

Thurs. Nov. 1. At home.

Frid. 2. Attended preaching at St. Peter's ch.

Sat. 3. Preached at St. Peter's ch. from Jam. 1:25.

Sund. 4. Preached at St. Stephen's church from Jam. 1:25.

Mond. 5. At home, a rainy day.

Tues. 6. Wed. 7. At home digging and storing away sweet potatoes.

Thurs. 8. At home, a rainy day.

Frid. 9. Went in forenoon to Gold Hill to to [repeated] Post Office & Shoemaker. In afternoon at home.

Sat. 10. Preached in Christiana ch. from 1 Cor. 9:24-27. Dinner at Nathan Brown's. Returned home.

Sund. 11. Preached at Christiana ch. from 2 Kings 5:12. After an intermission aided in the administration of the Lord's Supper. Returned home.

Mond. 12. Went to Salisbury. Dinner at Phebe Brown's.

Tues. 13. Brought sack salt home from Doctor Coleman's. In afternoon hauled corn home from field.

Wed. 14. Brought corn home from Mr. Frick's. In afternoon shucked & cribbed corn.

Thurs. 15. At home.

Frid. 16. In the morning went to M. A. Holshouser's to give instructions in relation to Ax handle. In afternoon went to Dr. Coleman's on business.

Sat. 17. At home. Dr. Coleman & wife dined with us in honor of my wife's birth day.

Sund. 18. Preached at Bethel ch. Stanly co. from Ps. 85:6. on the subject of revivals of religion. Baptized two infants. Returned home.

Mond. 19. At home.

Tues. 20. Went to John Earnheart's to engage weaving. In the afternoon went to M. A. Holshouser's & brought ax home.

Wed. 21. At home.

Thurs. 22. In afternoon went to D. Brady's to engage him to slaughter beef. Rainy day.

Frid. 23. At home. Rainy day.

Sat. 24. In forenoon called to see Dr. Coleman, he being sick. In afternoon at home. Lewis with us to night.

Sund. 25. Preached at Organ ch. Zech. 8:23. Returned home.

Mond. 26. At home. Prepared for slaughtering hogs.

Tues. 27. In forenoon went to mill. In afternoon In afternoon called to see Dr. Coleman.

Wed. 28. Went to Salisbury.

Thurs. 29. Had hogs slaughtered.

Frid. 30. Preached at St. Stephen's ch. from Acts 20:17-21. Returned home.

Sat. Dec. 1. Preached at St. Stephen's ch. from Eph. 6:1-4. Returned home.

Sund. 2. Preached at St. Stephen's ch. from 2 Tim. 1:13. Dinner & all night at Caleb L. Nussman's.

Mond. 3. Returned home by way of J. Powlass' & Gold Hill. Dinner at Mr. Powlass'.

Tues. 4. Went with wife to Dr. Coleman's & spent the day.

Wed. 5. Went to Gold Hill to the shoemaker.

Thurs. 6. Went to George Bayam's on business.

Frid. 7. At home.

Sat. 8. Started for Salem ch. All night at widow Joseph Colly's. Dinner to day at Phebe Brown's.

Sund. 9. Preached at Salem ch. from Is. 40:6-8. the fun[l] of Joseph Colly dec[d]. Dinner at Sam[l] Colly's. All night at Moses A. Bost's.

Mond. 10. Returned home.

Tues. 11. Attended to the funeral of David L., son of Joseph Lyerly at St. Peter's ch. preached from Is. 40:8. Dinner at H. A. Miller's. In afternoon went to Salisbury & returned.

Wed. 12. Went to Theophilus J. G. Trexler's and baptized his child. Baptized also six children for Henry Hohnberger. Returned home.

Thurs. 13. Went with wife to David Barringer's to witness the marriage of Lucy G. Barringer. Returned home after supper & left wife.

Frid. 14. Went to Bethel ch. Stanly co. & preached from Acts 20:17-21. All night at Alexander Misenheimer's.

Sat. 15. Preached at Bethel ch. Stanly Co. from James 1:25. Baptized 2 infants. All night at John A. Troutman's.

Sund. 16. Preached at Bethel ch, Stanly Co. from 2 Tim. 1:13. Dinner at Isom Misenheimer's. Returned home.

Mond. 17. At home till dinner, then went to Gold Hill to Post Office & to Mr. Powlass' shop.

Tues. 18. Went to Mt. Pleasant. All night at Lewis'.

Wed. 19. Attended an informal meeting of Board of Trustees of N. C. College. All night at Col. Shimpock's.

Thurs. 20. Returned home.

Frid. 21. Preached at Organ ch. from Jam. 1:12. Returned home.

Sat. 22. Preached at Organ ch. from Acts 20:17-21. Dinner at L. A. Heilig's. Baptized one infant.

Sund. 23. Preached at Organ ch. from 2 Tim. 1:13. Married to day Paul Holshouser & Catharine L. Hoffner.

Mond. 24. At home till evening, then went to Elm Grove to Christmas Tree.

Tues. 25. Went to St. Stephen's ch. & lectured on the subject of Christmas.

Wed. 26. Called to see Dr. Coleman.

Thurs. 27. At home.

Frid. 28. Went with Solomon Peeler to Salisbury & bought bureau for Emma.

Sat. 29. At home & slaughtered shoat.

Sund. 30. Had a conditional appointment to day for Bethel ch. Stanly Co., but the day being very inclement with rain, did not attend.

Mond. 31. Went to H. A. Miller's and paid a note of hand. Called by Dr. Coleman's and delivered Lottie's Shoe Buttoner.

Tues. Jan. 1, 1878. At home, wife & girls having gone visiting.
Wed. 2. At home. Joan & children called to see us.
Thurs. 3. Went with wife, Joan & children to Dr. Coleman's & spent the day.
Frid. 4. Accompanied Joan & children on their way home till beyond Mr. Bernhardt's. Called on the way home at John T. Lentz's & Luther C. Miller's.
Sat. 5. At home.
Sund. 6. Preached at Stephen's ch. from Deut. 5:3. the fun[1] of Jane Isenhour's child.
Mond. 7. Tues. 8. At home.
Wed. 9. Called to see Dr. Coleman & spent the day. Weather very inclement.
Thurs. 10. At home. D. Barringer called to see us.
Frid. 11. Sat. 12. At home.
Sund. 13. Preached at Organ ch. from Deut. 5:3. A very inclement day.
Mond. 14. At home till evening, then went to M. A. Holshouser's & brought Rose E. Fisher.
Tues. 15. Went to Mr. Powlass' & had shoeing done.
Wed. 16. Went to M. A. Holshouser's & bought some brick & engaged him to repair chimney.
Thurs. 17. At home. — had chimney repaired.
Frid. 18. Went to Salisbury.
Sat. 19. At home, had company.
Sund. 20. Bethel ch. Stanly Co. but the day being very inclement, had no congregation & did not preach. Dinner at Marvel Ritchey's. Returned home.
Mond. 21. Went to Mr. Grupy's. Dinner here. Called also at Dr. Coleman's.
Tues. 22. Went to Gold Hill to Post Office.
Wed. 23. Went to Moses Frick's & settled acct. & brought a load of pine. In afternoon went to saw mill & to Gold Hill.
Thurs. 24. Went to Eli Holshouser's to engage him to do some work. Called also to see Eliza, our former cook woman, she bring sick. Called also at Dr. Coleman's. Dinner here.
Mond. 28. Tues. 29. Wed. 30. At home, — had shed room recovered.
Thurs. 31. This morning wife slipped off dining room steps & broke her leg. Sent for Dr. Shimpock who managed the case. Went at 2 o'clock to M. A. Holshouser's & married Carson A. B. Beaver and Alice E. Beaver. Absent from home but a short time.

Frid. Feb. 1. Sent for Phebe Brown to nurse wife.
Sat. 2. At home.
Sund. 3. This my day for St. Stephen's ch. but did not attend in consequence of wife's affliction.
Mond. 4. Tues. 5. Wed. 6. Thurs. 7. Frid. 8. Sat. 9. At home.
Sund. 10. Preached at Organ ch. from 1 Pet. 5:8.9. Dinner at home.
Mond. 11. At home.
Tues. 12. In afternoon went to Mt. Pleasant. All night at Col. J. Shimpock.
Wed. 13. Attended meeting of Board of Trustees of N. C. College. In afternoon returned home.
Thurs. 14. Frid. 15. Sat. 16. At home.
Sund. 17. Preached at Bethel ch. Stanly Co. from 1 Pet. 5:8.9. Returned home.
Mond. 18. Tues. 19. Wed. 20. Thurs. 21. At home.
Frid. 22. Went to Salisbury. Dinner at Phebe Brown's.
Sat. 23. At home.
Sund. 24. Preached at Organ ch. from Luk. 8:18. Called to see Crawford A. Miller.
Mond. 25. At home.
Tues. 26. In the afternoon went to the colored grave yard to see Eliza Heilig buried.
Wed. 27. Went in afternoon to Mr. Grupy's to get come Still Beer for wife.
Thurs. 28. At home.

Frid. March 1. At home.

Sat. 2. In forenoon went to Gold Hill to Post Office. In afternoon at home.

Sund. 3. Peached at St. Stephen's ch. from Heb. 1:14. Returned home.

Mond. 4. At home.

Tues. 5. Went in the morning to Mrs. Lentz's to engage some corn. Balance of day at home.

Wed. 6. Thurs. 7. Frid. 8. Sat. 9. At home.

Sund. 10. Preached at Organ ch. from Matth. 4:1-11. Baptized 1 inf.t. Returned home.

Mond. 11. In forenoon went to Gold Hill to Post Office. In evening went to Mrs. Lentz's to engage corn.

Tues. 12. Wed. 13. Thurs. 14. At home.

Frid. 15. In afternoon brought corn home from Mrs. Lentz's.

Sat. 16. Called on Mr. Brady to lance mare, she having the distemper.

Sund. 17. Preached at Bethel ch. Stanly Co., from Luk. 15:25. Returned home.

Mond. 18. At home.

Tues. 19. Attended to the funeral of Henry Lentz at Union ch. — Preached from Matth. 5:6.

Wed. 20. At home.

Thurs. 21. Called in afternoon, by request, to see Edward Ruffty, he being very sick.

Frid. 22. At home.

Sat. 23. At home.

Sund. 24. Preached Organ ch. from Matth. 12:41.42. Baptized one infant. In afternoon went to St. Paul's ch. & attended to the funeral of Michael L. Brown. Preached from Matth. 5:6. Returned home.

Mond. 25. Tues. 26. Wed. 27. Thurs. 28. At home.

Frid. 29. Went to Gold Hill to Post Office. Also to Mauney's saw mill.

Sat. 30. At home.

Sund. 31. Preached at St. Stephen's ch. from Matth. 12:41.42. Dinner at Laurence Lingel's.

Mond. April 1. Went to Salisbury.

Tues. 2. Called in forenoon to see George Earnheart, he being sick. Went also to Gold Hill to Post Office. In afternoon went to H. A. Miller's to see his son Albert, he being sick.

Wed. 3. At home.

Thurs. 4. Went in the afternoon to Edward Ruffty's to attend to his funeral, but the day being very inclement, it was postponed one day.

Frid. 5. Attended to the funeral of Edward Ruffty at St. Matthew's ch.— preached from Amos 4:12. to a large congregation.

Sat. 6. Preached at St. Stephen's ch. from Ps. 116:12-14. preparatory to communion. Installed one Elder, baptized one infant, & confirmed four persons. Dinner at John Powlass' & baptized two of his children. Returned home.

Sund. 7. Preached at St. Stephen's ch. from Matth. 3:8. After an intermission administered the communion. Returned home.

Mond. 8. Went to Gold Hill to Post Office.

Tues. 9. Wed. 10. At home.

Thurs. 11. In the morning went to D. Brady's & had Lucy shod. Balance of day at home.

Frid. 12. In the morning went to M. A. Holshouser's to have scythe nead repaired. Balance of day at home.

Sat. 13. At home.

Sund. 14. Preached at Organ ch. from Matth. 21:10. Dinner at Crawford A. Millers.

Mond. 15. At home.

Tues. 16. Went to Salisbury. Dlnner at Phebe Brown's.

Wed. 17. Went to John T. Lentz's, to Mich. Miller's, to Jackson Bost's, & to Charlie Fisher's. Dinner at Jackson Bost's.

Thurs. 18. Went to Gold Hill in forenoon to Post Office. Balance of day at home.

Frid. 19. Good Friday. Preached at St. Stephen's ch. from John 19:30. Installed John Powlass as Elder, & baptized one infant. Returned home.

Sat. 20. Preached at Bethel ch. Stanly Co. preparatory to communion from Josh. 23:8. Installed Daniel Plyler as Elder. Returned home.

Sund. 21. Preached at Bethel ch. Stanly Co. from Luk. 13:24. Confirmed three persons. After intermission administered communion. Returned home.

Mond. 22. At home.

Tues. 23. Called in forenoon to see Albert Miller, he being sick.

Wed. 24. At home.

Thurs. 25. In the morning went to Dr. Coleman's for Books of Worship which he brought out from Salisbury for me. Balance of day at home,

Frid. 26. Called in the morning to see Rev. Linn & paid him salary for Wife & Emma.

Sat. 27. Had preparatory service at Organ Church — Prof. Rahn preached, Baptized one infant.

Sund. 28. Had communion at Organ Church — Prof. Rahn preached.

Mond. 29. Started for Synod. All night at Phebe Brown's in Salisbury.

Tues. 30. Took the train for Gibsonville. All night at Widow Ludwig Summers'.

Wed. May 1. At Frieden's Church attending Synod. All night at Simeon Wagoner's.

Thurs. 2. Attended Synod. All night at Peter Summers'.

Frid. 3. Attended Synod. All night at Simeon Wagoner's.

Sat. 4. Attended Synod. All at Simeon Wagoner's.

Sund. 5. Attended preaching at the church. All night at Widow Ludwig Summers'.

Mond. 6. Synod adjourned at 2 P.M. Went to Gibsonville & took the train for Winston. All night at Calvin Miller's.

Tues. 7. Went to Caleb Peeler's. Dinner at Mrs. Esther Stafford's. All night at C. Peeler's.

Wed. 8. In afternoon went to Lexington and took the train for Salisbury. All night at Mr. B. F. Fraley's.

Thurs. 9. Returned home.

Frid. 10. In afternoon went to Mr. Grupy's.

Sat. 11. In forenoon went to Gold Hill to Post Office.

Sund. 12. Preached at Organ ch. from Luk. 19:1-10. Baptized one infant. Dinner at Jesse Miller's. Called to see Albert Miller, he being very sick.

Mond. 13. In forenoon went to Gold Hill to Post Office. In afternoon at home.

Tues. 14. Went to Mt. Pleasant to College Commencement. Dinner at Lewis'. Supper at Col. Shimpock's. All night at Lewis'.

Wed. 15. Attended meeting of Board & College exercises. Dinner at Col. Shimpock's. In returned home.

Thurs. 16. In afternoon called to see Albert Miller he being very sick.

Frid. 17. Had catechization at St. Stephen's ch.

Sat. 18. Had catechization at Bethel ch. Stanly co. All night at Marvel Ritchies.

Sund. 19. Preached at Bethel ch. Stanly co. from Matth. 12:41.42. Dinner at Harter Ridenhour's. Returned home.

Mond. 20. At home.

Tues. 21. Went to Salisbury. In afternoon married at my house Rufus P. Roseman & Sarah E. Lyerly, daughter of George Lyerly.

Wed. 22. Went to Adam Earnheart's on business. In afternoon went to Mr. Grupy's, wife being there on a visit.

Thurs. 23. Went to Salisbury.

Frid. 24. At home.

Sat. 25. Had catechization at Organ ch. Dinner at Mrs. Seaford's, (widow).

Sund. 26. Preached at Organ ch. from Numb. 14:24. Baptized 2 inf^{ts}.

Mond. 27. Went to Gold Hill to post office.

Tues. 28. Went to mill (Mrs. Lentz's).

Wed. 29. At home.

Thurs. 30. Preached (Asension Day) at Elm Grove School House from Acts 1:9-11. Dinner at Jacob Miller's.

Frid. 31. Had catechization at Bethel ch. Stanly Co.

Sat. June 1. Had catechization at St. Stephen's ch.

Sund. 2. Preached at St. Stephen's ch. from Jer. 5:26. Returned home.

Mond. 3. Went to Salisbury. Dinner at Mrs. Brown's.

Tues. 4. In forenoon went to Gold Hill to post office. In afternoon at home.

Wed. 5. At home. Thurs. 6. At home.

Frid. 7. Went to Tax returning & to Gold Hill to Post Office.

Sat. 8. Had catechization at Organ Church.

Sund. 9. Preached at Organ ch. from Acts 17:11.12. Dinner at George Bernhardt's. In afternoon preached at Elm Grove School House from Phil. 3:20.21.

Mond. 10. Tues. 11. At home.

Wed. 12. Went to Salisbury.

Thurs. 13. At home.

Frid. 14. Had catechization at St. Stephen's ch.

Sat. 15. Had catechization at Bethel ch. Stanly. All night at Clayborn Misenheimer's.

Sat. 16. Preached Bethel ch. Stanly, from John 7:37. Dinner at Victor Melchor's. In afternoon preached at St. Stephen's ch. from John 7:37. Returned home.

Mond. 17. Tues. 18. At home.

Wed. 19. Went to Gold Hill to Post Office.

Thurs. 20. Went to J. Powlass', got a scythe snath, & had scythe hung.

Frid. 21. Went, in afternoon, to Gold Hill to Post Office.

Sat. 22. Had catechization at Organ ch.

Sund. 23. Preached at Organ ch. from John 7:37. Dinner at C. L. Brown's. In afternoon preached at Elm Grove from Matth. 13:33.

Mond. 24. Went to G. M. Bernhardt's to see Mrs. Bernhardt, she being sick. Dinner here. In afternoon called at Boyden Miller's to see Mrs. Miller, she being sick. Returned home by way of Post Office at Gold Hill.

Tues. 25. Wed. 26. Thurs. 27. At home.

Frid. 28. In forenoon went to Gold Hill to Post Office.

Satd. 29. At home.

Sund. 30. Preached at St. Stephen's ch. from Josh. 7:12. Baptized one infant. Dinner Peter J. Lentz's. In the afternoon preached at Bethel ch. Stanly Co. from Josh. 7:12. All night at David Lyerly's.

Mond. July 1. Returned home by way of John Powlass'. Took dinner here and had shoeing done.

Tues. 2. In forenoon went to Gold Hill to Post Office and to shoemaker's. In afternoon In afternoon went to G. M. Bernhardt's & found his wife a corpse. Called also to see Mrs. Boyden Miller.

Wed. 3. At home.

Thurs. 4. Attended to the funeral of Mrs. Mary A. Bernhardt at Organ ch. — preached from Ps. 34:19.

Frid. 5. Had catechizatlon at Bethel ch. Stanly Co.

Sat. 6. In the afternoon had catechlzation at St. Stephen's ch. All night at Sol. Nussman's.

Sund. 7. Preached at St. Stephen's ch. from 2 Kings 5:12. Dinner at Peter J. Lentz's. In the afternoon preached at Bethel ch. Stanly co. from 2 Kings 5:12. Returned home.

Mond. 8. Went to J. Powlass' & had mare shod.

Tues. 9. In forenoon went to Gold Hill to Post Office.

Wed. 10. Thurs. 11. At home.

Frid. 12. Went to Gold Hill to Post Office.

Sat. 13. Had catechization at Organ ch. Called to see Mrs. Boyden Miller, she being sick. Dinner here.

Sund. 14. Preached at Organ ch. from 2 Kings 5:12. Baptized three infants. Dinner at A. W. Klutts'. In afternoon preached at Rymer's School House from Phil. 3:20.21. Returned home.

Mond. 15. At home.

Tues. 16. Went in forenoon to Gold Hill to Post Office.

Wed. 17. Thurs. 18. At home, had wheat threshed.

Frid. 19. Went to St. Stephen's ch. to meet catechumens. Suspended catechization for want of attendance.

Sat. 20. At home. Dr. Bernheim & Rev. Linn with me. Dr. B. staid over night.

Sund. 21. Went to Bethel ch. it being my regular day. Rev. Thornwell, Presbyterian, being present, preached for me. Baptized one infant. Dinner at Clayborn Misenheimer's. In afternoon preached at St. Stephen's ch. from Acts. 17:11.12. Returned home.

Mond. 22. At home.

Tues. 23. Went to Gold Hill to shoemaker & to Post Office.

Wed. 24. Went to Gold Hill to Post Office and heard candidates speak.

Thur. 25. Frid. 26. At home.

Sat. 27. Had catechization at Organ ch.

Sund. 28. Preached at Organ church from Ps. 40:1-3. Dinner at Mary A. Heilig's. Had an appointment for afternoon at Elm Grove School House but did not attend in consequence of rain.

Mond. 29. Tues. 30. At home.

Wed. 31. Attended to the fun[1] of Anna L. Miller, at Organ ch. — preached from Eccl. 7:14.

Thurs. Aug. 1. In forenoon went to Morgan's to election. In afternoon at home.
Frid. 2. In afternoon went to Gold Hill to Post Office & sent $59.40 to Henkel & Co. for printing & mailing minutes. Sent also $2.40 to W. J. Duffie for L. G. Holshouser to pay for his Luth. Visitor.
Sat. 3. At home.
Sund. 4. Preached at St. Stephen's ch. from Ps. 40:1-3. Dinner at Peter J. Lentz's. In the afternoon preached at Bethel ch., Stanly co. from Ps. 103:1-4. Returned home.
Mond. 5. At home.
Tues. 6. In forenoon want to Gold Hill to Post Office. In afternoon at home.
Wed. 7. Went to Salisbury.
Thurs. 8. At home.
Frid. 9. At home.
Sat. 10. Had catechization at Organ ch.
Sund. 11. Preached at Organ ch. from Neh. 10:39. Dinner at William Beaver's. In afternoon preached at Rymer's School House from 2 Cor. 5:17. Returned home.
Mond. 12. At home.
Tues. 13. Went to Gold Hill & brought Small's horse home on trial.
Wed. 14. Went to saw mill to get a little lumber but failed. D. Barringer & wife with us to night.
Thurs. 15. Went to Salisbury.
Frid. 16. Went to Bethel ch. Stanly Co. and attended meeting of Western Conference. All night at David Lyerly's.
Sat. 17. At Conference. All night at William Blackwelder's.
Sund. 18. At Bethel ch. — All night at Philip Ridenhour's.
Mond. 19. Returned home.
Tues. 20. Attended at the burial of Moses Frick's child at St. Peter's ch. Rev. J. A. Linn officiated.
Wed. 21. In the afternoon went to Gold Hill to Post Office.
Thurs. 22. At home.
Frid. 23. Attended to the funeral of David L. Brown at Christiana ch. preached from 2 Tim. 4:7.8. Dinner at Nathan Brown's.
Sat. 24. Had catechization at Organ ch. Dinner at Albert Heilig's.
Sund. 25. Preached at Organ ch. from Ez. 33:5. Baptized two infants. Dinner at Crawford A. Miller's. In afternoon preached at Elm Grove School House from John 5:40.
Mond. 26. At home.
Tues. 27. In forenoon went Gold Hill to Post Office. In afternoon at home.
Wed. 28. Went to Charles Fisher's & had saddle repaired. Dinner here. Called also to see Paul Cruse. J. F. Rueckert with us to night.
Thurs. 29. At home. Rosa Fisher with us to night.
Frid. 30. Went to Steam Mill.
Sat. 31. Had catechization at Organ Church.

Sund. Sept. 1. Preached at St. Stephen's ch. from Ez. 33:5. Dinner at Moses Troutman's.

Mond. 2. In forenoon went to Mr. Powlass' shop.

Tues. 3. In forenoon went to Gold Hill to Post Office. In afternoon at home.

Wed. 4. At home. Commenced hay making.

Thurs. 5. In the morning went to Gold Hill to Post Office. Balance of day at home.

Frid. 6. At home.

Sat. 7. Had catechization at Organ church.

Sund. 8. Preached at Organ ch. from Deut. 32:46.47. Baptized one infant. Dinner at Dan[l] Miller's. In afternoon preached at Elm Grove from John 14:22.

Sund. 9. In afternoon went to Gold Hill to Post Office.

Tues. 10. Went to Salisbury.

Wed. 11 Thurs. 12. At home.

Frid. 13. Had catechization at Organ ch.

Sat. 14. Attended Sund. Sch. celebration at Lower Stone ch.

Sund. 15. Went to Bethel ch. Rev. Efird preached. Dinner at Reed Misenheimer's. In afternoon Efird (Rev.) preached at St. Stephen's ch. Rev. Efird & wife with us to night.

Mond. 16. At home.

Tues. 17. Went with wife to Mt. Pleasant. All night at Lewis'.

Wed. 18. Returned home. Dinner at Cha[s] Fisher's. B. Arey with us to night.

Thurs. 19. In afternoon walked to D. Barringer's & brought wife home.

Frid. 20. Had catechization at Organ Church. Dinner at Boyden Miller's. Then went to Jacob Morgan's and staid over night.

Sat. 21. Preached the funeral of David Morgan dec[d] at Corinth (Baptist) Church from 2 Tim. 4:7.8. Returned home.

Sund. 22. Preached at Organ ch. from Matt. 11:29.30. Dinner at Albert Heilig's. In afternoon preached at Elm Grove from Matt. 11:29.30.

Mond. 23. Went in forenoon to Jno. Powlass' & brought wagon home.

Tues. 24. Called in afternoon to see Cass Arey, he being home.

Wed. 25. Went to Salisbury.

Thurs. 26. Went to Mr. Shemwell's, Mrs. S. being sick.

Frid. 27. Attended Special Conference at Organ ch. Rev. Petrea preached. All night at D. L. Bost's.

Sat. 28. At Conference. Rev. Julian preached. All night at Paul Cruse's.

Sund. 29. At Organ ch. Preaching by Revds. Rahn & Bikle.

Mond. 30. At home.

Tues. Oct. 1. Went to Mt. Pleasant. In the evening baptized Lewis' infant daughter, Helen Amelia. All night at Col. Shimpock's.

Wed. 2. Attended meeting of Board of Trustees of N. C. College. Board & lodging at Col. Shimpock's.

Thurs. 3. Returned home.

Frid. 4. Had catechization at Organ ch. Very unwell with cold.

Sat. 5. Had preparatory service at St. Stephen's ch. — Did not preach in consequence of a severe cold. Confirmed one person, baptized one adult, & one infant. Dinner at J. W. Lentz's. Returned home.

Sund. 6. Preached at St. Stephen's ch. from Matt. 25:13. and administered the Lord's Supper.

Mond. 7. Attended to the funeral of John Misenheimer's child at St. Peter's ch.— preached from Matth. 25:13.

Tues. 8. Went to Wilson Kistler's on business in behalf of N. C. College. Returned home by way of David Barringer's.

Wed. 9. Went to Salisbury.

Thurs. 10. Went to Mt. Pleasant & brought Lottie Coleman home.

Frid. 11. At home.

Sat. 12. Had catechization at Organ church.

Sund. 13. Preached at Organ ch. from 1 Cor. 4:2. Very unwell. Returned home.

Mond. 14. Tues. 15. Wed. 16. Thurs. 17. At home.

Frid. 18. Had catechization at Organ ch.

Sat. 19. Had preparatory service at Bethel church Stanly co. — Baptized one infant. All night at John A. Troutman's.

Sund. 20. Preached at Bethel ch. Stanly Co. from 1 Cor. 4:2. Confirmed two persons. After intermission, administered the communion. All night at Alex. Misenheimer's.

Mond. 21. Returned home. In afternoon went with Phebe Brown to Salisbury. All night Mrs. Brown's.

Tues. 22. Attended to business for Mrs. Brown. Dinner at B. F. Fraley's. Returned home bringing Mrs. Brown along.

Wed. 23. At home.

Thurs. 24. In forenoon went to Gold Hill to Post Office.

Frid. 25. At home.

Sat. 26. Had preparatory services at Organ Church. Rev. R. L. Brown preached. Confirmed 24 persons. Returned home.

Sund. 27. At Organ church — Rev. R. L. Brown preached. After an intermission administered the communion. Returned home.

Mond. 28. Started for Davidson Co. Dinner at Mr. Grupy's. All night at Mr. Shemwell's.

Tues. 29. Went to Caleb Peeler's. All night here.

Wed. 30. Called to see H. Beckerdite's family. Dinner here. All night at Caleb Peeler's.

Thurs. 31. Went to Hopewell Church & after a Reformation Sermon by Rev. C. H. Bernheim, married Rev. William A. Lutz & Esther C. Stafford. Went to Mrs. Stafford's & took dinner. After dinner returned to Caleb Peeler's & staid over night.

Frid. Nov. 1. Returned home.

Sat. 2. In forenoon went to Gold Hill to Post Office. In afternoon at home.

Sund. 3. Preached at St. Stephen's ch. from 1 Cor. 4:2. Baptized 2 infants. Returned home.

Mond. 4. Went to Salisbury. Dinner at Phebe Brown's.

Tues. 5. Went to Gold Hill to Post Office, then to the election at Morgan's precinct.

Wed. 6. At home.

Thurs. 7. Frid. 8. Sat. 9. Attended the Western Conference at Luther's Church. Preached on Friday from 1 Cor. 4:2.

Sund. 10. In the morning married Adam M. Nussman and Ellen Klutts at Dr. Coleman's. Then went to Organ ch. Rev. Wm A. Lutz preached for me. At night went to Elm Grove School House. Rev. Lutz preached again.

Mond. 11. Went to Salisbury. Dinner at Mrs. Brown's.

Tues. 12. Wed. 13. At home.

Thurs. 14. Went to Gold Hill to Post Office & paid mine and Lewis' Tax to Sheriff.

Frid. 15. In afternoon went to Mt. Pleasant. All night at Lewis'.

Sat. 16. At one o'clock P.M. attended a meeting at St. Stephen's ch. on the subject of building a new church. All night at Peter J. Lentz's.

Sund. 17. Preached at Bethel ch. Stanly Co. from 1 Tim. 6:6. Dinner at Wm. Lyerly's. Returned home.

Mond. 18. Went to Salisbury. All night at Phebe Brown's.

Tues. 19. Returned home. Brought Phebe Brown with me.

Wed. 20. In afternoon went to Wilson Kesler's on business connected with N. C. College.

Thurs. 21. At home. Wife at Mr. Grupy's.

Frid. 22. Attended to the funeral of Nancy Solena, wife of John Carter at Rumple's Old Field Arbor. — preached from Amos 4:12.

Sat. 23. At home.

Sund. 24. Preached at Organ ch. from Dan. 6:10. Dinner at Dr. Coleman's.

Mond. 25. Tues. 26. Wed. 27. At home.

Thurs. 28. At home. Had winter hogs slaughtered.

Frid. 29. Preached at St. Stephen's ch. from 2 Cor. 4:7.

Sat. 30. Preached at St. Stephen's ch. from John 14:15. All night at C. L. Nussman's.

Sund. Dec. 1. Preached at St. Stephen's ch: from Dan. 6:10. Returned home.
Mond. 2. Started for Davidson Co. All night at Phebe Brown's in Salisbury.
Tues. 3. Took the cars at 5½ for Lexington. Took breakfast at Sour's Hotel. Then made my way to Caleb Peeler's. All night here.
Wed. 4. At Caleb Peeler's.
Thurs. 5. Went with Mrs. Peeler (sister Salome) to Anderson Bodenhamer's & took dinner. Then went to Andrew Motsinger's and married Michael C. Bodenhamer and Eliza J. Beckerdite. All night here.
Frid. 6. Went to Anderson Bodenhamer's to infare. Then returned to Caleb Peeler's & staid over night.
Sat. 7. Pleasant Nifong took me in his buggy to Lexington to meet the Cars. Took the train at 8½ for Salisbury. Then returned home.
Sund. 8. Preached at Organ ch. from 2 Cor. 4:7. Baptized one infant. Returned home.
Mond. 9. Went in forenoon to Wilson Kesler's for borrowed money for N. C. College.
Tues 10. Wed. 11. At home. Col. Shimpock with us to night.
Thurs. 12. At home.
Frid. 13. Went to Bethel ch. Stanly Co. & preached from Gen. 6:9. All night at Claborn Misenheimer's.
Sat. 14. Preached at Bethel ch. Stanly Co. from Acts 2:37. All night at David Lyerly's. Baptized to day one infant.
Sund. 15. Preached at Bethel ch. from Dan. 6:10. Dinner at Isom Misenheimer's. Returned home.
Mond. 16. Tues. 17. Wed. 18. Thurs. 19. At home.
Frid. 20. Preached at Organ ch. from Acts 2:37. Baptized one inft. Returned home.
Sat. 21. Had an appointment for to day at Organ ch. but the day being very inclement did not attend.
Sund. 22. Preached at Organ ch. from Is. 9:6. Baptized 2 infts. Returned home.+
Mond. 23. Went to Salisbury.
Tues. 24. Attended the Christmas Tree at St. Peter's church. At night attended Christmas Tree at Elm Grove School House.
Wed. 25. Attended the Christmas Tree at St. Stephen's Church. Dinner at Elizabeth Klutts' (widow). Then went to Organ church to Christmas Tree at night. Received a pair of boots, Shirt and Candies. All night at C. A. Miller's.
Thurs. 26. Returned home.
Frid. 27. At home.
Sat. 28. Went to Lower Stone Church to Christmas Tree. Dinner at W. C. Culp's.
Sund. 29. Preached at Elm Grove School from Deut. 5:3.
Mond. 30. Wrote sundry letters, then went to Gold Hill to Post Office registered the same.
Tues. 31. Went to Stanly Co. All night at Philip Ridenhour's.

+ Dinner to day at John W. Miller's. Baptized his child, it being in feeble health.

Jan. 1, 1879. Preached at Bethel ch. Stanly Co. from Deut. 5:3. last clause. Dinner at Dan¹ Lefler's. Returned home.

Thurs. 2. Attended to the funeral of James Owens' child at St. Stephen's ch.— preached from Matt. 25:13. Dinner at Mrs. Jacob Isenhour's.

Frid. 3. Sat. 4. At home.

Sund. 5. Preached at St. Stephen's ch. from Gen. 3:9. A very cold day.

Mond. 6. At home.

Tues. 7. In afternoon went to J. Powlass' & to Gold Hill.

Wed. 8. At home.

Thurs. 9. Went Mrs. Leah Holshouser's and married George W. Park & Laura Jane Holshouser.

Frid. 10. In afternoon went to Mr. Grupy's.

Sat. 11. At home.

Sund. 12. Started for Organ Church to fill my my [repeated] appointment, but failed to get there in consequence of rain & high water.

Mond. 13. At home. Had beef (Pigeon) slaughtered. Sent a quarter to Lewis at Mt. Pleasant.

Tues. 14. Went to Salisbury.

Wed. 15. Went to Gold Hill & had Lucy shod.

Thurs. 16. Went to George Peeler's on business connected with Bettie's estate. Dinner at Mr. Shemwell's.

Frid. 17. Went to Gold Hill to Post Office.

Sat. 18. Went to Stanly Co. All night at Caleb Lefler's.

Sund. 19. Preached at Bethel Church from Acts 11:26. last clause. Returned home.

Mond. 20. Rev. Linn & his mother called to see us. In the evening went to Salisbury. All night at Phebe Brown's.

Tues. 21. Attended to some settlements for Phebe Brown. Returned home.

Wed. 22. Went to Gold Hill to Post Office, and had bed-stead repaired.

Thurs. 23. At home.

Frid. 24. Went to cotton gin & Post Office.

Sat. 25. At home.

Sund. 26. Preached at Organ ch. from Acts 11:26. Dinner at Luther A. Heilig's.

Mond. 27. At home.

Tues. 28. Went to Gold Hill & had boots repaired.

Wed. 29. Went to Salisbury for White Lead, Oil, &c. to have house repainted. Dinner at Phebe Brown's.

Thurs. 30. Went to Paul Cruse's, by request, to write his will. Dinner here. Returned home & wrote his will.

Frid. 31. Returned to Mr. Cruse's & witnessed his will. Dinner here. Returned home.

Sat. Feb. 1. At home. Lewis called to see us.

Sund. 2. Preached at St. Stephen's ch. from Acts 11:26. Weather cold & inclement.

Mond. 3. Tues. 4. Wed. 5. Thurs. 6. At home having dwelling house re-painted.

Frid. 7. In afternoon went to Post Office.

Sat. 8. At home.

Sund. 9. Preached at Organ ch. from Gen. 3:15. Dinner at Uriah Miller's.

Mond. 10. At home. Tues. 11. Wed. 12. At home.

Thurs. 13. Went with Mr. Cauble in the evening to Mrs. Lentz's. Mr. C. contracted to paint her house.

Frid. 14. At home.

Sat. 15. Went to Bethel ch., Stanly Co. & had a meeting of Church Council. Compromised a case of delinquency of duty on the part of D. Plyler, Elder. All night at Philip Ridenhour's.

Sund. 16. Preached at Bethel ch. Stanly Co. from Gen. 3:15. Returned home.

Mond. 17. Tues. 18. At home.

Wed. 19. Went to Salisbury.

Thurs. 20. At home.

Frid. 21. In afternoon went to Gold Hill to Post Office.

Sat. 22. At home.

Sund. 23. Preached at Organ ch. from Luk. 10:25-37. Returned home.

Mond. 24. Went to Salisbury.

Tues. 25. Went to Danl Goodman's for feathers.

Wed. 26. At home.

Thurs. 27. In afternoon went to Nussman's Foundry.

Frid. 28. At home.

Sat. March 1. At home.

Sund. 2. Preached from St. Stephen's ch. from Luk. 10:25-37. Dinner at John Powlass'.

Mond. 3. At home.

Tues. 4. Started for the Free Diet at Mt. Moriah Church. All night at Michael Bostian's.

Wed. 5. Went to Mt. Moriah ch. to the Diet. Presided over the Diet. All night at Rev. Cone's.

Thurs. 6. At the Diet. All night at Rev. Cone's.

Frid. 7. At the Diet. Meeting adjourned at 4 p.m. Returned home.

Sat. 8. At home.

Sund. 9. Preached at Organ ch. from Prov. 1:24-26. Dinner at Eli Holshouser's.

Mond. 10. Called to see Paul Cruse, he being sick. Dinner here. Called also to see L. A. Heilig, he having cut his foot badly with hatchet.

Tues. 11. Went to Gold Hill to Post Office, thence to John T. Lentz's to have shoes repaired, thence home by way of J. Powlass' shop.

Wed. 12. Thurs. 13. At home very unwell with cold.

Frid. 14. Attended the closing exercises of Martin E. Miller's School.

Sat. 15. In forenoon attended preaching at St. Peter's ch. by Rev. L. A. Bikle, D.D. At night heard Dr. Bikle again.

Sund. 16. Preached at Bethel ch., Stanly Co. from Prov. 1:24-26. Dinner at Clab. Misenheimer's. In the afternoon preached at St. Stephen's ch. from Ps. 73:1. Returned home.

Mond. 17. At home.

Tues. 18. Went to Salisbury. Dinner at Phebe Brown's.

Wed. 19. Went to Gold Hill to Post Office, & took chair to Willie Jenkins to have repaired.

Thurs. 20. Called to see Paul Cruse, he being sick. Dinner here.

Frid. 21. Sat. 22. At home.

Sund. 23. Preached at Organ ch. from Prov. 22:6. Dinner at G. M. Bernhardt's. Baptized one infant.

Mond. 24. Went to Gold Hill & had frame made for cow's neck to prevent from sucking herself.

Tues. 25. At home.

Wed. 26. In afternoon went to Gold Hill for some Powder, Shot &c.

Thurs. 27. Went to Mt. Pleasant. Called to see Paul Cruse, he being very sick. Dinner here. Called by Dan[l] Goodman's & paid balance on feathers. Called also at Foil's Tan Yard. All night at Lewis'.

Frid. 28. In Mt. Pleasant, the day set for the meeting of Western Conference, Preached at night from Acts 9:6. All night at Col. Shimpock's.

Sat. 29. At Conference. Preached at 11 o'clock from Jam. 1:25. In the afternoon went to Paul Cruse's, he having died, & having been sent for to officiate at his burial. All night here.

Sund. 30. Attended to the funeral of Paul Cruse at Organ church — preached from Gen. 5:24. Returned home.

Mond. 31. Tues. Apr. 1. At home.

Wed. 2. Went to Gold Hill to Post Office.

Thurs. 3. Went to Salisbury.

Frid. 4. At home.

Sat. 5. Went St. Matthew's Church and preached for Rev. J. A. Linn, from Jam. 1:25. Returned home.

Sund. 6. Preached at St. Stephen's Church from Prov. 22:6.

Mond. 7. At home till dinner, then started for Concord as far as Mrs. Rachel Cruse's. All night here.

Tues. 8. Went to Concord to prove the Will of Paul Cruse, dec^{d}. Dinner at Moses Klutts'. Returned home.

Wed. 9. At home.

Thurs. 10. Started for Salem Church. All night at John Lingel's.

Frid. 11. Preached at Salem ch. from John 19:30. Dinner at Saml Colly's. All night at Moses A. Bost's.

Sat. 12. Preached at Salem ch. from Prov. 22:6. All night at Daniel Seaford's.

Sund. 13. Preached at Salem ch. from Job 7:37. Dinner at Danl Menius'. All night at Mrs. Sarah Miller's.

Mond. 14. Returned home.

Tues. 15. In afternoon went to M. A. Holshouser's & Jacob Holshouser's to put a handle in a hoe.

Wed. 16. In forenoon went to Organ ch. to examine Church Book.

Thurs. 17. Frid. 18. At home.

Sat. 19. Had preparatory service at St. Stephen's ch. — Preached from John 1:8.9. Baptized 3 inf^{ts}.

Sund. 20. Preached at St. Stephen's ch. from Ps. 133:1-3. & administered the communion. Dinner at Peter J. Lentz's. In the afternoon preached at Bethel ch. Stanly co. from 2 Cor. 5:17. Made some arrangements for Synod. All night at Alexander Misenheimer's.

Mond. 21. Returned home.

Tues. 22. Went to Salisbury & bought sack of Coffee, Barrel Sugar, & Fish.

Wed. 23. Went to John A. Troutman's & several other places making arrangements for Synod. Dinner at John A. Troutman's.

Thurs. 24. At home.

Frid. 25. Went to Gold Hill to Post Office & to John Powlass'.

Sat. 26. Had preparatory service at Organ ch. Baptized four infants. Rev. Stickley preached.

Sund. 27. Had communion at Organ ch. Rev. Stickley preached. Baptized & confirmed one adult.

Mond. 28. At home. Parson Stickley & wife with us to night.

Tues. 29. Started to Bethel Church to Synod. All night at Alexander Misenheimer's.

Wed. 30. At Bethel ch. Stanly Co. at Synod. All night at David Lyerly's.

Thurs. May 1. At Bethel ch. at Synod. All night at Alex.^r Palmer's.

Frid. 2. Called in the morning to see Mrs. Parker, she being very sick. Balance of the day in Synod. All night at Isom Misenheimer's.

Sat. 3. In synod at Bethel ch. All night at Caleb Lefler's.

Sund. 4. Called in the morning to see Mrs. Misenheimer (widow) she being sick. Attended divine service at Bethel ch. Returned home.

Mond. 5. Called at Elizabeth Klutts' (widow) and at J. Powlass'.

Tues. 6. Called at C. L. Nussman's & registered a letter with money at Gold Hill to O. C. Paper.

Wed. 7. Went to Salisbury.

Thurs. 8. At home.

Frid. 9. Sat. 10. At home.

Sund. 11. Preached at Organ ch. from Heb. 10:25. Dinner at J. Albert Heilig's. In afternoon preach^d at Elm Grove from Ex. 23:2.

Mond. 12. At home.

Tues. 13. Went to Gold Hill & registered a letter to W. J. Duffie, Columbia, S. C. with money ($9.83). Then went to Mt. Pleasant & attended the closing exercises of Female Seminary. All night at Mrs. Martha A. Dreher's.

Wed. 14. Returned home.

Thurs. 15. Frid. 16. Sat. 17. At home.

Sund. 18. Preached at St. Stephen's church from Heb. 10:25. Dinner at Peter J. Lentz's. In afternoon preached at Bethel ch., Stanly Co. from Heb. 10:25. Baptized one infant and then resigned the charge of the congregation. All night at Philip Ridenour's.

Mond. 19. Called to see Mrs. Isom Misenheimer, she being very sick. Then went to Wm. Lyerly's & baptized his child. Then went to Mt. Pleasant. Dinner & all night at Col. Shimpock's.

Tues. 20. In Mt. Pleasant. Attended meeting of College Trustees & College exercises. Dinner at Dr. Barrier's. All night at Col. Shimpock's. Unwell.

Wed. 21. Attended Commencement exercises and meeting of College Trustees. Dinner at John Harkey's. All night at Col. Shimpock's.

Thurs. 22. Returned home.

Frid. 23. Went to Gold Hill to Post-Office and Registered a money letter to New Market, Va. to Rev. S. Henkel D.D.

Sat. 24. At home. Very unwell.

Sund. 25. This my day at Organ church, but did not attend in consequence of indispostion.

Mond. 26. Tues. 27. Wed. 28. Thurs. 29. Frid. 30. Sat. 31. At home & part of the time quite unwell.

Sund. June 1. Went to St. Stephen's ch. and lectured to the congregation from Acts 2nd chapter. Returned home. In afternoon married John Leonard & Laura Noah.

Mond. 2. At home.

Tues. 3. Went to Gold Hill to post office and had Lucy shod.

Wed. 4. Thurs. 5. At home.

Frid. 6. Went to Kirk's school house and returned taxable property.

Sat. 7. At home.

Sund. 8. Preached at Organ ch. from Heb. 2:3. Dinner at Crawford Culp's. In afternoon Rev. Linn preached for me at Elm Grove School House.

Mond. 9. to Sat. 14. At home making hay, but the weather very unfavorable.

Sund. 15. Preached at St. Stephen's ch. from Heb. 2:3. Very unwell. Dinner at C. L. Nussman's.

Mond. 16. Went to Salisbury.

Tues. 17. Wed. 18. At home.

Thurs. 19. Went in forenoon to Gold Hill to post office & also had Lucy shod.

Frid. 20. Sat. 21. At home.

Sund. 22. Preached at Organ ch. from Luk. 14:15-24. Baptized one infant. Dinner at Calvin L. Brown's. In afternoon preached at Elm Grove from 1 John 1:8.9.

Mond. 23. In forenoon went to Gold Hill to post office.

Tues. 24. Went to Mt. Pleasant & brought Lottie Coleman home to Dr. Coleman's. Dinner at son Lewis'.

Wed. 25. In forenoon went to D. Barringer's mill.

Thurs. 26. Started for Conference at St. Michael's ch. Supper at Phebe Brown's. Took the train at 11 o'clock P.M. for Statesville.

Frid. 27. Took the train at 4 A.M. for Troutman. Breakfast at Joseph Leonard's. Went to St. Michael's ch. & preached from 1 Cor. 4:2. Not having a quorum, Conference did not organize. Returned to Troutman. Supper at Rev. Anthony's. All night at J. Leonard's.

Sat. 28. At St. Michael's ch. Organized Conference. Returned to Troutman. At Mr. Leonard's.

Sund. 29. At St. Michael's ch. Dr. Bikle preached. Went to Benjamin Arey's. Remained here till 12 o'clock at night, then went to Elm Wood to meet the train.

Mond. 30. Took the train at 2½ o'clock for Salisbury. Breakfast at Phebe Brown's. Took a seat in mail hack & returned home. In afternoon went to Gold Hill to Post Office.

Tues. July 1. Went with wife to L. A. Heilig's & spent the day.

Wed. 2. Thurs. 3. At home, not well.

Frid. 3. At home.

Sat. 5. Started for Ebenezer ch. All night at J. L. Graeber's.

Sund. 6. Preached at Ebenezer ch. from 1 Cor. 4:2. Dinner at J. L. Graeber's. Returned home.

Mond. 7. At home.

Tues. 8. Went to Jac. Miller's, his son Jerry being sick.

Wed. 9. In forenoon went to Gold Hill to post office.

Thurs. 10. At home. Had wheat & oats threshed.

Frid. 11. Sat. 12. At home.

Sund. 13. Preached at Organ ch. from Acts 17:30. Dinner at Daywalt Beaver's. In afternoon preached at Elm Grove from John 9:4. Returned home and married William T. R. Jenkin's & Margaret Ann Northern. Good rain this evening.

Mond. 14. At home.

Tues. 15. In forenoon went to Gold Hill to post office. In afternoon went to Salisbury in mail hack. All night at Phebe Brown's.

Wed. 16. Took excursion train for the top of mountain. All night at Henry city.

Thurs. 17. Returned to Salisbury. All night at Phebe Brown's.

Frid. 18. Returned home in mail hack.

Sat. 19. In afternoon started for Ebenezer ch. — All night at Michael Bostian's.

Sund. 20. Preached at Ebenezer ch. from 1 Tim. 6:6. Dinner at Jer. Eddleman's. Returned home.

Mond. 21. Tues. 22. Wed. 23. Thurs. 24. At home.

Frid. 25. Sat. 26. At home.

Sund. 27. Preached at Organ ch. from 1 Tim. 2:8. Installed church council. Dinner at J. A. Heilig's. In afternoon preached at Elm Grove from Rom. 8:9. last clause.

Mond. 28. Went to Gold Hill to post office & to John T. Lentz's to shoemaker.

Tues. 29. Went to Salisbury.

Wed. 30. Thurs. 31. At home.

Frid. Aug. 1. At home.

Sat. 2. Started for Ebenezer ch. All night at Dr. P. A. Seaford's.

Sund. 3. Preached at Ebenezer ch. from Rom. 10:1. Dinner at P. A. Sloop's. Returned home.

Mond. 4. Tues. 5. At home.

Wed. 6. Attended to the fun[1] of Y. G. Engelberg at Baptist ch. Gold Hill — preached from Ps. 90:12.

Thurs. 7. Went to election at Morgan's and voted for Stock Law.

Frid. 8. Went to Salisbury.

Sat. 9. Started for Bethel ch. Stanly Co. All night at Isom Misenheimer's.

Sund. 10. Preached at Bethel ch. Stanly Co. from Numb. 10:29. the fun[1] of Mary L. Misenheimer, wife of Isom Misenheimer. Dinner at Alex. Misenheimer's. Returned home.

Mond. 11. Went to St. Paul's ch. Rowan, & attended to the fun[1] of Cora May, daughter of A. F. Graeber. Preached from Heb. 4:9. All night at J. L. Graeber's.

Tues. 12. Went to Luther's Chapel & attended the Rowan Co. Sund. School Association. All night at Rev. Cone's.

Wed. 13. At Luther's Chapel till 2 o'clock P.M. then returned home.

Thurs. 14. Frid. 15. At home.

Sat. 16. Attended Sund. School Celebration at Elm Grove.

Sund. 17. Went to Ebenezer ch. & preached from Num. 10:29. Baptized one infant. Dinner at J. L. Graeber's. Returned home.

Mond. 18. Went to B. C. Arey's on business. Dinner at Mr. Grupy's.

Tues. 19. At home.

Wed. 20. Went to Laurence Lingel's for Peaches. Dinner here.

Thurs. 21. Went to Salisbury.

Frid. 22. At home.

Sat. 23. Attended Sunday School celebration at St. Luke's German Reformed Church.

Sund. 24. Preached at Organ ch. From Ps. 7:9. Baptized one infant. Dinner at Dan[1] Miller's. In the afternoon preached at Elm Grove from Ps. 48:14.

Mond. 25. Went to Salisbury & settled with Reuben (colored) in full of Indenture Bond.

Tues. 26. Wed. 27. At home.

Thurs. 28. Went to Andrew Cruse's & married Reuben W. Bost & Crissie C. Cruse.

Frid. 29. Sat. 30. At home.

Sund. 31. Preached at St. Matthew's ch. from Numb. 10:29. the fun[1] of Jonathan Stoner. Parson Adolphus Linn filled my appointment at Organ ch.

Mond. Sept. 1. Went to J. Powlass' Shop & had scythe set. Dinner here. Returned home by way of Gold Hill.

Tues. 2. At home.

Wed. 3. Went to Salisbury. Dinner at R. J. Holmes & baptized his child Ernest Lee.

Thurs. 4. Went to E. Foil's Tan Yard. Returned home by way of Boyden A. R. Miller's.

Frid. 5. At home.

Sat. 6. In afternoon went to Moses Eddleman's and staid over night.

Sund. 7. Preached at Ebenezer ch. from Jam. 1:25. Dinner at Widow Dan$^{\underline{l}}$ Eddleman's. Returned home.

Mond. 8. Attended to the fun$^{\underline{l}}$ Ador Enora, infant daughter of James C. Sides, at St. Stephen's church. Preached from Rev. 14:13.

Tues. 9. Went in forenoon to Gold Hill to post office.

Wed. 10. At home.

Thurs. 11. Went to Mrs. Heilig's mill. Dinner at Mrs. Heilig's.

Frid. 12. Sat. 13. At home.

Sund. 14. Preached at Organ ch. from Gen. 45:28. Dinner at C. A. Miller's. In afternoon preached at Elm Grove from Mark 10:46-52.

Mond. 15. Went to Gold Hill to Post Office.

Tues. 16. Went to Salisbury. Dinner at Phebe Brown's.

Wed. 17. At home.

Thurs. 18. Went to Gold Hill to Post Office.

Frid. 19. Went in afternoon to Gold Hill to post office.

Sat. 20. In the morning went D. Brady's & had Lucy shod. Then attended Sunday School Celebration at Lower Stone Church. Afterwards went to George Ketner's & staid over night.

Sund. 21. Preached at Ebenezer ch. from Gen. 6:22. Dinner at Widow Peter Ketner's. Returned home.

Mond. 22. Went to Calvin Pool's & brought wife & Bettie Thomas home. Dinner here.

Tues. 23. In afternoon hauled molasses cane to M. A. Holshouser's.

Wed. 24. Attended to the funeral of J. M. Cross' little daughter at Gold Hill Baptist Church. Preached from Matth. 5:8.

Thurs. 25. Brought molasses home from M. A. Holshouser's in forenoon. In afternoon at home.

Frid. 26. Sat. 27. At home.

Sund. 28. Preached at Organ ch. from Ps. 122:7. Took preliminary steps for the formation of a co-operative Bible Society. Dinner at John Fisher's. In afternoon preached at Elm Grove from Matth. 22:12.

Mond. 29. Went to Salisbury. Dinner at Ph. Brown's.

Tues. 30. Went with wife to Mt. Pleasant. All night at son Lewis'.

Wed. Oct. 1. Attended meeting of Board of Trustees of College. Dinner at Col. Shimpock's. Supper at Mrs. Dreher's. All night at son Lewis'.

Thurs. 2. Returned home.

Frid. 3. Went to Rev. Cone's & staid over night. Called also to see Frederic Stirewald & wife, they being old & feeble.

Sat. 4. Went with Rev. Cone's to Center Grove and assisted in laying corner Stone of church. Preached from Ps. 122:7. After intermission preached from 2 Cor. 5:17. Returned to Rev. Cone's.

Sund. 5. Preached at Ebenezer ch. from Ps. 7:9. Dinner at Jeremiah Eddleman's. Returned home.

Mond. 6. At home. Had company.

Tues. 7. Took Phebe Brown home to Salisbury. Dinner here.

Wed. 8. Thurs. 9. At home. Had some-------& shucked on Thursday evening.

Frid. 10. Started for Luther's---[page torn]--at Lena Bostian's.

Sat. 11. Went to Luther's Chapel and preached from Acts 9:6. All night at Rev. Cone's.

Sund. 12. Preached at Luther's chapel from Heb. 1:14. After an intermission assisted Rev. Cone in the administration of the Communion. All night at J. L. Graeber's.

Mond. 13. Returned home.

Tues. 14. Went to Salisbury. Dinner at Ph. Brown's.

Wed. 15. Went to Reed's mill on the river.

Thurs. 16. Went to Gold Hill to Post Office & to Mr. Crowell's & had shoes repaired (Emma's).

Frid. 17. At home.

Sat. 18. Went to Ebenezer ch. & preparatory service. Rev. Cone preached. All night at Paul Stirewalt's.

Sund. 19. Called in the morning at Frederic Stirewalt's & administered to communion to him & his wife, they being old & infirm. Then went to Ebenezer ch. & after a sermon by Rev. Cone, administered the communion. Had an intermission, after whieh Rev. Kimball-[page torn]-- Returned home.

------------------at home.

-------------------[page torn]

Wed. 22. Thurs. 23. At home.

Frid. 24. At home till afternoon then went to Gold Hill to post office.

Sat. 25. Had preparatory service at Organ ch. baptized one infant. Rev. Cone preached. Organized a co-operative Bible Society to co-operate with the County Society in the circulation of the Scriptures.

Sund. 26. At Organ ch. Rev. Cone preached. After an intermission administered the communion.

Mond. 27. Went to Mt. Pleasant and took grand-son Tommy home.

Tues. 28. At home digging Irish Potatoes.

Wed. 29. In ihe evening went to Mrs. Lentz's to Rev. Linn's reception. Rev. Lutz & wife with us to night.

Thurs. 30. At home, very much indisposed with something like chills.

Frid. 31. At home quite unwell.

Sat. Nov. 1. Sund. 2. Was under promise to assist Rev. Cone at a communion meeting at St. Paul's Church, but was too sick to attend.

Mond. 3. Tues. 4. Wed. 5. Thurs. 6. Frid. 7. At home.

Sat. 8. Preached at St. Stephen's ch. from Hos. 14:1.2. preparatory to communion.

Sund. 9. This my regular day for Organ ch. Rev. Smith of Salisbury filled the appointment. Preached at St. Stephen's ch. from 1 Thes. 2:11.12. & administered the Communion.

Mond. 10. In afternoon went to Wilson Kesler's & settled a note of hand.

Tues. 11. Attended to the funeral of Magdalene Brown, wife of Henry Brown, at Christiana Church — preached from Matth. 5:6. Dinner at Rev. R. L. Brown's. Called by H. A. Miller's & made some settlements. Called in evening at Mrs. Lentz's & brought wife home.

Wed. 12. In the morning went to mill. In the afternoon went to Gold Hill and paid Tax to Sheriff, also to the Post Office.

Thurs. 13. Went to Salisbury.

Frid. 14. Went to Gold Hill to post office & to mill.

Sat. 15. Started for Ebenezer ch. — all night at A. W. Klutts' Esq.

Sund. 16. Preached at Ebenezer ch. from 1 Thes. 2:11.12. Baptized two infants. Dinner at Frederick Stirewald's. Returned home.

Mond. 17. Tues. 18. At home.

Wed. 19. At home. Had winter hogs slaughtered.

Thurs. 20. Went to Smith Shuping's to dinner, thence to George M. Ketner's and married Rufus T. Lippard & Maggie C. Ketner. All night here.

Frid. 21. Returned home. In afternoon went to Gold Hill to post office.

Sat. 22. At home.

Sund. 23. Preached at Organ ch. from Matth. 16:26. Baptized one infant. Dinner at J. A. Heilig's.

Mond. 24. Went to Mt. Pleasant & took some sausages &c to Lewis.

Tues. 25. Went to Mr. Powlass' & had mare shod.

Wed. 26. In the morning went to mill. In the afternoon went to Gold Hill to post office.

Thurs. 27. This being Thanksgiving Day, had an appointment at Organ ch. — preached from Ps. 103:1-4. Then went to J. L. Graeber's & staid all night.

Frid. 28. Went to Ebenezer ch., this being the day for the Western Conference to meet at this place. Rev. Cone preached the opening sermon. All night at J. L. Graeber's.

Sat. 29. In conference at Ebenezer church. All night at Dr. P. A. Sifferd's.

Sund. 30. At Ebenezer ch. Rev. R. W. Petrea preached. After sermon returned home.

Mond. Dec. 1. At home.

Tues. 2. Wed. 3. At home.

Thurs. 4. Went to Moses Klutts' & married Caleb M. Troutman & Sarah A. Klutts. Then went to Elizabeth Trexler's & married David M. Lyerly & Charlotte C. Trexler. Returned home.

Frid. 5. Attended to the funeral of Sarah Josey (widow) — preached the funeral at the house from Heb. 4:9. & buried at Organ church.

Sat. 6. At home till afternoon then went to mill.

Sund. 7. Attended the dedication of Union Ev. Luth. Church. Participated in the dedication & communion services.

Mond. 8. At home.

Tues. 9. At home. B. Arey, his daughters Alice & Ellen & Ellen Grupy with us to night.

Wed. 10. At home, J. T. Goodman and wife with us to night.

Thurs. 11. In the evening went to Dr. Coleman's & brought wife home.

Frid. 12. At home, sick with cold.

Sat. 13. At home. Much indisposed. Lewis & children with us to night.

Sund. 14. This my day to preach at Organ ch. but not turn out in consequence of a severe cold & the inclemency of the weather.

Mond. 15. At home. Had Mrs. Lentz & daughter-in-law & Idy Miller to spend the day with us. Pleasant weather.

Tues. 16. Wed. 17. At home.

Thurs. 18. In forenoon went to Gold Hill to post office. Afternoon at home.

Frid. 19. In forenoon went to mill. Afternoon at home.

Sat. 20. Started for Ebenezer ch. Called to see Andrew Cruse, he being sick. All night at P. A. Sloop's.

Sund. 21. Preached at Ebenezer ch. from 1 Pet. 4:18. Dinner at J. L. Graeber's. All night at William Beaver's.

Mond. 22. Called to see Andrew Cruse, he being still sick & very feeble & infirm. Then returned home.

Tues. 23. In the afternoon went to Gold Hill to Post office.

Wed. 24. At home till evening then went to Elm Grove to Christmas Tree & addressed the audience.

Thurs. 25. Christmas Day. Went to Adolphus Heilig's to dinner. Then went to Organ. ch. to Christmas Tree. Addressed the audience. In the evening went to Mrs. Eddleman's (widow of Daniel Eddleman) & staid over night.

Frid. 26. Went to Ebenezer Church to Christmas entertainment. Sundry speakers addressed the audience. All night at Moses Eddleman's.

Sat. 27. Called to see Andrew Cruse, he being very feeble. Then went to Lower Stone Church to Christmas Tree. Addressed the audience. Returned home.

Sund. 28. Preached at Organ ch. from Ex. 23:2. Baptized one infant.

Mond. 29. Attended to the funeral of Andrew Cruse at Organ ch. Preached from 1 Thes. 4:14.

Tues. 30. Went to Gold Hill to post office, then to Laurence Lingel's, Mrs. Lingel being very sick. Dinner here.

Wed. 31. In afternoon called to see Mrs. Laurence Lingel, she being still very sick.

Thurs. Jan. 1, 1880. At home. Pleasant weather. Had some friends to spend the day with us. Married to day John A. F. Earnheart and Nancy Jane Hemphill.

Frid. 2. Attended to the fun[1] of Mrs. Elizbeth Lingel at Lower Stone Church. Preached from Rev. 2:10. last clause. Large attendance. Dinner Boyden A. R. Miller.

Sat. 3. Started for Ebenezer Church. All night at Jeremiah Eddleman's.

Sund. 4. Preached at Ebenezer ch. from Deut. 5:3. Dinner at J. L. Graeber's. Returned home.

Mond. 5. In forenoon went to mill. In afternoon went to Gold Hill to post office.

Tues. 6. Went to Salisbury.

Wed. 7. Attended to the funeral of William R. Stoner at St. Matthew's ch. Preached from Deut. 5:3. Large attendance. Dinner at Wilson Kesler's.

Thurs. 8. In forenoon went to mill. In afternoon went to H. A. Miller's and paid a note of hand.

Frid. 9. At home.

Sat. 10. At home.

Sund. 11. Preached at Organ ch. from Eph. 5:18. Subject Drunkenness. Dinner at Joseph Miller's. Baptized to day two infants.

Mond. 12. Went in forenoon to Milas A. Holshouser's to sale of Jake Ingram's corn. In the afternoon went to Post Office.

Tues. 13. Wed. 14. At home.

Thurs. 15. Went to Elizabeth Trexler's and married Jesse F. Park & Margaret J. Trexler. Returned home.

Frid. 16. At home.

Sat. 17. In the morning went to Gold Hill to post office. In afternoon started for Ebenezer ch. — All night at Moses Stirewalt's.

Sund. 18. Preached at Ebenezer from Jer. 17:9. 2 Cor. 13:5. Baptized one infant. Dinner at J. L. Graeber's. Returned home.

Mond. 19. Went to Salisbury.

Tues. 20. Wed. 21. At home.

Thurs. 22. In afternoon went to mill.

Frid. 23. At home till dinner, then went to Gold Hill to post office.

Sat. 24. At home. Lewis & children with us to night.

Sund. 25. Preached at Organ church from Josh. 7:12. — Baptized one infant. Returned home.

Mond. 26. At home.

Tues. 27. In forenoon went to Gold Hill to post office. In afternoon went to Wilson Kesler's on business.

Wed. 28. Went to Salisbury.

Thurs. 29. Went to George M. Fisher's and married Geo. A. Bost & Sarah E. Fisher.

Frid. 30. Went in forenoon to Gold Hill to post office & had Lucy Shod.

Sat. 31. Started for Ebenezer ch. All night at William Korf's.

Sund. Feb. 1. Preached at Ebenezer ch. from Prov. 14:34. Dinner at Mr. Sloop's, Esq. All night at Edmond E. Klutts'.

Mond. 2. Returned home. A very snowy inclement day.

Tues. 3. Wed. 4. Thurs. 5. At home.

Frid. 6. Went to cotton gin & to post office.

Sat. 7. At home.

Sund. 8. Preached at Organ ch. from Is. 32:11. Returned home.

Mond. 9. In afternoon went to Wilson Kesler's & paid $32 interest on a note by Jonas Cook as College Treasurer.

Tues. 10. In afternoon went to Gold Hill to post office.

Wed. 11. Went to Gold Hill for some oats. In afternoon went to mill.

Thurs. 12. At home. Married to day Mr. Calvin A. Fisher & Miss Eliza A. E. Miller, daughter of the late George A. Miller.

Frid. 13. In the morning went to mill, then to Gold Hill to Post Office.

Sat. 14. Started for Ebenezer ch. All night at widow Andrew Bostian's.

Sund. 15. Preached at Ebenezer ch. from Matth. 4:10. Dinner at J. L. Graeber's. Returned home.

Mond. 16. At home. Wife & girls went visiting to Dr. Coleman's.

Tues. 17. Went in forenoon to Gold Hill for some Oats & to Post Office.

Wed. 18. At home.

Thurs. 19. Went to Salisbury.

Frid. 20. At home. Made final settlement to day with Wm. P. Arey, Ward.

Sat. 21. In the morning went to Post Office. In afternoon at home.

Sund. 22. Preached at Organ ch. from Matth. 15:25. Baptized one infant. Dinner at Dr. Coleman's.

Mond. 23. Went to Gold Hill to Post Office.

Tues. 24. At home. In evening took Mrs. Coleman home.

Wed. 25. Started for Salem ch. to attend for a few days, the meeting of Eastern Conference. All night at Phebe Brown's in Salisbury.

Thur. 26. Went to Salem ch. All night at Abner Gheen's.

Frid. 27. At Salem ch. — Preached to day from Acts 26:17.18. All night at John Lingel's.

Sat. 28. Returned home. Lewis & children with us to night.

Sund. 29. Preached at St. Paul's church from Matth. 21:28-32. Dinner at Charles Fisher's.

Mond. March 1. In the morning went to mill. Rev. Smith & family with us over night.

Tues. 2. Went to Parson Linn's with Parson Smith & took dinner. Returned home by way of Dr. Coleman's. J. C. Miller with us over night.

Wed. 3. In the morning went to mill. In afternoon went to Post Office.

Thurs. 4. Went to Salisbury. Phebe Brown having sold her house & lot, made a transfer of title to the same.

Frid. 5. In the morning went to mill. In afternoon went to Gold Hill to Post Office & settled some store accounts.

Sat. 6. Started for Ebenezer ch. Over night at Moses A. Ketner's.

Sund. 7. Preached at Ebenezer ch. from Matth. 21:28. Dinner at J. L. Graeber's. Returned home.

Mond. 8. At home.

Tues. 9. In forenoon went to Gold Hill to Post Office. M. A. Ketner and J. R. Troutman with us to night.

Wed. 10. Sold a cow & calf to Mr. Troutman & 1 pig, & 3 pigs to Mr. Ketner, also made a conditional sale of Flora to Mr. Ketner.

Thurs. 11. Went to Salisbury.

Frid. 12. At home.

Sat. 13. In forenoon went to Gold Hill to Post Office.

Sund. 14. A very inclement day. Went to Organ ch. but did not preach as the congregation did not assemble in consequence of rain.

Mond. 15. Tues. 16. At home.

Wed. 17. Went to Post Office & to mill.

Thurs. 18. At home.

Frid. 19. In forenoon went to Mr. Frick's & had frame made for cow to prevent her from sucking herself.

Sat. 20. In forenoon went to mill. Lewis and children called to see us. In afternoon started for Ebenezer ch. All night at Rufus Troutman's.

Sund. 21. Preached at Ebenezer ch. from Matth. 21:10.11. Dinner at Dan[l] Eddleman's. Returned home.

Mond. 22. Went to Mr. Powlass' & had Lucy shod. Returned home by way of Post Office.

Tues. 23. In morning went to Post Office. In afternoon went to D. Barringer's & for Phebe Brown, settled with Lucy Philips.

Wed. 24. Attended to the funeral Mary Barbara, widow of John Lentz, at St Stephen's ch. — preached the fun[l] at the house from Matt. 5:6. Dinner at Caleb Nussman's.

Thurs. 25. In the morning went to Gold Hill. In the afternoon went to mill.

Frid. 26. Started for Bethel Church, Rowan, to assist Rev. H. M. Brown. All night at Rev. Brown's.

Sat. 27. Preached at Bethel ch. from Matth. 21:28. Dinner Alexander Lentz's. Supper at Mr. Reeves'. Preached again at night from Luk. 13:3. All night at H. G. Miller's.

Sund. 28. Preached at Bethel church from John 7:37. & aided in the admistration of the Lord's Supper. All night at Andrew Shuping's.

Mond. 29. Returned home. Dinner at Phebe Brown's in Salisbury.

Tues. 30. Went to Salisbury & brought wife home, she having gone thither on a visit.

Wed. 31. At home. Quite unwell.

Thurs. April 1. Went to Salisbury & brought Bureau & Bed Stead home for Bettie.

Frid. 2. At home.

Sat. 3. Preached at Luther's ch. from Matth. 21:28. for Rev. J. A. Linn. Returned home.

Sund. 4. Preached at Luther's ch. from John 7:37. Dinner at widow Caleb Shaver's. Returned home.

Mond. 5. Attended to the funeral of Mrs. Isaac Earnheart at Lower St. church — preached from Eccl. 9:5. Returned home by way of Albert Heilig's.

Tues. 6. In afternoon went to Moses Eagle's to get him to spay hogs.

Wed. 7. Had hogs spayed. Went to mill & Gold Hill to Post Office.

Thurs. 8. Frid. 9. Sat. 10. At home.

Sund. 11. Preached at Organ ch. from Acts 24:25. Baptized 3 infants. Dinner at Dr. Coleman's.

Mond. 12. In the morning went to mill. Balance of day at home.

Tues. 13. In the forenoon went to Gold Hill to Post Office & registered a letter to W. J. Duffie in Columbia, S. C. In afternoon went to David Ketchie's below St. Matthew's ch. on the subject of curing a heifer of warts.

Wed. 14. In the morning went to mill. In the afternoon at home & married Henry A. C. Ketner & Alice Caldwell.

Thurs. 15. At home.

Frid. 16. Started for Ebenezer ch. Called at James Eller's & baptized his child, his wife being afflicted & child in feeble health. All night at John Pless'.

Sat. 17. Called at Frederick Stirewald's, his wife being in bad health, then went to Ebenezer church. Rev. J. A. Linn preached for me. Baptized 2 infants & had preparatory service. All night at Dr. P. A. Sifferd's.

Sund. 18. In the morning called at Frederick Stirewald's & administered the communion to him & his wife. Then went to Ebenezer ch. Rev. J. A. Linn preached. After preaching administered the communion. Dinner at J. L. Graeber's. Returned home.

Mond. 19. At home.

Tues. 20. In afternoon went to Gold Hill to Post Office.

Wed. 21. Went to Salisbury.

Thurs. 22. Clerked sale for David Brady.

Frid. 23. In forenoon went to Gold Hill to Post Office. In afternoon went to mill.

Sat. 24. Had preparatory services at Organ ch. Rev. H. M. Brown preached. Confirmed one person. Baptized one infant at the church. Called at Uriah Miller's & took dinner and baptized two children for John H. Lentz & wife.

Sund. 25. At Organ church. Rev. Brown preached. After an intermission administered the communion. In afternoon went to Lower St. Church & attended to the fun[l] of Elizabeth Hampton. Preached from Heb. 9:27.

Mond. 26. In the morning went to H. A. Holshouser's for Rosa Fisher. Balance of day at home.

Tues. 27. In the morning went to M. A. Holshouser's for sewing machine. Balance of day at home making preparations for Synod.

Wed. 28. Went to Mt. Pleasant to attend meeting of Synod. Was elected President.

Thurs. 29. Frid. 30. At synod.

Sat. May 1. To day, being aided by the other officers of Synod, Ordained James Koontz (colored) to labor among the colored people.

Sund. 2. Much indisposed with cold. Attended preaching and communion.

Mond. 3. Returned home.

Tues. 4. Went with wife to Gold Hill to the shoemaker and to the Post Office.

Wed. 5. At home.

Thurs. 6. Ascension Day. Went to Ebenezer ch. and lectured to the people being too unwell to preach. Dinner at J. L. Graeber's. On the way home called at C. A. Miller's & baptized his child, the child being in bad health.

Frid. 7. Went to Salisbury with Rosa Fisher. Dinner at Phebe Brown's. Sent Postal Money Order to Our Church Paper.

Sat. 8. At home.

Sund. 9. Attended to the funeral of Licette Jane Eller at Organ ch. − preached from Heb. 11:16. Very unwell. Returned home.

Mond. 10. Went to Salisbury.

Tues. 11. Went to Gold Hill to Post Office.

Wed. 12. In forenoon went to mill. In afternoon at home, had Dr. Coleman & wife, & Rev. Linn & wife with us.

Thurs. 13. Went by way of Gold Hill to Laurence Lingel's for Oats. Dinner here. In afternoon went to mill.

Frid. 14. In afternoon went to Post Office.

Sat. 15. Went to Ebenezer ch. and had catechization. All night William Eddleman's.

Sund. 16. Preached at Ebenezer ch. from 1 Thes. 5:19. Dinner at Dr. P. A. Sifferd's. Returned home.

Mond. 17. Went to Salisbury. Dinner at Ph. Brown's.

Tues. 18. In afternoon went to mill.

Wed. 19. Went to Mt. Pleasant & took Tommy home. Returned by way of Foil's Tan Yard & Danl Goodman's.

Thurs. 20. In forenoon went to Wilson Kestler's & paid him some money on College Note. In afternoon went to mill.

Frid. 21. In forenoon engaged hands to mow grass. In afternoon went to Post Office.

Sat. 22. Went to Uriah Miller's & had shoeing done. Dinner here. Then went to Organ ch. & formed a class of catechumens. All night at Henry Klutts'.

Sund. 23. Preached at Organ ch. from 1 Thes. 5:19. Returned home.

Mond. 24. Went by way of Gold Hill, Danl Goodman's &c. to Mt. Pleasant to attend Commencement exercises of N. C. College. All night at Lewis'.

Tues. 25. In Mt. Pleasant. Dinner at Col. Shimpock's. All night at Lewis'.

Wed. 26. In Mt. Pleasant. Dinner at Col. Shimpock's. Supper at Danl Barrier's. All night at Lewis'.

Thurs. 27. Returned home.

Frid. 28. Started for Concord to attend meeting of Western Conference. All night on the way at Mrs. Rachel Cruse's.

Sat. 29. Went into Concord & attended meeting of Conference. Dinner at Mrs. Winecoff's. All night at Mr. Fetzer's.

Sund. 30. After an address by Dr. L. A. Bikle, installed Rev. S. T. Hallman as pastor of St. James Church. Dinner & supper at Alex^{r} Foil's. All night at Mr. Fetzer's.

Mond. 31. Returned home. Dinner at Caleb Cruse's.

Tues. June 1. At home making hay.

Wed. 2. In afternoon went to Gold Hill to Post Office.

Thurs. 3. At home.

Frid. 4. Went to Kirk's School House and made return of Taxes.

Sat. 5. Went to Ebenezer & had catechization in the afternoon. All night widow Mos. Bostian's.

Sund. 6. Preached at Ebenezer from Prov. 3:6. Dinner at J. M. Eddleman's. Returned home.

Mond. 7. Went to Salisbury.

Tues. 8. In forenoon went to mill. In afternoon at home.

Wed. 9. Went to Mr. J. Powlass' & had mare shod. Dinner here.

Thurs. 10. In afternoon went to mill.

Frid. 11. At home.

Sat. 12. Had catechization at Organ church.

Sund. 13. Preached at Organ ch. from Luk. 15:2. Baptized 2 infants. Very unwell. Dinner at Jacob Miller's.

Mond. 14. Tues. 15. At home.

Wed. 16. Went with son Lewis to Salisbury.

Thurs. 17. Went to Gold Hill & mailed some letters. Afternoon at home.

Frid. 18. In afternoon went to Post Office at Gold Hill.

Sat. 19. Went to Ebenezer ch. & in afternoon had catechization. All night at David Bostian's.

Sund. 20. Rev. Kimball preached to day. Dinner at Widow Ketner's. Returned home.

Mond. 21. Went to Gold Hill to post office.

Tues. 22. Wed. 23. Thurs. 24. Frid. 25. At home.

Sat. 26. Dinner to day at J. Allen Miller's. In afternoon had catechization at Organ ch.

Sund. 27. Preached at Organ ch. from John 5:6. Dinner at C. L. Brown's. In afternoon preached at Elm Grove from Jam. 1:25.

Mond. 28. Tues. 29. Wed. 30. At home.

Thurs. July 1. Went to Enochville. Dinner at J. Graeber's. All night at James Plaster's.

Frid. 2. Met the Councils of St. Enoch's and Trinity Churches to settle difficulties in the way of getting a preacher. All night at Alex.ᵗ Bostian's.

Sat. 3. Had catechization at Ebenezer ch. Dinner at Mr. Shinn's. All night at Calvin Leip's.

Sund. 4. Preached at Ebenezer ch. from Is. 32:11. Dinner at J. L. Graeber's. Returned home.

Mond. 5. Tues. 6. Wed. 7. Thurs. 8. At home.

Frid. 9. Went to Gold Hill to Post Office.

Sat. 10. Had catechization at Organ ch.

Sund. 11. Preached at Organ ch. from 1 Pet. 5:5. Dinner at Moses A. Fesperman's. In the afternoon preached to Sunday School at Peeler's School House from Ps. 34:11.

Mond. 12. Tues. 13. Wed. 14. Thurs. 15. At home.

Frid. 16. At home — had wheat & oats threshed.

Sat. 17. Had catechization at Ebenezer ch. Dinner at widow Cline's. All night at Jacob Pless'.

Sund. 18. Preached at Ebenezer ch. from John 7:37. Baptized one infant. Dinner at Augustus Ketner's. Returned home.

Mond. 19. At home.

Tues. 20. Went to the Misenheimer Springs.

Wed. 21. At the Springs.

Thurs. 22. In the afternoon returned home.

Frid. 23. At home.

Sat. 24. Went to Organ ch. meet catechumens, but the day being rainy the class did not attend. Dinner at L. A. Heilig's.

Sund. 25. Preached at Organ ch. from Is. 35:8-10. Installed Church Council. Dinner at G. A. Bernhardt's. In the afternoon preached at Elm Grove from Luk. 12:16-21.

Mond. 26. In forenoon went to Gold Hill to Post Office. Lewis with us to night.

Tues. 27. In the morning went to Dr. Coleman's. Balance of day at home.

Wed. 28. Went to Salisbury.

Thurs. 29. At home.

Frid. 30. At home.

Sat. 31. Had catechization at Ebenezer ch. All night at J. L. Graeber's.

Sund. Aug. 1. Preached at Ebenezer from Acts. 9:6. Dinner at J. A. Eddleman's.

Mond. 2. In afternoon went to Dr. Coleman's.

Tues. 3. Went to the spring at A. Misenheimer's. Returned home & got wet.

Wed. 4. Thurs. 5. At home.

Frid. 6. In afternoon went to Gold Hill to Post Office.

Sat. 7. At home.

Sund. 8. Preached at Organ ch. from Acts 9:6. Dinner at Daniel Miller's. In afternoon preached at Elm Grove from Luk. 11:1-10.

Mond. 9. At home.

Tues. 10. Attended the annual meeting of the Rowan County Sunday School Association at Organ Church.

Wed. 11. Attended the annual meeting of the Rowan County Bible Society at Organ Church. Both meetings were interesting.

Thurs. 12. At home.

Frid. 13. Went to D. Barringer's mill.

Sat. 14. Had catechization at Ebenezer ch. All night at Sandy Stirewalt's.

Sund. 15. Preached at Ebenezer from Ex. 14:15. Dinner at Moses Eddleman's. Returned home.

Mond. 16. Went to Salisbury.

Tues. 17. At home.

Wed. 18. Went to J. Powlass' & had mare shod.

Thurs. 19. At home.

Frid. 20. In afternoon went to Gold Hill to Post Office.

Sat. 21. Had catechization at Organ Church.

Sund. 22. Preached at Organ ch. from Rom. 12:2. Baptized one infant. Dinner at C. A. Miller's. In afternoon preached at Elm Grove from Is. 3:10.

Mond. 23. At home.

Tues. 24. Went to Salisbury.

Wed. 25. Thurs. 26. Frid. 27. Sat. 28. At home.

Sund. 29. Attended singing at Mt. Olive Church.

Mond. 30. Tues. 31. At home.

Wed., Sep. 1. Thurs. 2. Frid. 3. At home.

Sat. 4. Went by request to Rev. W. H. Cone's, he being in trouble about evil report's concerning him. All night here.

Sund. 5. Preached at Ebenezer ch. from Prov. 22:2. Dinner at George Troutman's. Returned home.

Mond. 6. Went to Salisbury. Dinner at P. N. Heilig's.

Tues. 7. Went to Gold Hill to Post Office and had Lucy shod. In afternoon called to see Rev. Linn, he being sick.

Wed. 8. At home.

Thurs. 9. Frid. 10. At home.

Sat. 11. Attended the laying of the Corner Stone for a new church at St. Stephen's.

Sund. 12. Preached at Organ ch. from Gal. 4:5. Dinner at C. L. Brown's. In afternoon preached at Elm Grove from Luk. 7:11-17.

Mond. 13. At home.

Tues. 14. Went to Gold Hill to post office.

Wed. 15. Thurs. 16. At home.

Frid. 17. Attended singing at Elm Grove. Returned home by way of post office at Gold Hill. Lewis with us to night.

Sat. 18. Had catechization at Ebenezer ch. All night at Dr. P. A. Sifferd's.

Sund. 19. Rev. Calvin Sifferd preached for me to day. Baptized 2 infants. Dinner at J. L. Graeber's. Returned home.

Mond. 20. Went to Gold Hill to post office.

Tues. 21. At home.

Wed. 22. Went to Gold Hill to post office.

Thurs. 23. In forenoon aided in surveying off a portion of Morgan Township to be attached to Gold Hill Township. In afternoon went to Gold Hill & heard Armfield, Democratic candidate for Congress speak. Also T. F. Klutts, democratic elector and Dr. Ramsey, Radical elector.

Frid. 24. In the morning went to mill, then to Gold Hill to post office.

Sat. 25. Had catechization at Organ ch. In afternoon late went to mill.

Sund. 26. Preached at Organ ch. from 1 King 19:9. Dinner at Joseph Miller's. In afternoon preached at Elm Grove from Matth. 4:10.

Mond. 27. Went with wife to Salisbury.

Tues. 28. In the morning went to mill. In afternoon went to Gold Hill to shoemaker & in the evening went to mill.

Wed. 29. Went to Salisbury under summons by David Barringer, as witness.

Thurs. 30. In the morning went to Gold Hill to have shoeing done, & went to mill. In afternoon went to M. A. Holshouser's and brought ax home.

Frid. Oct. 1. Had catechization at Ebenezer ch. Returned home.

Sat. 2. Attended Sunday School Entertainment at Organ Church. Returned home.

Sund. 3. Preached at Ebenezer ch. from Josh. 24:15. Dinner at P. A. Sifferd's. In the afternoon attended to the funeral of Catharine Ketner. Preached at the house from Matth. 5:6. Buried at Ebenezer. All night at J. M. Eddleman's.

Mond. 4. Went to Salisbury to attend meeting of County Commissioners. Returned home.

Tues. 5. Went to Gold Hill to the shoemaker & to the post office.

Wed. 6. Went to Mt. Pleasant to attend meeting of Board of Trustees. Did nothing, a quorum not being present. Returned home.

Thurs. 7. At home.

Frid. 8. Went to Gold Hill to the shoemaker & to the post office.

Sat. 9. Had catechization at Organ ch.

Sund. 10. Preached at Organ ch. from Prov. 14:34. Baptized one infant. Dinner at Mary A. Heilig's. In the afternoon preached at Elm Grove from 1 Sam. 12:23.24.

Mond. 11. Tues. 12. At home making hay.

Wed. 13. Went to Clerk's office in Salisbury as witness Arey vs. Barringer. Parties compromised without trial.

Thurs. 14. Went to D. Barringer's mill in forenoon. In afternoon at home.

Frid. 15. Had catechization at Ebenezer ch. All night at Moses A. Ketner's.

Sat. 16. Preached at Ebenezer from 2 Cor. 13:5. Baptized two infants & confirmed four persons. Held preparatory service. In afternoon went to George Troutman's to see his little son who was sick. Returned George M. Ketner's and staid over night.

Sund. 17. At Ebenezer ch. Rev. Calvin Sifferd preached morning & afternoon. Administered the Communion. Dinner at J. L. Graeber's. Returned home.

Mond. 18. Went to Gold Hill to post office & the shoemaker.

Tues. 19. Called to see Harvey Bernhardt at Rev. Crook's shop on the subject of buying corn. Had horseshoeing done by Haines.

Wed. 20. Brought rent corn home from Solomon Peeler's.

Thurs. 21. Frid. 22. Attended to the dividing of the corn for the Bernhardts at the Fullenwider place. Having bought the rent corn had it brought home. Graeber & Williamson (candidates) with us to night.

Sat. 23. Had catechization at Organ ch.

Sund. 24. Preached at Organ ch. from Col. 1:28. Dinner at R. W. Bost's. Then went to Mt. Pleasant & preached at night from Luk. 13:3. All night at Lewis'.

Mond. 25. Went to St. John's ch. by request of Church Council, to deliberate upon some irregularities in church usages on the part of Rev. Petrea, the pastor. He promised amendment. Returned home.

Tues. 26. Went to Morgan's to hear candidates.

Wed. 27. Went to Salisbury.

Thurs. 28. At home.

Frid. 29. Went early in the morning to George Troutman's & preached the funeral of his little son, 8 yrs. old, from Eccl. 12:1. Then went to Organ church & buried him. Then attended meeting of Western Conference in the church. Rev. W. J. Smith preached. Returned home.

Sat. 30. Conference at Organ church. Rev. S. T. Hallman preached. Baptized one infant, confirmed thirteen persons & then held preparatory service. Over night at Wm. Beaver's.

Sund. 31. At Organ Church. Confirmed one person. Rev. Hallman preached a Reformation sermon. After an intermission the communion was administered. Returned home.

Mond. Nov. 1. At home.

Tues. 2. Went to the election at Morgan's precinct and voted. Returned home by way of post office at Gold Hill.

Wed. 3. Went to Salisbury. A rainy day.

Thurs. 4. In forenoon went to Linn's mill. In afternoon at home.

Frid. 5. In forenoon went to Gold Hill to post office. In afternoon went to mill.

Sat. 6. At home. Had Mr. Frick in afternoon to build pig-pen.

Sund. 7. Went to Ebenezer ch. and preached from Prov. 14:32. Dinner at J. L. Graeber's. Returned home.

Mond. 8. At home. Penned pigs.

Tues. 9. Called to see Laurence Lingel.

Wed. 10. Went to Gold Hill to post office, then to Elm Grove to singing.

Thurs. 11. In forenoon helped to haul up some firewood. In afternoon went to St. Peter's ch. to singing.

Frid. 12. In forenoon went to Gold Hill to post office. In afternoon at home.

Sat. 13. At home.

Sund. 14. Preached at Organ ch. from Matth. 25:14-30. An inclement day.

Mond. 15. At home. Revds. Sifferd & Linn and families spent the day with us.

Tues. 16. In the morning went to Gold Hill to post office. In afternoon at home.

Wed. 17. Went to Salisbury with wife & Bettie.

Thurs. 18. In forenoon went to mill. In afternoon at home.

Frid. 19. In forenoon went to Gold Hill to post office. In afternoon went to mill.

Sat. 20. Started for Ebenezer ch. Over night at P. A. Sloop's Esq.

Sund. 21. Preached at Ebenezer from Mark 10:40-52. Baptized one infant. Dinner at P. A. Sloop's. Returned home.

Mond. 22. At home, had winter hogs slaughtered.

Tues. 23. At home.

Wed. 24. At home till afternoon, then went to Dr. Coleman's for Books of Worship which he brought from Salisbury for me.

Thurs. 25. At home.

Frid. 26. This is my birthday being now 71 years old. Went to Gold Hill to post office.

Sat. 27. At home.

Sund. 28. Went to Organ ch. An inclement day. Attendance very small. Lectured from Matth. 21:1-11.

Mond. 29. At home.

Tues. 30. Went with Moses Frick to Salisbury.

Wed. Dec. 1. At home.

Thurs. 2. Went to mill.

Frid. 3. In forenoon went to post office.

Sat. 4. Had catechization at Ebenezer ch. All night at Jeremiah Eddleman's.

Sund. 5. At Ebenezer ch. Rev. C. W. Sifferd preached. All night at Dr. P. A. Sifferd's.

Mond. 6. Returned home.

Tues. 7. Attended to the funeral Mrs. Nancy Melton at Gold Hill, preached from Matth. 25:10. Dinner at James Gill's.

Wed. 8. At home.

Thurs. 9. Went to Dr. Coleman's. Dinner here. In the evening went to mill.

Frid. 10. Went in forenoon to Gold Hill to post office. In afternoon at home.

Sat. 11. Went in morning to M. A. Holshouser's for Books of Worship. Then at home.

Sund. 12. Preached to day at St. Matthew's ch. the funeral of Mrs. Sandy Pool, she having died some time before. Rev. C. W. Sifferd filled my appointment at Organ ch. Dinner at Wilson Kesler's.

Mond. 13. At home.

Tues. 14. At home.

Wed. 15. Attended to the funeral of Peter Axam Ribelin at St. Matthew's ch. Preached from Eccl. 12:1.

Thurs 16. Went to Salisbury.

Frid. 17. Went by way of Gold Hill to Mt. Pleasant. All night at Col. Shimpock's.

Sat. 18. Dinner at son Lewis'. In afternoon went to Albemarle. Preached at night in Methodist church from Matth. 5:6. All night at Mr. Lilly's.

Sund. 19. Aided in laying the corner stone of Albemarle Ev. Luth. Church. Rev. L. A. Bikle, D.D. delivered the address. Dinner at Mr. Lilly's. Preached at night in the Methodist church from James 1:25. All night at Mrs. Hearne's (Widow).

Mond. 20. Returned home. A very inclement day.

Tues. 21. Went to D. Barringer's mill.

Wed. 22. Went to Gold Hill to Post office & to shoemaker.

Thurs. 23. In forenoon went to Dr. Coleman's.

Frid. 24. Attended to the funeral of Charles A. Miller at Organ ch. – preached from Heb. 9:27. Dinner at Dr. Coleman's. At night attended Christmas Tree at Elm Grove.

Sat. 25. Christmas Day. Spent the day with wife at Mrs. Lentz's. Snowed all day.

Sund. 26. This my day at Organ ch., but did not attend in consequence of deep snow. Son Lewis & children with us.

Mond. 27. Went to Gold Hill to post office.

Tues. 28. At home.

Wed. 29. Thurs. 30. Frid. 31. Snow in abundance.

Sat. Jan. 1, 1881. At home. Weather inclement.

Sund. 2. This was my day to preach at Ebenezer, but did not attend in consequence of heavy snow on the ground.

Mond. 3. At home.

Tues. 4. At home. Had two hogs slaughtered.

Wed. 5. At home.

Thurs. 6. In afternoon went to H. A. Miller's mill.

Frid. 7. Went to Gold Hill to post office.

Sat. 8. At home.

Sund. 9. This was my day to preach at Organ ch. but the day being very inclement & the roads very icy & slippery, did not attend.

Mond. 10. At home.

Tues. 11. Went to Salisbury.

Wed. 12. At home.

Thurs. 13. Went to D. Barringer's mill.

Frid. 14. In forenoon went to D. Barringer's mill. In afternoon to Gold Hill to post office.

Sat. 15. Started for Ebenezer ch. All night at widow Dan$^{\underline{l}}$ Eddleman's.

Sund. 16. Preached at Ebenezer ch. from Josh. 23:8. Dinner & all night at Henry T. Graeber's.

Mond. 17. Returned home. Called to see widow Charlie A. Miller & widow Moses Linn. Dinner at Dr. Coleman's.

Tues. 18. At home. Cleaned stables.

Wed. 19. At home.

Thurs. 20. At home.

Frid. 21. In forenoon went to Gold Hill to post office. In afternoon at home.

Sat. 22. At home preparing for Sunday.

Sund. 23. Preached at Organ ch. from Neh. 7:2. latter clause. Baptized three infants. Dinner at M. A. Holshouser's and baptized John F. Beatty's child.

Mond. 24. At home.

Tues. 25. Went to Moses Klutts' & baptized Calvin M. Troutman's child, it being sick. Dinner at Caleb Cruse's.

Wed. 26. At home.

Thurs. 27. Started for Conference at Ebenezer church. All night at Zwingle Roseman's. Suffered cold during the night.

Frid. 28. At Conference. Rev. B. S. Brown preached. Over night at J. M. Eddleman's.

Sat. 29. At Conference. Rev. W. J. Smith preached. All night at J. L. Graebers.

Sund. 30. At Ebenezer ch. Confirmed one person & received one by letter. Revds. Lutz and Kimball preached. All night at Mr. Sloop's.

Mond. 31. Returned home.

Tues. Feb. 1. Went to Gold Hill to Post Office.

Wed. 2. At home.

Thurs. 3. At home till evening, then went to M. A. Holshouser's & brought wife home, she having gone there on a visit. Snow & cold.

Frid. 4. Went to Gold Hill to post office.

Sat. 5. Went to Ebenezer & had catechization. All night at Mr. Korf's.

Sund. 6. Preached at Ebenezer ch. from Matth. 13:24-30. Dinner at Smith Shuping's. In the afternoon preached at Rymer's School House from Rev. 2:4.5. All night at Caleb Cruse's.

Mond. 7. Called to see widow Nancy Cruse. Called also to see Widow Mary Cruse. Dinner at latter place. Returned home.

Tues. 8. Called on sundry persons to sign a petition to the Legislature to prohibit the sale of Spirituous Liquors within three miles of St. Peter's Church, except under medical prescription.

Wed. 9. In forenoon went to post office at Gold Hill.

Thurs. 10. Went to widow Paul Yost's & married John M. Clarke & Lundy M. Yost. All night at Paul Stirewalt's.

Frid. 11. Called at George Troutman's, also at Henry Klutts'. Dinner here. Called to see David Beaver, he being in bad health. Then returned home.

Sat. 12. Went to Gold Hill to post office. Then at home.

Sund. 13. Preached at Organ church from Matth. 20:6. Dinner at G. M. Bernhardt's.

Mond. 14. In afternoon went to Linn's mill to see whether it was in running order.

Tues. 15. Went to Linn's mill & had horse feed ground.

Wed. 16. Went to Salisbury.

Thurs. 17. Went to Gold Hill to post office & to Elm Grove to singing.

Frid. 18. Went to Gold Hill to Post Office.

Sat. 19. Had catechization at Ebenezer ch. All night at widow Andrew Bostian's.

Sund. 20. Preached at Ebenezer ch. from Matth. 20:6. Returned home.

Mond. 21. Went to Mrs. Lentz's mill.

Tues. 22. Went to Salisbury & made return of Bettie Thomas' Estate as Guardian.

Wed. 23. Went to Gold hill to Post Office.

Thurs. 24. Went to Joseph Miller's, his wife being sick.

Frid. 25. Went to John T. Lentz's to shoe maker & to Rev. Crooks' & had mare shod.

Sat. 26. At home.

Sund. 27. Preached at St. Stephen's ch. from Acts 16:13-15. Dinner at John Powlass'. Rev. Kimball filled my appointment at Organ ch. Very inclement in afternoon.

Mond. 28. In forenoon went to Dr. Coleman's. In afternoon at home.

Tues. March 1. Went to Gold Hill to Post Office & to John T. Lentz's to have shoes made.

Wed. 2. Went to J. Allen Miller's. Dinner here.

Thurs. 3. Frid. 4. At home.

Sat. 5. Had catechization at Ebenezer ch. All night at George Ketner's.

Sund. 6. Preached at Ebenezer from Acts 16:13-15. Dinner at Sandy Stirewalt's. Had devotional exercises for the benefit of Mrs. Fred Stirewalt. All night at George Troutman's.

Mond. 7. Returned home. Called on the way to see Mrs. Seaford, widow of John Seaford. Dinner at L. A. Heilig's. In the evening went to mill.

Tues. 8. In forenoon went to Gold Hill to Post Office. In afternoon at home.

Wed. 9. In morning went to mill, — then at home.

Thurs. 10. In the morning went to Dr. Coleman's. In afternoon went with Albert Earnheart to see his mother to compromise difficulties, but failed to do anything.

Frid. 11. In forenoon went to Gold Hill to Post Office. In afternoon at home.

Sat. 12. Went to China Grove. All night with Rev. B. S. Brown.

Sund. 13. Preached at Luther's Chapel from 2 Tim. 1:13. & then aided in the installation of Rev. B. S. Brown. After an intermission, Rev. W. J. Smith, of Salisbury, preached, setting forth the duty of the people to the pastor. All night at Rev. W. H. Cone.

Mond. 14. Returned home.

Tues. 15. At home.

Wed. 16. Went to Salisbury.

Thurs. 17. Went around in afternoon to engage hands to split wood, but failed.

Frid. 18. At home.

Sat. 19. Went to Ebenezer ch. & had catechization. All night at Moses Stirewalt's.

Sund. 20. Rev. W. H. Cone being present preached at Ebenezer. Dinner at J. L. Graeber's. Preached in afternoon at Rymer's school House from 2 Cor. 5:17. All night at Rachel Cruse's.

Mond. 21. Called to see Mrs. Elias Beaver, she being very sick. Dinner here. In afternoon returned home by way of H. A. Miller's.

Tues. 22. Went to Linn's Mill.

Wed. 23. Thurs. 24. At home.

Frid. 25. In afternoon went to Gold Hill to Post Office.

Sat. 26. At home. Lewis with us to night.

Sund. 27. Preached at Organ ch. from Acts 16:16-34. Baptized three infants. Returned home.

Mond. 28. Went to Mr. Powlass' & had Lucy shod. Dinner here.

Tues. 29. Attended to the fun[1] of Mrs. Nelly Beaver, widow of Elias Beaver, at Organ ch. — preached Micah 2:10. Dinner at Reuben W. Bost's.

Wed. 30. At home.

Thurs. 31. Went to Salisbury. Dinner at Dr. Coleman's.

Frid. April 1. At home.

Sat. 2. At catechization at Ebenezer ch. All night at Jeremiah Eddleman's.

Sund. 3. Preached at Ebenezer ch. from Matt. 6:33. Baptized two infants. Dinner at J. L. Graeber's. Returned home.

Mond. 4. Went to Linn's mill.

Tues. 5. At home.

Wed. 6. At home, hauled hay into the barn.

Thurs. 7. Went to Salisbury.

Frid. 8. In afternoon went to Gold Hill to Post Office.

Sat. 9. Went to Salisbury under subpoena, State vs. Mary C. Earnheart et al. Case continued.

Sund. 10. Attended to the fun[1] of Nelly, wife of Joseph Miller, at Lower Stone Church. Preached from 2 Tim. 1:12. Then went to Organ church & preached from Matt. 6:33. Returned home.

Mond. 11. Went to Salisbury under subpoena Mary C. Earnheart vs. Albert Earnheart.

Tues. 12. In afternoon went to Jacob Lyerly's & brought home buggy wheels.

Wed. 13. In afternoon went to Gold Hill to Post Office. Returned by way of Mr. Powlass'.

Thurs. 14. At home.

Frid. 15. This being Good Friday, preached at Ebenezer ch. from John 19:30. Called in the afternoon at R. H. Klutts' & baptized his sick child. Dinner here. Went to Pleasant Pless' & staid over night.

Sat. 16. Went to J. L. Graeber's for dinner. In afternoon went to Ebenezer ch. & had preparatory service. Confirmed two persons. Rev. Cone preached. Returned to J. L. Graeber's & staid over night. Son Lewis here also.

Sund. 17. At Ebenezer ch. & had communion. Rev. Cone preached. Returned home.

Mond. 18. Went to Linn's mill.

Tues. 19. At home preparing for Synod.

Wed. 20. Went to Salisbury.

Thurs. 21. At home.

Frid. 22. In afternoon went to Gold Hill to post office.

Sat. 23. Preached at Organ ch. from 2 Cor. 13:5. Baptized one infant, confirmed one person & held preparatory service. All night at Henry Klutts'.

Sund. 24. Preached at Organ ch. from Acts. 18:21. & administered the communion without any intermission. After service called at widow Wm. Bost's to see Jane Crowell, who was very sick. Read a Scripture lesson and had prayer. Returned home, very tired.

Mond. 25. In forenoon took buggy to Mr. Powlass' for repair. In afternoon went to John F. Lentz's for Shoes, & to Gold Hill to Post Office.

Tues. 26. Started for Synod at Sandy Creek ch. Davidson Co. All night at Robert Thomson's. Had lodgings assigned here.

Wed. 27. Thurs. 28. Frid. 29. Sat. 30. At Synod.

Sund. May 1. Attended preaching & communion in the church. In afternoon started for home as far as John C. Miller's. All night here. Very unwell with bad cold.

Mond. 2. Returned home.

Tues. 3. Wed. 4. At home very unwell.

Thurs. 5. Went to Salisbury. Dinner at Rev. Smith's.

Frid. 6. At home.

Sat. 7. In afternoon went to Gold Hill to Post Office.

Sund. 8. Went to Organ ch. Unable to preach in consequence of severe cold. Read service & baptized two infants & dismissed.

Mond. 9. Went to Salisbury.

Tues. 10. In forenoon went to Dr. Coleman's for fire back & grate for stove. In afternoon went to mill.

Wed. 11. In forenoon went to mill & to Mr. J. Powlass'. In afternoon at home.

Thurs. 12. Frid. 13. At home.

Sat. 14. Started for Ebenezer ch. All night at Dr. P. A. Sifferd's.

Sund. 15. Preached at Ebenezer ch. from Matt. 11:28. Very unwell with severe cold. Dinner and over night at J. L. Graeber's.

Mond. 16. Returned home by way of Monroe Troutman's. Called at Carson A. B. Beaver's and baptized his sick child.

Tues. 17. In the morning went to Dr. Coleman's & went with him & acted as interpreter for him to administer medicine to a sick child in a Polish family.

Wed. 18. At home.

Thurs. 19. Went to Gold Hill to Post Office & to Mr. Powlass' & had Lucy shod.

Frid. 20. In forenoon went to Bernhardt's mill to Stock Law election. In afternoon a sick Polish family.

Sat. 21. At home.

Sund. 22. Preached at Organ ch. from Acts 16:13-15. Dinner at Joseph Miller's. In afternoon preached at Lower St. Church from Heb. 3:7.8. the funeral of Daywalt Beaver.

Mond. 23. Went to Mt. Pleasant to attend meeting of Board of Trustees of College & Commencement exercises. All night at Col. Shimpock's.

Tues. 24. In Mt. Pleasant. Dinner at Col. Shimpock's. All night at Lewis'.

Wed. 25. In Mt. Pleasant. Dinner & all night at Col. Shimpock's.

Thurs. 26. In forenoon returned home. In afternoon went to J. Powlass' & brought Buggy home.

Frid. 27. Went to Wilson Kesler's & paid him interest on College note. Returned by way of Gold Hill to get my mail.

Sat. 28. At home.

Sund. 29. Preached at St. Matthew's ch. from Is. 3:10. the funeral Lovina Hartman dec[d].

Mond. 30. In afternoon went to Gold Hill to Post Office.

Tues. 31. In forenoon went to Gold Hill to Post Office.

Wed. June 1. Went to Salisbury.

Thurs. 2. In forenoon went to Ribelin School House & made tax return. In afternoon went to mill.

Frid. 3. In the morning went to Dr. Coleman's. In afternoon went to mill. Lewis called to see us.

Sat. 4. At home.

Sund. 5. Went to Ebenezer ch. — Mr. Charlie Rose, a Student of Theology, preached in my staid. Baptized one infant. Dinner Augustus Ketner's. After baptized his child. Called to see James Roseman, he being sick. All night at A. F. Graeber's.

Mond. 6. Went to Salisbury. Attended meeting of County Magistrate's & had portion of Morgan Township attached to Gold Hill Township.

Tues. 7. Wed. 8. At home.

Thurs. 9. Went to Salisbury. Dinner at Dr. Coleman's.

Frid. 10. Sat. 11. At home, haying.

Sund. 12. Preached at Organ ch. from Ez. 36:27. Dinner at C. A. Miller's. In afternoon preached at Elm Grove from first Psalm.

Mond. 13. At home.

Tues. 14. Went to mill.

Wed. 15. At home.

Thurs. 16. In afternoon went to mill.

Frid. 17. Sat. 18. At home.

Sund. 19. Went to Ebenezer ch. Rev. Kimball bring present, preached & solicited money for Albemarle Church. Dinner H. T. Graeber's. Returned home & married James H. Jenkins & Laura V. Rouse.

Mond. 20. At home.

Tues. 21. At home. Dr. Coleman & family called to see us.

Wed. 22. In afternoon went to Volentine Zacherias, a Polish family, to witness the burial of a dead child, but did not bury till following morning.

Thurs. 23. In the morning went to see the Polish child buried at St. Peter's ch.

Frid. 24. In the morning went to Dr. Coleman's. In afternoon at home.

Sat. 25. At home.

Sund. 26. Preached at Organ ch. from 1 John 5:21. Dinner at L. G. Holshouser's. In afternoon preached at Elm Grove from Luk. 16:19-31.

Mond. 27. Tues. 28. Wed. 29. Thurs. 30. At home.

Frid. July 1. At home.

Sat. 2. Started for Ebenezer ch. All night at Mr. Korf's.

Sund. 3. Preached at Ebenezer ch. from 1 John 5:21. Dinner at John Pless'. In afternoon preached at Rymer's School House from Luk. 16:19-31. Returned home.

Mond. 4. Went to Salisbury to hear addresses on the subject of Prohibition.

Tues. 5. In afternoon went to Gold Hill to Post Office & to Wilson Kesler's on business.

Wed. 6. At home. This morning old horse Charley died.

Thurs. 7. At home.

Frid. 8. In afternoon went to Post Office.

Sat. 9. Went to Mr. Powlass' & had shoeing done. Dinner here.

Sund. 10. Preached at Organ ch. from Prov. 4:18. Dinner at Jesse Miller's. Preached in afternoon at Elm Grove from Luk. 19:1-10.

Mond. 11. Went to Salisbury.

Tues. 12. At home.

Wed. 13. Went to Post Office at Gold Hill, & rode around hunting my bull, which had broke out from my pasture.

Thurs. 14. Rode around some in search of bull.

Frid. 15. Went to Gold Hill to Post Office.

Sat. 16. Went to Ebenezer ch. & preached at 2 o'clock P.M. from Mark 13:37. preparatory. Dinner at P. A. Sloop's, Esq. All night at M. J. Eddleman's.

Sund. 17. Preached at Ebenezer ch. from Ex. 32:26. & administered the communion. Dinner at Rufus Troutman's. Returned home.

Mond. 18. In afternoon went to Gold Hill to Post Office & to mill.

Tues. 19. Went to Wilson Kesler's & borrowed some money.

Wed. 20. Went to Gold Hill & heard the question of prohibition discussed pro and con. Dinner at Frank Mauney's.

Thurs. 21. At home.

Frid. 22. In the evening with with Lewis to Gold Hill.

Sat. 23. Preached at Organ ch. in afternoon from Jam. 3:2. preparatory. Baptized two infants.

Sund. 24. Preached at Organ ch. from Matt. 5:44. & administered the Communion. Returned home.

Mond. 25. At home.

Tues. 26. In the morning went to Dr. Coleman's to engage a hand to thresh wheat.

Wed. 27. Attended to the funeral of Harvey A. Bernhardt's child at Organ ch. — preached from Ps. 87:3.

Thurs. 28. Started for Conference at Trinity ch. All night at Enochville with Rev. Lutz.

Frid. 29. Went to Conference. All night at Ephriam Fisher's.

Sat. 30. At Conference. All night at Philip Correll's.

Sund. 31. At Trinity. Revds. Hallman and Petrea preached. All night at Rev. Lutz'.

Mond. Aug. 1. Returned home. Dinner at Jerry Basinger's.

Tues. 2. Went to J. W. Miller's to get certificate of transfer to Gold Hill Township. Dinner at David Parker's.

Wed. 3. Went to Salisbury.

Thurs. 4. Went to George Troutman's & married J. M. Hipp & S. M. Troutman.

Frid. 5. At home.

Sat. 6. Started for Ebenezer ch. All night at Geo. M. Ketner's.

Sund. 7. Preached at Ebenezer ch. from Ps. 73:1. Baptized one infant. A rainy day & small congregation. Dinner at George Troutman's. In afternoon preached at Rymer's School House from Matt. 25:10. Returned home.

Mond. 8. Went to Salisbury.

Tues. 9. Went to Henry Klutts' for an old horse on trial.

Wed. 10. Went to Nussman's mill. Dinner here.

Thurs. 11. Took H. Klutts' horse home.

Frid. 12. Went to Salisbury.

Sat. 13. In the afternoon went to Mt. Pleasant. All night at Lewis'.

Sund. 14. Preached at St. John's church from Prov. 3:6. Dinner at Mr. Cline's, Returned home.

Mond. 15. Tues 16. Wed. 17. Thurs. 18. Frid. 19. At home.

Sat. 20. Went to Albemarle. Dinner at Sandy Misenheimer's at the Springs. All night at Mrs. Josephine's Hearne's. Preached at night from Acts 9:6.

Sund. 21. In forenoon Dr. Davis preached. Aided in dedication of the church & administration of the Holy Supper. Preached in afternoon from 2 Tim 1:13. Supper at Mr. Lilly's. Preached at night from [Prov.] 3:6. All night at Mr. Bostian's.

Mond. 22. Returned home.

Tues. 23. Attended Rowan County Sunday School Association at Union Church.

Wed. 24. Went to James Bernhardt's to look for a buggy horse. Did not buy.

Thurs. 25. At home.

Frid. 26. In forenoon went to Gold Hill to Post Office. In afternoon went to Rev. R. L. Brown's & staid over night.

Sat. 27. Attended Sund. Sch. celebration at Christiana church. Returned home

Sund. 28. This my day at Organ ch. Rev. S. T. Hallman preached. Dinner at C. A. Miller's. In afternoon preached at Elm Grove from Is. 55:6. Returned home.

Mond. 29. Called to see Zachariah Lyerly, he being in feeble health. Dinner here. Called also at Milas Miller's & got an old mare on trial.

Tues. 30. Wed. 31. At home.

Thurs. Sept. 1. At home, in my study.

Frid. 2. In forenoon went to Gold Hill to Post Office.

Sat. 3. Went to Concord. Dinner at Rachel Cruse's. Supper at Phebe Brown's. All night at Rev. Hallman's.

Sund. 4. Preached German from 2 Cor. 5:17. in Concord & administered the Communion to some German immigrants. Dinner at A. Foil's. Supper at Rev. Hallman's. Preached at night, Engl. from 2 Cor. 5:17. All night at Mr. Propst's.

Mond. 5. Returned home.

Tues. 6. At home.

Wed. 7. Went to Laurence Lingel's & wrote his will.

Thurs. 8. Went to Reid Misenheimer's mill.

Frid. 9. At home.

Sat. 10. In forenoon went to Gold Hill to Post Office. In afternoon at home. Son Lewis with us to night.

Sund. 11. Preached at Organ ch. from 1 Chron. 4:9.10. Baptized one infant. Dinner at Luther C. Miller's. In afternoon preached at Elm Grove from Luk. 17:11-19.

Mond. 12. At home.

Tues. 13. In the morning went to Henry A. Miller's in Emma Peter's behalf.

Wed. 14. Went to Joseph Lyerly's in forenoon to try & sell beef.

Thurs. 15. In the morning went to Dr. Coleman's. Balance of day at home.

Frid. 16. At home.

Sat. 17. In the morning went to Gold Hill to Post Office. In afternoon started for Ebenezer ch. All night at J. L. Graeber's.

Sund. 18. Preached at Ebenezer ch. from Eccl. 9:5. the funeral of Pleasant Pless' deceased child. Dinner at P. A. Sloop's. Returned home.

Mond. 19. Went to Salisbury.

Tues. 20. Attended to the funeral of William Lefler at Lower St. ch. — preached from Eccl. 9:5.

Wed. 21. At home, unwell.

Thurs. 22. In the morning went to Peter Miller's & left $20 to pay to Milas Miller for old mare. In afternoon went to John T. Lentz's to have shoes made. Returned home & cleaned wheat.

Frid. 23. Went to Reid Misenheimer's mill.

Sat. 24. In the morning went to Gold Hill & sold some butter. Balance of day at home.

Sund. 25. Preached at Organ ch. from Gen. 3:13. Dinner at C. L. Brown's. In afternoon preached at Elm Grove from 1 Tim. 4:7.

Mond. 26. Tues. 27. At home.

Wed. 28. In the morning went to Linn's mill.

Thurs. 29. At home making hay.

Frid. 30. Went to Gold Hill to post office. Very unwell.

Sat. Oct. 1. Started for Ebenezer ch. All night at Moses A. Ketner's.

Sund. 2. Preached at Ebenezer ch. from 1 Chron. 4:9.10. Dinner at J. L. Graeber's. Returned home.

Mond. 3. At home.

Tues. 4. Went to Salisbury under sub pena to attend Inferior Court.

Wed. 5. Went to Mt. Pleasant to attend meeting of Board of Trustees of N. C. College. Dinner at Col. Shimpock's. Supper at son Lewis'. All night at Col. Shimpock's.

Thurs. 6. Returned home.

Frid. 7. In forenoon went to Gold Hill to Post Office. Quite unwell. Then at home.

Sat. 8. In the morning took butter to Gold Hill. Then at home.

Sund. 9. Preached at Organ ch. from Acts. 9:36-42. Baptized one infant. Dinner at Boyden Miller's. Had an appointment this afternoon at Elm Grove but did not fill it in consequence of indisposition.

Mond. 10. Went on visit to H. A. Miller's.

Tues. 11. Wed. 12. Thurs. 13. At home.

Frid. 14. Started for Ebenezer ch. Called to see old Mrs. Basinger at her son Caleb's. Dinner here. All night at Lindsey Clark's (Rev).

Sat. 15. Preached at Ebenezer from Gen. 5:24. preparatory. Dinner at John Clark's. All night at Rufus Lippard's.

Sund. 16. At Ebenezer ch. Rev. Cone preached. Administered the communion. Dinner at Jeremiah Eddleman's. Returned home.

Mond. 17. Went to Gold Hill to Post Office.

Tues. 18. Went to Linn's mill.

Wed. 19. Went to J. Klutts' sale & bought some corn.

Thurs. 20. Had my corn brought home.

Frid. 21. In the morning went to mill. Then went with Rev. Strohecker to Gold Hill to Post Office.

Sat. 22. Had preparatory service at Organ ch. Rev. Strohecker preached. Baptized one infant.

Sund. 23. At Organ ch. Rev. Cone preached. Administered the communion.

Mond. 24. Tues. 25. At home.

Wed. 26. Went to Salisbury.

Thurs. 27. In afternoon started for Conference at Bethel ch. Stanly Co. All night at Sandy Misenheimer's.

Frid. 28. At conference. All night at David Lyerly's.

Sat. 29. At Conference. All night at John A. Troutman's,

Sund. 30. At Conference. Preached in afternoon from Matth. 11:28. All night at Sandy Misenheimer's.

Mond. 31. Returned home.

Tues. Nov. 1. In forenoon went to Gold Hill. In afternoon went to Cotton Gin.

Wed. 2. Thurs. 3. At home.

Frid. 4. Went to Gold Hill to Post Office.

Sat. 5. Preached at St. Peter's ch. from Gen. 5:24. and held preparatory service for Rev. Strohecker.

Sund. 6. Went to Ebenezer ch. & preached from John 5:6. Dinner at J. L. Graeber's. Returned home.

Mond. 7. At home.

Tues. 8. Went to Salisbury.

Wed. 9. Went to Jacob Klutts' & had old mare shod.

Thurs. 10. At home.

Frid. 11. Went to Post Office.

Sat. 12. Started for Trinity Church. Dinner at Rev. Cone's. All night at James Fisher's.

Sund. 13. Preached at Trinity ch. German from 2 Cor. 5:17. Dinner at James Fisher's. In the afternoon attended to the funeral of John Litaker at St. Enoch's ch. — preached from Gen. 5:24. All night at Rev. Lutz's.

Mond. 14. Returned home. Dinner at J. L. Graeber's.

Tues. 15. Went to Post Office in afternoon.

Wed. 16. In afternoon went to mill.

Thurs. 17. Went to Salisbury with Bettie & Emma & bought them cloaks.

Frid. 18. Went to Mt. Pleasant. All night at Lewis'.

Sat. 19. Went to G. M. Ketner's near Ebenezer ch. All night here.

Sund. 20. Preached at Ebenezer ch. from 1 Tim. 4:7. Dinner at J. L. Graeber's. Returned home.

Mond. 21. Tues. 22. At home.

Wed. 23. Went to Paul A. Miller's & baptized his child, it being sick.

Thurs. 24. At home. Slaughtered winter hogs.

Frid. 25. In forenoon went to Post Office. Then at home.

Sat. 26. Went to Corinth Baptist Church and preached the funeral of Ally Morgan from Gen. 5:24. Dinner at William Kesler's.

Sund. 27. Attended the Installation of Rev. Strohecker at St. Matthew's Church.

Mond. 28. At St. Matthew's Church. Preached in forenoon from 2 Tim. 1:13. & in afternoon from Acts. 9:6. Rev. Strohecker with us to night.

Tues. 29. At home.

Wed. 30. At home. Mr. Carter & wife with us to night.

Thurs. Dec. 1. At home.

Frid. 2. In forenoon went to Post Office. In afternoon at home.

Sat. 3. Went to Salisbury under sub pena as a witness. Then went to Dr. P. A. Sifferd's and staid over night.

Sund. 4. Preached at Ebenezer ch. from Acts 3:1-11. Dinner and all night at J. W. Misenheimer's. Baptized also his sick child.

Mond. 5. Returned home. Called to see Charlie Basinger. Called also to see Mrs. Fesperman (widow of John). Dinner here.

Tues. 6. At home.

Wed. 7. Went to Salisbury under sub pena as witness. All night with G. M. Gray, Esq.

Thurs. 8. Returned home in afternoon.

Frid. 9. Attended to the funeral Geo. Henry Eagle at Organ ch. preached from Gen. 5:24. Returned home by way of Gold Hill Post Office.

Sat. 10. Went to Salisbury under sub pena.

Sund. 11. Preached at Organ ch. from Acts 3:1-11. Baptized one infant.

Mond. 12. Went to Gold Hill to Post Office.

Tues. 13. At home

Frid. 14. At home.

Thurs. 15. Went to J. M. Faggart's, Esq. and married Augustus L. Pless & Mary E. Faggart. All night here.

Frid. 16. Returned home by way of Gold Hill.

Sat. 17. Started for Ebenezer church. All night at M. J. Eddleman's.

Sund. 18. Preached at Ebenezer ch. from Eph. 5:15.16. Dinner & all night at J. A. Eddleman's.

Mond. 19. Returned home.

Tues. 20. Wed. 21. At home. Lewis with us.

Thurs. 22. Went to Gold Hill to Post Office.

Frid. 23. At home.

Sat. 24. In the forenoon attended Christmas Tree at Elm Grove & addressed the audience. In the afternoon attended Christmas Tree at Organ Church & addressed the audience. All night at Reuben W. Bost's.

Sund. 25. Christmas day. Preached at Organ ch. from Is. 9:6. Dinner at Joseph Miller's. Returned home.

Mond. 26. Went to Wilson Kesler's & paid note of hand. Dinner here. Returned by way of Post Office at Gold Hill.

Tues. 27. Went to Salisbury.

Wed. 28. In the morning went to mill. Then at home. In the afternoon married Adolphus A. Miller & Margaret A. Powlass.

Thurs. 29. In afternoon went to Jesse Miller's & married John A. Peeler & Mary L. J. Miller.

Frid. 30. In the morning went to widow Linker's & allotted to her a year's provision. Then at Solomon Peeler's at infare.

Sat. 31. Had a meeting of Church Council of Organ church at 1 o'clock P.M. Then went to Paul Stirewalt's & staid over night.

Sund. January 1, 1882. Pretty deep snow this morning. Baptized Paul M. Stirewalt's child. Then went to Ebenezer ch. & preached from 2 Kings 4:26. Dinner and all night at J. L. Graeber's.

Mond. 2. Returned home.

Tues. 3. At home.

Wed. 4. Went to Gold Hill to Post Office.

Thurs. 5. At home.

Frid. 6. Went to Gold Hill to Post Office.

Sat. 7. At home.

Sund. 8. Preached at Organ ch. from Is. 30:10. In afternoon buried Luther Barringer's wife. Returned home.

Mond. 9. At home. A rainy day.

Tues. 10. Called to see Jacob Miller. Dinner here.

Wed. 11. At home.

Thurs. 12. Went to Gold Hill to Post Office.

Frid. 13. In forenoon went to Gold Hill to Post Office. In afternoon at home.

Sat. 14. Started for Ebenezer ch. All night at George Troutman's.

Sund. 15. Preached at Ebenezer ch. from Zech. 4:10. Dinner at J. L. Graeber's. All night at J. Allen Miller's.

Mond. 16. Returned home by way of J. Albert Heilig's.

Tues. 17. Went to Mt. Pleasant. Dinner at Geo. H. Bost's. All night at Col. Shimpock's.

Wed. 18. Attended meeting of Board of Trustees of N. C. College. Supper at Lewis'. All night at Col. Shimpock's.

Thurs. 19. Returned home. In afternoon went to mill.

Frid. 20. In forenoon went to mill. In afternoon went to Gold Hill to Post Office.

Sat. 21. In the morning went to Dr. Coleman's. In afternoon at home.

Sund. 22. Preached at Organ ch. Mark 13:37. Returned home.

Mond. 23. Went to Salisbury.

Tues. 24. At home.

Wed. 25. At home, very inclement weather.

Thurs. 26. Was to have gone some 15 miles to marry Robert Patterson, but not being well & mare lame, prevailed on J. Adolphus Linn to go in my place.

Frid. 27. Was to have gone to St. John's Church to Conference, but not being well did not attend. In afternoon went to Gold Hill to Post Office.

Sat. 28. At home, weather very inclement.

Sund. 29. Went to St. Peter's Church & heard Rev. T. H. Strohecker preach.

Mond. 30. Tues. 31. At home.

Wed. Feb. 1. At home.

Thurs. 2. At home.

Frid. 3. Went to Gold Hill to Post Office.

Sat. 4. At home, a very rainy day.

Sund. 5. Preached at Ebenezer ch. from Deut. 18:15. Baptized one infant. Dinner at J. L. Graeber's. Returned home.

Mond. 6. Went to Salisbury.

Tues. 7. Went to see Joseph Miller, he being sick. Wrote his will. Dinner here.

Wed. 8. Went to Gold Hill to Post Office & to J. Powlass'. Dinner here. Called also at Widow Daywalt Beaver's & C. A. Miller's.

Thurs. 9. At home.

Frid. 10. Went to Gold Hill to Post Office.

Sat. 11. Went to St. Peter's & heard Rev. Strohecker. Son Lewis & Rev. Strohecker with us over night.

Sund. 12. Preached at Organ ch. from Deut. 18:15. Called at Joseph Miller's who was very sick. Read a Scripture lesson & had prayer at his bed side. Dinner here. In afternoon preached the funeral of Paul A. Miller's deceased child at Lower St. ch. from Jer. 8:6. Returned home.

Mond. 13. Went to Jacob Klutts's & had mare shod.

Tues. 14. Attended to the funeral of Joseph Miller at Lower St. ch. – preached from Gen. 5:5. Dinner at L. A. Heilig's.

Wed. 15. Went to mill and Post Office.

Thurs. 16. At home.

Frid. 17. Went to Gold Hill to Post Office.

Sat. 18. Went to the residence of the late Joseph Miller & read his Will to the heirs. Baptized Alfred Klutts' child. Dinner here. Then went to J. L. Graeber's & staid over night.

Sund. 19. Preached at Ebenezer ch. from Rom. 6:22. Dinner at J. L. Graeber's. Returned home.

Mond. 20. At home.

Tues. 21. Went to Salisbury & proved Joseph Miller's Will & sent Money Order to W. P. Houseal, Crider & Bro. & to Luth. Book Store.

Wed. 22. At home.

Thurs. 23. Went to Allen Miller's Mill. Dinner here.

Frid. 24. Went to Gold Hill to Post Office.

Sat. 25. At home.

Sund. 26. Preached a very short sermon at Organ ch. from 1 Cor. 10:31. & then retired to give the congregation an opportunity to hold an election. Returned home.

Mond. 27. In the morning went to Wilson Kesler's by request to meet with building committee of St. Matthew's Church. Afternoon at home.

Tues. 28. At home.

Wed. March 1. At home.

Thurs. 2. Went in forenoon to Linn's Mill.

Frid. 3. In the morning went to Linn's mill. Then went to Gold Hill to Post Office.

Sat. 4. Attended to the funeral of Martha Jane, wife of Nathan Brown at Christiana ch. — preached from Ps. 50:15. All night at Moses Lingel's.

Sund. 5. Preached at Ebenezer ch. from John 4:28.29. Dinner at J. M. Eddleman's. Over night at Michael Bostian's.

Mond. 6. Returned home by way of Salisbury.

Tues. 7. In the morning went to M. A. Holshouser's & brought home window glass & Russian Oats.

Wed. 8. At home. An inclement day.

Thurs. 9. Went to Linn's mill

Frid. 10. Went to Gold Hill to Post Office.

Sat. 11. At home. Sowed some Russian oats.

Sund. 12. Preached at Organ ch. from Neh. 10:39. Baptized one infant. Went to J. L. Graeber's & staid over night.

Mond. 13. Attended to the funeral of Elizabeth Ketner, relict of Peter Ketner, at Ebenezer ch. — preached from Prov. 16:31. Dinner at J. L. Graeber's. Returned home.

Tues. 14. Went to Gold Hill to Post Office.

Wed. 15. Called to see Sally Holshouser, she being in feeble health.

Thurs. 16. At home.

Frid. 17. Went to Gold Hill to Post Office.

Sat. 18. Attended the closing exercises of our free school taught by Martin Miller.

Sund. 19. Went to Ebenezer church. preached from Matth. 12:38-41. Dinner & all night at Dr. P. A. Sifferd's.

Mond. 20. Called at Absalom Cress' & baptized his child, the mother being in bad health. Called at George Fisher's & took dinner. Called also at Mary A. Heilig's.

Tues. 21. Went to Gold Hill to Post Office.

Wed. 22. Went to Salisbury for Books Worship & Church Register.

Thurs. 23. Attended to the funeral of Paul Beaver at Lower St. Church — preached from Phil. 1:21.

Frid. 24. Went to Gold Hill to Post Office.

Sat. 25. Went to St. Matthew's ch. to laying of corner stone of new church. Corner stone laying postponed.

Sund. 26. Preached at Organ ch. from John 4:28.29. Dinner at Mrs. Ellen Miller's. All night at Eli Holshouser's. Baptized one infant to day.

Mond. 27. Called at Widow John Fesperman's, at Edmond Fesperman's, & Crawford Peeler's.

Tues. 28. Attended to the fun¹ of Peter Peck at St. Stephen's ch. — preached from Amos 4:12.

Wed. 29. Went to Salisbury & sent Postal Money Orders to W. J. Duffie, H. S. Boner, & S. Henkel.

Thurs. 30. At home.

Frid. 31. Went to Gold Hill to Post Office.

Sat. April 1. Started for Ebenezer ch. All night at Augustus Ketner's.

Sund. 2. Preached at Ebenezer from Gen. 41:9. Dinner at J. A. Eddleman's. All night at Mrs. Sena Bostian's.

Mond. 3. Went to Salisbury & handed a petition to County Commissioners for an election for Stock Law. Sent Postal Money Order to W. H. Houseal.

Tues. 4. Went to Gold Hill & had Lucy shod.

Wed. 5. Thurs. 6. At home.

Frid. 7. Good Friday. Preached to day at Organ ch. from John 19:30.

Sat. 8. Preached at Organ ch. from 2 Cor. 13:5. preparatory to Communion.

Sund. 9. Preached at Organ ch. from Col. 3:1 and administered the Communion.

Mond. 10. Went to Salisbury.

Tues. 11. Went to St. Matthew's ch. to the laying of the Corner Stone of the new church & breaking.

Wed. 12. Went to Mt. Pleasant. All night at Col. Shimpock's.

Thurs. 13. Returned home. In afternoon went to mill.

Frid. 14. In forenoon went to mill. In afternoon attended to funeral of Andrew A. Lyerly at St. Peter's ch. — preached from Eccl. 9:10.

Sat. 15. Preached at Ebenezer ch. at 2 P.M. from Acts 11:26. last clause, preparatory to communion. All night at Robert Patterson's.

Sund. 16. Preached at Ebenezer ch. from Matth. 22:5. & administered the Lord's Supper. All night at Mrs. Eddleman's, widow of Dan⁻ Eddleman.

Mond. 17. Attended to the funeral of Charles Basinger at Organ ch. Preached the funeral at the house from Heb. 4:9. Dinner at J. Allen Miller's.

Tues. 18. Went to Gold Hill to Post Office.

+

Thurs. 20. Went to Salisbury & baptized in German Frederick Reimer's child, the parents being native German's & unacquainted with the English language.

Frid. 21. At home.

Sat. 22. Had catechization at Organ ch. at 10 o'clock A.M. Then went to Mrs. Wm. Bost's (widow) to dinner. In afternoon preached here in Germ. from 2 Cor. 5:17. All night here.

Sund. 23. Preached at Organ ch. from Gen. 41:9. Dinner at George Bost's. In afternoon preached at Elm Grove from Luk. 13:24.

Mond. 24. At home.

Tues. 25. Went to John T. Lentz's, Shoemaker, & to Gold Hill to Post Office.

Wed. 26. Thurs. 27. At home.

Frid. 28. Went to Gold Hill to Post Office.

Sat. 29. Started for Ebenezer ch. — All night at Moses A. Stirewalt's.

Sund. 30. Preached at Ebenezer ch. from Is. 30:10. Dinner at H. T. Graeber's. Returned home.

+Wed. 19. At home.

Mond. May. 1. Went to John T. Lentz's, Shoemaker & to Gold Hill to Post Office.

Tues. 2. Started for Concord to Synod. All night at Mrs. Rachel Cruse's.

Wed. 3. Went to Concord. In Synod. Had lodgings assigned at Mrs. Phebe Brown's.

Thurs. 4. Frid. 5. Sat. 6. In Synod.

Sund. 7. Preached at night in the church of Scotia Seminary, colored, from Matt. 5:6.

Mond. 8. Returned home. Dinner at Caleb Cruse's.

Tues. 9. At home.

Wed. 10. Went to Reid Misenheimer's mill.

Thurs. 11. At home.

Frid. 12. Went to Salisbury.

Sat. 13. Had catechization at Organ church.

Sund. 14. Preached at Organ ch. from Eph. 5:15.16. Dinner at Calvin L. Brown's. Preached in the af afternoon at Elm Grove from Is. 48:18.

Mond. 15. Went to Gold Hill to Post Office.

Tues. 16. At home. Moses Miller, wife & daughter from Illinois with us to night.

Wed. 17. In afternoon took Moses Miller wife & daughter to L. G. Holshouser's.

Thurs. 18. Ascension Day. Preached at Elm Grove from Mark 16:19.

Frid. 19. In afternoon went to Gold Hill to Post Office.

Sat. 20. Attended to the funeral of Martha C. E. Foutz, wife of Columbus Foutz, at Lower Stone Church —preached from 1 Cor. 7:29. Then went to Ebenezer ch. by 2 o'clock P.M. and had catechization. All night at G. M. Ketner's.

Sund. 21. Preached at Ebenezer ch. from Is. 48:18. Dinner at J. A. Eddleman's. In the afternoon preached the funeral of widow Montford Holshouser, dec^d at her late residence from 1 Cor. 7:29. Returned home.

Mond. 22. Went to Mt. Pleasant. All night at Lewis'.

Tues. 23. In Mt. Pleasant. Attended meeting of College Trustees. Dinner & all night at Col. Shimpock's.

Wed. 24. Inaugurated Rev. G. D. Bernheim, D.D. as President of College. Returned home.

Thurs. 25. Went in forenoon to Wilson Kesler's & paid some money on College debt. Afternoon at home.

Frid. 26. Went to Gold Hill to Post Office, & in afternoon had catechization at our free Sch. house.

Sat. 27. Had catechization at Organ ch. Called in afternoon at Jesse Miller's & voted for Stock law. Dinner here.

Sund. 28. Preached at Organ ch. from Eccl. 11:9. Dinner at C. A. Miller's. In afternoon preached at Elm Grove from Titus 3:1.

Mond. 29. Tues. 30. Wed. 31.+ At home.

+In morning went to mill.

Thurs. Jun. 1. In the morning went to Jos. Beaver's to engage hands to mow grass. In afternoon engaged hands to mow grass.

Frid. 2. Went to Salisbury under sub pena as witness, R. A. Shimpock vs. Mary C. Earnheart.

Sat. 3. Went to Ebenezer ch. & had catechization at 2 o'clock P.M. Over night at F. W. Karf's.

Sund. 4. Preached at Ebenezer ch. from Eccl. 11:9. Dinner at H. T. Graeber's. All night at Edmond E. Klutts'.

Mond. 5. Returned home. In afternoon raked hay.

Tues. 6. Engaged in hay making.

Wed. 7. In forenoon went to Gold Hill to Post Office. In afternoon hauled hay.

Thurs. 8. Went with Dr. Shimpock, under subpena, to Salisbury. Dinner at McNeely's Hotel.

Frid. 9. Went to Gold Hill to Post Office & in afternoon had catechization at our free School House. A large class in attendance.

Sat. 10. Had catechization at Organ church.

Sund. 11. Preached German at Organ church from 1 Thes. 2:11.12. Dinner at Luther C. Miller's. In afternoon preached at Elm Grove from James 1:25. Good attendance.

Mond. 12. Went with wife & Bettie to Salisbury.

Tues. 13. Went to Gold Hill to Post Office.

Wed. 14. Thurs. 15. At home.

Frid. 16. At home.

Sat. 17. Called at Mr. Drake's to see old Mrs. Ludwig, supposed to be 100 yrs. old. Then went to Ebenezer ch. & had catechization at 2 o'clock P.M. All night at J. M. Eddleman's.

Sund. 18. Preached at Ebenezer ch. from Dan. 12:3. Baptized one infant. Dinner at Mr. Sloop's Esq. Returned home.

Mond. 19. Went to Gold Hill & made tax return.

Tues. 20. Went to Salisbury.

Wed. 21. Thurs. 22. At home.

Frid. 22. At home till 12 o'clock. Then went to our free School house & had catechization.

Sat. 24. Went to Christiana church & preached at 2 P.M. from Matt. 22:5. & baptized Rev. R. L. Brown's child. All night at Charles Lyerly's.

Sund. 25. Preached at Christiana ch. from 1 Thes. 2:11.12. & aided in the administration of the Eucharist. Dinner at Nathan Brown's. Returned home.

Mond. 26. Tues. 27. At home, haying.

Wed. 28. Went to Uriah Miller's & had shoeing done. Dinner here. In afternoon attended to the fun[1] of widow C. A. Miller's child at Organ ch. — preached from Phil. 1:21. last clause.

Thurs. 29. At home.

Frid. 30. Went to Gold Hill to Post Office.

Sat. July 1. Had catechization at Ebenezer ch. All night at J. L. Graeber's.

Sund. 2. Preached at Ebenezer from Ps. 116:12. Dinner at H. T. Graeber's. Returned home.

Mond. 3. Tues. 4. At home.

Wed. 5. Went to Gold Hill to Post Office.

Thurs. 6. At home

Frid. 7. Went to Gold Hill to Post Office. At 2 o'clock P.M. had catechization at our free School house.

Sat. 8. Had catechization at Organ church.

Sund. 9. In the morning addressed the Sunday School at Organ ch. Afterwards preached from Mark 6:52. Baptized one infant. Dinner at Reuben W. Bost's. In the evening attended to the funeral of L. Thames Yates child at Organ ch. Preached the funeral at the house from Matt. 5:8.

Mond. 10. Went with Lewis to Salisbury.

Tues. 11. Surveyed land for Lewis.

Wed. 12. In forenoon engaged threshing hands. In afternoon attended to the burial of Elizabeth Seaford at Organ ch.

Thurs. 13. At home.

Frid. 14. At home, had Wheat threshed.

Sat. 15. Had preparatory service at Ebenezer ch. at 2 P.M. Preached from Deut. 11:16. Baptized one infant. All night at Robert Patterson's.

Sund. 16. Preached at Ebenezer ch. from 1 Cor. 5:7.8. Administered the Communion. Installed 2 Deacons. Dinner at J. A. Eddleman's. In afternoon preached at a Stand near Frick's Saw mill from Luk. 13:3. All night at Alexander Lyerly's.

Mond. 17. Returned home.

Tues. 18. At home.

Wed. 19. Went to Salisbury.

Thurs. 20. At home.

Frid. 21. Went to Gold Hill to Post Office, then to our district school house & had catechization at 2 P. M.

Sat. 22. Went to Organ Church to have preparatory service at 2 P.M. but the day being rainy, the congregation was very small. Postponed the preparatory services to Sunday morning. Rev. R. L. Brown preached. All night at G. M. Fisher's.

Sund. 23. Rev. R. L. Brown preached. Then held preparatory service & administered the communion. Returned home.

Mond. 24. At home. Not well.

Tues. 25. Went to Misenheimer Springs. All night here.

Wed. 26. In afternoon returned home.

Thurs. 27. Started for Concord to attend meeting of Western Conference. All night at Mrs. Rachel Cruse's.

Frid. 28. Went to Concord. Dinner at Rev. Hallman's. All night at Mr. Fisher's, Esq.

Sat. 29. At Conference. Dinner at Mr. Fisher's Esq. All night at Philip Correll's. Preached this evening from Is. 30:10.

Sund. 30. At conference. Rev. Strohecker preached. Dinner at Alex. Foil's. in afternoon Rev. D. J. Koonts, colored, preached in Court House. All night at Rev. Hallman's.

Mond. 31. Returned home by way of Mt. Pleasant. Dinner at Col. Shimpock's. Borrowed $150.00 of Col. S. for Lewis.

Tues. Aug. 1. At home.

Wed. 2. At home.

Thurs. 3. Went to Gold Hill to Post Office.

Frid. 4. In the morning went to John Miller's to see M. A. Holshouser on the subject of his Organ. Then went to Gold Hill to Post Office.

Sat. 5. Had catechization at Ebenezer ch. All night at Mrs. Mary A. C. Beaver's, widow of Jeremiah Beaver.

Sund. 6. Preached at Ebenezer ch. from Gal. 6:9. Dinner at J. L. Graeber's. In afternoon preached at the Arbor near Frick's Saw mill from Luk. 13:24. All night at Crawford Peeler's.

Mond. 7. Returned home by way of Salisbury.

Tues. 8. At home. Moses Miller, wife and daughter from Illinois with us to night.

Wed. 9. At home.

Thurs. 10. Went to Salisbury on business for David Brady. In afternoon went to Catie Baily's and married Rufus A. Taylor & Laura M. Miller.

Frid. 11. Had catechization at our district school house. Returned home by way of Post Office at Gold Hill.

Sat. 12. Had catechization at Organ church.

Sund. 13. Preached the funeral of Abram Lentz, dec^d at St. Matthew's ch. from Ps. 71:9.

Mond. 14. Went to Moses Earnheart's & wrote an agreement between Mrs. Frances D. Earnheart & M. W. Stikeleather. Then went to Jeremiah Earnheart's & had shoeing done.

Tues. 15. Took Lewis to Salisbury for him to attend to the colored Teacher's Istitute.

Wed. 16. Went into the neighborhood of the river to see James Reid on business.

Thurs. 17. At home.

Frid. 18. Got a hard fall in the hog pen which disabled me for several days.

Sat. 19. Had an appointment for the afternoon at the arbor near Frick's saw mill, but was not able to fill it, (physically).

Sund. 20. This my day to preach at Ebenezer but was unable physically to fill it.

Mond. 21. Took Lewis to Salisbury, then went to John Lingel's for dinner. Then went to Danl Seaford's & staid over night.

Tues. 22. Went to Moses A. Bost's for dinner, then took Calvin Bost in the buggy and went to D. M. Barrier's & married Ferdinand J. Barrier & Jennie Krider. All night here.

Wed. 23. Returned home. Dinner in Salisbury at Mrs. Crawford's.

Thurs. 24. Went in the morning to Milas A. Holshouser's & had shoeing done.

Frid. 25. Attended to the funeral of Mattie Melona, daughter of Henry Williams, who got entangled in the machinery at Misenheimer's mill & got killed. Buried her at Gold Hill & preached from 1 Sam. 20:3. In afternoon had catechization at our free School house.

Sat. 26. Had catechization at Organ ch. at 2 o'clock P.M. Called to see Mrs. Barringer, her daughter, Mrs. Miller, being sick. All night at Eli Holshouser's.

Sund. 27. Preached at Organ ch. from Ex. 14:15. & installed 2 Deacons, & 1 Elder. Returned home.

Mond. 28. At home.

Tues. 29. Went to Gold Hill to Post Office.

Wed. 30. Went to Salisbury. A rainy day.

Thurs. 31. In forenoon went to Mrs. Lentz's mill. Then at home.

Frid. Sept. 1. Went to Gold Hill to Post Office in forenoon. Then at home.

Sat. 2. Started for Ebenezer ch. All night at Alexander Powlass'.

Sund. 3. Preached at Ebenezer ch. from Gal. 6:12. Dinner at J. L. Graeber's. All night at J. M. Eddleman's.

Mond. 4. Returned home. Dinner at widow John Fesperman's. Called on the way to see sundry members of the church.

Tues. 5. In the morning went to Dr. Coleman's, my wife being sick. Then at home.

Wed. 6. Thurs. 7. At home.

Frid. 8. Had catechization at our free school house at 2 P.M.

Sat. 9. Had catechization at Organ church.

Sund. 10. A very rainy day. This was my regular day to preach at Organ church, but no person attended. Went to Organ ch. and rode around it & then returned home.

Mond. 11. At home.

Tues. 12. Went to Gold Hill to Post Office.

Wed. 13. Went to mill in forenoon, then went to Jacob Klutts' and had shoeing done.

Thurs. 14. In the morning went to mill. Then went to Post Office, & also engaged hands to mow grass.

Frid. 15. Went to Gold Hill to Post Office.

Sat. 16. Started for Ebenezer Church. All night at A. Monroe Propst's.

Sund. 17. Preached at Ebenezer from 2 Chron. 33:12.13. Dinner at P. A. Sloop's, Esq. Returned home.

Mond. 18. Tues. 19. Wed. 20. Thurs. 21. At home haying.

Frid. 22. Went to Post Office, then to School house & had catechization.

Sat. 23. Had catechization at Organ ch. at 2 P.M. Returned home.

Sund. 24. This my day at Organ ch. Rev. J. A. Linn called by & took me in his buggy and preached to the congregation & solicited aid in building a church at Hickory. Baptized one infant and installed an Elder of the church.

Mond. 25. At home.

Tues. 26. Went to Post Office.

Wed. 27. At home.

Thurs. 28. In afternoon went with wife to M. A. Holshouser's to Molasses Factory.

Frid. 29. Went to M. A. Holshouser's and brought Molasses home. Then went to Gold Hill to Post Office.

Sat. 30. Started for Ebenezer. All night at Paul Stirewalt's.

Sund. Oct. 1. Preached at Ebenezer from Josh. 7:25. Dinner at J. A. Eddleman's. Returned home.

Mond. 2. At home.

Tues. 3. Went to Mt. Pleasant. All night at Col. J. Shimpock.

Wed. 4. Attended meeting of Board of Trustees of N. C. College. All night at Col. Shimpock's.

Thurs. 5. Returned home.

Frid. 6. Went to Gold Hill to post office, & in afternoon had catechization at Sch. house.

Sat. 7. In afternoon had catechization at Organ ch. Returned home.

Sund. 8. Preached at Organ ch. from Ps. 71:9. the funeral of Elizabeth Seaford, dec[d]. Dinner at C. L. Brown's. Called at Eli Miller's to see Martha Wagoner, who was sick. Called also at L. G. Holshouser's.

Mond. 9. Went with Lewis to Salisbury.

Tue. 10. Wed. 11. Thurs. 12. At home.

Frid. 13. Had catechization at Ebenezer ch. at 2 P.M. Dinner at Augustus Ketner's. All night at Dr. P. A. Sifferd's.

Sat. 14. Dinner at G. M. Ketner's. Had preparatory service at Ebenezer ch. at 2 P.M. Dr. L. A. Bikle preached. Baptized one adult & confirmed three persons. All night at Dr. P. A. Sifferd's.

Sund. 15. Had communion at Ebenezer. Rev. Bikle, D.D. preached. Dinner at P. A. Sloop's, Esq. In the afternoon called to see John Pless, he being very sick. All night at George Troutman's.

Mond. 16. Returned home.

Tue. 17. Went in forenoon to mill and to Gold Hill. In afternoon at home.

Wed. 18. In forenoon went to Gold Hill to post office.

Thurs. 19. Went to Geo. M. Fisher's & married Albert L. Lingel & Martha G. Fisher. Returned home.

Frid. 20. At home.

Sat. 21. Had preparatory services at Organ ch. at 2 o'clock P.M. Confirmed 17 persons.

Sund. 22. Had communion at Organ church. Baptized one infant. Prof. Dysinger from Mt. Pleasant preached. All night at Laurence Klutts'.

Mond. 23. Went to Mt. Pleasant. Dinner at Col. Shimpock's. Returned home.

Tues. 24. In afternoon went to George Troutman's & staid all night.

Wed. 25. Attended to the funeral of John Pless at Ebenezer ch. Preached from 2 Tim. 4:7.8. Dinner at J. L. Graeber's. Returned home.

Thurs. 26. In the morning went to Dr. Coleman's, my wife being sick. Then at home.

Frid. 27. Was to have gone to Albemarle to Conference, but could not leave home on account of sickness of wife.

Sat. 28. At home.

Sund. 29. Mond. 30. At home.

Tues. 31. Went to Gold Hill to post office, thence to J. T. Lentz's, the shoemaker.

Wed. Nov. 1. At home.

Thurs. 2. Went to Salisbury to get fruit trees.

Frid. 3. Went to Gold Hill to post office. At night attended political speaking.

Sat. 4. Started for Ebenezer ch. All night at Rufus Troutman's.

Sund. 5. Preached at Ebenezer from John 3:3. Dinner at H. T. Graeber's. Returned home.

Mond. 6. Went with Lewis to Salisbury.

Tues. 7. Went early in morning to Gold Hill to election, then at home.

Wed. 8. Went to Gold Hill to post office, then Laurence Lingel's & took dinner, then to John T. Lentz's the shoemaker & returned home.

Thurs. 9. Went to Jacob Klutts' & had Lucy shod. In afternoon went to mill.

Frid. 10. Went to mill in forenoon. Afternoon at home.

Sat. 11. Went to Salisbury.

Sund. 12. Preached at Organ ch. from Matt. 26:41. Baptized 2 infants. Then went to Jacob Barger's, his wife being very sick. Read a Psalm and had prayer. Dinner here. Returned home.

Mond. 13. At home.

Tues. 14. Went to sale of property of Zachariah Lyerly. Dinner here.

Wed. 15. Went to Gold Hill to Post Office.

Thurs. 16. At home.

Frid. 17. Went to Gold Hill to Post Office.

Sat. 18. Went to Salisbury & Expressed money to Mrs. Quantz, Richmond. Then went to Michael Bostian's & staid over night.

Sund. 19. Preached at Ebenezer from Matt. 26:41. Dinner at J. L. Graeber's. Called to see Mrs. Jacob Berger, she being very sick. Returned home.

Mond. 20. Tues. 21. Wed. 22. At home.

Thurs. 23. Went to Salisbury.

Frid. 24. At home.

Sat. 25. Went to cotton gin.

Sund. 26. Preached at Organ ch. from 1 Cor. 13:1-7.

Mon. 27. At home.

Tues. 28. At home. An icy day.

Wed. 29. Went to Crawford A. Miller's and confirmed his invalid daughter and administered the communion to her & to the parents. Dinner here. In the afternoon went to Mrs. Elizabeth Klutts' & staid over night.

Thurs. 30. Went to Rufus W. Misenheimer's & married George C. Klutts & Mattie C. Misenheimer. Dinner here. Then went to Lawson Troutman's and married William C. Troutman Mary Ann C. V. Weaver. Supper here. All night at George Troutman's.

Frid. Dec. 1. Returned home.

Sat. 2. Started for Ebenezer ch. Dinner at L. A. Heilig's. All night at J. A. Eddleman's.

Sund. 3. Preached at Ebenezer from 1 Cor. 13:1-7. Baptized one infant. Dinner at J. L. Graeber's. Returned home.

Mond. 4. At home.

Tues. 5. Went to Salisbury under sub-pena to attend Court. Dinner at Mills' Oyster Saloon. All night at Rev. W. J. Smith's.

Wed. 6. In Salisbury. Dinner at Snyder's Oyster Saloon. All night at Mrs. Crawford's.

Thurs. 7. In Salisbury. Dinner at Snyder's Oyster Saloon. All night at C. T. Bernhardt's.

Frid. 8. Returned home.

Sat. 9. Engaged hands to slaughter hogs. Went also to Jacob Holshouser's & engaged corn.

Sund. 10. Preached at Organ ch. from Matt. 14:15-21. Dinner at Alfred Miller's.

Mond. 11. At home. Had hogs slaughtered.

Tues. 12. At home.

Wed. 13. In afternoon went to mill.

Thurs. 14. Attended to the funeral of Anna E., wife of J. M. Eddleman, at Ebenezer ch., preached from 2 Tim. 1:12. Dinner at J. L. Graeber's. Then went to Lovina Beaver's & married James M. Eller & Ellen S. Beaver. Returned home after night.

Frid. 15. At home, very unwell with a severe cold.

Sat. 16. Started for Ebenezer church. All night at J. L. Graeber's. Cold weather.

Sund. 17. Preached at Ebenezer from Matt. 14:15-21. Dinner at H. T. Graeber's. Returned home.

Mond 18. Went to Gold Hill to Post Office.

Tues. 19. In forenoon went to mill, then at home.

Wed. 20. At home.

Thurs. 21. In afternoon went to Joseph Beaver's & Married Charles E. Bost & Martha R. C. Beaver.

Frid. 22. At home.

Sat. 23. Went to Gold Hill to post office, then to Elm Grove to Christmas Tree.

Sund. 24. Preached at Organ ch. from Jer. 6:16. giving some history of Organ ch. in order to stir up the people. Dinner at Jesse Miller's.

Mond. 25. Christmas Day. Called to see Moses Lingel, he being sick. Had some devotional exercises at his bedside. Dinner here. Returned home.

Tues. 26. Went to Martin A. Weaver's and baptized his sick child. In afternoon went to Jacob Holshouser's about corn.

Wed. 27. Took Bettie to Salisbury to sign deed.

Thurs. 28. At home. Had intended to start for Conference at Center Grove but wife's health being infirm & my mare having distemper did not go.

Frid. 29. In afternoon went to Gold Hill to Post Office. Rev. Anthony with us to night.

Sat. 30. At home. A deep snow on the ground.

Sund. 31. At home. Snow on the ground.

Mond. Jan. 1, 1883. New Year's Day. Made some arrangements to have corn hauled.

Tues. 2. Busy in having corn hauled. Rev. J. B. Anthony with us to night.

Wed. 3. In afternoon went to Jac. Holshouser's to pay for corn, but failed he not having change to break my bill.

Thurs. 4. Frid. 5. At home. Not very well.

Sat. 6. Had intended to start for Ebenezer but the day being very rainy & not being very well, did not go.

Sund. 7. This my day to preach at Ebenezer but failed to attend on account of distance, muddy roads, & not being very well.

Mond. 8. Went to Gold Hill to post office & to the shoemaker. Rev. G. D. Bearnheim, D.D. with us to night.

Tues. 9. In afternoon went to Mr. Morgan's, the shoemaker.

Wed. 10. At home. Snow on the ground.

Thurs. 11. At home.

Frid. 12. Went to Gold Hill to Post Office.

Sat. 13. At home.

Sund. 14. Preached at Organ ch. from John 2:1-11.

Mond 15. In afternoon went to Jacob Holshouser & paid for corn purchased from him.

Tues. 16. Wed. 1. At home. Sleety weather.

Thurs. 18. Went to Gold Hill to Post Office.

Frid. 19. At home.

Sat. 20. Had intended to start for Ebenezer ch. but the incessant rain during the day kept me at home.

Sund. 21. Went to Ebenezer ch. & preached from 2 Kings 5:1-14. Dinner & over night at J. L. Graeber's.

Mond. 22. Returned home.

Tues. 23. Went to Mt. Pleasant. All at Col. Shimpock's.

Wed. 24. Attended meeting of Board of Trustees of N. C. College. All night at Col. Shimpock's.

Thurs. 25. Returned home.

Frid. 26. Went to Gold Hill to Post Office.

Sat. 27. Met Church Council at Organ ch.

Sund. 28. Preached at Organ ch. from Eph. 6:1-4. Baptized one infant.

Mond. 29. At home.

Tues. 30. Went to Salisbury.

Wed. 31. In afternoon went to Mr. Shemwell's & staid over night.

Thurs. Feb. 1. Went John H. Long's & married Luther C. Sowers & Fannie F. Long. Returned home. Dr. Bernheim with us over night.

Frid. 2. After dinner took Dr. Bernheim to Gold Hill to meet mail hack.

Sat. 3. Started for Ebenezer ch. Over night at Geo. M. Ketner's.

Sund. 4. Preached at Ebenezer from Eph. 6:1-4. Baptized one infant. Dinner at J. A. Eddleman's. Returned home.

Mond. 5. In forenoon went to Gold Hill for horse shoes. In afternoon went to Jacob Klutts' & had Lucy shod.

Tues. 6. Wed. 7. At home.

Thurs. 8. At home.

Frid. 9. Went to Gold to Post Office.

Sat. 10. At home.

Sund. 11. Preached at Organ ch. from Ex. 20:14. 1 Cor. 6:18. Baptized 1 infant.

Mond. 12. At home.

Tues. 13. Went to Gold Hill to post office.

Wed. 14. At home.

Thurs. 15. Went to Organ ch. where the members are at work to build a Council Room. Dinner at Mrs. Catharine Barringer's. In the afternoon called at Alfred Miller's to see his sick wife. Read some Scripture lessons at her bed side & had prayer.

Frid. 16. In forenoon went to cotton gin. In afternoon went to Gold Hill to post office.

Sat. 17. In afternoon started for Ebenezer. All night at widow Moses Bostian's. Rain to night in abundance.

Sund. 18. Preached at Ebenezer from Is. 55:7. Dinner at J. L. Graeber's. Returned home.

Mond. 19. Tues. 20. Wed. 21. At home.

Thurs. 22. Went to Salisbury.

Frid. 23. Sat. 24. At home. Saturday a rainy day.

Sund. 25. Went to Organ ch. Rev. Cone being present preached for me. Baptized one inft.

Mond. 26. Started after dinner for A. F. Graeber's. All night at Allison Misenheimer's.

Tues. 27. Called to see A. F. Graeber, who had attempted suicide. Dinner here. Returned home.

Wed. 28. Went to mill.

Thurs. March 1. Went to Organ ch. where the members were engaged in erecting a Council house.

Frid. 2. Went to Gold Hill to post office.

Sat. 3. Started for Ebenezer ch. All night at J. M. Eddleman's.

Sund. 4. At Ebenezer ch. — Revds. Cone and Bikle being present, Rev. Bikle preached. Dinner at J. L. Graeber's. Returned home.

Mond. 5. Went to Salisbury.

Tues. 6. In the morning went to the shoemaker. In afternoon at home.

Wed. 7. Went to Gold Hill to post office.

Thurs. 8. Frid. 9. Sat. 10. At the raising of St. Peter's Church.

Sund. 11. Preached at Organ ch. from Micah 6:8. Baptized one infant. Returned home.

Mond. 12. Attended to the funeral Catherine Lentz, widow of Bostian Lentz, dec^d, at Lower St. Church. Preached from Prov. 16:31.

Tues. 13. In afternoon went to M. A. Holshouser's & spent the evening. Supper here. Returned home.

Wed. 14. In afternoon went to C. L. Brown's & spent the evening. Supper here. Returned home.

Thurs. 15. At home.

Frid. 16. Went to Gold Hill to post office.

Sat. 17. Started for Ebenezer ch. All night at F. W. Korf's.

Sund. 18. Preached at Ebenezer from Micah 6:8. Dinner at J. L. Graeber's. Returned home.

Mond. 19. Went to Mathias Miller's & Davie Co. All night here.

Tues. 20. Went with M. Miller in his buggy to the widow Haines, & examined the German records of Dutchman Creek Church-book. Had a sumptuous dinner & spent the day very pleasantly. Returned to Mathias Miller's & staid all night.

Wed. 21. Returned home.

Thurs. 22. At home. Had snow this morning.

Frid. 23. Preached on this Good Friday at Elm Grove from John 19:30. Dinner at Eli Miller's. Called also at L. G. Holshouser's.

Sat. 24. At home.

Sund. 25. Easter. Preached at Organ ch. from 1 Cor. 15:20. An inclement day. Snow in the afternoon.

Mond. 26. Snow till 12 o'clock. In afternoon started for Hickory, as far as Salisbury. All night at National Hotel.

Tues. 27. Took the train to Hickory. Met the joint committee of N.C. & Tennessee Synods. Dinner at Rees' Hotel. Took the afternoon train back to Salisbury. Returned home.

Wed. 28. At home.

Thurs. 29. Went to Gold to post office.

Frid. 30. At home. Rolled some logs after dinner. Rain, some hail, & heavy wind this afternoon.

Sat. 31. Went to St. Matthew's ch. to assist Rev. Strohecker at a communion. Did not preach the day being very rainy. All night at Michael Eller's.

Sund. Apr. 1. At Matthew's ch., preached from Matth. 21:28-32. & aided in the administration of the communion. Returned home. Rev. Strohecker with us to night.

Mond. 2. At home.

Tues. 3. Wed. 4. Thurs. 5. At home.

Frid. 6. In the morning went to Mr. Morgan's to have Emma's shoes repaired.

Sat. 7. At St. Peter's ch. & aided in the laying of the corner stone of the new church.

Sund. 8. Preached at Organ ch. from Ps. 103:1-4.

Mond. 9. At home.

Tues. 10. Went in morning to Mr. Morgan's for Emma's Shoes. Then at home.

Wed. 11. Went to Salisbury. Called in the afternoon at Christiana Church and witnessed the burial of Moses Lingel.

Thurs. 12. Went in forenoon to Gold Hill to post office. Then at home.

Frid. 13. At home till afternoon, then went to Gold Hill to post office.

Sat. 14. Went to Ebenezer ch. & had preparatory services. Baptized one infant. Rev. Strohecker preached. All night at G. M. Ketner's.

Sund. 15. At Ebenezer ch. Rev. Strohecker preached. Administered the communion. Dinner at H. T. Graeber's. Administered the communion to Mrs. J. L. Graeber who was sick. Returned home in the evening.

Mond. 16. In afternoon went to Gold Hill to post office.

Tues. 17. At home.

Wed. 18. Went to Jacob Klutts' & had mare shod. Dinner at H. A. Miller's.

Thurs. 19. At home.

Frid. 20. Went to Gold Hill to post office.

Sat. 21. Had preparatory service at Organ ch. Prof. Dysinger preached. Returned home.

Sund. 22. Had communion at Organ church. Prof. Dysinger preached. Congregation large.

Mond. 23. At home.

Tues. 24. Went to Gold Hill & registered a letter to W. P. Houseal, Newberry, S.C.

Wed. 25. At home.

Thurs. 26. Went to Mr. Powlass' shop. Dinner here.

Frid. 27. Went to Gold Hill to post office.

Sat. 28. Had catechization at Ebenezer ch. Called to see several member's of church. All night at widow Andrew Bostian's.

Sund. 29. Preached at Ebenezer from Ps. 103:1-4. Called in afternoon to see Mrs. Jacob Pless, she being sick. Returned home.

Mond. 30. Went in afternoon to Gold Hill to Post Office.

Tues. May 1. Went to Gold Hill to Post Office.

Wed. 2. Went to St. Stephen's church to Synod. Returned home.

Thurs. 3. At Synod. All night at C. L. Nussman's.

Frid. 4. At Synod. Returned home.

Sat. 5. At Synod. Returned home.

Sund. 6. At St. Stephen's ch. Rev. Peschau preached.

Mond. 7. At Synod.

Tues. 8. Went to Wilson Kesler's & paid note he held against N. C. College.

Wed. 9. At home.

Thurs. 10. Went to mill.

Frid. 11. Went to R. Misenheimer's Saw mill and to Gold Hill to Post Office.

Sat. 12. Had catechization at Organ Church. Called to see Mrs. Cath. Barringer & her daughter, Mrs. Ellen E. A. Miller. All night at Al. Bost's.

Sund. 13. Preached at Organ ch. from Is. 35:8-10. Baptized John A. Peeler's child. Dinner at C. L. Brown's. In afternoon preached at Elm Grove from Luk. 12:16-21. Called to see Mr. D. Brady, he being afflicted.

Mond. 14. Tues. 15. Wed. 16. At home.

Thurs. 17. Went to Gold Hill to Post office.

Frid. 18. Went to Gold Hill to Post Office.

Sat. 19. Had catechization at Ebenezer church. All night at Robert A. Patterson's.

Sund. 20. In the morning baptized Mr. Patterson's sick child. Preached at Ebenezer ch. from 1 Tim. 6:12. Addressed also the Sund. School. Dinner at J. A. Eddleman's. In afternoon Preached at Frick's Stand from Luke 12:16-21. Returned home.

Mond. 21. In forenoon went to J. Earnheart's and settled for weaving carpet.

Tues. 22. Went to Gold Hill to Post Office, thence to Laurence Lingel's. Dinner here. After dinner baptized Paul A. Miller's child. In afternoon went to Mt. Pleasant. All night at Col. J. Shimpock's.

Wed. 23. Attended a meeting of Board of Trustees of N. C. College. Dinner & all night at Col. J. Shimpock's.

Thurs. 24. Returned home.

Frid. 25. Went to Gold Hill to Post Office.

Sat. 26. Had catechization at Organ ch. at 2 P.M. All night at Eli Holshouser's.

Sund. 27. Preached at Organ ch. from 1 Tim. 6:12. Dinner at Moses Klutts'. In afternoon preached at Fisher's school-house from Eccl. 12:13. Returned home,

Mond. 28. Went to Salisbury.

Tues. 29. In forenoon engaged hands to mow grass. In the evening went to mill.

Wed. 30. At home.

Thurs. 31. Went to Post Office. Then engaged hands to mow grass.

Frid. June 1. Went to Post Office. Then at home.

Sat. 2. Started for St. Luke's ch. Dinner at Rev. Stickley's. All night at D. M. Barrier's.

Sund. 3. Preached at St Luke's ch. from 1 Tim. 6:12. Dinner at John Harkey's. All night at Dan[l] Seaford's.

Mond. 4. Returned home.

Tues. 5. Went to Gold Hill to Post Office.

Wed. 6. Went to Jacob Klutts' & had Lucy shod.

Thurs. 7. Went to Gold Hill to Post Office.

Frid. 8. Went to Gold Hill to Post Office.

Sat. 9. Had catechization at Organ ch. Called to Mrs. Nancy Cruse, she be afflicted. All night at A. W. Klutts'.

Sund. 10. Preached at Organ ch. from Gen. 28:17. Baptized one infant. Dinner at C. A. Miller's. In afternoon preached at Elm Grove from Luk. 12:32.

Mond. 11. In afternoon went to Jacob Pless' and staid over night.

Tues. 12. Attended to the funeral of P. M. Stirewalt's child at Ebenezer — preached from Mark 10:14. Dinner at J. L. Graeber's. Returned home.

Wed. 13. At home haying.

Thurs. 14. Went to Gold Hill to Post Office, thence to Michael Bostian's, thence to Absolem Cress' & staid over night.

Frid. 15. Went to China Grove & attended a meeting of the Executive Committee on Missions. Dinner at Frank T. Patterson's. All night at Moses A. Ketner's.

Sat. 16. Baptized M. A. Ketner's child. Then went to Dr. P. A. Sifford's & staid for dinner. In afternoon had catechization at Ebenezer ch. All night at J. M. Eddleman's.

Sund. 17. Preached at Ebenezer ch. from Ps. 119: 63. Baptized two infants. Dinner at Sena Bostian's. In afternoon preached at Frick's stand from Eccl. 12:13. All night at Mrs. Margaret Shinn's.

Mond. 18. Returned home.

Tues. 19. Went to Gold Hill to Post Office.

Wed. 20. In forenoon went to mill. In afternoon at home.

Thurs. 21. Went to Ebenezer ch. for some papers & a Minute which had been forgotten & left. Dinner at P. A. Sloop's Esq.

Frid. 22. Went to Gold Hill to Post office.

Sat. 23. Had catechization at Organ Church. All night at R. W. Bost's.

Sund. 24. Preached at Organ ch. from Ps. 119:63. Dinner at R. W. Bost's. In afternoon preached at Fisher's School House from Matt. 11:28. Called at widow Nancy Cruse's & baptized J. M. Hipp's child, it being sick. All night at Caleb Cruse's.

Mond. 25. Returned home.

Tues. 26. In forenoon went to Gold Hill to Post Office. In afternoon went to Jacob Klutts' and had shoeing done.

Wed. 27. At home.

Thurs. 28. Called to see Jacob Miller, an aged parishioner, & called also to see Mrs. Daywalt Beaver (widow) she being much afflicted.

Frid. 29. Went to Gold Hill to Post Office, & make return of taxable property.

Sat. 30. Had catechization at Ebenezer ch. All night at J. L. Graeber's.

Sund. July 1. Went to Mrs. Nancy Basinger's & preached her funeral from Ps. 90:12. The friends then carried her to Organ Church & buried her. Went to Ebenezer ch. & preached from Matth. 25:14-30. Dinner at Jeremiah A. Eddleman's. In the afternoon preached at the Arbor near Crawford Peeler's from Titus 3:1. All night at Albert Lingel's.

Mond. 2. Went to Salisbury.

Tues. 3. At home.

Wed. 4. Went to Gold Hill to Post Office.

Thurs. 5. Shelled corn & went to mill. Then at home.

Frid. 6. At home. Aided in hauling wheat. In the evening went to mill.

Sat. 7. Had catechization at Organ church. All night at C. A. Basinger's.

Sund. 8. Attended to the funeral of Sarah L. Eagle, widow of David Eagle, at Organ Church. Preached from Prov. 4:18. Dinner at Daniel Miller's. in the afternoon preached at Elm Grove from Titus 3:1. last clause.

Mond. 9. At home. Hauled manure on late Irish potato patch.

Tues. 10. Went to Gold Hill & registered letters to Columbia, Philadelphia & New Market.

Wed. 11. Went to Salisbury.

Thurs. 12. At home.

Frid. 13. Went to Gold Hill to Post Office.

Sat. 14. Had preparatory service at Ebenezer ch. Preached from Ps. 51:17. All night at J. L. Graeber's.

Sund. 15. At Ebenezer ch. — Rev. J. A. Linn preached. Baptized one infant. Administered the Communion. Dinner at P. A. Sloop's, Esq. Returned home.

Mond. 16. At home.

Tues. 17. In the morning went to M. A. Holshouser's & had some shoeing done. Then at home.

Wed. 18. Went to Concord. Dinner & supper at Phebe Brown's. In the evening married Rev. S. T. Hallman & Lilian L. Brown. All night at Phebe Brown's.

Thurs. 19. Returned home.

Frid. 20. Went to Gold Hill to Post Office.

Sat. 21. Had preparatory service at Organ ch. Preached from Ps. 51:17. Baptized three infants. Returned home.

Sund. 22. Preached at Organ ch. from John 14:15. & then administered the communion. Wife with me to day. Dinner at Dr. Coleman's.

Mond. 23. Went in forenoon to Jacob Klutts' but did not find him at home. In the afternoon went to John Powlass' & had shoeing done.

Tues. 24. At home. Shelled corn preparatory to goeing to mill.

Wed. 25. Went to Salisbury & brought Phebe Brown out.

Thurs. 26. In the morning went to mill. Then started for Center Grove to Conference. All night at William Eddleman's.

Frid. 27. At Conference. All night at Joseph Chamber's.

Sat. 28. At Conference. All night at Peter Glass'.

Sund. 29. At Centre Grove. Rev. Bikle preached at 10 o'clock A.M. Preached in the afternoon from Jam. 1:25. All night at Leroy Shullenberger's.

Mond. 30. Went to China Grove & attended meeting of Executive Committee on Missions. Dinner at Frank T. Patterson's. Returned home.

Tues. 31. At home, haying.

Wed. August 1. At home. Had wheat threshed.

Thurs. 2. At home, haying.

Frid. 3. Called to see John Ritchie, he being sick.

Sat. 4. Called in afternoon to see Havey A. Fesperman, he having died, however, a few hours before getting there.

Sund. 5. Attended to the funeral of Harvey A. Fesperman at Organ Church — preached from Heb. 3:7.8.

Mond. 6. Went to Misenheimer Springs.

Tues. 7. At the Misenheimer Springs.

Wed. 8. At the Springs till after dinner, then returned home.

Thurs. 9. At home.

Frid. 10. Went to Post Office.

Sat. 11. Attended preaching at St. Matthew's ch.

Sund. 12. Attended preaching at St. Matthew's ch.

Mond. 13. At home.

Tues. 14. Went to Gold Hill to Post Office.

Wed. 15. Went to Jacob Klutts' & had buggy tire shrunk.

Thurs. 16. Frid. 17. At home.

Sat. 18. Had catechization at Ebenezer ch. All night at G. M. Ketner's.

Sund. 19. Preached at Ebenezer ch. from Heb. 6:18. Dinner at Robert Patterson's. Called in afternoon to see John Clark, he being sick. All night at J. L. Graeber's.

Mond. 20. Called to see Rufus Troutman, he being sick. Returned home.

Tues. 21. Went to Gold Hill to Post Office.

Wed. 22. Took Phebe Brown to Salisbury & put her on the Train to Concord.

Thurs. 23. Went to Gold Hill to post office. Then at home.

Frid. 24. At home.

Sat. 25. Had catechization at Organ ch. at 2 P.M. Returned home.

Sund. 26. Preached at Organ ch. from Heb. 6:18. Baptized one infant. Returned home.

Mond. 27. Went to Mrs. Lentz's mill in afternoon.

Tues. 28. In afternoon went to mill & brought flour home.

Wed. 29. Went to Luther's Church & preached from Matth. 11:28. The painters not being done, the dedication was postponed.

Thurs. 30. Went to Luther's Church — preached from Jam. 1:25.

Frid. 31. Went to Gold Hill to Post Office.

Sat. Sept. 1. Had catechization at Ebenezer Church. All night at F. W. Korf's.

Sund. 2. Preached at Ebenezer from Luk. 10:25-37. Dinner at J. L. Graeber's. Returned home.

Mond. 3. Had mowing done. In afternoon called to see Jacob Holshouser, he being sick.

Tues. 4. Went to Gold Hill to Post Office, thence to J. T. Lentz's the shoemaker, thence to U. E. Miller's store, thence to widow Bost's (of William), thence to Mt. Pleasant. All night at Col. Shimpock's.

Wed. 5. In Mt. Pleasant. Had a meeting of Board of Trustees of N. C. College. All night at Col. Shimpock's.

Thurs. 6. Returned home. In afternoon went to Mr. Wilson Kesler's & negotiated a loan of money for Mt. Pleasant Female Seminary.

Frid. 7. Went to Luther's Church & dedicated the same. Preached from 2 Tim. 1:13.

Sat. 8. Had catechization at Organ ch. at 2 P.M. Returned home.

Sund. 9. Preached at Organ ch. from Luk. 10:25-37. Returned home.

Mond. 10. At home.

Tues. 11. In forenoon went to Post Office. In evening went to John Peeler's & brought wife home.

Wed. 12. In forenoon went to J. Klutts' & had shoeing done. In afternoon went to mill.

Thurs. 13. At home.

Frid. 14. Went to Post Office at Gold Hill.

Sat. 15. Attended to the funeral Margaret E. Bayam, wife of Charles Bayam. Preached the fun[1] at the house from Eccl. 9:10. Buried at Organ ch. Dinner at J. J. Basinger's. In afternoon had catechization at Ebenezer ch. All night at M. J. Eddleman's.

Sund. 16. At Ebenezer ch. Rev. Chas. Rose preached. Baptized one infant. Dinner at J. A. Eddleman's. Returned home.

Mond. 17. At home.

Tues. 18. Went to Salisbury. Supper at the Mt. Vernon Hotel. Went to hear Rev. Price, colored, make an address. Took the train at 12 at night for Statesville. Stopped at the St. Charles Hotel.

Wed. 19. This the day appointed for the Executive Committee on Missions to meet. None attended save myself & Rev. Lutz. Breakfast, dinner & supper at the St. Charles. Took the train at 12 at night & returned to Salisbury.

Thurs. 20. Breakfast at the Boyden House. Returned home.

Frid. 21. Went to Post Office & to mill.

Sat. 22. Had catechization at Organ church. Returned home.

Sund. 23. Preached at Organ ch. from Acts 20:21. Baptized one infant & confirmed Charles Bayam. Then went to widow John Fesperman's & baptized five children. Dinner here. Then called at Edmond Fesperman's to see his mother-in-law, Catharine Miller, who was old and sick. Returned home.

Mond. 24. Went to Gold Hill to Post Office.

Tues. 25. At home till afternoon then went to mill.

Wed. 26. Went to Salisbury & bought some corn & a sack of coffee.

Thurs. 27. Attended to the funeral of Catharine Miller at Lower Stone Church — preached from Heb. 4:9. Baptized Monroe Casper's child at Edmond Fesperman's. Dinner at Boyden Miller's.

Frid. 28. Attended Special Conference at St. Matthew's Church. Returned home. Rev. Hallman & wife with us to night & night before.

Sat. 29. At Conference. All night at Otho Pool's.

Sund. 30. At Conference. Returned home.

Mond. October 1. Attended to the funeral of Charles Bayam's twin children. Preached the funeral at Widow John Fesperman's from Matt. 19:14. Buried at Organ ch. Returned home.

Tues. 2. Went to Mt. Pleasant. All night at Col. Shimpock's.

Wed. 3. Attended meeting of Trustees of N. C. College. All night at Col. Shimpock's.

Thurs. 4. Went to Fair at St. John's Church. In afternoon went to J. L. Graeber's & staid over night.

Frid. 5. Went to China Grove & attended meeting of Ex. Committee on Missions. Dinner at T. Frank Patterson's. Returned to Moses Ketner's and staid all night.

Sat. 6. Went to George Ketner's, his daughter Rosa being sick. Dinner here. In afternoon had catechization at Ebenezer ch. All night at J. L. Graeber's.

Sund. 7. Preached at Ebenezer ch. from Prov. 29:1. Dinner at P. A. Sloop's. Returned home.

Mond. 8. At home.

Tues. 9. Went to Gold Hill to Post Office.

Wed. 10. At home.

Thurs. 11. Went with wife to H. A. Miller's & spent the day.

Frid. 12. Went to Albert Earnheart's on business for Lewis. Also to Gold Hill to Post Office.

Sat. 13. Went to George M. Ketner's & attended to the funeral of his daughter Rosetta V. at Ebenezer Church. Preached from Phil. 1:21. All night at J. L. Graeber's.

Sund. 14. Preached at Organ ch. from Jerm. 17:9. & 2 Cor. 13:5. Baptized one infant. Returned home.

Mond. 15. Went to Gold Hill to Post Office.

Tues. 16. At home.

Wed. 17. Took Bettie to Salisbury to select a Bedstead for Emma.

Thurs. 18. Had catechization at Organ Church.

Frid. 19. Had catechization at Ebenezer church. All night at Afred W. Klutts'.

Sat. 20. Had preparatory service at Ebenezer ch. Rev. R. L. Brown preached. Confirmed six persons. All night at J. A. Eddleman's.

Sund. 21. A very rainy day. Congregation could not assemble. Returned home. Postponed communion two weeks.

Mond. 22. At home. Rainy day.

Tues. 23. Went to M. A. Holshouser's to intercept mail carrier to send off a letter.

Wed. 24. Went to Gold Hill & paid tax.

Thurs. 25. At home.

Frid. 26. Had catechization at Organ Church.

Sat. 27. Had preparatory service at Organ Church. Rev. J. A. Linn preached. Baptized one adult. Confirmed twenty persons.

Sund. 28. Had Communion at Organ Church. Rev. G. F. Schaeffer preached.

Mond. 29. Went to Salisbury.

Tues. 30. Went to Calvin Pool's & bought some corn. Dinner here.

Wed. 31. Went to Lower St. Church and heard Rev. Gurley preach a Reformation sermon.

Thurs. November 1. At home.

Frid. 2. Went to Bethel Church in Stanly co. to meet Church Council, but Council failed to meet. Dinner at Alex. Misenheimer's. Returned home.

Sat. 3. Started for Ebenezer Church. All night at George Troutman's.

Sund. 4. Baptized Wm. C. Troutman's child at George Troutman's. Then went to Ebenezer Church & addressed the congregation from 1 Cor. 10:16. & administered the Communion. Dinner at Moses J. Eddleman's. Then went to Rufus Troutman's & administered the communion to him, he being greatly afflicted with consumption. Returned to M. J. Eddleman's & staid over night.

Mond. 5. Returned home.

Tues. 6. Went to Salisbury & settled with Smithdeal & Bernhardt for Oats. Returned by way of John C. Pool's & settled with him for Corn.

Wed. 7. Went to Gold Hill to Post Office.

Thurs. 8. In the morning went to Dr. Coleman's for cough medicine for wife. Then at home.

Frid. 9. Went to Concord to attend the celebration of 400th birthday of Dr. Martin Luther. All night at Rev. S. T. Hallman's.

Sat. 10. Attended celebration of 400th birthday of Luther. Dinner at Alex^r Foil's. All night at Rev. Hallman's.

Sund. 11. Attended preaching in Concord. All night at Rev. Hallman's.

Mond. 12. Returned home. In the evening went to Gold Hill to Post Office.

Tues. 13. Went to Mt. Pleasant. All night at Col. J. Shimpock's.

Wed. 14. Attended meeting of Board of Trustees of N. C. College. All night at Col. Shimpock's.

Thurs. 15. Returned home by way of Foil's Tanyard.

Frid. 16. Went to Bethel Church in Stanly Co. to meet Church Council, but did not have a quorum & could attend to no business. Returned home.

Sat. 17. At home.

Sund. 18. Having exchanged pulpits with Rev. T. H. Strohecker, preached to day at St. Matthew's Church, the funeral of Elizabeth Hill, who had died some months before, & also two of her children, from Ps. 73:26.

Mond. 19. Went to Gold Hill to Post Office.

Tues. 20. Went to Mrs. Moses Linn's & mended cord in her clock.

Wed. 21. Attended to the funeral of Joseph Pool at St. Matthew's ch. — preached from Gen. 5:24. In the evening went to Paul Stirewalt's, his son's wife being very sick. All night here.

Thurs. 22. Returned home.

Frid. 28. In the morning went to cotton gin. In the afternoon went to George Troutman's & staid over night.

Sat. 24. Attended to the funeral of Sarah Jane, wife of Paul M. Stirewalt, at Ebenezer ch. Preached from 2 Pet. 2:9. Large collection of people. Dinner at J. L. Graeber's. Returned home.

Sund. 25. In the morning went to J. T. Lentz's & married Brantly R. A. Beaver & Camilla E. Lentz. Then went to Organ ch. & preached from Ex. 33:14. Returned to M. Lentz's and took dinner.

Mond. 26. At home. This my birthday.

Tues. 27. Went in afternoon to Organ Church & buried Jacob Misenheimer's child.

Wed. 28. Slaughtered winter hogs. In afternoon went to Gold Hill to post office.

Thurs. 29. Attended to the funeral of Edward Pool at St. Matthew's Church. Preached from 2 Pet. 2:9. Dinner at Wilson Kesler's.

Frid. 30. Went to Gold Hill to Post Office.

Sat. Dec. 1. Started for Ebenezer Church. Visited several families on the way. All night at Geo. M. Ketner's.

Sund. 2. Preached at Ebenezer Church from John 3:14.15. Dinner at H. T. Graeber's. Returned home.

Mond. 3. Went to Gold Hill to Post Office.

Tues. 4. Went to Salisbury & sold the girls' cotton.

Wed. 5. Went to Gold Hill to Post Office.

Thurs. 6. At home.

Frid. 7. Went to Gold Hill to Post Office.

Sat. 8. Went to Salisbury & assisted in laying the corner stone of the new Lutheran Church. Dinner at Col. P. N. Heilig's.

Sund. 9. Preached at Organ Church from Joh. 3:14.15. Returned home.

Mond. 10. Went to Gold Hill to Post Office.

Tues. 11. At home.

Wed. 12. In forenoon went to Gold Hill to Post Office. In afternoon went to Calvin A. Fisher's and baptized his twin children, one of them being sick.

Thurs. 13. Frid. 14. At home.

Sat. 15. Started for Ebenezer Church. All night at Dr. P. A. Sifferd's.

Sund. 16. Preached at Ebenezer Church from 1 Cor. 4:2. Dinner & all night at J. A. Eddleman's.

Mond. 17. Returned home.

Tues. 18. In afternoon went to Mt. Pleasant. All night Col. John Shimpock's.

Wed. 19. In Mt. Pleasant. Attended meeting of Board of Trustees of N. C. College. At Col. Shimpock's.

Thurs. 20. Returned home. Dinner at Charles Fisher's.

Frid. 21. Went to Gold Hill to Post Office.

Sat. 22. At home.

Sund. 23. In the morning went to Peter Miller's & married Harvey B. Foutz & Emma. B. Miller. Then went to Organ Church & preached the fun[1] of Jacob Misenheimer's child which had died some weeks before from Matth. 5:8. Returned home.

Mond. 24. Went to Post Office at Gold Hill, and then to Elm Grove to Christmas Tree.

Tues. 25. Went to Organ Church to Christmas Festival. An inclement day.

Wed. 26. In afternoon went to mill.

Thurs. 27. Went to Salisbury. Returned by way of Cornelius Kestler's.

Frid. 28. Sat. 29. At home.

Sund. 30. Had no appointment for this day. At home.

Mond 31. At home.

Tues. Jan. 1. Went to Mt. Pleasant in afternoon. All night at Col. Shimpock's.

Wed. 2. Attended meeting of Board of Trustees of N. C. College. All night at Col. Shimpock's.

Thurs. 3. Returned home.

Frid. 4. In afternoon went to Post Office.

Sat. 5. Was to have attended a Sund. Sch. Convention at Organ Church, but the day being very inclement with snow storm, did not attend.

Sund. 6. This my regular day to preach at Ebenezer but the weather being very inclement, did not attend.

Mond. 7. Tues. 8. Wed. 9. Thurs. 10. At home, snow on the ground & weather cold.

Frid. 11. Went to Gold Hill to Post Office.

Sat. 12. At home.

Sund. 13. Preached at Organ Church from Rom. 12:1-5.

Mond. 14. At home.

Tues. 15. In afternoon went to M. A. Holshouser's to shoes half soled.

Wed. 16. Went to Salisbury.

Thurs. 17. At home.

Frid. 18. At home.

Sat. 19. Started for Ebenezer Church. All night at J. L. Graeber's.

Sund. 20. Preached at Ebenezer Church from Luk. 17:32. After preaching went to Calvin A. Lipe's & baptized his child. Dinner here. Returned to J. L. Graeber's & staid over night.

Mond. 21. Returned home. Weather cold.

Tues. 22. In afternoon went to M. A. Holshouser's to see David Campbell, who was sick & not of sound mind.

Wed. 23. Went to Gold Hill to Post Office.

Thurs. 24. Attended to the funeral of David Campbell at Liberty (Methodist) Church. Preached from Amos 4:12. latter clause.

Frid. 25. Went to Gold Hill to Post Office.

Sat. 26. Went to Rev. R. L. Brown's & baptized his infant child, it being in feeble health. Dinner here. Returned home.

Sund. 27. Preached at Organ church from Luk. 13:6-9. Returned home. Cold in the morning.

Mond. 28. In forenoon went to M. A. Holshouser's & settled for beef & shoe repairing. Then at home.

Tues. 29. Met two of the Elders of Organ Church at Jacob Holshouser's to restore peace & harmony between the said Holshouser & his wife. Dinner at Widow Daywald Beaver's.

Wed. 30. Had several stacks of hay hauled into the barn.

Thurs. 31. In the morning went to mill. Then to Gold Hill to Post Office.

Frid. Feb. 1. In forenoon went to Post Office. In afternoon at home.
Sat. 2. Started for Ebenezer Church. All night at Widow Moses Bostian's.
Sund. 3. Preached at Ebenezer Church from Gen. 22:1-3. Dinner at J. L. Graeber's. Returned home.
Mond. 4. In the morning went to mill. Then went to D. Barringer's to celebrate has matrimonial semi-centennial. All night here.
Tues. 5. Returned home.
Wed. 6. At home.
Thurs. 7. Went to mill morning & evening.
Frid. 8. In forenoon went to Post office. In afternoon went to mill.
Sat. 9. At home.
Sund. 10. Preached at Organ Church from Luk. 17:32. Returned home.
Mond. 11. Tues. 12. At home.
Wed. 13. Went to Post Office, then to Mr. Powlass' & had lock repaired. Dinner here.
Thurs. 14. Frid. 15. At home.
Sat. 16. Started for Ebenezer Church. All night at P. A. Sloop's, Esq.
Sund. 17. Preached at Ebenezer from Matth. 12:41. Dinner at J. A. Eddleman's. Returned home.
Mond. 18. Went to Wilson Kesler's on business for David Brady.
Tues. 19. Wed. 20. At home.
Thurs. 21. Went to Gold Hill to Post Office.
Frid. 22. At home.
Sat. 23. At home.
Sund. 24. Preached at Organ ch. from Matth. 12:42.
Mond. 25. Went to Gold Hill to Post Office.
Tues. 26. Started for special meeting of Synod at St. Enoch's Church. Stopped on the way at Absalom Cress' for dinner. Baptized his child. All night at Rev. Lutz's.
Wed. 27. In special meeting of Synod. All night at Rev. Lutz's.
Thurs. 28. Returned home. Dinner at Mich⁻ Bostian's.
Frid. 29. At home. Very cold weather.

Sat. March 1. Started for Ebenezer Church. All night at J. M. Eddleman's.

Sund. 2. Preached at Ebenezer from Matth. 12:42. Dinner at H. T. Graeber's. Returned home.

Mond. 3. At home — a very cold day.

Tues. 4. Went to Mt. Pleasant. All night at Col. Shimpock's.

Wed. 5. Had appointed a meeting for the Board of Trustees of N. C. College, but failed to have a quorum. Dinner & all night at Col. Shimpock's.

Thurs. 6. Returned home. Dinner at Laurence Lingel's.

Frid. 7. Went to Post Office.

Sat. 8. At home.

Sund. 9. Preached at Organ ch. from 1 Tim. 4:8. Heavy rains in the morning.

Mond. 10. At home.

Tues. 11. Went to Salisbury.

Wed. 12. Thurs. 13. At home.

Frid. 14. Went to Gold Hill to Post Office.

Sat. 15. Started for Ebenezer Church. All night at Robert Patterson's.

Sund. 16. Went to John Clark's & baptized his child. Then to Ebenezer Church & preached from 1 Tim. 4:8. Dinner at J. L. Graeber's. Returned home.

Mond. 17. In forenoon went to mill. In afternoon to J. Powlass' & had shoeing done.

Tues. 18. Went to Mt. Pleasant to attend meeting of Board of Trustees of N. C. College. All night at Col. Shimpock's.

Wed. 19. Attended meeting of Board of Trustees. Dinner & all night at Col. Shimpock's.

Thurs. 20. Returned home.

Frid. 21. Went to Gold Hill to Post Office.

Sat. 22. At home.

Sund. 23. Preached at Organ Church from 1 Thes. 5:6. Then went to Edmond E. Klutts' & baptized his sick child. Dinner here. Returned home.

Mond. 24. Tues. 25. At home.

Wed 26. Went to James A. Miller's. Dinner here. In afternoon went to Eli Holshouser's. Then returned home.

Thurs. 27. Started for Mt. Pleasant to Special Conference. All night at Laurence Klutts'.

Frid. 28. Went to Mt. Pleasant. Stopped at Col. Shimpock's. Preached from 1 Cor. 4:2. Dinner at Col. Shimpock's, & all night.

Sat. 29. At conference. Dinner to day at Capt. Jonas Cook's.

Sund. 30. Rev. Petrea preached. Consecrated the elements & aided in the administration of the communion. Preached at night from Prov. 29:1.

Mond. 31. Returned home.

Tues. April 1. At home.

Wed. 2. Took Bettie Thomas to Salisbury.

Thurs. 3. At home.

Frid. 4. Went to Gold Hall to Post Office.

Sat. 5. Went to Union Church and preached for Rev. R. L. Brown from Matt. 21:28. Dinner at Edward Wise's. Returned home.

Sund. 6. Preached at Union Church from Matth. 21:10. last clause. Assisted in administration of the Communion. Returned home.

Mond. 7. Went to Calvin Pool's & engaged some corn. Dinner here.

Tues. 8. Went to Montgomery & Co's. Saw mill.

Wed. 9. At home.

Thurs. 10. Went to Gold Hill to Post Office.

Frid. 11. Good Friday. Preached at Organ Church from John 19:30. Baptized one infant. Returned home.

Sat. 12. Preached at Organ Church from Matth. 21:28. Baptized one infant. Confirmed two persons. Had preparatory service. Returned home.

Sund. 13. Preached at Organ Church from John 7:37. Administered the Communion. Returned home.

Mond. 14. Tues. 15. At home.

Wed. 16. At home.

Thurs. 17. Went to mill morning & evening.

Frid. 18. Went to Gold Hill to Post Office.

Sat. 19. At home.

Sund. 20. Went to Ebenezer ch. & preached from 1 Thes. 5:6. Baptized one infant. Dinner at J. L. Graeber's. Returned home.

Mond. 21. Tues. 22. At home.

Wed. 23. Went to Gold Hill to Post Office.

Thurs. 24. At home.

Frid. 25. Went to Gold Hill to Post Office.

Sat. 26. Went in forenoon to J. A. Miller's to see his mother, Eliza Miller, having written her will for her.

Sund. 27. Preached at Organ ch. from John 10:11.

Mond. 28. At home making preparations for Synod.

Tues. 29. Started for Ebenezer Church to attend meeting of Synod. All night at J. L. Graeber's.

Wed. 30. At meeting of Synod. All night at Frederic Stirewalt's

Thurs. May 1. At Synod. All night at David Bostian's

Frid. 2. At Synod. Supper at Mrs. Cline's. At night heard Rev. Koonts (colored) preach. All night at R. A. Patterson's.

Sat. 3. At Synod. All night at Mrs. Beaver's.

Sund. 4. At Ebenezer Church. Had preaching & Communion. Returned home.

Mond. 5. At home.

Tues. 6. Wed. 7. At home.

Thurs. 8. Went to Salisbury.

Frid. 9. Sat. 10. At home.

Sund. 11. This my day at Organ Church. Rev. J. A. Linn being present preached in my stead. Baptized one infant. Returned home.

Mond. 12. At home.

Tues. 13. Went to mill, then at home.

Wed. 14. Attended to the funeral of Eve Elizabeth Trexler, wife of Lawson Trexler, at St. Peter's Church. Preached from Ps. 50:15.

Thurs. 15. At home.

Frid. 16. Went to Salisbury.

Sat. 17. Started for Ebenezer Church. Called to see Jacob Miller. All night at P. A. Sloop's, Esq.

Sund. 18. At Ebenezer Church. Rev. J. A. Linn preached. Dinner at H. T. Graeber's. Returned home.

Mond. 19. At home.

Tues. 20. Started for Mt. Pleasant to attend closing exercises of College. Called at Haynes' Shop & had shoeing done. Dinner at Jackson Bost's. All night at Col. Shimpock's.

Wed. 21. Thurs. 22. In Mt. Pleasant. Home at Col. Shimpock's.

Frid. 23. Returned home.

Sat. 24. At home.

Sund. 25. Preached at Organ Church from Prov. 14:32. Baptized one infant. Dinner at C. A. Miller's. In afternoon preached at Elm Grove from Matt. 22:11.12.

Mond. 26. At home.

Tues. 27. Went to Gold Hill to Post Office, and then went to engage hands to mow grass.

Wed. 28. Thurs. 29. At home. Had Lewis to build a hog pen.

Frid. 30. Went to Gold Hill to Post Office.

Sat. 31. Started for Ebenezer. All night at J. M. Eddleman's.

Sund. June 1. Preached at Ebenezer from Hos. 14:1.2. Dinner at J. M. Eddleman's. Returned home.

Mond. 2. Tues. 3. Wed. 4. At home, haying.

Thurs. 5. Went to And. Berger's to get some brandy for wife. Called also to see Mrs. Peter Earnheart, she being sick.

Frid. 6. Went to Gold Hill to Post Office.

Sat. 7. At home.

Sund. 8. Preached at Organ church from Gal. 6:7. Dinner at William Beaver's. In afternoon preached widow Nancy Cruse's from Ps. 37:3. All night at Jackson Bost's.

Mond. 9. Returned home.

Tues. 10. Went to Gold Hill to Post Office.

Wed. 11. At home.

Thurs. 12. In forenoon went to Rockwell Post Office & mailed some letters.

Frid 13. Went to Gold Hill to Post Office.

Sat. 14. Had intended to start for Ebenezer ch. but the weather being showery, did not go. Was taken unwell during the night.

Sund. 15. Not being well, sent Lewis to Ebenezer to render an excuse for my absence.

Mond. 16. At home.

Tues. 17. Went to Salisbury & sent off money for communion ware for St. Peter's Church.

Wed. 18. Thurs. 19. Frid. 20. Sat. 21. At home.

Sund. 22. Preached at Organ Church from Ps. 144:15. Dinner at Boyden A. R. Miller's. In afternoon preached at Elm Grove from Acts 13:26. Returned home.

Mond 23. At home.

Tues. 24. Went to Salisbury & brought out Communion ware for St. Peter's Church.

Wed. 25. At home.

Thurs. 26. Went with Lewis to Peeler's School House & returned taxes.

Frid. 27. Sat. 28. Sund. 29. Attended Special Conference at St. Peter's Church.

Mond. 30. At home.

Tues. July 1. Went in afternoon to see Dr. Coleman, he being sick.

Wed. 2. At home.

Thurs. 3. Frid. 4. At home wife sick.

Sat. 5. Started for Ebenezer. All night at Jacob Misenheimer's.

Sund. 6. Preached at Ebenezer from Ps. 144:15. Baptized one infant. Dinner at H. T. Graeber's. Returned home.

Mond. 7. to Sat. 12. At home, wife sick.

Sund. 13. Preached at Organ Church from Acts 16:16-34. Baptized two infants. Dinner at widow Cruse's. In afternoon preached at Fisher's School House from Eccl. 12:13.14. Returned home.

Mond. 14. At home.

Tues. 15. Went with Lewis to Salisbury.

Wed. 16. At home.

Thurs. 17. Went to Mr Powlass' & had shoeing done.

Frid. 18. At home.

Sat. 19. Went to Ebenezer Church. Rev. R. L. Brown preached. Baptized one infant. Held preparatory service. All night at G. M. Ketner's.

Sund. 20. At Ebenezer Church. Rev. R. L. Brown preached. Administered the Holy Lord's Supper. Dinner at J. A. Eddleman's. Returned home.

Mond. 21. At home, had wheat threshed.

Tues. 22. In afternoon went to Mt. Pleasant. All night at Col. Shimpock's.

Wed. 23. Attended meeting of Board Trustees. Dinner at Col. Shimpock's. Returned home.

Thurs. 24. Frid. 25. At home.

Sat. 26. Had preparatory service at Organ Church. Rev. J. D. Shirey preached. Installed two Elders & two Deacons. Baptized one infant. All night at William Beaver's.

Sund. 27. At Organ Church. Rev. Shirey preached. Administered the Holy Supper. Returned home.

Mond. 28. Went to Salisbury.

Tues. 29. Wed. 30. Thurs. 31. At home.

Frid. Aug. 1. Went to Gold Hill to post office.

Sat. 2. Started for Ebenezer Church. All night at Absalom Cress'.

Sund. 3. Preached at Ebenezer Church from Ps. 37:1-3. Dinner at J. L. Graeber's. Returned home.

Mond. 4. At home.

Tues. 5. In afternoon went to mill.

Wed. 6. Went to Gold Hill to Post Office & brought flour home for Lewis.

Thurs. 7. In forenoon called to see William Beaver, who had been hurt some by the thresher. In afternoon went to mill.

Frid. 8. Started for Salem Church to assist Rev. Shirey at communion meeting. All night at John Lingel's.

Sat. 9. Preached at Salem Church from Ps. 37:1-3. In afternoon called with Rev. Shirey to see Dan$^{\underline{l}}$ Menius who was sorely afflicted with Cancer. Dinner & all night at Moses A. Bost's.

Sund. 10. Preached at Salem ch. from Rev. 2:4.5. Assisted in the communion. Dinner & all night at Dan$^{\underline{l}}$ Seaford's.

Mond. 11. Returned home.

Tues. 12. At home.

Wed. 13. Went to Mt. Pleasant & took flour to Lewis. Returned home.

Thurs. 14. Frid. 15. At home.

Sat. 16. Started for Ebenezer ch. Called at Mr. Pless'. All night at Paul Stirewalt's.

Sund. 17. Preached at Ebenezer ch. from Acts 16:30.31. Baptized one infant. Dinner at widow Dan$^{\underline{l}}$ Eddleman's. Returned home.

Mond. 18. Had Mr. Crowell to haul hay in afternoon.

Tues. 19. At home.

Wed. 20. Went to widow Edward Pool's and bought some Oats. Dinner here.

Thurs. 21. At home.

Frid. 22. Went to Mrs. Pool's & had Oats hauled by M. A. Holshouser. Dinner here.

Sat. 23. Attended Gold Hill Township Sunday School Association at Organ Church. Called also to see Jeremiah Miller who had been severely hurt by the kick of a horse. Returned home.

Sund. 24. Preached at Organ Church from Ps. 37:1-3. Baptized two infants. Called to see Henry Klutts, he being sick. Dinner here. Returned home.

Mond. 25. Started, in afternoon, for Rowan Co. Sund. School Association at Harris Chapel. All night at J. L. Graeber's.

Tues. 26. Attended Sund. Sch. Association at Harris Chapel. All night at Rosena Bostian's (widow).

Wed. 27. Returned home. Called on the way to see Henry Klutts, he being sick. Dinner at Allison Bost's. Called also to see Jerry Miller, he being badly hurt by kick of horse.

Thurs. 28. Went to Gold Hill to Mill & to post office.

Frid. 29. Went to Salisbury.

Sat. 30. At home.

Sund. 31. Went to St. Peter's church & heard Rev. Strohecker preach.

Mond. Sep. 1. Went to Catharine Bailey's and assisted in laying off her dower, and dividing the land among legatees. Dinner & supper here.

Tues. 2. In afternoon went to Mt. Pleasant to attend meeting of Board of Trustees. All night at Col. Shimpock's.

Wed. 3. Attended meeting of Board of Trustees of N. C. College. Dinner at Lewis' — All night at Col. Shimpock's.

Thurs. 4. Returned home.

Frid. 5. Went to J. Powlass' & had shoeing done.

Sat. 6. Started for Ebenezer Church. Called to see Henry Klutts, he being sick. All night at George Troutman's.

Sund. 7. Preached at Ebenezer Church from Prov. 3:9.10. Dinner at J. A. Eddleman's. Returned home.

Mond. 8. Tues. 9. At home, haying.

Wed. 10. Attended to the funeral of Christena Canup. Preached the funeral at Littleton Lingel's, the place of her residence, from Heb. 4:9. Buried at Lower St. Church.

Thurs. 11. Frid. 12. At home.

Sat. 13. Buried Henry Klutts, an aged member, at Organ Church. Preaching of the funeral postponed on account of sickness of his son Edmond. All night at R. W. Bost's.

Sund. 14. Preached at Organ Church from Prov. 3:9.10. Returned home.

Mond. 15. Went to Gold Hill to post office. Then called to see Mrs. C. L. Brown, she being very sick. Called at Mrs. Ellen E. A. Miller's, & went to Organ Church for some documents which had been forgotten.

Tues. 16. In the afternoon went with wife to see Mrs. Calvin L. Brown, she being sick.

Wed. 17. Went to Salisbury.

Thurs. 18. At home.

Frid. 19. Went to Gold Hill to post office and to mill.

Sat. 20. Started for Ebenezer Church. Called to see E. E. Klutts, he being sick. All night at Chaˢ Powlass'.

Sund. 21. In the morning called a Thornton R. Powlass' & baptized his child. Preached at Ebenezer Church from John 4:14. Baptized one infant. Dinner at H. T. Graeber's. Returned home.

Mond. 22. At home.

Tues. 23. Called to see Mrs. Calvin L. Brown, she being sick. Called also at the post office at Gold Hill.

Wed. 24. Went to J. C. Pool's & paid acct. for Oats.

Thurs. 25. Went with Rev. Strohecker to Misenheimer's Springs. Dinner here.

Frid. 26. Went to Gold Hill to post office.

Sat. 27. At home.

Sund. 28. Preached at Organ Church from 1 Sam. 12:23.24. Dinner at J. A. Miller's. Returned home.

Mond. 29. Went to Gold Hill to post office.

Tues. 30. Went to Mt. Pleasant. Called on the way to see Mrs. Calvin L. Brown. Called also to see Laurence Lingel. Dinner here. All night at son Lewis'.

Wed. Oct. 1. Attended meeting of Board of Trustees of N. C. College. Dinner at son Lewis'. All night at Col. Shimpock's.

Thurs. 2. Returned home.

Frid. 3. Went to Gold Hill to post office & heard the candidates speak.

Sat. 4. Went to St. Paul's Church to aid Rev. Rose at a communion. Preached from Acts 9:6. All night at Allison Misenheimer's.

Sund. 5. Preached at St. Paul's Church in the forenoon from Rom. 10:1. Aided in Communion. Preached in afternoon from Neh. 6:3. Returned home.

Mond. 6. At home.

Tues. 7. Went to Tobias Lyerly's & brought Lewis' hack home.

Wed. 8. At home.

Thurs. 9. Went to Gold Hill & heard Mr. Coke make a political speech.

Frid. 10. Went to Gold Hill to post office & to mill.

Sat. 11. In forenoon called to see Mrs. C. L. Brown, she being sick. In afternoon at home.

Sund. 12. Preached at Organ ch. from Col. 2:6.7. Baptized one infant. Returned home.

Mond. 13. Took wife on a visit to James A. Miller's.

Tues. 14. Attended to the funeral of John Richie's daughter. Preached the funeral at the house and buried at Organ Church. Preached from Heb. 3:15.

Wed. 15. Went to mill at Gold Hill & had some wheat ground for Lewis.

Thurs 16. Went to Gold Hill and heard John Henderson & Dr. Ramsey, candidates for Congress, address the people. Returned home and married Julius A. A. Earnheart and Martha E. Powlass at my house.

Frid. 17. At home.

Sat. 18. Went to Ebenezer Church & had services preparatory to communion Rev. Rose preached. All night at F. W. Korf's.

Sund. 19. Called in the morning at Frederick Stirewalt's at administered the communion to him and his wife, they being old & infirm. Then went to Ebenezer Church & had communion. Rev. Rose preached. Dinner at Paul Stirewalt's. Then went to Peter Cruse's to see his wife, she being very sick. Returned to Paul Stirewalt's & staid all night.

Mond. 20. Returned home by way of Edmond Fesperman's.

Tues. 21. Attended to the funeral of Mititia Brown at Organ Church. Preached from Is. 3:10. Attended to the funeral also of Mary Ann Cruse, wife of Peter Cruse. Preached from Rev. 14:13.

Wed. 22. Went to Cornelius Ketner's & got some brandy.

Thurs. 23. At home.

Frid. 24. Went to Salisbury. Dinner at Col. P. N. Heilig's.

Sat. 25. Went to Organ Church & had services preparatory to communion. Rev. Prof. Rupp preached. Baptized one infant & confirmed three persons. Returned home.

Sund. 26. At Organ Church. Rev. Prof. Rupp preached. Administered the communion.

Mond. 27. Went to Gold Hill to mill.

Tues. 28. Divided corn at Sol. Peeler's.

Wed. 29. In the morning went to Andr. Berger's & engaged him to spay shoats.

Thurs. 30. At home, divided Geo. Park's corn.

Frid. 31. At home, divided John A. Peeler's corn.

Sat. Nov. 1. Started for Ebenezer Church. All night at Dr. E. E. Klutts'. Indisposed with severe cold.

Sund. 2. Went to Ebenezer Church. Was not able to preach in consequence of severe cold. J. L. Graeber conducted some devotional exercises. Dismissed the congregation. Dinner at P. A. Sloop's, Esq. Returned home.

Mond. 3. At home.

Tues. 4. In forenoon went to Gold Hill to election, then at home.

Wed. 5. At home.

Thurs. 6. Went to Salisbury.

Frid. 7. In afternoon helped to take the girl's cotton to the gin.

Sat. 8. In forenoon brought the girl's cotton and seed home.

Sund. 9. Preached at Organ Church from Heb. 11:13. the last clause, the funeral of Henry Klutts, dec[d].

Mond. 10. Tues. 11. At home.

Wed. 12. Went to Salisbury to attend the Diet composed of delegates from the various Synods of the South. Had lodgings assigned at B. F. Fraley's.

Thurs. 13. Attended the Diet.

Frid. 14. Returned home.

Sat. 15. Started for Ebenezer Church. All night at Dr. P. A. Sifferd's.

Sund. 16. Preached at Ebenezer from Eph. 6:18. Dinner at J. L. Graeber's. Returned home.

Mond. 17. In forenoon went to Gold Hill to post office, then at home.

Tues. 18. Wed. 19. At home.

Thurs. 20. At home. Married, at my house, Mr. Henry J. Bost & Miss Margaret D. Bost.

Frid. 21. In forenoon went to Gold Hill to post office. In afternoon at home.

Sat. 22. At home.

Sund. 23. Preached at Organ ch. from Mark 13:24.

Mond. 24. Tues. 25. At home.

Wed. 26. Went to Salisbury. This my 75th birth day.

Thurs. 27. At home. Lewis called to see us.

Frid. 28. Was to have gone to Conference at Union ch. but the day very rainy and inclement did not go.

Sat. 29. Went to Conference at Union Church. Rev. Petrea preached. Had a short session in afternoon. All night at George Lyerly's.

Sund. 30. At Union Church. Assisted in the services of the day. Returned home.

Mond. Dec. 1. At home, made preparations for slaughtering hogs.
Tues. 2. Had Hogs slaughtered.
Wed. 3. Went to David Barringer's to buy corn, but failed. Dinner here.
Thurs. 4. At home.
Frid. 5. Went to Gold Hill to post office.
Sat. 6. Started in afternoon for Ebenezer church. All night at J. L. Graeber's.
Sund. 7. Preached at Ebenezer ch. from Mark 13:34. Dinner at J. A. Eddleman's. Returned home.
Mond. 8. Called to see Rev. R. L. Brown, he being sick.
Tues. 9. At home.
Wed. 10. Went in forenoon to post office.
Thurs. 11. At home.
Frid. 12. Went to Gold Hill to post office.
Sat. 13. In the morning went to Mr. Grupy's to engage corn.
Sund. 14. Preached at Organ Church from 1 Cor. 4:2. Baptized on infant. Returned home. Very rainy.
Mond. 15. Went at 12 M. & employed Mr. Taylor to cut wood short for fire.
Tues. 16. At home.
Wed. 17. Thurs. 18. Went to Ellen Grupy's plantation & had corn brought home.
Frid. 19. At home.
Sat. 20. A very cold day. Started for Ebenezer. All night at J. M. Eddleman's.
Sund. 21. A very inclement day. Went to Ebenezer. Congregation very small. Lectured from Luk. 13:6-9. Dinner & all night at J. L. Graeber's.
Mond. 22. Attended to the fun[1] of Laurence Lingel at Lower Stone Church. Preached from Ps. 37:37. Went back to Mr. Lingel's late residence & staid over night.
Tues. 23. Returned home. In afternoon went to M. A. Holshouser's on business, but found him not at home.
Wed. 24. At home.
Thurs. 25. Went in forenoon to Solomon Peeler's and married John S. Beaver & Mary Jane Peeler. Went in afternoon to M. A. Holshouser's and married W. M. Linker & Camilla C. Earnheart. Returned home.
Frid. 26. Attended Christmas Tree at Elm Grove.
Sat . 27. Attended Christmas Sunday School Festival at Organ Church. All night at Paul Klutts'.
Sund. 28. Preached at Organ ch. from Luk. 13:6-9.
Mond. 29. In afternoon went to Gold Hill to post office.
Tues. 30. Went to Mr. Grupy's & paid Mrs. Grupy for corn. Then went to Salisbury.
Wed. 31. Attended to the funeral of John Lentz's child at Organ ch.– preached from Matth. 25:13. Dinner at L. A. Heilig's.

Jan. 1, 1885. New Year's day. At home. Weather mild & cloudy, with some rain, till the after part of the day, the wind then veered to N.W. & turned cold.

Frid. 2. At home, clear & cold.

Sat. 3. Started for Ebenezer ch. All night at widow Charles Miller's. Weather cold & inclement.

Sund. 4. Preached at Ebenezer from 1 Pet. 4:18. Weather very inclement. All night at G. M. Ketner's.

Mond. 5. Returned home. Cold and rainy.

Tue. 6. At home.

Wed. 7. Went to Gold Hill to Post Office.

Thurs. 8. At home.

Frid. 9. Sat. 10. At home.

Sund. 11. Preached at Organ Church from Ex. 20:7. Returned home.

Mond. 12. Went to Salisbury.

Tues. 13. In afternoon went to Gold Hill to Post Office.

Wed. 14. In afternoon went to Michael Bostian's & staid over night.

Thurs. 15. In the morning baptized an orphan child adopted by Solomon Yost & Wife. Then went to Mrs. Troutman's & married Milas Safrit & Laura M. Troutman. In afternoon went to Mrs. Mary Cruse's & married Paul J. Klutts & Margaret A. Cruse. All night here.

Frid. 16. Returned home by way of G. M. Bernhardt's.

Sat. 17. Started for Ebenezer ch. All night at George Troutman's. Weather cold & blustering.

Sund. 18. Preached at Ebenezer ch. from Ex. 20:7. Dinner at J. L. Graeber's. All night at William Beaver's.

Mond. 19. Called to see Charles Fisher, who is old & infirm. Called also to see Dr. Coleman, he being sick. Then returned home.

Tues. 20. At home.

Wed. 21. In forenoon went to Gold Hill to Post Office. Then at home.

Thurs. 22. At home.

Frid. 23. Sat. 24. At home, weather inclement.

Sund. 25. Preached at Organ Church from Ex. 20:15. Dinner at Paul J. Klutts'. Returned home.

Mond. 26. Went to Gold Hill to Post Office. Called to see John Powlass, he being afflicted with asthma. Dinner here.

Tues. 27. Called to see Rev. R. L. Brown, he being sick. Dinner here. Called also to see Mrs. Peter Miller, she being sick. Read a Scripture lesson & prayed at her bed-side. Returned home.

Wed. 28. At home. Cold and windy.

Thurs. 29. Went to Jacob Holshouser's in company C. L. Brown, to restore harmony in said Holshouser's family, but failed. Mrs. H. being partially deranged. Dinner at C. L. Brown's.

Frid. 30. Went to Laurence Lingel's dec^d sale for an hour. Returned home by way of Post Office at Gold Hill. In the evening went to mill.

Sat. 31. Started for Ebenezer ch. All night at Robert A. Patterson's.

Sund. Feb. 1. Preached at Ebenezer ch. from Ex. 20:15. Dinner at Dr. P. A. Sifferd's. Returned home.

Mond. 2. At home.

Tues. 3. Went to Rockwell Post Office & mailed some letters. Then called to see G. M. Bernhardt, he being sick. Dinner here. Returned home.

Wed. 4. Went to Salisbury. Called also to see Rev. R. L. Brown.

Thurs. 5. At home.

Frid. 6. Went to Gold Hill to Post Office.

Sat. 7. At home.

Sund. 8. Preached at Organ Church from Ex. 20:12. Returned home. Afternoon inclement.

Mond. 9. Attended the burial of G. M. Bernhardt at Organ Church. Assisted Rev. Heller in the services. A very rainy day. Returned home.

Tues. 10. Wed. 11. At home. Thurs. 12. At home.

Frid. 13. An inclement day. In afternoon went to Gold Hill to Post Office.

Sat. 14. This my day to start for Ebenezer ch. but it snowed all day so that I did not turn out.

Sund. 15. This my day to preach at Ebenezer ch., but did not leave home on account of snow.

Mond. 16. At home till afternoon, then went to mill.

Tues. 17. Went to M. A. Holshouser's & had shoes repaired. Dinner here.

Wed. 18. Attended to the funeral of Sally Shuping at St. Peter's Church — preached from Ps. 71:9.

Thurs. 19. Frid. 20. Sat. 21. At home.

Sund. 22. Preached at Organ Church from Ex. 20:8-11. Returned home.

Mond. 23. At home.

Tues. 24. Went to Mt. Pleasant. All night at Col. Shimpock's.

Wed. 25. Attended meeting of Board of Trustees of College. Dinner at Col. Shimpock's. All night at Lewis'.

Thurs. 26. Returned home.

Frid. 27. Went to John T. Lentz's to shoemaker. Returned home by way of Post Office at Gold Hill.

Sat. 28. Started far Ebenezer Church. All night at widow Tempe Bostian's.

Sund. March 1. Preached at Ebenezer ch. from Ex. 20:12. Dinner at J. L. Graeber's. Then called in company with Mr. Graeber to see Frederick Stirewald, he being afflicted. The evening inclement. Returned to Mr. Graeber's and staid over night.

Mond. 2. Returned home.

Tues. 3. Went to Salisbury. Called also to see R. L. Brown.

Wed. 4. Went in the morning to M. A. Holshouser's. Then at home.

Thurs. 5. At home.

Frid. 6. In afternoon went to Gold Hill to Post Office.

Sat. 7. At home.

Sund. 8. Preached at Organ Church from Ex. 20:16. Baptized one infant. Called at M. A. Holshouser's, his father being sick. Read a Scripture lesson & had prayer. Dinner here.

Mond. 9. In afternoon called to see Mr. Holshouser. Read a Scripture lesson & had prayer.

Tues. 10. In afternoon called to see Mr. Holshouser, who was rapidly approaching his latter end.

Wed. 11. Attended to the funeral of Isaac Earnheart, preached the funeral at D. Brady's from Job 16:22. Buried him at Lower Stone Church.

Thurs. 12. Attended to the funeral of Jacob Holshouser at Lower Stone Church — preached from Job 5:26. Called to see L. A. Heilig, who was suffering from hemorrhage of the lungs. Baptized his child.

Frid. 13. At home. Sent to Post Office to day.

Sat. 14. Started for Ebenezer ch. Called to see L. A. Heilig. All night at Moses Stirewalt's.

Sund. 15. At Ebenezer Church. Had a severe cold & was very hoarse. — Did not preach, but talked some on the subject of raising money for Synod. Dinner at P. A. Sloop's, Esq. Returned home.

Mond. 16. Called at D. Brady's by request. Then at home.

Tues. 17. Went to Gold Hill to Post Office. Then at home.

Wed. 18. At home. Had a deep snow.

Thurs. 19. Went to D. Brady's to witness a deed. In the afternoon went by way of J. T. Lentz's to Caleb Cruse's & staid over night.

Frid. 20. Attended to the funeral of Charles Fisher at Organ Church. Preached from Job 16:22. Returned home.

Sat. 21. At home.

Sund. 22. This my day to preach at Organ ch. but the day being very inclement with snow did not attend.

Mond. 23. In the afternoon went to Gold Hill to Post Office.

Tues. 24. At home.

Wed. 25. At home, in my study all day.

Thurs. 26. Went to Salisbury.

Frid. 27. Went to Gold Hill to Post Office.

Sat. 28. Started for Ebenezer ch. Called by to see L. A. Heilig. All night at Augustus Ketner's.

Sund. 29. Preached at Ebenezer ch. from Ex. 20:16. Dinner at H. T. Graeber's. Returned home.

Mond. 30. In afternoon went to Klutts' blacksmith shop.

Tues. 31. In the morning went to Klutts' shop. In afternoon went to Mt. Pleasant. All night at Col. Shimpock's.

Wed. Apr. 1. Attended meeting of Board of Trustees of N. C. College. Dinner at Col. Shimpock's. All night at son Lewis'.

Thurs. 2. Returned home. In afternoon married Paul S. Klutts & Mary D. Miller at my house.

Frid. 3. Had intended to start for Ebenezer, but the afternoon being very rainy, did not go.

Sat. 4. Started very early for Ebenezer Church & preached from Prov. 23:26. Preparatory to Communion. All night at F. W. Korf's. Called also to see Frederick Stirewald, who is old & afflicted.

Sund. 5. Called in the morning & administered the communion to Frederick Stirewald, his wife and son's wife. Prof. Schaeffer preached. Baptized one infant. Administered the Communion to the congregation being assisted by Prof. Schaeffer. Dinner at J. A. Eddleman's. Returned home.

Mond. 6. Went to Salisbury.

Tues. 7. Wed. 8. At home.

Thurs. 9. To day married Jacob Jeremiah Miller and Lottie S. Trexler at my house. In the evening went to mill.

Frid. 10. At home.

Sat. 11. At home.

Sund. 12. Preached at Organ ch. from Ex. 20:14. 1 Cor. 6:18. Baptized 1 inft. Dinner at Boyden Miller's. Called to see John Lentz, he being sick. Returned home.

Mond. 13. Called to see Alexander Trexler & paid him his part in cotton bale.

Tues. 14. Went to Gold Hill to Post Office & registered several letters.

Wed. 15. Attended to the funeral of Elizabeth Basinger at Organ ch., supposed to be 101 years old.

Thurs. 16. At home.

Frid. 17. At home hauling hay into barn till dinner. In afternoon went to Gold Hill to Post Office.

Sat. 18. At home.

Sund. 19. Went to Ebenezer Church & preached from Ex. 20:14. 1 Cor. 6:18. Dinner at H. T. Graeber's. Returned home & married Albert D. Thomas and Eve Ann Miller at my house.

Mond. 20. In forenoon went to Wilson Kesler's on business for David Brady.

Tues. 21. Wed. 22. Thurs. 23. At home.

Frid. 24. Called to see John T. Lentz he being sick. Read Scripture lesson & had prayer. Returned home by way of Gold Hill & Post Office.

Sat. 25. Preached at Organ Church from Ps. 7:9. preparatory to Communion. Baptized three infants & had preparatory service.

Sund. 26. In the morning went to C. L. Brown's & married Harvey A. Holshouser & Dovie D. Brown. Then went to Organ church. Prof. Rupp preached. Together then administered the communion. Dinner at C. L. Brown's. Returned home.

Mond. 27. Started for Synod at Bethel Church. All night at John C. Miller's. Had lodgings assigned at J. C. Miller's & remained there till adjournment of Synod.

Tues. May 4. Returned home.

Tues. 5. Wed. 6. Thurs. 7. At home.

Frid. 8. In forenoon went to Gold Hill to post office. In afternoon at home.

Sat. 9. Had catechization at Organ church in afternoon. Returned home.

Sund. 10. Preached at Organ church from 1 Cor. 15:58. Dinner at Eli Holshouser's. Returned home.

Mond. 11. At home.

Tues. 12. Wed. 13. At home.

Thurs. 13. Preached at Corinth from Job 16:22. the funeral of Catharine Casper, wife of Levi Casper, who had died some months previous. Ascension Day. Dinner at John Trexler's. Returned home.

Frid. 15. Went to Gold Hill to Post Office. In afternoon at home.

Sat. 16. In the morning went to Gold Hill & had shoeing done. In the afternoon started for Ebenezer ch. All night at J. L. Graeber's.

Sund. 17. Preached at Ebenezer from Ps. 133:1-3. Called in the morning to see Frederic Stirewald. Dinner at H. T. Graeber's. Returned home.

Mond. 18. Called to see Luther Barringer, he being sick. Called also at John T. Lentz's. Returned home by way of post office at Gold Hill.

Tues. 19. In afternoon went to Mt. Pleasant to at attend Commencement of N. C. College & meeting of Board of Trustees. All night at Col. Shimpock's.

Wed. 20. In Mt. Pleasant. Dinner &c at Col. Shimpock's.

Thurs. 21. In Mt. Pleasant till 3 P.M., then went to Catharine Barringer's & married Monroe M. Ketner & Ellen E. A. Miller. Started for home after night but stopped by rain. All night at Green Eller's.

Frid. 22. Returned home.

Sat. 23. In the afternoon had catechization at Organ Church. Returned home.

Sund. 24. Preached at Organ ch. from 1 Tim. 6:6. Dinner at R. W. Bost's. All night at Rachel Cruse's.

Mond. 25. Went to Concord to execute a Deed by appointment of Synod for some land willed to Synod by a Mr. Blackwelder. Dinner at Mr. Blum's. All night at G. E. Ritchie's, Esq.

Tues. 26. Returned home.

Wed. 27. Called around in the neighborhood to engage hands to make hay.

Thurs. 28. Started for St. John's Church to attend meeting of Southern Conference. All night at G. H. Bost's.

Frid. 29. Went to Conference at St. John's Church. Had home assigned at Archibald Cline's. All night here.

Sat. 30. At Conference. All night at Arch^{d} Cline's.

Sund. 31. At St. John's Church. Preached in afternoon from 1 Tim. 6:6. Returned home.

Mond. June 1. Went to Mr. Stikeleather's, to Gold Hill, & to Uriah Miller's, arranging to meet Dr. Shimpock's damaging reports about me.

Tues. 2. In the morning went to Gold Hill to have notice served on Dr. Shimpock to confront me at M. A. Holshouser's on Frid. June 5, 1885, at 2 o'clock P.M., & substantiate his damaging reports.

Wed. 3. Went to see L. G. Holshouser, L. C. Miller, C. L. Brown, Brantly Beaver, & Joseph Beaver, arranging to meet Dr. Shimpock's damaging reports about me. Called at Post Office at Gold Hill, and at Noe's Shop & had shoeing done.

Thurs. 4. Went to Salisbury.

Frid. 5. Met Dr. R. A. Shimpock at Milas A. Holshouser's & refuted the damaging reports which Dr. Shimpock circulated against me.

Sat. 6. Went to Ebenezer ch. & had catechization at 2 o'clock P.M. Then called to see Frederick Stirewald, he being sick. All night at Dr. P. A. Sifferd's.

Sund. 7. Preached at Ebenezer ch. from 1 Thes. 2:11.12. Baptized one infant. Dinner at J. L. Graeber's. Returned home.

Mond. 8. At home, haying.

Tues. 9. At home, haying.

Wed. 10. Went to Mrs. Green Heilig's to attend to the funeral of Catharine Eagle. Being in advance of the time for the coffin, went to A. W. Klutts' Esq. to regulate about taxes. Returned & took dinner & preached the funeral at the house from Matth. 25:13. Then buried at Organ Church.

Thurs. 11. At home, had haying finished.

Frid. 12. Went to Gold Hill to post office, then to our free School house & had catechization.

Sat. 13. Had catechization at Organ Church at 2 P.M. All night at A. W. Klutts' Esq.

Sund. 14. Preached at Organ Church from Numb. 14:24. Baptized one infant. Dinner at U. E. Miller's.

Mond. 15. Went to Salisbury.

Tues. 16. In afternoon went to Gold Hill to Post Office.

Wed. 17. Thurs. 18. At home.

Frid. 19. At home.

Sat. 20. Went to Ebenezer church & had catechization at 2 o'clock P.M. Called afterwards to see Frederick Stirewald & wife, they being sick. All night at G. M. Ketner's.

Sund. 21. At Ebenezer church. Rev. Calvin Sifford preached in my stead. Dinner at P. A. Sloop's Esq. Returned home.

Mond. 22. At home.

Tues. 23. Wed. 24. At home.

Thurs. 25. In the morning went Dr. Coleman's to get medicine for wife.

Frid. 26. In afternoon had catechization at our free school house. Returned home by way of post office at Gold Hill. Rainy evening.

Sat. 27. Had catechization at Organ ch. at 2 P.M. Rainy evening. All night at Mrs. Bost's, widow of Wm.

Sund. 28. Preached at Organ ch. from Luk. 13:6-9. Dinner at C. L. Brown's. In afternoon preached at Elm Grove from Ex. 14:15. Returned home.

Mond. 29. Went to Misenheimer Springs.

Tues. 30. In afternoon returned home.

Wed. July 1. Thurs. 2. Frid. 3. At home.

Sat. 4. Started for Ebenezer ch. Called to see R. Henry Klutts he being sick. Dinner at P. A. Sloop's, Esq. In afternoon had catechization at Ebenezer. All night at Moses Ketner's.

Sund. 5. At Ebenezer ch. Rev. Calvin Sifford being present, preached in my stead. Dinner & all night at J. A. Eddleman's. Rainy evening.

Mond. 6. Returned home.

Tues. 7. At home.

Wed. 8. In afternoon called to see Jacob Miller, he being old & infirm.

Thurs. 9. At home.

Frid. 10. Had catechization at our free school house at 2 P.M. Returned home by way of post office at Gold Hill.

Sat. 11. Had catechization at Organ church at 2 P.M. All night at R. W. Bost's.

Sund. 12. At Organ church. Rev. Stoudenmire being present, preached in my stead. Dinner at Dan^{1} Miller's. In afternoon at Elm Grove. Rev. Stoudenmire preached.

Mond. 13. Tues. 14. Wed. 15. At home haying.

Thurs. 16. Went to Salisbury.

Frid. 17. At home. Quite unwell.

Sat. 18. Went to Ebenezer ch. — dispensed with catechization at 11 A.M. being unwell. Preached at 2 P.M. from Ex. 14:15. & held preparatory service. All night at J. L. Graeber's.

Sund. 19. Called in the morning at Frederick Stirewalt's, he and his wife being old & afflicted & administered to them the communion. Preached at Ebenezer from Luk. 13:10-17. & administered the communion. Returned home.

Mond. 20. Tues. 21. Wed. 22. Thurs. 23. At home.

Frid. 24. At 2 o'clock P.M. had catechization at free school house. Returned home by way of post office at Gold Hill.

Sat. 25. Had catechization at Organ ch. at 11 o'clock A.M. In the afternoon preparatory service. Preached from Hosea 14:1.2. Baptized two infants. Installed Church Council. All night at Caleb Cruse's.

Sund. 26. Baptized Anderson A. Cruse's child at Caleb Cruse's. Preached at Organ ch. from Acts 18:21. Administered the communion. Dinner at Eli Holshouser's. Returned home.

Mond. 27. Tues. 28. Wed. 29. Thurs. 30. At home. Not very well.

Frid. 31. In afternoon went to post office at Gold Hill.

Sat. Aug. 1. At home.

Sund. 2. Went to St. Peter's ch. & heard Mr. Trexler, Theo. student preach.

Mond. 3. At home.

Tues. 4. Went to Rev. R. L. Brown's in forenoon & took Mrs. Mary Eddleman's watch to him to repair.

Wed. 5. In the afternoon buried Washington Brady's child. at St. Peter's ch.

Thurs. 6. At home.

Frid. 7. Went to Gold Hill to post office.

Sat. 8. At home.

Sund. 9. Went to Christiana Church & heard Mr. Yarger, Theo. Student, preach. Baptized Mr. Milas Miller's child. Installed Church Council. Dinner at Rev. R. L. Brown's. Returned home.

Mond. 10. Tues. 11. Wed. 12. Thurs. 13. At home.

Frid. 14. At home.

Sat. 15. Attended the Gold Hill Township Sunday School Convention at Elm Grove.

Sund. 16. Went to Lower Stone Church & heard Rev. Heller preach. Dinner at L. G. Holshouser's.

Mond. 17. At home. Tues. 18. At home.

Wed. 19. Called to see Mrs. Crawford A. Miller, she being in bad health. Called also to see Mrs. Daywalt Beaver (widow), she being old & infirm. Dinner here. Returned home by way of Gold Hill post office.

Thurs. 20. In the afternoon went to Rev. R. L. Brown's for some watches he had repaired.

Frid. 21. Went to Gold Hill to post office.

Sat. 22. At home.

Sund. 23. Went with family to Christiana ch. & heard Rev. Junius B. Fox preach. Dinner at Peter Miller's. Returned home.

Mond. 24. Tues. 25. At home.

Wed. 26. Went to Rowan County Sunday School Convention at St. Matthew's ch. Returned home.

Thurs. 27. At Sund. School Convention at St. Matthew's ch. Returned home. Dr. Rumple with us to night.

Frid. 28. Attended to the funeral of Amanda C. Safret at Christiana ch. — Preached from Job. 16:22. Then went to Organ ch. to attend meeting of Southern Conference. Returned home.

Sat. 29. At Conference at Organ ch. All night at A. W. Klutts' Esq.

Sund. 30. At Organ ch. Baptized one infant. Returned home.

Mond. 31. Went to Gold Hill & had Lucy shod.

Tues. Sep. 1. Went to Salisbury.

Wed. 2. Engaged hands to make hay.

Thurs. 3. Frid. 4. At home, haying.

Sat. 5. Went to Ebenezer ch. & had catechization at 2 P.M. Dinner to day at Moses J. Barger's. All night at J. L. Graeber's.

Sund. 6. Preached at Ebenezer from Heb. 1:14. Dinner at J. A. Eddleman's. Returned home.

Mond. 7. Went to Gold Hill to post office & to Andrew Berger's for brandy for wife.

Tues. 8. Called in forenoon to see David Barringer who had his thigh broken.

Wed. 9. Thurs. 10. At home.

Frid. 11. Had catechization at 2 P.M. at our school house.

Sat. 12. Had catechization at Organ Church.

Sund. 13. Preached at St. Peter's Church from Luk. 5:32. Baptized 7 inf[ts], confirmed 3 persons, had preparatory service, & administered the holy Communion.

Mond. 14. Called to see Jacob Miller, he being old and infirm.

Tues. 15. Went to Salisbury.

Wed. 16. At home.

Thurs. 17. In the afternoon called at L. G. Holshouser's to examine his shingle's with of having some made.

Frid. 18. Went to Stanly County to see John Knup to engage shingles to cover my house. Dinner at Henry Arey's. Went across the country to Whitson Miller's to engage timber for shingles. Returned home.

Sat. 19. Went to Ebenezer ch. Took sick on the way. Dismissed the catechumens. All night at Widow Dan[l] Eddleman's.

Sund. 20. Unable to preach. Returned home. At home the balance of the month sick.

Thurs. Oct. 1. Had Solomon Peeler to take me in the buggy to Crawford A. Miller's. Married Eli. D. A. Beaver & Martha R. Miller.

Frid. 2. Sat. 3. At home.

Sund. 4. At home. Sent Tobie Brown with a note to Ebenezer, stating that I was unable to preach that day.

Mond. 5. At home.

Tues. 6. Went to post office at Gold Hill.

Wed. 7. Attended to the funeral of Sarah C. wife of John Berger, at St. Peter's ch., preached from Eccl. 9:6.

Thurs. 8. At home.

Frid. 9. Had catechization in the afternoon at our free School house.

Sat. 10. Had catechization at Organ church.

Sund. 11. Preached at Organ church from Matt. 12:22-37.

Mond. 12. At home. Rainy & Stormy day.

Tues. 13. Went to Mt. Pleasant. All night at Lewis'.

Wed. 14. Attended meeting of Board of Trustees. Dinner at Jonas Cook's. All night at Lewis'.

Thurs. 15. Returned home. Dinner at L. A. Heilig's.

Frid. 16. Went to Mr. Parker's for some brandy.

Sat. 17. Had catechization at Ebenezer church. At night at J. L. Graeber's.

Sund. 18. Preached at Ebenezer church from Matt. 12:22-37. Dinner at H. T. Graeber's. Returned home.

Mond. 19. Went to Salisbury.

Tues. 20. At home. Divided Geo. Park's corn.

Wed. 21. At home.

Thurs. 22. Went to Mrs. Joicy C. Linn's & married Dr. C. M. Pool & Mary E. Linn. All night at Mr. Shemwell's.

Frid. 23. Returned home, & in the afternoon had catechization at our free School house.

Sat. 24. Had catechization at Organ church.

Sund. 25. Went to C. L. Brown's at 8 o'clock A.M. & married Caleb L. Klutts & Ellen A. Brown, then went to Organ church & preached from Matt. 22:1-14. Baptized one infant. Returned to C. L. Brown's for dinner.

Mond. 26. In the afternoon went to Gold Hill to Post Office.

Tues. 27. In forenoon went John Peeler's & divided Lewis' corn. In afternoon went to Mt. Pleasant. All night at Lewis'.

Wed. 28. Had meeting of Trustees of College. Dinner & supper at Col. Shimpock's. All night at Lewis'.

Thurs. 29. Returned home.

Frid. 30. Started for Ebenezer ch. in afternoon. All night at J. A. Eddleman's.

Sat. 31. Preached at Ebenezer from Acts 28:15. Confirmed one person & held preparatory service. All night at Geo. M. Ketner's.

Sund. Nov. 1. Called in the morning at Frederick Stirewalt's, he & his wife being old & afflicted, & administered the holy communion. Then went to Ebenezer & preached from Prov. 3:6. & administered the holy communion. Dinner at P. A. Sloop's. Returned home. Rainy evening.

Mond. 2. At home.

Tues. 3. In forenoon went to Gold Hill to post office.

Wed. 4. At home, divided Hampton's corn.

Thurs. 5. Went to Salisbury & sent Money Order to the Luth. Book Store.

Frid. 6. At home making some preparations for Saturday & Sunday.

Sat. 7. Preached at Organ ch. from 1 Cor. 15:58. Baptized one infant, confirmed twenty four persons, & held preparatory service. Returned home.

Sund. 8. At Organ ch. Prof. Rupp preached. We then together administered the communion. The councils of Organ & Ebenezer met jointly and declined to accept my resignation.

Mond. 9. In the morning went to M. A. Holshouser's on business. Then at home.

Tues. 10. At home.

Wed. 11. Called to see Solena Bost she being sick. Read a scripture lesson & had prayer. Returned home by way post office.

Thurs. 12. Called in forenoon to see Rev. R. L. Brown. In afternoon at home.

Frid. 13. Went to Gold Hill to post office.

Sat. 14. Started for Ebenezer church. All night at F. W. Korf's.

Sund. 15. Preached at Ebenezer from 1 Cor. 15:58. Dinner at H. T. Graebers. Returned home.

Mond. 16. At home.

Tues. 17. Went to M. A. Holshouser's & brought saw home. Then went to mill.

Wed. 18. At home.

Thurs. 19. Went to Salisbury.

Frid. 20. After dinner went to post office.

Sat. 21. At home.

Sund. 22. Preached at Organ ch. from Prov. 1:24-26. Baptized one infant. Returned home.

Mond. 23. At home till after dinner then went to Barbara Brady's to harmonize difficulties between her and Moses G. Brady.

Tues. 24. In forenoon went to Gold Hill and brought home sack of coffee.

Wed. 25. At home.

Thurs. 26. Attended to the funeral of Rev. R. L. Brown's child at Christiana Church. Preached from Matt. 19:14. Dinner at Rev. R. L. Brown's.

Frid. 27. Went to Mt. Olive church to Conference. All night at John Moose's.

Sat. 28. At Conference. All night at Wellington Moose's.

Sund. 29. At Mt. Olive church. Took part in the communion services. All night at Laurence Klutts'.

Mond. 30. Went to Caleb M. Troutman's and bought four pigs. Dinner at widow Charlie Fisher's. Returned home.

Tues. Dec. 1. At home. Received my pigs. Had wood hauled.

Wed. 2. Hauled cotton to the gin.

Thurs. 3. Had winter hogs slaughtered.

Frid. 4. Attended to the funeral of Lula Joana Stikeleather at Lower St. Church. Preached from Eccl. 12:1. Dinner at Boyden Miller.

Sat. 5. Attended to the funeral of Solina Bost at Organ Church. Preached from Phil. 1:21. All night at J. L. Graeber's.

Sund. 6. Preached at Ebenezer ch. from Ez. 33:5. Dinner at Tempe Bostian's. All night at J. A. Eddleman's.

Mond. 7. Returned home.

Tues. 8. Went to Mt. Pleasant to attend special meeting of Synod. Assigned to Col. Shimpock's.

Wed. 9. Thurs. 10. Attended Synod. Not very well.

Frid. 11. Returned home.

Sat. 12. Went to Salisbury with Geo. Parks.

Sund. 13. This my day at Organ church, but did not attend in consequence of incessant rain.

Mond. 14. In the morning went to Geo. Park's then at home.

Tues. 15. At home.

Wed. 16. At home.

Thurs. 17. Attended to the funeral of Margaret Maria Fisher at Organ church. Preached from Prov. 14:32. latter clause. Then went to Allison Bost's & married David C. Holshouser & Sarah E. A. Bost. Returned home.

Frid. 18. Went to Gold Hill to post office.

Sat. 19. Started for Ebenezer church. Called to see Frederick Stirewalt & wife, they being old & afflicted. All night at G. M. Ketner's.

Sund. 20. Preached at Ebenezer church from Acts 20:32. Baptized one infant. Closed my pastoral administration. Dinner at J. L. Graeber's. Returned home.

Mond. 21. At home.

Tues. 22. After dinner went to M. A. Holshouser's & had settlement. Then went to Gold Hill to post office & registered several letters.

Wed. 23. Thurs. 24. At home.

Frid. 25. Went to Organ ch. to Christmas Tree.

Sat. 26. At home.

Sund. 27. Preached at Organ ch. from Acts 20:32. and closed my pastoral administration. Dinner and all night at R. W. Bost's.

Mond. 28. Called at Moses Klutts' & took dinner. Returned home.

Tues. 29. Went to Solena Bost's sale & to Gold Hill to post office.

Wed 30. At home.

Thurs. 31. Went to David C. Parker's & married Henry W. Cauble & Beneter C. Parker. Returned home.

Frid. Jan. 1, 1886. At home. Pleasant day.

Sat. 2. Had catechization at St. Matthew's church.

Sund. 3. Preached at St. Matthew's ch. from 1 Thes. 2:11.12. An inclement day. Very rainy.

Mond. 4. At home.

Tues. 5. Went to Rockwell post office and mailed some letters. Called at Dr. Coleman's.

Wed. 6. Went to Salisbury. All night at Tobias Lyerly's.

Thurs. 7. Returned home by way of Rev. R. L. Brown's.

Frid. 8. Went to Gold Hill to post office. Snow in afternoon.

Sat. 9. Went to St. Peter's ch. to fill an appointment for catechization, but no one attended. A very cold day with snow on the ground.

Sund. 10. A cold day. Preached at St. Peter's church from 1 Thes. 2:11.12.

Mond. 11. At home.

Tues. 12. Went to M. A. Holshouser's. Looked over sale account. Dinner here.

Thurs. 13. Went to John T. Lentz's to bury him, he having died very suddenly, but the coffin did not arrive till very late in the evening. Had some short religious exercises & left for home. Called to see old Mrs. Stikeleather, she being very sick.

Thurs. 14. In afternoon went to M. A. Holshouser's.

Frid. 15. Went to Jeremiah Earnheart's & had Lucy shod. Dinner here. Returned home by way of post office at Gold Hill.

Sat. 16. Had an appointment for catechization at St. Matthew's ch., but the day being very inclement with rain, did not attend.

Sund. 17. Preached at St. Matthew's church from Prov. 3:6. Returned home.

Mond. 18. Attended to the burial of Mrs. Stikeleather (an old lady) at Lower St. Church.

Tues. 19. Went to Mt. Pleasant. All night at Lewis'.

Wed. 20. Attended meeting of Board of Trustees. At Lewis'.

Thurs. 21. Returned home by way of Mrs. M. A. Heilig's.

Frid. 22. Went to Gold Hill to post office.

Sat. 23. Started for Luther's church. All night at David C. Parker's.

Sund. 24. A very inclement day with cold and sleet. Went to the church, but nobody attending, returned home.

Mond. 25. Tues. 26. Wed. 27. At home.

Thurs. 28. Went to B. P. Basinger's & married Mr. George W. Culp & Miss Julia A. Basinger. Returned home.

Frid. 29. Went to Gold Hill to post office.

Sat. 30. Had catechization at St. Peter's ch.

Sund. 31. Preached at St. Peter's ch. from Prov. 3:6.

Mond. Feb. 1. At home.

Tues. 2. Went to Jos. A. Brown's to post office. Dinner here. A very inclement day.

Wed. 3. Thurs. 4. Frid. 5. At home. Weather very cold.

Sat. 6. Had catechization at St. Matthew's church, but few attended, the weather being inclement.

Sund. 7. Preached at St. Matthew's church from James 1:25. Baptized 3 children. Attendance good. Dinner at W. Kesler's.

Mond. 8. At home.

Tues. 9. Went to Rockwell post office, thence to Peter Miller's. Dinner here.

Wed. 10. At home.

Thurs. 11. In afternoon went to Gold Hill to post office.

Frid. 12. Went to Lower Stone Church to preach the funeral of John T. Lentz, who had died some time previous, but the widow being sick & unable to attend, the funeral was postponed to a future day.

Sat. 13. Had catechization at St. Peter's church.

Sund. 14. Preached at St. Peter's ch. from Matth. 21:28-32. Baptized 2 infts. Dinner at H. A. Miller's. Returned home.

Mond. 15. Went to Salisbury. All night at Col. P. N. Heilig's.

Tues. 16. Returned home.

Wed. 17. At home.

Thurs. 18. At home.

Frid. 19. Went to Organ church & gave a short lecture to a few persons from Matth. 5:6. Baptized one infant. Returned home by way of Gold Hill.

Sat. 20. Had catechization at St. Peter's church.

Sund. 21. Preached at St. Peter's church from Prov. 29:1.

Mond. 22. Went to Rockwell to post office & Registered a letter to Capt. Cook, Mt. Pleasant, & mailed others.

Tues. 23. At home.

Wed. 24. Went to Rockwell post office & Registered a letter to W. P. Houseal, Newberry & mailed others. In afternoon took Church Books to M. A. Holshouser.

Thurs. 25. At home, a rainy day.

Frid. 26. Went to Gold Hill to post office.

Sat. 27. Started for Luther's Church. All night at B. P. Basinger's.

Sund. 28. Preached at Luther's church from Prov. 29:1. Dinner at Jacob C. Earnheart's. Baptized his child. Returned home.

Mond. March 1. At home. Had wood hauled.

Tues. 2. Went to M. A. Holshouser's in afternoon to settle account with him for acid &c. Then went to where the new school house was being built.

Wed. 3. Went to Jacob Klutts' to have shoeing done, but he not being at home, failed to have it done.

Thurs. 4. Went in forenoon to Mr. Klutts' & had shoeing done, In afternoon went to Rockwell post office & registered a letter to W. P. Houseal & sent stamps to Duffie for Book Worship.

Frid. 5. Went to Wilson Kesler's & wrote a letter for him to Rev. T. H. Strohecker.

Sat. 6. At home.

Sund. 7. Preached at Matthew's ch. from Prov. 29:1. Had a full audience. Returned home.

Mond. 8. In forenoon took coffee mill to L. C. Miller's to have it repaired.

Tues. 9. Went to J. A. Brown's to post office. Took dinner here. Returned home by way of H. A. Miller's.

Wed. 10. At home. Rainy day.

Thurs. 11. Went to Salisbury.

Frid. 12. Went to Gold Hill to post office.

Sat. 13. At home.

Sund. 14. Preached at St. Peter's Church from Jam. 1:25. In afternoon preached the fun[1] of Christina Stikeleather at Elm Grove from Job 14:14.

Mond. 15. After dinner went to M. A. Holshouser's and brought shingle nails home.

Tues. 16. Went to Rockwell post office, & then to John Miller's. Took dinner here. Called also at H. A. Miller's and had a colloquism with his daughter-in-law, C. M. Miller's wife, on the subject of being confirmed, to which she assented. She came from Franklin Presbyterian Church.

Wed. 17. Thurs. 18. At home.

Frid. 19. Went to Gold Hill to post office.

Sat. 20. At home, a rainy day.

Sund. 21. Preached at St. Matthew's ch. from 1 Cor. 4:2. Returned home.

Mond. 22. Went in afternoon to see Mrs. Jacob Holshouser, wife of Jacob Holshouser, she being sick.

Tues. 23. Went to Solomon Peeler's & engaged him to haul stove wood. Went also to M. A. Holshouser's to engage him to haul wood, but found him not at home.

Wed. 24. At home , had stove wood hauled home.

Thurs. 25. Had firewood hauled home. In afternoon went to Gold Hill to post office.

Frid. 26. At home.

Sat. 27. Went to Luther's ch. to have catechization, but key of the church not being there, & the weather inclement, had to dispense with it. All night at John E. Shaver's.

Sund. 28. Preached at Luther's ch. from Jam. 1:25. Dinner at David C. Parker's. Returned home.

Mond. 29. Went in forenoon to Jerry Earnheart's & had Lucy shod. Rainy day.

Tues. 30. Rainy in forenoon. In afternoon took Lewis' wheat to mill.

Wed. 31. Went to David C. Parker's for sweet potatoe plantings. Dinner here.

Thurs. April 1. At home.

Frid. 2. At home.

Sat. 3. Preached at St. Matthew's ch. from 2 Cor. 13:5. preparatory to communion. All night at O. V. Pool's.

Sund. 4. Preached at St. Matthew's ch. from Matt. 21:28-32. & administered the communion. Dinner at Wilson Kesler's. Returned home.

Mond. 5. At home. Cloudy & rainy.

Tues. 6. At home.

Wed. 7. Went to Rockwell post office. Called at Dr. Coleman's to engage him to call & see my wife, she being sick.

Thurs. 8. Went to Salisbury for medicine for my wife. Took sick returning home. Called at Dr. Coleman's & ate a biscuit & drank a cup of coffee.

Frid. 9. Went to Gold Hill to post office.

Sat. 10. Went to St. Peter's church & lectured from 2 Cor. 13:5. preparatory to communion. Baptized one infant & held preparatory service. Was very unwell with cold.

Sund. 11. At St. Peter's church. Baptized one infant & confirmed Mrs. Mary S. Miller who came well recommended from Franklin Presbyterian Church. Was unable to preach in consequence of severe cold. Administered the holy communion. In the afternoon went to D. Brady's & administered the communion to Mrs. Brady, she being much afflicted with cancer.

Mond. 12. At home. Very unwell.

Tues. 13. Went to Tobias Lyerly's, he having been burnt out by some incendiary.

Wed. 14. After dinner went to Solomon Peeler's and paid John Beaver for ditching.

Thurs. 15. Went in forenoon to Tobias Lyerly's & carried a hen & young chickens to him. In afternoon at home & had bellows put up in shop.

Frid. 16. Went to Gold Hill to post office.

Sat. 17. At home.

Sund. 18. Preached at St. Peter's ch. from Mark 13:34.

Mond. 19. In the morning went to Andrew Berger's on business. Returned home & then went to Pinckney Cauble's. Dinner here. Rev. G. F. Schaeffer & son called & sent for me. In the evening piloted Rev. S. & son into the Beaty's for reoad.

Tues. 20. At home.

Wed. 21. Went with Bettie to Salisbury.

Thurs. 22. At home.

Frid. 23. Good Friday. Went to Luther's church and preached from John 19:30. Baptized one infant. All night at Conrad Miller's.

Sat. 24. Preached at Luther's church from Prov. 23:26. Baptized one infant & held preparatory service. Went to George Wilhelm's to dinner. Then went to Daniel Richie's, his wife being afflicted. Returned to Mr. Wilhelm's & staid over night.

Sund. 25. Preached at Luther's church from 2 Tim. 1:18. Baptized one infant & administered the communion. Dinner at Jacob C. Earnheart's. Returned home.

Mond. 26. At home till 10 o'clock, then went to Frederick Stirewalt's, he and his wife being old & afflicted. Administered to them the holy communion. All night at J. L. Graeber's.

Tues. 27. Returned home.

Wed. 28. At home.

Thurs. 29. In afternoon went to Alexander Lyerly's & married John H. A. Barger & Catharine S. Lyerly. Returned home.

Frid. 30. Went to Union church to meeting of Synod. Had home assigned at Duglas Roseman's.

Sat. May 1 to Wed. 5. At Synod. Staid on Tuesday night at Mr. Shemwell's. Returned home on Wed. afternoon.

Thurs. 6. Went to R. W. Bost's & married George A. Bean & Susan L. Bost. Returned home.

Frid. 7. Went in forenoon to Rockwell post office. In afternoon at home.

Sat. 8. Went in forenoon to Gold Hill to post office. In afternoon at home.

Sund. 9. Being without a charge at present, had no appointment for this day. Called to see David Barringer, he being afflicted with broken leg.

Mond. 10. Went to Salisbury & Expressed Seal of Synod to Rev. F. W. E. Peshau, Wilmington. In afternoon made arrangements for recovering my house.

Tues. 11. Had hands to recover my house. Hurried to Gold Hill for nails.

Wed. 12. Thurs. 13. At home, had house recovered.

Frid. 14. Went to Gold Hill & to Jer. Earnheart's & had Lucy shod.

Sat. 15. Went to Gold Hill in the morning with butter & eggs.

Sund. 16. At home. Spent the day reading Bible &c.

Mond. 17. In the morning went to Rockwell post office. Returned by way of H. A. Miller's. In afternoon took M. A. Holshouser's ladder home. Then went to And. Barger's on business.

Tues. 18. At home. A very rainy day.

Wed. 19. Thurs. 20. At home, rainy weather.

Frid. 21. Went to Rev. R. L. Brown's to get J. L. Eddleman's watch. In afternoon at home.

Sat. 22. At home. Lewis called to see us.

Sund. 23. At home, had no appointment for this day. Spent the day in reading Scriptures.

Mond. 24. At home.

Tues. 25. Went to Mt. Pleasant. All night at Lewis'. At night attended Academic exercises.

Wed. 26. Attended declamation exercises. In afternoon attended meeting of Board of Trustees. Dinner to day & all night at Col. Shimpock's.

Thurs. 27. Went with Prof. Schaeffer to Misenheimer Springs. Dinner here. Returned to Mt. Pleasant. All night at Lewis'.

Frid. 28. Returned home.

Sat. 29. Went to Andr. Barger's on business. In afternoon at home.

Sund. 30. Had no appointment for this day. At home. Spent the day in reading.

Mond. 31. Went to Salisbury. Baptized Harvey A. Bernhardt's child.

Tues. June 1. Went to Gold Hill to post office & to Mr. Crowell's, the shoemaker.

Wed. 2. Thurs. 3. At home.

Frid. 4. Went to Gold Hill to post office and made return of taxes.

Sat. 5. At home.

Sund. 6. At home, had no appointment to day.

Mond. 7. At home haying.

Tues. 8. At home haying.

Wed. 9. At home, a rainy day.

Thurs. 10. Attended to the fun[1] of Mrs. David Brady at Lower St. Church, preached from Heb. 9:27. Returned by way of Rockwell post office.

Frid. 11. At home, haying.

Sat. 12. At home.

Sund. 13. Preached at St. Peter's ch. from 2 Cor. 5:17.

Mond. 14. Went to Wilson Kesler's & borrowed money for N. C. College.

Tues. 15. Went with Lewis to Salisbury.

Wed. 16. Went to Gold Hill to mill & post office.

Thurs. 17. At home.

Frid. 18. Went to Gold Hill to post office.

Sat. 19. At home.

Sund. 20. Went to Lower St. church & heard Rev. Heller preach. Then went to Wesley C. Propst & baptized his three children. Returned home.

Mond. 21. Went to Salisbury on the way to Gen[l] Synod in Roanoke city. Dinner at J. A. Randleman's. All night at Col. P. N. Heilig's.

Tues. 22. Took the train for Roanoke City. Breakfast in Greensborough, 75 cts. Dinner in Lynchburg, 50 cts. Reached Roanoke City & had home assigned at G. A. Turner's Esq.

Wed. 23. Thurs. 24. Frid. 25. Sat. 26. In Synod.

Sund. 27. Attended preaching in Baptist Church by Rev. Gilbert, D.D. In afternoon attended Sunday School meeting in Luth. church. In the evening went to the country to Mr. Earnheart's & staid over night.

Mond. 28. Returned to Gen[l] Synod which closed its sessions at night.

Tues. 29. In afternoon started for home. Supper in Danville, 75 cts. Reached Salisbury at One A.M. Took lodging at the Mt. Vernon Hotel till day, 50 cts.

Wed. 30. Returned home on mail hack.

Thurs. July 1. At home, a very rainy day.

Frid. 2. At home.

Sat. 3. Went to Gold Hill to post office.

Sund. 4. At home, had no appointment.

Mond. 5. Went to Jer. Earnheart, thence to John Powlass' & had shoeing done.

Tues. 6. Attended to the funeral of Catharine Bailey at St. Peter's church — Text 2 Kings 20:1.

Wed. 7. Went to Rev. R. L. Brown's & had clock repaired.

Thurs. 8. Went to John Richie's, he being sick & wrote a will for him. Dinner here.

Frid. 9. At home.

Sat. 10. Went to Foutz's & Alfred Klutts' to arrange about wheat threshing. Afternoon at home.

Sund. 11. At home, had no appointment.

Mond. 12. At home, had wheat threshed.

Tues. 13. Went to Wilson Kesler's & refunded him some money which he had paid to me in mistake. Then went to J. C. Earnheart's to saw mill to have lumber sawed for steps. Dinner here.

Wed. 14. Thurs. 15. At home.

Frid. 16. Went to Gold Hill to post office.

Sat. 17. At home. In afternoon help to divide the property of Cath. Bailey, dec[d].

Sund. 18. Went to Luther's church & heard Rev. Staemy (Methodist) preach a fun[l]. Very sensational. Made announcements for myself. Dinner at Parker Basinger's. Returned home.

Mond. 19. At home.

Tues. 20. Went to Jacob Klutts' & had shoeing done.

Wed. 21. Attended to the funeral of Geo. A. Bean at Organ church. Spoke from Luke 7:11-17.

Thurs. 22. At home.

Frid. 23. In afternoon called to see Stephen Brady, he being sick. Had prayer at his bed-side.

Sat. 24. At home.

Sund. 25. Had no appointment for this day. Spent the day at home reading Bible.

Mond. 26. Made arrangements for haymaking.

Tues. 27. Wed. 28. Thurs. 29. At home haying.

Frid. 30. At home.

Sat 31. Attended the Township Sunday School convention at Lower St. church.

Sund. Aug. 1. Preached at Luther's Church from 2 Cor. 5:17. Dinner at David C. Parker's. Returned home.

Mond. 2. In the morning went to Gold Hill for horse shoes & nails.

Tues. 3. At home.

Wed. 4. Went in evening with Lewis to see the free School house.

Thurs. 5. At home. Lewis took wife and Emma to Misenheimer Springs.

Frid. 6. At home.

Sat. 7. Went to Organ church in afternoon & aided Rev. Brown in his preparatory service. All night at Moses Klutts' sen.

Sund. 8. At Organ church. Aided Rev. Brown in his communion service. Dinner at Eli Holshouser's.

Mond. 9. At home.

Tues. 10. Went with Lewis to Rev. R. L. Brown's & had my clock regulated.

Wed. 11. At home.

Thurs. 12. Went to Gold Hill to mill & post office.

Frid. 13. At home.

Sat. 14. Had catechization at Luther's church at 2 P.M. All night at Jacob C. Earnheart's.

Sund. 15. Preached at Luther's church from Matt. 11:28. Returned home.

Mond. 16. Tues. 17. Wed. 18. At home. D. Barringer & wife called to see us & staid over night.

Thurs. 19. At home.

Frid. 20. Sat. 21. At home.

Sund. 22. At home, had no appointment for this day. At home reading Bible,

Mond. 23. Went to Salisbury. Heard Judge Boykin's charge to the Grand Jury.

Tues. 24. At home.

Wed. 25. Went to Organ church to adjudicate the case of Amanda E. Klutts against Wellington C. Klutts for seduction. The Council found W. C. Klutts guilty & suspended him indefinitely.

Thurs. 26. At home.

Frid. 27. Sat. 28. Sund. 29. Attended Conference at St. Peter's church.

Mond. 30. Went to Saw mill at J. C. Earnheart's and brought lumber home for house steps.

Tues. 31. Went to O. M. Holshouser's to engage him to put up house steps. In afternoon went to Rockwell post office. Earthquake to night at 9½ o'clock.

Wed. Sep. 1. Went to Gold Hill for some nails.

Thurs. 2. At home.

Frid. 3. Went to Gold Hill to post office and to mill.

Sat. 4. Had catechization at Luther's church. All night at John E. Shaver's.

Sund. 5. Preached at Luther's church from Ex. 20:7. Baptized one infant. Dinner at J. C. Earnheart's. Returned home.

Mond. 6. Tues. 7. Wed. 8. At home.

Thurs. 9. Went to Andrew Barger's to get him to spay hogs. Had hogs spayed in afternoon.

Frid. 10. In forenoon engaged H. A. Holshouser to mow grass. Then went to Gold Hill to post office. In afternoon sowed turnip seed.

Sat. 11. Attended Sunday School picnic at St. Peter's church.

Sund. 12. Had no appointment for this day. At home reading Bible.

Mond. 13. At home. Had M. A. Holshouser to mow with his mower.

Tues. 14. At home, haying.

Wed. 15. At home. a cloudy day.

Thurs. 16. Frid. 17. At home, haying.

Sat. 18. Had catechization at Luther's church. All night at Whitson Miller's.

Sund. 19. Preached at Luther's church from Prov. 3:9.10. Dinner at Alexander Shaver's. All night at David C. Parker's.

Mond. 20. Attended to the fun[1] of Philipena Hodge at Luther's church. Preached from Matt. 5:6. Dinner at David C. Parker's. Returned home.

Tues. 21. In afternoon went to Andr. Barger's for hoes, but the work was not done.

Wed. 22. Went to Rockwell post office & registered a letter containing money for Luth. Visitor.

Thurs. 23. At home. Had seed wheat cleaned.

Frid. 24. Went to Gold Hill to post office.

Sat. 25. In afternoon called to see the widow Charles Fisher, she being sick. All night at Laurence Klutts'.

Sund. 26. In the morning went to Alfred Klutts' & married Albert S. Miller & Anna E. L. Klutts. Returned home.

Mond. 27. Went to Salisbury.

Tues. 28. In forenoon went to Rockwell post office & mailed sundry letters. Then at home.

Wed. 29. In forenoon went to Rockwell post office & mailed some letters. Then at home.

Thurs. 30. Went to Gold Hill to mill. In afternoon at home.

Frid. Oct. 1. At home.

Sat. 2. Had catechization at Luther's church. All night at Jacob Cruse's.

Sund. 3. Preached at Luther's church from Act. 9:6. Baptized two adults & two infants. Dinner at B. P. Basinger's. Returned home.

Mond. 4. Went in afternoon to Rockwell post office, thence to Andrew Barger's & settled for hoe handles.

Tues. 5. Went to Mt. Pleasant to attend meeting of Board of Trustees of N. C. College. All night at Lewis'.

Wed. 6. In Mt. Pleasant. Failed to have a quorum for the transaction of business. Supper at Col. J. Shimpock's. All night at Lewis'.

Thurs. 7. Returned home.

Frid. 8. Went to Gold Hill to pay Taxes, to post office & hear candidates speak.

Sat. 9. At home.

Sund. 10. Had no appointment for this day. At home reading Bible.

Mond. 11. Tues. 12. At home haying.

Wed. 13. In forenoon went to Daniel Miller's by his request & wrote his will. In afternoon at home.

Thurs. 14. At home cribbing corn.

Frid. 15. At home.

Sat. 16. Preached at Luther's church from Ps. 51:2. preparatory to communion. Baptized one adult, & confirmed ten persons. Held preparatory service. Had a chill this afternoon. All night at B. P. Basinger's.

Sund. 17. At Luther's church. Rev. Kimball being present, preached. After preaching administered the holy communion. All night at Danl Ritchies.

Mond. 18. Returned home. Quite sick in afternoon & night with chill. Sent for the doctor & took medicine & broke it up.

Tues. 19. Wed. 20. Thurs. 21. Frid. 22. At home.

Sat. 23. In the morning went to John Peeler's & divided corn for Lewis. Then at home. Lewis called to see us.

Sund. 24. Had no appointment for this day, hence at home.

Mond. 25. At home.

Tues. 26. In afternoon went to Mt. Pleasant. All night at Lewis'.

Wed. 27. Attended meeting of Board of Trustees of N. C. College. Supper at Col. Shimpock's. All night at Lewis'.

Thurs. 28. Returned home.

Frid. 29. Attended conference at Christiana church. All night at Rev. R. L. Brown's.

Sat. 30. At Conference. All night at Milas Miller's.

Sund. 31. At Conference. Returned home.

Mond. Nov. 1. Went to Salisbury.

Tues. 2. Went to Gold Hill to election. Also to David C. Parker's for some brandy.

Wed. 3. At home.

Thurs. 4. In afternoon went to Mrs. Lentz's mill.

Frid. 5. At home.

Sat. 6. Had catechization at Luther's church. In afternoon called at John E. Shaver's, his wife's mind being unbalanced. Dinner here. All night at Rufus Taylor's.

Sund. 7. Preached at Luther's ch. from Matt. 21:28-32. Baptized thirteen adults & afterwards admitted them to the communion of the church by confirmation. Dinner at Jacob C. Earnheart's. Returned home.

Mond. 8. Very unwell. Went with wife to Osborn M. Holshouser's.

Tues. 9. Went to Rockwell post office. Unwell.

Wed. 10. Thurs. 11. At home, sick with cold.

Frid. 12. Sat. 13. At home, quite unwell.

Sund. 14. At home & unwell.

Mond. 15. At home, getting up some wood.

Tues. 16. At home. Unwell.

Wed. 17. Went to Gold Hill to post office.

Thurs. 18. At home. Unwell.

Frid. 19. Called to see Jacob Miller. Dinner here.

Sat. 20. Had catechization at Luther's church. All night at widow Conrad Miller's.

Sund. 21. Preached at Luther's church from Matt. 4:16. on the subject of the Reformation. Baptized one adult & then confirmed him. Dinner at J. C. Earnheart's. Returned home.

Mond. 22. Tues. 23. Wed. 24. At home. Unwell.

Thurs. 25. Thanksgiving day. Went to St. Peter's church — heard Rev. Peschau preach.

Frid. 26. This is my birthday. At home. 77 years old.

Sat. 27. At home. Lewis with us over night.

Sund. 28. At home. No appointment for this day.

Mond. 29. At home. Tues. 30. At home.

Wed. Dec. 1. Went to Gold to post office & had Lucy shod.
Thurs. 2. At home, had winter hogs slaughtered.
Frid. 3. Went to Gold Hill to post office.
Sat. 4. This my day for catechizing at Luther's church but the day being very inclement with snow & sleet did not attend.
Sund. 5. At home. This my day to preach at Luther's church, but the day being very inclement, did not attend.
Mond. 6. At home, inclement weather.
Tues. 7. Wed. 8. At home, snow on the ground.
Thurs. 9. Went to Gold Hill to post office.
Frid. 10. Sat. 11. At home, snow on the ground.
Sund. 12. At home, had no appointment for this day.
Mond. 13. Tues. 14. At home.
Wed. 15. Went to Gold Hill. Took seed cotton to Jenkin's store. Bought honey of Montgomery.
Thurs. 16. At home.
Frid. 17. Went to Gold Hill to post office.
Sat. 18. At home.
Sund. 19. Preached at Luther's church from Eph. 6:18. Returned home.
Mond. 20. Went to Salisbury & sold bale cotton.
Tues. 21. Went to Gold Hill & voted for subscription to Rail Road.
Wed. 22. Thurs. 23. At home.
Frid. 24. In afternoon went to Elm Grove to Christmas Tree. Rainy afternoon.
Sat. 25. Christmas Day. Went to St. Peter's church to Christmas Tree.
Sund. 26. At home. No appointment for this day.
Mond. 27. Went to Gold Hill to post office.
Tues. 28. Went with wife to David Barringer's on visit.
Wed. 29. At home.
Thurs. 30. Went in afternoon to Rockwell post office. A rainy evening.
Frid. 31. At home.

Sat. Jan. 1, 1887. New Year's day. At home. Lewis called to see us.

Sund. 2. Went to Luther's church & preached from Luk. 18:9-14. Cold day & congregation small. Dinner at J. C. Earnheart's. Returned home.

Mond. 3. In afternoon went to Jacob Holshouser's & sent to A. Berger's for brandy for wife, she being sick.

Tues. 4. Went to see Dr. Coleman for wife.

Wed. 5. At home, a very snowy day.

Thurs. 6. Frid. 7. Sat. 8. At home. Snow on the ground.

Sund. 9. At home. Had no appointment.

Mond. 10. In the morning went to Solomon Peeler's & engaged a sack of flour.

Tues. 11. Wed. 12. At home.

Thurs. 13. Went to D. Barringer's on business.

Frid. 14. Went to Gold Hill to post office.

Sat. 15. Went to John E. Shaver's & staid over night.

Sund. 16. Preached at Luther's ch. from Mark 1:40-45. Dinner at David C. Parker's. Returned home.

Mond. 17. Tues. 18. Wed. 19. At home.

Thurs. 20. In forenoon went to Joseph Beaver's to engage him to repair chimney backs. In afternoon had chimney backs repaired.

Frid. 21. Went to Gold Hill to post office.

Sat. 22. At home, quite unwell. Ellen Grupy & daughter called to see us & staid over night.

Sund. 23. At home, had no appointment.

Mond. 24. At home, cold and windy.

Tues. 25. Went to mill (Lentz's) and to Crawford Earnheart's for splits to hang up meat.

Wed. 26. In forenoon went to mill, then at home.

Thurs. 27. Went to Jeremiah Earnheart's & had buggy wheel repaired. Returned home by way of post office Gold Hill.

Frid. 28. In afternoon went to Rockwell post office & registered a letter to W. P. Houseal containing money for L. G. Holshouser's subscription to Luth. Visitor.

Sat. 29. At home.

Sund. 30. At home. Had no appointment.

Mond. 31. Went to Gold Hill to post office.

Tues. Feb. 1. Went to James A. Miller's for cabbage seed for wife. Dinner here. Returned by way of Milas Miller's.

Wed. 2. Went in afternoon to Gold Hill to post office.

Thurs. 3. Went to Dr. L. W. Coleman's and married Egbert B. C. Hambley of London, Egland, & Lottie C. Coleman.

Frid. 4. At home.

Sat. 5. In afternoon went to John Cannup's and & staid over night.

Sund. 6. Preached at Luther's church ch. from 1 Cor. 9:24-27. Dinner at J. C. Earnheart's. Then returned home.

Mond. 7. Went to Rockwell to post office.

Tues. 8. Went to Salisbury.

Wed. 9. At home.

Thurs. 10. Went to Dr. Coleman's to deliver Marriage Certif^e. Then to Gold Hill to post office.

Frid. 11. Went to Gold Hill to post office.

Sat. 12. At home. Lewis called to see us.

Sund. 13. At home, had no appointment.

Mond. 14. At home.

Tues. 15. Went to Gold Hill to post office.

Wed. 16. Thurs. 17. At home.

Frid. 18. Went to Gold Hill to post office.

Sat. 19. Went to free School House to attend a debate on Prohibition of manufacturing intoxicating liquors.

Sund. 20. A very rainy day. Did not go to my appointment.

Mond. 21. Went to Salisbury under subpoena as witness in court.

Tues. 22. Went to Jeremiah Earnheart's and had horse shod. Returned by way of post office at Gold Hill.

Wed. 23. Went to Salisbury to court under subpoena.

Thurs. 24. Went to Allen Miller's to mill.

Frid. 25. In forenoon went to Allen Miller's mill & brought flour home. In afternoon went to Gold Hill to post office.

Sat. 26. At home.

Sund. 27. At home. Had no appointment.

Mond. 28. At home.

Tues. March 1. Went to Mrs. Lentz's mill.

Wed. 2. In afternoon went to mill & brought my horse-feed home.

Thurs. 3. At home.

Frid. 4. Went to Gold Hill to Post Office.

Sat. 5. In afternoon went to Jacob C. Earnheart's and staid over night.

Sund. 6. Preached at Luther's ch. from Eph. 6:1-4. Dinner at Charles Glover's. Returned home.

Mond. 7. At home. Dr. Coleman & family called to see us.

Tues. 8. At home. Sowed clover seed.

Wed. 9. At home. A rainy day.

Thurs. 10. At home.

Frid. 11. Went to Gold Hill to post office.

Sat. 12. At home.

Sund. 13. Had no appointment for this day. In the morning went to Dr. Coleman's for some medicine for wife.

Mond. 14. Tues. 15. Had manure hauled in the garden & had it plowed, & planted potatoes.

Wed. 16. At home. In afternoon went to Gold Hill to post office.

Thurs. 17. Frid. 18. Went both days to Gold Hill to post office.

Sat. 19. At home.

Sund. 20. Went to Luther's church & preached from Luk. 10:30-37. Dinner at John E. Shaver's. Returned home.

Mond. 21. Tues. 22. At home.

Wed. 22. In forenoon went to John Earnheart's & brought carpet home. In afternoon at home.

Thurs. 24. Went to Salisbury.

Frid. 25. In the morning went to Lentz's mill. Then went to Gold Hill to post office. Lewis called to see us.

Sat. 26. In the afternoon went to George Wilhelm & staid over night.

Sund. 27. Went to Luther's church & organized Sunday School. Afterwards preached from Mark 13:34. Dinner at David C. Parker's. Returned home.

Mond. 28. In afternoon went to Lentz's mill.

Tues. 29. At home.

Wed. 30. In afternoon went to Lentz's mill & to Jacob Holshouser's.

Thurs. 31. At home , a rainy day.

Frid. April 1. At home.

Sat. 2. In afternoon went to Daniel Ritchie's & staid over night.

Sund. 3. Preached at Luther's ch. from Matt. 21:1-11. Dinner at Richard Glover's. Returned home.

Mond. 4. Went to Gold Hill to post office.

Tues. 5. At home.

Wed. 6. Went to Gold Hill to have shoeing done, but failed, the smith not in his shop.

Thurs. 7. At home in my study.

Frid. 8. Good Friday. Went to Luther's ch. & preached from John 1:29. All night at Joseph W. Miller's.

Sat. 9. Preached at Luther's ch. from 1 Cor. 5:7.8. Preparatory. All night at B. P. Basinger's.

Sund. 10. Preached at Luther's ch. from Ps. 71:9. the fun[1] of Conrad Miller. Administered the communion. Dinner at J. C. Earnheart's. Returned home.

Mond. 11. Went with wife to David Barringer's.

Tues. 12. Went to Salisbury.

Wed. 13. At home.

Thurs 14. Went to Gold Hill to post office.

Frid. 15. Went to Gold Hill to Smith Shop & Post office.

Sat. 16. In the morning went to Lentz's mill. In afternoon went to J. N. C. Morgan's & staid over night.

Sund. 17. Preached at Luther's ch. from Gen. 6:22. David C. Parker's. Returned home.

Mond. 18. At home.

Tues. 19. Went to Salisbury.

Wed. 20. In forenoon went to Wilson Kesler's on business relating to Rev. Strohecker.

Thurs. 21. At home, had Tobia Brown to adjust my straw cutter.

Frid. 22. Went to Gold Hill to mill & to post office.

Sat. 23. At home.

Sund. 24. At home. Had no appointment for this day.

Mond. 25. At home in my study. A rainy day.

Tues. 26. Wed. 27. At home making preparations to go to Synod.

Thurs. 28. Went to Salisbury on my way Synod. Thence by Rail Road to Statesville. Thence by by private conveyance to Mr. Williamson. All night here.

Frid. 29. Conveyed to St. Michael's church, the seat of Synod. Had home assigned at James Patterson's Esq.

Sat. 30. In Synod. In the evening was conveyed by Augustus Brown to his residence. All night here.

Sund. May 1. Was conveyed back to church. Consecrated the elements for Communion. All night at Mr. Patterson's.

Mond. 2. Tues. 3. In Synod. Both nights at Mr. Patterson's. Synod adjourned Tuesday night.

Wed. 4. Went by private conveyance to Statesville. Dinner at Lansing White's. Called also to see Mrs. Kelly. Took the train at 5 P.M. for Salisbury. Thence by private conveyance to David Barringer's. All night here.

Thurs. 5. In the morning Mr. Barringer brought me home in his buggy.

Frid. 6. At home.

Sat. 7. Went in forenoon to Gold Hill to post office.

Sund. 8. At home, no appointment for to day.

Mond. 9. Went to Salisbury for coat & vest. Brought Dr. Coleman out.

Tues. 10. Took wife to L. G. Holshouser's to spend the day. After dinner went Rockwell to post office. In evening brought wife home.

Wed. 11. At home.

Thurs. 12. Attended to the burial of Stephen Brady dec^d at St. Peter's ch. The fun^l to be preached hereafter. Wife, Emma & Tobia Brown went visiting to Calabria.

Frid. 13. At home.

Sat. 14. In the morning went to Gold Hill to post office.

Sund. 15. Preached at Luther's ch. from Luke 13:24. Dinner at J. C. Earnheart's. Returned home.

Mond. 16. Went to Misenheimer's mill.

Tues. 17. Went to Salisbury.

Wed. 18. At home.

Thurs. 19. Ascension Day. Preached at Luther's ch. from Mark 16:19. Dinner at B. P. Basinger's. Returned home.

Frid. 20. Went to Gold Hill to post office.

Sat. 21. Took Tobia Brown to Salisbury. Lewis with us over night.

Sund. 22. At home, had no appointment for to day.

Mond. 23. Went to Mr. Lentz's & had shaft put into my buggy. In afternoon at home.

Tues. 24. Went to Gold Hill to post office.

Wed. 25. Went to Rockwell post office. Returned by way of M. A. Holshouser's on business.

Thurs. 26. Went to Salisbury & bought corn & had it hauled home.

Frid. 27. Went to Gold Hill to post office.

Sat. 28. Went to Gold Hill to mill.

Sund. 29. Whitsuntide. Preached at Luther's church from Ez. 36:27. Returned home.

Mond. 30. Went to Jerry Earnheart's & had Lucy shod.

Tues. 31. In afternoon went to Mt. Pleasant. At Lewis'.

Wed. June 1. Attended meeting of Board of Trustees. Dinner, Supper & all night at Col. Shimpock's.

Thurs. 2. Attended Commencement exercises. Dinner at Lewis'. Returned home.

Frid. 3. Sat. 4. At home.

Sund. 5. Preached at Luther's church from Micah 2:10. the fun[1] of Joseph Miller's child which had died some before. Returned home.

Mond. 6. Tues. 7. At home haying.

Wed. 8. Thurs. 9. At home, indisposed.

Frid. 10. At home. Sat. 11. Went to Jerry Earnheart's & had Charley shod.

Sund. 12. At home. Had no appointment for this day.

Mond. 13. In the morning went to Dr. Coleman's. Returned home, & then went to Salisbury for medicine for wife.

Tues. 14. Wed. 15. Thurs. 16. At home & unwell.

Frid. 17. Sat. 18. At home.

Sund. 19. Went to Luther's church, but being very unwell, did not preach. Read service, a scripture lesson, & a few words to Sunday School, & dismissed. Dinner at J. C. Earnheart's. Returned home. Lewis with me to day.

Mond. 20. In the morning went to Geo. Parks' & bought a sack of flour.

Tues. 21. Wed. 22. Thurs. 23. At home.

Frid. 24. At home till afternoon, then went to Lentz's mill.

Sat. 25. Went to Gold Hill & made tax return.

Sund. 26. At home, had no appointment.

Mond. 27. In the morning went to Dr. Coleman's in relation to my wife's case, she being sick.

Tues. 28. Went to see Frederick Stirewald & wife. they being old and infirm. Dinner at P. A. Sloop's, Esq. All night at J. L. Graeber's.

Wed. 29. Returned home.

Thurs. 30. At home, had well cleaned.

Frid. July 1. Sat. 2. At home.

Sund. 3. Preached at Luther's ch. from Luk. 16:19-31. Dinner at William Kirk's. Returned home.

Mond. 4. Went to Geo. Parks' in forenoon and had shoeing.

Tues. 5. Went to Mt. Pleasant. Dinner on the way at Caleb Cruse's. Called to see widow Chas. Fisher. Called also at Laurence Klutts', he having a sick son. All night at Col. Shimpock's.

Wed. 6. Attended meeting of Board of Trustees of N. C. College. Board & over night at Col. Shimpock's.

Thurs. 7. Met Rev. A. D. L. Moser at Mt. Carmel church in committee to reconcile some disharmony between Mt. Carmel & Luther Union Churches. Committee recommended to the best of their judgement & dismissed. Dinner at Martin Shoe's. Returned home. Baptized at Mt. Carmel Rufus O. Barringer's child.

Frid. 8. At home. Sat. 9. At home.

Sund. 10. At home. Had no appointment for this day.

Mond. 11. Tues. 12. Wed. 13. Thurs. 14. At home.

Frid. 15. Went to Organ church and buried Peter Cruse. Preached from Ex. 33:14.

Sat. 16. At home, had wheat threshed.

Sund. 17. This my day Luther's church. Did not attend. Sent Lewis to explain my non attendance & read service. Went to Organ ch. in afternoon & buried John Jacob Miller. Preached from Heb. 4:9.

Mond. 18. Tues. 19. At home haying.

Wed. 20. Went to James A. Miller's mill. Dinner here. Baptized also Mr. Miller's child.

Thurs. 21. At home.

Frid. 22. Went to Gold Hill to post office.

Sat. 23. At home.

Sund. 24. Had no appointment for this day. Went to see Daniel Miller, he bring sick. Dinner here.

Mond. 25. At home.

Tues. 26. In afternoon went to Widow Jacob Miller's & read the will of J. Jacob Miller, dec^d.

Wed. 27. Went to Salisbury to witness the Will of J. Jacob Miller but the Probate Judge or Clerk being absent nothing could be done.

Thurs 28. Went to Organ church to Gold Hill Township Sunday School Association & intended thence to go to Conference in Concord, but being very unwell returned home.

Frid. 29. Sat. 30. At home & sick.

Sund. 31. At home & indisposed.

Mond. Aug. 1. Tues. 2. Wed. 3. Thurs. 4. At home.
Frid. 5. Went to Reid Misenheimer's mill.
Sat. 6. At home.
Sund. 7. Preached at Luther's church from Prov. 3:6. Dinner at Richard Glover's. Returned home.
Mond. 8. Tues. 9. Wed. 10. Thurs. 11. Frid. 12. At home.
Sat. 13. At home.
Sund. 14. At home, had no appointment to day.
Mond. 15. Started after dinner for St. Enoch's Church. Staid over night at J. A. Eddleman's.
Tues. 16. Went to St. Enoch's church. Had home assigned at Rev. W. A. Lutz's.
Wed. 17. Attended the semi-centennial of St. Enoch's church by special request & delivered an address to the people. Was followed by other speakers. At Rev. Lutz's.
Thurs. 18. Returned home.
Frid. 19. At home. Sat. 20. At home.
Sund. 21. Preached at Luther's ch. from 1 Pet. 4:18. Dinner at Jacob C. Earnheart's.
Mond. 22. Went to Salisbury to prove Jacob Miller's Will.
Tues. 23. At home.
Wed. 24. In afternoon went to Gold Hill to post office.
Thurs. 25. Took wife on a visit to David Barringer's.
Frid. 26. At home
Sat. 27. At home.
Sund. 28. Preached at Luther's church from Luk. 15:11-24. Dinner at David C. Parker's. Returned home.
Mond. 29. In forenoon went to John Earnheart's & brought Carpet home. Then at home.
Tues. 30. Went to William Basinger's and had Charley shod.
Wed. 31. Went to Misenheimer's mill. Edwin Arey & daughter called to see us.

Thurs. Sept. 1. Frid. 2. Sat. 3. At home.

Sund. 4. Went to St. Peter's ch. & heard Rev. H. A. Trexler preach.

Mond. 5. Went to Salisbury to prove John Ritchie's will.

Tues. 6. Went to Gold Hill to post office, & then called to see Danl Miller, he being sick.

Wed. 7. In the morning went to Sol. Peeler's & to M. A. Holshouser's. Then at home.

Thurs. 8. Frid. 9. At home.

Sat. 10. Went to John E. Shaver's & staid over night.

Sund. 11. Preached at Luther's ch. from Josh. 23:8. Dinner at Whitson Arey's. Returned home.

Mond. 12. Attended the burial of Danl Miller at Organ church. Rev. W. R. Brown preached the funeral.

Tues. 13. At home.

Wed. 14. Celebrated to day our Golden Wedding. Many friends were present. Received many golden gifts & congratulations. Brother Adam came from Oregon to see us.

Thurs. 15. Frid. 16. Sat. 17. At home.

Sund. 18. Went with wife to St. Peter's church & heard Rev. H. A. Trexler preach.

Mond. 19. At home.

Tues. 20. Went to Mt. Pleasant to attend meeting of Board of Trustees of N. C. College. Over night at Col. J. Shimpock's.

Wed. 21. In meeting of Board of Trustees. Dinner at Capt. J. Cook's. Over night at Col. Shimpock's.

Thurs. 22. Returned home.

Frid. 23. Went to Gold Hill to post office.

Sat. 24. Went to George Wilhelm's & staid over night.

Sund. 25. Preached at Luther's ch. from Eccl. 11:9. Dinner at Stokes Hill's. Returned home.

Mond. 26. Tues. 27. At home.

Wed. 28. Went to Gold Hill to post office in the afternoon. Br. Adam with me.

Thurs. 29. At home.

Frid. 30. Took Br. Adam to Salisbury for him to take the train for his home in Oregon.

Sat. Oct. 1. At home.

Sund. 2. At home. Had no appointment for to day.

Mond. 3. Went to Allen Miller's mill. Thence to Augustus Sifford's. Dinner here. Then went to widow Ritchie's to examine deeds for land willed to N. C. College. Returned by way Allen Miller's mill & brought flour home.

Tues. 4. In forenoon hauled cane to M. A. Holshouser's to cane mill. In afternoon at home.

Wed. 5. At home.

Thurs. 6. Went to Salisbury to prove Dan[l] Miller's Will.

Frid. 7. In the morning went to M. A. Holshouser's & brought Corn Sheller home sent by Tobie Brown from Richmond, Va. a Golden Wedding present. Then at home.

Sat. 8. Went to Luther's church & preached from Ps. 51:2. preparatory to communion. All night at Whitson Miller's.

Sund. 9. Preached at Luther's church from Acts 11:26. Dinner at Jacob C. Earnheart's. Returned home.

Mond. 10. Went to Salisbury & took the train for Charlotte. Dinner at the Central Hotel. Supper at Rev. Brown's. Took the train at 8½ P.M. for Wilmington.

Tues. 11. Arrived in Wilmington at 8½ A.M. Staid with Rev. Peschau during my sojourn in Wilmington. Met with met with [written twice] a great deal of kindness from the good people in Wilmington.

Wed. 12. In Wilmington.

Thurs. 13. Preached at night in the Lutheran church from James 1:25.

Frid. 14. In the afternoon went to the Sound & across to the Beach to see the Ocean.

Sat. 15. In Wilmington.

Sund. 16. In the morning preached in English in the Luth. church from Prov. 3:6. & assisted in the administration of the Holy Supper. Preached again at night in German from 2 Cor. 5:17. & assisted in the Eucharist.

Mond. 17. In Wilmington.

Tues. 18. At night lectured in Memorial Hall on the times and customs of 50 years ago.

Wed. 19. In Wilmington.

Thurs. 20. In the afternoon went to the sound and across to the beach to see the Ocean.

Frid. 21. Took the train for Charlotte & arrived in Charlotte same evening. Took the train for Salisbury.

Sat. 22. Took mail hack for home & reached home 12 M.

Sund. 23. Preached Luther's ch. from Matt. 22:1-14. Dinner at G. W. Arey's. Returned home.

Mond. 24. Tues. 25. At home. Wed. 26. At home.

Thurs. 27. Went to Gold Hill to post office. In afternoon went to St. Peter's church to see Rev. H. A. Trexler married.

Frid. 28. At home.

Sat. 29. Went to Ebenezer church to Conference. All night at Geo. M. Ketner's.

Sund. 30. In the morning called to see Frederick Stirewalt & wife, they being old & frail. Then went to Ebenezer ch. & heard Prof. Schaidt preach a Reformation sermon. Very inclement day. All night at J. A. Eddleman's.

Mond. 31. A very inclement day. All day and over night at J. A. Eddleman's.

Tues. Nov. 1. Returned home.

Wed. 2. At home

Thurs. 3. Went to Salisbury.

Frid. 4. Sat. 5. At home.

Sund. 6. Went to St. Peter's ch. & heard Rev. Trexler preach.

Mond. 7. Took wife to Dr. Coleman's, then went to Rockwell post office. Returned to Dr. Coleman's & took dinner. Brought wife home.

Tues. 8. At home.

Wed. 9. Went to Mt. Pleasant. All night at Col. Shimpock's.

Thurs. 10. Attended meeting of Board of Trustees & inauguration of Pres. Schaidt. All night at Col. Shimpock's.

Frid. 11. Returned home.

Sat. 12. At home.

Sund. 13. Preached at Luther's church from Ps. 7:9. Dinner and all night at John E. Shaver's.

Mond. 14. Returned home. In afternoon went to Wilson Kesler's on business.

Tues. 15. Went to Solomon Peeler's & divided corn.

Wed. 16. Went to Salisbury & paid Tax.

Thurs. 17. Went to Dr. Coleman's in morning for medicine for wife.

Frid. 18. Went to Gold Hill to post office.

Sat. 19. Went to Jerry Earnheart's & Geo. Bost's & had Charley shod. Dinner at Mr. Bost's. Returned by way of post office.

Sund. 20. At home, had no appointment.

Mond. 21. Tues. 22. At home.

Wed. 23. Went to Gold Hill to post office & to Misenheimer's mill.

Thurs. 24. At home, hauled wood.

Frid. 25. Went to Gold Hill to post office.

Sat. 26. In afternoon went to John Canup's & staid over night.

Sund. 27. Preached at Luther's church from Prov. 14:34. Dinner at B. P. Basinger's. Returned home.

Mond. 28. Went to Andrew Berger's & got some cider oil for wife.

Tues. 29. Went to Jacob Holshouser's & engaged some corn.

Wed. 30. At home, made preparations to have hogs slaughtered.

Thurs. Dec. 1. Had winter hogs slaughtered.
Frid. 2. Sat. 3. At home.
Sund. 4. Went to St. Peter's ch. & heard Rev. Trexler preach.
Mond. 5. In the morning, went to Gold Hill. Then took wife to Dr. Coleman's.
Tues. 6. Went Allen Miller's mill. Dinner here.
Wed. 7. Took some lard to Dr. Coleman in the afternoon.
Thurs. 8. At home. A rainy day.
Frid. 9. At home.
Sat. 10. In afternoon went to Joseph W. Miller's and staid over night.
Sund. 11. Preached at Luther's ch. from 1 Cor. 4:2. Dinner at David C. Parker's. Returned home.
Mond. 12. At home.
Tues. 13. Had cotton hauled to the gin.
Wed. 14. Went to Gold Hill to mill.
Thurs. 15. Went to cotton gin & had cotton seed & cotton bale brought home.
Frid. 16. In afternoon went to M. A. Holshouser's & bought a quarter of beef.
Sat. 17. At home. Cloudy & rainy.
Sund. 18. Had no appointment for to day. In afternoon went to J. L. Graeber's & staid over night.
Mond. 19. Attended to the funeral of Frederick Stirewalt. Preached the fun[1] at the house from 2 Tim. 4:7.8. &
      buried at Ebenezer ch. Dinner at Henry Graeber's. Returned home.
Tues. 20. Wed. 21. Thurs. 22. At home.
Frid. 23. Went to Gold Hill to post office.
Sat. 24. At home, a very rainy day. Had in= to be at St. Stephen's ch. but inclement weather prevented me from
      going.
Sund. 25. Christmas Day. Had promised to be at St. Stephen's ch. to participate in the semi-centennial
      celebration of the organization of the congregation, but was prevented by inclement weather. Snow on
      the ground.
Mond. 26. At home.
Tues. 27. At home, hauld wood on one horse wagon.
Wed. 28. Received word in the morning of Mrs. David Barringer's death. In afternoon took wife to Mr.
      Barring's. Returned home.
Thurs. 29. Went to Mr. Barringer's and brought wife home.
Frid. 30. Sat. 31. At home.

Sund. Jan. 1. Had no appointment for this day. At home reading Bible. A very rainy day.

Mond. 2. At home.

Tues. 3. Took watch to Rev. R. L. Brown's to have it repaired. Br. Brown not at home. Dinner here.

Wed. 4. Thurs. 5. At home.

Frid. 6. Went to Gold Hill to post office.

Sat. 7. In forenoon went to Rev. R. L. Brown's and & brought watch home.

Sund. 8. Preached at Luther's ch. from Heb. 10:24. Dinner at J. C. Earnheart's. Returned home.

Mond. 9. Tues. 10. At home.

Wed. 11. Attended to the funeral of John Luther Barringer. Preached the funeral at the house from Ps. 144:15. & buried at Lower Stone Church. Dinner at Boyden Miller's. Returned home by way of Dr. Coleman's.

Thurs. 12. Frid. 13. Sat. 14. At home. Bad weather.

Sund. 15. At home. Had no appointment.

Mond. 16. Tues. 17. At home. Bad weather.

Wed. 18. Went to M. A. Holshouser's & had shoes half soled. Dinner here.

Thurs. 19. Frid. 20. At home.

Sat. 21. At home.

Sund. 22. Had an appointment for this day at Luther's ch., but the day being very inclement, with snow on the ground, did not attend.

Mond. 23. At home.

Tues. 24. Went to Gold Hill to Post office.

Wed. 25. At home.

Thurs. 26. Took turnips to Gold Hill. Went also to post office.

Frid. 27. Had intended to go to Conference at St. John's church, but owing to the unsettled state of the weather & bad roads did not attend.

Sat. 28. Went to D. Barringer's mill.

Sund. 29. At home. Had no appointment.

Mond. 30. Went to Gold Hill to post office.

Tues. 31. At home. Had wood hauled.

Wed. Feb. 1. In the morning went to F. Crowell's to see him about renting land to him. Then at home.

Thurs. 2. Frid. 3. Sat. 4. At home.

Sund. 5. Had no appointment. At home.

Mond. 6. At home.

Tues. 7. Went to Gold Hill to post office.

Wed. 8. Went to D. Barringer's mill.

Thurs. 9. Took wife to Dr. Coleman's & spent the day.

Frid. 10. Sat. 11. At home.

Sund. 12. At an appointment for this day at Luther's ch., but the weather being unfavorable & the roads bad, did not attend.

Mond. 13. In the morning took some chickens to Gold Hill. Then at home.

Tues. 14. Called to see Rev. H. A. Trexler, then went to W. M. Linker's & baptized his child. Dinner here. Returned home, & then brought wife home from Mrs. Linn's.

Wed. 15. At home.

Thurs. 16. In the morning went to Jacob Holshouser's & engaged some corn. Then at home.

Frid. 17. Went to Gold Hill to post office.

Sat. 18. At home.

Sund. 19. Preached at St. Peter's ch. from 1 Sam. 12:23.24.

Mond. 20. At home.

Tues. 21. Went to Geo. Park's to engage oats for seed. Then went to Rockwell P. O. & then to And. Berger's & returned home.

Wed. 22. In the morning went to Geo. Park's for oats, & then to Gold Hill and delivered potatoes.

Thurs. 23. At home, rainy day.

Frid. 24. Went to Gold Hill to post office. a very rainy day.

Sat. 25. In afternoon went to J. C. Earnheart's & staid over night.

Sund. 26. Preached at Luther's ch. from 1 Sam. 12:23.24. Dinner at J. C. Earnheart's. Returned home.

Mond. 27. Went to Gold Hill to post office.

Tues. 28. Wed. 29. At home.

Thurs. March 1. Went to James A. Mill. Dinner here.

Frid. 2. Went to Gold Hill to post office.

Sat. 3. Went to G. W. Linker's & baptized his child. Called also at Dr. Coleman's. Returning called at M. A. Holshouser's. Dinner here.

Sund. 4. At home. Had no appointment.

Mond. 5. Went to Jerry Earnheart's & had shoeing done. Returned by way of Gold Hill.

Tues. 6. Went to Salisbury.

Wed. 7. Went to Gold Hill for package of books.

Thurs. 8. Frid 9. At home.

Sat. 10. In the afternoon went to Whitson Arey's & staid over night.

Sund. 11. Had an appointment at Luther's ch. but the forenoon being very rainy did not attend. In the afternoon returned home.

Mond. 12. Went in forenoon to Wilson Kesler on business. In afternoon at home.

Tues. 13. At home. Very cold & rainy.

Wed. 14. Went to Gold Hill to post office.

Thurs. 15. At home.

Frid. 16. Attended closing exercises of School at our free school house.

Sat. 17. At home.

Sund. 18. Went to St. Peter's church & heard Rev. H. A. Trexler preach.

Mond. 19. At home.

Tues. 20. Went to Gold Hill in the afternoon to the post office.

Wed. 21. Went with wife to Dr. Coleman's and confirmed Dr. L. W. Coleman, Jane Coleman, and Lottie C. Hambley. Baptized also E. B. C. Hambley's child. Dinner here.

Thurs. 22. At home.

Frid. 23. Sat. 24. At home.

Sund. 25. Went to Luther's church but could not preach in consequence of severe cold & hoarseness. Had short religious services & returned home.

Mond. 26. At home.

Tues. 27. Went to Gold Hill & purchased envelopes. Balance of the day at home.

Wed. 28. Went to Rockwell post office & mailed a number of circulars. Dinner here.

Thurs. 29. Frid. 30. At home.

Sat. 31. Went to Luther's church & had preparatory service. Rev. R. L. Brown preached. Staid over night at J. N. C. Morgan's. Baptized his child at home.

Sund. Apr. 1. At Luther's church. Rev. R. L. Brown preached. Administered the Lord's Supper. Staid over night at J. C. Earnheart's.

Mond. 2. Returned home.

Tues. 3. Wed. 4. At home.

Thurs. 5. Frid. 6. Sat 7. At home.

Sund. 8. Went to Luther's church & preached from 1 Kings 19:13. Dinner at Richard Glover's. Returned home.

Mond. 9. At home.

Tues. 10. Wed. 11. Thurs. 12. At home.

Frid. 13. Went to Gold Hill to mill & post office.

Sat. 14. Attended preaching at St. Peter's church. Rev. Strickler preached.

Sund. 15. Preached at Luther's ch. from Jerm. 17:9. 2 Cor. 13:5. Dinner at David C. Parker's. In afternoon went to Zion ch. (Methodist) and heard Rev. Rowe preach. Returned home.

Mond. 16. to Sat. 21. At home.

Sund. 22. Preached at Luther's ch. from 1 Pet. 5:4. Baptized one infant. Dinner at J. C. Earnheart's. Returned home.

Mond. 23. Tues. 24. Wed. 25. At home. Thurs. 26. At home.

Frid. 27. Went to Salisbury.

Sat. 28. Went to D. Barringer's mill.

Sund. 29. Had no appointment. At home.

Mond. 30. Tues. May 1. At home.

Wed. 2. Went to Salisbury to attend the Woman's Home & Foreign Missionary Society. All night at Wilborn Fraley's.

Thurs. 3. Went by R. Road to Concord to attend meeting of Synod. Had home assigned at G. W. Patterson's.

Frid. 4. Sat. 5. Sund. 6. Mond. 7. At Synod. In the evening of Monday returned to Salisbury by R. Road. All night at Wilborn Fraley's.

Tues. 8. Returned home on the mail hack.

Wed. 9. Went to George M. Fisher's & married Joseph W. Holshouser & Emma U. Fisher.

Thurs. 10. Went to Rockwell post office & registered several letters. Dinner here.

Frid. 11. Sat. 12. At home.

Sund. 13. Had no appointment for this day. At home reading.

Mond. 14. to Frid. 18. At home.

Sat. 19. At home.

Sund. 20. Had an appointment for this day at Luther's church, but the day very rainy, did not attend.

Mond. 21. In the morning went to Dr. Coleman's & took his umbrella home.

Tues. 22. At home.

Wed. 23. In forenoon went to Gold Hill to mill.

Thurs. 24. In the morning took wife to Milas A. Holshouser's to spend the day. In evening brought her home.

Frid. 25. At home.

Sat. 26. Went to J. A. Miller's mill.

Sund. 27. Attended to the funeral of Elizabeth L. Trexler, widow of Caleb Trexler, dec^d at St. Peter's church —preached from 2 Tim. 1:12. A large audience.

Mond. 28. At home.

Tues. 29. In the morning went to Boyden Beaver's, his infant child having died. Conducted the services at the house. Rev. Heller attended to the burial.

Wed. 30. Went to Mt. Pleasant to attend meeting of the board of N. C. College & commencement exercises. Stopped at Col. Shimpock's.

Thurs. 31. In Mt. Pleasant.

Frid. June 1. Returned home.

Sat. 2. At home.

Sund. 3. At home. Had no appointment for this day.

Mond. 4. Tues. 5. At home.

Wed. 6. In forenoon engaged hands to mow grass.

Thurs. 7. At home.

Frid. 8. In afternoon went to Gold Hill & listed taxes.

Sat. 9. In afternoon went to Rev. Isaac Shaver's and staid over night.

Sund. 10. Preached at Luther's ch. from John 20:23. Dinner at B. P. Bassinger's. Returned home.

Mond. 11. At home.

Tues. 12. Went to Gold Hill to post office.

Wed. 13. In forenoon went to Rockwell post office.

Thurs. 14. At home.

Frid. 15. Sat. 16. Went to Gold Hill both days to post office.

Sund. 17. Went to St. Peter's ch. and heard Rev. Trexler preach.

Mond. 18. Tues. 19. At home.

Wed. 20. Took wife to Dr. Coleman's to spend the day. Then went to Gold Hill to post office. In the evening went & brought wife home.

Thurs. 21. Frid. 22. At home.

Sat. 23. At home.

Sund. 24. Preached at Luther's ch. from Matt. 11:29.30. Dinner at J. C. Earnheart's. Returned home.

Mond. 25. At home haying. In the evening went to Geo. Linker's to engage him to haul hay.

Tues. 26. At home. Haying.

Wed. 27. Thurs. 28. Frid. 29. At home.

Sat. 30. In the morning went Gold Hill to post office. Then at home.

Sund. July 1. Went to St Peter's church & heard Rev. Trexler preach.

Mond. 2. At home.

Tues. 3. Went to J. Allen Miller's mill.

Wed. 4. At home.

Thurs. 5. Frid. 6. At home.

Sat. 7. In afternoon went to John E. Shaver's and staid over night.

Sund. 8. Preached at Luther's church from Gen. 41:9. Dinner at G. W. Arey's. Returned home.

Mond. 9. At home.

Tues. 10. Went to William Basinger's & had shoeing done. Called at post office at Gold Hill.

Wed. 11. At home.

Thurs. 12. Took wife to Dr. Coleman's & spent the day.

Frid. 13. At home.

Sat. 14. Went to St Peter's ch. & preached for Rev. H. A. Trexler from John 20:23. preparatory to communion.

Sund. 15. Went to St. Peter's ch. & preached for Rev. H. A. Trexler from John 7:37. & assisted in the administration of the Lord's Supper.

Mond. 16. At home.

Tues. 17. In the afternoon attended the burial of Augusta Stikeleather at St. Peter's ch. Services conducted by Rev. H. A. Trexler.

Wed. 18. Took wife to H. A. Miller's & spent the day. Called also to see Mrs. Anna Trexler.

Thurs. 19. Frid. 20. At home, had wheat threshed.

Sat. 21. At home.

Sund. 22. Went to Luther's church and preached from Matt. 12:39. Dinner at David C. Parker's. Returned home.

Mond. 23. In the morning took my buggy to Jerry Earnheart's shop to have repaired.

Tues. 24. At home. Wed. 25. At home.

Thurs. 26. In the morning went to Jerry Earnheart's & brought my buggy home. Then went to Dr. Coleman's on business. Dinner here.

Frid. 27. Went to Bethel church, Stanly co. to Special Conference. Dinner at Rev. Cox's. Had home assigned at David Lyerly's. All night here.

Sat. 28. At Conference. All night at Mr. Lyerly's.

Sund. 29. At Conference. After divine service returned home.

Mond. 30. At home.

Tues. 31. Went to Salisbury.

Wed. Aug. 1. At home.
Thurs. 2. Went in afternoon to Dr. Coleman's for medicine for wife.
Frid. 3. Sat. 4. At home.
Sund. 5. At home, wife being sick.
Mond. 6. At home. Prof. Turner took dinner with us.
Tues. 7. Went to J. Allen Miller's mill.
Wed. 8. In the morning went to Gold Hill.
Thurs. 9. Went to Salisbury.
Frid. 10. At home. Sat. 11. At home.
Sund. 12. Preached at Luther's ch. from 1 Thes. 2:11.12. Dinner at J. C. Earnheart's. Returned home.
Mond. 13. At home.
Tues. 14. In forenoon went to Gold Hill to post office.
Wed. 15. Took wife to Dr. Coleman's, then returned to M. A. Holshouser's. Dinner here.
Thurs. 16. At home.
Frid. 17. Sat. 18. At home.
Sund. 19. Took wife to St. Peter's ch. to hear Rev. H. A. Trexler preach. Returned home.
Mond. 20. At home.
Tues. 21. Went to St. Matthew's church to attend the semi-centennial of the congregation. Lectured twice to the people. Returned home.
Wed. 22. Thurs. 23. Frid. 24. At home.
Sat. 25. At home.
Sund. 26. Preached at Luther's ch. from Is. 30:10. Returned home.
Mond. 27. In the morning went to Gold Hill to post office.
Tues. 28. Went to John E. Shaver's for some oats. Dinner here.
Wed. 29. At home.
Thurs. 30. At home.
Frid. 31. Went to Gold Hill to post office.

Sat. Sep. 1. At home.

Sund. 2. Went wife to St. Peter's ch. and heard Rev. H. A. Trexler preach. Returned home.

Mon 3. At home.

Tues: 4. Went to Jerry Earnheart's & had Charley shod.

Wed. 5. Went to Allen Miller's mill. Dinner here.

Thurs. 6. Frid. 7. At home.

Sat. 8. Went to Gold Hill to post office.

Sund. 9. Preached at Luther's ch. from Ex. 20:15. Dinner at B. P. Basinger's. Returned home.

Mond. 10. At home, a rainy day.

Tues. 11. In the morning went to M. A. Holshouser's for a bag of chop. Then at home.

Wed. 12. Went to John Earnheart's and brought tubs home. In afternoon went to John Miller's for a little brandy.

Thurs. 13. In afternoon went to Jeremiah J. Miller's by request & baptized his two children.

Frid. 14. Went to Gold Hill to post office.

Sat. 15. In the afternoon went to Geo. M. Barringer & staid over night.

Sund. 16. Preached at Union church from John 20:23. All night at Dugal L. Arey's.

Mond. 17. Returned home. Rainy day.

Tues. 18. Wed. 19. Thurs. 20. At home haying.

Frid. 21. In afternoon went to Gold Hill to post office.

Sat. 22. At home.

Sund. 23. Preached at Luther's ch. from Jerm. 22:29. Dinner at Richard Glover's. Returned home.

Mond. 24. Engaged hands to mow grass.

Tues. 25. Wed. 26. At home, haying.

Thurs. 27. Went in the afternoon to Geo. Wilhelm's & staid over night.

Frid. 28. Went to Luther's church to attend the meeting of the Southern Conference. Rev. Cox preached the opening sermon. All night at Wm. A. Kirk's.

Sat. 29. At Conference. Rev. Strickler preached.

Sund. 30. At Conference. Rev. Cox preached. Baptized & confirmed one adult, viz, Martitia Catharine Fraley. Then baptized her eight children. Then confirmed two persons. Administered the holy communion being assisted by the ministers of Conference. Returned home.

Mond. Oct. 1. Tues. 2. At home.

Wed. 3. Went to Gold Hill to post office, and also to pay my tax. Heard the candidates speak.

Thurs. 4. At home.

Frid. 5. Went to Gold Hill to post office.

Sat. 6. At home.

Sund. 7. Went to St. Peter's ch. & Rev. H. A. Trexler being absent, on account of family afflictions, preached, by request of council, from 1 Pet. 4:18. Dinner at widow Moses Linn's.

Mond. 8. Went to Salisbury.

Tues. 9. In afternoon went to Rev. H. A. Trexler's, his wife being sick.

Wed. 10. Thurs. 11. Frid. 12. At home.

Sat. 13. Went to David C. Parker's & staid over night.

Sund. 14. Preached at Luther's ch. from Mark 6:52. Dinner at Jacob C. Earnheart's. Married here Moselle Earnheart & Sarah Jane Basinger. Returned home.

Mond. 15. Went to Misenheimer's mill.

Tues. 16. Wed. 17. At home.

Thurs. 18. Had corn shucked at night. At home.

Frid. 19. Sat. 20. At home.

Sund. 21. Took wife to St Peter's ch. Heard Rev. Trexler preach. Assisted in the administration of communion.

Mond. 22. In afternoon went to Gold Hill to post office.

Tues. 23. At home.

Wed. 24. Thurs. 25. Frid. 26. At home.

Sat. 27. In forenoon went to Dr. Coleman's, Mr. Hambley's child being very sick. In afternoon went to Jacob C. Earnheart's & staid over night.

Sund. 28. Preached at Luther's ch. from Matt. 25:14-30. Dinner at Whitson Arey's. Returned home.

Mond. 29. In forenoon went to Dr. Coleman's to see Mr. Hambley's sick child. In afternoon went to Gold Hill to post office.

Tues. 30. At home.

Wed. 31. Went to mill at Gold Hill.

Thurs. Nov. 1. At home.

Frid. 2. Went to Gold Hill to post office. In the afternoon took wife to Dr. Coleman's to see the sick.

Sat. 3. At home.

Sund. 4. Went to St. Peter's ch. & heard Rev. Trexler preach.

Mond. 5. Went in forenoon to Rev. H. A. Trexler's & baptized his child, his wife being sick.

Tues. 6. Went in forenoon to Gold Hill to the election. In afternoon at home.

Wed. 7. Thurs. 8. Frid. 9. At home.

Sat. 10. Went to Organ ch. & participated in the centennial of Rev. Charles A. G. Storch's taking charge of Organ ch.

Sund. 11. Attended to the funeral of Mrs. Elizabeth L. Klutts, wife of Moses Klutts, at Lower St. church. Addressed the large concourse of people from Job 14:14. Dinner at Boyden A. Miller's. Returned home.

Mond. 12. In the morning went to M. A. Holshouser's & sent some money by him to Jonas Cook, Treasurer of N. C. College. In afternoon went to Gold Hill to post office.

Tues 13. Wed. 14. Thurs. 15. At home.

Frid. 16. Went to Gold Hill to post office.

Sat. 17. At home.

Sund. 18. Preached at Luther's ch. from Eph. 5:18. Returned home after preaching.

Mond. 19. Tues. 20. Wed. 21. Thurs. 22. At home.

Frid. 23. At home, cold weather.

Sat. 24. Attended to the funeral of Joseph A. Powlass at Lower Stone church. — preached from Ex. 33:14.

Sund. 25. Preached at Luther's ch. from Ex. 23:2. Dinner at J. C. Earnheart's. Returned home.

Mond. 26. My birthday. 79 yrs. old. Had winter hogs slaughtered.

Tues. 27. Wed. 28. Thurs. 29. At home.

Frid. 30. Went to Mrs. Linn's to Rosses infare.

Sat. Dec. 1. At home.

Sund. 2. Had no appointment for this day. At home.

Mond. 3. Tues. 4. At home. Shelled corn & sent to mill.

Wed. 5. In the morning went to Jacob Lyerly's & engaged some pigs. Then at home.

Thurs. 6. In the morning went to Jacob Lyerly's & 4 pigs home.

Frid. 7. At home.

Sat. 8. In afternoon went to B. P. Basinger's & staid over night.

Sund. 9. Preached at Luther's ch. from Deut. 18:15. Dinner at Jacob C. Earnheart's. Returned home. Had a chill this evening.

Mond. 10. Tues. 11. At home warding off the chill.

Wed. 12. Went to Gold Hill. In afternoon took wife to see her sister, Mrs. Coleman.

Thurs. 13. Frid. 14. At home.

Sat. 15. Went to Joseph A. Brown's (Rockwell) post office. Dinner here.

Sund. 16. Had no appointment. At home with wife. she being infirm. Read my Bible.

Mond. 17. At home, a rainy day.

Tues. 18. Wed. 19. Thurs. 20. At home.

Frid. 21. Went to Gold Hill to post office.

Sat. 22. In afternoon went to John E. Shaver's and staid over night.

Sund. 23. Preached at Luther's Church from Matt. 1:21. Dinner at Richard Glover's. Returned home.

Mond. 24. Went to John C. Pool's on business. Dinner here.

Tues. 25. Christmas. At home.

Wed. 26. After dinner went to Rockwell post office & mailed some letters. then went to Alexander Lyerly's & staid over night.

Thurs. 27. Went to Dr. Milo A. J. Roseman's and married Albert L. Lyerly and Fannie E. Roseman. After dinner returned home.

Frid. 28. At home.

Sat. 29. Sund. 30. Mond. 31. At home.

Tues. Jan. 1, 1889. New Year's Day. At home.

Wed. 2. At home.

Thurs. 3. Went to Salisbury. Returned as far as Joseph A. Brown's & staid over night.

Frid. 4. Returned home.

Sat. 5. At home, a very day.

Sund. 6. Had no appointment for this day. At home.

Mond. 7. Tues. 8. Wed. 9. At home in my study.

Thurs. 10. In the afternoon went to Mrs. Linker's, widow of Isaac Linker, & married John D. Brown and Laura M. Linker.

Frid. 11. At home in my study.

Sat. 12. Went to David C. Parker's & staid over night.

Sund. 13. Preached at Luther's ch. from Numb. 10:29. Dinner at Jacob C. Earnheart's. Returned home.

Mond. 14. In forenoon went to Rockwell post office. Then at home.

Tues. 15. At home. Mrs. Frick & Mrs. Alexander Peeler called to see us.

Wed. 16. At home, a rainy day.

Thurs. 17. At home.

Frid. 18. Went to Gold Hill to post office.

Sat. 19. At home.

Sund. 20. Had no appointment for this day. At home a very rainy day.

Mond. 21. Went to Wilson Kesler's & paid over some money on College note.

Tues. 22. Wed. 23. Thurs. 24. At home.

Frid. 25. Went to Gold Hill to post office.

Sat. 26. At home, a very inclement day.

Sund. 27. This was my day to preach at Luther's church, but did not attend in consequence of the inclemency of weather.

Mond. 28. Tues. 29. At home.

Wed. 30. Went to Dr. Coleman's. Dinner here.

Thurs. 31. In the morning went to Mr. Trexler's cotton gin. Mrs. Henry Miller & daughter in law called to see us.

Frid. Feb. 1. At home. Sent to Allen Miller's mill.

Sat. 2. At home.

Sund. 3. Had home with wife while others went to preaching.

Mond. 4. Went to Dr. Coleman's & collected some money for the relief of Rev. J. H. Fesperman & family. Then went Rockwell post office & sent seven dollars by Registered Letter to Mrs. C. A. Fesperman.

Tues. 5. Wed. 6. At home.

Thurs. 7. Frid. 8. At home.

Sat. 9. In afternoon went to Geo. L. Wilhelm's & staid over night over night.

Sund. 10. Preached at Luther's church from Luk. 18:35-43. Dinner at J. C. Earnheart's. Returned home.

Mond. 11. Tues. 12. At home.

Wed. 13. Walked to Gold Hill to post office & to have shoes repaired.

Thurs. 14. Took some turnips to Gold Hill & exchanged for sugar & coffee. Cass Arey with us to night.

Frid. 15. Went in the morning to Dr. Coleman's and brought Mrs. Nancy Shemwell to spend some time with us.

Sat. 16. Attended to the funeral of George Park's child, preached the fun[1] at the house & buried at St. Peter's ch. A very inclement day with rain.

Sund. 17. At home, a very rainy day.

Mond. 18. In afternoon went to Gold Hill to post office.

Tues. 19. Wed. 20. At home.

Thurs. 21. At home, this afternoon & during the night had a deep snow.

Frid. 22. At home. Snow on the ground.

Sat. 23. In the afternoon went to Whitson Arey's & staid over night.

Sund. 24. This was my day to preach at Luther's ch., but the day being very cold & inclement, did not attend. Returned home.

Mond. 25. Tues. 26. Wed. 27. Thurs. 28. At home.

Frid. March 1. Went to Gold Hill to post office.

Sat. 2. At home, a rainy day.

Sund. 3. Had no appointment. At home with wife.

Mond. 4. Went to Salisbury & sold bale cotton.

Tues. 5. Wed. 6. At home.

Frid. 8. Went to Misenheimer's mill & to post office.

Sat. 9. At home.

Sund. 10. Went to Luther's ch. & preached from Math. 6:33. Dinner at J. C. Earnheart's.

Mond. 11. At home.

Tues. 12. Went to Gold Hill & Registered 2 letters.

Wed. 13. At home.

Thurs. 14. In afternoon took Mrs. Phebe Brown to J. C. Pool's.

Frid. 15. Sat. 16. At home.

Sund. 17. Had no appointment for this day. At home.

Mond. 18. Tues. 19. Wed. 20. At home.

Thurs. 21. Went to Salisbury.

Frid. 22. At home.

Sat. 23. In the afternoon went to J. C. Earnheart's & staid over night.

Sund. 24. Preached at Luther's ch. from Gen. 5:24. Dinner at J. C. Earnheart's. Returned home.

Mond. 25. Tues. 26. At home.

Wed. 27. At home. Rev. W. R. Brown's wif & Ellen Holshouser called to see us.

Thurs. 28. At home.

Frid. 29. Attended the closing exercising of our free school by Bina Lingel.

Sat. 30. At home.

Sund. 31. At home. Had no appointment for this day.

Mond. April 1. At home.
Tues. 2. Took Phebe Brown to Salisbury.
Wed. 3. Thurs. 4. At home.
Frid. 5. Went to Gold to post office.
Sat. 6. At home, a very windy cold day.
Sund. 7. Had any an appointment at Luther's ch. but did not attend, the weather being cold and blustering. Sent Lewis to read service & lecture.
Mond. 8. At home.
Tues. 9. In afternoon went to Gold Hill to post office.
Wed. 10. Went to Misenheimer's mill.
Thurs. 11. At home.
Frid. 12. At home.
Sat. 13. In afternoon went with Lewis to B. P. Basinger's & staid over night.
Sund. 14. Preached at Luther's ch. from 1 Tim. 6:6. Returned home. Rain the evening.
Mond. 15. Tues. 16. Wed. 17. Thurs. 18. At home.
Frid. 19. Went to Gold Hill to post office.
Sat. 20. Went to preaching at St. Peter's ch.
Sund. 21. Preached at St. Peter's church from Col 3:1. & assisted Rev. Trexler in the communion.
Mond. 22. Tues. 23. At home.
Wed. 24. Went to Jerry Earnheart's to have horse shod &c., but failed he having gone to Salisbury.
Thurs. 25. Frid 26. At home.
Sat. 27. Went to Luther's ch. & preached from Luke 10:25-37. preparatory to communion. Over night at John E. Shaver's.
Sund. 28. Preached at Luther's ch. from Acts 24:25. and administered to communion. Dinner at J. C. Earnheart's. Returned home.
Mond. 29. At home.
Tues. 30. Went to Gold Hill to post office.

Wed. May 1. At home.

Thurs. 2. Went to Daniel Ritchie's & staid over night.

Frid. 3. Went with Geo. L. Wilhelm to St. John's ch. to attend meeting of Synod. Had home assigned at Mrs. M. M. Miller's.

Sat. 4. Sund. 5. At Synod . Overnight at Mrs. Miller's.

Mond. 6. At Synod. Went with Col. Shimpock to Mt. Pleasant & staid over night.

Tues. 7. Returned to Synod. At Mrs. Miller's.

Wed. 8. At Synod. At Mrs. Miller's.

Thurs. 9. Returned home.

Frid. 10. Went to Gold Hill to post office.

Sat. 11. At home.

Sund. 12. Went to Luther's church and preached from Acts 20:32. & resigned the pastoral charge of the congregation. Dinner at J. C. Earnheart's. Returned home.

Mond. 13. Tues. 14. Wed. 15. Thurs. 16. At home.

Frid. 17. Went to Gold Hill to post office.

Sat. 18. Went to Salisbury to attend the dedication of Luth. church on Sunday. All night at Wilborn Fraley's.

Sund. 19. Dr. Bowman, of Savannah, Ga. preached the dedication sermon. By request of pastor & council I performed the act of dedication. Dinner at Mr. Fraley's. By request of Reuben J. Holmes, he being too indisposed to go to church, went to his house & baptized & confirmed him, & admitted him to the communion of the church in Salisbury. I then baptized his two grand children, the children of Charles H. Holmes & wife. Supper at Mr. Fraley's. All night at Robert Lenear's.

Mond. 20. Returned home.

Tues. 21. Wed. 22. Thurs. 23. At home. Wife sick.

Frid. 24. Went in the morning to Dr. Coleman's for medicine for wife. Then at home.

Sat. 25. At home.

Sund. 26. At home. Read Scriptures.

Mond. 27. Tues. 28. Wed. 29. At home.

Thurs. 30. Ascension day. At home. Had company. Mrs. John Earnheart & Mrs. Linn called to see wife. Rain.

Frid. 31. Went to Jerry Earnheart's & had buggy wheels repaired. Dinner here. Called to see Joseph Beaver he being sick. Returned by way of Gold Hill.

Sat. June 1. In the morning went to Gold Hill to store. Then at home.

Sund. 2. Took wife to St. Peter's ch. & heard Rev. H. A. Trexler preach. Returned home.

Mond. 3. At home.

Tues. 4. In afternoon went to Mt. Pleasant. All night at Col. Shimpock's.

Wed. 5. Attended meeting of Board of Trustees of College & College exercises. At Col. Shimpock's.

Thurs. 6. Attended meeting of Board of Trustees and College exercises. In afternoon returned home.

Frid. 7. In afternoon went to Gold Hill to post office.

Sat. 8. At home.

Sund. 9. At home.

Mond. 10. In the morning went Dan Linn's (Colored) to get him to work but failed to see him.

Tues. 11. Wed. 12. At home.

Thurs. 13. Went to see Sarah J. Ritchie, widow of John Ritchie on business. Then to A. W. Klutts' Esq. & made my tax return, then home.

Frid. 14. Sat. 15. At home.

Sund. 16. At home, had no appointment.

Mond. 17. Tues. 18. Wed. 19. Thurs. 20. At home.

Frid. 18. Attended to funeral of Rev. H. A. Trexler's child at St. Peter's ch. preached from Gen. 3:19.

Sat. 22. Attended to the funeral of David M. Lyerly's child at St. Peter's ch. — preached from Matt. 25:13.

Sund. 23. At home, no appointment.

Mond. 24. At home, haying by M. A. Holshouser.

Tues. 25. Married to at my house Mr. Julius A. Castor & Mrs. Sarah Jane Ritchie. Rainy day.

Wed. 26. Thurs. 27. At home. Rev. Cox & son took dinner with us to day.

Frid. 28. Sat. 29. At home. Rainy weather.

Sund. 30. At home, plenty of rain & high water.

Mond. July 1. At home. Rev. S. L. Keller & wife took dinner with us to day.

Tues. 2. Wed. 3. At home. Rainy weather.

Thurs. 4. Attended the annual meeting of H. & F. Missionary Society at Organ church.

Frid. 5. Went to Gold Hill to post office. Revds. W. Brown & Berley took dinner with us to day.

Sat. 6. Attended the burial of Boyden Beaver's child at Lower St. church. Rev. W. R. Breached the fun[1].

Sund. 7. Went to St. Peter's ch. & heard Rev. Trexler preach.

Mond. 8. Tues. 9. Wed. 10. At home. Had wheat threshed on Wednesday.

Thurs. 11. In the morning went to Dr. Coleman's for medicine for Emma's eye. Called to see Mrs. Linker who is sorely afflicted with cancer.

Frid. 12. Went to Gold Hill to post office.

Sat. 13. At home.

Sund. 14. At home, had no appointment for this day.

Mond. 15. Tues. 16. At home.

Wed. 17. Went to Misenheimer's mill.

Thurs. 18. At home.

Frid. 19. Went to Gold Hill to post office.

Sat. 20. Went to St. Peter's church and preached for Rev. H. A. Trexler from Josh 23:8.

Sund. 21. At St. Peter's church and preached for Rev. H. A. Trexler from Gen. 5:24. & aided in the administration of Lord's Supper.

Mond. 22. At home.

Tues. 23. Went to Jerry Earnheart's & had shoeing done.

Wed. 24. At home.

Thurs. 25. At home.

Frid. 26. Went to Gold Hill to post office.

Sat. 27. At Organ ch. at Gold Hill S. S. School Convention.

Sund. 28. At home, had no appointment.

Mond. 29. Went to Gold Hill for pair of shoes.

Tues. 30. Went to Mt. Pleasant. All night at Col. John Shimpock's.

Wed. 31. Attended meeting of Board of Trustees of N. C. College. All night at Col. Shimpock's.

Thurs. Aug. 1. Returned home.
Frid. 2. Went to Gold Hill to post office.
Sat. 3. At home.
Sund. 4. Went to St. Peter's ch. & heard Rev. Trexler preach.
Mond. 5. Went to Mrs. Castor's (formerly widow Ritchie) to get a copy of Deed for her land.
Tues. 6. Took Sam$^{\underline{l}}$ to Salisbury.
Wed. 7. At home.
Thurs. 8. Want to Charley Misenheimer's to get his son to work, but failed to get him.
Frid. 9. Went to Jacob Beaver's Sale and to the post office at Gold Hill.
Sat. 10. Went to Joseph Beaver's late residence & brought some wheat home.
Sund. 11. At home.
Mond. 12. Went to Gold Hill to mill.
Tues. 13. At home. Had turnip ground plowed.
Wed. 14. In the morning went to Henry Hill's to engage a hand to work. In afternoon went to mill at Gold Hill
 & brought a bag of chop home.
Thurs. 15. At home. Sowed turnip seed.
Frid. 16. Went to Gold Hill to post office.
Sat. 17. In afternoon went to Elm Grove and heard Lewiss Mauney and Shober on subject of rail road.
Sund. 18. At home taking care of wife.
Mond. 19. Tues. 20. At home.
Wed. 21. Thurs. 22. At home.
Frid. 23. Started for Davie County to attend Sunday School day at Reformation church. All night at Matthias
 Miller.
Sat. 24. Attended Sunday School Day at Reformation church. An interesting day. In afternoon returned to Rev.
 Rose's at Zeb or Franktown. All night here.
Sund. 25. Preached at Bethel Church from Neh. 6:3. Dinner at Rev. Rose's. All night at John C. Miller's.
Mond. 26. Went to Salisbury to attend Special meeting of Synod. Had home assigned at Wilborn Fraley's.
Tues. 27. Attended special meeting of Synod.
Wed. 28. Returned home.
Thurs. 29. At home.
Frid. 30. Went to Gold Hill to post office.
Sat. 31. At home.

Sund. Sept. 1. Went to St. Peter's ch. with wife & heard Rev. H. A. Trexler preach.

Mond. 2. Tues. 3. Wed. 4. At home.

Thurs. 5. Frid. 6. At home.

Sat. 7. Went to Gold Hill to post office.

Sund. 8. Went with Lewis to St. Stephen's church & Rev. Cox preach.

Mond. 9. At home.

Tues. 10. In the morning went to Gold Hill & voted for Rail Road. In afternoon went to Rufus Fisher's & bought one bushel Pennsylvania Foltz wheat.

Wed. 11. Thurs. 12. Frid. 13. Sat. 14. At home.

Sund. 15. Took wife to St Peter's ch. & heard Rev. H. A. Trexler preach.

Mond. 16. Tues. 17. Wed. 18. Thurs. 19. At home.

Frid. 20. Went to Gold Hill to post office.

Sat. 21. At home.

Sund. 22. Took wife to see Mrs. Linker who is very much afflicted. Also to see Lottie L. Hambly, her niece, who had recently been confined.

Mond. 23. At home.

Tues. 24. Wed. 25. At home, had house rolled for Mr. Hill.

Thurs. 26. Frid. 27. Sat. 28. At home haying. Conference at St. Stephen's ch. but could not attend.

Sund. 29. Went to St. Peter's ch. & heard Rev. Allen Holshouser preach.

Mond. 30. Went to Gold Hill to post office and to mill, then to Jerry Earnheart's & had buggy repaired.

Tues. Oct. 1. At home.
Wed. 2. Thurs. 3. At home.
Frid. 4. Went to Salisbury.
Sat. 5. Went to Gold Hill to post office & to mill.
Sund. 6. Went to St. Peter's ch. & heard Rev. Trexler.
Mond. 7. At home.
Tues. 8. In afternoon went to Mt. Pleasant. All night at Col. Shimpock's.
Wed. 9. Attended meeting of Board of Trustees of N. C. College. In afternoon returned home.
Thurs. 10. Frid. 11. At home.
Sat. 12. Went to Pinkney Brady's & engaged him to repair floor of house for Mr. Hill to live in. Then went to Gold Hill to post office.
Sund. 13. At home.
Mond. 14. Attended to the funeral of Mrs. Linker, preached the funeral at the house from Matt. 5:6. and buried at Liberty.
Tues. 15. At home preparing to build a chimney.
Wed. 16. Went to Dr. Coleman's for medicine for wife and engaged Jos. A. Brown to build a chimney.
Thurs. 17. Frid. 18. At home. Had chimney built.
Sat. 19. Went to Gold Hill to post office.
Sund. 20. Went to St. Peter's ch. & heard Rev. Trexler preach, & assisted in the administration of the Lord's Supper.
Mond. 21. Tues. 22. Wed. 23. Thurs. 24. At home.
Frid. 25. In the morning went to Mrs. Linn's for a quarter of beef. Shucked corn to night.
Sat. 26. At home, a rainy day.
Sund. 27. At home.
Mond. 28. Went to Gold Hill to Store for glass &c.
Tues. 29. Went to Gold Hill to meet the mail from Salisbury. Dinner at Frank Mauney's.
Wed. 30. At home.
Thurs. 31. At home.

Frid. Nov. 1. Sat. 2. At home.

Sund. 3. Went to St. Peter's ch. to preach for Rev. Trexler, but the day being very inclement, the congregation did not turn out.

Mond. 4. Went to Earnheart's Saw mill to engage lumber for kitchen for Mr. Hill.

Tues. 5. At home.

Wed. 6. Went to Gold Hill to mill.

Thurs. 7. Went to Jerry Earnheart's & had buggy repaired. Brought grapevines home from Col. Miller's.

Frid. 8. Took waggon to Jerry Earnheart's to have it repaired.

Sat. 9. In afternoon brought home from Jerry Earnheart's.

Sund. 10. At home.

Mond. 11. At home.

Tues. 12. Went to Pink Brady's & engaged him to build kitchen for Mr. Hill.

Wed. 13. At home.

Thurs. 14. At home, had hands getting out timber for kitchen for Mr. Hill.

Frid. 15. Took wife to M. A. Holshouser's to spend the day, then went to Dr. Coleman's to see Mrs. Coleman, who had been badly hurt by being thrown out of the buggy. Brought wife home in the evening.

Sat. 16. In afternoon went to Dr. Coleman's.

Sund. 17. At home, a very rainy day.

Mond. 18. At home. This wife's birthday.

Tues. 19. Wed. 20. Thurs. 21. Frid. 22. Went to Gold Hill.

Sat. 23. In the evening went to Dr. Coleman's in relation to Mrs. Coleman's Will.

Sund. 24. At home, had no appointment.

Mond. 25. At home.

Tues. 26. At home. This my 80th birthday.

Wed. 27. At home. Had intended to slaughter my winter hogs, but the day unfavorable, had to put off.

Thurs. 28. Had winter hogs slaughtered.

Frid. 29. At home.

Sat. 30. Went to Gold Hill for glass & putty.

Sund. Dec. 1. At home reading.

Mond. 2. Went to Jacob Lyerly's to engage some pigs, but did not find him at home.

Tues. 3. At home.

Wed. 4. Went to Jacob Lyerly's & bought three pigs.

Thurs. 5. Went to Dr. Coleman's to see the sick.

Frid. 6. Went to Gold Hill to post office.

Sat. 7. Went to Salisbury.

Sund. 8. At home.

Mond. 9. Went to C. A. Basinger's to have him prove a deed. Dinner here. Then to took Mr. Basinger in my buggy & went to W. A. Klutts', Esq. to prove a Deed. Returned home.

Tues. 10. Went to Salisbury & had Deed registered.

Wed. 11. Went to Gold Hill to mill.

Thurs. 12. At home.

Frid. 13. Went in forenoon to John Earnheart's to have coat made.

Sat. 14. Took Mrs. Wadkins & sister to Gold Hill, then went to Elm Grove & joined the Alliance.

Sund. 15. Took wife to St. Peter's ch. and Rev. H. A. Trexler preach.

Mond. 16. Tues. 17. At home.

Wed. 18. Went in the afternoon to Gold Hill to the post office & to get Horse Shoes & nails.

Thurs. 19. Went in the afternoon to Jerry Earnheart's & had Horse shod.

Frid. 20. Went to Gold Hill to post office.

Sat. 21. In the morning went to Gold Hill to the Store.

Sund. 22. At home reading.

Mond. 23. Tues. 24. At home.

Wed. 25. Christmas Day. Weather warm & pleasant. Went to Organ Church & heard Rev. W. R. Brown preach.

Thurs. 26. At home. Paul Philips, wife & others called & spent the day.

Frid. 27. Took a pair of chickens to Calvin Pool's. Dinner here.

Sat. 28. Sund. 29. At home.

Mond. 30. In the afternoon went to John A. Peeler's to engage him to do some work to smoke house. Rain & turned cold.

Tues. 31. At home.

Wed. Jan. 1, 1890. New Year. Went to Wilson Kesler's and paid over a check by Cook & Foil on the National Bank of Concord, for forty dollars as interest on Kesler's Note against N. C. College.

Thurs. 2. Went with family to Solomon Peeler's & took dinner. In afternoon at home.

Frid. 3. At home.

Sat. 4. Went to Gold Hill to post office.

Sund. 5. At home, wife frail & infirm.

Mond. 6. Went to A. Trexler's Saw mill to engage some lumber but found him not at home. Then went to the Alliance Store & bout some Sugar and Cheese.

Tues. 7. Wed. 8. Thurs. 9. Frid. 10. At home, weather warm.

Sat. 11. Went to Gold Hill to post office.

Sund. 12. At home reading.

Mond. 13. Tues. 14. At home.

Wed. 15. Went to Misenheimer's mill.

Thurs. 16. At home, weather turned cold.

Frid. 17. At home.

Sat. 18. In afternoon attended Elm Grove Alliance meeting.

Sund. 19. Married at my house John W. Linker and Mary A. L. Brown. Then at home.

Mond. 20. Went to Jerry Earnheart's & had clevis made. Dinner here. Returned home by way of Gold Hill.

Tues. 21. Went to Salisbury.

Wed. 22. Thurs. 23. At home.

Frid. 24. Sat. 25. At home. Weather cold for several days.

Sund. 26. At home.

Mond. 27. Went in the forenoon to M. A. Holshouser's & brought Phebe Brown to see us.

Tues. 28. At home. Wed. 29. At home.

Thurs. 30. Took wife & Mrs. Brown to Mrs. Linn's on a visit. In the evening brought them home again.

Frid. 31. Went to Gold Hill to mill & post office.

Sat. Feb. 1. At home.

Sund. 2. At home with wife, she being very frail.

Mond. 3. At home.

Tues. 4. In forenoon went to Dr. Coleman's and to Trexler's saw mill. In afternoon took my wife to St. Peter's ch. to burial of old Mrs. Earnheart.

Wed. 5. Went to Salisbury for medicine for wife.

Thurs. 6. Frid. 7. Sat. 8. At home.

Sund. 9. At home, day inclement.

Mond. 10. At home.

Tues. 11. Went to the Alliance store for sugar & coffee, but the store keeper not being at home, failed in getting the articles.

Wed. 12. At home. Thurs. 13. Frid. 14. At home.

Sat. 15. Went to the Alliance Store & bought some Coffee & Sugar.

Sund. 16. Took wife to St Peter's ch. & heard Rev. H. A. Trexler preach.

Mond. 17. Went to Trexler's Saw Mill & bought some lumber.

Tues. 18. At home.

Wed. 19. Went to Gold Hill to mill.

Thurs. 20. Frid. 21. Sat. 22. At home.

Sund. 23. At home, had no appointment.

Mond. 24. Tues. 25. Wed. 26. At home.

Thurs. 27. From this time up to March 24. At home confined to house & bed together, being sick with deep seated cold, or la grippe.

March. 25. Went to Gold Hill to post office.

Wed. 26. Took wife to Mrs. Linn's to spend the day. Then went to Dr. Coleman's for seed sweet potatoes. In the evening brout wife home.

Thurs. 27. In forenoon went to Gold Hill to post office.

Frid. 28. Attended examination at our School House.

Sat. 29. In afternoon went to George Troutman's and staid over night. Had an attack of cholic and spent a very restless night.

Sund. 30. Married Mr. Robert J. Coleman and Miss Laura C. Troutman. Very indisposed to day, so much so that I could not return home.

Mond. 31. Mr. Troutman brought in his buggy as far as Trexler's Cotton gin.

Tues. April 1. to Sat. 5. At home quite unwell.

Sund. 6. At home quite unwell. Baptized to day at my home the infant child of Rev. H. A. Trexler & wife.

Mond. 7. At home.

Tues. 8. Went to mill & post office at Gold Hill.

Wed. 9. At home.

Thurs. 10. Took wife to M. A. Holshouser's to spend the day. Then went to Jerry Earnheart's and had horse shod. In the evening brought wife home.

Frid. 11. Went to Gold Hill to post office.

Sat. 12. At home.

Sund. 13. At home reading Bible.

Mond. 14. Went to Salisbury.

Tues. 15. Went to Alliance Store & bought fish &c.

Wed. 16. At home.

Thurs. 17. Frid. 18. At home.

Sat. 19. In afternoon attended Alliance meeting at Elm Grove.

Sund. 20. Mond. 21. At home.

Tues. 22. In afternoon went to Trexler's Saw mill for lumber to make chicken coop.

Wed. 23. Went to Gold Hill to post office.

Thurs. 24. At home.

Frid. 25. Went to Gold Hill to post office.

Sat. 26. Sund. 27. At home, wife sick.

Mond. 28. At home, wife sick.

Tues. 29. At home. wife still sick.

Wed. 30. Wife died this morning at 3 o'clock.

Thurs. May 1. Buried my wife at Union Church. Could not attend the burial being sick with derangement of the bowels.

Frid. 2. At home. quite unwell.

Sat. 3. Sund. 4. At home, not well.

Mond. 5. Went to Dr. Coleman's & brought Mrs. C. who staid over night.

Tues. 6. Had wife's clothing &c. divided. Took Mrs. Coleman home.

Wed. 7. Went to Gold Hill to mill.

Thurs. 8. Frid. 9. Sat. 10. At home, not well.

Sund. 11. Mond. 12. At home, not well.

Tues. 13. to Sat. 17. At home.

Sund. 18. Attended preaching at St. Peter's church. To day Rev. H. A. Trexler preached wife's funeral from Phil. 1:21. A large congregation of people.

Mond. 19. Tues. 20. Wed. 21. At home.

Thurs. 22. At home.

Frid. 23. Went to Gold Hill to mill and post office.

Sat. 24. Took some chickens to Gold Hill. Then went to Alliance Store. Dinner at Eli Beaver's.

Sund. 25. At home reading Bible.

Mond. 26. Tues. 27. At home.

Wed. 28. Went to Gold Hill to attend to some business for W. L. Shaver.

Thurs. 29. At home.

Frid. 30. Went to Gold Hill to post office. In the evening brought a borrowed cow home from M. A. Holshouser's.

Sat. 31. In afternoon attended Alliance Meeting at Elm Grove.

Sund. June 1. Went to St. Peter's ch. and heard Rev. H. A. Trexler preach.

Mond. 2. Went with Lewis to Mt. Pleasant. All night at Col. Shimpock's.

Tues. 3. In afternoon returned home.

Wed. 4. At home.

Thurs. 5. In the morning went to Gold Hill and made tax return. In afternoon went to Jacob C. Earnheart's & staid over night.

Frid. 6. Returned home.

Sat. 7. At home.

Sund. 8. At home reading Bible &c.

Mond. 9. Tues. 10. At home.

Wed. 11. Went to Salisbury & engaged tomb stones for wife's grave.

Thurs. 12. Went to Union Church to the pick-nic of the Salisbury Lutheran Sunday School.

Frid. 13. At home.

Sat. 14. At home.

Sund. 15. Preached at St. Peter's ch. from Prov. 23:17.18.

Mond. 16. Tues. 17. Wed. 18. At home.

Thurs. 19. Went to Jerry Earnheart's & had horse shod. In afternoon went to M. A. Holshouser's on business.

Frid. 20. At home.

Sat. 21. At home.

Sund. 22. Went to Christiana ch. and heard Rev. Wertz preach. Dinner at Albert Thomas'.

Mond. 23. Went to Trexler's Saw mill on business.

Tues. 24. Went to Gold Hill to post office.

Wed. 25. Thurs. 26. At home.

Frid. 27. Went to Organ ch. to Meeting of Southern Conference. Returned home.

Sat. 28. At Southern Conference. Returned home.

Sund. 29. At Southern Conference. Returned home.

Mond. 30. My Alliance friends met and made my hay.

Tues. July 1. At home.
Wed. 2. Thurs. 3. At home.
Frid. 4. Went to Gold Hill to post office.
Sat. 5. In afternoon went Elm Grove Alliance.
Sund. 6. Went to St. Peter's ch. and heard Rev. H. A. Trexler preach.
Mond. 7. Went to Gold Hill to post office.
Tues. 8. At home.
Wed. 9. Went to H. A. Miller's and engaged a sack of flour. Dinner here.
Thurs. 10. Went to H. A. Miller's and brought sack flour home.
Frid. 11. Went to Gold Hill to post office. In afternoon went to Franklin Crowell's to see wheat threshers. Supper here.
Sat. 12. At home. Had wheat threshed.
Sund. 13. Preached at Christiana from John 20:23. Had a good & attentive congregation. Dinner at Nathan Brown's.
Mond. 14. At home.
Tues. 15. Went to Gold Hill to post office.
Wed. 16. At home.
Thurs. 17. At home. Frid. 18. At home.
Sat. 19. In forenoon attended meeting of Alliance at Elm Grove. Dinner at Boyden A. Miller's. Then went to primary meeting at Bernhardt's mill. Then went to J. L. Graeber's & staid over night.
Sund. 20. In the morning called to see Mrs. Frederic Stirewalt who has been afflicted for a long time. Administered to her the communion. Then went to Ebenezer & preached from Prov. 23:17.18. Assisted Rev. W. R. Brown in the administration of the communion. All night at J. A. Eddleman's.
Mond. 21. Returned home.
Tues. 22. At home.
Wed. 23. Called to see Mrs. Sally Holshouser, mother of L. G. Holshouser, she being sick. Then called at C. L. Brown's. In afternoon called to see Jacob Holshouser, he being palsy stricken & helpless. Had devotional exercises at his bedside.
Thurs. 24. Went to Gold Hill to post office.
Frid. 25. Went to Gold Hill to post office.
Sat. 26. Went to Alliance Store for sugar & coffee.
Sund. 27. At home reading Bible.
Mond. 28. Went to L. G. Holshouser's, his mother having died, & had devotional services at the house. Returned home. A rainy day.
Tues. 29. At home.
Wed. 30. Went to R. R. Commissary & bartered some bacon for coffee and sugar.
Thurs. 31. Took some cabbage to Dr. Coleman's & to the Commissary at Mr. Hambley's farm.

Frid. Aug. 1. Went to Gold Hill to mill and post office.

Sat. 2. Attended Missionary Meeting at St. Peter's ch.

Sund. 3. Went to St. Peter's ch. & heard Rev. Trexler preach.

Mond. 4. In afternoon went to Moses Frick's and staid over night.

Tues. 5. Employed Mr. Frick to go to Salisbury & haul Wife's Grave Stones to Union church. Then went to Mrs. Shemwell's & staid over night.

Wed. 6. Went to Union Church Grave Yard and had B. C. Arey & Thomas Eller to set up Wife's Grave Stones to her grave. Returned home.

Thurs. 7. At home.

Frid. 8. Went to Gold Hill to post office.

Sat. 9. After dinner went to Dr. Coleman's and baptized E. B. C. Hambley's child. Then went to Charles Lyerly's and staid over night.

Sund. 10. Preached at Christiana from Jam. 1:25. Dinner at Milas Miller's. Returned home.

Mond. 11. Went to Jerry Earnheart's, in forenoon & had horse shod. Then at home.

Tues. 12. At home.

Wed. 13. Thurs. 14. At home writing.

Frid. 15. Went to Gold Hill to post office. Then to the Alliance at Elm Grove.

Sund. 16. Went to Lower Stone ch. to Township (of Gold Hill) Sunday School Convention. Emma sister Kate an her husband with us to night.

Sund. 17. At home reading.

Mond. 18. Went to William Wilkinson's & brought Emma home, she having gone there with her sister. In evening attended arbitration meeting at our free school house.

Tues. 19. In afternoon went to Michael Reinhardt's & staid over night. Mr. R. gave a half bushel of Folcaster wheat for seed.

Wed. 20. Called at John Foil's & bought some seed wheat (Folcaster). Then returned home.

Thurs. 21. At home, made sour crout.

Frid. 22. Sowed turnip seed. Then to went R. R. Commissary & sold some chickens. Then went to Gold Hill to post office.

Sat. 23. At home.

Sund. 24. At home reading the New Testament.

Mond. 25. Went to Geo. Park's, to Trexler's Saw mill &c. on business.

Tues. 26. Took some onions, potatoes, & cabbage to the R. R. Commissary at Hambley's farm. Sold Molly & calf to day to Jacob Holshouser.

Wed. 27. Went to Jerry Earnheart's Shop. Then to Gold Hill to post office.

Thurs. 28. At home.

Frid. 29. Went to Gold Hill to post office, but high water prevented the mail from arriving.

Sat. 30. Went to Jerry Earnheart's to shop, & then to Gold Hill to post office.

Sund. 31. At home reading.

Mond. Sep. 1. At home.

Tues. 2. Went R. R. Commissary to sell apples, but failed to sell then.

Wed. 3. At home. Wrote Mrs. Freeman's will at her request.

Thurs. 4. Brought some lumber home for gate.

Frid. 5. At home.

Sat. 6. Attended Elm Grove Alliance.

Sund. 7. Went to St. Peter's ch. and heard Rev. H. A. Trexler preach.

Mond. 8. At home. Mrs. Phebe Brown left to day for Richmond.

Tues. 9. Went to Gold Hill to post office.

Wed. 10. Went to R. R. Commissary and sold some apples.

Thurs. 11. At home.

Frid. 12. Went to Gold Hill to mill and to post office.

Sat. 13. Went to Rock quarry & to see culvert at L. G. Holshouser's.

Sund. 14. At home, a very rainy day.

Mond. 15. Rode around to engage hands to make hay the following week.

Tues. 16. At home.

Wed. 17. Went to Gold Hill to post office & to buy shoes for myself & Emma.

Thurs. 18. At home

Frid. 19. Went to Gold Hill to post office.

Sat. 20. At home.

Sund. 21. At home reading.

Mond. 22. At home haying.

Tues. 23. Wed. 24. At home haying.

Thurs. 25. Started for Salisbury as far as Rockwell, but returned home on account of rain.

Frid. 26. In forenoon went to Gold Hill to post office. In afternoon went to R. R. Commissary and sold some apples & watermelon.

Sat. 27. At home.

Sund. 28. At home reading.

Mond. 29. Tues. 30. At home.

Wed. Oct. 1. At home. Rev. Calvin Sifferd gave me a short call.

Thurs. 2. In afternoon went to R. Road Commissary and sold some apples.

Frid. 3. Went to Gold Hill to post office.

Sat. 4. At home.

Sund. 5. Went to St. Peter's church & Rev. Trexler being sick, preached from James 1:25.

Mond. 6. Went to R. Road Commissary and sold some apples.

Tues. 7. At home.

Wed. 8. Preached the funeral of Diana Misemer at the house from Heb. 9:27. Friends buried her at Union church.

Thurs. 9. At home.

Frid. 10. Went to Gold Hill to post office. In afternoon took apples to R. R. Commissary.

Sat. 11. Took ham of meat to Commissary at Mr. Hambley's plantation. Called also at Dr. Coleman's, then returned home.

Sund. 12. At home reading bible.

Mond. 13. At home.

Tues. 14. Went in morning to Gold Hill and registered. In afternoon took apples to R. Road Commissary.

Wed. 15. Thurs. 16. At home.

Frid. 17. Went to Gold Hill to post office.

Sat. 18. Went to St. Peter's ch. & heard Rev. Prof. Fisher preach.

Sund. 19. Went to St. Peter's ch. & heard Rev. Prof Fisher preach. Assisted in the services and the administration of the Communion.

Mond. 20. Went to Jerry Earnheart's and had shoeing done. Returned by way of post office at Gold Hill.

Tues. 21. Wed. 22. Thurs. 23. At home.

Frid. 24. Went to Gold Hill to post office, paid Tax, & heard candidates speak.

Sat. 25. At home.

Sund. 26. At home reading Bible.

Mond. 27. At home.

Tues. 28. Attended to the funeral Fannie L. Linker, daughter of George W. & Mary E. Linker. Preached the funeral at the house from Eccl. 12:1. & buried at St. Peter's church.

Wed. 29. Thurs. 30. At home.

Frid. 31. Divided Mr. Hill's corn. Then went to Gold Hill to post office.

Sat. Nov 1. At home.

Sund. 2. Preached at St. Peter's ch. from 1 Kings 19:9. the pastor, Rev. Trexler being sick & absent.

Mond. 3. Went to Alliance Store for Kerosene Oil.

Tues. 4. In forenoon went to Gold Hill & voted. In afternoon called to see Geo. Linker, he being sick. Called also at Dr. Coleman's.

Wed. 5. Went to Dr. Coleman's & went with Mrs. Coleman to John Miller's on business. Dinner at Dr. Coleman's.

Thurs. 6. At home.

Frid. 7. In forenoon went to Boyden Miller's and bought one & half bushels Fulcaster Wheat to sow. In afternoon went to Gold Hill to post office.

Sat. 8. At home.

Sund. 9. At home reading Bible.

Mond. 10. Tues. 11. Wed. 12. Thurs. 13. At home.

Frid. 14. Went to Gold Hill to mill and the the post office.

Sat. 15. At home.

Sund. 16. Went to St. Peter's church and heard Rev. H. A. Trexler preach.

Mond. 17. At home.

Tues. 18. Went to Rockwell post office, thence to Rail Road & down the road to Second Creek, to view the road & tressel across the creek. Dinner at Jesse Miller's.

Wed. 19. Went to see the mud cut back of Mr. Crowell's & called at Lyl's commissary. In afternoon went to Gold Hill for sack salt.

Thurs. 20. Went to Gold Hill & sold side of bacon.

Frid. 21. In afternoon went to Gold Hill to post office.

Sat. 22. At home.

Sund. 23. At home reading.

Mond. 24. Intercepted the mail & sent off a letter of excuse for non-attendance at Conference. Then at home.

Tues. 25. In forenoon went to Gold Hill & bought a pair of shoes. Then at home.

Wed. 26. This my 81st birthday. Went to Ellen Grupey's & married Benjamin E. Sumner and Sophie Kesler. All night here.

Thurs. 27. Went to Union church expecting thanksgiving services, but no such appointment had been made. Dinner at Rev. Wertz's. Returned home.

Frid. 28. Went to Gold Hill to post office.

Sat. 29. Called to see some neighbors to arrange for slaughtering hogs. Then at home.

Sund. 30. At home reading.

Mond. Dec. 1. Had hogs slaughtered.

Tues. 2. Went in forenoon to Rail Road to see convicts work.

Wed. 3. Went in forenoon to Jacob Lyerly's to engage some pigs, & in afternoon went to bring them home, but fail to bring them.

Thurs 4. Married at my house James M. Wood & Emma J. Small. In afternoon went to Jacob Lyerly's & brought pigs home.

Frid. 5. Went to Gold Hill to post office. In afternoon called to George Linker, he being sick.

Sat. 6. At home till after dinner, then went to Rockwell & mailed some letters.

Sund. 7. A rainy day. At home reading.

Mond. 8. Attended to the funeral of George W. Linker at St. Peter's ch. – preached from Job 14:14.

Tues. 9. At home.

Wed. 10. Went to Gold Hill to mill.

Thurs. 11. Went in forenoon to George Bost's & had some work done to buggy. In afternoon went to Jacob Holshouser's to engage some corn but failed.

Frid. 12. Went to Gold Hill to post office.

Sat. 13. At home.

Sund. 14. At home reading.

Mond. 15. At home. Capt. J. Fisher & Mr. Ramsey (Editor Watchman) with us to night.

Tues. 16. Wed. 17. At home, inclement weather.

Thurs. 18. In forenoon went to Gold Hill to store & bought 4 lbs coffee. In afternoon took Lilly Patterson to Dr. Coleman's.

Frid. 19. Went to Gold Hill to post office.

Sat. 20. At home.

Sund. 21. Went to St. Peter's ch. & heard Rev. H. A. Trexler preach.

Mond. 22. Went to Gold Hill to post office.

Tues. 23. Wed. 24. At home.

Thurs. 25. Christmas Day. At home reading, the weather being cold and inclement.

Frid. 26. At home.

Sat. 27. Went to Gold Hill to Post office.

Sund. 28. At home reading.

Mond. 29. At home. Tobie Brown called to see me.

Tues. 30. Wed. 31. At home.

Thurs. Jan. 1, 1891. At home, reading.
Frid. 2. Went to Gold Hill to mill & Post office.
Sat. 3. At home.
Sund. 4. At home reading.
Mond. 5. Tues. 6. At home.
Wed. 7. Went to M. A. Holshouser's to intercept the mail carrier to send off a letter.
Thurs. 8. At home.
Frid. 9. Went to St Peter's ch. to the burial of Mrs. John D. Brown. Rev. Trexler preached.
Sat. 10. Went to Gold Hill to Post office.
Sund. 11. At home, reading.
Mond. 12. Tues. 13. Wed. 14. Thurs. 15. Frid. 16. At home and very unwell with cold.
Sat. 17. to Tues. 27. Confined to the house.
Wed. 28. to Sat. 31. At home — not stout.

Feb. 1. to Mond. 9. At home — not stout.
Tues. 10. Frid. 13. At home, health feeble.
Sat. 14. In the afternoon went in my buggy to Franklin Crowell's, who was badly hurt by the falling of a piece
    of timber.
Sund. 15. At home. Married to day Mr. Joseph A. Basinger & Miss Minnie E. Stikeleather.
Mond. 16. At home.
Tues. 17. Wed. 18. Thurs. 19. Frid. 20. At home.
Sat. 21. Attended to the funeral of L. J. Hampton's infant child at St. Peter's church. Preached from Mark
    10:13-16.
Sund. 22. Mond. 23. At home.
Tues. 24. In the afternoon called to see Franklin Crowell in his afflicted condition.
Wed. 25. Went to Gold Hill to mill & post office.
Thurs. 26. Frid. 27. At home.
Sat. 28. At home.

Sund. March 1. At home.

Mond. 2. Tues. 3. Wed. 4. At home.

Thurs. 5. Called to see Mrs. David Brady. she being much afflicted. Had devotional exercises at her bed side.

Frid. 6. Sat. 7. At home.

Sund. 8. At home.

Mond. 9. At home.

Tues. 10. In afternoon went to see Mr. F. Crowell, he being much afflicted.

Wed. 11. At home.

Thurs. 12. Mr. Crowell having died, went to his residence to see him carried off to be buried.

Frid. 13. Sat. 14. Sund. 15. At home.

Mond. 16. Went in forenoon to Gold Hill to mill.

Tues. 17. At home very unwell with cold.

Wed. 18. Thurs. 19. Frid. 20. At home.

Sat. 21. Attended the closing exercises of Bethany Academy.

Sund. 22. Mond. 23. At home.

Tues. 24. Wed. 25. Thurs. 26. At home.

Frid. 27. Good Friday. At home.

Sat. 28. At home.

Sund. 29. Easter. At home reading.

Mond. 30. Tues. 31. At home.

Wed. April 1. Went to Gold Hill to post office.

Thurs. 2. Went to Gold Hill & married Mr. Thomas R. Sheets and Jennie Crowell, daughter of W. H. Crowell.

Frid. 3. Sat. 4. At home.

Sund. 5. At home. Married to day at my house James R. Sparnell & Ida C. McAllister.

Mond. 6. At home.

Tues. 7. Went to Rockwell post office and mailed some letters.

Wed. 8. Went to C. L. Brown's, Mrs. Ribelin having died. In the absence of the pastor, attended, by request, to religious services at the house. Then went to Gold Hill to post office.

Thurs. 9. At home.

Frid. 10. Went to Gold Hill to post office.

Sat. 11. Sund. 12. At home.

Mond. 13. Tues. 14. Wed. 15. At home.

Thurs. 16. Took Mrs. Lilly to Rockwell Depot, then went to Alliance Store at Elm Grove.

Frid. 17. Went to Gold Hill to post office.

Sat. 18. In afternoon went to Elm Grove Alliance.

Sund. 19. Went to St. Peter's ch. & heard Rev. Trexler preach. Assisted in the administration of the Lord's Supper.

Mond. 20. Tues. 21. Wed. 22. At home.

Thurs. 23. Went to Dr. Coleman's & had tooth extracted.

Frid. 24. Went to Gold Hill to post office.

Sat. 25. Went to Alliance Store & attended a meeting at Elm Grove of the neighbors to consult about building a church.

Sund. 26. At home.

Mond. 27. At home.

Tues. 28. At home.

Wed. 29. Started for Synod at Enockville. Went Rail Road to China Grove. Over night at J. M. Eddleman's.

Thurs. 30. Went by private conveyance to seat of Synod. Home assigned by Pastor Lutz at his house.

May 1-5. In Synod.

Wed. 6. Rev. Lutz had me conveyed to China Grove. Over night at Mr. Winecoff's.

Thurs. 7. By R. R. to Salisbury. Stopped with W. C. Fraley's till following day.

Frid. 8. Heard Ben Ferrel speak, then returned home with Lewis.

Sat. 9. In forenoon went to Gold Hill to post office. In afternoon went to Alliance Store, then to Rockwell Depot & brought barrell of Sugar home.

Sund. 10. At home.

Mond. 11. In the morning went to John V. Fisher's in relation to dividing barrel of Sugar.

Tues. 12. At home. Divided barrel sugar.

Wed. 13. Went to Jerry Earnheart's and had horse shod & buggy tire shrunk. Rainy afternoon.

Thurs. 14. At home.

Frid. 15. Went to Gold Hill to post office.

Sat. 16. Attended Alliance at Elm Grove, in the afternoon.

Sund. 17. Went to St. Peter's church and heard Rev. H. A. Trexler preach.

Mond. 18. Tues. 19. Wed. 20. Thurs. 21. At home.

Frid. 22. Went to Gold Hill to mill & post office.

Sat. 23. At home.

Sund. 24. Went to Organ church & heard Rev. W. R. Brown preach. Dinner at Rev. Brown's.

Mond. 25. At home.

Tues. 26. At home. Baptized to day at my house G. W. Linker's child & John W. Linker's child.

Wed. 27. Thurs. 28. At home.

Frid. 29. Went to Gold to post office.

Sat. 30. At home, had gates & fence made and milk box covered.

Sund. 31. Went to Elm Grove to hear Rev. Cox preach but he failed to attend. Rev. H. A. Trexler preached.

Mond. June 1. Tues. 2. At home.

Wed. 3. Went to Rockwell & made tax return. Dinner at Dr. Coleman's.

Thurs. 4. At home.

Frid. 5. Went to Alliance Store, and then to Gold Hill to post office.

Sat. 6. At home.

Sund. 7. Preached the funeral of Geo. Bame at St. Matthew's church from 2 Tim. 4:6-8. Dinner at Mr. Bame's a son of deceased. Returned home.

Mond. 8. Took the train at Rockwell to Salisbury. Stopped at Mr. W. C. Fraley's & remained over night.

Tues. 9. Took the train in the morning for Lexington and was met here by Caleb Peeler who carried me to his house. Remained here till next day.

Wed. 10. Went with Sister Salome Peeler to Winston. Stopped at Calvin Miller's and remained till Friday 12th. Here met with Sister Mary, probably for the last time.

Frid. 12. Returned to Caleb Peeler's. Called to see Eliza & Anna Rothrock. Dinner here. Called also to see Charles Rothrock. Supper here. Returned to C. Peeler's.

Sat. 13. Went with Sister Salome to see Hugh Beckerdite's daughters, thence to Mich[l] Bodenhamer's. Dinner here. Returned to C. Peeler's.

Sund. 14. Went with Esther Lutz to Friedburg & heard Rev. Hall preach. Visited also the Grave Yard where my parents are buried. Returned to C. Peeler's.

Mond. 15. Started for home. Master Peeler Nifong brought me Lexington, there took the train for Salisbury, there took the train for Gold Hill, thence returned home.

Tues. 16. At home.

Wed. 17. In afternoon called to see Mrs. H. A. Miller, she being sick.

Thurs. 18. At home.

Frid. 19. Went to Gold Hill to post office.

Sat. 20. In afternoon attended Alliance at Elm Grove.

Sund. 21. Went to St. Peter's ch. and heard Rev. J. A. Linn preach.

Mond. 22. Tues. 23. Wed. 24. At home.

Thurs. 25. Called to Mrs. H. A. Miller, she being sick.

Frid. 26. Went to Gold Hill to post office.

Sat. 27. Sund. 28. Mond. 29. At home.

Tues. 30. At home.

Wed. July 1. Thurs. 2. At home.

Frid. 3. In afternoon went to Gold Hill to post office.

Sat. 4. Went to Organ church to W. H. and F. Missionary Meeting. All night at William Beaver's.

Sund. 5. Went to Lower Stone Church and heard Rev. Heller preach. Dinner at Boyden Miller's.

Mond. 6. At home.

Tues. 7. Wed. 8. Thurs. 9. At home.

Frid. 10. In the morning went to Rockwell post office. In afternoon went to Gold Hill to post office.

Sat. 11. At home.

Sund. 12. At home reading.

Mond. 13. Tues. 14. At home.

Wed. 15. In forenoon went to Gold Hill to post office. In afternoon went to Mich^{l} Morgan's & bought some tar for milk box.

Thurs. 16. At home.

Frid. 17. Buried Wilson Kesler at St. Matthew's ch. preached from Matth. 25:13.

Sat. 18. Went with Mrs. Coleman to Mrs. Nancy Shumwell's. Dinner at Calvin Pool's. All night at Mrs. Shemwell's.

Sund. 19. Preached at Union church from Prov. 23:17.18. Returned home.

Mond. 20. At home. Had wheat threshed.

Tues. 21. Wed. 22. At home.

Thurs. 23. Went to Adam Holshouser's and had horse shod.

Frid. 24. Went to Salisbury. Dinner at W. C. Fraley's.

[August 1891]

Miller's daughter Maggie.

Mond. 31. Went to Gold Hill to mill.

Tues. Sept. 1. Went to Salisbury.

Wed. 2. Went to H. A. Miller's mill.

Thurs. 3. Started for Albemarles. Stopped at Ritchie's mill and staid over night, at Daniel Ritchie's.

Frid. 4. Boarded the train in the evening & went to Albemarle. Stopped at Mrs. Lilly's.

Sat. 5. At Mrs. Lilly's.

Sund. 6. Preached at Luth. Church from Ex. 20:7. Took supper at Mr. Sydny Hearne's. Preached again at night from Prov. 23:17.18. All night at Mrs. Lilly's.

Mond. 7. Returned home.

Tues. 8. At home.

Wed. 9. Went to Gold Hill to post office.

Thurs. 10. Went to Jerry Earnheart's and had buggy wheel repaired.

Frid. 11. Sat. 12. At home.

Sund. 13. Went to Luther's church & heard Rev. C. C. Lyerly preach the funeral of David C. Parker & daughter dec[d]. Dinner at Crasa Ann Parker's, widow of David C. Parker. Returned home.

Mond. 14. Went to Alliance Store & bought horse shoes & nails. Then went to Jerry Earnheart's and had shoeing done.

Tues. 15. Went to Joseph Kesler's in forenoon in relation to a note oweing by N. C. College. In afternoon went to M. A. Holshouser's to see old lady Peeler.

Wed. 16. At home.

Thurs. 17. In the afternoon went to Rockwell post office & mailed some letters. Called also at Dr. Coleman's.

Frid. 18. At home.

Sat. 19. In afternoon attended Elm Grove Alliance.

Sund. 20. Went to St. Peter's ch. & heard Rev. H. A. Trexler preach.

Mond. 21. At home.

Tues. 22. Started for Nazareth ch. in Forsyth co. as far as Salisbury. All night at Jacob Randleman's.

Wed. 23. Boarded the train for Greensboro and Winston. Reached Winston at 12 M. & stopped with J. C. Miller & remained till next day.

Thurs. 24. Went by R. R. to Rural Hall. Staid over night at Mrs. Payne's.

Frid. 25. Preached at Nazareth ch. from Prov. 23:17.18. All night at A. P. Styer's.

Sat. 26. Preached at Nazareth ch. from James 1:25. Installed Church Council. All night at W. W. Kapp's.

Sund. 27. Preached Nazareth ch. from Ex. 20:7. All night James W. Newsom's.

Mond. 28. Returned by R. R. to Winston. All night at J. Calvin Miller's.

Tues. 29. Returned home by R. Road.

Wed. 30. At home.

Thurs. Oct. 1. At home.

Frid. 2. Went to Gold Hill to post office.

Sat. 3. Went to Gold Hill to post office.

Sund. 4. Preached at St. Peter's ch. from Neh. 6:3.

Mond. 5. At home.

Tues. 6. In afternoon went with Lewis to Mt. Pleasant. All night at Col. Shimpock's.

Wed. 7. Attended meeting of Trustees of N. C. College. At night attended inauguration of Rev. J. D. Shirey as President of College. Home assigned at Col. Shimpock's.

Thurs. 8. Returned home.

Frid. 9. At home.

Sat. 10. In the morning went to Dr. Coleman's to see Kate Quantz.

Sund. 11. At home. Rainy day.

Mond. 12. In the morning to Joseph W. Kesler's and turned over a check from Jonas Cook, Treasurer B. Trust. of N. C. College.

Tues. 13. Wed. 14. At home.

Thurs 15. At home.

Frid. 16. Went to Gold Hill to post office.

Sat. 17. Went to St. Peter's ch. & heard Rev. H. A. Trexler preach. In afternoon went to Alliance at Elm Grove.

Sund. 18. Took Mrs. J. J. Quantz to St. Peter's ch. & heard Rev. H. A. Trexler preach & assisted in the administration of the Lord's Supper.

Mond. 19. Went to H. A. Miller's mill.

Tues. 20. At home.

Wed. 21. Went to Gold Hill to post office.

Thurs. 22. Went to H. A. Miller's mill.

Frid. 23. Went to Gold Hill to post office.

Sat. 24. Went to Gold Hill to post office. In afternoon went to M. A. Holshouser's & brought Mrs. Kate Quantz to Lewis'.

Sund. 25. At home.

Mond. 26. Took Mrs. Quantz to Calvin Pool's. Dinner here.

Tues. 27. Wed. 28. At home.

Thurs. 29. At home.

Frid. 30. Buried Mrs. Margaret Trexler at St. Peter's church. Preached from Heb. 4:9.

Sat. 31. Went to Gold Hill to post office.

Sund. Nov. 1. Went to St. Peter's ch. and heard Rev. H. A. Trexler preach.

Mond. 2. In afternoon went to Rockwell P. Office.

Tues. 3. Went to Danl Ritchie's. Dinner here. In afternoon went to Danl Cassel's for honey, but failed to get any. Returned home.

Wed. 4. Thurs. 5. At home.

Frid. 6. Went to Gold Hill to mill & post office.

Sat. 7. At home.

Sund. 8. Went to Organ church and heard Rev. W. R. Brown preach. Dinner at Eli Holshouser's.

Mond. 9. Called to see Peter Miller, he being over four years my senior & somewhat afflicted. Dinner here.

Tues. 10. At home.

Wed. 11. Went to Jacob Lyerly's and engaged two pigs.

Thurs. 12. At home.

Frid. 13. At home.

Sat. 14. In the morning went to Gold Hill to post office, in afternoon attended Elm Grove Alliance.

Sund. 15. Went to Lower Stone church & heard Rev. Heller preach. Returned home.

Mond. 16. Tues. 17. At home.

Wed. 18. In afternoon went to M. A. Holshouser's to engage him to help slaughter my hogs.

Thurs. 19. At home. Had my hogs slaughtered.

Frid. 20. At home.

Sat. 21. At home.

Sund. 22. At home. Married at my house Dr. L. N. Burleyson & Ella M. Parker.

Mond. 23. At home.

Tues. 24. Went to Gold Hill to mill.

Wed. 25. In afternoon went to M. A. Holshouser's, to Dr. Coleman's, & to A. Trexler's saw mill.

Thurs. 26. This my 82nd birthday. Mrs. Jane Coleman & Lottie Hambley & children took dinner with us. In the evening, Lewis & family took supper with us.

Frid. 27. Sat. 28. At home.

Sund. 29. At home, a snowy day.

Mond. 30. Went to Rockwell Depot in the afternoon preparatory to boarding the train next morning for Salisbury. All night at Mrs. Mary Peeler's.

Tues. Dec. 1. Boarded to train & went to Salisbury under subpena as witness for Joseph Kesler. The case was postponed to following Court. Returned home.

Wed. 2. At home.

Thurs. 3. At home. Frid. 4. At home.

Sat. 5. Went to Gold Hill to post office.

Sund. 6. Sund. 6. Went to St. Peter's ch. and heard Prof. C. L. T. Fisher preach. Prof. Fisher took dinner with me.

Mond. 7. At home.

Tues. 8. Went to Dr. Coleman's & took dinner, then went to Mr. Hambley's farm to see his fine stock.

Wed. 9. Went to Alex. Trexler's saw mill, in the forenoon, to engage some lumber.

Thurs. 10. Had Mr. M. A. Holshouser & Solomon Peeler to haul corn for me from Mr. J. McAnless' farm. Went with the wagons. Dinner at Mr. McAnless'.

Frid. 11. Sat. 12. At home. Sick with a severe cold.

Sund. 13. Mond. 14. Tues. 15. At home. sick with cold.

Wed. 16. Thurs. 17. Frid. 18. At home, sick with cold.

Sat. 19. Sund. 20. Mond. 21. At home.

Tues. 22. Wed. 23. Thurs. 24. At home.

Frid. 25. Christmas Day. At home. Weather pleasant. Girls went to Christmas Tree at St. Peter's church.

Sat. 26. Sund. 27. At home.

Mond. 28. Tues. 29. Wed. 30. At home.

Thurs. 31. At home. To day Adol. Earnheart moved in as tenent.

Frid. Jan. 1. At home. New Year's Day. The day cloudy but not cold.
Sat. 2. At home. Cloudy & some rain but not cold.
Sund. 3. Mond. 4. Tues. 5. Wed 6. At home.
Thurs. 7. Frid. 8. At home. Weather cold.
Sat. 9. At home, inclement weather.
Sund. 10. At home, considerable snow on the ground.
Mond. 11. Tues. 12. Wed. 13. Inclement weather.
Thurs. 14. At home. Weather moderated.
Frid. 15. Sat. 16. At home. Weather cold & snow.
Sund. 17. At home. Weather cold.
Mond. 18. Tues. 19. At home. Abundance of rain.
Wed. 20. From this time up to Feb. 25 in very infirm health, part of the time confined to bed & in the hands of the doctor. Am still taking medicine.
Feb. 25. Am still confined to the house & in feeble health.
" 26. to Thurs. March 3. Confined to the house.

March 4. Rode out in my buggy over the plantation.
Sat. 5. At home.
Sund. 6. Mond. 7. Tues. 8. At home.
Wed. 9. Thurs. 10. Frid. 11. Sat. 12. At home.
Sund. 13. At home. Baptized to day at my house John S. M. Miller's child.
Mond. 14. Tues. 15. Wed. 16. At home.
Thurs. 17. At home. Had the mIsfortune to sprain one of my ankles very badly which has disabled me very much.
Frid. 18. to Thurs. 31. Confined to home and room with sprained ankle.

Frid. April 1 to Tues. 12. At home with sprained ankle.
Wed. 13. Thurs. 14. Frid. 15. At home.
Sat. 16. Went in my buggy to M. A. Holshouser's to see old lady Peeler, she being sick. Dinner here.
Sund. 17. At home, weather cloudy.
Mond. 18. Went to M. A. Holshouser's, Mrs. Peeler having died. Rev. W. R. Brown buried her.
Tues. 19. to Wed. 27. At home, confined to the house. Health more or less infirm.
Thurs. 28. At home, not very well.
Frid. 29. Went to St. Paul's church with Lewis to attend Synod. All night at Mrs. Julia Heilig's.
Sat. 30. At Synod. All night at Adam Earnheart's.

Sund. May 1. At Synod. All night at Solomon Yost's.

Mond. 2. At Synod. All night at Julia Heilig's.

Tues. 3. At Synod till afternoon then returned home.

Wed. 4. Thurs. 5. Frid. 6. At home.

Sat. 7. Went to burial of Sarah Brown at St. Peter's ch. In afternoon went with Lewis to Gold Hill.

Sund. 8. At home.

Mond. 9. In afternoon went to Gold Hill and Expressed Electropoise to Charleston. Then called at Dr. Coleman's & Trexler's saw mill & settled bill for sawing.

Tues. 10. Wed. 11. Thurs. 12. At home.

Frid. 13. Sat. 14. At home.

Sund. 15. Went to St. Peter's ch. and heard Rev. H. A. Trexler preach.

Mond. 16. Tues. 17. Wed. 18. At home.

Thurs. 19. Frid. 20. Sat. 21. At home.

Sund. 22. At home, a rainy day.

Mond. 23. Tues. 24. Wed. 25. At home.

Thurs. 26. Went to Gold Hill & heard Mr. Shuford deliver and Alliance address.

Frid. 27. Went to Gold Hill to post office.

Sat. 28. Sund. 29. At home. Sunday a rainy day.

Mond. 30. Went to Mt. Pleasant to attend meeting of Trustees of College & College Commencement. Stopped & Col. Shimpock's.

Tues. 31. Attended meeting of Board &c. Dinner at Prof. C. L. T. Fisher's. Supper at Rev. B. S. Brown's. Over night Col. Shimpock's.

Wed. June 1. Attended commencement &c. All night at Col. Shimpock's.
Thurs. 2. Returned home.
Frid. 3. Sat. 4. Sund. 5. At home.
Mond. 6. Tues. 7. Wed. 8. At home.
Thurs. 9. Went to Gold Hill and made Tax return.
Frid. 10. In forenoon went to Rufus Ridenour's to look at a cow. In afternoon went to Gold Hill to post office.
Sat. 11. In forenoon went to Andrew Berger's on business. Called also to see Jacob Holshouser in his affliction.
Sund. 12. At home.
Mond. 13. Went to H. A. Miller's to spend a few hours with Dr. P. A. Seaford. Dinner here. In afternoon went
        to Rockwell depot & brought Carrie home.
Tues. 14. Wed. 15. Thurs. 16. At home.
Frid. 17. In afternoon went to Gold Hill to post office.
Sat. 18. Attended to the funeral of Thomas Holshouser's child at St. Peter's church — addressed the people from
        Matt. 19:14.
Sund. 19. Mond. 20. At home.
Tues. 21. Went to Rockwell depot & brought Mrs. Wadkins to Lewis'.
Wed. 22. Thurs. 23. At home.
Frid. 24. Went to Rockwell and brought Emma home.
Sat. 25. Sund. 26. At home.
Mond. 27. At home.
Tues. 28. Wed. 29. Thurs. 30. At home.

Frid. July 1 to Wed. July 20. At home in bad health, confined to room & sometimes in bed.
Thurs. 21. Went in cool of the morning to Gold Hill & returned.
Frid. 22. Sat. 23. At home.
Sund. 24. At home. Baptized at my house William A. Earnheart's child.
Mond. 25. Tues 26. Wed. 27. At home.
Thurs. 28. Went in the cool of the morning to Gold Hill and returned.
Frid. 29. Sat. 30. At home.
Sund. 31. Attended to the funeral of Delia Holshouser, wife of Jacob Holshouser at St. Peter's church. Preached
        the funeral at the house from Heb. 4:9.

Mond. Aug. 1. Went In the morning to H. A. Miller's to look at a cow.

Tues. 2. Went to Salisbury. Dinner at W. C. Fraley's. All night at Mrs. Shemwell's.

Wed. 3. Returned home.

Thurs. 4. Frid. 5. At home.

Sat. 6. In afternoon attended preparatory service at St. Peter's church. Rev. W. R. Brown with me over night.

Sund. 7. Attended communion at St. Peter's ch. Rev. W. R. Brown preached. Gave some assistance in communion.

Mond. 8. Went to Gold Hill.

Tues. 9. Went to Gold Hill.

Wed. 10. Thurs. 11. At home.

Frid. 12. At home.

Sat. 13. Attended Gold Hill Township Sunday School Convention at Gold Hill. Dinner at Ephriam Mauney's.

Sund. 14. At home.

Mond. 15. At Home.

Tues. 16. Went to Gold Hill to meet delegates to W. H. and F. Missionary Convention.

Wed. 17. Thurs. 18. At W. H. & F. Convention at St. Peter's church.

Frid. 19. Took delegates to Rockwell.

Sat. 20. At home.

Sund. 21. Went to St. Peter's ch. & heard Mr. Miller Theo[1] Student preach.

Mond. 22. Tues. 23. At home.

Wed. 24. Took the train at Rockwell and went to Salisbury. Returned by train.

Thurs. 25. Frid. 26. Sat. 27. At home.

Sund. 28. Preached at Organ church from Prov. 23:17.18. Baptized one infant. Dinner at C. R. Lyerly's & baptized his child.

Mond 29. Went in forenoon to John Earnheart's to have clothes made.

Tues. 30. At home.

Wed. 31. Went to Dr. Coleman's & brought Jane Coleman to see us. Spent the day & night with us.

Thurs. Sep. 1. At home. Married to day at my house Mr. Robert C. Pool and Mrs. Margaret E. Crowell.

Frid. 2. Went in forenoon to Mr. Hambley's creamery & farm. Dinner at Dr. Coleman's. In afternoon went to Rockwell & heard candidates speak.

Sat. 3. Went to Gold Hill & to Alliance at Elm Grove.

Sund. 4. Went to St. Peter's ch. & heard Mr. Miller, student, preach.

Mond. 5. In forenoon went to Dr. Coleman's, and in afternoon to Gold Hill to post office.

Tues. 6. At home.

Wed. 7. At home. Mrs. Phebe Brown, Mrs. Nancy Shemwell, & Paul Barringer called to see us.

Mond. 14. At home.

Thurs. 8. Frid. 9. At home.

Sat. 10. After dinner went to Gold Hill & heard candidates speak.

Sund. 11. At home.

Mond. 12. In the morning went to Gold Hill to post office. In afternoon went to John Earnheart's & brought clothes home which Mrs. E. made for me.

Tues. 13. Wed. 14. At home.

Thurs. 15. After dinner went to M. A. Holshouser's to have door lock repaired, but failed.

Frid. 16. Went to John Powlass' & had door lock repaired. Dinner here. Then went to Gold Hill to post office.

Sat. 17. Attended Alliance in afternoon.

Sund. 18. At home. reading Bible.

Mond. 19. Tues. 20. Wed. 21. At home.

Thurs. 22. Went to Gold Hill for nails.

Frid. 23. Went to Gold Hill to post office.

Sat. 24. At home.

Sund. 25. Attended to the funeral of Peter Earnheart at St. Peter's church. Preached from Eccl. 9:5.

Mond. 26. At home.

Tues. 27. In forenoon went to Dr. Coleman's & took some vinegar to Lottie Hambley.

Wed. 28. Thurs. 29. At home.

Frid. 30. Went to Gold Hill to post office.

Sat. Oct. 1. In afternoon attended Elm Grove Alliance.

Sund. 2. Preached at St. Peter's ch. from John 20:23. Baptized one infant.

Mond. 3. At home.

Tues. 4. Went to Mt. Pleasant. All night at Col. J. Shimpock's.

Wed. 5. Attended meeting of Board of Trustees of College. Dinner at Rev. Geo. H. Cox's. All night at Col. Shimpock's.

Thurs. 6. Returned home. Dinner at Caleb Cruse's.

[Different handwriting]

Fri. 7. Sat. 8. Sun. 9. At home.

Mon. 10. Tues. 11. At home.

Wed. 12. At home. Got my fingers badly cut in the straw cutter.

Thurs. 13. Fri. 14. At home.

Sat. 15. In the afternoon had preparatory service at St. Peter's ch.

Sun. 16. Preached at St. Peter's ch. from James I Chapt. verse 25 and administered the communion.

Mon. 17. of Oct to Sat. Nov. 5. At home.

Sun. 6. Preached at St. Peter's Ch. from Prov. XXIX.1. and baptized two infants.
Mond. 7. At home.
Tues. 9. Went to Gold Hill to attend presidential election and voted for Cleveland.
Wed. 9. to Sat. 12. At home.
Sat. 12. to Sat. 19. At home.
Sun. 20. Preached at St. Peter's Ch. from Matt. 8:1-4. and baptized one infant.
Mon. 21 to Dec. 3. At home.
Sun. 4. Preached at St. Peter's Ch. from Jer. 17:9.
Mon. 5. to Sat. 17. At home.
Sun. 18. Preached at St. Peter's Ch. from Ex. 20:7.
Mon. 19. to 28. At home.

[Original handwriting resumes]

~~Frid. 29. Sund. 31. At home.~~
Thurs. 29. to Sat. 31. At home.
                    1893
Sund. 1 to Thurs. 19. At home. Snow in abundance.
Frid. 20. to Tues. 31. At home.

Wed. Feb. 1. At home.
Thurs. 2. Went to Gold Hill to post office.
Frid. 3. to Mond. 6. At home.
Tues. 7. to Wed. 15. At home.
Thurs. 16. to Sat. 18. At home.
Sund. 19. Went to St. Peter's ch. and heard Rev. Huddle preach his introductory sermon.
Mond. 20. At home.
Tues. 21. At dinner time walked to Solomon Peeler's & spent an hour.
Wed. 22. to Tues. 28. At home.

Wed. March 1. to Thurs. 9. At home.
Frid. 10. In the afternoon went to the School House & spent the afternoon.
Sat. 11 to Sat. April 1. At home.

Sund. 2. Went to St. Peter's church & heard Rev. Huddle preach.
Mond. 3. to Frid. 14. At home.
Sat. 15. Went to St. Peter's church and heard Rev. Huddle preach. Prof. Shirey with us over night.
Sund. 16. Went to St. Peter's ch. & heard Prof. Shirey preach. Communed with the congregation.
Mond. 17. At home. Rev. W. R. Brown and family with us to night.
Tues. 18. At home.
Wed. 19. Went to Salisbury by R. R.
Thurs. 20. At home.
Frid. 21. At home.
Sat. 22. Attended to the burial of Jacob Holshouser at St. Peter's ch. — Burial service rendered by Rev. Huddle.
Sund. 23. Went to Mariah Miller's and married John L. Holshouser and Laura C. Miller. Then went to
        Christiana Church & heard Rev. Wertz preach. Dinner at Julius Holshouser's.
Mond. 24. Tues. 25. Wed. 26. Thurs. 27. At home.
Frid. 28. Went to Gold Hill to post office.
Sat. 29. At home.
Sund. 30. Went to St. Peter's ch. and heard Rev. Huddle preach.

May Mond. 1. Started for Synod. Went with Lewis in buggy to Salisbury, thence by R. R. to China Grove. Over night at M. A. Eddleman's.

Tues. 2. In Synod at Luther's Chapel. All at Sam$^{\underline{l}}$ Roberts'.

Wed. 3. In Synod. Rainy day. All night at Montfort Kirk's.

Thurs. 4. Returned home.

Frid. 5. Sat. 6. At home.

Sund. 7. Preached at St. Peter's church from Prov. 3:9.10. How to make money.

Mond. 8. Tues. 9. At home.

Wed. 10. Thurs. 11. Frid 12. At home.

Sat. 13. In afternoon attended Woman's Miss. Meeting at L. G. Holshouser's.

Sund. 14. Mond. 15. Tues. 16. Wed. 17. At home.

Thurs. 18. Frid. 19. Sat. 20. At home.

Sund. 21. Went to St. Peter's ch. & heard Rev. W. P. Huddle preach. D. L. Arey and Mr. Lester took dinner with us.

Mond. 22. At home.

Tues. 23. Went to Dr. Coleman's & to Mr. Hambly's farm. Dinner at Dr. Coleman's.

Wed. 24. Thurs. 25. At home.

Frid. 26. In forenoon went to M. A. Holshouser's & to L. G. Holshouser's. In afternoon went to Gold Hill.

Sat. 27. At home.

Sund. 28. At home.

Mond. 29. Went to Mt. Pleasant. All night at Col. Shimpock's.

Tues. 30. In Mt. Pleasant attending commencement exercises. Heard Dr. Gotwald's address. Dinner to day at Prof. Fisher's. All night at Col. Shimpock's.

Wed. 31. Attend meeting of Trustees of N. C. C. & graduating exercises.

Thurs. June 1. Returned home.

Frid. 2. Sat. 3. Sund. 4. At home, sick.

Mond. 5. Tues. 6. Wed. 7. At home, not well.

Thurs. 8. Frid. 9. Sat. 10. Sund. 11. At home.

Mond. 12. Went to Misenheimer Springs.

Tues. 13. Wed. 14. Thurs. 15. At Springs.

Frid. 16. Returned home.

Sat. 17. to 26. At home.

Tues. 27. to Frid. 30. At home.

Sat. July 1. At home.

Sund. 2. Went to St. Peter's church and heard Rev. Huddle preach.

MEMOIR
OF
Rev. SAMUEL ROTHROCK, D. D.

On Nov. 2, 1894, this godly man, a father in the Ministerium of the E. L. Synod of North Carolina, died, in his 86th year, full of good works, and leaving to his family a rich legacy of good and wholesome precept and example, and to the Synod a great number of baptized and confirmed members, 1700 of the former and 1229 of the latter, therefore your committee would submit the following:

WHEREAS, It hath pleased Almighty God, who in his providence gave us this pure and consecrated man, to remove him from our midst to be with him in the church triumphant.

Resolved 1. That we render praise and thanksgiving to God for sparing this his servant to go in and out before Synod so long, having preached 61 years.

Resolved 2. That we bow in submission to the will of our Heavenly Father, in the removal of his servant.

Resolved 3. That we earnestly commend his example in preparing to enter the Gospel ministry, to all of our beneficiaries, (a) That he, like his Savior, worked with his hands to become useful; (b) That he regarded all help from Synod, in getting an education, as only a loan, which he scrupulously returned with interest; (c) That he was content to give his life to the cause of God in the Synod in which he was born.

Resolved 4. That we will ever cherish and hold in sacred remembrance all his labors of love as a minister of the Gospel, in our Synod, and in the entire church, both in preaching and writing.

Resolved 5. That we honor his memory for the chaste, pure, and useful life which he led; for his invincible will and unswerving devotion to the educational institutions of Synod, and his loyalty to the Bible and the Confessions of our Church; for his uncompromising opposition to fanaticism, error, and schism.

Resolved 6. That we extend to his family in their bereavement our sympathies, and invoke heaven's rich blessings upon them continually.

Resolved 7. That the Secretary be requested to send a copy of these resolutions to his bereaved family.

W. A. LUTZ,
G. D. BERNHEIM,
W. KIMBALL.

Reproduced from page 35, Minutes, North Carolina E. L. Synod, May 2-6, 1895 at St. Michael's Church, Iredell County, N.C.

The following is not part of the Rothrock Diaries, but an Account Book kept by Rev. Rothrock for a period of time. "Page" numbers refer to original Account Book page numbers.

Page 1

Account Book
Feb. 20, 1833

Page 2 [All crossed out but readable.]
~~Commenced boarding at~~
~~Mr. Arey's Sept. 18th 1834~~

_____

~~Commenced School Oct. 6, 1834.~~
~~My list St. Thomas~~
~~July 22, 1836 Rec^d of L. Jones $5.00~~

Page 3

Money expended since my residence in Salisbury	
Lamp 60 Jug & Oil 30	0 90
10 bush corn at 30 [?]. b. of Mr. Bell	3 60
Box of wafers 10 & hair dress-- [?] 25	0 35
Letter to Revd Morris	0 15¾
Pulpits Assistant 2 Vol.	0 75
Natural Philosophy	0 60
Curry Comb	0 12½
Straw to bed my stable	0 6¼
Paper 10 Quills 2½	0 12½
Altering my bridle	1 56¼
Toll at the bridge	0 20
Saddle Pad	0 50
20 bush oats 20 per bush.	4 00
16½ [?] corn at 30 [?]	4 95
For [?] living animals	0 25
Paid to the Tract Society	2 00
Nights Lodg. in Lexington	1 00
Crossing the bridge twice	0 20
To the shoe blacker	0 30
Tuk.[?] Va.[?] & the Fair	0 37½
A cloth coat	20 00
Shoe brushes	0 20
Discount in exchanging money	0 60
Pint of oil	0 18

Page 4

Clothes brush 20 Na 18¾ paper 10	0 48¾
Pair of shoes	2 25
Expended to Synod	1 37½
Shoeing my mare	1 00
Saddle girt & Salem paper for Jacob	1 75
Pad lock	0 37½
Pattern for pantaloons & vest	6 75
Postage at the Post office	5 00
A jaunt to Father's	0 50
To shoeing a horse	0 50
To making pants & vest	3 00
To four pills	0 25
Discount	1 00
Trip to Pennsylvania & back	115 12½
to Profess. S. S. Schmucker	12 00

to Benjamin Airey	27 50
April 11th to Airey & Harkey	45 00
Trunk in Lexington	2 25
Sundries	2 43⅓
Looking-glass	0 50
Sundries	0 45
Sundries	0 30
Pair of shoes	1 75
3 bushels corn at 35 cts.	1 5
Articles towards house keeping	17 77

Page 5

Tin Ware	2 80
Money expended from the present date,	
Feb. 17th 1835	$ cts
To B. Fraley for tayloring	21 00
To Dr Burns Adm^r of Wm Hughes Dec^d	16 27
To Jacob Brown for corn	3 00
Borrowed money replaced	3 00
To J. Murphy store Accounts	10 00
To one Venison ham	00 40
To paper & discount in money	00 18¾
To P. Arey for boarding	20 00
To one pound of coffee	00 18¾
To five pounds of cheese	00 62½
To 12 lbs. of at 10 per lb.	1 20
To 46 lbs. of bacon at 12½ pr lb	5 75
To 4 lbs sugar + 2 lbs. coffee	0 87½
To J. Murphy store accounts	16 6¼
To Mr. Buis, shop accounts	7 50
To B. Fraly, tailoring	6 00
To Jac. Brown, house rent, etc.	21 40
To G. Vogler butter etc.	6 21¼
To 3 dozen eggs	0 25
Sundries	1 00

Page 6

To H. W. Cauffman, Chancy, Pa.	10 00
To Luth. Obs.	2 00
To Henry's Exposition	13 00
To coffee, sugar etc.	1 31¼
To [?] shad	0 40
To Post office accounts	13 74
To check & cloth	1 36
To 1 bottle of Tonic mixture	1 00
To Waistcoat Pattern $1.25 paper 25	1 50
To making Waistcoat	0 62½
To eggs 1½ doz	0 9
To Sundries	0 30
To Borrowed money refunded	27 00
To Borrowed money refunded	22 00
To Revd G. Shober for books	19 00
To Hoffman's Arndt	1 00
Calico etc. for frock	2 82½
Silk etc for frock	11 28¾
Shoes, stockings etc.	2 00

Page 7

Commencement of the year
~~line marked through July~~
In Mercersburg July 19th, 1835
In McConnelsburg July 26th, 1835
In St. Thomas August 2nd, 1835
In Grossman's January 18th, 1836

Page 8

May 25, 1836 Received of Mr. Nead on my
Second list, St. Thos. $5.00
_____

Sept. 15, 1836. Received of Mr. Sackman
on first list St. Thomas - $1.00
July 22, 1836. Received of T. Jones
on first list St. Thomas - $5.00
Sept. 19, 1836. Received of Hannah
Lawcker list St. Thomas - 50 cts.
Sept. 21, 1836. Received on my list
St. Thomas - $17.00
Sept. 1836 Received of John Butler on
my list St. Thomas. - 5.00
Sept. 30, 1836. Received on my list
St. Thomas - 27.31¼
Sept. 30, 1836. Received on my list
St. Thomas - 20.44
Sept. 1836. Received Geo. Cradler on my
list St. Thomas - 1.00
Sept. 1836. Received of D. Hadler on my
list St. Thomas - 2.00
Sept. 1836. Recieved of J. Coble on my
list St. Thomas - 2.00
Sept. 1836. Received of P. Spence on my
list St. Thomas - 1.00

Page 9

April 30, 1836. Received on my list
at Grossman's church - $14.50
October 1, 1836. Received on my list
at Grossman's church - $25.37½
_____

My list in St. Thomas
Oct. 3rd. Received of Mr. Maden one
Dollar
Oct. 3rd. Received of Mr. John Kissil
$1.50

Page 10

March 27, 1836. Received on my
list in Mercersburg $34.00
Sept. 10, 1836. Received on my list
in Mercersburg. $50.50
Sept. 12, 1836. $1.00
Sept. 29, 1836. Received on my list
in Mercersburg $49.00

Page 11

Nov. 30. Received on my list in
M'Connellsburg $22.46

Decembr 27. Recevd. on my list in
McConnellsburg $13.25
Jan. 25, 1836. Received $1.00
Feb. 23rd - Received $11.50
May 15, 1836. Received - 5.00
July 10, 1836. Received - 17.50
Sept. 5, 1836. Received - - 22.77¼
Sept. 13, 1836. Received - 11.21½

Page 12

Sept. 29, 1835. Received of Mr. Walh
Mr. Nead $3.75 on my list St. Thomas.
Oct. 15, 1835. Received of Mr. Baker for Mr.
Nead $5.00 on my list in St. Thomas.
Oct. 28, 1835. Received of J. Butler for Mr.
Nead $2.00 on my list in St. Thomas.
_____ _____ Received of Mr. Butler drwn. out
of the church Treasury $10.00 to be
refunded out of my Salary.
Nov. 6th, 1835. Received of Mr. M'Garvy on
my list St. Thomas $5.00 in tayloring.
Nov. 11, 1835. Received of J. Butler on
my list St. Thomas $10.50
Nov. 28. Received of Mr. Polsgrove on my
list St. Thomas $3.00 in shoemaking.
Jan. 9, 1836. Received of J. Butler on
my list St. Thomas $6.50
March 15th, 1836. Received of J. Butler
on my list St. Thomas $6.50
Received for Mr. Baker from persons
in his employment $2.00
April 4, 1836. Recve^d of Rothrauff
& Patton on my list St. Thos. 6.50
May 21, 1836. Received of J. Kissel on my
list St. Thomas $11.00
May 25, 1836. Received of Mr. Nead on my
list St. Thomas $5.00
July 9, 1836. of Mr. Pence 1.00 St. Thomas

Page 13

[Everything on this page marked through with
"X's", some readable and some not. What is
readable is shown below.]

~~Commenced boarding with Mr. Nead~~
~~Myself Aug. 2, 1835~~
~~Mrs. Rothrock Aug. 21st, 1835~~
~~   Days absent~~
~~Myself~~ [here are 69 marks in groups of four marks
           with a fifth crossing to indicate five]
~~Mrs. R.~~ [10 marks, followed by:] 3 weeks. 6 weeks.
~~Moved to Mrs. Hoffman's May 2, 1836~~
_____

1836
~~March 23rd D^r to Rev. M'Knight - - $31.37½~~
~~   24. [?] to the [?] - - - - - - 16.85¼~~
~~D^r to Ruthrauff & Patton - - 10.00~~
~~D^r to Ruthrauff & Patton - - 3.50~~

~~D^r to Ruthrauff & Patton - - - 1.44~~
April 19, 1836. Paid to Editor Luth. Obs.
See Luth. Obs. Apr. 29, 1836
for B. Fraly, Salisbury, N.C. - $2.00
~~D^r to Ruthrauff & Patton - -   2.00~~
~~D^r to D. Hodtin[?] to furniture -   25.00~~
~~D^r to Mr. Seifert[?] to [?] - -   19.50~~
~~D^r to [?] Treasury - - -   [?.??]~~
~~D^r to D. Dechirt[?] Chaub[?] - - - -   31.50~~
~~D^r to Mr. [?] - hay - - -   1[?].00~~
~~D^r to Mr. Hough - bacon [?] lbs. -   .12½~~
~~D^r to Mr. C[?] - flour   .50~~
~~D^r to Ruthrauff & Patton - Hogshead   .75~~
~~D^r to Missionary Treasury - - -   .87½~~
~~D^r to Missionary Treasury - - -   .55~~

Page 14

Received on my second list in Salis.
My second list in Salisbury - - - - -$6.00
Second list in Salisbury - - - - -   2.00
Second list in Salisbury - - - - - - 31.00
Second list in Salisbury - - - - - - 3.00
1, 2, & 3rd list in Salisbury - - - - -18.00
Second list in Salisbury - - - - - - -35.21¼
1 & 2nd lists in Salisbury - - - - - 20.95
2nd list in Salisbury - - - - - - 11.00
2nd list in Salisbury - - - - - - 10.00
2nd list in Salisbury- - - - - - 31.00
2nd list in Salisbury - - - - - - 13.37½

~~D^r to Rothrauth & Patton, dishes, etc.- [?].40~~
~~D^r to Missionary Treasury- - - - - -3.00~~
~~D^r to Mr. Nead - boarding - - - -70.00~~
~~June 15 to Mrs. Hoffman - borrowed -- 3.00~~

~~D^r to Mr. Ho[?]sey - Chamb[?] - - - 1.00~~
~~D^r to J. [?] [?] - - - 3.86½~~
~~D^r to Rothrauth & Patton, [?] - - 1.30~~
~~D^r to Polsgrove[?] shoes~~

Page 15

Received from Union Congregation
Second list at Union - - - $3.00
Second list at Union - - -   2.00
Second list at Union - - -   30.00
Second list at Union - - -   6.00
Second list at Union - - -   44.00

Page 16

~~Indebted to the Miss. Treas. $2.00~~
~~Synodical Treas.   7.00~~
~~-- Miss. Treas.   5.00~~
~~Synodical Treas.   10.00~~
~~Synodical Treas.   20.00~~
~~Synodical Treas.   22.00~~
~~D^r to the Book Committee at Gettysburg~~
~~for 63 Luth. Hymn Books, small, at~~
~~62½ cts. per book - - $39.37½^{pd}~~

Holshousers.
Second list at Holshousers ——— $6.50
Second list at Holshousers ———   27.75
[Note: Strikeouts represent that that part was crossed out, but not necessarily line-by-line or word-by-word.]

Page 17

D^r at the Post office
~~to one letter   0.25~~
~~1 letter   0.25~~
~~1 letter   0.25~~
~~2 letters   0.25~~
~~1 letter   0.25~~
~~1 letter   0.25~~
~~1 letter   0.25~~
~~1 letter   0.25~~
~~2 letters   0.50~~
~~1 letter   0.25~~

~~2 letters   0.20~~
~~1 letter   0.25~~
~~1 letter   0.25~~
~~4 letters   0.62½~~
~~Paid the above April 16th, 1835~~

Hartman's
Second list at Hartman's - - - $4.25

Page 18

[Note: Strikeouts represent parts crossed out, mostly by large "X's".]

~~March 18th. Lent to Mr. Rousy 3 bush corn.~~
~~Lent to Mr. Price 4 bush. & ½ gal corn[?]~~
~~Lent to Mr. Buice 3½ bushels corn.~~
~~-- -- -- -- 4 boxes of corn~~
~~Lent to Mr. Buise $8.50~~
~~dr to Mr. Buis for boarding $45.[?]~~
~~Recevd of Thomas Mull Junr~~
~~one load of wood $1.00~~
~~one load of hay   4.00~~
~~Paid to Mr. Buise $25.00~~
~~to Mr. Mull -   7.00~~
~~to Mr. Buise 20.00~~
65 cts per bush.
~~Received of Mr. Trexler 3½ bush. corn~~
~~Sold to Mr. J. Brown 29 lbs of~~
~~bacon at 10 cts per lb. - 2.90~~
~~Received of H. Trexler 3½ bush. corn~~
~~Received of P. Arey 2 bushels of corn~~
~~Received of Jacob Brown 4 bush. corn~~
~~Received of Mr. Mowry 1 load of wood~~
~~Mt. Mowry 2 loads of wood~~
~~Sold to Mr. J. Brown ¾ load of hay~~

Page 19

~~d^r to Mr. Buise to 12 bush. corn   2.00~~
~~d^r at the post office to 2 letters   0.50~~
~~to 2 letters   0.50~~
~~to 5 letters   1.37½~~

d^r to Mr. D. Fraly for a coat ~~20.00~~
d^r to B. Fraley for money borrowed ~~40.00~~
~~at the post office to one letter 0.25~~
~~to 3 letters 0.75~~
~~to 2 letters 0.50~~
~~to 2 letters 0.12½~~
~~to 1 letter 0.18¾~~
~~to 1 letter 0.25~~
~~to 1 letter 0.18¾~~
~~Dues to the Post office paid.~~
~~June 21, 1835~~

d^r at the Post office for pamph. ~~0.7~~
~~to 1 letter 0.25~~
~~to 1 letter 0.18¾~~
~~to 1 pamphlet 0.6~~
~~to 3 letters 0.75~~
~~to 3 letter 0.75~~
~~to 1 letter 0.18¾~~
~~to 1 letter 0.18¾~~
~~to 2 letters 0.3[?]¾~~
~~to 1 letter 0.25~~
~~to 1 letter 0.25~~
~~to 2 letters 0.50~~
~~to 1 letter 0.18¾~~
~~to 1 letter 0.25~~
~~to 1 letter 0.25~~
~~to 1 letter 0.18¾~~
~~to 1 letter 0.10~~

page 20

April 11th Sent to Messrs. Arey &
Harkey forty five dollars to Gettysburg.
~~on my new list in Salis. 4.00~~
~~on my new list in Salis. 1.00~~
~~on my new list in Salis. 1.00~~
~~D^r to Mr. Butler Senr to 6 bushels~~
~~of oats~~
~~to one bag of corn in the ears.~~
~~to ½ ton hay.~~
~~D^r to Jacob Butler to 7 bush. oats.~~
~~D^r to Rothrauff & Patten to store~~
~~accounts $25.00~~
~~D^r to S. Butler Gettysburg to Creden's~~
~~Concordance $5.00~~
~~D^r to Mr. M'Garvy $1.00~~
~~D^r to J. Butler to 7 bush. oats~~
~~D^r to Mr. Jones to 6 bush. corn~~
~~Jan 9, 1836 D^r to Mr. Jones to 9 bush. oats.~~
~~D^r to Mr. Butler, Senr to 1 or 2 bags~~
~~of corn in the ears.~~
~~D^r to Jacob Butler to 5 or 6 bush. of~~
~~oats.~~
~~D^r to Jacob Butler to 14 bush. oats & 3~~
~~bush. potatoes.~~

Page 21

Money received
on my subscription list 3.00

on my subscription list 7.30
on my list at Union 0.95
For attending Mrs. Sink's funeral 2.00
For preaching Mr. Wilhelm's funeral 1.00
On my list in Salisbury 3.00
For marrying Jeremiah Barringer 2.00
for missionary labors 25.00
donation 1.00
on my list in Salisbury 1.00
on my list at Union 16.00
on my list in Salisbury 4.00
on my list at Union 17.00
on my list at Union 3.00
on my list in Salisbury 31.00
on my list at Union 19.75
on my list in Salisbury 24.50
on my list at Union 27.50
on my list in Salisbury 6.00
on my list at Union 9.00
on my list at Holshouser's 28.00
on my list in Salisbury 15.00
on my list at Union 2.75
on my list in Salisbury 13.00

Page 22

From Mr. File on my list at
Union ——— ——— ——— $ 2.50
on my list at Union __ __ 5.75
on my list at Union __ __ 5.00
on my list at Holshouser's 4.50

~~May 15, 1836 Received of Geo. Rinedaler~~
~~McConnellsburg. $2.00 for Luth.~~
~~Obs.~~

Page 23

~~Came to Mr. Buise Feb. 14th, 1833~~
~~Commenced washing with Mrs. Buise~~
~~Feb. 20th, 1833.~~

~~Absent days [?].1.4.9.4.1.9.1.3.3.3.2.3.~~
~~4 weeks. days 3.3.3.2.~~
~~Mrs. R. days 5.3.5.2. Settled~~

Page 24 [Blank]

Page 25

1850 CONFIRMATIONS
Oct. 12 Organ Church 1 person

1851
March 23. Organ ch. 1 person
Apr. 26. Organ ch. 46 persons

Dec. 7. St. Stephen's ch. 3 persons

1853
Apr. 23. Organ ch 61 persons

May 14. St. Stephen's ch. 19 persons

1853
Oct. 16 St. Stephen's ch. 1 person

1855
Apr. 21. Organ Ch 53 persons

Oct. 19, 1856 Confirmed at
             Luther's Chapel 1 person
1857
Apr. 25. Organ ch. 62 persons

1858. Apr. 17. at
St. Peter's Ch. 17 persons

Page 26

ADULT BAPTISMS
1853
May 14. St. Stephen's ch. 1 person

1857
Apr. 25. Organ ch. 3 persons

1858
Apr. 17. St. Peter's Ch. 6 persons

Page 27

1850 Infant Baptisms
March 24. Organ ch. 2 inf^{ts}
Apr. 7. St. Stephen's ch. 2 inf^{ts}
" 14. Organ ch. 1 inf^t
" 20. St. Stephen's ch. 1 inf^t
" 21. St. Stephen's ch. 1 inf^t
" 27. Organ ch. 4 inf^{ts}
1850
May 12. Organ ch. 2 inf^{ts}
" 26. Organ ch. 1 inf^t
July 14. Organ ch. 2 inf^{ts}
" 28. Organ ch. 2 inf^{ts}
Aug. 11. Organ ch. 1 inf^t
Sept. 2. Concord - Revd Harter's child.
" 5. John Bost's his child
" 8. Organ ch. 3 inf^{ts}
" 15. St. Stephen's ch. 1 infant
" 20. Organ ch. 1 inf^t
Oct. 12. Organ ch. 5 infts
" 13. Organ ch. 1 inft

Page 28

Infant Baptisms continued
1850
Oct. 13. David Lentz's, Danl. Moyer's child
" 27. Organ ch. 1 inf^t
Nov. 2. St. Stephen's ch. 4 inf^{ts}
" 4. Tice Barringer's 5 inf^{ts}
" 10. Organ ch. 5 inf^{ts}

" 16. Peter Troutman's 4 inf^{ts}
Dec. 29. Organ ch. 1 inf^t
1851
Jan. 12. Organ ch. 3 inf^{ts}
" 26. Organ ch. 2 inf^{ts}
Feb. 9. Organ ch. 1 inf^t
" 23. Organ ch. 1 inf^t
March 16. St. Stephen's ch. 1 inf^t

May 11. Organ ch. 2 inf^{ts}
June 8. Organ ch. 2 inf^{ts}
" 22. Organ ch. 1 inf^t
July 13. Organ ch. 4 inf^{ts}
" " Peter Lentz's dec^d his child
" 27. Organ ch. 1 inf^t

Page 29

Infants Baptized continued
Aug. 3. St. Stephen's ch. 1 inf^t
Sept. 14. Organ ch. 2 inf^{ts}
Oct. 25. Organ ch. 3 inf^{ts}
Dec. 6. St. Stephen's ch. 3 inf^{ts}
" 14. Organ ch. 2 infan^{ts}
1852
Jan. 11. Organ ch. 1 inf^t
" 26. P. N. Heilig's his child
" 30. John Bost's his child
Feb. 1. St. Stephen's ch. 3 inf^{ts}
" 8. Organ ch. 4 inf^{ts}
" 22. Organ ch. 1 inf^t
Mar. 14. Organ ch. 1 inf^t
Apr. 11. Organ ch. 4 inf^{ts}
Apr. 24. Organ ch. 3 inf^{ts}
May 16. St. Stephen's ch. 1 inf^t
Jun. 7. St. Stephen's ch. 1 inf^t
" 13. Organ ch. 1 inf^t

Page 30

Infant Baptisms continued
1852
June 27. Organ ch. 1 inf^t
July 11. Organ ch. 1 inf^t
" 18. St. Stephen's ch. 1 inf^t
" 25. Organ ch. 1 inf^t
Aug. 15. St. Stephen's ch. 1 inf^t
Sept. 12. Organ ch. 1 inf^t
" 19. St. Stephen's ch. 1 inf^t
Oct. 1. Jacob Goodman's his child
" 16. St. Stephen's ch. 1 inf^t
" 23. Organ ch. 4 inf^{ts}
Nov. 14. Organ ch. 2 inf^{ts}
" 28. Organ ch. 1 inf^t
1853
Jan. 4. George Mayer's his child
" 9. Organ ch. 2 inf^{ts}
" 16. St. Stephen's ch. 1 inf^t
Feb. 13. Organ ch. 1 inf^t

" 27. Organ ch. 2 infts
Page 31

Infant Baptisms continued

__1853__
March 6. St. Stephen's ch. 1 inft
" 20. St. Stephen's ch. 1 inft
" 27. Organ ch. 5 infts
Apr. 10. Organ ch. 2 infts
" 23. Organ ch. 2 infts
May 14. St. Stephen's ch. 2 infts

May 22. Organ ch. 2 infts
June 12. Organ ch. 1 inft
" 26. Organ ch. 4 infts
July 10. Organ ch. 3 infts
Aug. 14. Organ ch. 2 infts
Sep. 11. St. Stephen's ch. 1 inft
" 25. Organ ch. 2 infts
" 27. Paul Beaver's his child
Oct. 1. Mathias Barringer's 3 children
" 9. Organ ch. 1 inft
" 15. St. Stephen's ch. 2 infts

Page 32

__1833__ Infant Baptisms
Oct. 22. Organ ch. 2 infts
Nov. 20. Organ ch. 1 inft
" 27. St. Stephen's ch. 1 inft
Dec. 16. St. Stephen's ch. 1 inft
" 25. Organ ch. 2 infts
__1854__
Jan. 22. Organ ch. 1 inft
Mar. 12. Organ ch. 5 infts
Apr. 3. Cross Roads/Shepd. Revd Arey's child
" 9. Organ ch. 1 inft
Apr. 23. Organ ch. 1 inft
Apr. 29. Organ ch. 2 infts

__1854__
May 20. St. Stephen's ch. 3 infts
" 28. Organ ch. 3 infts
June. 25. Organ ch. 1 inft
July 9. Organ ch. 1 inft
" 23. Organ ch. 1 inft
" 24. Organ ch. 1 inft
Sept. 10. Organ ch. 1 inft

Page 33

__1854__ Infant Baptisms
Sept. 17. St. Stephen's ch. 1 inft
Dec. 23. Organ ch. 1 inft
" 30. St. Stephen's ch. 1 inft
__1855__
Jan. 28. Organ ch. 1 inft
Feb. 11. Organ ch. 4 infts
" 18. St. Stephen's ch. 1 inft
March 4. At David Bostian's 1 inft
" " at Frederick Stirewald's 1 inft
" 11. Organ ch. 2 infts

Apr. 1. St. Stephen's ch. 1 inft
" 21. Organ ch. 3 infts

__1855__
May 13. Organ ch. 3 infts
" 27. Organ ch. 1 inft
June 2. Union ch. 2 infts
" 3. Union ch. 1 inft
" 10. Organ ch. 1 inft

Page 34

__1855__ Infant Baptisms
June 24. Organ ch. 1 inft
July 8. Organ ch. 1 inft
Aug. 26. Organ ch. 2 infts
Sep. 9. Organ ch. 1 inft
Oct. 10. Henry Seaford's his child
" 14. Organ ch. 1 inft
" 27. Organ ch. 4 infts
Nov. 4. St. Peter's ch. 1 inft
Dec. 23. Organ ch. 5 infants
__1856__
Feb. 24. Organ ch. 3 infants
March 2. St. Peter's ch. 1 inft
" 9. Organ ch. 1 inft
" 23. Organ ch. 1 inft
" 24. Paul Beaver's his child
Apr. 13. Organ ch. 4 infants
" 26. Organ ch. 4 infts

__1856__
June 8. Salem 1 inft
" 13. Organ ch. 1 inft

Page 35

__1856__ Infant Baptisms
June 15. Luther's Chapel 1 inft
" 22. Organ ch. 1 inft
" 29. St. Peter's ch. 1 inft
July 5. Union ch. 3 infts
" 6. Luther's Chapel 1 inft
" 27. Organ ch. 1 inft
Aug. 3. Luther's Chapel 1 inft
" 24. Organ ch. 2 infts
Sept. 22. David Bost's, his child
Sept. 28. Organ ch. 2 infts
Oct. 12. Organ ch. 2 infts
" " St. Peter's ch. 1 inft
" 17. Tobias Cruse's, his 2 children
" 18. Luther's Chapel 1 inft
Nov. 2. Luther's Chapel 1 inft
" 16. Luther's Chapel 2 infts
Dec. 7. Luther's Chapel 1 inft

Page 36

Infant Baptisms
Dec. 28 Organ ch. 1 inft
1857
Feb. 8. Organ ch. 2 infts

Feb. 22. Organ ch. 2 inf^{ts}
Feb. 11. Jeremiah Beaver's his child
March 8. Organ ch. 2 inf^{ts}
   " 22. Organ ch. 1 inf^t
Apr. 12. Organ ch. 1 inf^t
   " 25. Organ ch. 1 inf^t

June 7. St. Peter's ch. 1 inf^t
   " 14. Organ ch. 4 inf^{ts}
   " 21. St. Peter's ch. 3 inf^{ts}
   " 28. Organ ch. 1 inf^t
   " 28. Fred. Stirewalt's his son's child
Aug. 22. St. John's ch. 1 inf^t
   " " At C. Melchor's 2 inf^{ts}
   " 29. Organ ch. 7 inf^{ts}
Sept. 13. Organ ch. 1 inf^t

Page 37
   1857   Infant Baptisms
Sept. 27. Organ ch. 6 inf^{ts}
Oct. 11. Organ ch. 1 inf^t
   " 24. Organ ch. 2 inf^{ts}
Nov. 15. St. Stephen's ch. 1 inf^t
Dec. 13. Rufus Miller's child
   " 20. St. Peter's ch. 1 inf^t
   " 27. Organ ch. 1 inf^t
   1858
Jan. 10. Organ ch. 1 inf^t
Feb. 28. Organ ch. 1 inf^t
March 13. Organ ch. 1 inf^t
   " 14. Organ ch. 2 inf^{ts}
Apr. 17. St. Peter's ch. 1 inf^t
   " 24. Organ ch. 9 inf^{ts}

Page 38
   [This page blank]

Page 39
   1850   Burials
May 14. Organ ch. Michael Bostian, Sen.
   " 30. Lower St. ch. James F. Fraley
June 2. Organ ch. Christena Troutman
July 3. Organ ch. Solomon Cruse
Sept. 7. Lower St. ch. Paul Beaver's child
   " 11. Organ ch. John Bost's child
Oct. 8. Organ ch. Mrs. Pasinger
Nov. 1. Lower St. ch. Wm. Holshouser's child
   " 4. Tice Barringer's Sim. Hofman's step child
   " 11. Lower St. ch. William Holshouser
Dec. 6. Stone House Sarah Brown
   " 15. St. Stephen's ch. Old Mrs. Culp

   1851
Jan. 3. Organ ch. Mrs. Richie
   " 4. Mathias Barringer at his residence
   " 17. Lower Stone ch. Saml Powlass
Feb. 4. Lower Stone ch. Leah Trexler
   " 25. St. Stephen's ch. John Lentz's child

Page 40
   1851   Burials
Apr. 25. Jacob Smith's Wm. Smith, Sen.

   1851
June 9. St. Stephen's ch. Paul Nussman
Aug. 7. Lower Stone ch. J. Trexler's child
Oct. 3. Union ch. Alex. Kesler's child
   " 8. Union ch. Widow Walton (Jesse)
Nov. 3. Isaac Kesler's, Elizabeth Linn
   " 18. Peter Walton's, Lewis Walton
   " 27. Organ ch. Mrs. Sam'l Linn
Dec. 24. Organ ch. Mrs. Mowry's child
   1852
Jan. 26. Organ ch. Mrs. Mich^l Overcash
Feb. 2. Organ Ch. John Bost's child
   " 5. Lower St. ch. Mrs. Fraley
   " 16. Organ ch. Mrs. Zaceriah Lyerla
March 18. Organ ch. Mrs. Danl Brown
Apr. 21. Lower St. ch. Peter Mowry
   " 27. Organ ch. Alex. Cauble

Page 41
   1852   Burials
May 25. Organ ch. David Lentz (of Jacob)
   " 30. Lower St. ch. Old Mrs. Troutman
July 24. Lower St. ch. Alex. Holshouser
Aug. 3. Organ ch. Melchor Troutman
   " 11. Lower St. ch. Andr. Berger's child
Sep. 26. Organ ch. Martha Klutts
   " 30. Lower St. ch. Mrs. Danl Peeler
Oct. 12. Organ ch. Barbara M. Patterson
Nov. 10. Lower St. ch. Moses Klutts' child
Dec. 27. Lower St. ch. Mrs. Jacob Fisher
   1853
Feb. 18. Lower St. ch. Mrs. Eli Klutts
March 15. Organ ch. Old Mrs. Josey
Apr. 18. Lower St. ch. Regina Klutts
May 10. Lower St. ch. Henry Holshouser

May 27. Lower St. ch. Solomon Klutts' child
July 12. Organ ch. John Lingle's daughter
   " 13. Organ ch. Frederick Yost

Page 42
   1853   Burials
July 21. Organ ch. George Safret
Aug. 31. Organ ch. Tobias Stirewald
Sep. 29. Lower St. ch. Paul Beaver's child
   " 30. Organ ch. Widow Boger
Oct. 4. Lower St. ch. Leonard Klutts
   " 8. Organ ch. Dawalt Ketner
   " 11. Lower St. ch. Andrew Berger's child
   " 15. Organ ch. George Bost
   " 19. Organ ch. Paul Stricker
   " 20. Organ ch. Mrs. John Rimer
Dec. 10. Organ ch. Mrs. Barbara Klutts
   " 13. Lower St. ch. Mrs. Eve Peeler

1854
Feb. 10. Lower St. ch. James Holshouser's child
Apr. 26. Phanuel's ch. Eliz. C. Shuping
May 18. Organ ch. Laurence Misenheimer's child
" 28. Organ ch. Solomon Ketchey's child
June 3. Lower St. ch. Stephen Brady's son

Page 43
Burials
1854
~~July 8. Union ch.~~
July 8. Union ch. Bostian Lentz
" 24. Organ ch. John Yost
Sept. 4. Organ ch. Dan^1 Eddleman's child
" 4. Organ ch. Margaret Fisher
" 13. Organ ch. P. A. Seaford's child
" 26. Organ ch. Mich^1 Goodman's child
Oct. 1. St. Stephen's ch. P. Troutman's child
" 4. Lower St. ch. Simeon Earnheart
" 4. St. Stephen's ch. Henry Peck
" 23. Organ ch. John Louder's child
" 23. Organ ch. John Smith
" 26. Organ ch. Sam^1 Linn
Nov. 1. Organ ch. Peter Cruse's child
Dec. 8. Organ ch. Philip Eddleman
1855
Jan. 18. Organ ch. R. N. Heilig's child

Page 44
1855   Burials
Feb. 22. Lower St. ch. Margaret S. Miller
" 26. Organ ch. Peter Eagle
March 2. Lower St. ch. Asa Miller
Apr. 11. Union ch. Mrs. Cath. Barringer
_____

1855
May 13. Lower St. ch. J. Montgomery's child
May 21. Organ ch. Mrs. Catharine Miller
" 28. Union ch. Louisa N. Boger
June 10. Organ ch. Polly Holshouser
" 13. Organ ch. Elenora Holshouser
" 15. Organ ch. John Bostian's child
July 4. Organ ch. Eli Seaford's child
" 4. Organ ch. J. J. Miller's child
" 28. Organ ch. Polly Ann Troutman
Aug. 28. Organ ch. David Brown
Sept. 14. Organ ch. Polly C. Overcash
" 17. Organ ch. Mary A. Bostian

Page 45
1855   Burials
Sept. 18. Lower St. ch. J. W. Earnheart
" 30. Lower St. ch. Valentine Pence
Oct. 20. Organ ch. Henry Seaford's child
" 29. Organ ch. John T. Lentz's child
Nov. 24. Organ ch. Chas. Bostian's child
" 27. Organ ch. Z. Lyerly's child
" 28. St. Peter's Ch. H. A. Miller's child
Dec. 11. Lower St. ch. Mrs. Sam^1 Beaver

1856
Jan. 22. Mt. Pleasant Mrs. Haines
March 27. Lower St. ch. Paul Beaver's child
Apr. 4. St. Paul's ch. Moses A. Brown
" " " " Mrs. Wilson Fisher
" 6. Organ ch. Jacob Bostian
_____

1856
May 4. St. John's ch. Mrs. Cath. Probst
" 6. St. Enoch's ch. Mrs. Anna Smith

" 19. Organ ch. Mrs. David Casper

Page 46
1856   Burials
May 26. Organ ch. Wilie Holshouser
June 3. Organ ch. Susanne Reimer
" 4. Union ch. H. A. Walton's child
" 13. Organ ch. J. A. Patterson's child
" 18. Organ ch. John Basinger's child
July 1. Organ ch. Geo. M. Ketner's child
" 4. Mt. Zion Philip Correl's child
" 7. Organ ch. Geo. A. Eagle's child
Aug. 14. St. Paul's ch. Elizabeth,
    wife of Mich^1 L. Brown
" 24. Lower St. ch. Susanna,
    wife of Henry Klutts
" 25. Lower St. ch. Moses Trexler's child
" 26. St. Paul's ch. Henry L. Brown's child
Sept. 25. Union ch. Martin L. Walton
Oct. 2. Organ ch. Charles Fisher's child
" 4. Organ ch. Martha, wife of
    Joseph Barringer

Page 47
1856   Burials
Oct. 27. Organ ch. Peter Cruse's child
Nov. 23. Organ ch. Mrs. Elizabeth,
    Wife of Philip Cruse
" 28. Organ ch. P. M. Heilig's child
Dec. 4. Organ ch. Susanne Seaford
" 9. Organ ch. Jesse Beaver's child
" 16. Lower St. ch. Conrad Casper
" 22. Organ ch. Clementine Harkey
1857
Jan. 11. Organ ch. Sally Garner
" 19. St. Peter's ch. Thornton R.,
    Son of David & Mary Barringer
" 24. Organ ch. Catharine Cruse
Jan. 31. Organ ch. John J. Miller
Feb. 2. Union ch. Polly Brown
" 10. St. Peter's ch. Alex. Trexler
March 4. Lower St. ch. Elizab. Pence
" 11. Union ch. Isaac Kesler

Page 48
1857   Burials
Apr. 20. Eliza. Kesler at home
" 21. St. John's ch. John K. Miller's son

<u>1857</u>
May 27. Widow Earnheart at home
June 15. John Eller at home.
  " 18. Lower St. ch. Alex. Cope
  " 19. Organ ch. Mrs. McCombs
July 16. Organ ch. Mary Holshouser
  " 21. Lower St. ch. A. M. Miller's child
  " 27. Organ ch. M. Fesperman's child
  " 30. Lower St. ch. Mrs. Amelia Miller
Aug. 8. St. Stephen's ch. Revd. L. C.
              Groseclose's child
  " 10. Lower St. ch. P. Earnheart's child
Sept. 1. St. Stephen's ch. Revd. L. C.
              Groseclose's child
Sept. 12. St. John's ch. Jacob Moose's child

Page 49
    <u>1857</u>
    Oct. 16. St. Paul's ch. Mr. Young's child
    " 24. Organ ch. Moses A. Seaford
    " 27. Organ ch. Joseph Seaford
    " 30. Luther's Chapel John Beaver
    Nov. 23. St. Mathew's ch. Mrs. Ellick Casper

    Nov. 30. Organ ch. John Eagle
    Dec. 1. St. Mathew's ch. J. E. Hoffman
    " 6. Organ ch. Geo. H. Ketner
    <u>1858</u>
    Feb. 6. Organ ch. Sarah Ann E. B. Goodman
    " 8. Organ ch. Mary S. F. Graeber
    " 10. Lower St. ch. Amy Powlass
    " 14. Organ ch. Mrs. Graeber, relict
         of Revd Henry Graeber
    " 22. Organ ch. Louisa M. H. Leppard
    March 11. Organ ch. Peter Weaver
    Apr. 15. Stone House Sol. Brown's daughter

GOLDEN WEDDING

---OF---

REV. AND MRS. S. ROTHROCK,

------NEAR------

GOLD HILL, N. C.,

September 14, 1887.

BY REV. F. W. E. PESCHAU,
WILMINGTON, N. C.

Golden Wedding of Rev. and Mrs. Rothrock.

Bright and charming was the day of the golden wedding celebration of Rev. and Mrs. S. Rothrock, in their comfortable home near Gold Hill, Rowan County, N. C. And bright and happy were the relatives, friends and acquaintances of the aged couple, and all who had the privilege of being with them. An occurrence so rare in ministerial life should be properly observed, and so it was.

Any church body could be proud to have in its ministry, so good and grand an old man as Pastor Rothrock, whose life is without a stain or blame. His life has been a pure one. His labors have been constant, faithful and successful. For over fifty-four years he has preached Christ and him crucified, and in his life has set an example ever worthy of imitation by both clergy and laity. His devotion to our Church, his gentle, unassuming demeanor, his faithfulness as a friend, his wisdom as a counsellor, his ever ready response to aid in every good work, his plain, pointed, gospel preaching, and his holy life, has ever endeared him to all he has associated with, and hence he has, and has had, friends not only by the dozen or score, but by the hundreds and thousands. Many were the testimonials of honor, and appreciation and love bestowed upon him and his bride of fifty years ago, on Wednesday, September 14th.

" Father Rothrock," as he is lovingly and familiarly called by ministers and laymen who know him, was born in Rowan County, N. C. He spent nearly all his life in his native State, North Carolina, and expects to die in it, and to rest in its soil till the resurrection morn. Considering his old age, he is remarkably well preserved, but in the last two years a decided change has come over him and his strength is waning. He is

A Grand, Good Old Man.

He is universally popular, and is loved and revered by old and young. For fifty-five long years he has been in the ministry and, until two years ago, always in charge of a church or a charge. He has held many prominent positions of honor and trust in our Church, and is a grand, good old man because he was a grand, good young man. When a student he walked all the way from his North Carolina home to Gettysburg, Pa., where the oldest Lutheran college in the country is located. In his summer vacation he walked back home. This simple incident shows the make-up of this noble son of North Carolina.

Mrs. Rothrock bears the marks of age more than her husband. Her hair has turned quite white. She has a pleasant, attractive face, and must have been a handsome young woman in her earlier years. Of all the children born in their family, only one—Professor Louis Rothrock, once county superintendent, and for many years a professor in our college at Mt. Pleasant—was present, all the rest being dead.

List of Contributions from North Carolina.

Each of the persons here named gave $1, in gold, except when otherwise specified:

3

Midway—Caleb Peeler, Mrs. Caleb Peeler.

Kappa—Rev. W. R. Ketchie.

Zeb—Rev. C. A. Rose.

Raleigh—Governor Scales.

Bear Poplar—Rev. J. D. Shirey.

Watsonville—C. B. Miller.

Smaller Contributions.

Zeb—J C Miller, 50 cents.

Providence—David Fink, 25 cents.

$5 Contributions.

Salisbury—J. R. Holmes and wife; Mrs. J. Linn and son.

Gold Hill—Mrs. Jane Coleman, Mrs. Lottie C. Hambley.

Contributions from other States.

From South Carolina—Wm. P. Houseal, publisher LUTHERAN VISITOR.

From Pennsylvania—Rev. Prof. M. Valentine, D. D., President of the Theological Seminary, Gettysburg; Rev. S. Stall, editor *Lutheran Year Book*, Lancaster; Rev. M. Sheeleigh, editor *Lutheran S. S. Herald*.

From Kentucky—Mr. J. S. Bean, Louisville.

From Virginia—Rev. S. Henkel, D. D., New Market.

From Ohio—Rev. H. C. Haithcox, Ashland.

LETTERS.

Besides the contributions sent, nearly every contributor sent a congratulatory letter, a list of which may not be in place as the most of the names already appear in the "List of Contributions." We would add, however, the names of Prof. J. D. Dreher, Ph.D., President Roanoke College; Mrs. A. Knobloch, Wilmington, and Rev. Joel Swartz, D. D., Gettysburg, Pa.

The letters from the consuls bore the seals of the various countries represented, as Hon. Edward Peschau, * German Empire; Hon. James Sprunt, British Empire, and Hon. R. E. Heide, Kingdoms of Denmark, Norway and Sweden.

Wilmington — Hon. Edward Peschau, German consul*; Hon James Sprunt, British vice-consul; Hon. R. E. Heide, consul of Denmark, Norway, Sweden; Dr. F. C. Miller, German druggist; Julius A. Bonitz, Esq., editor *Daily Messenger;* Henry Haar, sr., and wife, E. Schulken, sr., and wife, Chas. Schulken and wife, A. D. Wessell and wife, Edward Wessell, F. W. Ortman and wife, F. Henry Krahnke and wife, H. Rehder and wife, George Tiencken and wife, J. William Tiencken, Mrs. F. W. E. Peschau, Rev. Father Charles F. Burns, assistant priest, J. D. H. Klander, J. D. Oldenbuttel, and a $2.50 gold piece from the Hon. Charles M. Stedman, Lieutenant-Governor of North Carolina.

Charlotte — Captain T. L. Seigle, Captain W. A. Barrier, Major S. E. Linton, Rev. T. S. Brown.

Mount Pleasant—Rev. Prof. J. G. Schaidt, President North Corolina College; Rev. Prof. J. A. Linn, President Female Seminary; Captain Jonas Cook, Major L. G. Heilig, Prof. H. T. J. Ludwig, Mr. E. D. Lentz, Col. J. Shimpock, Rev. W. R. Petrea.

Salisbury—Rev. C. B. King, Dr. J. C. Pool, Mrs. J. C. Pool, Geo. H. Shaver, Mrs. P. N. Heilig, Col. P. N. Heilig, J. A. Randleman, Paul M. Barringer, Mrs. D. Barringer, Rev. R. L. Brown.

Gold Hill—Milas. A. Holshouser, O. M. Holshouser, Mrs. M. A. Holshouser, John S. Beaver, Dr. L. W. Coleman.

Enochville—Rev. W. A. Lutz, Mrs. W. A. Lutz, H. W. Ludwig, Prof. F. B. Brown, Aaron Yost, Mrs. A. Yost.

China Grove—Rev. W. R. Brown, I. J. Patterson.

Jerusalem—Matthias Miller.

---

* A relative of Rev. F. W. E. Peschau and son of Rev. C. A. D. Peschau, Lutheran Pastor in Hanover over 50 years and died at the advanced age of 80 years in 1883.

4

All the letters written to the happy couple were read by persons appointed for that purpose. The German letters were read by Rev. Prof. J. G. Schaidt, President North Carolina College. The Danish letter from Hon. R. E. Heide, consul of Denmark, Norway and Sweden, was read by Rev. F. W. E. Peschau.

We herewith publish the letters of the Lieutenant-Governor and the Governor of North Carolina, and we are proud of such testimonials to a Lutheran pastor. We wish we could publish all the letters:

Letter From Lieutenant-Governor Chas. M. Stedman.

WILMINGTON, N. C., Sept. 8, 1887.
Rev. S. Rothrock, Gold Hill, N. C:

MY DEAR SIR: My good and esteemed friend, Rev. F. W. E. Peschau, has called my attention to the fact that you will have been married fifty years on September 14th, 1887. I congratulate you most heartily, and trust that many years may still be added to your long life of virtue, of honor and of usefulness. Be kind enough to present my best wishes to your good lady, Mrs. Rothrock.

Please find enclosed a piece of gold, as a slight testimony of esteem and regard.

Very truly yours,
CHAS. M. STEDMAN.

—

Letter From His Excellency, Governor A. M. Scales.

STATE OF NORTH CAROLINA,
EXECUTIVE DEPARTMENT,
RALEIGH, N. C., Sept. 1, '87.
Rev. and Mrs. S. Rothrock:

ESTEEMED FRIENDS—I have known you and most favorably for a number of years. I have heard of the efforts for Zion on the part of the Rev. S. Rothrock, in preaching the gospel and persuading men everywhere to repent, and by every means in his power, in season and out of season, in urging them through the grace of God to become good men, good citizens, and most of all heirs of God and joint heirs with the Lord Jesus Christ. I desire to contribute my mite on the occasion of your golden wedding, not for its intrinsic value but to honor the good man and good woman who have so long and faithfully served and honored God and their country. May the day be a happy one to both.

May your lives be spared for many more years of usefulness, and when death shall come may you find an abundant entrance at the right hand of the Father.

Your friend and well wisher,
A. M. SCALES.

—

Other Favors Shown.

Not only were congratulatory letters and golden coins sent, but other favors were shown from among which we mention the following:

A pass over the Carolina Central Railroad for both Mr. and Mrs. Rothrock, from Charlotte to Wilmington and return, good for sixty days. An invitation from Mr. H. C. Eccles, proprietor of the Central Hotel of Charlotte, to a free use of their hotel while on their trip. Tickets for a free trip on steamer Passport, Captain J. W. Harper, from Wilmington to the sea shore and return. Two huge loaves of bread for the aged pair and a huge "German coffee cake, two feet by four, for the son, Prof. L. Rothrock, from P. Blomme, Wilmington. Fifty pieces of candy for Pastor Rothrock, and fifty for his wife, from Messrs. Haar and Stolter, Wilmington. Besides this, two young orphan ladies, for many years cared for by the couple, presented Mrs. Rothrock with a very handsome black silk apron, and friends and neighbors sent in baskets of provisions, books, etc.

Mr. F. H. Krahnke, of Wilmington, wrote a German poem for the occasion, and Rev. Joel Swartz, D. D., so well and favorably known throughout our Church and throughout our country as a superior poet, wrote for the happy occasion the following highly appropriate and charming lines, which were most highly appreciated:

5

Golden Wedding Poem.

BY REV. JOEL SWARTZ, D. D., GETTYSBURG, PA.

I.

The years have worn the wedding ring
  Which pledged us young and binds us
    old,
And it has proved no gilded thing,
  But to its centre gold--pure gold.

II.

Our love, a half a hundred years
  We've worn and tried and tested, too;
And toils, and cares, and mingled tears
  Have proved it golden, through and
    through.

III.

What, though love's symbols wear away,
  And hands that gave and wore grow cold,
The souls it bound shall not decay,
  And love itself will not grow old.

IV.

Ah, no! it rather shall grow more,
  And more and more our souls possess
As we approach the golden shore,
  As time, and sense, and earth grow less.

V.

And we, in love shall still be one
  Beyond the storm, beyond the calm;
Reunited at the great white throne,
  And at the marriage of the lamb.

The object of the gathering, a condensed sketch of the marriage, of the officiating minister, the time, place, etc., of fifty years ago, was stated by Rev. W. A. Lutz.

The Scripture lessons, consisting of selections of God's promises of long life to His children were made and read by Rev. R. W. Petrea. Prayer was offered at different times by the various ministers present.

Address of congratulations and golden wedding ceremony by the President of Synod.

A beautiful and touching address of congratulations was made by Prof. Lewis Rothrock, to his aged mother and venerable father, the one 76, the other 79 years old.

There were present the members and immediate relatives of the family, friends, acquaintances and neighbors, and the following Lutheran pastors: Revs. R. L. Brown, W. R. Brown, R. W. Petrea, J. A. Linn, W. R. Ketchie, W. A. Lutz, J. G. Schaidt and F. W. E. Peschau.

In carrying out the programme, Rev. Professor Linn, represented the Northern Conference and Rev. W. A. Lutz, the Southern Conference of the North Carolina Synod and turned over to the president of the synod, through a committee of two ladies (Mrs. Rev. Lutz and Mrs. Prof. Rothrock, who had arranged the gold coins so as to make out the words "God held you") the monies contributed and by him they were handed to the aged pair. Quite a history could be given in connection with some of these coins. One was a war relic, another was the only gold dollar a loving child had owned when it died, etc.

The committees having affairs in charge, were: Committee on letters, etc., F. W. E. Peschau, president North Carolina Synod ; J. L. Buck, secretary ; H. M. Brown, corresponding secretary. Committee on arrangements : W. A. Lutz, C. A. Rose, Col P. N. Heilig, Capt. T. L. Seigle.

A Touching Incident.

A very delightful surprise awaited the couple, when Mr. Adam Rothrock, a brother of the old pastor, whom he had not seen for forty years, put in an appearance, having traveled all the way from Weston, Oregon, a distance of over three thousand miles. The scene of the meeting can be better imagined than described, it was as touching as it was rare. Mr. A. Rothrock stated that before two hours had elapsed after he received the invitation in his far off Northwestern home,

6

he was on board of the train for old North Carolina and the Golden Wedding.

The *Daily Messenger* of Wilmington has the following to say regarding the wedding, and with this quotation we close :

"In every way and every sense of the word the golden wedding was a decided success. The day was a most charming one, the attendance was large and more than could have been expected, and proved to be a most congenial and happy crowd. Nothing in any way, shape or form transpired that could mar the unbroken pleasure and happiness of the entire day. Both those that came from near and from far left the happy couple full of most pleasant memories of the unusually joyous occasion. The gifts were appropriate, and nothing was left undone to complete the arrangements. The dinner was a sumptuous feast, and all that could be desired, both for its variety and its delicacies. There was music, instrumental and vocal; the addresses were alike characterized by a touching pathos and a pleasant vein of humor, and both speakers and hearers entered fully into the joys of the day. The venerable aged couple manifested a most decided appreciation of the kindness, love and honor shown them, and were at times moved to tears. We venture to say that there was no happier home or happier couple in Rowan county, or any other county, than this.

Truly, the venerable couple, so worthy of the highest esteem, were thus honored in a befitting manner, and all those who participated in, and all those who contributed towards the festive occasion, also honored themselves, and will long remember and with pleasure, the golden wedding of Rev. and Mrs. S. Rothrock, near Gold Hill, Rowan county, N. C., September 14th, 1887."

FATHER ROTHROCK

A Sketch of the Life of this Good Old Man, Written by One Who Knew and Loved Him.

Father Rothrock is dead! Last Friday, November 2nd, as the day was waning, he fell asleep, and his soul was wafted to its eternal abode. He had not been seriously ill. No fell disease played upon him, but while in his usual state of health death claimed him as his own. As he lived, so he died in peace.

On Sunday, the 4th inst., the funeral and burial obsequies were solemnized at Union Lutheran Church, five miles east of Salisbury. This day was one of autumn in her glory, of silvery skies and mellow sunshine, of nestling leaves and moaning breezes — one of those days whose glory subdues our vaunting spirits and bathes our souls in sweet solemnity.

An immense congregation assembled at the church to participate in the sad funeral rites and to offer a last tribute of love and respect to the dead. The congregation was composed largely of those among whom he lived and moved during the greater part of his life — of those he had consecrated in holy baptism, laid hands upon in confirmation and united in sacred marriage — and these, by their hushed voices, their noiseless footsteps and tear stained cheek — gave expression to the great love and deep devotion they cherished for their leader and benefactor.

The beautiful and soul inspiring form of burial service, according to the liturgy of the Lutheran church, was read in full by Revs. Lutz, King, Huddle and C. A. Brown. Then with a depth of pathos unknown to any but the loving and sympathetic hearts, the congregation, with bowed heads and subdued voices, joined in singing the sweet old hymnn: "Asleep in Jesus, blessed sleep."

Then followed a memoir of the deceased by Rev. W. A. Lutz, who also preached the funeral sermon. It was brief, yet eloquent, and contained, among many other things, the following facts:

Rev. Samuel Rothrock, D. D., familiarly known as "Father Rothrock", was born eight miles south of Salem, N. C., on November 26, 1809, being the fifth of a family of nine children. His ancestors were Huguenots. The early years of his life were spent on the farm and in the shop with his father.

He possessed a burning desire to obtain an education, but his advantages were exceedingly limited. Almost by chance he learned, through a newspaper, of the college at Gettysburg, Pa., and afterwards conceived the idea of taking a course at this institution. This vague idea grew into a strong determination and on March 7, 1829, at the age of 19 years, clad in a suit of home-spun jeans, with the meagre sum of fifty cents in his pocket and bearning a haversack which contained naught but a home-made suit of clothing and a Bible, he set out afoot for Gettysburg. After twenty days of walking, in sunshine and rain, through mud and mire, through valley and over mountain, he made the whole distance of nearly four hundred miles, arriving at Gettysburg on March 27th. He made one visit home, remaining 18 days, then returning to Gettysburg, thus walking the whole distance four times, counting his last return home.

He began preaching in 1832, acting as a supply for the pastorate of Dr. Kurtz, who at that time was prevented from serving his churches on account of ill health. He was licensed to preach in 1833, and was ordained in Virginia in 1834. He was pastor of the Lutheran church in Salisbury for two years, from 1833 to 1835. Afterward he was engaged in ministerial work in Pennsylvania for a period of one year. With the exception of this one year his whole ministerial life was spent in North Carolina. For 32-1/2 years he was pastor of historic Organ church, Rowan County, and during that time received more than 600 into that church. Twice he had the honor of being chosen president of the Southern General Lutheran Synod, in which position he exhibited unusual executive power and ability.

He was very business like and systematic and kept a strict record of all his transactions. From his papers we cull the following: He baptized 1,605 infants and 117 adults; confirmed 1,229 persons; married 470 couples; buried 922 persons and preached as many funerals. During his whole ministerial life, of more than 60 years, he preached upwards of 4,000 sermons. He was even systematic in his works of benevolence, and though he was by no means wealthy, he always gave one-twentieth of all his income to charitable and religious objects.

To demonstrate the nobility and purity of spirit which actuated and characterized the deceased in his latter years, it is not irrelevant to note a few expressions which he made shortly before his death. Prior to the war he was a slave owner and is said to have been one of the kindest and best of masters. Unlike many, he instructed his slaves in the principles of Christianity and had them baptised, himself becoming their sponsor. How superior was their lot to that of the majority of the race since their emancipation! Nevertheless, in conversing with his friends just before his death, he said: "I have but few things to regret, but if I could live my life over, I would never own a slave."

He was married twice, and lived with his second wife more than 50 years. In giving directions as to how he should be buried he said: "I buried my dear wife in a walnut coffin, but do not make my coffin of walnut, for I do not deserve as good as she." How free from vanity! Yet again while talking to Rev. Lutz with reference to his funeral obsequies he said, "When I die let no one eulogize me beyond what I deserve; tell my weaknesses as well as my virtues, if I possess any; say "There goes a sinner saved by grace." But, in the language of the churchyard Elegy

> "No farther seek his merits to disclose
> Or draw his frailities from their dread abode
> (There they alike in trembling hope repose)
> The bosom of his Father and his God."

Taking for his text the passage in the parable of the talents — "Well done, thou good and faithful servant; thou hast been faithful over a few things, I will make thee ruler over many things: enter thou into the joy of thy Lord," Rev. Lutz preached a powerful sermon. Using the facts given above as a basis, he pointed out in a clear and forcible manner how faithful Father Rothrock had been with the talent entrusted to his keeping and how rich would be his heritage in the kingdom of his Lord.

The sermon completed, while the congregation sang "How blest the righteous when he dies," the lid was removed from the coffin and the immense audience slowly and reverently filed by to take a last look at the dead. The procession then moved on to the grave and the body was committed to the soil that bore and cherished it. And it was then, as we heard the preacher say "Ashes to ashes and dust to dust," and heard the clods rattle upon the coffin lid, that we fully realized that Father Rothrock was really dead. So quiet and unpretentious had been his life, so numerous were the living monuments of his labors, so impressed were we with the record of his life, and so quiet and peaceful was his end, that it was hard to believe that we were burying from sight his mortal remains, and we tried to hush the stinging thought that called him dead.

Thus ends a memorable life — a life which is a blessing to the good and a reproach to the evil. Surely he shall not be reckoned the least in the history of the world nor receive the reward of the slothful in the great reckoning of the Master. Father Rothrock is dead, yet he lives! His influence pervades the lives of the thousands to whom he has ministered in perpetual benediction. Nor shall it cease when they, too, shall have entered "the bourne from whence no traveler returns;" but their children and their children's children shall reap the golden fruits of his righteousness. We might rear a column o'er his silent grave that would feel the kiss of every dawn and would be bathed in the glories of all sunsets, yet the good that he has done, the weary lives he has comforted, the troubled hearts he has consoled, the wayward souls he has reclaimed and blessed — all these speak in mightier tones — tones attuned to loving hearts and souls redeemed.

This obituary is from *The Daily Herald,* Salisbury, NC, Friday Evening, November 9, 1894.

APPENDIX D

Last Will and Testament

From Book #3, Pages 70, 71, 72 of Rowan County NC Wills.

Rowan County — In the Superior Court
State of North Carolina

    To all whom these Presents shall come - Greeting: It being satisfactorily proven to the undersigned Clerk of the Superior Court for Rowan County, that S. S. Rothrock late of the said County is dead, having made his last Will and Testament, which has been admitted to Probate, (a true copy whereof is hereunto annexed,) and Sam'l. F. Wiley one of the Executors therein named, having qualified as such according to law:

    Now these are therefore to empower the said Executor to enter in and upon all and singular the goods and chattels, rights and credits of the said deceased and the same to take into possession wheresoever to be found, and all the just debts of the said deceased to pay and satisfy: and the residue of said estate to distribute according to the directions of said Will.

    Witness my hand and the seal of the Court, this 16 day of January, 1895.

      W. G. Watson, Clerk of Superior Court.

State of North Carolina } In the Superior Court
    Rowan County   }

    A paper writing purporting to be the Last Will and Testament of Samuel Rothrock deceased is exhibited before me, the undersigned Clerk of the Superior Court for said County, by L. H. Rothrock. The Executor therein mentioned, and the due execution thereof by the said Samuel Rothrock is proved by the oath and examination of Lawson G. Holshouser and Milas A. Holshouser the subscribing witnesses thereto who being duly sworn, doth depose and say, and each for himself, deposeth and saith that he is a subscribing witness to the paper writing now shown him purporting to be the last will and testament of Samuel Rothrock that the said Samuel Rothrock in the presence of this deponent, subscribed his name at the end of such paper writing now shown as aforesaid, and which bears date of the 24 day of May, 1893. And the deponent saith that the said Samuel Rothrock the testator aforesaid, did at the time of the subscribing his name as aforesaid, declare the said paper writing so subscribed by him and exhibited to be his Last Will and Testament, and this deponent did thereupon subscribe his name at the end of said will as an attesting witness thereto, and at the request and in the presence of the said testator. And this deponent further saith that at the said time when the said testator subscribed his name to the said will as aforesaid, and at the time of the deponents subscribing his name as an attesting witness thereto, as aforesaid, the said Samuel Rothrock was of sound mind and memory, of full age to execute a will and was not under any restraint to the knowledge, information or belief of this deponent and further these deponents saith not.

        Lawson G. Holshouser {Seal)
        Milas A. Holshouser   {Seal}

Severally Sworn and subscribed
this 13 day of December, 1894 before me

      W. G. Watson
      Clerk Superior Court

Upon the evidence here deduced it is adjudged that the paper writing exhibited and every part and clause thereof is the Last Will and Testament of Samuel Rothrock deceased, which said Will and Testament is in the words and figures following to wit:

In the name of Almighty God, Amen.

I Samuel Rothrock, of Rowan County and State of North Carolina, being of disposing mind and memory, and considering the uncertainty of life, do make and publish this my last will and testament in manner following, that is to say:

1. I bequeath my body to the earth to be decently buried.

2. I commend my soul into the hands of a merciful God.

3. I direct all my just and burial expenses to be paid out of my estate. Among my just debts I include the following: One note of hand to Emma Peters for one hundred dollars bearing date May 15, 1890. One note of hand to Bettie Thomas for one hundred dollars bearing date of May 15, 1890. Said notes to be paid according to their true intent and meaning.

4. I give and bequeath my library, including all my books, pamphlets, and periodicals, to pass into the possession, immediately after my death, of my son, Lewis H. Rothrock.

5. I have already given to Emma Peters and to Bettie Thomas, to each of them, one bureau, one bed, and furniture as their absolute property.

6. Whereas Emma Peters and Bettie Thomas have, for a long time, lived in my family as members of the same, were kind and good to my wife during her life, are good and kind to me in my declining years, now if the said Emma Peters and Bettie Thomas shall continue with me as heretofore, then and in that case, I devise and bequest to them jointly my dwelling house and house furniture, my kitchen and utensils, necessary out buildings, all the provisions and poultry on hand, my sow, horse and garden to have and to hold the same without molestation, for the term of six months, next succeeding my death. My reason for making the foregoing bequest is to provide for the said Emma Peters and Bettie Thomas a home and comfortable support for the term specified, and to give them ample time to arrange for their future homes thereafter. The said Emma Peters and Bettie Thomas may at their option and for consideration satisfactory to them, transfer any or all of the foregoing bequest to my son Lewis H. Rothrock but not transfer or aliene to any other person.

All the residue of my estate, real and personal after the expiration of six months next succeeding my death, to pass into the hands of my son, L. H. Rothrock executor of this my last will and testament to execute the same according to the true intent and meaning thereof.

In testimony whereof I herewith set my hand and seal, this 24th day of May, 1893.

Samuel Rothrock   {Seal}

Signed as witnesses at the   }
request of the testator, and   }
in his presence.
Lawson G. Holshouser
Milas A. Holshouser

INDEX TO BAPTISMS

A List of Rev. Rothrock's Baptisms Wherein He Named the Child/Person (Arranged alphabetically):

Sat. Sund. August 5, 1838. Baptized Rev. **Arey**'s child in connection with 2 others.
Mond. April 3, 1854. Baptized Rev'd **Arey**'s child.

Tues. November 22, 1842. Baptized D. **Barringer**'s 3 children.
Thurs. July 7, 1887. Baptized Rufus O. **Barringer**'s child.
Frid. October 31, 1845. Baptized Sam'l. **Barrier**'s child
Thurs. April 9, 1874. Baptized and confirmed Dan'l. C. **Basinger**.
Thurs. June 27, 1844. Baptized Sam'l. **Bayam**'s child.
Sund. January 23, 1881. Baptized John F. **Beatty**'s child.
Mond. May 16, 1881. Baptized Carson A. B. **Beaver**'s child.
Tues. September 27, 1853. Baptized Paul **Beaver**'s child.
Mond. March 24, 1856. Baptized Paul **Beaver**'s child.
Frid. 16. Baptized H. **Beckerdite**'s child.
Frid. July 14, 1876. Baptized Jacob **Berger**'s infant child.
Sat. April 16, 1836. Baptized Mr. **Bermong**'s child.
Mond. May 31, 1886. Baptized Harvey A. **Bernhardt**'s child.
Mond. September 22, 1856. Baptized **David Bost**'s child.
Thurs. September 5, 1850. Baptized John **Bost**'s child.
Sat. December 13, 1862. Baptized Chas. **Bostian**'s child.
Mond. 6. Baptized B. **Braddy**'s child.
Tues. June 28, 1836. Baptized Mr. **Brech**'s child.
Frid. March 24, 1848. Baptized David **Brown**'s child.
Frid. August 5, 1870. Baptized Michael L. **Brown**'s child.
Sund. May 16, 1875. Baptized Pleasant M. **Brown**'s child.
Sund. May 30, 1875. Baptized Revd. R. L. **Brown**'s child.
Sat. June 24, 1882. Baptized Revd. R. L. **Brown**'s child.
Sat. January 26, 1884. Baptized Revd. R. L. **Brown**'s infant child.

Thurs. September 27, 1883. Baptized Monroe **Casper**'s child.
Frid. September 19, 1834. Baptized John **Cawble**'s wife.
Sat. March 21, 1835. Baptized 3 of John **Cawble**'s children.
Tues. November 28, 1843. Baptized John **Cawble**'s child.
Sund. December 19, 1841. Baptized the widow Moses **Cawble**'s child.
Sund. March 16, 1884. Baptized John **Clark**'s child.
Frid. April 15, 1836. Baptized Mr. **Cotz**'s child.
Sund. August 20, 1871. Baptized Mr. **Cozort**'s child.
Sund. July 24, 1836. Baptized 4 infts. Baptized Mr. **Cradler**'s child.
Mond. March 20, 1882. Baptized Absalom **Cress**' child.
Tues. February 26, 1884. Baptized Absalom **Cress**' child.
Sund. July 26, 1885. Baptized Anderson A. **Cruse**'s child.
Frid. October 17, 1856. Baptized Tobias **Cruse**'s 2 children.

Sat. September 20, 1834. Baptized 1 adult viz Camilla **Earnhart**.
Thurs. December 25, 1834. Baptized 4 children for Elias **Earnhart**.
Sund. February 28, 1886. Baptized Jacob C. **Earnheart**'s child.
Sat. May 13, 1871. Baptized and confirmed Leah **Earnheart**.
Sund. July 24, 1892. Baptized William A. **Earnheart**'s child.
Sat. July 15, 1843. Baptized the deceased Charles **Eller**'s child.
Frid. April 16, 1880. Baptized James **Eller**'s child.
Sat. April 25, 1874. Baptized 3 of Sam'l. **Elliott**'s children.

Wed. December 12, 1883. Baptized Alvin A. **Fisher**'s twin children.
Sund. November 27, 1859. Baptized and confirmed Mrs. Rebecca, wife of Peter E. **Foutz**.
Sat. Feb. 8, 1834. Baptized 7 children, 6 of whom were Wm. **Foltz**'s.
Sat. April 26, 1834. Baptized Alexander **Fraley**'s wife. Confirmed 4 others.
Sund. September 30, 1888. Baptized and confirmed 1 adult, viz, Martitia Catharine **Fraley**. Then Baptized her eight
children.
Thurs. January 7, 1836. Baptized **Frederick**'s the barber's child.

Sund. October 19, 1862. Baptized Adam **Goodman**.
Frid. October 1, 1852. Baptized Jacob **Goodman**'s child.

Sat. December 19, 1846. Baptized H. **Hahnberger**'s child.
Wed. March 21, 1888. Baptized E. B. C. **Hambley**'s child.
Sat. August 9, 1890. Baptized E. B. C. **Hambley**'s child.
Mond. January 8, 1877. Baptized O. W. **Hampton**'s 2 children.
Sat, March 1, 1834. Baptized Mr. **Harris**'s child.
Sund. September 1, 1850. Baptized Revd. **Harter**'s child.
Sund. October 7, 1849. Baptized Mr. **Hegler**'s 6 children.
Thurs. March 12, 1885. Baptized L. A. **Heilig**'s child.
Mond. January 26, 1852. Baptized Paul N. **Heilig**'s child.
Sund. July 31, 1836. Baptized Sarah **Hemphill**.
Thurs. September 29, 1836. Baptized five of Henry **Hickman**'s children.
Sund. June 24, 1883. Baptized J. M. **Hipp**'s child.
Mond. May 18, 1874. Baptized R. J. **Holmes**' child.
Wed. September 3, 1879. Baptized R. J. **Holmes**' child Ernest Lee.
Frid. May 25, 1860. Baptized Reuben J. **Holmes**' child.
Tues. February 14, 1871. Baptized 2 of Mr. R. J. **Holmes**' children.
Sund. May 19, 1889. Baptized and confirmed Reuben J. **Holmes** then his 2 grandchildren, the children of Charles H.
   Holmes and wife.
Wed. December 12, 1877. Baptized 6 children for Henry **Hohnberger**.
Sund. August 24, 1862. Baptized Eli **Holshouser**'s child.
Sund. March 31, 1844. Baptized Henry **Holshouser**'s child.
Mond. February 19, 1872. Baptized Michael **Holshouser**'s 2 children.

Sund. June 5, 1881. Baptized Augustus **Kerner**'s child.
Frid. March 10, 1843. Baptized Lony **Kesler**'s child.
Sund. April 10, 1859. Baptized Mr. **Ketchey**'s child (and another infant).
Mond. May 14, 1860. Baptized Mr. **Ketner**'s child.
Sat. June 16, 1883. Baptized M. A. **Ketner**'s child.
Sat. May 13, 1871. Baptized and confirmed Tiney Eliz. **Kirk**.
Sat. February 18, 1882. Baptized Alfred **Klutts**' child.
Sund. March 23, 1884. Baptized Edmond E. **Klutts**' child.
Sund. February 7, 1847. Baptized Tobias **Klutts**' child.
Frid. April 15, 1881. Baptized R. H. **Klutts**' child.

Sund. April 13, 1834. Baptized Mrs. **Lamb** and 7 children.
Sund. June 25, 1843. Baptized Moses **Lemly**'s child.
Thurs. March 23, 1871. Baptized Abram **Lentz**'s son.
Sat. April 24, 1880. Baptized 2 children for John H. **Lentz** and wife.
Wed. January 19, 1859. Baptized Mathias **Lentz**'s child.
Sat. December 25, 1858. Baptized Wilson **Lentz**'s child (and another infant).
Sund. April 7, 1872. Baptized Mr. Wilson **Lentz**'s grand-child.
Sund. Febuary 20, 1870. Baptized Mr. **Lingel**'s child.
Sat. March 3, 1888. Baptized G. W. **Linker**'s child.
Tues. May 26, 1891. Baptized G. W. **Linker**'s child.
Tues. May 26, 1891. Baptized John W. **Linker**'s child.
Tues. February 14, 1888. Baptized W. M. **Linker**'s child.
Mond. November 15, 1875. Baptized Mr. **Linton**'s child.
Sund. January 20, 1884. Baptized Calvin A. **Lipe**'s child.
Sund. August 28, 1892. Baptized C. R. **Lyerly**'s child.
Mond. May 19, 1879. Baptized Wm. **Lyerly**'s child.

Mond. February 17, 1873. Baptized Sam'l. M. **Martin**'s child.
Thurs. May 6, 1880. Baptized C. A. **Miller**'s child.
Thurs. September 13, 1888. Baptized Jeremiah J. **Miller**'s 2 children.
Sund. April 13, 1892. Baptized John S. M. **Miller**'s child.
Sund. August 9, 1885. Baptized Mr. Milas **Miller**'s child.
Wed. November 23, 1881. Baptized Paul A. **Miller**'s child.

Frid. April 18, 1845. Baptized Daywald **Miller**'s child.
Sund. November 28, 1869. Baptized Mr. Graber **Miller**'s child.
Wed. July 20, 1887. Baptized James A. **Miller**'s child.
Sund. December 22, 1878. Baptized John W. **Miller**'s child.
Tues. May 22, 1883. Baptized Paul A. **Miller**'s child.
Wed. January 19, 1848. Baptized Widow **Miller**'s (of Wm.) son.
Sund. December 4, 1881. Baptized J. W. **Misenheimer**'s child.
Sat. March 31, 1888. Baptized J. N. C. **Morgan**'s child.
Tues. January 4, 1853. Baptized Mr. **Moyer**'s child.
Sund. October 13, 1850. Baptized Dan'l. **Moyer**'s child.

Sat. April 4, 1846. Baptized William J. **McDaniel**.

Sund. May 20, 1883. Baptized Mr. **Patterson**'s child.
Sund. March 4, 1855. Baptized Joseph A. **Patterson**'s child.
Frid. June 13, 1856. Baptized Mr. Joseph A. **Patterson**'s child.
Sund. May 13, 1883. Baptized John A. **Peeler**'s child.
Sat. April 6, 1878. Baptized 2 of John **Powlass**' children.
Sund. September 21, 1884. Baptized Thornton R. **Powlass**' child.
Thurs. October 4, 1877. Baptized Wesley T. **Propst**'s child.
Sund. June 20, 1886. Baptized Wesley **Propst**'s 3 children.

Thurs. June 23, 1842. Baptized S. **Ribelin**'s child.
Sat. June 11, 1836. Baptized Mr. **Riechart**'s child.
Thurs. April 20, 1882. Baptized Frederick **Reimer**'s child.
Sat. April 20, 1872. Baptized Mr. **Robison**'s child.
Sund. March 28, 1847. Had our daughter, Charlotte Lucetta Jane [**Rothrock**] baptized by Revd. Anthony.
Sund. September 14, 1873. Baptized Lewis' [**Rothrock**] child.
Sund. October 31, 1875. Baptized Thomas, Lewis' [**Rothrock**] third child.
Tues. October 1, 1878. Baptized Lewis' [**Rothrock**] infant daughter.
Sund. March 4, 1855. Baptized Mr. **Rumple**'s child.

Thurs. May 17, 1860. Baptized Eli **Seaford**'s twin children.
Wed. October 10, 1855. Baptized Henry **Seaford**'s child.
Sund. July 13, 1862. Baptized Dan'l. S. **Sides**' child and two others.
Mond. May 29, 1874. Baptized Mr. and Mrs. **Simpson**'s child.
Mond. April 12, 1875. Baptized George H. **Shaver**'s child.
Sund. April 8, 1860. Baptized 3 infants and Adam and Eve C. **Stirewald**'s child.
Sund. January 1, 1882. Baptized Paul M. **Stirewalt**'s child.
Sund. Thurs. August 18, 1859. Baptized Jacob **Stirewalt**'s child.
Sund. April 17, 1836. Baptized Mr. **Stouer**'s child.

Mond. December 11, 1876. Rev'd. R. L. Brown baptized my ward, Elizabeth **Thomas**.
Thurs. August 15, 1844. Baptized H. **Thomas**' child.
Wed. September 21, 1836. Baptized 2 children, of whom Mr. **Tool** has the raising.
Mond. November 5, 1888. Baptized Rev'd. H. A. **Trexler**'s child.
Sund. April 6, 1890. Baptized infant child of Rev'd. H. A. **Trexler**.
Wed. October 30, 1844. Baptized Peter **Trexler**'s child.
Wed. July 28, 1847. Baptized Peter **Trexler**'s child.
Wed. December 12, 1877. Baptized Theophilus J. G. **Trexler**'s child.
Tues. January 25, 1881. Baptized Calvin M. **Troutman**'s child.
Sund. November 4, 1883. Baptized Wm. C. **Troutman**'s child.

Thurs. April 14, 1836. Baptized Mr. **Vondersmith**'s child.

Sund. January 19, 1862. Confirmed Amelia **Waller**.
Sund. May 5, 1839. Baptized Jacob **Walton**'s infant child.
Tues. December 26, 1882. Baptized Martin A. **Weaver**'s child.
Mond. November 30, 1835. Baptized Mrs. **Wunderlich** & child.

Mond. July 24, 1854. Baptized 1 of John **Yost**'s children.
Thurs. January 15, 1885. Baptized orphan child adopted by Solomon **Yost** and wife.

There were three instances where Rev. Rothrock did not specify either the name or number of baptized:

Sund. June 23, 1844, Sund. July 9, 1846 and Sund. December 28, 1862.

Rev. Rothrock did not name the person/child listed below:

Baptized 13 adults and confirmed them on Sund. November 7, 1886.

Baptized 8 infants on Sat. April 22, 1848.

Baptized 7 children or infants on Sund. August 20, 1843; Sat. April 23, 1859, and Sund. September 13, 1885.

Baptized 6 adults or infants on Sat. April 16, 1836; Sat. October 2, 1847; Sat. October 20, 1849; and Sat. April 21, 1860.

Baptized 5 adults or infants on Sund. May 17, 1835; Sund. July 24, 1836; Sat. April 6, 1839; Sund. April 3, 1842; Sat. May 6 and Mond. December 25, 1843; Sund. April 14 and Sund. June 2, 1844; Sat. April 25, 1846; Sat. June 3 and Sat. October 21, 1848; Sund. September 8; Sat. October 12; Mond. November 4 and Sund. November 10, 1850; Sund. March 27, 1853; Sund. March 12, 1854; Sund. December 23, 1855. Sat. May 3, 1862; Sund. March 26, 1876 and Sund. September 23, 1883.

Baptized 4 children, infants or adults on Sat. August 30, 1834; Sund. March 6, 1842; Sund. June 4 and Sat. October 21, 1843; Sund. April 5 and Sund. July 23, 1846; Sund. February 13, 1848; Sat. April 27; Sat. November 2 and Sat. November 16, 1850; Sund. July 13, 1851; Sund. February 8; Sund. March 11 and Sat. October 23, 1852; Sund. June 26, 1853; Sund. February 11 and Sat. October 27, 1855; Sund. April 13 and Sat. April 26, 1856; Sund. December 14, 1862; Sund. April 15, 1866; Sat. October 26, 1872; Sund. June 11, 1876; Sat. April 28, 1877 and Sat. April 26, 1879.

Baptized 3 children, infants or adults on Sund. October 18, 1835 (Baptized 3 children, 2 of whom were of Roman Catholic parents); Thurs. January 21; Sund. June 12 and Sat. September 24, 1836; Sund. August 5, 1838, (Baptized Rev. Arey's child in connection with 2 others); Sund. April 10; Sat. April 23; Sat. May 28 and Sat. October 1, 1842; Sat. May 20 and Sat. October 14, 1843; Sund. March 24 and Sund. May 26, 1844; Sund. October 19, 1845; Sat. April 17; Sund. June 6; Sund. July 11; Sund. November 28, 1847; Sund. February 27; Sund. August 13, 1848; Sund. February 25; Sund. April 8, 1849; Sund. January 12; Sat. December 6, 1851; Sund. February 1; Sat. March 24, 1852; Sund. July 10; Sat., October 1, 1853; Sat. May 20; Sund. May 28, 1854; Sat. April 21; Sund. May 13, 1855; Sund. February 24; Sat. July 5, 1856; Sund. May 8; Sat. July 9, 1859; Sund. April 8, 1860, (Baptized 3 infants and Adam and Eve C. Stirewald's child); Sund. March 8, 1863; Sat. October 21, 1865; Sund. February 27, 1876; Sat. April 19, 1879; Sund. April 11, 1880; Sund. January 23; Sund. March 27, 1881; Sat. July 21, 1883; Sat. April 25, 1885 and Sund. February 7, 1886.

Baptized 2 children, infants or adults on Sat. Feb. 15; Sund. March 9; Sat. March 1; Sund. March 16; Sund. July 13; Sund. August 17, 1834; Sund. March 15, 1835; Mond. February 22; Sat. April 30; Sund. May 15; Sund. May 22, 1836; Sund. February 24; Sund. June 16; Wed. July 31; Sund. October 20, 1839; Sund. January 23; Sund. March 20; Sat. April 9; Sat. April 16; Sund. September 4, 1842; Sund. April 9; Sund. April 23; Sat. May 13; Sat. October 28; Sat. November 11; Sund. November 12, 1843; Sund. January 14 (Twins); Sund. March 10; Sat. April 6; Sund. June 9; Sat. October 19, 1844; Sund. April 13; Sat. April 26; Sund. May 11; Sund. July 20; Sund. September 28, 1845; Sund. March 22; Sund. May 10; Sund. June 14; Sund. June 21; Sund. August 13; Sat. August 19, 1846; Sund. February 14; Sund. April 11; Sund. July 4; Sund. September 19; Sund. December 12, 1847; Sund. March 26; Sund. May 14; Sund. September 3; Sat. October 14, 1848; Sat. March 10; Sund. June 10; Sund. June 24; Sat. October 27, 1849; Sund. February 10; Sund. March 24; Sund. April 7; Sund. May 12; Sund. July 28; Sund. September 15, 1850; Sund. January 26; Sund. May 11; Sund. June 8; Sat. September 25; Sund. September 14, 1851; Sund. November 14, 1852; Sund. January 9; Sund. January 16; Sund. February 27; Sund. April 10; Sat. May 14; Sund. May 22; Sund. August 14; Sund. September 25; Sat. October 15; Sat. October 22; Sund. December 25, 1853; Sat. June 2; Sund. August 26; Sund. March 11, 1855; Sund. March 9; Sund. August 24; Sund. September 28; Sund. November 16, 1856; Sund. February 8; Sund. February 22; Sund. March 8, 1857; Sund. March 27; Sund. June 5; Sund. June 12; Sund. June 26; Sund. July 24; Sat. October 15; Sat. October 22; Sund. November 13, 1859; Sund. February 26;

Baptized 2 children, infants or adults (Continued):

Sund. March 25; Sund. April 15; Sund. May 27, 1860; Sund. July 13; Sund. September 14; Sat. October 18, 1862; Sund. September 24, 1865; Mond. May 21, 1866; Sund. November 7, 1869; Sat. April 23; Sund. September 25, 1870; Sund. July 16; Sund. September 3, 1871; Sund. August 11, 1872; Sat. April 12, 1873; Sund. May 10, 1874; Sat. April 24, 1875; Sund. February 20; Sund. October 15; Sat. November 4, 1876; Sund. March 18; Sund. March 25; Sat. April 20; Sund. June 3; Sund. August 26; Sund. November 18; Sat. December 15, 1877; Sund. May 26; Sund. August 25; Sund. November 3; Sund. December 22, 1878; Sund. November 16, 1879; Sund. January 11; Sat. April 17; Sund. June 13; Sund. September 19; Sat. October 16, 1880; Sund. April 3; Sund. May 8; Sat. July 23, 1881; Sund. November 12, 1882; Sund. June 17, 1883; Sund. July 13; Sund. August 24, 1884; Sat. July 25, 1885; Sund. February 14; Sund. October 3; Sund. October 3, 1886; Sund. December 6, 1893.

Baptized 1 child, infant or adult on Sund. March 2; Sat. March 15; Sund. March 23; Sund. April 20, (a colored man); Sund. June 8; Sat. June 14; Sat. September 20; Sat. September 20, (Baptized & confirmed 1 colored man); Sund. October 5; Sund. October 12; Sat. October 18, 1834; Sund. January 4; Sund. Feb. 1; Frid. September 25; Sund. October 11, 1835; Tues. March 29; Sat. April 9; Sund. April 10; Sund. May 29; Sat. August 13; Sund. September 11, (adult); Sund. September 11, (infant); Sund. September 18; Sund. October 22; Sund. October 29, 1836; Sund. August 12, (infant); Sund. August 12, (child); Sund. August 19; Sat. September 29; Sund. October 7, 1838; Sat. January 5; Sund. January 13; Sund. March 3; Sund. March 10; Sund. May 5; Wed. May 29; Sat. August 24; Sat. October 5; Sund. October 27; Sund. November 3; Sund. December 8, 1839; Sund. February 16, 1840; Sund. December 12; Sund. December 19, 1841; Sund. January 16; Sat. March 12; Sat. May 7; Sund. May 8; Sund. June 5; Sund. June 12; Sund. August 14; Sund. September 11; Sund. October 23, 1842; Sund. March 26; Sund. April 2; Sat. May 27; Sat. May 27; Sund. June 4; Sat. June 17; Sund. June 18; Sund. June 25; Sund. July 9; Sund. September 3; Sund. September 10; Sat. September 16; Sund. September 17; Frid. September 22; Sund. September 24; Sat. October 21; Sat. November 18; Frid. November 24; Frid. December 15, 1843; Frid. January 26; Sund. February 25; Sat. March 2; Sund. March 3; Sund. April 7; Sund. April 21; Sat. April 27; Sund. June 16; Sund. July 7; Sund. September 8; Sund. October 27; Frid. November 8; Sat. November 9; Sund. November 10; Sund. December 8; Wed. December 25; Thurs. December 26; Sat. December 28, 1844; Sund. February 9; Sund. February 16; Sund. March 9; Sund. March 16; Sund. April 6; Sund. June 8; Sund. July 13; Sund. October 12; Sat. October 25; Sund. November 16; Sund. November 23; Sund. November 30; Sund. December 7; Sund. December 28, 1845; Sund. January 25; Sund. February 8; Sund. February 15; Sund. February 22; Sund. March 1; Sat. April 4; Sund. April 12; Sund. May 31; Sund. July 12; Sund. August 6; Sat. August 26; Sund. August 27; Sund. November 8; Sund. December 13, 1846; Sund. January 3; Sund. January 24; Sund. February 7; Sund. February 21; Sund. February 28; Thurs. April 29; Sund. July 25; Sund. August 22; Sund. September 5; Sat. October 2; Sat. October 2; Sat. October 9; Sund. December 26, 1847; Sund. January 9; Sund. March 5; Sund. March 12; Sat. April 15; Sat. April 15; Sund. June 25; Sund. July 9; Sund. September 10; Sund. October 8; Sund. October 22; Sund. November 19; Sund. December 17, 1848; Sund. March 18, [1] Sund. March 18, [2] Sund. March 25; Sat. April 14; Sat. April 21; Sund. May 27; Sund. June 17; Sund. August 12; Sund. August 19; Sund. August 26; Sund. September 9; Sund. October 14; Frid. October 26; Sund. November 11; Sund. December 9; Sund. December 23, 1849; Sund. January 27; Sund. April 14; Sat. April 20; Sund. April 21; Sund. May 26; Sund. August 11; Frid. September 20; Sund. October 13; Sund. October 27; Sund. November 29, 1850; Sund. February 9; Sund. February 23; Sund. March 16; Sund. June 22; Sund. July 13; Sund. July 27; Sund. August 3; Sat. September 25, 1851; Sund. January 11; Sund. February 22; Sund. March 14; Sund. April 16; Sund. June 13; Sund. June 27; Sund. July 11; Sund. July 18; Sund. July 25; Sund. August 15; Sund. September 12; Sund. September 19; Sat. October 16; Sund. November 28; Sat. October 27, 1852; Sund. February 13; Sund. March 6; Sund. March 20; Sat. May 14; Sund. June 12; Sund. September 18; Sund. October 9; Sund. November 20; Sund. November 27; Frid. December 16, 1853; Sund. January 22; Sund. April 9; Sund. April 23; Sund. June 25; Sund. July 9; Sund. July 23; Sund. September 17; Sat. December 23; Sat. December 30, 1854, Sund. February 18; Sund. April 1; Sund. May 27; Sund. June 3; Sund. June 10; Sund. June 24; Sund. July 8; Sund. September 9; Sund. October 14; Sund. November 4, 1855, Sund. March 2; Sund. March 23; Sund. June 8; Sund. June 15; Sund. June 22; Sund. June 29; Sund. July 6; Sund. July 27; Sund. August 3; Sund. October 12 [1]; Sund. October 12 [2]; Sat. October 18; Sund. November 2; Sund. December 7; Sund. December 28, 1856; Sund. March 22; Sund. April 12; Sat. December 25, 1858 (also Wilson Lentz's child), January 8; Sund. April 10, (also Mr. Ketchey's child); Sat. April 16 [1]; Sat. April 16 [2]; Sat. April 23; Sund. July 10, 1859; Sund. January 15; Sund. January 22; Sat. January 28; Sund. March 11; Sund. May 13; Sund. June 3; Sund. June 10, 1860; Sund. January 12; Sund. January 26; Sund. February 2; Sund. February 9; Sund. February 23; Sund. May 11; Sund. September 7; Sund. September 21; Sund. October 12, 1862; Sund. May 21; Sund. June 11, July 28; Sund. August 27; Sund. October 1; Sat. October 21; Sat. October 21, 1865; Sat. April 14; Sat. April 14; Sund. April 15; Mond. May 21, 1866; Sund. November 7; Sat. December 4, 1869; Sund. January 16; Sund. January 23; Sund. March 6; Sund. June 26; Sund. October 16; Sund. December 18, 1870; Sund. February 5; Sund. April 16; Sund. April 23; Sund. May 7;

Baptized 1 child, infant or adult (Continued):

Sund. September 24, 1871 Sat. April 20; Sund. May 5; Sat. May 11; Sund. June 23; Sund. September 8; Sund. September 22, 1872; Sund. January 19; Sat. October 18; Sund. November 16; Sund. December 21, 1873; Sund. January 25; Sat. April 18; Sund. August 9; Sund. August 23; Sund. November 8; Sund. December 13, 1874; Sund. March 28; Sund. April 11; Sund. September 5, 1875; Sund. January 2; Sund. March 5; Sund. March 19; Sat. April 15; Sat. April 22; Sund. May 14; Sund. May 28; Sund. June 18; Sund. July 16; Sund. September 3; Sund. September 17; Sund. September 24; Sat. October 21, 1876; Sund. January 14; Sund. February 25; Sund. April 22; Sund. May 27; Sund. June 24; Sund. July 15; Sund. September 2; Sund. September 16; Sund. September 23; Sat. October 6; Sund. October 14; Sat. December 22, 1877; Sund. March 10; Sund. March 24; Sat. April 6; Frid. April 19; Sat. April 27; Sund. May 12; Sund. June 30; Sund. July 21; Sund. September 8; Sat. October 5; Sat. October 5; Sat. October 19; Sund. December 8; Sat. December 14; Frid. December 20, 1878; Sund. March 23; Sund. April 27, (Baptized and confirmed 1 adult). Sund. May 18; Sund. June 22; Sund. August 17; Sund. August 24; Sat. October 25; Sund. November 23; Sund. December 28, 1879; Sund. January 18; Sund. January 25; Sund. February 22; Sat. April 24; Sund. July 18; Sund. August 22; Sund. October 10; Sat. October 30; Sund. November 21, 1880; Sat. April 23; Sund. June 5; Sund. August 7; Sund. September 11; Sund. October 9; Sat. October 22; Sund. December 11, 1881; Sund. February 5; Sund. March 12; Sund. March 26; Sund. June 18; Sund. July 9; Sat. July 15; Sund. September 24; Sat. October 14; Sund. October 22; Sund. December 3, 1882; Sund. January 28; Sund. February 4; Sund. February 11; Sund. February 25; Sund. March 11; Sat. April 14; Sund. June 10; Sund. July 15; Sund. August 26; Sund. September 16; Sund. September 23; Sund. October 14; Sat. October 27, 1883; Frid. April 11; Sat. April 12; Sund. April 20; Sund. May 11; Sund. May 25; Sund. July 6.; Sat. July 19; Sat. July 26; Sund. August 17; Sund. September 21; Sund. October 12; Sat. October 25; Sund. December 14, 1884; Sund. March 8; Sund. April 5; Sund. April 12; Sund. June 7; Sund. June 14; Sund. August 30; Sund. October 25; Sat. October 31; Sat. November 7; Sund. November 22; Sund. December 20, 1885; Frid. February 19; Sat. April 10; Sund. April 11; Frid. April 23; Sat. April 24; Sund. April 25; Sund. September 5; Sat. October 16; Sund. November 21, 1886 (Baptized 1 adult and then confirmed him); Sund. April 22, 1888; Sund. August 28, 1892; Sund. October 2, and Sund. December 20, 1892.

INDEX TO CONFIRMATIONS

(By Date, where identified):

Sat. October 6, 1838. Confirmed 1 person, Mr. **Wade**.
Sund. October 21, 1838. Confirmed Mr. C. **Fisher**.
Sund. November 27, 1859. Baptized and confirmed Mrs. **Rebecca**, wife of Peter E. **Foutz**.
Sat. May 13, 1871. Baptized and confirmed Leah **Earnheart**.
Sat. May 13, 1871. Baptized and confirmed Tiney Eliz. **Kirk**.
Sund. September 23, 1883. Confirmed Charles **Bayam**.
Sund. April 11, 1886. Confirmed Mrs. Mary S. **Miller**.
Wed. March 21, 1888. Confirmed Dr. L. W. **Coleman**, Jane **Coleman**, and Lottie C. **Hambley**.

Confirmations, Not Named (By Date):

Sat. April 19, 2 males and 5 females; Sat. April 26, 4 persons; Sat. September 20, 33 persons, viz 18 females & 15 males; Sat. September 20, 1834, Baptized & confirmed 1 colored man; Sat. April 9, 13 persons; Sat. April 16, 18 persons; Sund. April 24, 1 person; Sund. September 11, 1836, 3 persons; Sund. September 30, 1838, 1 person; Sat. April 6, 1839, 1 person; Sund. April 10, 20 persons; Sat. April 30, 2 persons; Sat. October 1, 1842, 2 persons; Sat. May 6, 1 person; Sat. October 14, 13 persons; Sat. October 21, 9 persons; Sund. November 12, 1843, 10 persons; Sund. April 28, 1 person; Sat. November 9, 1 person; Thurs. December 26, 53 persons; Sat. December 28, 1844, 1 person; Sat. April 26, 15 persons; Sund. October 19, 1845, 24 persons; Frid. August 18, 1 person; Sat. August 19, 1846, 1 person; Thurs. April 29, 1847, 48 persons; Sund. July 8, 3 persons; Frid. April 20, 51 persons; Sat. October 20, 1849, 16 persons; Sat. October 12, 1850, 1 person; Sat. April 26, 46 persons; Sund. December 7, 1851, 3 persons; Sat. April 23, 61 persons; Sat. May 14, 19 persons; Sat. October 15, 1853, 1 person; Sund. May 21, 1854, 1 person; Sat. April 21, 1855, 53 persons; Sund. October 19, 1856, 1 person; Sat. April 16, Baptized and confirmed 2 persons; Sund. October 9, 1 person; Sat. April 23, 1859, 42 persons; Sund. April 30, 2 persons; Sund. May 7, 1 person; Sund. May 28, 1865, 2 persons; Sat. April 14, 1 person; Sund. April 15, 1866, 7 persons; Sund. October 23, 3 persons; Sund. December 11, 1870, 1 person; Sund. April 16, 5 persons; Sund. October 15, 1871, 6 persons; Sat. May 11, 1 person; Sund. October 20, 2 persons; Sat. October 26, 1872, 3 persons; Sat. April 19, 1873, 2 persons; Sund. April 26, 2 persons; Sund. October 25, 1874, 5 persons; Sund. April 16, 1876, 1 person; Sund. October 24, 1875, 4 persons; Sat. April 22, 3 persons; Sat. October 21, 8 persons; Sund. October 15, 2 persons; Sat. November 4, 1876, 1 person; Sat. April 20, 18 persons; Sat. October 6, 1877, 4 persons; Sat. April 6, 4 persons; Sund. April 21, 3 persons; Sund. October 20, 2 persons; Sat. October 26, 1878, 24 persons; Sund. April 27, 1879, Baptized and confirmed 1 adult; Sund. October 31, 1 person; Sat. October 16, 4 persons; Sat. October 30, 1880, 13 persons; Sund. January 30, 1 person; Sat. April 16, 2 persons; Sat. April 23, 1881, 1 person; Sat. October 14, 3 persons; Sat. October 21, 1882, 17 persons; Sat. October 20, 6 persons; Sat. October 27, 1883, 20 persons; Sat. October 25, 3 persons; Sat. April 12, 1884, 2 persons; Sund. September 13, 3 persons; Sat. November 7, 1885, 24 persons; Sat. October 16, 10 persons; Sund. November 21, 1886, Baptized 1 adult and then confirmed him; Sund. September 30, 1888, 2 persons.

INDEX TO MARRIAGES

During the period from 1834 through 1893 covered by the diaries now available to us, Samuel Rothrock recorded some 351 marriages, of which he apparently did not actually perform four, but witnessed. In one instance, he did not leave a record of the bridegroom's name.

For quick reference, we here note those 351 marriages in alphabetical order, first by the bride's surname, then by the groom's surname. Please refer to the actual diaries for more details.

INDEX TO MARRIAGES — BRIDE
Alphabetical by Bride's Surname

Wed. Jan. 31, 1866	Richard L. Brown	and	Nancy E. **Agner**
Tues. Feb. 13, 1849	John Miller	and	Eliz. A. **Air**
Wed. Apr. 17, 1850	John Clarke	and	Charlotte **Arey**
Tues. May 26, 1835	Charles Barringer	and	Elizabeth **Arey**
Sund. Mar. 22, 1846	Wilie Knup	and	Elizabeth **Arey**
Thurs. Nov. 24, 1853	Dr. Littleton W. Coleman	and	Jane **Arey**
Tues. Feb. 4, 1834	David Barringer	and	Mary **Arey**
Thurs. Mar. 25, 1852	John S. Long	and	Esther **Barger**
Wed. Jan. 31, 1855	Daniel M. Moose	and	Anna Louisa **Barrier**
Thurs. Jan. 25, 1872	Jesse W. Miller	and	Laura M. **Barrier**
Thurs. May 11, 1843	Caleb Heilig	and	Mary **Barrier**
Thurs. Mar. 13, 1856	John J. Barringer	and	Mary L. **Barrier**
Thurs. Oct. 26, 1848	Edward Moss	and	Christiana **Barringer**
Thurs. Dec. 9, 1875	Charles A. Miller	and	Ellen E. A. **Barringer**
Thurs. Jan. 15, 1835	Ambrose Eddleman	and	Elizabeth **Barringer**
Thurs. Dec. 13, 1877	Groom Unknown	and	Lucy C. **Barringer**
	(Witnessed the marriage)		
Sund. Nov. 30, 1851	William A. Lentz	and	Lunda M. **Barringer**
Thurs. May 26, 1853	Osborne M. Klutts	and	Mary C. **Barringer**
Thurs. Aug. 10, 1848	John D. Gadlin	and	Rebecca **Barringer**
Thurs. Jun. 24, 1847	John Lowder	and	Sarah L. **Barringer**
Thurs. Jan. 28, 1886	George W. Culp	and	Julia A. **Basinger**
Sund. Oct. 14, 1888	Moselle Earnheart	and	Sarah Jane **Basinger**
Thurs. Jan. 31, 1878	Carson A. B. Beaver	and	Alice E. **Beaver**
Thurs. Apr. 25, 1850	Jacob Holshouser	and	Anna **Beaver**
Thurs. Jun. 6, 1850	Moses A. Bost	and	Caroline **Beaver**
Thurs. Oct. 12, 1854	Reuben W. Bost	and	Catherine E. **Beaver**
Thurs. Apr. 12, 1877	Luther W. S. Bost	and	Ella Maria **Beaver**
Thurs. Dec. 14, 1882	James M. Eller	and	Ellen S. **Beaver**
Thurs. Feb. 6, 1862	David Earnheart	and	Eve L. **Beaver**
Thurs. Jul. 17, 1873	Levi J. Hampton	and	Leah **Beaver**
Thurs. Feb. 26, 1857	Andrew A. Bostian	and	Louisa **Beaver**
Thurs. Dec. 21, 1882	Charles E. Bost	and	Martha R. C. **Beaver**
Sund. Jun. 1, 1856	Joseph Cruse	and	Rachel **Beaver**
Thurs. Dec. 5, 1878	Michael C. Bodenhamer	and	Eliza J. **Beckerdite**
Thurs. Jan. 30, 1845	Henry L. Brown	and	Magdalene **Berger**
Wed. Aug. 22, 1849	Rev. J. A. Linn	and	Margaret A. **Bernhardt**
Wed. Jan. 14, 1852	William Safret	and	Catherine **Blackwelder**
Thurs. Jun. 1, 1843	Daniel Techour	and	Leah **Boger**
Thurs. Jul. 7, 1859	Henry M. Miller	and	Melinda **Boogs**
Thurs. Dec. 9, 1852	Jesse Beaver	and	Catherine L. **Bost**
Wed. Dec. 28, 1859	Tobias Miller	and	Jemima E. **Bost**
Thurs. Nov. 30, 1876	Luther C. Miller	and	Laura A. **Bost**
Thurs. Nov. 20, 1884	Henry J. Bost	and	Margaret D. **Bost**
Thurs. Dec. 17, 1885	David C. Holshouser	and	Sarah E. A. **Bost**

Thurs. May 6, 1886	George A. Bean	and	Susan L. **Bost**
Thurs. Dec. 16, 1852	George Smith	and	Margaret A. **Bostian**
Sund. Dec. 1, 1853	Joseph A. Patterson	and	Margaret L. **Bostian**
Thurs. Dec. 13, 1855	Danl. Troutman	and	Catharine **Brady**
Thurs. Jan. 21, 1836	John Bates	and	Barbara **Bricken**
Sund. Apr. 26, 1885	Harvey A. Holshouser	and	Dovie D. **Brown**
Thurs. Mar. 27, 1834	Paul Miller	and	Elizabeth **Brown**
Tues. Jul. 27, 1852	Peter A. Fisher	and	Elizabeth C. **Brown**
Sund. Oct. 25, 1885	Caleb L. Klutts	and	Ellen A. **Brown**
Wed. Jul. 18, 1883	Rev. S. T. Hallman	and	Lilian L. **Brown**
Thurs. Mar. 1, 1860	Alfred W. Rusher	and	Malissa C. **Brown**
Thurs. Jun. 11, 1846	Edward Baim	and	Margaret **Brown**
Thurs. Feb. 22, 1844	Henry Barringer	and	Maria **Brown**
Thurs. Aug. 16, 1849	Geo. A. Brown	and	Maria S. **Brown**
Thurs. May 8, 1856	Paul Misenheimer	and	Maria S. **Brown**
Wed. Oct. 16, 1872	Charles N. Simpson	and	Martha R. **Brown**
Thurs. Sep. 6, 1855	David Fisher	and	Mary A. L. **Brown**
Sund. Jan. 19, 1890	John W. Linker	and	Mary A. L. **Brown**
Tues. Apr. 14, 1846	John J. Miller	and	Mary Ann **Brown**
Tues. Feb. 12, 1839	John L. Randleman	and	Nancy **Brown**
Tues. Mar. 4, 1834	Elexandre Hulen	and	Sophia **Brunner**
Thurs. Apr. 23, 1835	David Miller	and	Eliz. **Butner**
Wed. Apr. 14, 1880	Henry A. C. Ketner	and	Alice **Caldwell**
Sund. Jan. 2, 1859	Henry Troutman	and	Rachel **Casper**
Tues. Dec. 21, 1852	Milas Shuping	and	Mary **Cauble**
Thurs. Aug. 22, 1839	Moses Trexler	and	Margaret **Cawble**
Thurs. Feb. 3, 1887	Egbert B. C. Hambley	and	Lottie C. **Coleman**
Tues. Dec. 27, 1870	Julius B. Sheets	and	Louisa H. **Colly**
Thurs. Mar. 5, 1840	Richard Julin	and	Sophia **Creason**
Tues. May 27, 1845	Joseph Miller	and	Nuly **Cress**
Sund. Jan 3, 1875	John W. Fisher (colored)	and	Anna **Crowell** (colored)
Thurs. Apr. 2, 1891	Thomas R. Sheets	and	Jennie **Crowell**
Thurs. Dec. 22, 1870	Richard C. Horton	and	M. P. **Crowell**
Thurs. Sep. 1, 1892	Robert C. Pool	and	Mrs. Margaret E. **Crowell**
Thurs. Oct. 1, 1846	Danl. Klutts	and	Catherine **Cruse**
Thurs. Aug. 28, 1879	Reuben W. Bost	and	Crissie C. **Cruse**
Thurs. Oct. 26, 1865	John Fisher	and	Leah **Cruse**
Thurs. Jan. 15, 1885	Paul J. Klutts	and	Margaret A. **Cruse**
Tues. Feb. 28, 1854	Solomon Klutts	and	Maria, widow of Danl. **Cruse**
Thurs. Mar. 18, 1852	Danl. Fisher	and	Rose Ann **Cruse**
Thurs. Sep. 27, 1855	L. Calvin Miller	and	Lovina **Culp**
Sund. Dec. 3, 1848	Henry Dry	and	Mary Ann **Culp**
Wed. Sep. 10, 1856	John Eddleman	and	Mary C. **Culp**
Thurs. Apr. 25, 1872	David R. Julian	and	Bettie **Culverhouse**

(Attended the marriage by Rev. Neiffer)

Thurs. Sep. 19, 1844	Ambrose Lentz	and	Polly Caroline **Dry**
Wed. Mar. 28, 1860	Caleb A. Basinger	and	Catherine Ann **Eagle**
Thurs. Feb. 12, 1846	Charles Bostian	and	Sena **Eagle**
Wed. Aug. 10, 1859	Allison Misenheimer	and	Sophia L. **Eagle**
Thurs. Dec. 25, 1884	W. M. Linker	and	Camilla C. **Earnheart**
Tues. Aug. 5, 1851	James Montgomery	and	Leah **Earnheart**
Thurs. Aug. 12, 1869	J. M. Cross	and	Rachel C. **Earnheart**
Tues. Oct. 26, 1847	Wiley Kirk	and	Susan **Earnheart**
Tues. May 22, 1849	Jeremiah L. Graeber	and	Mrs. E. **Eddleman**
Tues. Oct. 27, 1846	Wilson A. Lentz	and	Polly **Eddleman**

Thurs. Dec. 15, 1881	Augustus L. Pless	and	Mary E. **Faggart**
Thurs. Mar. 22, 1866	Henry H. Clark	and	Camilla **Fesperman**
Tues. Jul. 31, 1849	Jacob Lyerly, jr.	and	Anna **Fisher**
Thurs. Nov. 11, 1852	William A. Houck	and	Catherine L. **Fisher**
Thurs. Mar. 5, 1857	John Klutts	and	Elizabeth C. **Fisher**
Wed. May 9, 1888.	Joseph W. Holshouser	and	Emma U. **Fisher**
Thurs. Jul. 10, 1873	Rev. Henry M. Brown	and	Lucetta J. **Fisher**
Thurs. Oct. 19, 1882	Albert L. Lingel	and	Martha G. **Fisher**
Thurs. Apr. 21, 1859	Jacob Berger	and	Mary A. L. **Fisher**
Thurs. May 25, 1843	Franklin Smith	and	Mary Ann **Fisher**
Thurs. Jan. 29, 1880	Geo. A. Bost	and	Sarah E. **Fisher**
Wed. Jun. 29, 1870	W. L. Kistler	and	Lucy **Foster**

(Married by Rev. Pharr)

Wed. Sep. 4, 1872	Pleasant M. Brown	and	Maria C. **Foster**
Thurs. Mar. 23, 1848	Jesse Barrier	and	Elizabeth C. **Fouts**
Thurs. Feb. 14, 1850	Geo. A. Barger	and	Rebecca C. **Fouts**
Thurs. Jun. 30, 1853	Joseph Beaver	and	Rachel M. **Foutz**
Sund. Jan. 12, 1845	Michael Goodman	and	Sarah **Foutz**
Thurs. Jun. 19, 1856	Henry M. Beaver	and	Susanna **Foutz**
Wed. Apr. 23, 1845	Rev. John Lantz	and	Nancy **Fraley**

(Witnessed marriage by Rev. Crooks)

Thurs. May 23, 1844	Goodman Spencer	and	Elis. **Gadlin**
Thurs. Dec. 28, 1848	James Klutts	and	Matty **Garner**
Tues. Sep. 27, 1859	Solomon Ketchey	and	Susanna **Garner**
Thurs. Jan. 18, 1844	George Basinger	and	Anna **Ghentz**
Mond. Sep. 21, 1835	Henry Swink	and	Barbara **Gitz**
Wed. Oct. 4, 1871	Saml. M. F. Martin	and	Altisa C. **Goodman**
Thurs. Apr. 25, 1850	John E. Miller	and	Elizabeth **Goodman**
Tues. Feb. 26, 1850	Aaron Richie	and	Leah **Goodman**
Thurs. Mar. 3, 1870	Adam Holshouser	and	Lydia **Goodman**
Wed. May 12, 1852	John Lippard	and	Louisa R. H. **Graeber**
Wed. Oct. 22, 1856	Michael Goodman	and	Sarah A. **Graeber**
Thurs. Feb. 13, 1873	Moses Cress	and	Jane **Graham**

Sund. Oct. 6, 1850	George Goodman	and	Catherine **Hahnberger**
Thurs. Oct. 8, 1835	Abraham Crider	and	Margaret Ann **Hamilton**
Sund. Nov. 12, 1865	Crawford Holshouser	and	Elizabeth **Harkey**
Wed. Mar. 26, 1845	William McDaniel	and	Susanne **Harkey**
Thurs. Apr. 16, 1835	David Beaver	and	Abaline **Hartman**
Tues. Aug. 5, 1856	John W. Fisher	and	Christena L. **Hartman**
Wed. Jul. 27, 1859	Paul Peeler	and	Mary C. **Hartman**
Tues. Aug. 22, 1843	Milas Arey	and	Sophia **Hartman**
Thurs. Nov. 28, 1844	John H. Miller	and	Camilla C. **Heilig**
Thurs. Aug. 21, 1834	Peter Peck	and	Catherine **Heilig**
Wed. Oct. 10, 1877	John J. Quantz	and	Catharine M. **Heilig**
Thurs. Jul. 17, 1856	Milas Rusher	and	Mary Ann M. **Heilig**
Thurs. Aug. 19, 1852	Reuben Y. Holmes	and	R. S. Caroline **Heilig**
Thurs. Jan. 1, 1880	John A. F. Earnheart	and	Nancy Jane **Hemphill**
Thurs. Apr. 7,1853	Aaron W. Miller	and	Rachel L. **Henly**
Thurs. Apr. 21, 1859	James W. Rymer	and	Lydia Ann **Hill**
Tues. Apr. 12, 1859	Saml. M. Rymer	and	Sarah J. **Hill**
Thurs. Nov. 21, 1872	A. R. Shoaf	and	Malinda C. **Hoffman**
Sund. Dec. 23, 1877	Paul Holshouser	and	Catharine L. **Hoffner**
Tues. May 14, 1844	John Bullen	and	Tena **Hoffner**
Wed. Nov. 16, 1870	John Brady	and	Barbara **Holshouser**
Wed. Feb. 14, 1866	John V. Fisher	and	Catharine L. **Holshouser**
Thurs. Jul. 21, 1853	Jacob Klutts	and	Eliza M. **Holshouser**
Thurs. Jan. 9, 1879	George W. Park	and	Laura Jane **Holshouser**

Wed. Dec. 29, 1852	Eli Seaford	and	Margaret **Holshouser**
Thurs. Feb. 23, 1854	Jesse Miller	and	Margaret **Holshouser**
Thurs. May 18, 1871	Moses G. Brady	and	Mary L. **Holshouser**
Thurs. Dec. 16, 1852	Charles Lyerly	and	Sarah **Holshouser**
Thurs. Oct. 15, 1835	Henry Unger	and	Susannah **Hotzhe**
Wed. Apr. 7, 1852	Eli A. Propst	and	Amelia A. **House**
Thurs. Apr. 13, 1854	Henry G. Lentz	and	Elizabeth **Hudgins**
Thurs. Aug. 17, 1876	James C. Sides	and	Martha J. **Isenhour**
Thurs. Feb. 28, 1850	Michael A. Bostian	and	Rachel **Icehour**
Thurs. Nov. 4, 1847	Thomas Reimer	and	Sally **Icehour**
Thurs. Nov. 3, 1870	Henry Clay Loftin (colored)	and	Amy **Ingram** (colored)
Thurs. Aug. 30, 1877	James Owens	and	Ellen M. **Isenhour**
Thurs. Dec. 24, 1874	Nathen R. Morgan	and	Mary M. **Isenhour**
Thurs. Jun. 5, 1873	D. L. Parker	and	Ellen **Jenkins**
Thurs. Sep. 29, 1836	John Keler	and	Myring **Johns**
Thurs. Mar. 26, 1857	Joseph Basinger	and	Crissa F. **Josey**
Thurs. Sep. 22, 1836	Geo. Dick	and	Cath. **Keler**
Tues. Oct. 30, 1855	Benjamin F. Walton	and	Widow Catharine **Kesler**
Wed. Nov. 26, 1890	Benjamin E. Sumner	and	Sophie **Kesler**
Thurs. Feb. 6, 1851	Elam A. Patterson	and	Barbara M. **Ketner**
Thurs. Oct. 9, 1856	Alexander Leip	and	Elizabeth L. **Ketner**
Thurs. Sep. 4, 1856	George W. Misenheimer	and	Susanna **Ketner**
Thurs. Jul. 31, 1851	Ellick M. Miller	and	Edith **Kirk**
Thurs. Dec. 2, 1847	Eli Lentz	and	Elizabeth **Kirk**
Thurs. Mar. 12, 1846	Simon P. Eddleman	and	Eve **Kirk**
Thurs. Nov. 29, 1849	Peter E. Fouts	and	Rebecca **Kirk**
Tues. May 11, 1847	David Holshouser	and	widow Sally **Kistler**
Thurs. Jun. 2, 1853	George M. Fisher	and	Amy **Klutts**
Sund. Sep. 26, 1886	Albert S. Miller	and	Anna E. L. **Klutts**
Thurs. Apr. 6, 1848	Geo. E. Bost	and	Caroline **Klutts**
Thurs. May 8, 1851	Mathias M. Lentz	and	Caroline **Klutts**
Tues. Dec. 5, 1843	Laurence Misenheimer	and	Christena L. **Klutts**
Sund. Nov. 10, 1878	Adam M. Nussman	and	Ellen **Klutts**
Thurs. Aug. 22, 1850	Moses Trexler	and	Eve C. **Klutts**
Thurs. Dec. 22, 1853	John D. Miller	and	Eve Elizabeth **Klutts**
Thurs. Mar. 20, 1856	John P. Eagle	and	Leah **Klutts**
Thurs. Nov. 3, 1870	Caleb L. Nussman	and	Margaret C. F. **Klutts**
Thurs. Mar. 24, 1870	Osborn M. Holshouser	and	Martha C. **Klutts**
Sund. Jun. 9, 1844	Alexander Corl	and	Mary **Klutts**
Wed. Mar. 5, 1856	Moses A. Fesperman	and	Mary **Klutts**
Thurs. Dec. 15, 1859	Danl. W. Propst	and	Mary E. **Klutts**
Thurs. Dec. 4, 1879	Caleb M. Troutman	and	Sarah A. **Klutts**
Tues. Mar. 29, 1836	John Bachman	and	Esther **Krider**
Thurs. Sep. 24, 1874	Thomas J. Bashford	and	Lucy A. **Krimminger**
	(Aided Rev. Neiffer)		
Sund. May 21, 1865	Samuel Snider	and	Ann **Layton**
Thurs. Jul. 14, 1842	John Powless	and	Amey **Lentz**
Sund. Nov. 25, 1883	Brantly R. A. Beaver	and	Camilla E. **Lentz**
Thurs. Apr. 24, 1851	Paul Holshouser	and	Elenora **Lentz**
Sund. Jan. 7, 1872	Daniel Harkey	and	Harriet E. **Lentz**
Thurs. Oct. 23, 1856	Monroe Troutman	and	Margaret A. **Lentz**
Thurs. Nov. 18, 1869	Jesse A. Cozort	and	Mary J. **Lentz**
Thurs. Jan. 6, 1859	John A. Barrier	and	Sophia L. **Lentz**
Thurs. Sep. 29, 1853	Jacob Klutts	and	Catharine L. **Leppard**
Thurs. Oct. 20, 1853	Archibald M. A. Klutts	and	Clarissa M. **Leppard**
Thurs. Mar. 20, 1856	William Beaver	and	Crissa E. **Leppard**

Wed. Nov. 26, 1856	Peter A. Brown	and	Eliza. S. **Leppard**
Thurs. Sep. 20, 1855	David A. Bost	and	Sophia L. **Leppard**
Thurs. Apr. 22, 1852	John Trexler Esq.	and	Anna **Lingle**
Thurs. Jun. 24, 1875	Calvin H. Bost	and	Laura R. **Lingle**
Thurs. Jun. 12, 1856	George A. Miller	and	Louisa **Lingel**
Thurs. Jun. 13, 1850	Andrew Berger	and	Sarah C. **Lingle**
Thurs. Jul. 20, 1848	Isaac Kessler	and	Mrs. Eliza **Linn**
Thurs. Dec. 24, 1874	Frank Heilig (colored)	and	Julia **Linn** (colored)
Thurs. Oct. 22, 1885	Dr. C. M. Pool	and	Mary E. **Linn**
Tues. Jul. 31, 1849	George A. Rusher	and	Louisa M. **Lippard**
Thurs. Aug. 10, 1848	Moses Seaford	and	Sarah M. **Lippard**
Thurs. Feb. 1, 1883	Luther C. Sowers	and	Fannie F. **Long**
Wed. Sep. 2, 1874	Thomas H. Kirk	and	Eliza Jane **Ludwick**
Thurs. Feb. 5, 1852	Caleb Trexler	and	Elizabeth L. **Lyerla**
Thurs. Apr. 29, 1886	John H. A. Barger	and	Catharine S. **Lyerly**
Thurs. May 2, 1844	Moses Klutts	and	Leah **Lyerly**
Thurs. Jan. 4, 1844	Adam Trexler, jr.	and	Margaret **Lyerly**
Thurs. Nov. 30, 1843	Danl. Brown	and	Polly **Lyerly**
Tues. May 21, 1878	Rufus P. Roseman	and	Sarah E. **Lyerly**
Tues. Oct. 19, 1875	John F. Eagle	and	Addie H. **Miller**
Thurs. Feb. 20, 1851	Pinkney Summit	and	Barbara B. **Miller**
Thurs. Apr. 12, 1860	Jacob W. Bost	and	Catharine **Miller**
Sund. Dec. 23, 1883	Harvey B. Foutz	and	Emma B. **Miller**
Thurs. Feb. 12, 1880	Calvin A. Fisher	and	Eliza A. E. **Miller**
Thurs. Apr. 16, 1835	Peter Trexler	and	Eliz. C. **Miller**
Thurs. May 21, 1885	Monroe M. Ketner	and	Ellen E. A. **Miller**
Sund. Apr. 19, 1885	Albert D. Thomas	and	Eve Ann **Miller**
Wed. Dec. 7, 1859	Eli Holshouser	and	Laura C. **Miller**
Sund. Apr. 23, 1893	John L. Holshouser	and	Laura C. **Miller**
Thurs. Aug. 10, 1882	Rufus A. Taylor	and	Laura M. **Miller**
Sund. Oct. 20, 1844	Harris M. Ridenhour	and	Levina **Miller**
Wed. Jan. 19, 1848	Edmond Fesperman	and	Margaret D. **Miller**
Tues. Jun. 21, 1836	John Rensch	and	Margaretta **Miller**
Thurs. Oct. 1, 1885	Eli. D. A. Beaver	and	Martha R. **Miller**
Thurs. Jan. 24, 1856	Richard C. Brown	and	Mary C. **Miller**
Thurs. Apr. 2, 1885	Paul S. Klutts	and	Mary D. **Miller**
Thurs. Dec. 29, 1881	John A. Peeler	and	Mary L. J. **Miller**
Thurs. Feb. 13, 1845	David Knup	and	Philpena **Miller**
Thurs. Oct. 21, 1847	Ambrose Lentz	and	Rebecca E. **Miller**
Thurs. Apr. 14, 1842	Peter L. Barringer	and	Rose Ann **Miller**
Thurs. Jun. 25, 1846	Moses Trexler	and	Widow **Miller**
Sund. Dec. 1, 1853	Moses Safret	and	Widow Christena L. **Misenheimer**
Wed. Oct. 16, 1850	Augustus F. Graeber	and	Margaret A. **Misenheimer**
Thurs. Nov. 30, 1882	George C. Klutts	and	Mattie C. **Misenheimer**
Tues. Jul. 5, 1836	William Smith	and	Mary **Morgan**
Thurs. May 7, 1874	Geo. A. Canup	and	Mary C. **Morgan**
Thurs. May 24, 1866	Lewis M. Brady	and	Philpena E. **Morgan**
Sund. Jun. 24, 1855	Rufus Miller	and	Elizabeth C. **Moyer**
Thurs. Dec. 19, 1872	David L. Elliott	and	Licetta J. **Moyer**
Sund. Apr. 5, 1891	James R. Sparnell	and	Ida C. **McAllister**
Thurs. Aug. 31, 1843	Jack Garner	and	Marg. **Newman**
Thurs. May 24, 1860	Julius A. Coleman	and	Elizabeth A. **Nichols**
Sund. Jun. 1, 1879	John Leonard	and	Laura **Noah**
Sund. Jul. 13, 1879	William T. R. Jenkins	and	Margaret Ann **Northern**
Sund. Nov. 9, 1845	Peter Earnheart	and	Catherine **Nussman**
Wed. Dec. 30, 1846	Rev. W. G. Harter	and	Margaret V. **Nuttall**

Thurs. Jan. 3, 1856	Jeremiah Beaver	and	Mary Ann C. **Overcash**
Thurs. Oct. 31, 1850	J. A. Troutman	and	Amelia **Parham**
Thurs. Dec. 31, 1885	Henry W. Cauble	and	Beneter C. **Parker**
Sund. Nov. 22, 1891	Dr. L. N. Burleyson	and	Ella M. **Parker**
Tues. May 25, 1852	George Moyer	and	Mrs. **Peacock** (widow)
Thurs. Mar. 27, 1834	Solomon Sifford	and	Mary **Pealer**
Thurs. Sep. 23, 1847	Edmond Honeycut	and	Caroline **Peck**
Thurs. Aug. 18, 1853	John Lingle	and	Eve Ann **Peeler**
Thurs. Dec. 25, 1884	John S. Beaver	and	Mary Jane **Peeler**
Wed. Feb. 23, 1859	Alexander Peeler	and	Sarah Ann E. **Peeler**
Tues. Aug. 1, 1854	Peter Trexler Esq.	and	Sarah C. **Peeler**
Thurs. Jan. 23, 1840	Adam Casper	and	Sophia **Peeler**
Thurs. Apr. 13, 1854	Milas A. Holshouser	and	Sophia L. **Peeler**
Thurs. Mar. 29, 1866	Solomon Wotzman	and	Harriet E. **Pool**
Wed. Dec. 28, 1881	Adolphus A. Miller	and	Margaret A. **Powlass**
Thurs Oct. 16, 1884	Julius A. A. Earnheart	and	Martha E. **Powlass**
Thurs. Dec. 10, 1874	Joseph T. Carson	and	Martha L. **Quillman**
Tues. Nov. 1, 1859	John C. Miller	and	Mary Ann **Redwine**
Thurs. Dec. 19, 1872	Caleb Lentz	and	Maggie **Reeves**
Thurs. Apr. 27, 1854	Tobias Cruse	and	Catherine L. **Reimer**
Sund. Aug. 13, 1876	John W. Miller	and	Eve Ann Maria **Reimer**
Thurs. Apr. 27, 1854	Alexander M. Miller	and	Clotilda **Ribelin**
Tues. Jan. 30, 1866	Calvin L. Brown	and	Mititia **Ribelin**
Thurs. Dec. 2, 1869	John Eagle	and	Amanda J. **Riles**
Thurs. Oct. 28, 1852	Danl. Beaver	and	Anna C. **Rimer**
Tues. Jun. 25, 1889	Julius A. Castor	and	Mrs. Sarah Jane **Ritchie**
Thurs. Dec. 21, 1871	James H. Hodges	and	Lizzie M. **Ritz**

(Attended ceremonies by Rev. J. G. Neiffer)

Thurs. Oct. 9, 1834	George Randleman	and	Eliza **Rosamon**
Thurs. Dec. 27, 1888	Albert L. Lyerly	and	Fannie E. **Roseman**
Thurs. Apr. 7, 1842	Jacob Brown	and	Eliza **Rothrock**
Sund. Jun. 19, 1881	James H. Jenkins	and	Laura V. **Rouse**
Thurs. Feb. 11, 1836	John Bechdole	and	Sarah **Sachman**
Wed. Feb. 4, 1852	Geo. H. Ritchie	and	Eliza **Safret**
Thurs. Apr. 9, 1857	Jacob P. Goodman	and	Margaret **Safret**
Wed. Feb. 18, 1857	George V. Bost	and	Rosina C. **Safret**
Tues. Feb. 8, 1842	John Yost	and	Sarah **Safret**
Tues. Nov. 15, 1859	Thomas Sapp	and	Sarah **Safret**
Thurs. Jan. 8, 1846	Guy Hill	and	Anna **Seaford**
Wed. Mar. 28, 1866	Dr. James P. Porter	and	Lovinia B. **Seaford**
Sund. May 23, 1852	George M. Ketner	and	Margaret **Seaford**
Thurs. Jun. 12, 1845	Henry Kluts	and	Susan **Seaford**
Tues. May 1, 1855	Moses Bostian	and	Temperance L. **Seaford**
Thurs. Jul. 28, 1836	Nicholas Mourer	and	Sarah Ann **Sellers**
Tues. Dec. 26, 1848	Danl. C. Kirk	and	Mary **Shaver**
Tues. Aug. 4, 1846	Jacob Stirewalt	and	Mary K. **Shaver**
Thurs. Oct. 23, 1856	Jacob Probst	and	Rebecca **Shaver**
Sund. Nov. 21, 1869	J. F. Watts	and	Martha Ann **Sheets**
Thurs. Oct. 9, 1856	Peter A. Bostian	and	Barbara C. **Shive**
Thurs. Jun. 1, 1865	Peter A. Ritchey	and	Elizabeth C. **Shuping** (widow)
Thurs Dec. 4, 1890	James M. Wood	and	Emma J. **Small**
Thurs. May 17, 1877	George W. Barringer	and	Mrs. Mary A. **Smith**
Thurs. May 20, 1852	Alexander Bostian	and	Mary E. **Smith**
Tues. Aug. 5, 1845	John Hartman	and	Nancy Ann **Smith**
Sund. Apr. 15, 1855	Charles S. Patterson	and	Rose Anna **Smith**

Sund. Aug. 23, 1835	John Marshal	and	Sarah **Spitle**
Thurs. Oct. 31, 1878	Rev. William A. Lutz	and	Esther C. **Stafford**
Sund. Feb. 15, 1891	Joseph A. Basinger	and	Minnie E. **Stikeleather**
Sund. May 11, 1845	John Smith	and	Catharine **Stirewalt**
Thurs. Jan. 6, 1842	John Ingram	and	Jane **Stokes**
Thurs. Jun. 10, 1847	D. Setzer	and	Fanny **Thomas**
	(Attended wedding)		
Thurs. Dec. 4, 1879	David M. Lyerly	and	Charlotte C. **Trexler**
Thurs. Apr. 9, 1885	Jacob Jeremiah Miller	and	Lottie S. **Trexler**
Thurs. Feb. 25, 1847	Moses Lingle	and	Louisa **Trexler**
Thurs. Jan. 15, 1880	Jesse F. Park	and	Margaret J. **Trexler**
Thurs. Aug. 31, 1865	James P. Earnheart	and	Sophia C. **Trexler**
Sund. May 18, 1845	Adam Cruse	and	Catherine **Troutman**
Sund. Mar. 30, 1890	Robert J. Coleman	and	Laura C. **Troutman**
Thurs. Jan. 15, 1885	Milas Safrit	and	Laura M. **Troutman**
Thurs Aug. 14, 1851	Danl. Brown	and	Leah **Troutman**
Thurs. Jul. 31, 1856	Jeremiah Basinger	and	Margaret **Troutman**
Thurs. Aug. 4, 1881	J. M. Hipp	and	S. M. **Troutman**
Thurs. Jan. 7, 1875	Eli Holshouser	and	Leah **Wagoner**
Sund. Dec. 16, 1838	Alexander Brown	and	Elizabeth **Walton**
Tues. Jun. 30, 1874	George Achenbach	and	Melinda F. **Walton**
Thurs. Apr. 17, 1834	Robert Ramsy	and	Mary **Walton**
Tues. Aug. 12, 1845	Levi Thomas	and	Susan **Walton**
Sund. Apr. 24, 1842	Asa Ribelin	and	Susan C. **Walton**
Thurs. Apr. 7, 1836	John Croft	and	Martha **Wartz**
Tues. Mar. 8, 1859	Paul Yost	and	Adaline **Weaver**
Thurs. Aug. 26, 1852	Alexander Yost	and	Elizabeth S. **Weaver**
Thurs. Nov. 30, 1882	William C. Troutman	and	Mary Ann C. V. **Weaver**
Thurs. Jan. 12, 1843	(br). Adam Rothrock	and	Elizabeth **Whitlow**
Sund. Dec. 7, 1856	Moses Linn	and	Elizabeth **Wormington**
Thurs. Feb. 10, 1881	John M. Clarke	and	Lundy M. **Yost**
Tues. Dec. 24, 1844	John Bostian	and	Polly Eliza **Yost**
Tues. Apr. 27, 1847	George Troutman	and	Sophia C. **Yost**
Wed. Dec. 22, 1869	Jacob A. Berger	and	Elizabeth C. **Young**

INDEX TO MARRIAGES — GROOM
Alphabetical by Groom's Surname

Thurs. Dec. 13, 1877	Groom Unknown	and	Lucy C. Barringer
	(Witnessed the marriage)		
Tues. Jun. 30, 1874	George **Achenbach**	and	Melinda F. Walton
Tues. Aug. 22, 1843	Milas **Arey**	and	Sophia Hartman
Tues. Mar. 29, 1836	John **Bachman**	and	Esther Krider
Thurs. Jun. 11, 1846	Edward **Baim**	and	Margaret Brown
Thurs. Feb. 14, 1850	Geo. A. **Barger**	and	Rebecca C. Fouts
Thurs. Apr. 29, 1886	John H. A. **Barger**	and	Catharine S. Lyerly
Thurs. Mar. 23, 1848	Jesse **Barrier**	and	Elizabeth C. Fouts
Thurs. Jan. 6, 1859	John A. **Barrier**	and	Sophia L. Lentz
Tues. May 26, 1835	Charles **Barringer**	and	Elizabeth Arey
Tues. Feb. 4, 1834	David **Barringer**	and	Mary Arey
Thurs. May 17, 1877	George W. **Barringer**	and	Mrs. Mary A. Smith
Thurs. Feb. 22, 1844	Henry **Barringer**	and	Maria Brown
Thurs. Mar. 13, 1856	John J. **Barringer**	and	Mary L. Barrier
Thurs. Apr. 14, 1842	Peter L. **Barringer**	and	Rose Ann Miller
Thurs. Sep. 24, 1874	Thomas J. **Bashford**	and	Lucy A. Krimminger
	(Aided Rev. Neiffer)		
Wed. Mar. 28, 1860	Caleb A. **Basinger**	and	Catherine Ann Eagle
Thurs. Jan. 18, 1844	George **Basinger**	and	Anna Ghentz
Thurs. Jul. 31, 1856	Jeremiah **Basinger**	and	Margaret Troutman
Thurs. Mar. 26, 1857	Joseph **Basinger**	and	Crissa F. Josey
Sund. Feb. 15, 1891	Joseph A. **Basinger**	and	Minnie E. Stikeleather
Thurs. Jan. 21, 1836	John **Bates**	and	Barbara Bricken
Thurs. May 6, 1886	George A. **Bean**	and	Susan L. Bost
Sund. Nov. 25, 1883	Brantly R. A. **Beaver**	and	Camilla E. Lentz
Thurs. Jan. 31, 1878	Carson A. B. **Beaver**	and	Alice E. Beaver
Thurs. Oct. 28, 1852	Danl. **Beaver**	and	Anna C. Rimer
Thurs. Apr. 16, 1835	David **Beaver**	and	Abaline Hartman
Thurs. Oct. 1, 1885	Eli. D. A. **Beaver**	and	Martha R. Miller
Thurs. Jun. 19, 1856	Henry M. **Beaver**	and	Susanna Foutz
Thurs. Jan. 3, 1856	Jeremiah **Beaver**	and	Mary Ann C. Overcash
Thurs. Jun. 30, 1853	Joseph **Beaver**	and	Rachel M. Foutz
Thurs. Dec. 9, 1852	Jesse **Beaver**	and	Catherine L. Bost
Thurs. Dec. 25, 1884	John S. **Beaver**	and	Mary Jane Peeler
Thurs. Mar. 20, 1856	William **Beaver**	and	Crissa E. Leppard
Thurs. Feb. 11, 1836	John **Bechdole**	and	Sarah Sachman
Thurs. Jun. 13, 1850	Andrew **Berger**	and	Sarah C. Lingle
Thurs. Apr. 21, 1859	Jacob **Berger**	and	Mary A. L. Fisher
Wed. Dec. 22, 1869	Jacob A. **Berger**	and	Elizabeth C. Young
Thurs. Dec. 5, 1878	Michael C. **Bodenhamer**	and	Eliza J. Beckerdite
Thurs. Jun. 24, 1875	Calvin H. **Bost**	and	Laura R. Lingle
Thurs. Dec. 21, 1882	Charles E. **Bost**	and	Martha R. C. Beaver
Thurs. Sep. 20, 1855	David A. **Bost**	and	Sophia L. Leppard
Thurs. Jan. 29, 1880	Geo. A. **Bost**	and	Sarah E. Fisher
Thurs. Apr. 6, 1848	Geo. E. **Bost**	and	Caroline Klutts
Wed. Feb. 18, 1857	George V. **Bost**	and	Rosina C. Safret
Thurs. Nov. 20, 1884	Henry J. **Bost**	and	Margaret D. Bost
Thurs. Apr. 12, 1860	Jacob W. **Bost**	and	Catharine Miller
Thurs. Apr. 12, 1877	Luther W. S. **Bost**	and	Ella Maria Beaver
Thurs. Jun. 6, 1850	Moses A. **Bost**	and	Caroline Beaver
Thurs. Oct. 12, 1854	Reuben W. **Bost**	and	Catherine E. Beaver
Thurs. Aug. 28, 1879	Reuben W. **Bost**	and	Crissie C. Cruse
Thurs. May 20, 1852	Alexander **Bostian**	and	Mary E. Smith
Thurs. Feb. 26, 1857	Andrew A. **Bostian**	and	Louisa Beaver
Thurs. Feb. 12, 1846	Charles **Bostian**	and	Sena Eagle

Tues. Dec. 24, 1844	John **Bostian**	and	Polly Eliza Yost
Thurs. Feb. 28, 1850	Michael A. **Bostian**	and	Rachel Icehour
Tues. May 1, 1855	Moses **Bostian**	and	Temperance L. Seaford
Thurs. Oct. 9, 1856	Peter A. **Bostian**	and	Barbara C. Shive
Wed. Nov. 16, 1870	John **Brady**	and	Barbara Holshouser
Thurs. May 24, 1866	Lewis M. **Brady**	and	Philpena E. Morgan
Thurs. May 18, 1871	Moses G. **Brady**	and	Mary L. Holshouser
Sund. Dec. 16, 1838	Alexander **Brown**	and	Elizabeth Walton
Tues. Jan. 30, 1866	Calvin L. **Brown**	and	Mititia Ribelin
Thurs. Nov. 30, 1843	Danl. **Brown**	and	Polly Lyerly
Thurs. Aug. 14, 1851	Danl. **Brown**	and	Leah Troutman
Thurs. Aug. 16, 1849	Geo. A. **Brown**	and	Maria S. Brown
Thurs. Apr. 7, 1842	Jacob **Brown**	and	Eliza Rothrock
Thurs. Jan. 30, 1845	Henry L. **Brown**	and	Magdalene Berger
Thurs. Jul. 10, 1873	Rev. Henry M. **Brown**	and	Lucetta J. Fisher
Wed. Nov. 26, 1856	Peter A. **Brown**	and	Eliza. S. Leppard
Wed. Sep. 4, 1872	Pleasant M. **Brown**	and	Maria C. Foster
Thurs. Jan. 24, 1856	Richard C. **Brown**	and	Mary C. Miller
Wed. Jan. 31, 1866	Richard L. **Brown**	and	Nancy E. Agner
Tues. May 14, 1844	John **Bullen**	and	Tena Hoffner
Sund. Nov. 22, 1891	Dr. L. N. **Burleyson**	and	Ella M. Parker
Thurs. May 7, 1874	Geo. A. **Canup**	and	Mary C. Morgan
Thurs. Dec. 10, 1874	Joseph T. **Carson**	and	Martha L. Quillman
Tues. Jun. 25, 1889	Julius A. **Castor**	and	Mrs. Sarah Jane Ritchie
Thurs. Dec. 31, 1885	Henry W. **Cauble**	and	Beneter C. Parker
Thurs. Jan. 23, 1840	Adam **Casper**	and	Sophia Peeler
Thurs. Mar. 22, 1866	Henry H. **Clark**	and	Camilla Fesperman
Wed. Apr. 17, 1850	John **Clarke**	and	Charlotte Arey
Thurs. Feb. 10, 1881	John M. **Clarke**	and	Lundy M. Yost
Thurs. May 24, 1860	Julius A. **Coleman**	and	Elizabeth A. Nichols
Thurs. Nov. 24, 1853	Dr. Littleton W. **Coleman**	and	Jane Arey
Sund. Mar. 30, 1890	Robert J. **Coleman**	and	Laura C. Troutman
Sund. Jun. 9, 1844	Alexander **Corl**	and	Mary Klutts
Thurs. Nov. 18, 1869	Jesse A. **Cozort**	and	Mary J. Lentz
Thurs. Feb. 13, 1873	Moses **Cress**	and	Jane Graham
Thurs. Oct. 8, 1835	Abraham **Crider**	and	Margaret Ann Hamilton
Thurs. Apr. 7, 1836	John **Croft**	and	Martha Wartz
Thurs. Aug. 12, 1869	J. M. **Cross**	and	Rachel C. Earnheart
Sund. May 18, 1845	Adam **Cruse**	and	Catherine Troutman
Sund. Jun. 1, 1856	Joseph **Cruse**	and	Rachel Beaver
Thurs. Apr. 27, 1854	Tobias **Cruse**	and	Catherine L. Reimer
Thurs. Jan. 28, 1886	George W. **Culp**	and	Julia A. Basinger
Thurs. Sep. 22, 1836	Geo. **Dick**	and	Cath. Keler
Sund. Dec. 3, 1848	Henry **Dry**	and	Mary Ann Culp
Thurs. Dec. 2, 1869	John **Eagle**	and	Amanda J. Riles
Tues. Oct. 19, 1875	John F. **Eagle**	and	Addie H. Miller
Thurs. Mar. 20, 1856	John P. **Eagle**	and	Leah Klutts
Thurs. Feb. 6, 1862	David **Earnheart**	and	Eve L. Beaver
Thurs. Aug. 31, 1865	James P. **Earnheart**	and	Sophia C. Trexler
Thurs. Jan. 1, 1880	John A. F. **Earnheart**	and	Nancy Jane Hemphill
Thurs. Oct. 16, 1884	Julius A. A. **Earnheart**	and	Martha E. Powlass
Sund. Oct. 14, 1888	Moselle **Earnheart**	and	Sarah Jane Basinger
Sund. Nov. 9, 1845	Peter **Earnheart**	and	Catherine Nussman
Thurs. Jan. 15, 1835	Ambrose **Eddleman**	and	Elizabeth Barringer
Wed. Sep. 10, 1856	John **Eddleman**	and	Mary C. Culp
Thurs. Mar. 12, 1846	Simon P. **Eddleman**	and	Eve Kirk

Thurs. Dec. 14, 1882	James M. **Eller**	and	Ellen S. Beaver
Thurs. Dec. 19, 1872	David L. **Elliott**	and	Licetta J. Moyer
Wed. Jan. 19, 1848	Edmond **Fesperman**	and	Margaret D. Miller
Wed. Mar. 5, 1856	Moses A. **Fesperman**	and	Mary Klutts
Thurs. Feb. 12, 1880	Calvin A. **Fisher**	and	Eliza A. E. Miller
Thurs. Mar. 18, 1852	Danl. **Fisher**	and	Rose Ann Cruse
Thurs. Sep. 6, 1855	David **Fisher**	and	Mary A. L. Brown
Thurs. Jun. 2, 1853	George M. **Fisher**	and	Amy Klutts
Thurs. Oct. 26, 1865	John **Fisher**	and	Leah Cruse
Sund. Jan 3, 1875	John W. **Fisher** (colored)	and	Anna Crowell (colored)
Tues. Aug. 5, 1856	John W. **Fisher**	and	Christena L. Hartman
Wed. Feb. 14, 1866	John V. **Fisher**	and	Catharine L. Holshouser
Tues. Jul. 27, 1852	Peter A. **Fisher**	and	Elizabeth C. Brown
Thurs. Nov. 29, 1849	Peter E. **Fouts**	and	Rebecca Kirk
Sund. Dec. 23, 1883	Harvey B. **Foutz**	and	Emma B. Miller
Thurs. Aug. 10, 1848	John D. **Gadlin**	and	Rebecca Barringer
Thurs. Aug. 31, 1843	Jack **Garner**	and	Marg. Newman
Sund. Oct. 6, 1850	George **Goodman**	and	Cathcrine Hahnberger
Thurs. Apr. 9, 1857	Jacob P. **Goodman**	and	Margaret Safret
Sund. Jan. 12, 1845	Michael **Goodman**	and	Sarah Foutz
Wed. Oct. 22, 1856	Michael **Goodman**	and	Sarah A. Graeber
Wed. Oct. 16, 1850	Augustus F. **Graeber**	and	Margaret A. Misenheimer
Tues. May 22, 1849	Jeremiah L. **Graeber**	and	Mrs. E. Eddleman
Wed. Jul. 18, 1883	Rev. S. T. **Hallman**	and	Lilian L. Brown
Thurs. Feb. 3, 1887	Egbert B. C. **Hambley**	and	Lottie C. Coleman
Thurs. Jul. 17, 1873	Levi J. **Hampton**	and	Leah Beaver
Sund. Jan. 7, 1872	Daniel **Harkey**	and	Harriet E. Lentz
Wed. Dec. 30, 1846	Rev. W. G. **Harter**	and	Margaret V. Nuttall
Tues. Aug. 5, 1845	John **Hartman**	and	Nancy Ann Smith
Thurs. May 11, 1843	Caleb **Heilig**	and	Mary Barrier
Thurs. Dec. 24, 1874	Frank **Heilig** (colored)	and	Julia Linn (colored)
Thurs. Jan. 8, 1846	Guy **Hill**	and	Anna Seaford
Thurs. Aug. 4, 1881	J. M. **Hipp**	and	S. M. Troutman
Thurs. Dec. 21, 1871	James H. **Hodges**	and	Lizzie M. Ritz
	Ceremony by Rev. J. G. Neiffer		
Thurs. Aug. 19, 1852	Reuben Y. **Holmes**	and	R. S. Caroline Heilig
Thurs. Mar. 3, 1870	Adam **Holshouser**	and	Lydia Goodman
Sund. Nov. 12, 1865	Crawford **Holshouser**	and	Elizabeth Harkey
Tues. May 11, 1847	David **Holshouser**	and	widow Sally Kistler
Thurs. Dec. 17, 1885	David C. **Holshouser**	and	Sarah E. A. Bost
Wed. Dec. 7, 1859	Eli **Holshouser**	and	Laura C. Miller
Thurs. Jan. 7, 1875	Eli **Holshouser**	and	Leah Wagoner
Sund. Apr. 26, 1885	Harvey A. **Holshouser**	and	Dovie D. Brown
Thurs. Apr. 25, 1850	Jacob **Holshouser**	and	Anna Beaver
Sund. Apr. 23, 1893	John L. **Holshouser**	and	Laura C. Miller
Wed. May 9, 1888	Joseph W. **Holshouser**	and	Emma U. Fisher
Thurs. Apr. 13, 1854	Milas A. **Holshouser**	and	Sophia L. Peeler
Thurs. Mar. 24, 1870	Osborn M. **Holshouser**	and	Martha C. Klutts
Thurs. Apr. 24, 1851	Paul **Holshouser**	and	Elenora Lentz
Sund. Dec. 23, 1877	Paul **Holshouser**	and	Catharine L. Hoffner
Thurs. Sep. 23, 1847	Edmond **Honeycut**	and	Caroline Peck
Thurs. Dec. 22, 1870	Richard C. **Horton**	and	M. P. Crowell
Thurs. Nov. 11, 1852	William A. **Houck**	and	Catherine L. Fisher
Tues. Mar. 4, 1834	Elexandre **Hulen**	and	Sophia Brunner
Thurs. Jan. 6, 1842	John **Ingram**	and	Jane Stokes

Sund. Jun. 19, 1881	James H. **Jenkins**	and	Laura V. Rouse
Sund. Jul. 13, 1879	William T. R. **Jenkins**	and	Margaret Ann Northern
Thurs. Apr. 25, 1872	David R. **Julian**	and	Bettie Culverhouse

(Attended the marriage by Rev. Neiffer)

Thurs. Mar. 5, 1840	Richard **Julin**	and	Sophia Creason
Thurs. Sep. 29, 1836	John **Keler**	and	Myring Johns
Thurs. Jul. 20, 1848	Isaac **Kessler**	and	Mrs. Eliza Linn
Tues. Sep. 27, 1859	Solomon **Ketchey**	and	Susanna Garner
Sund. May 23, 1852	George M. **Ketner**	and	Margaret Seaford
Wed. Apr. 14, 1880	Henry A. C. **Ketner**	and	Alice Caldwell
Thurs. May 21, 1885	Monroe M. **Ketner**	and	Ellen E. A. Miller
Tues. Dec. 26, 1848	Danl. C. **Kirk**	and	Mary Shaver
Wed. Sep. 2, 1874	Thomas H. **Kirk**	and	Eliza Jane Ludwick
Tues. Oct. 26, 1847	Wiley **Kirk**	and	Susan Earnheart
Wed. Jun. 29, 1870	W. L. **Kistler**	and	Lucy Foster

(Married by Rev. Pharr)

Thurs. Feb. 13, 1845	David **Knup**	and	Philpena Miller
Sund. Mar. 22, 1846	Wilie **Knup**	and	Elizabeth Arey
Thurs. Jun. 12, 1845	Henry **Kluts**	and	Susan Seaford
Thurs. Oct. 20, 1853	Archibald M. A. **Klutts**	and	Clarissa M. Leppard
Sund. Oct. 25, 1885	Caleb L. **Klutts**	and	Ellen A. Brown
Thurs. Oct. 1, 1846	Danl. **Klutts**	and	Catherine Cruse
Thurs. Nov. 30, 1882	George C. **Klutts**	and	Mattie C. Misenheimer
Thurs. Jul. 21, 1853	Jacob **Klutts**	and	Eliza M. Holshouser
Thurs. Sep. 29, 1853	Jacob **Klutts**	and	Catharine L. Leppard
Thurs. Dec. 28, 1848	James **Klutts**	and	Matty Garner
Thurs. Mar. 5, 1857	John **Klutts**	and	Elizabeth C. Fisher
Thurs. May 2, 1844	Moses **Klutts**	and	Leah Lyerly
Thurs. Jan. 15, 1885	Paul J. **Klutts**	and	Margaret A. Cruse
Thurs. Apr. 2, 1885	Paul S. **Klutts**	and	Mary D. Miller
Thurs. May 26, 1853	Osborne M. **Klutts**	and	Mary C. Barringer
Tues. Feb. 28, 1854	Solomon **Kluttz**	and	Maria, widow of Danl. Cruse
Wed. Apr. 23, 1845	Rev. John **Lantz**	and	Nancy Fraley

(Witnessed marriage by Rev. Crooks)

Thurs. Oct. 9, 1856	Alexander **Leip**	and	Elizabeth L. Ketner
Thurs. Sep. 19, 1844	Ambrose **Lentz**	and	Polly Caroline Dry
Thurs. Oct. 21, 1847	Ambrose **Lentz**	and	Rebecca E. Miller
Thurs. Dec. 19, 1872	Caleb **Lentz**	and	Maggie Reeves
Thurs. Dec. 2, 1847	Eli **Lentz**	and	Elizabeth Kirk
Thurs. Apr. 13, 1854	Henry G. **Lentz**	and	Elizabeth Hudgins
Thurs. May 8, 1851	Mathias M. **Lentz**	and	Caroline Klutts
Sund. Nov. 30, 1851	William A. **Lentz**	and	Lunda M. Barringer
Tues. Oct. 27, 1846	Wilson A. **Lentz**	and	Polly Eddleman
Sund. Jun. 1, 1879	John **Leonard**	and	Laura Noah
Thurs. Oct. 19, 1882	Albert L. **Lingel**	and	Martha G. Fisher
Thurs. Aug. 18, 1853	John **Lingle**	and	Eve Ann Peeler
Sund. Feb. 25, 1847	Moses **Lingle**	and	Louisa Trexler
Thurs. Jan. 19, 1890	John W. **Linker**	and	Mary A. L. Brown
Thurs. Dec. 25, 1884	W. M. **Linker**	and	Camilla C. Earnheart
Wed. Aug. 22, 1849	Rev. J. A. **Linn**	and	Margaret A. Bernhardt
Sund. Dec. 7, 1856	Moses **Linn**	and	Elizabeth Wormington
Wed. May 12, 1852	John **Lippard**	and	Louisa R. H. Graeber
Thurs. Nov. 3, 1870	Henry Clay **Loftin** (colored)	and	Amy Ingram (colored)
Thurs. Mar. 25, 1852	John S. **Long**	and	Esther Barger
Thurs. Jun. 24, 1847	John **Lowder**	and	Sarah L. Barringer
Thurs. Oct. 31, 1878	Rev. William A. **Lutz**	and	Esther C. Stafford
Thurs. Dec. 27, 1888	Albert L. **Lyerly**	and	Fannie E. Roseman

Thurs. Dec. 16, 1852	Charles **Lyerly**	and	Sarah Holshouser
Thurs. Dec. 4, 1879	David M. **Lyerly**	and	Charlotte C. Trexler
Tues. Jul. 31, 1849	Jacob **Lyerly**, jr.	and	Anna Fisher
Sund. Aug. 23, 1835	John **Marshal**	and	Sarah Spitle
Wed. Oct. 4, 1871	Saml. M. F. **Martin**	and	Altisa C. Goodman
Thurs. Apr. 7, 1853	Aaron W. **Miller**	and	Rachel L. Henly
Wed. Dec. 28, 1881	Adolphus A. **Miller**	and	Margaret A. Powlass
Sund. Sep. 26, 1886	Albert S. **Miller**	and	Anna E. L. Klutts
Thurs. Apr. 27, 1854	Alexander M. **Miller**	and	Clotilda Ribelin
Thurs. Dec. 9, 1875	Charles A. **Miller**	and	Ellen E. A. Barringer
Thurs. Apr. 23, 1835	David **Miller**	and	Eliz. Butner
Thurs. Jul. 31, 1851	Ellick M. **Miller**	and	Edith Kirk
Thurs. Jun. 12, 1856	George A. **Miller**	and	Louisa Lingel
Thurs. Jul. 7, 1859	Henry M. **Miller**	and	Melinda Boogs
Thurs. Apr. 9, 1885	Jacob Jeremiah **Miller**	and	Lottie S. Trexler
Thurs. Feb. 23, 1854	Jesse **Miller**	and	Margaret Holshouser
Thurs. Jan. 25, 1872	Jesse W. **Miller**	and	Laura M. Barrier
Tues. Feb. 13, 1849	John **Miller**	and	Eliz. A. Air
Tues. Nov. 1, 1859	John C. **Miller**	and	Mary Ann Redwine
Thurs. Dec. 22, 1853	John D. **Miller**	and	Eve Elizabeth Klutts
Thurs. Apr. 25, 1850	John E. **Miller**	and	Elizabeth Goodman
Thurs. Nov. 28, 1844	John H. **Miller**	and	Camilla C. Heilig
Tues. Apr. 14, 1846	John J. **Miller**	and	Mary Ann Brown
Sund. Aug. 13, 1876	John W. **Miller**	and	Eve Ann Maria Reimer
Tues. May 27, 1845	Joseph **Miller**	and	Nuly Cress
Thurs. Sep. 27, 1855	L. Calvin **Miller**	and	Lovina Culp
Thurs. Nov. 30, 1876	Luther C. **Miller**	and	Laura A. Bost
Thurs. Mar. 27, 1834	Paul **Miller**	and	Elizabeth Brown
Sund. Jun. 24, 1855	Rufus **Miller**	and	Elizabeth C. Moyer
Wed. Dec. 28, 1859	Tobias **Miller**	and	Jemima E. Bost
Wed. Aug. 10, 1859	Allison **Misenheimer**	and	Sophia L. Eagle
Thurs. Sep. 4, 1856	George W. **Misenheimer**	and	Susanna Ketner
Tues. Dec. 5, 1843	Laurence **Misenheimer**	and	Christena L. Klutts
Thurs. May 8, 1856	Paul **Misenheimer**	and	Maria S. Brown
Tues. Aug. 5, 1851	James **Montgomery**	and	Leah Earnheart
Wed. Jan. 31, 1855	Daniel M. **Moose**	and	Anna Louisa Barrier
Thurs. Dec. 24, 1874	Nathen R. **Morgan**	and	Mary M. Isenhour
Thurs. Oct. 26, 1848	Edward **Moss**	and	Christiana Barringer
Thurs. Jul. 28, 1836	Nicholas **Mourer**	and	Sarah Ann Sellers
Tues. May 25, 1852	George **Moyer**	and	Mrs. Peacock (widow)
Wed. Mar. 26, 1845	William **McDaniel**	and	Susanne Harkey
Sund. Nov. 10, 1878	Adam M. **Nussman**	and	Ellen Klutts
Thurs. Nov. 3, 1870	Caleb L. **Nussman**	and	Margaret C. F. Klutts
Thurs. Aug. 30, 1877	James **Owens**	and	Ellen M. Isenhour
Thurs. Jan. 9, 1879	George W. **Park**	and	Laura Jane Holshouser
Thurs. Jan. 15, 1880	Jesse F. **Park**	and	Margaret J. Trexler
Thurs. Jun. 5, 1873	D. L. **Parker**	and	Ellen Jenkins
Sund. Apr. 15, 1855	Charles S. **Patterson**	and	Rose Anna Smith
Thurs. Feb. 6, 1851	Elam A. **Patterson**	and	Barbara M. Ketner
Sund. Dec. 1, 1853	Joseph A. **Patterson**	and	Margaret L. Bostian
Thurs. Aug. 21, 1834	Peter **Peck**	and	Catherine Heilig
Wed. Feb. 23, 1859	Alexander **Peeler**	and	Sarah Ann E. Peeler
Thurs. Dec. 29, 1881	John A. **Peeler**	and	Mary L. J. Miller
Wed. Jul. 27, 1859	Paul **Peeler**	and	Mary C. Hartman
Thurs. Dec. 15, 1881	Augustus L. **Pless**	and	Mary E. Faggart

Thurs. Oct. 22, 1885	Dr. C. M. **Pool**	and	Mary E. Linn
Thurs. Sep. 1, 1892	Robert C. **Pool**	and	Mrs. Margaret E. Crowell
Wed. Mar. 28, 1866	Dr. James P. **Porter**	and	Lovinia B. Seaford
Thurs. Jul. 14, 1842	John **Powless**	and	Amey Lentz
Thurs. Oct. 23, 1856	Jacob **Probst**	and	Rebecca Shaver
Thurs. Dec. 15, 1859	Danl. W. **Propst**	and	Mary E. Klutts
Wed. Apr. 7, 1852	Eli A. **Propst**	and	Amelia A. House
Wed. Oct. 10, 1877	John J. **Quantz**	and	Catharine M. Heilig
Thurs. Apr. 17, 1834	Robert **Ramsy**	and	Mary Walton
Thurs. Oct. 9, 1834	George **Randleman**	and	Eliza Rosamon
Tues. Feb. 12, 1839	John L. **Randleman**	and	Nancy Brown
Thurs. Nov. 4, 1847	Thomas **Reimer**	and	Sally Icehour
Tues. Jun. 21, 1836	John **Rensch**	and	Margaretta Miller
Sund. Apr. 24, 1842	Asa **Ribelin**	and	Susan C. Walton
Tues. Feb. 26, 1850	Aaron **Richie**	and	Leah Goodman
Sund. Oct. 20, 1844	Harris M. **Ridenhour**	and	Levina Miller
Thurs. Jun. 1, 1865	Peter A. **Ritchey**	and	Elizabeth C. Shuping (widow)
Wed. Feb. 4, 1852	Geo. H. **Ritchie**	and	Eliza Safret
Tues. May 21, 1878	Rufus P. **Roseman**	and	Sarah E. Lyerly
Thurs. Jan. 12, 1843	(br) Adam **Rothrock**	and	Elizabeth Whitlow
Thurs. Mar. 1, 1860	Alfred W. **Rusher**	and	Malissa C. Brown
Tues. Jul. 31, 1849	George A. **Rusher**	and	Louisa M. Lippard
Thurs. Jul. 17, 1856	Milas **Rusher**	and	Mary Ann M. Heilig
Thurs. Apr. 21, 1859	James W. **Rymer**	and	Lydia Ann Hill
Tues. Apr. 12, 1859	Saml. M. **Rymer**	and	Sarah J. Hill
Thurs. Jan. 15, 1885	Milas **Safrit**	and	Laura M. Troutman
Sund. Dec. 1, 1853	Moses **Safret**	and	Widow Christena L. Misenheimer
Wed. Jan. 14, 1852	William **Safret**	and	Catherine Blackwelder
Tues. Nov. 15, 1859	Thomas **Sapp**	and	Sarah Safret
Wed. Dec. 29, 1852	Eli **Seaford**	and	Margaret Holshouser
Thurs. Aug. 10, 1848	Moses **Seaford**	and	Sarah M. Lippard
Thurs. Jun. 10, 1847	D. **Setzer**	and	Fanny Thomas
	Attended the wedding		
Tues. Dec. 27, 1870	Julius B. **Sheets**	and	Louisa H. Colly
Thurs. Apr. 2, 1891	Thomas R. **Sheets**	and	Jennie Crowell
Thurs. Nov. 21, 1872	A. R. **Shoaf**	and	Malinda C. Hoffman
Tues. Dec. 21, 1852	Milas **Shuping**	and	Mary Cauble
Thurs. Aug. 17, 1876	James C. **Sides**	and	Martha J. Isenhour
Thurs. Mar. 27, 1834	Solomon **Sifford**	and	Mary Pealer
Wed. Oct. 16, 1872	Charles N. **Simpson**	and	Martha R. Brown
Thurs. May 25, 1843	Franklin **Smith**	and	Mary Ann Fisher
Thurs. Dec. 16, 1852	George **Smith**	and	Margaret A. Bostian
Sund. May 11, 1845	John **Smith**	and	Catharine Stirewalt
Tues. Jul. 5, 1836	William **Smith**	and	Mary Morgan
Sund. May 21, 1865	Samuel **Snider**	and	Ann Layton
Thurs. Feb. 1, 1883	Luther C. **Sowers**	and	Fannie F. Long
Sund. Apr. 5, 1891	James R. **Sparnell**	and	Ida C. McAllister
Thurs. May 23, 1844	Goodman **Spencer**	and	Elis. Gadlin
Tues. Aug. 4, 1846	Jacob **Stirewalt**	and	Mary K. Shaver
Thurs. Feb. 20, 1851	Pinkney **Summit**	and	Barbara B. Miller
Wed. Nov. 26, 1890	Benjamin E. **Sumner**	and	Sophie Kesler
Mond. Sep. 21, 1835	Henry **Swink**	and	Barbara Gitz
Thurs. Aug. 10, 1882	Rufus A. **Taylor**	and	Laura M. Miller
Thurs. Jun. 1, 1843	Daniel **Techour**	and	Leah Boger
Sund. Apr. 19, 1885	Albert D. **Thomas**	and	Eve Ann Miller

Tues. Aug. 12, 1845	Levi **Thomas**	and	Susan Walton
Thurs. Jan. 4, 1844	Adam **Trexler**, jr.	and	Margaret Lyerly
Thurs. Feb. 5, 1852	Caleb **Trexler**	and	Elizabeth L. Lyerla
Thurs. Apr. 22, 1852	John **Trexler**	and	Anna Lingle
Thurs. Aug. 22, 1839	Moses **Trexler**	and	Margaret Cawble
Thurs. Jun. 25, 1846	Moses **Trexler**	and	Widow Miller
Thurs. Aug. 22, 1850	Moses **Trexler**	and	Eve C. Klutts
Thurs. Apr. 16, 1835	Peter **Trexler**	and	Eliz. C. Miller
Tues. Aug. 1, 1854	Peter **Trexler**	and	Sarah C. Peeler
Thurs. Dec. 13, 1855	Danl. **Troutman**	and	Catharine Brady
Thurs. Dec. 4, 1879	Caleb M. **Troutman**	and	Sarah A. Klutts
Tues. Apr. 27, 1847	George **Troutman**	and	Sophia C. Yost
Sund. Jan. 2, 1859	Henry **Troutman**	and	Rachel Casper
Thurs. Oct. 23, 1856	Monroe **Troutman**	and	Margaret A. Lentz
Thurs. Oct. 31, 1850	J. A. **Troutman**	and	Amelia Parham
Thurs. Nov. 30, 1882	William C. **Troutman**	and	Mary Ann C. V. Weaver
Thurs. Oct. 15, 1835	Henry **Unger**	and	Susannah Hotzhe
Tues. Oct. 30, 1855	Benjamin F. **Walton**	and	Widow Catharine Kesler
Sund. Nov. 21, 1869	J. F. **Watts**	and	Martha Ann Sheets
Thurs Dec. 4, 1890	James M. **Wood**	and	Emma J. Small
Thurs. Mar. 29, 1866	Solomon **Wotzman**	and	Harriet E. Pool
Tues. Feb. 8, 1842	John **Yost**	and	Sarah Safret
Tues. Mar. 8, 1859	Paul **Yost**	and	Adaline Weaver
Thurs. Aug. 26, 1852	Alexander **Yost**	and	Elizabeth S. Weaver

Index to Funerals and Burials

Not Named

Sund. March 23, 1834. Attended to a funeral. (Not named)
Sund. March 26, 1854. Funeral at Widow Garner's. (Not named)
Sund. June 23, 1844. Funeral of an aged colored person at Michael Heilig's.
Sund. April 13, 1834 Funeral at Holshouser's. (Not named)
Sund. October 12, 1834. Funeral at Holshouser's. (Not named).
Thurs. June 23, 1881. Saw Polish child buried at St. Peter's ch.
Sund. June 27, 1847. Funeral at Organ ch. (Not named)
Sund. August 13, 1843. Funeral at St. Stephen's ch. (Not named)
Sat. March 2, 1844. Funeral at St. Mathew's ch. (Not named)
Sund. May 12, 1844. Funeral at Organ ch. (Not named)
Sund. August 9, 1846. Funeral of 2 colored persons in the grove near Organ ch.
Sund. August 19, 1849. Funeral at St. Stephen's ch. (Not named)
Thurs. January 15, 1863. Burial service for a colored boy.
Wed. December 29, 1869. Buried a colored woman at the Grave Yard for colored persons.
Sat. April 1, 1876. Funeral at St. Stephen's ch. (Not named)

NAMED

Sund. December 23, 1838. Funeral of Henry **Agner**'s child at Union Church.
Sund. April 16, 1843. Burial service of Mrs. **Agner** at Union.
Sund. May 21, 1843. Funeral of Mrs. Henry **Agner** at Union ch.
Sund. December 27, 1835. Funeral of Mr. **Arb**'s child.
Wed. January 3, 1844. Funeral of Abram **Arey** at Union.
Mond. February 16, 1846. Burial of Sophia, wife of Milas **Arey** at Union ch.
Thurs. October 31, 1844. Funeral of Mrs. Arey, widow of Abram **Arey**, decd., at Union ch.
Mond. October 6, 1845. Burial of Mrs. **Arey**, at Union ch. Sermon by Revd. J. B. Anthony.
Sund. June 1, 1834. Peter **Aronhart**'s child at Union Ch.
Thurs. April 20, 1876. Burial of Rev. Wm. **Artz**, at St. John's ch.
Sund. June 11, 1876. Funeral of Rev. William **Artz** at Organ ch.

Tues. July 6, 1886. Funeral of Catharine **Bailey** at St. Peter's church.
Sat. August 25, 1877. Funeral of Patsy **Baily** at St. Peter's ch.
Sund. June 7, 1891. Funeral of Geo. **Bame** at St. Matthew's church.
Wed. March 10, 1847. Funeral of Susanna **Bame** at Paul Cruse's.
Mond. February 11, 1850. Funeral of Old Mrs. **Barger** at Lower St. ch.
Thurs. November 2, 1843. Funeral of Mathias **Barrier**'s child at St. Stephen's ch.
Sund. August 21, 1870. Funeral of Monroe **Barrier**'s child.
Sund. February 19, 1871. Funeral of the child (9 yrs. old) of Monroe **Barrier** at Salem Ch.
Tues. December 26, 1843. Funeral of Saml. **Barrier**'s child at Lower Stone ch.
Sund. April 4, 1847. Funeral of widow **Barrier** at Lower Stone ch.
Sat. January 13, 1844. Funeral of Widow **Barrier**'s child (Tobias) at Lower Stone church.
Sund. June 12, 1845. Funeral of Mrs. **Barringer**'s negro girl at the house.
Wed. April 11, 1855. Funeral of Catharine **Barringer**, widow of John P. Barringer, at Union ch.
Frid. March 1, 1850. Funeral of Charles **Barringer** at Organ ch.
Sund. November 5, 1854. Funeral of Charles **Barringer** at St. Stephen's ch.
Tues. November 7, 1843. Funeral of D. **Barringer**'s child at Union ch.
Tues. June 14, 1853. Burial of D. **Barringer**'s child at Union ch.
Sund. January 18, 1857. Funeral of Mr. D. **Barringer**'s child St. Peter's ch.
Mond. January 19, 1857. Burial of Mr. D. **Barringer**'s child at St. Peter's ch.
Sund. February 1, 1857. Funeral of David & Mary **Barringer**'s child at St. Peter's ch.
Sund. November 17, 1872. Funeral of Elizabeth **Barringer** at Bethesda ch.
Tues. December 1, 1846. Funeral of Henry **Barringer** at Organ ch.
Thurs. January 9, 1845. Funeral of John **Barringer** at Organ ch.
Thurs. November 21, 1844. Funeral of John **Barringer**'s child at Organ ch.
Wed. January 11, 1888. Funeral of John Luther **Barringer** at the house & buried at Lower Stone Church.
Sund. January 8, 1882. Buried Luther **Barringer**'s wife at Organ ch.

Sat. October 4, 1856. Funeral of Martha, wife of Joseph **Barringer** at Organ ch.

Tues. January 14, 1851. Funeral of Mathias **Barringer** at his residence.

Frid. March 29, 1844. Funeral of Moses **Barringer**'s child at Organ ch.

Wed. April 15, 1885. Funeral of Elizabeth **Basinger** at Organ ch.

Tues. July 22, 1862. Funeral of Jeremiah **Basinger**'s child at Organ ch.

Tues. February 20, 1866. Funeral of John **Basinger** at the house, buried at Organ ch.

Wed. June 18, 1856. Funeral of John **Basinger**'s child at Organ ch.

Sund. July 1, 1883. Mrs. Nancy **Basinger**'s funeral at her house, buried at Organ Church.

Sund. January 21, 1844. Burial of Mrs. **Bayam** at St. Mathew's ch.

Mond. October 1, 1883. Funeral of Charles **Bayam**'s twin children at Widow John Fesperman's, buried at Organ ch.

Sat. September 15, 1883. Funeral Margaret E. **Bayam**, wife of Charles Bayam house, buried at Organ ch.

Wed. July 5, 1843. Funeral of Stufle **Bayam**'s child at St. Mathew's ch.

Sund. July 16, 1843. Funeral of Tice **Bayam**'s child at St. Mathew's ch.

Wed. July 21, 1886. Funeral of Geo. A. **Bean** at Organ church.

Tues. May 29, 1888. Funeral of Boyden **Beaver**'s infant child at the house. Rev. Heller buried.

Sat. July 6, 1889. Burial of Boyden **Beaver**'s child at Lower St. church. Rev. W. R. Brown preached the funeral.

Wed. September 14, 1859. Funeral of Charles **Beaver**'s child at Lower St. ch.

Sund. May 22, 1881. Funeral of Daywalt **Beaver** at Lower St. Church.

Sat. July 5, 1845. Funeral of Daywald **Beaver**'s child at his house.

Sund. December 29, 1872. Funeral of Elias **Beaver** at Organ ch.

Tues. April 15, 1845. Funeral of Mr. Henry **Beaver** at the Lower Stone ch.

Mond. April 7, 1845. Funeral of Mrs. Henry **Beaver** at the Lower Stone ch.

Tues. December 9, 1856. Funeral of Jesse **Beaver**'s child at Organ Church.

Sat. October 23, 1875. Funeral of Mrs. Joseph **Beaver** at Salem ch.

Thurs. October 14, 1847. Funeral of Moses **Beaver**'s child at the Lower Stone ch.

Sund. December 7, 1856. Funeral of Moses **Beaver**'s child at Luther's Chapel.

Tues. March 29, 1881. Funeral of Mrs. Nelly **Beaver**, widow of Elias Beaver, at Organ ch.

Thurs. March 23, 1882. Funeral of Paul **Beaver** at Lower St. Church.

Sat. September 7, 1850. Funeral of Paul **Beaver**'s child at Lower Stone Church.

Thurs. September 29, 1853. Funeral of Paul **Beaver**'s child at L. St. church.

Thurs. March 27, 1856. Funeral of Paul **Beaver**'s child at Lower St. Ch.

Tues. December 11, 1855. Funeral of Mrs. Saml. **Beaver** at Lower St. ch.

Wed. September 3, 1834. Funeral of Mr. **Beever**'s child at Holshouser's.

Wed. August 11, 1852. Funeral of Andr. **Berger**'s child at Lower St. ch.

Tues. October 11, 1853. Funeral of Andrew **Berger**'s child at L. St. ch.

Frid. January 10, 1862. Funeral of Andrew **Berger**'s child at Lower St. ch.

Thurs. October 4, 1877. Funeral of Andrew **Berger**'s child, Charlie, at Lower St. Church.

Frid. July 14, 1876. Funeral of Mrs. Jacob **Berger** at Organ ch.

Thurs. December 7, 1871. Burial of John **Berger** at Salem Ch.

Frid. April 16, 1875. Funeral of Mrs. John **Berger** at Salem ch.

Tues. December 25, 1849. Funeral of Saml. **Berger** at Lower St. ch.

Thurs. June 12, 1862. Funeral of Sarah C. **Berger**, wife of Andrew Berger, at Lower St. ch.

Wed. October 7, 1885. Funeral of Sarah C. wife of John **Berger**, at St. Peter's ch.

Thurs. April 18, 1872. Funeral of Thomas F. **Berger** at Salem ch.

Mond. February 9, 1885. Burial of G. M. **Bernhardt** at Organ Church. Assisted Rev. Heller.

Wed. July 27, 1881. Funeral of Harvey A. **Bernhardt**'s child at Organ ch.

Thurs. July 4, 1878. Funeral of Mrs. Mary A. **Bernhardt** at Organ ch.

Sat. July 26, 1862. Funeral of Alexander **Blackwelder** at Pless' School house, who fell in battle May 31, 1862.

Sat. July 5, 1856. Funeral of Mrs. **Blackwell** at Union ch.

Mond. May 28, 1855. Funeral of Danl. **Boger**'s daughter at Union ch.

Frid. September 30, 1853. Funeral of Widow **Boger** at Organ ch.

Sat. October 16, 1869. Funeral of Mrs. **Bogle** at Salem ch.

Sund. September 9, 1877. Funeral of Catharine E. daughter of Reuben W. **Bost**, at Organ Church.

Thurs. November 23, 1876. Funeral of D. L. **Bost**'s child at Lower Stone Church.

Wed. January 29, 1862. Funeral of David A. **Bost** at Organ church.

Sund. September 11, 1853. Funeral of Mrs. George **Bost** at the residence.

Sat. October 15, 1853. Funeral of George **Bost** at Organ ch.

Wed. September 11, 1850. Funeral of John **Bost**'s child at Organ ch.

Mond. February 2, 1852. Funeral of John **Bost**'s child at Organ ch.

Sund. August 14, 1859. Funeral of John **Bost** at Organ church.
Frid. July 14, 1876. Funeral of John A. W. **Bost** at Organ ch.
Mond. February 19, 1877. Funeral Moses **Bost**'s child at Organ ch.
Mond. June 26, 1876. Funeral of Mrs. Reuben **Bost**.
Mond. July 10, 1876. Funeral of Reuben **Bost**'s child at Organ ch.
Sat. December 5., 1885 Funeral of Solina **Bost** at Organ Church.
Tues. June 24, 1862. Funeral of William **Bost**.
Sund. June 14, 1846. Funeral of Wm. **Bost**'s child at Organ ch.
Sund. July 22, 1877. Funeral of Andrew **Bostian** at Ebenezer ch.
Sund. May 27, 1877. Funerals of Catharine **Bostian** & her son Moses Bostian at Ebenezer Church.
Sat. December 13, 1862. Funeral of Chas. **Bostian** at his late residence.
Sat. November 24, 1855. Funeral of Charles **Bostian**'s child at Organ ch.
Sund. October 19, 1856. Funeral of Eli **Bostian**'s child at Luther's Chapel.
Sund. April 6, 1856. Funeral of Jacob **Bostian** at Organ ch.
Frid. January 2, 1846. Funeral of John **Bostian**'s infant child at Organ ch.
Frid. June 15, 1855. Funeral of John **Bostian**'s child at Organ ch.
Frid. December 19, 1862. Funeral of John M. **Bostian**, Soldier, at David Bostian's, who died at Charlottesville, Va.
Mond. September 17, 1855. Funeral Mary Ann **Bostian**, an orphan child, at Organ ch.
Thurs. March 28, 1850. Funeral of Michael **Bostian** at the house, buried at Luther's Chapel.
Tues. May 14, 1850. Burial of Michl. **Bostian**, Sen. at Organ ch.
Sund. May 26, 1850. Funeral of Michl. **Bostian**, Sen. at Organ ch.
Sat. December 27, 1873. Funeral of Mrs. **Boyden**, widow of Dr. Boyden, services at Gold Hill & buried at Organ. church.
Tues. September 7, 1847. Funeral of Mr. **Braddy**'s child at Lower St. ch.
Thurs. June 10, 1886. Funeral of Mrs. David **Brady** at Lower St. Church.
Sat. September 22, 1855. Funeral of John **Brady**'s child.
Thurs. December 9, 1869. Funeral of Mrs. John **Brady** at the house, buried on the premises.
Thurs. May 12, 1887. Burial of Stephen **Brady** at St. Peter's ch. Funeral to be hereafter.
Sat. June 3, 1854. Funeral of Stephen **Brady**'s son at Lower St. Church.
Wed. August 5, 1885. Buried Washington **Brady**'s child. at St. Peter's ch.
Sund. November 6, 1842, Funeral of Mrs. **Bringle** at Union.
Tues. February 22, 1848. Funeral of Christian **Bringle**'s wife at the home.
Wed. July 2, 1834. Funeral of Mr. Andrew **Brown** at his residence.
Tues. September 19, 1843. Funeral of Andrew **Brown** at Union ch.
Sund. August 18, 1839. Funeral of Cruso **Brown** at Union ch.
Thurs. February 14, 1850. Funeral of Mrs. Danl. **Brown** at Organ ch.
Thurs. March 18, 1852. Funeral of Mrs. Danl. **Brown** at Organ Church.
Sat. June 7, 1834. Funeral of Mr. David **Brown** Senr at his house.
Tues. August 28, 1855. Funeral of David **Brown** at Organ ch.
Sund. March 26, 1848. Funeral of Mrs. David **Brown** at Organ ch.
Frid. August 23, 1878. Funeral of David L. **Brown** at Christiana ch.
Tues. June 28, 1842. Funeral of Eliza **Brown**, wife of Jacob Brown, Jr. at Union ch.
Thurs. August 14, 1856. Funeral of Elizabeth, wife of Michl. L. **Brown** at St. Paul's ch.
Wed. May 3, 1843. Funeral of Mrs. Henry **Brown** at the Stone house.
Tues. August 26, 1856. Funeral of Henry L. **Brown**'s child at St. Paul's ch.
Mond. March 16, 1835. Funeral of Mrs. **Brown**, consort of James Brown, at his residence.
Thurs. December 14, 1843. Funeral of Jacob **Brown**, Sen. at Union church.
Sund. January 28, 1844. Funeral of Jacob **Brown**'s child at the Stone House.
Mond. December 11, 1843. Funeral of Jeremiah **Brown** at Union ch.
Frid. January 9, 1891. Burial of Mrs. John D. **Brown** at St Peter's ch. Rev. Trexler preached.
Frid. February 6, 1835. Philip **Brown**'s wife's funeral.
Tues. December 11, 1838. Funeral of Elizabeth **Brown**, wife of Allen at Union ch.
Sat. March 6, 1852. Funeral of George **Brown** at his late residence.
Tues. November 11, 1879. Funeral of Magdalene **Brown**, wife of Henry Brown, at Christiana Church.
Sat. March 4, 1882. Funeral of Martha Jane, wife of Nathan **Brown** at Christiana ch.
Sund. March 24, 1878. Funeral of Michael L. **Brown**. St. Paul's ch.
Tues. October 21, 1884. Funeral of Mititia **Brown** at Organ Church.
Mond. December 13, 1841. Funeral of Moses **Brown**, sen, at his house.
Frid. April 4, 1856. Funerals of Moses A. **Brown** at St. Paul's ch.

Frid. April 17, 1835. Was to have funeral of Philip **Brown**'s child, but did not attend.
Thurs. July 2, 1874. Funeral of Pleasant **Brown**'s child at St. Luke's ch.
Mond. February 2, 1857. Funeral of Polly **Brown** at Union ch.
Thurs. November 26, 1885. Funeral of Rev. R. L. **Brown**'s child at Christiana Church.
Frid. December 6, 1850. Funeral of Widow Sarah **Brown** at the house. Buried her at Stone house.
Sat. May 7, 1892. Went to burial of Sarah **Brown** at St. Peter's ch.
Thurs. November 2, 1865. Funeral of Sophia M. **Brown** at St. Paul's ch.
Sat. January 20, 1844. Funeral of Mrs. **Bullen** at St. Mathew's ch.
Mond. February 3, 1840. Funeral of Mrs. **Butner**.

Sund. March 19, 1871. Funeral of Nancy **Camel** at Salem ch.
Tues. September 30, 1845. Funeral of Mrs. **Cameron**.
Sund. July 17, 1870. Funeral of Mr. **Campbell** at Salem ch.
Thurs. January 24, 1884. Funeral of David **Campbell** at Liberty (Methodist) Church.
Wed. February 28, 1877. Funeral of Mrs. Polly **Canup**, relict of Dr. John Canup, at St. Matthew's ch.
Wed. September 10, 1884. Funeral of Christena **Canup** at Littleton Lingel's, buried at Lower St. Church.
Frid. November 22, 1878. Funeral of Nancy Solena, wife of John **Carter** at Rumple's Old Field Arbor.
Mond. December 1, 1845. Funeral of old Mr. Adam **Casper** at the Lower St. ch.
Mond. July 7, 1834. Funeral of Adam **Casper**'s child at the Germ. Reformed Church called the Stone church.
Frid. July 12, 1839. Funeral of Mrs. Adam **Casper**, at the Stone Church.
Sat. September 20, 1862. Funeral of Alexander **Casper** at St. Mathew's ch.
Mond. May 19, 1856. Funeral of Amelia Ann, wife of David **Casper** at Organ ch.
Thurs. May 13, 1885. Funeral of Catharine Casper, wife of Levi **Casper** at Corinth.
Tues. December 16, 1856. Funeral of Conrad **Casper** at Lower St. ch.
Frid. June 25, 1847. Funeral of Mrs. David **Casper** at the Lower Stone ch.
Mond. November 6, 1871. Funeral of John **Casper** in Salisbury.
Tues. March 10, 1846. Funeral of Mr. **Castor**'s son at Organ church.
Tues. April 27, 1852. Funeral of Alex. **Cauble** at Organ ch.
Sund. November 8, 1874. Funeral of the infant daughter of the Widow Nancy **Cauble** at Salem ch.
Tues. January 2, 1849. Funeral of Christena **Cawble** at Mr. Butner's.
Thurs. November 27, 1845. Funeral of Danl. **Cawble**'s daughter at Fullenwider's ch.
Frid. December 1, 1843. Funeral of John **Cawble**'s child, did not attend.
Sund. December 3, 1843. Funeral of John **Cawble**'s child.
Tues. April 5, 1842. Funeral of John **Cawble**'s wife at Union.
Frid. April 17, 1846. Funeral of Peter **Cawble** at Fullenwider's ch.
Sat. November 4, 1843. Funeral of Peter **Cawble**'s child at Union ch.
Frid. September 10, 1847. Funeral of Rachel **Cawble** (widow) at Fullenwider's ch.
Sund. June 1, 1834. Widow **Cawble** at Union ch.
Wed. April 8, 1846. Funeral of Widow P. **Cawble**'s child at home.
Sund. February 16, 1840. Funeral of Wilie **Cawble**'s child at Union.
Thurs. July 14, 1836. Funeral of Mrs. **Chranister** in St. Thomas.
Sund. October 9, 1859. Funeral of Mrs. Charlotte **Clark** at St. Michael's ch.
Thurs. October 27, 1859. Funeral of Mr. and Mrs. **Clark**'s child at St. Michael's ch. in Iredell.
Sund. July 10, 1859. Funeral of John **Clarke** at St. Michael's ch.
Frid. April 5, 1872. Funeral of Adam **Cline** at Ebenezer ch.
Sund. December 9, 1877. Funeral of Joseph **Colly** at Salem ch.
Wed. June 18, 1873. Funeral of Saml. **Colly**'s child at Salem ch.
Sat. February 6, 1875. Funeral of Mrs. **Cone** at Organ.
Thurs. October 23, 1873. Funeral Mrs. Cath. C. **Coon** at Salem ch.
Wed. April 16, 1834. Funeral of Sally **Corl** in Salis.
Frid. July 4., 1856 Funeral of Philip **Correll**'s child at Mt. Zion.
Sund. September 12, 1869. Funeral of Henry **Cress** at Bethel.
Mond. July 21, 1873. Burial service of John **Cress**' child at Salem ch.
Sund. October 12, 1873. Funeral of John **Cress**'s child at Salem ch.
Wed. September 24, 1879. Funeral of J. M. **Cross**' little daughter at Gold Hill Baptist Church.
Thurs. March 12, 1891. Mr. F. **Crowell** having died, went to his residence to see him carried off to be buried.
Sat. February 17, 1849. Funeral of 2 of James **Crowel**'s children at Kendall's church.
Sund. Sept. 10, 1865. Funeral of Ambrose **Cruse** at Organ ch., who died a prisoner of war.
Mond. December 29, 1879. Funeral of Andrew **Cruse** at Organ ch.

Sat. January 24, 1857. Funeral of Catherine **Cruse**, in the 89th year of her age at Organ ch.
Sund. March 13, 1853. Funeral of Danl. **Cruse** at Organ ch.
Sund. November 23, 1856. Funeral of Elizabeth, wife of Philip **Cruse** at Organ ch.
Sund. November 28, 1852. Funeral of Mrs. Jacob **Cruse** at Organ ch.
Sund. November 7, 1847. Funeral of John **Cruse** at Organ ch.
October 21, 1884. Funeral also of Mary Ann **Cruse**, wife of Peter Cruse.
Tues. Thurs. May 15, 1845. Funeral of Moses **Cruse** at Organ ch.
Sund. March 30, 1879. Funeral of Paul **Cruse** at Organ church.
Frid. July 15, 1887. Buried Peter **Cruse** at Organ church.
Wed. November 1, 1854. Funeral of Peter **Cruse**'s child at Organ ch.
Mond. October 27, 1856. Funeral of Peter **Cruse**'s Child at house, buried at Organ Church.
Wed. April 4, 1866. Funeral Philip **Cruse** at Organ ch.
Sund. September 30, 1877. Funeral of Sarah, wife of Andrew **Cruse** at Organ ch.
Wed. July 3, 1850. Funeral of Sol. **Cruse**, Organ ch.
Wed. June 4, 1845. Funeral of Sophia, wife of John **Cruse**, at Organ ch.
Sund. December 15, 1850. Funeral of old Mrs. **Culp** at St. Stephen's ch.
Sund. March 16, 1845. Burial service of David **Culp**'s child at St. Stephen's ch.
Mond. November 16, 1846. Funeral of Edmond **Culp** at St. Stephen's ch.
Tues. October 6, 1846. Funeral of Peter **Culp** at St. Stephen's ch.

Sund. September 16, 1877. Funeral of M. M. **Daniel**'s child at Bethel ch., Stanly.
Tues. August 4, 1835. Buried Mr. **Deckson** Esqr.
Sund. May 18, 1834. Funeral of Mr. James **Dun** in Salisbury.

Sund. February 11, 1844. Funeral of Mrs. **Eagle** & Alexr. **Eagle** at the Lower Stone Church.
Wed. June 10, 1885. Funeral of Catharine **Eagle** at Mrs. Green Heilig's, buried at Organ Church.
Mond. July 7, 1856. Funeral of George A. **Eagle**'s child at Organ ch.
Frid. December 9, 1881. Funeral Geo. Henry **Eagle** at Organ ch.
Mond. June 19, 1865. Funeral of Geo. H. **Eagle**'s child at the house, buried at Organ ch.
Wed. December 13, 1843. Funeral of Moses **Eagle**'s child at St. Stephen's ch.
Mond. Mond. February 26, 1855. Funeral of Peter **Eagle** at Organ ch.
Sund. July 8, 1883. Funeral of Sarah L. **Eagle**, widow of David Eagle, at Organ Church.
Tues. February 4, 1890. Burial of old Mrs. **Earnheart** at St. Peter's ch.
Wed. December 6, 1843. Funeral of Andrew **Earnheart**'s wife at the Lower Stone church.
Sund. February 15, 1863. Funeral C. W. **Earnheart** at St. Peter's ch.
Wed. February 11, 1863. Burial of Calvin **Earnheart** at St. Peter's Church.
Thurs. December 15, 1859. Funeral of Mrs. Catherine, wife of Jacob **Earnheart**. Buried on the plantation.
Tues. May 25, 1847. Funeral of Christopher **Earnheart** at Henry Earnheart's.
Sund. November 23, 1845. Funeral of David **Earnheart**'s child at the Lower Stone ch.
Sund. July 8, 1849. Funeral of Geo. **Earnheart**'s child at the Lower stone ch.
Wed. February 11, 1863. Burial Eli **Earnheart** at St. Peter's Church.
Sund. July 6, 1862. Funeral of Eli **Earnheart** at St. Peter's ch., a volunteer, who died in Hospital in Petersburg.
Sat. November 27, 1847. Funeral of Henry **Earnheart**, Sen. at his residence.
Thurs. January 20, 1859. Funeral of Henry **Earnheart**'s son at St. Peter's ch.
Sund. July 14, 1872. Funeral of Mrs. Henry **Earnheart** at Salem ch.
Wed. March 11, 1885. Funeral of Isaac **Earnheart** at D. Brady's. Buried him at Lower Stone Church.
Mond. April 5, 1880. Funeral of Mrs. Isaac **Earnheart** at Lower St. church.
Sund. January 29, 1843. Funeral at Jacob **Earnheart**'s.
Sund. August 5, 1877. Funeral of Jacob **Earnheart**, at Gold Hill.
Tues. September 18, 1855. Funeral of John W. **Earnheart** at Lower St. ch.
Wed. January 1, 1873. Funeral of Peggy **Earnheart** at Jesse Miller's.
Wed. November 29, 1843. Funeral of Peter **Earnheart** at Union ch.
Sund. September 25, 1892. Funeral of Peter **Earnheart** at St. Peter's church.
Thurs. May 28, 1846. Funeral of Peter **Earnheart**, at his residence.
Wed. April 25, 1860. Funeral of Philip **Earnheart** at Lower St. ch.
Sat. July 29, 1848. Funeral of Polly **Earnheart** at Organ ch.
Wed. October 4, 1854. Funeral of Simeon **Earnheart** at Lower St. ch.
Sund. December 25, 1853. Funeral of Mrs. **Eddleman** at Organ ch.
Thurs. December 14, 1882. Funeral of Anna E., wife of J. M. **Eddleman**, at Ebenezer ch.
Tues. June 29, 1847. Funeral of Ambrose **Eddleman** at Organ ch.

Mond. September 4, 1854. Funeral of Danl. **Eddleman**'s child at Organ ch.
Sund. July 27, 1862. Funeral of Jacob Alexr. **Eddleman**, at Organ ch. who also fell in battle May 31, 1862.
Frid. December 8, 1854. Funeral of Philip **Eddleman** at Organ ch.
Sat. April 13, 1850. Funeral of Widow **Eddleman** at Organ ch.
Sund. June 16, 1839. Funeral of old Mrs. **Eller** at Union church.
Tues. November 11, 1845. Funeral of Andrew **Eller** at Union ch.
Sund. January 22, 1843. Funeral of Andrew **Eller**'s Mother-in-law, at Union.
Sat. July 15, 1843. Funeral of Charles **Eller** at Union.
Sund. May 9, 1880. Funeral of Licette Jane **Eller** at Organ ch.
Tues. November 25, 1845. Funeral of Michael **Eller** at Union ch.
Frid. February 13, 1874. Funeral of Margaret Alice, the daughter of Saml. **Elliot** at Salem ch.
Wed. August 6, 1879. Funeral of Y. G. **Engelberg** at Baptist ch. Gold Hill.
Sund. September 17, 1876. Funeral Mr. **Ewing**'s child, at Bethel ch. Stanly.

Sund. October 9, 1870. Funeral of Cornelius **Fesperman** at Bethel ch.
Sund. August 5, 1883. Funeral of Harvey A. **Fesperman** at Organ Church.
Mond. March 3, 1845. Funeral of John **Fesperman** at St. Paul's ch.
Mond. March 4, 1844. Funeral of John **Fesperman**'s daughter at his home.
Sund. January 10, 1847. Funeral of Mrs. Philip **File** at Lower Stone ch.
Frid. March 20, 1885. Funeral of Charles **Fisher** at Organ Church.
Thurs. October 2, 1856. Funeral of Charles **Fisher**'s child at Organ ch.
Mond. December 27, 1852. Funeral of Mrs. Christena, wife of Jacob **Fisher** at Mr. Fisher's, Buried at Lower St. Church.
Mond. April 27, 1846. Funeral of John **Fisher** at St. Paul's ch.
Mond. September 4, 1854. Funeral of Margaret **Fisher** (widow) at Organ ch.
Thurs. December 17, 1885. Funeral of Margaret Maria **Fisher** at Organ church.
Thurs. June 29, 1876. Funeral of Mrs. Solomon **Fisher** at Organ ch.
Frid. April 4, 1856. Funeral of Mrs. Wilson **Fisher** at St. Paul's ch.
Thurs. October 2, 1856. Funeral of Solomon **Fisher**'s child at Organ ch.
Tues. February 26, 1839. Funeral of old Mr. **Folk** at his house.
Sat. May 20, 1882. Funeral of Martha C. E. **Foutz**, wife of Columbus Foutz, at Lower Stone Church.
Wed. October 24, 1838. Funeral of B. F. **Fraley**'s child in Salisbury.
Frid. August 3, 1849. Funeral of D. **Fraley** at the Lower St. ch.
Thurs. February 5, 1852. Funeral Mrs. Eleonor **Fraley** at Lower St. ch.
Thurs. May 30, 1850. Funeral of James F. **Fraley** at Lower St. ch.
Thurs. August 28, 1834. Funeral of Mr. Samuel **Fraley**'s child.
Sund. August 3, 1873. Funeral of Mr. **Freeze**'s daughter, Amanda, at the house.
Sund. January 11, 1874. Funeral of Philip **Freeze** at Salem ch.
Sat. February 15, 1834. Funeral of old Mr. **Frick** at Hartman's.
Sat. August 27, 1842. Funeral of Danl. **Frick**'s child at the Lower Stone Church.
Sat. February 25, 1860. Funeral of Joseph Alexander, son of Danl. **Frick**, at Lower St. Church.
Tues. August 20, 1878. Burial of Moses **Frick**'s child at St. Peter's ch. Rev. J. A. Linn officiated.
Mond. September 11, 1843. Funeral of Mr. **Fullenwider**'s child at Saml. Linn's.

Sat. April 24, 1847. Funeral of John **Garner** at Organ ch.
Sat. February 22, 1851. Funeral of Widow **Garner**'s daughter.
Sund. January 11, 1857. Funeral of Sally **Garner** Organ ch.
Wed. July 13, 1859. Funeral of Widow Catherine **Garner** at the house. Buried at Organ ch.
Frid. October 31, 1845. Funeral of Old Mr. **Ghents**, at Organ ch.
Mond. October 27, 1862. Funeral of Adam **Goodman** at the house, buried at Union ch.
Sund. May 13, 1877. Funeral of Crawford J. **Goodman** at Organ church.
Mond. April 5, 1847. Funeral of Widow Geo. **Goodman** at Phanuel's Church.
Sund. June 18, 1871. Funeral of Jacob C. **Goodman** at Kistler's Stand.
Thurs. March 2, 1843. Funeral of James **Goodman**'s child.
Wed. March 24, 1847. Funeral of John **Goodman** at Fullenwider's ch.
Sat. March 14, 1846. Went to John **Goodman**'s, one of his sons being buried [Evidently, did not conduct service].
Tues. September 26, 1854. Funeral of Michl. **Goodman**'s child at Organ ch.
Sund. October 15, 1865. Funeral of Moses A. **Goodman** at St. Peter's ch.
Sund. March 27, 1859. Funeral of Nancy **Goodman** (Thomas Goodman's widow) at Organ church.

Sund. August 26, 1877. Funeral of Sarah **Goodman** at Organ ch.
Thurs. November 6, 1862. Funeral of Widow **Goodman**, relict of Thomas Goodman Sen. at the house.
Sund. July 17, 1859. Funeral of Wm. **Goodman**'s child at St. Peter's ch.
Mond. August 11, 1879. Funeral of Cora May, daughter of A. F. **Graeber** at St. Paul's ch. Rowan.
Sund. October 29, 1843. Rev. Scheck preached Rev. **Graeber**'s Funeral.
Wed. September 13, 1843. Burial of Revd. H. **Graeber** at Organ ch.
Wed. April 13, 1836. Funeral of Mr. **Grossman**, Senr. at Grossman's ch.

Mond. September 4, 1843. Funeral of Mr. **Hahnberger**'s child at Organ ch.
Sat. December 19, 1846. Funeral of H. **Hahnberger** at Organ ch.
Tues. January 22, 1856. Funeral of Mrs. Christena, wife of Dr. **Haines** in Mt. Pleasant.
Sund. April 25, 1880. Funeral of Elizabeth **Hampton** at Lower St. Church.
Sat. April 19, 1834. Funeral of John **Hampton** in Salisbury.
Sat. February 21, 1891. Funeral of L. J. **Hampton**'s infant child at St. Peter's church.
Mond. December 22, 1856. Funeral of Clementine **Harkey** at Organ ch.
Sund. February 22, 1846. Funeral of Mrs. John **Harkey** at the Lower Stone ch.
Sund. July 13, 1834. Funeral of Mr. **Harris**' child in Salisbury.
Sund. January 18, 1835. Funeral of Mr. **Hartman**'s child at Union.
Sund. May 21, 1843. Funeral of Capt. J. **Hartman**, at his late residence.
Sund. May 29, 1881. the Funeral Lovina **Hartman** at St. Matthew's ch.
Thurs. May 18, 1843. Funeral of Peter **Hartman**'s son at Union ch.
Frid. July 15, 1842. Funeral of Sophia **Hartman**'s child at John Hartman's.
Sat. March 20, 1847. Funeral of Mr. Geo. **Hartzel** at Organ ch.
Mond. April 24, 1848. Preached the Funeral of John **Hays** at Jacob Austin's in Stanly County.
Sund. September 16, 1838. Funeral of Mr. **Hedrick** at Leonard's ch.
Sat., October 1, 1853. Funeral of old Mrs. **Hegler** at Mathias Barringer's old residence.
Sund. March 16, 1834. Funeral of Mr. **Heilig**'s child in Salis.
Tues. February 24, 1874. Burial of Augustus **Heilig** at Organ ch. Service by Rev. Strobel.
Sund. February 13, 1859. Funeral of C. A. **Heilig** at Organ ch.
Mond. March 2, 1866. Burial of Dave **Heilig**'s (colored) child at the African grave yard near the School house.
Tues. February 26, 1878. In the afternoon went to the colored grave yard to see Eliza **Heilig** buried.
Sat. July 26, 1845. Preached the Funeral of George **Heilig** at his late residence.
Sund. January 11, 1857. Burial service of Jane, a colored woman of Mrs. Sally **Heilig**'s.
Frid. May 9, 1845. Funeral of Mr. Michael **Heilig** at Organ Church.
Sat. August 12, 1843. Funeral of Michl. **Heilig**'s child at St. Paul's ch.
Thurs. January 18, 1855. Funeral of P. N. **Heilig**'s child at Organ ch.
Frid. November 28, 1856. Funeral of P. N. **Heilig**'s child at the house, buried at Organ ch.
Thurs. October 30, 1873. Burial of P. N. **Heilig**'s little daughter at Organ. Rev. Neiffer performed the Burial Wed.
October 10, 1877. Buried Col. P. N. **Heilig**'s infant child at Organ ch.
Thurs. March 7, 1844. Funeral of Widow **Heilig** at Organ ch.
Wed. May 1, 1844. Funeral of Eliza **Hill** at St. Mathew's ch.
Sund. November 18, 1883. Funeral of Elizabeth **Hill** & two of her children at St. Matthew's church.
Sat. March 28, 1846. Funeral of Eliz. Ann **Hill** at St. Paul's ch.
Thurs. January 13, 1848. Funeral of Guy **Hill** at St. Paul's ch.
Wed. March 15, 1843. Funeral of the Widow **Hill** at St. Paul's ch.
Mond. September 20, 1886. Funeral of Philipena **Hodge** at Luther's church.
Mond. June 12, 1843. Funeral of Mrs. **Hoffman** at St. Mathew's church.
Sat. January 8, 1842. Funeral of Danl. **Hoffman**'s child, coffin not ready in time.
Sat. December 9, 1843. Funeral of Danl. **Hoffman**'s child at St. Mathew's ch.
Sund. September 26, 1869. Funeral of Mary Jane **Hoffman** at the house, buried at Bethel ch.
Tues. April 2, 1844. Funeral of George **Hoffner** at St. Mathew's church.
Sat. December 25, 1841. Funeral of Martin **Hoffner** at his late residence.
Mond. November 4, 1850. Funeral of Simeon **Hoffner**'s step child at Tice Barringer's.
Sat. November 2, 1844. Funeral of Widow **Hoffner** at the Lower Stone ch.
Sat. August 23, 1834. Funeral of Mr. Henry **Hohnbarger**'s son at the Organ church.
Wed. March 27, 1839. Funeral of Andrew **Holdshouser**'s child at Union ch.
Frid. February 14, 1845. Funeral of Mr. **Hollman**, an English miner, at St. Stephen's ch.
Sat. July 24, 1852. Funeral of Col. A. **Holshouser** at Lower St. Church.

Sund. February 11, 1844. Funeral of Alexr. **Holshouser**'s daughter at the Lower Stone Church.
Thurs. October 23, 1862. Funeral of C. M. **Holshouser** at Lower St. church.
Mond. July 4, 1859. Funeral of David **Holshouser** at Organ ch.
Wed. February 3, 1847. Funeral of Mrs. David **Holshouser** at Organ ch.
Sat. August 25, 1849. Funeral of David **Holshouser**'s daughter at St. Paul's ch.
Sund. July 31, 1892. Funeral of Delia **Holshouser**, wife of Jacob Holshouser at St. Peter's church.
Wed. June 13, 1855. Funeral of Elenora, wife of Paul **Holshouser**, at Organ ch.
Sat. November 19, 1859. Funeral of Elihu **Holshouser** at Organ ch.
Thurs. October 12, 1848. Funeral of Elihu **Holshouser**'s child at Organ ch.
Sund. November 14, 1847. Funeral of Mrs. Hannah **Holshouser** at Lower St. ch.
Tues. May 10, 1853. Funeral of Henry **Holshouser** at Lower St. ch.
Sund. March 31, 1844. Funeral of Henry **Holshouser**'s child at Linn's School House.
Sat. May 10, 1845. Funeral of Jacob **Holshouser**, sen. at the Lower Stone ch.
Thurs. March 12, 1885. Funeral of Jacob **Holshouser** at Lower Stone Church.
Sat. April 22, 1893. Burial of Jacob **Holshouser** at St. Peter's ch. - Burial service rendered by Rev. Huddle.
Frid. February 10, 1854. Funeral of James **Holshouser**'s child at Lower St. ch.
Sund. May 21, 1882. Funeral of widow Montford **Holshouser**, at her late residence.
Mond. November 6, 1876. Funeral of Mrs. Paul **Holshouser** at Organ ch.
Frid. September 21, 1849. Funeral of Philpena **Holshouser**, wife of Frederic Holshouser at the Lower Stone ch.
Sund. June 10, 1855. Funeral of Polly **Holshouser**, wife of Elihu, at Organ ch.
Sat. June 18, 1892. Funeral of Thomas **Holshouser**'s child at St. Peter's church.
Frid. April 16, 1847. Funeral of Tobias **Holshouser** at Lower St. ch.
Mond. May 26, 1856. Funeral of Wilie **Holshouser** at Organ ch.
Mond. November 11, 1850. Funeral of William **Holshouser** at Lower St. ch.
Frid. October 29, 1847. Funeral of William **Holshouser**'s child at Lower St. ch.
Frid. November 1, 1850. Funeral of Wm. **Holshouser**'s child at Lower St. ch.
Wed. February 18, 1874. Burial of James **Honeycutt** Sen. at St. Stephen's ch.
Frid. July 13, 1849. Funeral of Wilson **Honeycutt**'s child at St. Stephen's.
Mond. January 21, 1839. Funeral of Danl. **Hottinger**'s wife at Union ch.
Tues. March 1, 1859. Funeral of James **House**'s child at Organ ch.
Mond. June 2, 1862. Funeral of James **House**'s child at Organ ch.
Sund. May 25, 1873. Funeral of Clementine **Hunter** at Salem ch.

Sund. January 6, 1878. Funeral of Jane **Isenhour**'s child at Stephen's ch.

Sat. November 16, 1844. Funeral of Mrs. Lewis **Jacobs** & her infant child at Jacob Walton's.
Mond. October 3, 1842. Burial service of Mrs. **Johnson** at Union ch.
Sund. June 4, 1843. Funeral of Mrs. **Johnson** at Union ch.
Sund. October 23, 1842. Funeral of Mr. **Josey**'s daughter.
Wed. January 28, 1846. Funeral of Mrs. **Josey** (Widow) at Organ ch.
Tues. March 15, 1853. Funeral of old Mrs. **Josey** at Organ ch.
Tues. April 3, 1860. Funeral of Anna Louisa **Josey** at Organ ch.
Sund. June 25, 1854. Funeral of Elizabeth **Josey** at Organ ch.
Sund. August 8, 1852. Funeral of John **Josey** at his residence.
Sund. April 29, 1855. Funeral of John **Josey** at Organ ch.
Tues. October 31, 1843. Funeral of John **Josey**'s son at Organ ch.
Sat. November 25, 1843. Funeral of John **Josey**'s child at Organ ch.
Sund. March 8, 1846. Burial service of John **Josey**'s infant child at Organ.
Tues. February 23, 1847. Funeral of Moses **Josey**'s child at Organ ch.
Mond. May 14, 1849. Funeral of Moses **Josey**'s child at Organ church.
Frid. December 5, 1879. Funeral of Sarah **Josey** (widow) at the house, buried at Organ church.
Sund. December 26, 1858. Funeral of the Widow **Josey**'s daughter at Organ ch.

Thurs. June 21, 1849. Funeral of Mr. **Keijnick**'s child, at Organ ch.
Mond. December 4, 1843. Funeral of Dr. **Kelley**'s child at St. Stephen's ch.
Sund. June 3, 1849. Burial of Dr. **Kelly**'s child at St. Stephen's ch.
Sund. July 1, 1849. Funeral of Dr. **Kelly**'s child at St. Stephen's ch.
Sund. March 29, 1835. Funeral of John **Kerns**' child at Peter Kerns'.
Tues. September 5, 1843. Funeral of John **Kern**'s child at his house.

Mond. March 11, 1844. Funeral of John **Kern**'s child at J. Kern's, buried Peter Kern's.
Tues. December 19, 1843. Funeral of Mrs. **Kesler** at Union.
Frid. October 3, 1851. Funeral of Alex. **Kesler**'s child at Union ch.
Sund. March 12, 1843. Funeral of Christena **Kesler**'s child at Union ch.
Sund. October 1, 1843. Funeral of Christian **Kesler** at Union ch.
Mond. April 20, 1857. Funeral of Eliza **Kesler** at the house.
Mond. March 4, 1844. Funeral of Geo. **Kesler** at Union ch.
Wed. February 26, 1834. Funeral of Mr. Geo. **Kesler**'s child at Union.
Wed. March 11, 1857. Funeral of Isaac **Kesler** at the house, buried at Union Ch.
Mond. October 4, 1847. Funeral of Jesse **Kesler** at St. Mathew's ch.
Sund. November 30, 1845. Funeral of old Mr. **Ketchey** at Organ ch.
Sat. September 10, 1842. Funeral of Mrs. **Ketchey** (widow) at Union Church.
Sund. May 28, 1854. Burial of Mr. Solomon **Ketchey**'s child at Organ ch.
Sund. April 10, 1859. Funeral at widow Garner's, of Solomon **Ketchey**'s wife.
Thurs. August 11, 1859. Funeral of Solomon **Ketchey**'s child at Organ Church.
Wed. November 26, 1845. Funeral of Mrs. **Ketchy** at Organ ch.
Sat. April 25, 1846. Funeral of Mrs. **Ketner** at Organ ch.
Frid. June 13, 1845. Funeral of Anna Louisa **Ketner** at Organ ch.
Sund. October 3, 1880. Funeral of Catharine **Ketner** at the house. Buried at Ebenezer.
Sat. October 8, 1853. Funeral of Dawalt **Ketner** at Organ ch.
Mond. March 13, 1882. Funeral of Elizabeth **Ketner**, relict of Peter Ketner, at Ebenezer ch.
Tues., July 1, 1856. Funeral of Geo. M. **Ketner**'s child at Organ ch.
Thurs. August 11, 1859. Funeral of John **Ketner**'s child at Organ ch.
Sat. September 10, 1859. Funeral of Peter **Ketner** at Organ.
Sat. October 13, 1883. Funeral of George M. **Ketner**'s daughter Rosetta V. at Ebenezer Church.
Frid. February 18, 1853. Funeral of Mrs. Eli **Klutts** at Lower St. ch.
Sat. December 10, 1853. Funeral of Barbara **Klutts** at Organ ch.
Mond. April 30, 1860. Funeral of Eli **Klutts**' child at the house, buried at Lower St. ch.
Sund. September 31, 1875. Funeral of Mrs. Elizabeth **Klutts** at St. Peter's ch.
Sund. November 11, 1888. Funeral of Mrs. Elizabeth L. **Klutts**, wife of Moses Klutts, at Lower St. church.
Sat. September 13, 1884. Buried Henry **Klutts**, an aged member, at Organ Church.
Sund. November 9, 1884. Funeral of Henry **Klutts**, at Organ Church.
Sat. March 1, 1845. Funeral of Henry **Klutts**' wife at the Lower Stone Church.
Frid. June 12, 1846. Funeral of James **Klutts**' wife at Organ ch.
Sat. January 30, 1847. Funeral of John **Klutts** at Lower Stone Church.
Mond. February 10, 1862. Funeral of John **Klutts** at Organ ch.
Tues. October 4, 1853. Funeral of Leonard **Klutts** at L. St. church.
Sund. September 26, 1852. Funeral of Martha **Klutts**, wife of James at Organ Church.
Sat. March 26, 1859. Funeral of Moses **Klutts** at Lower St. ch.
Wed. November 10, 1852. Funeral of Moses **Klutts**' child at Lower St. ch.
Sund. July 27, 1856. Funeral of Osborne **Klutts**' child at Organ ch.
Sat. July 2, 1859. Funeral of Osborn **Klutts**' child at the house, buried at Organ ch.
Sat. April 13, 1844. Funeral of Paul **Klutts**' child at the Lower Stone Church.
Wed. August 18, 1869. Funeral of R. J. **Klutts** at Bethel ch.
Mond. April 18, 1853. Funeral of Regina **Klutts** at Lower St. Church.
Sund. March 27, 1859. Funeral of Sally Emaline **Klutts** at Organ ch.
Frid. May 27, 1853. Funeral of Solomon **Klutts**' child at Lower St. ch.
Wed. February 4, 1846. Funeral of Sophia **Klutts** (daughter of Leonard Klutts) at the Lower Stone ch.
Sund. August 24, 1856. Funeral of Susanna, wife of Henry **Klutts**, at the Lower St. Ch.
Sund. March 15, 1863. Funeral of Tobias **Klutts** at St. Peter's ch., who fell in the battle of Fredericksburg.
Sund. May 26, 1844. Funeral of widow **Klutts**' child at Lower Stone ch.
Mond. February 12, 1844. Funeral of Mrs. David **Knup** at the Lower Stone Church.
Sund. December 1, 1844. Funeral of David **Knup**'s child.
Sund. November 24, 1872. Buried Jacob **Koon** at Salem ch.
Sund. December 8, 1872. Funeral of Jacob **Koon** at Salem ch.
Frid. March 24, 1848. Funeral of Mr. **Korf** at Organ ch.

Sund. August 28, 1842. Funeral of Mr. **Lee**'s child at St. Paul's ch.
Sund. May 14, 1871. Funeral of Aaron **Lefler** at St. Peter's ch.

Tues. September 20, 1881. Funeral of William **Lefler** at Lower St. ch.
Wed. August 2, 1843. Funl. of Col. **Lell** at Tice Barringer's.
Wed. November 27, 1839. Funeral of old Mrs. **Lemly** at St. Matthew's Ch.
Sat. December 23, 1843. Funeral of Moses **Lemly**'s child at St. Mathew's ch.
Thurs. March 14, 1844. Funeral of Philip **Lemly** at St. Mathew's ch.
Sund. August 13, 1882. Funeral of Abram **Lentz** at St. Matthew's ch.
Sat. October 27, 1877. Funeral of Adolphus Eugene, son of Eli **Lentz** at Organ ch.
Sat. August 15, 1846. Funeral of Ambrose **Lentz**'s child at John Lentz's, too indisposed to officiate.
Sund. November 15, 1846. Funeral of Ambrose **Lentz**'s child at St. Stephen's ch.
Sat. July 8, 1854. Funeral of Bostian **Lentz** at Union ch.
Mond. March 12, 1883. Funeral Catherine **Lentz**, widow of Bostian Lentz at Lower St. Church.
Tues. May 25, 1852. Funeral of David **Lentz** (son of Jacob) at Organ ch.
Mond. May 6, 1872. Funeral of Col. David **Lentz** at Bethel Ch.
Tues. March 19, 1878. Funeral of Henry **Lentz** at Union ch.
Tues. February 25, 1851. Funeral of John **Lentz**'s child at St. Stephen's ch.
Wed. December 31, 1884. Funeral of John **Lentz**'s child at Organ ch. in the services.
Frid. February 12, 1886. Funeral of John T. **Lentz** at Lower Stone Church.
Mond. October 29, 1855. Funeral of John T. **Lentz**'s child at Organ ch.
Wed. March 24, 1880. Funeral Mary Barbara, widow of John **Lentz**, at St. Stephen's ch.
Frid. January 21, 1859. Funeral of Mathias **Lentz**'s child at Lower St. ch.
Sund. July 13, 1851. Funeral of Peter **Lentz** at Organ ch.
Thurs. April 16, 1846. Funeral of Polly C. **Lentz**, wife of Ambrose Lentz, at St. Stephen's ch.
Wed. April 16, 1873. Funeral of R. W. **Lentz** at Organ ch.
Frid. March 21, 1834. Went to the burying of Revd. **Lerk**, German Reformed.
Sund. January 19, 1840. Funeral of Cornelius **Lineberger**'s child at Union.
Frid. January 2, 1880. Funeral of Mrs. Elizbeth **Lingel** at Lower Stone Church.
Mond. December 22, 1884. Funeral of Laurence **Lingel** at Lower Stone Church.
Wed. April 11, 1883. Witnessed the Burial of Moses **Lingel** at Christiana Church.
Sund. December 14, 1851. Funeral of Mrs. John **Lingle** at Organ Ch.
Tues. July 12, 1853. Funeral of John **Lingle**'s daughter at Organ ch.
Mond. October 14, 1889. Funeral of Mrs. **Linker** at the house and buried at Liberty.
Tues. October 28, 1890. Funeral Fannie L. **Linker**, daughter of George W. & Mary E. Linker at the house & buried at St. Peter's church.
Mond. December 8, 1890. Funeral of George W. **Linker** at St. Peter's ch.
Mond. December 25, 1843. Funeral of Mr. **Linn**'s colored woman.
Thurs.November 2, 18517. Funeral of Mrs. **Linn** at Organ ch.
Mond. November 3, 1851. Funeral of Elizabeth **Linn** at Isaac Kesler's.
Thurs. October 26, 1854. Funeral of Saml. **Linn** at Organ ch.
Sund. November 13, 1881. Funeral of John **Litaker** at St. Enoch's ch.
Tues. March 24, 1835. Funeral of Wm. **Loch**'s child in Salisbury.
Tues. May 15, 1860. Funeral of John S. **Long** at the house, buried family burying ground.
Mond. October 23, 1854. Burial of John **Louder**'s child.
Sat. February 8, 1845. Funeral of Nicholas **Ludwig**'s child at St. Stephen's ch.
Sund. September 30, 1877. Buried Elijah **Ludwig**'s child at Mt. Mitchell ch. (Methodist).
Frid. August 19, 1842. Milas **Luther** was buried at Union church.
Sund. August 28, 1842. Revd. Scheck preached the Funeral of Milas **Luther** at Union.
Sund. August 13, 1854. The Funeral of Charles **Lyerla**'s child.
Mond. September 12, 1859. Funeral of John **Lyerla**'s child at St. Peter's ch.
Mond. February 16, 1852. Funeral of Mrs. Zaceriah **Lyerla** at Organ ch.
Mond. December 26, 1853. Funeral of Zacheriah **Lyerla**'s child.
Tues. January 27, 1835. Funeral of Stuffle **Lyerlie**'s child at Union ch.
Sund. October 25, 1846. Funeral of old Mrs. **Lyerly** at Lower Stone ch.
Frid. April 14, 1882. Funeral of Andrew A. **Lyerly** at St. Peter's ch.
Wed. July 26, 1871. Funeral of Danl. **Lyerly** at Salem Ch.
Tues. December 11, 1877. Funeral of David L., son of Joseph **Lyerly** at St. Peter's ch.
Sat. June 22, 1889. Funeral of David M. **Lyerly**'s child at St. Peter's ch.
Sund. July 17, 1859. Funeral of Jacob **Lyerly**'s child at St. Peter's ch.
Frid. January 22, 1875. Funeral of Jesse **Lyerly** at Salem ch.
Frid. October 13, 1843. Funeral of Geo. **Lyerly**'s child at Union ch.

Frid. May 16, 1862. Funeral of Martin **Lyerly** at Organ ch.
Mond. August 24, 1846. Funeral of Moses **Lyerly**'s child at the Lower Stone ch.
Thurs. October 24, 1872. Funeral of Mrs. Nancy **Lyerly** at Salem ch.
Tues. November 27, 1855. Funeral of Zacheriah Lyerly's child at Organ ch.

Sat. February 15, 1873. Funeral of Mrs. Jacob Goodman's daughter, Mrs. Altira C. **Martin**.
Sund. February 16, 1873. Preached the Funeral of Mrs. **Martin**.
Mond. February 17, 1873. Buried Mrs. **Martin** according to the Burial service in the Book of Worship.
Sund. April 15, 1860. Widow John **May**'s Funeral at the house.
Wed. October 3, 1877. Heard Dr. Davis preach the Funeral of Mrs. C. **Melchor**.
Tues. December 7, 1880. Funeral of Mrs. Nancy **Melton** at Gold Hill.
Mond. May 21, 1855. Funeral of Mrs. **Miller** at Organ ch.
Wed. February 21, 1866. Funeral of Alexander M. **Miller** at Lower St. ch.
Wed. November 12, 1862. Funeral of Alex. M. **Miller**'s child. at Lower St. ch.
Wed. July 31, 1878. Funeral of Anna L. **Miller**, at Organ ch.
Frid. March 2, 1855. Funeral of Mr. Asa **Miller** at the house, buried Lower St. ch.
Wed. June 28, 1882. Funeral of widow C. A. **Miller**'s child at Organ ch.
Thurs. September 27, 1883. Funeral of Catharine **Miller** at Lower Stone Church.
Frid. December 24, 1880. Funeral of Charles A. **Miller** at Organ ch.
Sund. April 10, 1887. Funeral of Conrad **Miller** at Luther's ch.
Mond. August 13, 1877. Funeral of Cornelius W. **Miller** at Organ ch.
Mond. June 19, 1876. Funeral of Danl. **Miller** at St. John's church.
Mond. September 12, 1887. Burial of Danl. **Miller** at Organ church.
Sat. October 25, 1862. Eli **Miller**'s child at Lower St. ch.
Mond. July 18, 1859. Funeral of Elizabeth, wife of John **Miller**, at Organ ch.
Thurs. July 23, 1874. Funeral of Elizabeth R., wife of Alfred **Miller** at Lower St. Church.
Thurs. June 1, 1876. Funeral of Eve Ann **Miller** at Organ ch.
Thurs. January 12, 1871. Funeral of Francis Victor **Miller** at Bethel ch.
Thurs. October 2, 1845. Funerals of Geo. **Miller** & his son, Henry at Organ ch.
Sund. October 13, 1872. Funeral of H. **Miller**'s child at Salem ch.
Sund. November 23, 1862. Funeral of Henry **Miller** at Organ ch., who fell in the battle Sharpsburg.
Thurs. March 26, 1846. Funeral of Mrs. Henry **Miller**'s at Fullenwider's church.
Wed. November 28, 1855. Funeral of Henry A. **Miller**'s child at St. Peter's ch.
Thurs. October 20, 1842. Funeral of Jacob **Miller**, at his house.
Sund. March 9, 1845. Funeral of John **Miller**, son of George.
Thurs. December 30, 1869. Burial of John **Miller** at Organ ch. Burial service. Rev. Cone preached the Funeral.
Sat. January 31, 1857. Funeral of John J. **Miller** at Organ ch.
Wed. July 4, 1855. Funeral of John J. **Miller**'s child at Organ ch.
Sund. July 17, 1887. Buried John Jacob **Miller** at Organ ch.
Tues. February 14, 1882. Funeral of Joseph **Miller** at Lower St. ch.
Tues. March 18, 1845. Funeral of Joseph **Miller**'s wife at the Lower St. ch.
Wed. November 8, 1843. Funeral of Joseph **Miller**'s child at the Lower Stone ch.
Sund. June 5, 1887. Funeral of Joseph **Miller**'s child at Luther's church.
Wed. May 17, 1876. Funeral of Luther **Miller**'s child at Organ ch.
Thurs. February 22, 1855. Funeral of Margaret Solena **Miller** Asa Miller's, buried at Lower St. Church.
Sat. February 12, 1859. Funeral of Mary Ann, daughter of Peter **Miller**, at Organ ch.Sund. April 10, 1881. Funeral of Nelly, wife of Joseph **Miller**, at Lower Stone Church.
Frid. February 25, 1859. Funeral of Paul **Miller** at the house, buried at Organ ch.
Sund. February 12, 1882. Funeral of Paul A. **Miller**'s child at Lower St. ch.
Tues. October 17, 1843. Funeral of Peter **Miller**'s child at Organ ch.
Sat. June 8, 1850. Funeral of Peter **Miller**'s child.
Sund. March 10, 1844. Funeral of Peter **Miller**'s child at Organ ch.
Sat. December 16, 1843. Funeral of Polly **Miller** at St. Stephen's ch.
Sund. March 19, 1871. Funeral of Rose Sophia **Miller**, daughter of C. R. Miller.
Wed. March 19, 1845. Funeral of Miss Sybilla **Miller** at Organ ch.
Sat. November 20, 1847. Burial of William **Miller** at Lower Stone ch.
Wed. October 8, 1890. Funeral of Diana **Misemer** at the house, friends buried her at Union church.
Tues. November 27, 1883. Buried Jacob **Misenheimer**'s child at Organ Church.
Sund. December 23, 1883. Funeral of Jacob **Misenheimer**'s child at Organ Church.

Mond. October 7, 1878. Funeral of John **Misenheimer**'s child at St. Peter's ch.
Thurs. May 18, 1854. Funeral of Laurence **Misenheimer**'s child at Organ ch.
Sund. August 10, 1879. Funeral of Mary L. **Misenheimer**, wife of Isom Misenheimer at Bethel ch. Stanly Co.
Sund. May 13, 1855. Funeral of James **Montgomery**'s child at Lower St. ch.
Sat. November 26, 1881. Funeral of Ally **Morgan** at Corinth Baptist Church.
Sat. September 21, 1878. Funeral of David **Morgan** at Corinth (Baptist) Church.
Sund. October 14, 1877. Funeral of John **Morgan**'s child at St. Peter's ch.
Sund. December 26, 1847. Funeral of Jacob **Mowry**'s Son at the house.
Wed. April 21, 1852. Funeral of Peter **Mowry** at Lower St. ch.
Wed. December 24, 1851. Funeral of Widow **Mowry**'s child at Organ Church.
Sund. January 25, 1835. Mr. Tho. **Mull**'s funeral at his residence.

Mond. June 9, 1851. Funeral of Paul **Nussman** at St. Stephen's. - preached from Ps. 58:11.

Tues. April 8, 1845. Funeral of Catherine **Overcash** at Organ ch.
Mond. January 26, 1852. Funeral of Mrs. Michl. **Overcash**.
Frid. September 14, 1855. Funeral of Polly Caroline **Overcash** at Organ ch.
Thurs. January 2, 1879. Funeral of James **Owens**' child at St. Stephen's ch.

Sat. February 16, 1889. Funeral of George **Park**'s child at the house & buried at St. Peter's ch.
Sund. September 13, 1891. Went to Luther's church & heard Rev. C. C. Lyerly preach the funeral of David C. **Parker** & daughter decd.
Frid. March 25, 1842. Funeral of Mr. **Pasinger** at Union ch.
Tues. October 8, 1850. Funeral of Mrs. **Pasinger** at Organ ch.
Tues. October 12, 1852. Funeral of Barbara M. **Patterson** at Organ ch.
Mond. April 30, 1860. Funeral of Charles **Patterson**'s child at Organ ch.
Frid. June 13, 1856. Funeral of Joseph A. **Patterson**'s child at Organ ch.
Thurs. December 25, 1862. Funeral of Joseph A. **Patterson** at his residence. Mr. Patterson was wounded in the battle of Sharpsburg, Md. and returned home & died.
Frid. January 5, 1849. Funeral of Mrs. **Peacock** at St. Stephen's ch.
Mond. July 25, 1842. Funeral of Louisa **Pealer** at Union ch.
Sund. August 27, 1843. Funeral of Moses **Pealer** at St. Mathew's ch.
Sund. June 11, 1843. Funeral of John **Peck**, sen. at St. Stephen's ch.
Frid. December 4, 1846. Funeral of John **Peck**, jr. at St. Stephen's ch.
Wed. October 4, 1854. Funeral of Henry **Peck** Esq. at St. Stephen's ch.
Tues. March 28, 1882. Funeral of Peter **Peck** at St. Stephen's ch.
Mond. April 18, 1892. Rev. W. R. Brown buried Mrs. **Peeler** at M. A. Holshouser's.
Mond. June 5, 1876. Funeral of Crawford **Peeler**'s child at Lower Stone Church.
Thurs. September 30, 1852. Funeral of Mrs. Danl. **Peeler** at Lower St. ch.
Tues. December 13, 1853. Funeral of Eve, widow of Peter **Peeler**, at Lower St. ch.
Mond. December 6, 1847. Funeral of Lewis **Peeler** at Lower St. ch.
Sat. March 6, 1852. Funeral of Peter **Peeler**'s son Moses.
Mond. June 2, 1845. Burial of Mrs. Regina **Peeler** at the Lower St. ch.
Tues. November 14, 1843. Burial service of Saml. **Peeler**'s child at Union ch.
Sund. December 3, 1843. Funeral Saml. **Peeler**'s child at Union. Funeral of three of Mr. Peeler's children.
Sund. March 13, 1859. Funeral of Simeon **Peeler** at Lower St. ch.
Tues. June 8, 1875. Burial of Tobias **Peeler** at Lower St. ch. Rev. Trexler officiated.
Sund. September 30, 1855. Funeral of Valentine **Pence** at Lower St. ch.
Wed. March 4, 1857. Funeral of Elizabeth widow of Valentine **Pence**, at Lower St. ch.
Sund. May 22, 1859. Funeral of Mr. **Penninger**'s child at Organ ch.
Sat. December 4, 1847. Funeral of Mrs. **Penninger** at Lower St. ch.
Wed. October 25, 1882. Funeral of John **Pless** at Ebenezer ch.
Thurs. November 21, 1844. Funeral of Mrs. Louisa **Pless** at Organ ch.
Sund. September 18, 1881. Funeral of Pleasant **Pless**' child.
Thurs. January 18, 1844. Funeral of John **Plott**, at Organ ch.
Thurs. November 29, 1883. Funeral of Edward **Pool** at St. Matthew's Church.
Tues. April 13, 1847. Funeral of Mrs. Jacob **Pool** at the house.
Wed. November 21, 1883. Funeral of Joseph **Pool** at St. Matthew's ch.
Sund. December 12, 1880. Funeral of Mrs. Sandy **Pool** at St. Matthew's ch.

Wed. January 12, 1859. Funeral of Otho **Poole**'s child St. Matthews ch.
Sund. August 7, 1870. Funeral of Mr. **Porter**'s child at Salem ch.
Sat. November 24, 1888. Funeral of Joseph A. **Powlass** at Lower Stone church.
Frid. January 17, 1851. Funeral of Saml. **Powlass** at Lower St. Church.
Sund. November 12, 1876. Funeral of William **Powlass** at Lower Stone Church.
Sund. May 4, 1856. Funeral of Mrs. Catharine, wife of Henry **Probst** at St. John's ch.
Tues. September 13, 1859. Funeral of Mrs. Elizabeth, wife of Valentine **Propst**, at Organ ch.
Wed. July 20, 1859. Funeral of Valentine **Propst**'s, jr. child at Organ ch.
Mond. November 23, 1874. Funeral of Wisley **Propst**'s child at Salem ch.

Wed. January 24, 1844. Funeral of old Mrs. **Randleman**, decd, at St. Paul's ch.
Frid. December 31, 1847. Funeral of Jacob **Randleman**'s child at St. Stephen's church.
Sund. January 22, 1860. Funeral of George R. **Randleman** at St. Paul's ch.
Sat. February 10, 1844. Funeral of Mrs. **Rauch** at St. Mathew's ch.
Sat. February 28, 1846. Burial service of Valentine **Reimer**.
Sund. March 22, 1846. Funeral of Valentine **Reimer** at Organ ch.
Frid. November 24, 1843. Funeral of Mr. **Reimert** at Organ ch.
Wed. April 17, 1844. Funeral of old Mrs. **Reimert** at Organ church.
Sund. November 24, 1844. Funeral of Mrs. **Reimert** at Organ ch.
Sund. February 9, 1845. Funeral of Widow **Reimert** at Organ ch.
Sund. June 27, 1847. Funeral of old Mrs. **Ribelin** at the Lower St. ch.
Wed. December 15, 1880. Funeral of Peter Axam **Ribelin** at St. Matthew's ch.
Tues. April 1, 1845. Funl. of Saml. **Ribelin** at the house, buried Lower Stone ch.
Sund. January 7, 1849. Burial of John **Richard**'s at St. Stephen's ch.
Frid. January 3, 1851. Funeral of Mrs. **Richie** at Organ ch.
Sund. July 24, 1859. Funeral of Elizabeth, wife of George **Richey**, at Organ ch.
Tues. October 14, 1884. Funeral of John **Richie**'s daughter at the house and buried at Organ Church.
Frid. December 24, 1858. Funeral of Cath. L. **Rimer** at Organ ch.
Sund. January 10, 1847. Funeral of Elizabeth **Rimer** at Organ church.
Thurs. October 20, 1853. Funeral of Mrs. John **Rimer** at Organ ch.
Tues. June 3, 1856. Funeral of Susanna **Rimer** at Organ ch.
Sund. March 26, 1843. Funeral of Mr. Thomas **Rimert**'s wife.
Frid. June 22, 1877. Funeral of Margaret C. **Ritchie** at Organ ch.
Wed. May 30, 1877. Funeral of Solomon **Ritchie**, at his late residence.
Thurs. September 11, 1862. Funeral of James C. **Roseman**'s child at the house, buried at Lower St. Church.
Thurs. December 28, 1865. Funeral of James C. **Roseman**'s child at the house, buried at Lower Stone.
Sat. December 9, 1848. Burial of Father (**Rothrock**) at the Moravian Church. Funeral preached by Revd. Sensiman.
Sat. September 27, 1851. Lucetta's (**Rothrock**) funeral preached by Rev. Linn then buried her at Union Church Grave Yard.
Sat. August 23, 1845. Burial of Mother (**Rothrock**) at the Moravian Church, Funeral was preached by Rev. Mr. Sensamon.
Thurs. May 1, 1890. Buried my wife (Mrs. **Rothrock**) at Union Church.
Sund. June 1, 1834. Mr. **Ruffta**'s child at Union ch.
Frid. April 5, 1878. Funeral of Edward **Ruffty** at St. Matthew's ch.
Sund. December 19, 1869. Funeral of George **Ruffty** at Salem ch.
Sund. February 9, 1873. Funeral of Wilie **Ruffty** at Salem ch.
Sund. July 13, 1856. Funerals of two of Mr. **Rumple**'s children at Organ ch.

Frid. August 28, 1885. Funeral of Amanda C. **Safret** at Christiana ch.
Tues. June 24, 1845. Funeral of Charles **Safret** at Organ ch.
Thurs. July 21, 1853. Funeral George **Safret** at Organ ch.
Wed. May 25, 1836. Funeral of Mr. **Schaeffer** in St. Thomas.
Mond. July 25, 1859. Funeral of Christena **Seaford** at Organ ch.
January 25, 1863. Funeral of Eli **Seaford** at Organ ch., who fell in the battle of Fredericksburg.
Wed. July 4, 1855. Funeral of Eli **Seaford**'s child at Organ ch.
Wed. July 12, 1882. Burial of Elizabeth **Seaford** at Organ ch.
Sund. October 8, 1882. Funeral of Elizabeth **Seaford** at Organ ch.
Sat. June 20, 1846. Funeral of George **Seaford**'s wife at Organ ch.
Sat. October 20, 1855. Funeral of Henry **Seaford**'s child at Organ ch.

Sund. December 14, 1862. Funeral of Henry A. **Seaford** at Organ ch.
Sat. February 26, 1859. Funeral of Moses **Seaford** at the house, buried at Organ ch.
Wed. September 13, 1854. Funeral of P. A. **Seaford**'s child at Organ ch.
Thurs. July 12, 1877. Funeral of Samuel **Seaford** at Salem ch.
Mond. April 14, 1862. Funeral of Simeon **Seaford** at Organ ch.
Thurs. December 4, 1856. Funeral of Mrs. Susanna **Seaford** at Organ ch.
Thurs. April 3, 1845. Funeral of William **Seaford** at Organ ch.
Sat. March 18, 1848. Funeral of old Mrs. **Sell**'s at Mathias Barringer's.
Wed. September 23, 1835. Funeral of Mr. **Seller**'s, services performed by Revd. Rawhouser.
Tues. November 24, 1846. Funeral of John **Setzer** at Organ ch.
Sund. November 15, 1874. Burial of Caleb **Setzer** at Ebenezer ch. (Methodist).
Sund. April 18, 1875. Heard Rev. Triplett preach the Funeral of Mr. **Setzer** at Ebenezer ch.
Sund. May 8, 1870. Funeral of Crissa Ann **Sewell** at Bethel Ch.
Tues. August 26, 1873. Rev. Rumple preached J. T. **Shaver**'s Funeral in Salisbury.
Frid. January 23, 1874. Funeral of John **Shuman** at Union Church.
Sund. September 16, 1855. Funeral of David **Shuping**'s child at Bostian's School House.
Mond. 9. Funeral of Eli **Shuping** at Lower Stone ch.
Wed. April 26, 1854. Funeral of Mrs. Elizabeth **Caroline**, wife of Moses Shuping at Phanuel's Church.
Wed. 18. Funeral of Sally **Shuping** at St. Peter's Church.
Mond. September 8, 1879. Funeral Ador Enora, infant daughter of James C. **Sides**.
Sund. May 21, 1876. Funeral of Elizabeth **Sides** at Bethel ch.
Thurs. May 20, 1847. Funeral of Mrs. Lydia **Sides**, wife of Nelson Sides, at Organ church.
Sund. June 11, 1854. Funeral of Nelson **Sides**' son.
Mond. April 29, 1844. Funeral of Mrs. **Smith** at Organ church.
Tues. April 5, 1859. Funeral of Catherine, relict of John **Smith**, at Phanuel's ch.
Tues. May 6, 1856. Funeral of Mrs. G. W. **Smith** [St. Enoch's].
Tues. May 20, 1834. Funeral of Geo. **Smith**'s child at Jacob Smith's.
Mond. September 15, 1873. Funeral of George M. **Smith** at Union ch.
Wed. February 24, 1847. Funeral of Jacob **Smith** at Organ ch.
Sund. November 26, 1854. Funeral of John **Smith** at Organ ch.
Sund. March 8, 1846. Funeral of Mary Ann **Smith** at St. Paul's ch.
Frid. April 25, 1851. Funeral of William **Smith**, sen. at the house, buried at Jacob Smith's burying ground.
Frid. January 23, 1835. Funeral of Wm. **Smith**'s Junr.'s child at J. Smith's.
Sund. April 19, 1835. Was to have preached a Funeral at Wm. **Smith**'s Junr., could not attend.
Thurs. June 6, 1844. Funeral of Mr. **Smithdeal**'s child - at the house.
Sat. January 2, 18447. Funeral of Mr. **Speck**'s child at Organ ch.
Thurs. September 21, 1843. Funeral of old Mrs. **Starnes** at St. Mathew's ch.
Wed. April 25, 1877. Funeral of Saml. R. **Starnes** at St. Matthew's ch.
Mond. January 18, 1886. Burial of Mrs. **Stikeleather** (an old lady) at Lower St.
Tues. July 17, 1888. Burial of Augusta **Stikeleather** at St. Peter's ch.
Sund. March 14, 1886. Funeral of Christina **Stikeleather** at Elm Grove.
Frid. December 4, 1885. Funeral of Lula Joana **Stikeleather** at Lower St. Church.
Sat. July 19, 1856. Funeral of 2 of Jacob **Stirewald**'s children.
Wed. June 11, 1862. Funeral of Sandy **Stirewald**'s child at the house and buried at Organ Church.
Mond. December 19, 1887. Funeral of Frederick **Stirewalt** at the house & buried at Ebenezer ch.
Thurs. September 3, 1846. Funeral of Henry **Stirewalt**'s son at the church near Widow Greaber's.
Sat. November 11, 1848. Funeral of Jacob **Stirewalt**'s wife at Phanuel's ch.
Tues. June 12, 1883. Funeral of P. M. **Stirewalt**'s child at Ebenezer.
Sat. November 24, 1883. Funeral of Sarah Jane, wife of Paul M. **Stirewalt**, at Ebenezer ch.
Wed. August 31, 1853. Funeral of Tobias **Stirewalt** at Organ ch.
Sund. February 20, 1842. Funeral of Mrs. **Stoner** at St. Mathew's ch.
Sund. August 31, 1879. Funeral of Jonathan **Stoner** at St. Matthew's.
Wed. January 7, 1880. Funeral of William R. **Stoner** at St. Matthew's ch.
Tues. September 18, 1838. Funeral of David **Stork** in Salisbury.
Sat. April 7, 1860. Funeral of Leah C. **Stricker** at the house, buried at Organ ch.
Wed. October 19, 1853. Funeral of Paul **Striker** at Organ ch.
Sund. October 15, 1843. Funeral of Danl. **Swink** at Union ch.

Frid. January 17, 1840. Funeral of Jacob **Thomas**' wife.
Frid. December 12, 1856. Funeral at home of Levi **Thomas**' child.
Sund. February 4, 1855. Funeral of Sophia **Thomas** at Charles Earnheart's.
Frid. April 7, 1871. Funerals of Levi **Thomas** and wife at Union ch.
Sat. May 26, 1849. Funeral Adam **Trexler** at Union ch.
Sund. June 4, 1865. Funeral of Adam **Trexler** at his late residence.
Wed. December 20, 1843. Funeral of Mrs. Adam **Trexler** at Union church.
Tues. November 19, 1844. Funeral of Adam **Trexler**'s daughter at Union ch.
Tues. February 10, 1857. Funeral of Alexander, son of John **Trexler**, at St. Peter's church.
Sund. May 27, 1888. Funeral of Elizabeth L. **Trexler**, widow of Caleb Trexler at St. Peter's church.
conducted by Rev. H. A. Trexler.
Wed. May 14, 1884. Funeral of Eve Elizabeth **Trexler**, wife of Lawson Trexler, at St. Peter's Church.
Sund. 18, 1890. Funeral of Rev. H. A. **Trexler**'s wife at St. Peter's church.
Frid. June 18, 1889. Funeral of Rev. H. A. **Trexler**'s child at St. Peter's ch.
Sat. February 28, 1846. Funeral of Jacob **Trexler**, sen. at the Lower Stone ch.
Thurs. August 7, 1851. Funeral of Jacob **Trexler**'s child at Lower St. church.
Sat. July 29, 1876. Burial of James **Trexler**'s child at St. Peter's ch.
Sund. March 1, 1857. Funls. of two of John **Trexler**'s children at St. Peter's ch.
Tues. February 4, 1851. Funeral of Leah **Trexler**, wife of John, at the Lower St. ch.
Mond. July 24, 1871. Funeral of M. **Trexler**'s daughter at house, buried at Lower Stone Church.
Frid. October 30, 1891. Buried Mrs. Margaret **Trexler** at St. Peter's church.
Tues. February 8, 1876. Funeral of Moses **Trexler** at Salem ch.
Mond. December 17, 1849. Funeral of Moses **Trexler**'s wife at Organ ch.
Sat. September 25, 1875. Funeral of Moses **Trexler**'s wife.
Mond. August 25, 1856. Funeral of Moses **Trexler**'s child at Lower St. ch.
Sund. March 9, 1873. Funeral of Moses **Trexler**'s son, agd. 15 yrs at Salem ch.
Sat. April 24, 1852. Funeral of Peter **Trexler**'s wife at Lower St. ch.
Sat. July 19, 1845. Funeral of two of Peter **Trexler**'s children at the Lower Stone Church.
Sat. July 21, 1849. Funeral of Mr. **Troutman**'s child at St. Stephen's ch.
Tues. March 24, 1846. Funeral of Mrs. **Troutman** at St. Stephen's church.
Sund. May 30, 1852. Funeral of old Mrs. **Troutman** at the Lower Stone Church.
Tues. October 16, 1838. Funeral of Abel **Troutman** at the Stone ch.
Sund. June 2, 1850. Funeral of Christena **Troutman** (widow) at Organ Church.
Sund. October 19, 1845. Burial service of David **Troutman**'s wife at the Lower Stone Church.
Sund. November 2, 1845. Funeral David **Troutman**'s wife at the home.
Sund. December 4, 1853. Funeral of David **Troutman**'s daughter at St. Stephen's ch.
Sund. February 8, 1857. Funeral of Elizabeth **Troutman** at Organ ch.
Frid. October 29, 1880. Funeral of George **Troutman**'s little son, 8 yrs. old at the home, buried at Organ ch.
Sat. July 28, 1855. Funeral of Henry **Troutman**'s wife at the house, buried at Organ ch.
Wed. January 31, 1849. Burial of two of Henry **Troutman**'s children at St. Stephen's ch.
Sund. June 17, 1849. Funeral of three of Henry **Troutman**'s children at St. Stephen's ch.
Tues. March 27, 1849. Funeral of John **Troutman** at David Troutman's.
Sund. February 21, 1847. Funeral of John **Troutman**'s son at his house.
Tues. August 3, 1852. Funeral of Melchor **Troutman** at Organ ch.
Sund. October 1, 1854. Funeral of Peter **Troutman**'s little daughter at St. Stephen's ch.
Sund. June 25, 1866. Funeral of Saml. **Troutman** at Lower St. Church. Funeral of F. A. Stirewalt's child.
Sund. November 1, 1846. Funeral of Sophia **Troutman** at David Troutman's.
Mond. March 31, 1845. Funl. of Geo. **Troutman**'s at the house.

Sund. February 16, 1845. Funl. of J. **Udy**'s child.

Thurs. June 22, 1848. Funeral of Danl. **Waggoner**'s child at St. Stephen's ch.
Sat. May 19, 1860. Funeral of Philip **Wagner** at Widow Wagner's (of Philip).
Sund. Aug. 20, 1865. Funeral of John **Waller**, at St. Peter's ch.
Sund. July 17, 1859. Funeral of Milly **Waller**'s daughter Eve M. S. Waller & of Nancy Waller at St. Peter's ch.
Sat. June 30, 1855. Funeral at Nancy **Waller**'s, of John Waller.
Wed. June 4., 1856 Funeral of Arabella F. infant daughter of Henry A. & Ann **Walton** at Union ch.
Sund. May 5, 1839. Funeral of Mrs. W. at Jacob **Walton**'s.
Sund. January 7, 1844. Funeral of Mr. **Walton**'s child at Jacob Walton's

Tues. February 20, 1844. Funeral of Jacob **Walton**'s little daughter.
Wed. October 8, 1851. Funeral of Mrs. **Walton**, widow of Jesse, at Union ch.
Tues. November 18, 1851. Funeral of Lewis **Walton** at his residence. Buried at Peter Walton's.
Thurs. September 25, 1856. Funeral of Martin L. **Walton** at Union ch.
Sat. October 5, 1872. Burial of W. A. **Walton**, Sheriff of Rowan Co. at St. Luke's ch.
Mond. November 12, 1838. Funeral of Jacob **Weant** at his residence.
Sund. June 25, 1843. Funeral of Daniel **Weaver**'s son at St. Paul's ch.
Sat. March 30, 1844. Funeral of Esrom **Weaver**'s wife at the Lower Stone ch.
Frid. January 10, 1840. Funeral of Jacob **Weaver** at St. Paul's ch.
Sund. February 25, 1877. Funeral of Martin A. **Weaver**'s infant son at Organ ch.
Frid. March 22, 1850. Funeral of Sally **Weaver** at Organ ch.
Sat. April 6, 1850. Funeral of Mrs. Henry **Wilhelm** at St. Mathew's Church.
Frid. August 25, 1882. Funeral of Mattie Melona, daughter of Henry **Williams**, buried her at Gold Hill.
Wed. August 10, 1842. Funeral of Mrs. **Wise** at Union.
Tues. October 17, 1843. Burial of Charles **Wise**'s child at Union ch.
Sund. November 5, 1843. Funeral of Charles **Wise**'s child at Union ch.
Tues. September 4, 1838. Funeral of Robert **Wood** in Salisbury.
Tues. December 22, 1835. Funeral of Mrs. **Wunderlich** in St. Thomas.

Sund. July 9, 1882. Funeral of L. Thames **Yates** child at the house, buried at Organ ch.
Sund. July 8, 1855. Funeral of Frank **Yost**'s wife at Organ ch.
Wed. July 13, 1853. Funeral of Frederic **Yost** at Organ ch.
Mond. July 24, 1854. Burial of John **Yost** at Organ ch.
Sund. July 30, 1854. Funeral of John **Yost** at Organ ch.
Sund. June 17, 1855. Funeral at Mrs. **Yost**'s (widow of John Yost) of her child.
Sat. January 27, 1849. Funeral of John **Yost**'s child at Organ ch.

Wed. June 22, 1881. Witness the Burial of Volentine **Zacherias**' child.
Sund. August 10, 1862. Funerals of Solomon **Zimmerman** & his son, Julius at Hopewell.

INDEX TO BIBLICAL TEXTS

INDEX TO PERSONS

Note: Because of Rev. Rothrock's variations of notations in referring to the same person at different times, this index is not edited or combined in any way. The entries are as he wrote them in his diaries.

Rawhouser
    Rev. 21, 600
Ray
    Mr. 311
    Mrs., Old 340
Reck
    J., Rev. 19
Reckart
    Michael 110
Redwine
    A., Mrs. 209
    Mary Ann 576, 583
    Mary Ann, Mrs. 246
    Widow 80
Reeves
    Charles 310
    Maggie 310, 576, 582
    Mr. 396
Rehder
    H. and wife 555
Reid
    James 425
    Mr. 131
Reimer (see also Reimert, Rimer, Rimert, Rymer)
    Catherine L. 199, 576, 580
    Eve Ann Maria 354, 576, 583
    Frederick 565
    Frederick's child 421
    John 199
    Susanne 550
    Thomas 123, 574, 584
    Valentine 102, 103, 599
Reimert (see also Reimer, Rimer, Rimert, Rymer)
    Mr. 77, 599
    Mrs. 82, 87, 599
    Widow 90, 599
Reinhardt
    Michael 520
Rensch
    John 30, 575, 584
Repass
    S. A., Rev. 303
Reyns 18
Rhyne
    George L. iv
Ribelin
    Asa 59, 577, 584
    Clotilda 199, 576, 583
    Mititia 268, 576, 580
    Mrs. 91, 98, 122, 199, 223, 248, 268, 527
    Mrs., Old 118, 599
    Paul 216
    Peter Axam 405, 599
    S. 79, 565
    S.'s child 61
    Saml. 75, 88, 91-93, 599
    Widow 208
Richard [Richards?]
    John 137, 599

Richey (see also Richie, Richy, Ritchey, Ritchi, Ritchie)
    Elizabeth 242, 599
    George's wife 242, 599
Richie (see also Richey, Richey, Ritchey, Ritchi, Ritchie)
    Aaron 150, 573, 584
    Daniel's wife 469
    John 472
    John's daughter 451, 599
    Mrs. 161, 549, 599
    Solomon 349
Richy (see also Richey, Richie, Ritchey, Ritchi, Ritchie)
    John 135
Ridenhour (see also Ridenhower, Ridenhour)
    D. 151
    Danl. D. 77
    Frank 367
    Harris M. 86, 575, 584
    Harter 374
    Mr. 204
    Phil., Esq. 268
    Philip 347, 354, 377, 381, 383
    Rufus 338
Ridenhower (see also Ridenhour, Ridenhour)
    Philip 347, 348, 362
Ridenour (see also Ridenhour, Ridenhower)
    Philip 364, 386
    Rufus 537
Riechart
    Child 30
    Mr. 565
Right
    Mr. 285
Riles
    Amanda J. 274, 576, 580
    Mrs. 274
Rim
    Susanna 224, 599
Rimer (see also Reimer, Reimert, Rimert, Rymer)
    Anna C. 182, 576, 579
    Cath. L. 235
    Elizabeth 113, 599
    John, Mrs. 193, 549, 599
Rimert (see also Reimer, Reimert, Rimer, Rymer)
    Thomas' wife 69, 599
Rinedaler
    Geo. 546
    George 22
    Mr. 19
Riple (see also Ripple)
    Martin 96
Ripple (see also Riple)
    Christena, Aunt 156, 192
Ritchey (see also Richey, Richie, Richy, Richie, Ritchi, Ritchie)
    Marvel 371
    Mr. 317

INDEX TO CHURCHES, PLACES, EVENTS, AND MISCELLANEOUS INFORMATION

Note: This index has been edited to combine references to the same
items, so index may not agree word-for-word with indicated text.

NOTES

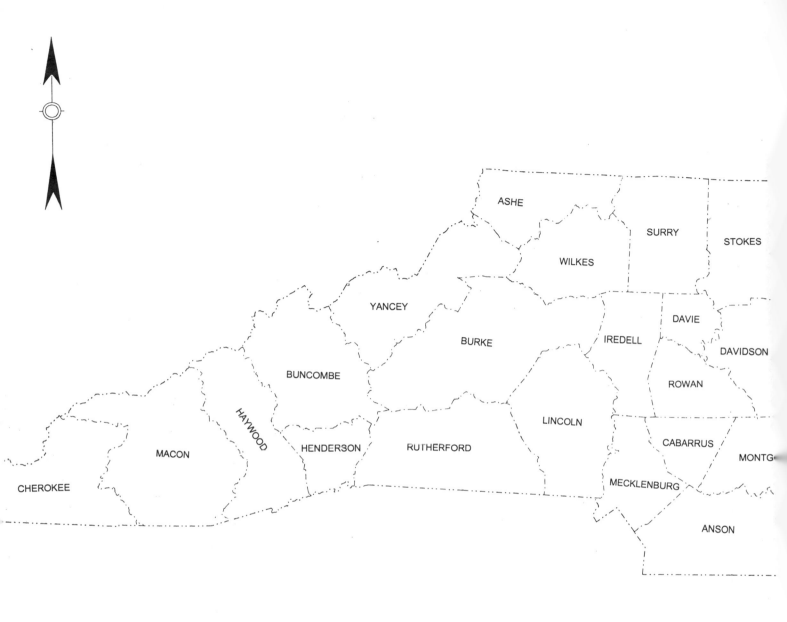

NORTH CAROLINA
AT THE BEGINNING OF
1840